CHARLES
DE GAULLE

BOOKS BY DON COOK

CHARLES DE GAULLE
TEN MEN AND HISTORY
THE WAR LORDS: EISENHOWER
(Edited by Field Marshal Lord Carver)
FLOODTIDE IN EUROPE

CHARLES DE GAULLE

A *Biography*

DON COOK

A Perigee Book

Perigee Books
are published by
The Putnam Publishing Group
200 Madison Avenue
New York, NY 10016

The author gratefully acknowledges permission from the following sources to
quote material in their control:
Brandt & Brandt Literary Agents Inc., for permission to quote from *Diplomat
Among Warriors,* by Robert D. Murphy.
Macmillan Publishers Limited, London and Basingstoke, for permission to quote
from volume 6 of *Macmillan Memoirs,* by Harold Macmillan, copyright ©1973 by
Times Newspapers, Ltd.
W.W. Norton & Compny, Inc., and Weidenfeld & Nicholson for permission to
quote from *Witness to History, 1929-1969,* by Charles E. Bohlen, copyright ©1973
by W.W. Norton & Company, Inc.
Simon & Schuster, a division of Gulf & Western Corporation and Weidenfeld &
Nicholson for permission to quote from *The Complete War Memoirs of Charles de
Gaulle* (British title *Memoirs of Hope*), copyright ©1955, 1959 by Simon &
Schuster, Inc.; copyright ©1959, 1960 by Charles de Gaulle; British edition
copyright ©1955 by Charles de Gaulle.

Designed by Richard Oriolo

Library of Congress Cataloging in Publication data

Cook, Don, date.
    Charles de Gaulle, a biography.

    Bibliography: p.
    Includes index.
    1. Gaulle, Charles de, 1890–1970.   2. France —
Politics and government — 20th century.   3. France —
Presidents — Biography.   4. Generals — France — Biography.
5. France. Armée — Biography.   I. Title.
[DC420.C66   1985]   944.083'6'0924 [B]   84-18922
ISBN 0-399-51143-1

Printed in the United States of America

1   2   3   4   5   6   7   8   9   10

TO THE FRIENDSHIP AND MEMORY OF
CHARLES E. BOHLEN
AMERICAN AMBASSADOR TO FRANCE, 1962–68

"It was the best of times, it was the worst of times. . . ."

CONTENTS

All my life I have thought of France in a certain way. This is inspired by sentiment as much as by reason. The emotional side of me tends to imagine France, like the princess in the fairy stories or the Madonna in the frescoes, as dedicated to an exalted and exceptional destiny. Instinctively I have the feeling that Providence has created her either for complete successes or for exemplary misfortunes. If, in spite of this, mediocrity shows in her acts and deeds, it strikes me as an absurd anomaly, to be imputed to the faults of Frenchmen, not to the genius of the land. But the positive side of my mind also assures me that France is not really herself unless in the front rank; that only vast enterprises are capable of counterbalancing the ferments of dispersal which are inherent in her people; that our country, as it is, surrounded by the others, as they are, must aim high and hold itself straight, on pain of mortal danger. In short, to my mind, France cannot be France without greatness.

CHARLES DE GAULLE

I

PREPARATION

O N E

A STUDY IN POWER

There is but one theme in the life of Charles de Gaulle, and that is power. His great agonizing devotion to France, his dreams and his exhortations to greatness, would have amounted to little more than the philosophical superpatriotism of a soldier-intellectual had he never been able to translate it all into the exercise of power.

From his earliest years in school and the French Army, he devoted himself consciously, instinctively and almost exclusively in everything that he did and the histories he so avidly read to the study of power, examining its roots and pondering its techniques, preparing for power, reaching for power and demonstrating his ability to exercise power at every opportunity and at whatever level presented itself. There were ups and downs in his life, to be sure. But there was no diversion from this single-minded absorption with power—no byways of intellectual exploration or curiosity, no change of direction, no side interests or lively social life, no diverting friends or cronies, no avocation or hobbies or devotion to sport, certainly no scandal and no pursuit of pleasures. There is a joylessness about de Gaulle's life—for him the pursuit of power was much too serious a matter for the intrusion of laughter or pleasure.

When France laid down its arms and asked for an armistice from the Germans in 1940, power lay at General de Gaulle's feet, and he was ready for it. He had not the slightest doubt, uncertainty, hesitation or surprise that he was a man of destiny. Empty though the vessel might be, he would fill it with his own extraordinary personality and ability, a self-confidence that far exceeded mere egotism, and above all a readiness in the name of France to demonstrate power and invent power where it had ceased to exist.

France throughout its history has moved in and out of national tragedy, declared wars and made peace, changed its constitutions, altered its foreign policy and shifted its allegiances under the personal dominance and leadership of one man—who often has emerged from nowhere. It is a nation that goes through periodic bouts of abrupt and often profound change in order to survive and progress. For General de Gaulle in 1940, the assumption of the mantle of French destiny was as natural as putting on his Army greatcoat. As in the past, French history again required a leader to come to the rescue of the nation, to revive France, to restore France's honor and regain for her a place among the victorious powers of Europe. De Gaulle's origins were no more obscure than those of Napoleon, and his intellect and ability to seize and exercise power ruthlessly was every bit as strong. In the past, *"l'État, c'est moi"* had been the watchword of the kings of France. However egocentric it might seem to the rest of the world, for Charles de Gaulle it was a matter of simple historical necessity to become the State.

This French experience is the antithesis of Anglo-Saxon democratic history, in which constitutional stability is paramount and change comes through continuity and evolution. For Anglo-Saxons, this made the de Gaulle phenomenon all the more difficult to accept and comprehend. Winston Churchill, a nineteenth-century romantic devoted to France, did understand it and at the outset embraced de Gaulle. Franklin D. Roosevelt could not. General de Gaulle was anachronistic, out of place in the American Century, and a little absurd. He was a brigadier general with few troops, an enormous ego and an uncooperative nature. France was prostrate, and that was that.

Roosevelt dismissed de Gaulle contemptuously with the oft-repeated remark, "Sometimes he thinks he's Joan of Arc and sometimes he thinks he's Clemenceau." It was beyond his comprehension that this austere general, whom few men had ever heard of before even in France, could create power for himself with nothing but his own rectitude, intelligence, personality and sense of destiny. In particular, Roosevelt had never before in all his political life been up against the power of intransigence. Steeped in politics, FDR was probably the greatest political manipulator in American history. But General de Gaulle refused to be manipulated. It was incomprehensible (and indeed often totally unreasonable) that a French general in the middle of a war could be so unyielding with his allies, so petty, so haughty, so deliberately antagonistic, troublesome and uncooperative. The great Churchill was prepared to play the Loyal Lieutenant and subjugate his national interests to the greater interests of the war effort as defined by Roosevelt. But de Gaulle's destiny was to fight for French interests, not subjugate them to the Anglo-Saxons. Intransigence was his prime weapon, often his only weapon, and it remained his prime instrument of power to the end of his days.

*

How does mere ambition in a man harden into a sense of destiny, and what gives a man a feel for power and an appetite for power? General de Gaulle, for all his vivid writing, discloses very little of himself apart from rather melancholy introspections about France and other subjects. He decided early on to enter the Army, convinced as many Frenchmen were at the turn of the century that another war with Germany was inevitable. The Army was a place where a man could exercise command and power, even at a young age and with a low rank, and perhaps even find destiny.

De Gaulle was perfectly suited in personality, temperament, intellect, courage and patriotic conviction to the molding of a military career. He was a loner from the start, all his life ready to embrace the loneliness of command that is a hallmark of great generals. He always remained remote, aloof, distant from his fellow officers. He was moody, brooding, dour and intensely intellectual in his approach to his career and the challenges and problems of military life. He devoured military history, always seeking out the details of the commanders who challenged the conventional, commanders who were original and made a success of disobeying. From the outset of his career, even when commanding platoons or companies on exercises, he made a habit of doing it his way, against the concepts and even the orders of those above him. He constantly sought to demonstrate his own independence and superiority at whatever level he was operating. His service records and stories about him from his early Army days are replete with tales and complaints about the arrogance, condescension, superiority and disregard of the opinions of others that marked his entire life. He was not popular and promotions were painfully slow. Nevertheless, on the premise that power begets power, de Gaulle continued to push and thrust at every opportunity to acquire power by demonstrating power, even on occasion deliberately putting his career in the French Army at risk. But his strong intellect and total dedication to his profession could not be ignored. Difficult and ambitious he was, but always exceptional.

On one occasion in those early years, a young fellow officer ventured in a rare moment of conversational reflection when they were out on a maneuver to say to de Gaulle: *"Mon cher ami,* I am going to say something that will probably make you smile, but I have a curious feeling that you are heading for a very great destiny." To this, de Gaulle simply gazed out into the distance and replied with toneless thought: *"Oui . . . moi aussi."* (Yes, I do too.)

In 1927, when he was thirty-seven and still only an Army captain, de Gaulle's pursuit of destiny developed decisively. He distilled and synthesized his historical readings and philosophical broodings about leadership and power into a remarkable series of lectures that he delivered to France's highest war college, the École Supérieure de Guerre, which were subsequently published in a slim little volume entitled *Le Fil de l'Épée* (The Edge of the Sword). At the time, it would have taken a very large stretch of anyone's imagination to guess that these lectures would turn out to be a kind of catechism in power by France's most dominant man of the century. The lectures were no great success with his audience, for all their brilliance of analysis, like much else in de Gaulle's prewar career. But they marked an annealing process in de Gaulle, a point at which he had equipped himself and rooted himself in a strong personal philosophy of power, along with the intellect and personality to go with it. His approach was strictly authoritarian and military—nothing whatsoever to do with politics, economics or social theory. As de Gaulle then moved slowly upward in his career in the 1930s, in staff assignments at the Ministry of War, his utter confidence in his own feel for power grew along with his disillusion with and contempt for politics and politicians. His task in those days was the overhaul of French war mobilization plans in the face of the revived menace from Nazi Germany. But his personal frustrations in trying to get action and decisions out of fourteen different governments of the Third Republic hardened him in his conviction that there was nothing wrong with France that strong leadership could not put right, and in his determination to act according to his own precepts if destiny ever offered him the chance. Although he was contemptuous of politicians, he set about rather unctuously seeking them out in this period and trying to cultivate them with the aim of achieving power for himself. It was an accident of war that landed him in London in June 1940—but what is destiny, if not opportunity seized.

*

No one who ever saw General de Gaulle in person was likely to forget—not merely his great height, but the powerful sense of authority and *presence* that he generated simply walking down a street, or when he stood up before a crowd with his arms stretched out and his fists clenched, or merely sitting behind a table passively and imperiously answering questions at a news conference. Much of this aura he deliberately cultivated and contrived in order to heighten the mystique of power—in accordance with precepts that he had laid down in *Le Fil de l'Épée*. "There can be no prestige without mystery," he had written, and he instilled automatically and deliberately in those who saw him or approached his desk a sense of deference, of awe, of fear and uncertainty, of inferiority, of care and hesitation. Dr. Henry A. Kissinger, something of a connoisseur in such matters, wrote that de Gaulle "dominated a room with an almost physical force of his authority" as he had never seen in any other man except China's Mao Tse-tung.

He was the most polite of men with his staff, with visitors, with guests—but it was the politeness and courtesy that a chief of state and man of power displays to subordinates and outside supplicants. Never, ever, did he permit any intimacy or sense of friendship. Always, with everyone, a distance was kept. His own son, Admiral Philippe de Gaulle, says that at an early age he sensed that his father was different, and that he had to keep his distance from him. René Capitant, who joined de Gaulle in London and was still with him as minister of justice in his last government in 1969, once remarked: "Between the hand that makes the move and the pieces on the chessboard, there can be no friendship." Georges Pompidou, who worked closely with de Gaulle for twenty-five years and was his premier for six years, went out of his way to write a journalist to deny a published report that the General had *ever* called him by his first name.

He was a user of men the way a commander has to commit troops to battle, allowing himself no interest or regard in the problems or personal attributes of those who served him, apart from their ability to serve him well. If anything interfered, they were soon dispatched elsewhere. Claude Mauriac, son of the famous French writer François Mauriac, served as a private secretary to de Gaulle, handling his personal correspondence for nearly two years after the liberation of Paris. He records how he once came out of de Gaulle's office rather puffed up by a particularly important and sensitive confidence the General had shared with him, to be told by one of the more hardheaded aides: "Don't delude yourself. He needs a mirror. Anybody else would have done just as well. In fact, Gaston Palewski [de Gaulle's long-time chef de cabinet], whom everybody believes to be so powerful, plays no other role than that. Listener to a man who thinks aloud but who pays no heed to the remarks of his interlocutor."

De Gaulle himself wrote: "Solitude was my temptation. It became my friend. What else could satisfy anyone who has been face to face with history?"

In such a man there was little to expect in lightheartedness or levity, and there was none. De Gaulle's humor, such as it was, was invariably sardonic, mordant and consisted largely of put-down remarks or pointed barbs. When one of his supporters, d'Astier de la Vigerie, once ventured to tell him that friends of his were worried about some particular government policy, de Gaulle's response was: "Then, *mon cher* d'Astier, change your friends!" Sometimes a witty cartoon or caricature would draw a smile from de Gaulle, but he was no man to approach with a joke or a funny story. It is rare indeed to find a photo of him smiling.

Does history make men, or do men make history? General de Gaulle is indisputably, powerfully and massively in the latter category. He fought constantly to impose himself on events, and he made history for France on a major scale. "He was a man—take him for all in all"—and there is a *totality* about de Gaulle's personality, the fashion in which he concentrated every facet of his character on the single-minded exercise of power. His strict moral rectitude became a kind of backbone for the French, not overly reputed for morality. The simplicity and austerity of his personal life and living habits, the lack of pleasure or diversion or humor or fun that enlivens other men's lives, served in de Gaulle to contribute to his total dedication to the art of power. What would be dullness in other men became part of the fascination and mystique of his power.

Imposing total austere dedication on himself, he automatically demanded it of others. Jean Belliard was a young Free French agent who became a French diplomat after the war. He related to the author how he and two other agents were paraded before General de Gaulle at Free French headquarters in London in 1943 before being parachuted back into France. It was Belliard's third espionage mission.

"We marched into the General's office and came to attention," he said. "He rose from behind his desk, looked us up and down and then simply said: '*Eh bien, messieurs. Vous allez en France. Si vous mourez, la France vivra! Au revoir, messieurs!*' (Well, gentlemen. You are going to France. Even if you die, France will live! Goodbye, gentlemen.) We marched out somewhat taken aback, but de Gaulle had said all that he needed to say."

Clement R. Attlee, the British Labour Party leader and postwar prime minister who had been wartime deputy prime minister to Winston Churchill, wrote a review of de Gaulle's War Memoirs in which he commented that de Gaulle was a great general but not a very good politician. Attlee then received a letter from de Gaulle thanking him for the review and remarking in a dry inversion of Clemenceau's famous epigram about wars and generals: "I have come to the conclusion that politics is far too serious a business to leave to the politicians."

He was a man of no personal indulgences whatsoever. For many years he was a heavy smoker, but he gave this up abruptly after the war, telling his son-in-law, General Alain de Boissieu: "I have succeeded in sticking to it by telling everyone I was not smoking anymore. De Gaulle cannot go back on his word!" Such third-person references to himself came naturally and spontaneously, as if he were constantly painting his own portrait or molding his own heroic sculpture.

Long walks in solitude with his wife or alone were his only exercise all his life. Often his aides, entering his office, would find him pacing up and down, deep in thought. His only other interest outside his closed family circle—and the exercise of power—was reading—an avid lifetime reading of history and literature and the classics. He took no interest in the theater or opera or music, except to attend and preside on state occasions as host to some distinguished visitor to France. He was utterly frugal in personal living habits, and took no emoluments from the State beyond his military pension when he was out of office. But he was a stickler for his rights of protocol, and declined to attend the funeral of King George VI in London in February 1952, because, out of office (at that time), he would have to be seated behind President Vincent Auriol instead of at the front.

*

"General de Gaulle is a simple man," Josef Stalin remarked to Britain's Lord Beaverbrook in a wartime conversation in Moscow. To Roosevelt at Yalta, the Soviet dictator repeated that he "did not find General de Gaulle a very complicated man." While this does not automatically leap to the mind in appraising de Gaulle, there nevertheless was a strong truth in Stalin's observation. There was indeed a monolithic simplicity about General de Gaulle's rectitude and character and personal life, and the single-mindedness with which he pursued his aims of power. In the case of his one and only meeting with Stalin, his objective was a treaty of friendship with the Soviet Union. But he wanted a treaty on his own terms and he was not prepared to bargain for it or pay Stalin's price—which at that time was recognition by France of the puppet Polish Communist National Committee. De Gaulle adopted his usual posture of intransigence, and in the end Stalin gave in—even with a murmur of congratulations to de Gaulle for his performance.

The General's favorite power stratagem was the simple, sudden *fait accompli*—monolithic, irreversible, non-negotiable unilateral decisions on behalf of France that were designed to disrupt the chessboard and change the game. Very early in the war, there was his secret order to the Free French Navy to occupy the little islands of Saint-Pierre and Miquelon near Newfoundland, against instructions from Roosevelt. There was his veto of British entry into the European Common Market, his abrogation of five defense cooperation agreements with the United States, and his withdrawal of French forces from the military command structure of the North Atlantic Treaty Organization. Having decided on one of these strategic moves, he would then resort to the tactics of a military commander, using every means at his disposal of wile, guile and deception to mislead and lull "the enemy" against the sudden launching of attack.

For General de Gaulle, rectitude and integrity in the single-minded defense and pursuit of "the interests of France" did not require him to be candid, open and above board in his dealings with anyone. He was secretive, deceptive and non-negotiable not only in diplomatic relations with other governments, but within his own government and with his own ministers as well. Cabinet meetings were invariably largely pro-forma sessions to endorse and carry out the mundane routines of government. De Gaulle made all his major foreign policy decisions alone, without advice and without discussion. There will be no great future disclosures of records showing him getting conflicting advice from this or that minister and having to trim his sails for some political consideration or agonize over what to do. But neither did he rush in hastily and shoot from the hip with decisions. That was not his style. He always sought to be a master of his own timing, of waiting and outwaiting events and the moves of others to choose his own moment to make his counterattack. All this he would ponder in solitude on his long walks in the countryside around his home at Colombey-les-Deux-Églises until ready to act. Ministers invariably would be informed when they watched his televised news conferences. Secrecy was vital to surprise, and surprise was vital to de Gaulle's exercise of power.

Jean Monnet, France's other great man of this century, once remarked in a conversation with the author: "You do not negotiate with de Gaulle. He does not negotiate, once his mind is made up. What you have to do is arrange conditions and set up hard facts and situations that he has to take into account in making his decisions. Then he can be very realistic and flexible." Monnet was the antithesis of de Gaulle in international outlook and flexibility, but as Frenchmen they understood each other.

*

There are indeed many examples of surprising flexibility on the part of de Gaulle in the face of hard facts and political realities. One was the composition of his postliberation government and its policies of sweeping social change. By no stretch of the imagination could General de Gaulle be placed on the left wing of the French political spectrum. Yet the 1944–45 government over which he presided was further to the left than any French government since 1848—further even than the Popular Front of Léon Blum in 1936, which had Communist support but no Communist ministers. Under de Gaulle in 1944, Communists entered the government, which then rapidly proceeded to nationalize the coal mines, the gas and electricity industries, four of the nation's largest banks, the Renault automobile works, to put in place a comprehensive social security system and, under Jean Monnet, the best and most effective national economic planning machinery of an industrialized democracy in the world.

De Gaulle, who had been so inflexible over taking control of the French colonies during the war and restoring the French Empire worldwide, then reversed field completely when he returned to power in 1958, and with almost breathtaking speed set virtually every piece of French overseas territory on the road to self-government and independence—albeit still with close economic ties to France. Above all he forced the entire French nation to adjust and accept the facts and realities and necessity of ending the fiction that Algeria was part of France, and setting that country free. In the face of outside challenges, or what he considered to be a threat to French interests, he was adamant. But if he could act independently on his own, and the situation required it, then he could be very flexible indeed. If it were possible to put any political label on de Gaulle, it probably would have to be something contradictory like "authoritarian liberal."

But General de Gaulle in the exercise of power always sought to create hard facts and realities of his own, to which others would have to respond. Often, however, these were simply declarations of his own prejudices, expressions of dubious logic or statements of political will that he would deploy as "facts" as a means of justifying his own ends. They would then be repeated and repeated in a kind of endless Gaullist litany of political action. The United States could not be counted on as an ally in the defense of Europe—therefore France had to have its own nuclear weapons and be ready to act alone. Great Britain is an island and not yet ready for membership in Europe. Yalta is the root of the division of Europe, imposed by the superpowers in the absence of France. Gold is the only realistic base for the world's monetary system. Soviet communism is becoming more benign. France is the natural leader of the Third World. Integration is evil—independence is strength. Europe can only be created through independent coop-eration of strong nation-states. Hegemony of the superpowers must be resisted and the power blocs made to fade away. France, serving herself, is serving the whole world.

De Gaulle viewed relationships between the superpowers and lesser powers rather like the planetary system, in which each planet has its own gravitational pull. But medium-sized planets have to stay well away from the big ones if they are to retain a place of their own and an orbit of their own in space, and not wind up as satellites. For de Gaulle, in political terms, the Soviet Union exercised no such gravitational pull on France—or at least none that he feared or acknowl-edged. But the United States did. This invariably pitted him against Washington in an endless, obsessive opposition to all things American in order to show that France had her own policy and place in orbit.

De Gaulle possessed two great assets enabling him to pursue goals of power that in lesser men would have looked like chasing butterflies or boxing shadows. His intelligence was formidable, and he had an extraordinary ability to create drama. With his enormous absorption of history, diplomacy and political theory, and his capacious memory, he could synthesize his thoughts and give even dubious ideas or theories a vitality, precision and endless stimulation in his news confer-ences, monologues, speeches, conversations or instructions for his subordinates. He had that famous French capacity for logic—although more often than not it could be based on a curious selection or adjustment of facts. But he was never superficial, and never dull. On top of that, his histrionic ability was unmatched on the world stage—certainly during his second era in power. The greats of the war years had faded or were gone—Roosevelt, Stalin, Churchill ("A great artist of a great history," de Gaulle wrote of him admiringly), Truman, Eisenhower. Then, for a while, he shared the stage with Macmillan, Adenauer, Kennedy, Khrushchev, and then he was alone.

Yet de Gaulle's foreign policy was in the final analysis the least successful aspect of his exercise of power. The drama of press conference announcements, the tactics of *fait accompli* and surprise attack, the intransigence, the persistence of slurs, doubts and invented misjudgments and mistrust of others may have served his ambitions for France, but they did not add up to a coherent or constructive foreign policy. De Gaulle in the end became a voice that declaimed at everyone but spoke only for himself. Jean Monnet made a more solid and constructive contribution to French leadership of Europe, to stability and peace, when he masterminded the plan for a European Coal and Steel Community in 1952, when Charles de Gaulle was in the political wilderness.

Nevertheless, in the narrower context of France itself, which was all that mattered to de Gaulle, his achievements place him on the highest plateau of his country's history.

The first was the restoration of France between 1940 and 1945 from a defeated nation to the ranks of the victorious Allied Powers of World War II. The legitimacy of his assertion or usurpation of power against Marshal Henri Philippe Pétain and the Vichy government will no doubt always be debated by tedious French constitutional historians. It did not happen overnight, but in the end, General de Gaulle prevailed as the State. If he had not, and Vichy had remained the only government of France, then France would have remained a defeated, disgraced, collaborationist nation, rescued by the Anglo-Saxons, with no voice or rights of her own in the occupation of Germany or the postwar reconstruction of Europe.

De Gaulle's second great achievement was the rescue of France from the brink of civil chaos in 1958, and with his return to power the skillful ending of the Algerian War and at the same time the conversion of the rest of the French Empire from a mounting liability into a political asset of free and independent self-governing states in the Third World.

Finally, he bequeathed to France genuine constitutional stability, with the institutions and structure of strong, stable and lasting government for the first time since Napoleon.

For the rest, the cult of Gaullism, with all its scribes and apostles and pharisees and interpreters from left to right, is a permanence in French politics. Frenchmen of every walk of life measure his greatness simply by asking, "Without de Gaulle, what would France be today?"

T W O

THE MOLDING OF
A SOLDIER

Charles André Marie Joseph de Gaulle was a child during the Belle Epoque, that time of extraordinary flowering of art, music, theater, literature and culture in France, the last romantic age of history.

He was born in northern France in the industrial city of Lille on November 22, 1890, midway between the Franco-Prussian War of 1870–71 and the awful carnage still to come in 1914. His father fought with the French Army against the Prussians at the siege of Paris, France's heroic epic in the bitterness of defeat. The war itself was relatively short and sharp, leaving the country at large intact and unscathed. The uprising of the Paris Commune which followed had been far worse, ending in a bloodbath in which 25,000 Frenchmen were killed by other Frenchmen. Still, the government of the new Third Republic survived with a precarious cachet of authority, and recovery was swift despite the loss of the provinces of Alsace and Lorraine to Germany and the peace terms dictated by Bismarck and Kaiser Wilhelm I at the Palace of Versailles. When the Kaiser's armies had gone, and peace and stability were restored, France took off on one of those periods of dramatic renewal and expansion that have marked its history. The year before de Gaulle was born, this boom of the new Industrial Age was climaxed and celebrated with the great Paris Exhibition of 1889, which also marked the beginning of the beautiful years of the Belle Epoque. The exhibition itself was crowned by the construction of Gustave Eiffel's soaring tower on the banks of the Seine. It remained the tallest structure in the world for the next forty years, until the completion of the Chrysler Building in New York in 1929.

On the surface, Europe during the Belle Epoque was peaceful and prosperous, its borders open, its commerce expanding, its dominance worldwide. It was ruled by five emperors, thirteen kings or queens, twenty-one minor dynasties and an uncounted galaxy of princes, archdukes, counts, viscounts, grafs and barons filling pages and pages of the Almanach de Gotha, to whom royal honors and protocol were due. War was still more or less as Karl von Clausewitz had defined it over fifty years before—a continuation of politics by other means. Armies were small bodies of low-paid recruits, officered by sons of the titled aristocracy and the new wealthy upper classes, who were supposed to bring along a private income to subsidize their careers, their uniforms and their living standards. Rulers and regiments vied with one another in the design of gaudy military dress, so that formal dinner-dances in any capital of the old Europe looked like scenes from *The Merry Widow* or *The Student Prince*.

The Great Powers were competing with each other mainly in distant places, in the imperial scramble for colonies in Africa, Southeast Asia, India, China and the Pacific. It was the time of the White Man's Burden, and with peace in Europe there was the glamorous diversion for military men of colonial skirmishes to be won on horseback against native tribesmen in a heady but fairly safe mixture of risk and romance. The machine gun had been invented only in 1883, and was barely a proven weapon—let alone had it yet changed the face of battle and the cost of war.

The old royalty and the new bourgeois barons of the burgeoning industrial world flocked to Paris by the thousands for the Great Exhibition and the view from the top of the Eiffel Tower. Although France was republican, and hence disturbing to the old monarchical order that had prevailed in Europe since the Congress of Vienna in 1815, Paris was indisputably the cultural center of Europe and therefore of the world.

In the 1890s, France overflowed with the greatest single national concentration of cultural talent in all history. There were the painters Monet, Degas, Cézanne, Gauguin, Seurat, Van Gogh, Matisse, Toulouse-Lautrec, Pissarro, le Douanier Rousseau, Sisley, Renoir and Rouault. Rodin towered over the world of sculpture. In music, it was the time of César Franck, Claude Debussy, Léo Delibes, Charles Gounod, Gustave Charpentier, Jules Massenet, Gabriel Fauré and Camille Saint-Saëns. In the theater, Edmond Rostand wrote *Cyrano de Bergerac,* Maurice Maeterlinck wrote *Pelléas et Mélisande* and the divine Sarah Bernhardt was the world's greatest actress. Major poets were Arthur Rimbaud, René Sully Prud-homme, Paul Verlaine and the young Paul Claudel. Henri Bergson was a dominant world figure in philosophy. Among the writers and novelists were Anatole France, Émile Zola, Guy de Maupassant, Edmond de Goncourt, J.-K. Huysmans, Maurice Barrès, Pierre Louÿs, Romain Rolland and Marcel Proust, who delicately nibbled on *madeleines* in the tea garden of the Ritz Hotel and remembered things past. In the 1890s the careers of André Gide, Colette and Jean Cocteau were just begin-ning.

But beneath the glitter and tinsel, the renaissance of achievement and cultural supremacy, for the French the currents of defeat and humiliation, bitterness and revanchism, continued to run deep. Whatever the prosperity and flowering of the nation, the republican regimes were habitually weak, and France was regularly seen to be the loser in power struggles and the imperial scramble with Great Britain and the German Empire. She had lost the Suez Canal to the British in a financial operation masterminded by Disraeli. Then Lord Kitchener forced the French to depart from the Upper Nile in the incident at Fashoda. The Kaiser waged gunboat diplomacy against French interests in Tangier and Morocco. All this added to the feelings of national disgrace ever since the loss of Alsace and Lorraine and the Franco-Prussian War.

As governments of the Third Republic floundered for lack of leadership, there was a strong revival of monarchist sentiments and political feeling. In the first thirty years of the Third Republic, not one president completed his term of office. There were scandals, resignations, one assassination, and the fifth in line of these illustrious gentlemen, Félix Faure, died of a heart attack in the amorous embrace of his mistress in the Élysée Palace in 1899. The Republic was almost overthrown by the gaudy and popular General Georges Boulanger in a brief, comic opera-like political revolt in 1889. Then the regime was rocked by the Panama Canal Company financial scandal, with accompanying suicides by its fraudulent promoters. Finally came the espionage charges against the Jewish Captain Alfred Dreyfus in 1894, which dominated and divided the nation for the next twelve years until Dreyfus was finally cleared and rehabilitated. But a wave of anti-Semitism in France continued right down to the Second World War. Charles Maurras, a prominent and influential royalist political philosopher early in the century who then turned Fascist-appeaser in his late years in the 1930s and was finally put on trial for collaboration after the liberation of France from the Nazis in 1945, proclaimed to the court: "This is the revenge of Dreyfus!"

Charles de Gaulle, eternally serious, eternally melancholy where France was concerned, grew up in this great cultural explosion of the Belle Epoque, but responded instead to the deeper currents of unrest and confusion. Of his youth, he wrote in his War Memoirs:

> Nothing affected me more than the evidence of our national successes: Popular enthusiasm when the Tsar of Russia passed through a review at Longchamp, the marvels of the Exhibition, the first flights of our aviators. Nothing saddened me more profoundly than our weaknesses and our mistakes, as revealed to my childhood gaze by the way people looked and the things they said: the surrender at Fashoda, the Dreyfus case, social conflicts, religious strife. As an adolescent, the fate of France, whether as a subject of history or the stake in public life, interested me above everything.

The de Gaulle family, which originated in northern France, goes back more than five centuries. An early ancestor, Jehan de Gaulle, fought against the English at the Battle of Agincourt in 1415. In the social structure of the Middle Ages, the de Gaulles ranked as *petite noblesse d'épée,* the sword-bearing officer class. They were not among the "great families," but by the eighteenth century they had moved up the ladder to become *petite noblesse de robe,* lesser nobility without title or land. By now, law was the principle family profession. Three generations of de Gaulles served the kings of France as Crown lawyers, until Jean-Baptiste-Philippe de Gaulle wound up imprisoned in the Bastille for a time during the French Revolution. Jean-Baptiste's son, who was born in 1801 and christened Julien-Philippe, turned to history, writing and teaching. He edited an official life of Saint

Louis and authored a long and erudite history of the city of Paris. He was Charles de Gaulle's grandfather.

Julien-Philippe had three sons. The first, named Charles, was paralyzed at an early age but devoted himself from his invalid's bed to a study of the Celts, published a work of Celtic history and wrote poems in the Breton language. A younger brother, Jules, became a member of the Institut de France and one of the foremost entomologists of his time, cataloguing and classifying more than 5,000 varieties of bees, wasps and other hymenoptera.

Henri, the middle son, born in 1848, was Charles de Gaulle's father. He was educated for the Army. At the age of twenty-two, serving as a lieutenant during the siege of Paris, he was wounded in a skirmish with the Prussians at Le Bourget, where the famous airport was later built. But he then had to take up a teaching career instead for economic reasons. In 1886, while teaching in Lille, Henri married a second cousin on his mother's side, Jeanne Maillot-Delannoy. Charles was the second child of the marriage, which produced four boys and a girl.

The de Gaulles were therefore a family of deep French roots, steeped in its history, service and traditional values, a family of learning and erudition, intensely Catholic and conservative in outlook. Henri de Gaulle as a teacher was austere, polite, gentle and stimulating, but also strict, and his pupils as well as his children stood in awe of him. He lived to the ripe old age of eighty-five. De Gaulle's mother died in Brittany in 1940 during the German occupation, soon after hearing of her son's "Call to Honor" to the French following his flight to London in the climactic days of World War II.

De Gaulle was close to both of his parents all his life. From his mother came the passionate, sensitive side of his nature, as well as his mask of reserve. His father, a very tall man who passed his height on to his four sons, gave him his intelligence, his deep and systematic way of thinking, his sense of history, his application and self-discipline and his great strength of character. He was also a stickler with his children and his pupils in the proper and elegant use of the French language. They were a close-knit and very private family, and life on a teacher's income offered no frills. Henri de Gaulle made up for this with strong intellectual discipline and was continuously stimulating and deeply informed with his children. "An anxious concern about the fate of our country came as second nature to my three brothers, my sister and myself," Charles later wrote.

Soon after the turn of the century, Jeanne de Gaulle having given birth to her family, as she desired, in her native city of Lille, they moved to Paris. Henri took a prestigious teaching position as lay headmaster of the Jesuit College of the Immaculate Conception. Then, after a major political upheaval when the republican regime enforced a law separating Church and State and closed the Jesuit schools, the elder de Gaulle managed to found a private school of his own in the rue de Grenelle.

When the Jesuit schools were closed down and the order expelled from France, Charles was sent by his father across the frontier into Belgium to continue his studies in another Jesuit school. By the time he returned home after a year, he had made up his mind on a military career. Apart from his father's early zest for soldiering and experiences in the Franco-Prussian War, there was nothing in particular in the family tradition to direct Charles toward the Army except his early-acquired devotion for and deep concern about France. But soldiering and military play constantly ran through his boyhood, when he had quickly come to dominate his brothers. One day his younger brother Pierre came crying to his mother with the tale: "Charles hit me—we were fighting a war and I was a spy and I was captured and was carrying a message and he was the general and instead of swallowing the message like he told me, I gave it to the enemy!"

Another time he and his older brother, Xavier, were playing toy soldiers and Xavier suddenly wanted to be "king of France" instead of "emperor of Germany." Charles retorted indignantly: "Never! France is mine!"

But to a thoughtful and serious teenager considering a career, it was increasingly clear the way the tides of history were running for France. Germany under Wilhelm II was becoming more and more belicose, and was now challenging not only France as a land power but Britain's sea power as well. Britain was drawing closer to France, and the Entente Cordiale had been proclaimed. Confrontation and showdown of the Great Powers had begun to sputter on a long fuse. In young de Gaulle's eyes, the State was weak, and the strong stabilizing institutions of France were the Church and the Army. He would go where strength and power and action for France would lie.

He had not been an exceptional student or as disciplined in his studies as his father would have liked. His interest lay in history, literature and philosophy, and he glided along successfully on the strength of an already prodigious memory. In later years, he told his grandchildren that to train his memory he spent hours memorizing French words and sentences spelled backward and that he could even repeat whole sentences backward in Latin. He memorized hundreds of lines of French poetry, the whole of *Cyrano de Bergerac* and even chunks of *Antigone* in classical Greek. But his father told him firmly that it would take more than that to make it into the military academy at Saint-Cyr, so Charles packed off to a preparatory school to spend two years buckling down to mathematics, science and other disciplines.

It was the requirement of the French Army of that day for officer candidates first to spend one year in the ranks—"to learn how to obey before learning how to command." So Charles enlisted in the 33rd Infantry Regiment stationed at Arras, near Lille, on October 10, 1909. One year later he entered Saint-Cyr Academy, on the outskirts of Paris beyond Versailles.

His great height of six feet five inches, even more exceptional among Frenchmen, promptly earned him nicknames like *"La Grande Asperge"* (Great Asparagus Stalk) and *"Double-mètre"* (Two Meters), and his long and prominent nose got him the label of "Cyrano"—to which he responded by mounting a table in the cadets' mess and reciting long passages from the Rostand classic. He took this ragging indifferently, and did not seem very interested in Saint-Cyr friendships or companionships. He remained aloof and distant from others all his life, first by nature and then as a conscious and cultivated style of leadership and exercise of power.

"Average in everything except height," an instructor noted on one of Charles de Gaulle's grading papers, but this was probably more a reaction to personality than ability. De Gaulle graduated from Saint-Cyr thirteenth in a class of 211, which was headed by Alphonse Juin, later an outstanding combat commander with the Free French, and the last marshal of France. Commissioned on October 1, 1912, de Gaulle asked to return to his old 33rd Infantry Regiment as a sublieutenant.

His new commanding officer was Colonel Henri Philippe Pétain.

*

"My first colonel showed me the meaning of the gift and art of command," de Gaulle wrote in his memoirs. Pétain, who was then already fifty-six years old, indeed possessed many of the basic qualities of a superior military commander that de Gaulle would emulate. He was a man of remarkably fine physical appearance and presence, but cold, glacial and aloof. He spoke rarely and briefly, usually with a sardonic twist to his comments, but he made his orders concise and clear. He had a direct and simple understanding of men and how to lead them, and he inspired courage and confidence with his efficiency, judgment and commands. He had another quality that certainly attracted de Gaulle—he was a maverick in his military thinking, a rebel as far as the French General Staff was concerned. For this reason Pétain had been held back at every promotion, and was old as a captain, a major, and now as an old colonel. It seemed that the 33rd Infantry in 1912 might be his last command before retirement.

The French Army, which had not fought a real war since 1870, was trained and committed at that time to a very simple doctrine of "attack, attack, attack"— come what may. It was a doctrine that took little or no account of the development of the machine gun and firepower. It relied simply on the *élan* of officers and men, and it led to ghastly slaughter in the First World War.

Pétain opposed this doctrine of the General Staff with a logic and persistency that almost cost him his career. His view was succinctly and repeatedly summarized in lectures he delivered well before the outbreak of war in 1914 to the École Supérieure de Guerre: "Let us first crush the enemy by artillery fire, and afterward we shall win our victory. An offensive is gunfire leading an advance. A defensive is gunfire stopping an advance. The gun wins ground, the infantry occupies it." For a time Pétain was without a military assignment. General Staff officers muttered grimly about his undermining the offensive spirit being drilled into the Army. And indeed, along with his nonconformity, Pétain's thinking and logic and his conclusions always seemed to reflect a kind of inevitability of pessimistic realism—perhaps his strongest quality, but one that enabled him to accept defeat calmly in 1940.

As for the terrible outcome of this doctrinal argument going on before the First World War, which was then fought out in the trenches and mud for four years, de Gaulle summarized in a book that he wrote in the 1930s, *La France et son Armée:*

> For two years [1914–16] we had to attack without the arms we needed. The
> 75 mm guns would not do everything for us. Apart from the fact that wide
> belts of ground were outside its trajectory, it hadn't enough power to do

effective damage to protected targets. Although in 1915 the High Command at last decided that they must have adequate heavy artillery, this did not go into service until the beginning of 1917. Hence the vast losses we suffered for so long as a result of our repeated assaults. In 1915 on the French front alone, we lost 1,350,000 men killed, wounded and taken prisoner in order to put out of action 550,000 Germans. Our country, so weak in manpower, had to pay for errors and delays with human lives.

Lieutenant de Gaulle quickly made his mark in the 33rd Infantry Regiment, as well as in the town of Arras, with his great height and stiff military bearing, his immaculate uniform, his single-minded and efficient devotion to his unit and his duties, and his impromptu discourses in the officers' mess on history, battles and tactics. Pétain, who knew everything going on in the regiment despite the distance he kept from his subordinates and his men, noted in de Gaulle's dossier at the end of the first year as an officer: "Has proved from the beginning to be an officer of real worth who raises high hopes for the future. Throws his whole heart into his job as an instructor. Gave a brilliant lecture on the causes of the conflict in the Balkan Peninsula."

Soon after came Pétain's order promoting de Gaulle to the rank of full lieutenant: "Very intelligent, passionately devoted to his profession. Handled his section perfectly on maneuvers. Worthy of all praise."

At the outbreak of war in August 1914, the 33rd Infantry moved forward at once across the frontier into Belgium, to take up battle on the flank of the great German wheeling movement from the north toward Paris and the heart of France. At the Belgian town of Dinant, the regiment was ordered to hold a bridge across the Meuse, already under fire from the advancing Germans. Lieutenant de Gaulle led his men on a dash through the streets to reach the bridge, later recording that "I felt I was two people—one running like a machine, the other anxiously looking at him." Then: "I had just covered the last twenty meters to the bridge when I felt what seemed to be a whiplash on my knee and missed my footing. The four who were with me were all brought down in the same instant. Sergeant Debout fell on top of me. A hail of bullets hit the pavement and walls around us and thumped with a duller sound into the dead and wounded on the ground."

De Gaulle was evacuated with a severe leg wound and spent seven months recovering. From his hospital bed, he wrote his mother complaining that "the British government bears a heavy responsibility for not making up their minds to go to war until the last minute, and having their army very ill-prepared." In another letter he wrote that "our own best interests require us not to lay down our arms until we have linked up with the Russians across Germany—otherwise we will have to start again in ten years' time."

By the time de Gaulle rejoined the 33rd Infantry, Pétain had shot ahead to take command of a division and then a corps. Under a new commander, de Gaulle became the regimental adjutant. But in March 1915, he was wounded again, and this time took five months to recover. One of the wounds was a shrapnel tear in his left hand, as a result of which he later wore his wedding ring on his right hand all his life. He was back with the 33rd Infantry when it was ordered to Verdun in February 1916, where Pétain was now in overall command of the French armies in the worse slaughter of the war, if not of all history.

Erich von Falkenhayn, the German commander, launched the Battle of Verdun quite simply as an action to bleed the French to death. He very nearly succeeded, but his own forces paid an appalling price as well. In six months of fighting around Verdun from February to August 1916, the French lost 315,000 killed, wounded and missing, while the Germans, who were attacking behind massive firepower, lost 281,000. This total of almost 600,000 casualties in one battle was about equal to the total of all French losses—military and civilian—in the entire six years of World War II.

De Gaulle's company went into line on March 2 at an early stage of the battle at the village of Douaumont, a key fortified height approximately at the center of the twenty-mile Verdun salient, which was shaped something like a fishhook along a ridge. At dawn on that first day, the Germans opened up with a tremendous barrage, plastering the French positions around Douaumont to a depth of two miles with 105-mm, 305-mm and 380-mm shells and mortars for more than six hours. It was the kind of firepower that Pétain had begged for but which the French did not have. At noon, the German infantry came out of the trenches with bayonets fixed.

De Gaulle's company was penetrated, with two islands of resistance holding out. According to an account of the action which he wrote in prison camp and sent to his regimental commander after the war, he decided to lead a few of the survivors with him along a communications trench to join up with the others. He related: "I had hardly gone ten meters when I came on a group of Boches crouching in a shellhole. They saw me at the same moment, and one of them ran his bayonet into me. The thrust went through my map-case and wounded me in the thigh. Another Boche shot my orderly dead. Seconds later a grenade exploded literally in front of my face, and I lost consciousness."

When de Gaulle came to, he was a prisoner of war. As he disappeared into Germany, another citation by Pétain listed him as "fallen in action" and in glowing terms gave a somewhat different account: "Captain de Gaulle, reputed for his great intellectual and moral worth, as his battalion was decimated by a frightful bombardment and the enemy reached its lines on a broad front, led his men in a fierce attack and savage hand-to-hand fighting—the only solution that met his sense of military honor. He fell in the fighting. A peerless officer in all respects."

At first de Gaulle's family was told that he was presumed dead, and it was several months before they learned through the Red Cross that he was alive in a prison camp. When he returned from the war, he received the Legion of Honor for the action at Douaumont.

De Gaulle made five escape attempts in Germany—none of them successful. His conspicuous height was no help. Finally he was shipped to a high-security punishment camp at Ingolstadt, on the banks of the Danube, where he did 120 days in solitary confinement in a dark cell.

Nevertheless, he had some exceptional fellow-officer-prisoners, including the

French air ace Roland Garros, and Colonel Georges Catroux, who would rally to the Free French in 1940. There was also a young Russian officer named Mikhail Tukachevsky, an out-and-out Marxist, who became a marshal of the Red Army and then was liquidated by Stalin in the great purge of the 1930s.

There was still an element of nineteenth-century chivalry in the treatment of prisoners of war, despite the awful carnage going on. German newspapers, which arrived regularly at Ingolstadt, even printed the uncensored texts of the French military communiqués. Now and then German-language Swiss papers also turned up for the PWs. De Gaulle was therefore able to follow in general terms the course of the war, and also improve his command of German. He had never seen a tank, but he learned of their emergence at the Battle of Cambrai in November 1917, and eventually got some satisfaction from reading in *Die Frankfurter Zeitung:* "Foch has tanks, we have not." Ever systematic and studious, de Gaulle made copious notes of military, strategic and political analysis, in particular the old arguments over attack versus firepower that had cost the French so dearly. When the armistice at last ended the war in November 1918, he returned home from thirty-two months as a PW with a suitcase full of material for future writings and lectures.

He was now twenty-eight years old, and he had missed more than half the war and all of the action and promotion that would have gone with it. Of course he might well not have survived had he not been taken prisoner, for the casualties among junior officers were by far the highest. But that was not much consolation for an ambitious young officer. Nevertheless, he still had a career ahead of him, and in some ways he probably was able to take a fresher and more detached view of the lessons to be drawn than were his war-weary contemporaries. At any rate, the chance to repair his loss in command of troops came when Poland called on the Allies early in 1919 for help in fighting off the Bolsheviks. France was glad to respond.

*

In April 1919 Polish General Joseph Haller arrived in France to begin recruiting among Polish refugees and such French as might want to join. Both the cause and the military opportunity appealed to de Gaulle, and he joined the 4th Division of Polish *chasseurs* with his rank of captain. By mid-1919 he was on his way to Warsaw.

De Gaulle's service in Poland lasted more than a year and a half. The first months were quiet and routine. His division was headquartered in a suburb of Warsaw, with the fighting going on far to the east, on the Ukrainian frontier below the famous Pripet Marshes. The Ukrainians and the Poles were fighting the Bolsheviks, with the dual aim of securing Poland's frontiers as far to the east as possible and establishing an independent Ukraine. De Gaulle's duties were fairly light, and for a time he lived in the Hotel Bristol, which still stands in the center of Warsaw in what used to be the city's elegant district of town houses. De Gaulle was acting in a long tradition of Franco-Polish friendship and historical links— Louis XV and his Polish bride, Napoleon and Maria Walewska, the scientists Pierre and Maria Curie, the interlarding of French society by Polish émigrés such as the Poniatowskis and the Palewskis. French was the second language of the Polish aristocracy, and Captain de Gaulle was a popular figure in Warsaw society. He was invited to lecture at the Polish Staff College. He first had his notes translated into Polish. Then, with his prodigious memory, he learned them phonetically. It was a gallant effort, but it didn't really work because pronunciation was one thing but intonation another. So he regretfully allowed an interpreter to take over.

By mid-1920 the military situation had begun to deteriorate. Exhausted by three years of struggle against the Bolsheviks with little outside help, the Ukrainian effort collapsed and the Red Army threw its weight against the Poles. Its commander was de Gaulle's old prison camp companion, Mikhail Tukachevsky.

In three weeks, Tukachevsky advanced to within fifteen miles of Warsaw. On July 23 the Poles sued for an armistice and the Allied governments moved hastily to forestall a total collapse by trying to get the Russians to a conference table. But, in a forerunner of the power play over Poland twenty-five years later, after World War II, the Bolsheviks immediately laid down conditions for a conference that would have imposed a Communist dictatorship on the Poles. The Allies, despite all their pledges and encouragements to the Poles, now suddenly found they no longer had the means or the political will to go through with their policy. They pressed the Poles to accept Russian terms for a conference, and arrangements were under way for a meeting to resolve the Polish question in the Russian city of Minsk. Then came what Winston Churchill called "the miracle of the Vistula."

While these negotiations were in progress, the Polish Army under Marshal Joseph Pilsudski suddenly struck at the flank of the Red Army across the Vistula, east of Warsaw. Meanwhile, the 4th Polish Division, with de Gaulle now promoted to major in the Polish Army and in command of an infantry battalion, had been moved to the Zubrucz River, southeast of Warsaw, and went into action to support Pilsudski with a diversionary attack to pull Russian troops away from the Warsaw front. In four days the battle was over. Some 70,000 Russian prisoners were taken by the Poles, the Red Army was routed and Poland was saved—at least until 1939. General Maxime Weygand was in charge of the French Military Mission to Warsaw at the time and played a key role in planning the Polish attack. Again de Gaulle was singled out for praise from a senior French commander for exceptional intelligence and courage in handling his unit. He was also awarded the Virtuti Militari, the highest military decoration Poland then offered. He had made up some of the lost time he spent in prison camp.

*

In June, before these climactic events in Poland, de Gaulle had been on leave in Paris, and there, by prearrangement of which he was unaware, he met a rather shy and reserved young lady named Yvonne Vendroux, whose father was a biscuit manufacturer in the town of Calais. It was a whirlwind courtship. The matchmaker was Madame Paule Denquin, a close friend of Yvonne's mother and also a godchild of de Gaulle's father, Henri de Gaulle.

Yvonne had already turned down one proposal of marriage from an Army officer, a general's son, because "traipsing from garrison town to garrison town is not for me." But Madame Denquin was suddenly struck by the idea that she would change her mind for Charles de Gaulle.

"The Vendroux were planning a trip to Paris, so we arranged a meeting at the Salon d'Automne, the big annual art exhibition, and the de Gaulles and the Vendroux just sort of bumped into one another," she later related. "It looked unplanned. I introduced Charles to Yvonne and they immediately walked ahead alone, talking about the paintings."

Two weeks later, Yvonne's brother Jacques was competing in a fencing tournament in Paris, and she traveled with him to watch the match. They were invited afterward to attend the annual ball of the École Polytechnique at the Palace of Versailles—and there was Captain de Gaulle in dress uniform. He asked Jacques if he might dance with Yvonne, and after the sixth waltz they returned and Yvonne announced to her brother: "Captain de Gaulle has just asked me to marry him. I said yes."

She was ten years younger than de Gaulle, and the engagement did not become official until after his return from Poland in February 1921. He was offered a post as lecturer at the Polish Staff College when the fighting was over, but instead received welcome orders to become a lecturer in military history at Saint-Cyr. He and Yvonne were married in Calais on April 7, 1921, and their first child, Philippe, was born promptly in December.

The de Gaulles settled down in a little apartment on the Left Bank on the boulevard des Invalides, and he commuted by train each day to Saint-Cyr. They kept very much to themselves and their own relatives instead of mixing in the military society surrounding the academy. Yvonne was dark, petite, pretty and well-educated. She was utterly self-effacing and devoted herself to her husband's career for the rest of her life. He was already absorbed with his feelings about France and destiny, and she was absorbed in him. Life for the de Gaulles was much too serious to be enlivened by humor or fun, but their devotion to each other was complete and constant to the end of their days.

At Saint-Cyr, de Gaulle was assigned to lecture on nineteenth-century history from the time of Napoleon—whom he judged harshly for having left France "crushed, invaded, drained of blood and of courage, smaller then when he took control, condemned to accept bad frontiers, the evils of which have never been redressed." Much of the material developed in his lectures was later incorporated into his book La France et son Armée. He could now give vent in an organized and systematic way to his own vast reading and study of authors such as Charles Maurras, with his pronounced monarchist views, Charles-Pierre Péguy, who had courageously supported the innocence of Dreyfus, and the nationalist historian Maurice Barrès. Above all, he was devoted to the philosophy of Henri Bergson, who had written:

> By what sign do we ordinarily recognize the man of action, who leaves his mark on the events into which fate throws him? Is it not because he embraces a more or less long succession in an instantaneous vision? The greater the share of the past that he includes in his present, the heavier the

mass he pushes into the future so as to put pressure on the events in preparation: his action, like an arrow, moves forward with a strength proportional to that with which its representation was bent backward.

De Gaulle was an impressive lecturer, with his height and commanding presence, his immaculate dress (white gloves washed and freshly pressed each evening by Yvonne), his lucid and beautifully phrased use of language, his unhesitating delivery always from memory without notes, yet full of detail, quotations, analysis and observation. He reveled, too, in patriotic rhetoric. Speaking of France's defeat in the Franco-Prussian War, he would call the class to stand at attention while he exalted the eternal spirit of the Army—no doubt with his father's service in the siege of Paris in mind:

> In that war without consolations, we lacked neither men nor courage. The many proofs of this testified to the precious heritage, still intact, of our military virtue. These valiant men tried by sheer courage to conquer an evil destiny. No defeat destroyed their will to fight. The unfair humiliations they suffered can never be forgotten or wiped out. They will remain a perpetual lesson for those who govern and those who command.

This was a turning period in de Gaulle's career. First of all, developing his Saint-Cyr lectures, he had begun to realize the gifts of intellect and leadership that he had always felt within himself, and his superiority over his fellow officers stood out for all to see. At the same time, the chance came to put renewed momentum into his military career, which had stagnated since prison camp during the war as far as the Army went.

The École Supérieure de Guerre, closed during the war when officers were needed elsewhere, reopened in 1919. De Gaulle was not automatically qualified to apply for entrance because he had never served as a General Staff officer, but he could gain admission by competitive examination. He was accepted in November 1922, and for a time was both a lecturer at Saint-Cyr and a student at the École Supérieure, adjacent to the Invalides in Paris. It was an exceptional class that he entered—206 officers from fourteen countries (including four Americans), all with strong records of wartime experience. The professors were men who had commanded in battle, and teaching and discussion was both informed and passionate.

This was particularly enlivened by the fact that French military dogma had undergone a 180-degree turn since the ghastly rejection of Pétain's theory of supportive firepower versus massive frontal attack. From overweening belief in attack and the invincibility of the bayonet in the hands of divisions of gallant infantrymen, the General Staff was now dedicated to a doctrine of the superiority of defense. The machine guns and artillery of the Great War had convinced the senior generals who had served with Pétain, Foch and Joffre that defensive firepower was now the key to battle.

But the younger officers were imbued with the new possibilities of the tank, which had made its appearance only in the late stages of the war. No real doctrine of tank warfare or employment of armor in battle had yet been developed, but it was already the fixed view of the General Staff that the role of the tank was defensive, to increase firepower and then support the infantry advancing behind a suitable artillery barrage.

De Gaulle was largely a listener to all this debate. Other officers in the course had had direct wartime experience with tanks, which de Gaulle had not. But he absorbed the arguments, and with his experience of the Pétain controversy over firepower, he quickly formed an intellectual disdain for the new theoretical rigidity of General Staff commanders and teachers. The success that his history lectures at Saint-Cyr were then having did not of course diminish de Gaulle's soaring egotism and self-confidence, and this quickly reflected in the comments on his record at the École Supérieure: "A very developed personality, great confidence in himself. Could achieve excellent results if he admitted mistakes with a little better grace, and if he consented more easily to allow his point of view to be disputed."

Then, a year later:

> A very intelligent officer, cultivated and serious, greatly gifted. Unfortunately spoils his incontestable qualities by his excessive assurance, his severity toward the opinions of others and his attitude of being a king in exile. Moreover, he appears to have more aptitude for general studies and for the synthesis of a problem than for its detailed examination and the practicalities of its execution.

De Gaulle was so antagonizing to the instructors and directors of the École Supérieure that he very nearly torpedoed his own career. It was here that the sifting process would determine which officers went on to higher command, and there were serious doubts among de Gaulle's instructors whether this brilliant but egotistical, haughty and unyielding man would be the right officer to entrust with higher responsibilities.

This reached a climax in a final full-scale field exercise, conducted in eastern France near the town of Bar-sur-Aube in the summer of 1924 under the school's chief lecturer in general tactics, Colonel Moyrand. He assigned de Gaulle the role of an opposing army corps commander, with staff officers and divisional commanders under him drawn from the rest of the student body. Moyrand then put de Gaulle through an intensive testing of tactical maneuvers and full-scale battlefield responses to a variety of rapidly changing situations. De Gaulle came through with calm, careful, sound decisions, and orders that were clear-headed and practical, and was judged in the end to have won the "battle." But the style of aloof superiority that went with his success got under Moyrand's skin. After the exercise, the officers were assembled in a local school for a critique, and one of de Gaulle's classmates later recalled what happened:

> The colonel presided on the rostrum, while de Gaulle sat opposite him with

his long legs cramped under a school desk. Next to de Gaulle sat Captain Châteauvieux, who had acted as his chief of staff. The questions which the colonel asked, and his rather sarcastic, aggressive tone made it seem like a severe cross-examination in a law court, but de Gaulle maintained his calm and answered with restraint.

The more serene he appeared, the more it irritated the colonel, who saw all his traps skillfully avoided. At last he burst out with an irrelevant question which seemed almost an admission of defeat, about where the supply services had been for one of the regiments of a division on the right. De Gaulle asked Captain Châteauvieux to answer.

The colonel then said furiously, "But I asked you, de Gaulle," and de Gaulle replied calmly: "Mon Colonel, you entrusted me with the responsibilities of an army corps command. If I had to assume those of my subordinates as well, I should not have my mind free to fulfill my assignment satisfactorily." De Gaulle then added a Latin phrase: *De minimis non curat praetor* (the law does not concern itself with small matters), and again said, "Please answer the colonel, Châteauvieux."

At this, Moyrand, barely able to control himself, retorted to de Gaulle: "We knew you considered many tasks beneath you. Very well. I am now clear in my mind about you."

Nor was that by any means the end of it. It was the last big exercise of the course, and the instructors gathered to decide final grades. There were only three rankings of the students: Very good, good or passable. Only with a "very good" grading could an officer be certain of a coveted appointment to the General Staff and a place on the ladder to top rank and high command. The majority of de Gaulle's instructors were in favor of cutting him down to size with a "passable" grade only.

Then came an unexpected intervention from de Gaulle's old commander, Pétain, now a marshal of France and inspector general of the Army, overseeing all officer appointments and promotions. The whole "de Gaulle controversy" had become so animated and prolonged, in particular the service gossip about the altercation with Colonel Moyrand, that Pétain descended on the school to review what had happened, inspect de Gaulle's records, interview him and Moyrand and make his findings. Magisterially, he pronounced that de Gaulle had been correct in his handling of the exercise, and that to give him merely a "passable" grade would be an incorrect judgment of his record.

But the school's commandant, General Dufieux, would not bow entirely to the Marshal's wishes. De Gaulle of course was certain that his record justified a top passing grade. But instead he was granted only a secondary rating of "good." The effect of this setback was immediate. Instead of an appointment to the General Staff, he was posted to a logistics assignment at headquarters of the French Army of Occupation in Germany, in the Rhineland city of Mainz, where he was to be responsible for supplies, rations, food storage and refrigeration.

Furious at his grading and the turn his Army career now seemed to be taking, he declaimed to his fellow officer-students in the courtyard of the École Supéri-eure "I will come back to this dirty hole only when I am commandant of it! Then you will see how things will change."

That was very nearly what in fact happened.

THREE

DE GAULLE AND PÉTAIN

When Charles de Gaulle left for his new posting in Germany in October 1924, he was thirty-four years old and had been a captain since 1915. He remained a captain until 1927. He was competing on the promotion list with other officers his age or younger with a great deal more wartime experience in command of combat troops. And he was also competing with himself—his personality, his arrogance and overweening sense of his own superiority, his "king in exile" manner that had been noted in his record at the École Supérieure, and the edge of haughty disdain that cut through so readily in his dealings with persons above or below him. Meanwhile, there were hundreds of other ambitious officers in the Army to choose from, and de Gaulle's career prospects at this stage were not particularly bright. He even talked about leaving the Army—but along with his undoubted intellectual abilities and his ambitions, he knew he had something else going for him: the esteem and patronage of Marshal Pétain.

He paid a formal call on the marshal before departing for Germany. There was certainly not much intellectual stimulation in the job of looking after problems of refrigeration and distribution of rations for the Army of Occupation. So de Gaulle settled down to refresh his knowledge of German, and produced his first book—a volume of essays on the collapse of Germany in 1918–19 titled *La Discorde Chez l'Ennemi* (Discord Among the Enemy), published at the end of 1924. It did not make much of a mark, and sold fewer than a thousand copies. Moreover, by its publication, de Gaulle further antagonized the military hierarchy by showing readiness to seek recognition and an audience for his views and literary talents outside the confines of staff lectures and official periodicals.

All the same, the timing of the book was propitious and it won praise from specialist readers. France was then facing the unpalatable fact that the whole of its policy toward Germany, based on the Versailles Peace Treaty, was rapidly coming unraveled. Heavy reparations charged against Germany had led to astronomical and uncontrolled inflation of the mark, bringing the German economy virtually to a standstill until an international rescue operation was organized under the Dawes Plan to inject hard-currency loans and restore stability and start recovery. Meanwhile the French were working actively in the Rhineland under the cover of their military occupation to promote a separatist movement and set up a puppet "Rhenish Republic" detached from Germany—but this had backfired and was stimulating revanchist German nationalism instead. French support for a strong anti-German military policy and occupation force was waning in Paris, simply because it was costing the taxpayers too much. France's relations with Great Britain were cooling because the British were showing less and less enthusiasm for pursuing the repressive provisions of the Versailles Treaty. In this turmoil and confusion, the shadow German General Staff had systematically begun to plan circumvention of the treaty in order to rebuild military strength. The myth that the war had been lost because the German Army had been stabbed in the back by leftist revolutionaries in Berlin was finding fertile ground.

De Gaulle, surveying the German collapse with his typical search for a broad historical synthesis of the political, psychological, military and national characteristics to be found in the shaping of events, prophetically singled out the Nietzschean cult at work in Germany, and wrote:

> The superman, with his exceptional character, his will to power, his taste for risk, his contempt for others, appears to these impassioned and ambitious Germans as the ideal to which they should aspire. They tend to belong to that formidable Nietzschean elite, which is convinced that it serves the general interest in pursuing its own glory, which would keep the masses enslaved while despising them, and which is not deterred by human suffering except to salute it as necessary and desirable.

While de Gaulle was brooding over the German scene, Pétain, as head of the Conseil Supérieur de Guerre, was shaping a political "grand design" for the future of the French Army. A Socialist government under Édouard Herriot and Léon Blum had taken over and was, in 1925, considering a reduction in military conscription from three years to two or even one to save money for social service. Pétain, urged by his staff, decided to mount a flank attack on the politicians by preparing a history of the role of French arms through the ages, which of course would conclude that three years of *service militaire* was fundamental to security. Someone was needed to take charge of researching and drafting the work—and the marshal's automatic first choice was the literary Captain de Gaulle. He was recalled from Germany after exactly one year and joined Pétain's staff in Paris in October 1925.

The history project ideally suited de Gaulle's interests and intellectual talents, and he went to work at high speed. Within a matter of months he had produced several chapters of what would later become *La France et son Armée*. But Pétain then interrupted the "great work" with another project. He instructed de Gaulle instead to prepare for immediate publication a shorter study on the role of permanent fortifications in the defense of France. Again Pétain's motive was political—an article to influence the politicians. It was also to de Gaulle's literary taste, and included sections on Sébastien Vauban's long line of frontier fortresses constructed during the reign of Louis XIV, and the neglect of strong defense positions such as Douaumont, where he had been captured in the Battle of Verdun.

The article appeared in the *Revue Militaire Française* in December 1925 under the title *"Rôle Historique des Places Françaises,"* and was immediately acclaimed for its lucidity and the logical strength of its conclusions. It charted the geographical weakness of the flat, open countryside of northeastern France, where wars had been fought for centuries, going back to Marlborough, the Hundred Years War, and beyond. It analyzed the power and ambitions of Germany since 1870 and concluded that with no natural barriers on its northeastern frontier, "fortification of its territory is a permanent national necessity for France."

Since the theme of the article was more or less dictated by Pétain, it is scarcely surprising that it was the most successful piece of writing that de Gaulle turned out between the two World Wars—if success had been simply a matter of enthusiasm of the Conseil Supérieur de Guerre of those years. But it is the ultimate irony that the article was used by Pétain as a major propaganda piece in persuading the French government to build the Maginot Line—those fortresses along the Rhine that became the defensive millstone around the French Army's neck in the catastrophe of 1940.

One of de Gaulle's few close friends in the Army, Captain Lucien Nachin, wrote to him questioning the wisdom of his conclusions—whether he might not be fostering a false sense of "defensive security" in France. De Gaulle and Nachin kept up a correspondence for a number of years, and Nachin subsequently produced one of the early de Gaulle biographies in 1944, with the letters as original source material. In this instance, de Gaulle responded with a somewhat limp explanation in which he tried to differentiate between what the State builds in the way of fortifications and what the Military then does with those forts in its defensive plans.

> In my humble opinion [de Gaulle wrote] the defensive organization must not be—as·many wish—part of the operational plan. The necessary and permanent defensive organization, which is related to the geographical, political and even state of morale in which the country finds itself, is a question for the government. The operational plan is a question for the command. The latter takes account of the strongholds (whatever their form) in its projects, as one of its means, exactly as it takes account of its forces, of the *matériel* and of economic power.

Whatever the validity of this exercise in logic, it certainly never worked out that way for France, Pétain, the new defensive doctrine of the General Staff and the vast sums of money subsequently poured into the Maginot Line. Once the forts were there and the money spent, they inevitably came to dominate not only military planning but the mentality and psychological state of the nation as well. It was short-sighted of de Gaulle to imagine it could be otherwise. Despite his ex-post-facto explanations, the article stood as an unvarnished piece of advocacy for a Maginot Line that he would later condemn with such scorn for saddling France with a defeatist mentality.

But in the meantime, Pétain and the military hierarchy were delighted, and the marshal now moved in his next act of "rehabilitation" of his protégé after the affair of the secondary grading he was given when he had left the École Supérieure de Guerre two years before. A new commandant, General Pierre Hering, had taken over at the École, and Pétain called him in to inform him that he still considered de Gaulle's grading a miscarriage of justice and that he wanted to "give a lesson to those professors that they will understand." Pétain proposed that Captain de Gaulle be invited to give a series of lectures to the professors and the officer-students at the school, in defiance of all precedent, and declared that he would preside over the lectures in person. Hering was a proclaimed nonconform-ist, and he fell in readily with the marshal's wishes. The first lecture took place on April 27, 1927.

*

De Gaulle's spectacular return to the École Supérieure de Guerre was a major event in his life—not, of course, a historic event, or even a particularly successful one, but one that nevertheless was decisive and fundamental to his military career and his eventual role on the world stage. Suddenly he was no longer languishing on the assignment lists in a backwater logistics job, waiting for the wheels of the military bureaucracy to turn. Pétain, partly for his own political reasons to be sure, had taken him from eclipse and placed him in the spotlight before the most prestigious military assembly France could muster, which he called to attention with the brief introductory remark: "Gentlemen, Captain de Gaulle is going to express his ideas to you. Kindly listen to them attentively."

For his part, de Gaulle responded with a histrionic performance of three lectures on the subject of military leadership. The first lecture was largely an elaborate tribute to the old marshal himself. But they were far more than that. The lectures were an intellectual shaping and annealing—a refining, distilling, sharpening and hardening—of de Gaulle's fascination with—indeed, obsession with—the mystique of power. He seized the opportunity to assemble from men and history a closely woven philosophical analysis of the qualities and attributes that produce outstanding leadership, and laid down a credo of the style and exercise of power by which he would live until the end of his days.

The marshal's presence of course ensured that the lecture hall was packed. The school staff assembled stiffly in an anteroom and Pétain motioned to de Gaulle, in full-dress uniform, to enter first—symbolic revenge for that humiliating final grade. "The honor is yours," the marshal said. "It is the lecturer's privilege to lead the way. And after entering he is entitled to teach what he wishes. That is how I applied it to myself, expressing ideas different from those of my time."

De Gaulle, with three bands of glittering braid on his sleeves, was the lowest-ranking officer in the room, preceding the marshal of France, with his seven stars. He mounted the platform, removed his *képi* and placed it on the table, unbuckled his dress sword and laid it down, and removed his white gloves. He then acknowl-edged the marshal's presence with a brief, stiff nod and launched without a note into an unhesitating, unhalting and closely reasoned discourse, on each occasion lasting just under an hour. The lectures were published by de Gaulle in 1932, slightly expanded, under the title *Le Fil de l'Épée.*

The first lecture was titled "Action in War and the Leader." By the time he had completed the three lectures, de Gaulle had quoted from memory references drawn from Socrates, Lucretius, Pericles, Julius Caesar, Frederick the Great, Napoleon, Scharnhorst, Goethe, Tolstoy, Victor Hugo, Anatole France, Francis Bacon, Henri Bergson, Bismarck and Moltke, Clemenceau, Marshal MacMahon and lesser-known figures.

Taking up the theme of the leader and what constitutes "the divine element of authority," de Gaulle paid this homage to Pétain—and to himself:

> Powerful personalities, preparing for conflict, crises, great events, do not always possess the easy manners and superficially attractive qualities which go down well in ordinary life. They are usually blunt and uncompromising, without social graces. Although deep down the masses may obscurely do them justice, recognizing their superiority, they are rarely loved and in consequence rarely find an easy path to the top. Selection boards are inclined to go more on personal charm than merit.

In the second lecture, "Character," de Gaulle stated that "when faced with the challenge of events, the man of character has recourse to himself, to leave his mark on action, to take responsibility for it, to make it his own business." He then had this somewhat prophetic praise for disobedience:

> We can go further and say that those who have done great deeds have often had to take the risk of ignoring the merely routine aspects of discipline. Examples are plentiful: Pélissier at Sebastopol stuffing the Emperor's threat-ening dispatches into his pocket unopened and reading them after the action was over; Lanrezac saving his army after Charleroi by breaking off the battle, contrary to orders; Lyautey keeping the whole of Morocco in 1914, in the teeth of instructions issued at a higher level. After the Battle of Jutland and the English failure to take the opportunity offered them of destroying the German fleet, Admiral [John] Fisher, then First Sea Lord, exclaimed in a fury after reading Jellicoe's dispatch: "He has all Nelson's qualities but one: He doesn't know how to disobey!"

And, in the final lecture, "Prestige," de Gaulle assuredly had himself as well as Pétain in mind when he declared that "certain men have, one might say almost from birth, the quality of exuding authority, as though it were a liquid, though it is impossible to say precisely of what it consists." He continued:

> First and foremost there can be no prestige without mystery, for familiarity breeds contempt. In saying this, I do not mean that a leader must shut

himself away in an ivory tower, remote from and inaccessible to his subordinates. On the contrary, if one is to influence men's minds, one must observe them carefully and make it clear that each has been marked out from its fellows, but only on condition that this goes with a determination to give nothing away, to hold in reserve some piece of secret knowledge which may, at any moment, intervene, the more effectively from being in the nature of a surprise.

There would even seem to be some relationship between a man's inner force and his outward seeming. No experienced soldier has ever underrated the importance of appearances. Every page of the *Commentaries* provides us with evidence of the studied manner in which Caesar moved and held himself in public. We know how much thought Napoleon gave to showing himself in such a manner as to impress his audience. What, above all else, we look for in a leader is the power to dominate events, to leave his mark upon them, and to assume responsibility for the consequences of his actions.

Apart from Marshal Pétain's impassive pleasure, the lectures were no great success. The brilliance of de Gaulle's performance was offset as far as his captive audience was concerned by the circumstances of the occasion as well as by the personality of the lecturer. The school commandant had to listen to a lot of sour complaining. The exhortation to leadership that de Gaulle was espousing went over the heads of most officers, who were left with a feeling that however excellent the synthesis of material had been, there was really nothing very new in what he had to say.

De Gaulle in his final lecture declared that "the hero cannot hope for the happiness of the common herd—he must fight, first of all, against himself." His loyal friend Captain Nachin later wrote of the reaction:

> He was well aware that despite their receptivity, the officers making up the audience had only partly understood his train of thought. They had been held by his extraordinary brilliance, by the training they had received, the mentality imbuing them, and their present environment, producing not only lack of comprehension but a sort of latent hostility, a state of resistance to his teaching. They and de Gaulle were really not on the same level.

In the autumn of 1927, de Gaulle obtained permission to repeat his lectures at the Sorbonne before an audience of academics, intellectuals and politicians, but his ideas drew no more response from civilians than they had from the military. Still, he had re-emerged in his career. Promotion from captain to major finally came through. Pétain, meanwhile, had lost interest in the historical project that had been his original excuse for bringing de Gaulle to Paris. Then, in December 1927, de Gaulle received a new assignment as commander of the 19th Battalion of Light Infantry, a unit of the famous Alpine Chasseurs, back in Germany at the town of Trier. The director of infantry at General Headquarters remarked: "I am posting a future generalissimo of the French Army." De Gaulle wrote gloomily to Nachin:

"It is nice to be promoted, but the real question is different. The important thing is to make one's mark."

*

Major de Gaulle was now back in command of troops in the French Army for the first time since his capture at Verdun in March 1916. His appointment, moreover, was an exception to a rule that only a former *chasseur* could command Alpine troops. De Gaulle at once proceeded to apply in a systematic way the theories and lessons of leadership he had outlined in his lectures. To begin with— "appearances . . . the studied manner in which Caesar moved and held himself in public." Those white gloves, washed with care each evening by Yvonne, were no longer reserved for formal occasions, but became part of the everyday apparel of the commanding officer as he walked from his quarters across a bridge over the Moselle each morning to his headquarters in Trier and carried out parades and inspections. The headgear of the Alpine Chasseurs is a beret, worn traditionally inclined to the left. But de Gaulle decided to wear his to the right—and 721 officers and men of his battalion followed suit. But he was an effective if rigorous commander, and within a few weeks after taking over, his men had acclaimed him with the title of *"chasseur d'honneur."*

Firmly settled in his new command, he next proceeded to try out his philosophy of disobedience. Within the confines of his battalion, he was determined to demonstrate to those above and below him that he was running his own show. He took his troops out on a winter field exercise one morning on a long march to a river crossing, and then received orders to stay in the field overnight. But it had been his intention to test the stamina of his men with a return to barracks that same night. He called his officers together and announced that troops were to lighten backpacks for a fast march home. There were objections that they were in a divisional column of march and should get authorization from the general commanding. De Gaulle curtly announced: "I take full responsibility."

They marched into Trier well after dark, the band playing the regimental tune of "Sidi-Brahim," much to the annoyance of the German citizens. For this deliberate breach of discipline and exercise orders, de Gaulle faced a penalty of two weeks' close arrest and severe censure in his dossier. But he blandly brushed aside warnings of the consequences with the remark "Everything will die down. I belong to the *maison Pétain.*" Moreover, he was right, although this scarely added to his popularity. An investigation was ordered, and against all precedent it was decided to take no action against the haughty major.

After that, an influenza epidemic hit the French Army in Germany, and de Gaulle's battalion—through no fault of his own—suffered the heaviest in the division to which it was attached. A parliamentary commission first descended on Trier to investigate, then Marshal Pétain turned up in person to reassure France and the Army. De Gaulle was personally cleared and praised for his rigorous efficiency and his relations with his men. But the aftermath was otherwise.

In the wake of the flu epidemic, conscripts began writing their Deputies in the National Assembly requesting transfer back to units in France. This began to reach an alarming proportion, harmful to discipline and training. De Gaulle, on his own, drew up a battalion order that any man who took steps to get a transfer would be immediately punished. A couple of days after the order was read to the troops, a telegram arrived transferring one of his men to an army corps in France. Instead of shipping the man out, de Gaulle put him on two weeks' detention. The man's Deputy in Paris at once lodged a strong complaint with the minister of war, Paul Painlevé. De Gaulle received a summons to appear before the commander in chief of the Army of Occupation, and faced sixty days' close arrest, transfer to the nonactive list and an end to his career.

Instead, before he was due to appear he took a train to Paris and presented himself at Marshal Pétain's office. He explained that he was in trouble over "a rather tricky business" and got in to see the marshal. Pétain heard the story and called Painlevé, with whom he was on close terms. Fortunately for de Gaulle, the soldier had petitioned his Deputy before the battalion order against further transfers had been issued, so there was an easy way out. The soldier was released, the headquarters summons canceled and the incident closed. "That was quite a thorn I pulled out of his side," Pétain remarked laconically to his staff. He had again changed de Gaulle's career.

All the same, de Gaulle had stretched his luck pretty far, and the old marshal, who didn't mind using others but resented being used, began to put distance between himself and his arrogant protégé. At the Ministry of War, there was open resentment against an officer who insisted on total discipline from those below him and appealed to those above him when he himself broke the rules. Years later, when de Gaulle was president of France, an interviewer asked him if he still held the same views on disobedience. He allowed himself a fleeting smile and replied: "Things have changed, for now I am the Chief."

In 1929, as his two-year assignment as battalion commander neared its end, de Gaulle had no wish to return to a headquarters job in Paris, so he applied for a direct transfer to the Army of the Levant in Beirut. Of the Germany which he was leaving, he wrote prophetically to Nachin:

> The French Army of Occupation on the Rhine will not be there much longer. The force of circumstances is knocking down what remains of Europe's vital, fixed frontiers. One should realize that the Anschluss is close at hand, and that Germany will soon take back, peacefully or by force, the territory seized from her for the benefit of Poland. After that, they will ask us to return Alsace. That seems to me to be written in the stars.

De Gaulle spent nearly two years in the Middle East, the first time he had been outside Europe. Duties were light, and he traveled during his tour at Beirut headquarters to Cairo, Baghdad, Aleppo, Jerusalem, Damascus and elsewhere. Basically, he only confirmed a conviction he had already formed—that policing a colonial empire was a waste of time for the Army and a diversion from its central mission of guaranteeing the security of France itself. He had expressed this view consistently in his early lectures on French history at Saint-Cyr, and it was also in line with Pétain's thinking. In those days the Army was more or less divided between the colonialists, who sought career assignments in the Levant, Algeria, Morocco, Indochina or the primitive backwaters of French Africa, and those like de Gaulle, whose focus was across the Rhine. From Beirut, he again wrote to Nachin:

> My impression is that we haven't really made much impact here, and that the people are as alien to us—and we to them—as they ever were. It is true that as a course of action we have adopted the worst possible system in this country, that is to try to get the people to do things for themselves. But nothing has ever been achieved out here without compulsion, neither the canals of the Nile nor the aqueduct of Palmyra nor a Roman road nor an olive grove. As far as I can see, our fate will be to go as far as that, or to get out.

Toward the end of 1931 he was posted back to Paris. Pétain had at last retired from active military service at the age of seventy-six, but he was still a powerful figure, not very far in the political background from which he would soon be recalled to government service. He had been succeeded as head of the Army by General Maxime Weygand, de Gaulle's superior officer in Poland in 1920. De Gaulle's new assignment was the General Secretariat of the National Defense Council, a new permanent policymaking body that Pétain had established directly under the prime minister with the task of preparation and organization of the nation for war.

*

The world had slumped into the Great Depression, Germany was rapidly succumbing to Nazi intimidation, and Pierre Laval was premier of France when de Gaulle returned to Paris. He wrote trenchantly in his War Memoirs:

> From 1932 to 1937, under fourteen governments, I found myself involved in a planning capacity in the whole range of political, technical and administrative activity concerning the country's defense. The work I had to do, the discussions at which I was present, the contacts I was obliged to make, showed me the extent of our resources, but also the feebleness of the State. For the disjointedness of government was rife all over this field. Not—certainly—that the men who figured there lacked intelligence or patriotism; on the contrary I saw men of incontestable value and sometimes of great talent come to the head of the ministries. But the political game consumed them and paralyzed them.

One of de Gaulle's first tasks on the Secretariat was the preparation of an updated study on full-scale mobilization of national resources and organization of the State in the event of war. But the problem and plans that he addressed formed a classic case of the "disjointedness of government" and political frustration which by 1939–40 had created an eggshell nation with a rotten egg inside. A national mobilization act had been introduced in the National Assembly in 1923, but was buried for five years. The study de Gaulle carried out was aimed at updating and intensifying the economic scope of mobilization in particular, but it took eighteen months before a government could even introduce it in parliament. Then it did not pass the committee stage of consideration until March 1936, and it was not brought to a vote until two years later, March 1938, the year of the Munich agreement. It became law after Senate approval that July—by which time Hitler had been mobilizing for five years and war was barely a year away.

De Gaulle, meanwhile, returned to writing and literary efforts to push his ideas and relieve the frustrations of watching governments come and go, unable to make coherent decisions. First he completed the expansion of his three lectures at the École Supérieure de Guerre into book form, adding to the original text various examples of leadership and flattering references to Pétain, and publishing it in 1932 with the dedication: "To Marshal Pétain: This essay, Monsieur le Maréchal, could only be dedicated to you, for nothing shows better than your glory how clear thought can lead to correct action."

De Gaulle then sent a first copy of Le Fil de l'Épée printed on special paper to Pétain with a handwritten inscription added: "Homage from C. de Gaulle in deepest respect and devotion." It is the ultimate irony that this copy was among the few personal possessions that Pétain took with him when he was transported on de Gaulle's orders to the bleak fortress on the Île d'Yeu in the open Atlantic off the Brittany coast to serve out a sentence of life imprisonment after World War II. It was still with him when he died there in 1951, at the age of ninety-five.

Meanwhile, thanks to his friend Captain Nachin, de Gaulle had come into contact with another aging but imaginative and vigorous-minded retired Army officer who was to influence his career. He was Colonel Émile Mayer, over eighty years old when he and de Gaulle first met in 1932, a Jewish officer who had served in the Army through the wrenching and nauseating period of the Dreyfus affair, never wavering in his faith in Dreyfus's innocence. For this reason, he never reached the rank of general, but he was a lively, intelligent and cultivated man who was the natural centerpiece of an informal group of military men who gathered regularly on Monday evenings at a brasserie on the boulevard Montparnasse, not far from the Ministry of War, for discussion and conversation.

At one of these sessions late in 1932, de Gaulle launched into a discussion of an article that had appeared in a military periodical on the handling of tanks in the French Army. He began outlining his own ideas for creating an elite and fully professional armored force of 100,000 men as part of the Army. The contingent would be highly mobile, in contrast to the static infantry formations of French conscripts. As the discussion progressed, Mayer proposed that de Gaulle write an article—"Not a book, it would take too long, a book can come later, let's be content with an article, an explosive article." De Gaulle set to work, but it took time since his staff duties were very time-consuming. The article appeared in May 1933, in the Revue Politique et Parlementaire under the title "Vers l'Armée de Métier" (Toward a Professional Army). It made little impact apart from still further irritating his superiors. They sent down word that de Gaulle would have to choose between his career and his efforts to reform the French Army. His answer was to expand the article into a book of the same title, which appeared exactly one year later, in May 1934. But again, like all his prewar literary efforts, the response was minimal and the book sold barely 750 copies in France.

It was a clarion call to the Army to revise its defensive doctrine, modernize its organization and recognize the new dimension of war that the tank was creating. But the book was accepted, and indeed glorified, only much later, after the collapse of 1940, when it was belatedly discovered that there had been a prophet in the ranks all along. In the creation of Gaullist legend, the picture of de Gaulle as a first apostle of armor was vastly overblown. He was far from original in his discovery, he was rather superficial in his analysis and he was late in joining the ranks of the writers and theoreticians. Indeed, it was not until after World War II, when *Vers l'Armée de Métier* was reprinted, that de Gaulle added some important afterthoughts on cooperation between tanks and air power in breaking through and exploiting armored mobility.

In Britain, both Captain B. H. Liddell Hart and Major General J. F. C. Fuller had begun writing at length on the role of armor and the new mobility of war fourteen years before de Gaulle's book appeared. In fact, Liddell Hart made an official visit to the French Army in 1926–27 at the invitation of Marshal Pétain and wrote a sympathetic but penetrating critique of French attitudes toward the advent of the tank. The report was officially circulated among French officers at Pétain's order. Since de Gaulle was on Pétain's personal staff at that time, he was certainly familiar with Liddell Hart's writings. Within the Army itself, a proposal for creation of armored divisions had been submitted to the General Staff by General Jean-Baptiste Estienne in 1923 and again by General Joseph Doumenc in 1928, and ignored. As for Gaullist legend that it was he who inspired General Heinz Guderian's creation of the Nazi Panzer divisions, in documents captured at the end of World War II there was not one mention of de Gaulle or his writings found in the reports of the German military attachés in Paris from 1932 to 1937. Guderian and his fellow officers had studied the British and the Austrian General Ritter von Eimmansberger much earlier than de Gaulle's book appeared. German General Wilhelm Ritter von Thoma, who was captured in North Africa in 1943, described de Gaulle's writings as "rather up in the clouds," and Liddell Hart wrote that "so far as can be deduced from his hazy outline, the division he pictured would have been a clumsy monstrosity, impossible to maneuver."

But without embellishing the legend, it is clear that de Gaulle perceived the impact that armor would have on French battle during the next war, the desperate need for armored divisions and the urgency of a drastic change in military outlook and doctrine. He was the only Frenchman who fought the military hierarchy, the politicians and the public in his attempts to force reforms and see that a sound, realistic and advanced concept in armored strategy was adopted.

De Gaulle's ideas on armored warfare were neither as original nor as well-developed and thoroughly thought-out as those of other theorists. But his convictions were, and above all he now had a great cause to encompass his heroic ideas and melancholy broodings over the fate of France, the power of men to influence events, his readings in military history, his studies of tactics and battle, and his theories of leadership and power. Far from being intimidated by warnings from on high about the effect of his heresies and political activism on his military career, he pressed on with his views wherever and whenever he could find someone in power to listen.

Early in 1934 Marshal Pétain came out of military retirement to take over as minister of war in a government headed by Gaston Doumergue. He briefly considered including de Gaulle in his personal Cabinet, but others hastily protested that his long-time protégé had too many newfangled and difficult ideas. In any case, Pétain was far more concerned about getting credits to build the Maginot Line than about new concepts of warfare. His sole effort now was to soothe the nation and its leaders with assurances of invulnerability. De Gaulle was no longer a member of the *maison Pétain.*

But at the end of 1934, one of the members of Colonel Mayer's little entourage of the boulevard Montparnasse *brasserie* introduced de Gaulle to Paul Reynaud, a lively and forceful exception to the lackluster prewar politicians. From the outset, he gained Reynaud's ear on the subject of armored divisions—partly by flattery ("I have already tried others—it is either you or no one")—and Reynaud took up the cause. De Gaulle later wrote: "He seemed to me, *par excellence,* qualified for this enterprise. His intelligence was of the caliber to understand the reasons; his talent to make them understood; his courage to sustain them. In addition, well known as he was, Paul Reynaud gave the impression of a man whose future was before him. I saw him, convinced him, and from then on worked with him."

When the Doumergue government fell and Pétain left the Ministry of War in March 1935, Reynaud went before the National Assembly with a long and eloquent speech calling for adoption of de Gaulle's plan for creation of an armored corps of 100,000 professional soldiers. But he was predictably defeated after a speech by the new minister of war, General Joseph-Léon-Marie Maurin, who asked how anyone could think of the French taking the offensive "when we have spent billions to establish a fortified barrier," and then declared: "The government, at least as far as I am concerned, knows perfectly well what the plan of the next war will be." De Gaulle, meanwhile, was denied permission to have his writings on the professional army appear in the official *Revue Militaire Française* on the grounds that "it is inopportune to publish in the *Revue* ideas that risk running counter to, or might induce others to run counter to, the views of the Ministry."

In 1936, when the Popular Front was in power, Premier Léon Blum sent for de Gaulle for a discussion of the ideas he had heard from Reynaud. It was Colonel Mayer, a friend of Blum's, who urged the meeting. Blum, writing his Memoirs in a Vichy prison during the war, recorded:

I saw enter with a calm and even placid ease a man whose height, breadth and frame had something gigantic about them. One felt in him at first contact a man "all of one piece." The man who thus presented himself, who looked at me so calmly, who spoke to me with his slow and measured voice, could by all evidence be occupied at any one time only by one idea, one design, one belief, but then he had to give himself up to it absolutely so that nothing else should enter into consideration. He was probably hardly capable of conceiving that his own convictions should not be fully shared by everyone else.

It was not a successful meeting—de Gaulle for his part recalled that phones kept ringing and Blum complained of the difficulty of concentrating on any one idea even for five minutes. He further depressed Blum by gloomily forecasting military disaster if the Germans succeeded in breaking through the French defenses. For de Gaulle, it was another dead-ended effort with one of the best and most humane of France's prewar premiers.

Blum did suggest to de Gaulle an appointment to the staff of the minister of war, where, presumably, he might be able to exercise more influence on decision-making and policy. But de Gaulle turned this down, telling Blum that he had already been accepted for the next course at France's "school for marshals," the Centre de Hautes Études Militaires. After five years in the corridors of power, he no longer saw much chance of forcing a change in attitudes. As often happened with de Gaulle throughout his career, when he reached a dead end with an idea or a cause, he would retire from that scene to wait for events to change and circumstances to form that would permit him to return to the attack.

He had been promoted to the rank of lieutenant colonel in 1932, after five years as a major, but when his name then came forward at the time of his entry into the Center for Higher Military Studies at the end of 1936 for promotion to full colonel, it was blocked by General Maurice Gamelin, who had succeeded Weygand as commander in chief of the Army and would lead France in war three years later. At this point, Paul Reynaud intervened on de Gaulle's behalf with Blum's minister of war, Édouard Daladier, but it was not until the end of 1937 that Daladier finally got the promotion through against the opposition of the High Command. De Gaulle was a pretty obstreperous case for the military to handle.

Meanwhile he embarked on another writing project that produced a frivolous and final controversy that ended his last ties with Pétain. Ever since Pétain had called him back to Paris from Germany in 1925, de Gaulle had kept the notes and early chapters he had written on the project of an official history of the French Army. Now, at the urging of his friend Colonel Mayer, he decided to resurrect the material, complete it and publish it—as he said in the preface, "as a final warning which, from my modest place, I address to my country on the eve of the cataclysm."

As military writing, La France et son Armée fell well short of this claim. But even before de Gaulle could proceed with the book, he had to seek Pétain's permission. At the outset the marshal objected vigorously that the early chapters were an official study and must remain unpublished and anonymous. De Gaulle paid his last personal call on the marshal, who was then eighty-two, and mollified him with a promise of a dedication. Pétain said he would write it himself. De Gaulle then prepared his own flowery dedication "To Marshal Pétain, who wanted this book written, who directed with his advice the writing of the first five chapters, and thanks to whom the last two are the history of our victory." The book went to press before he notified the marshal of what he had done. Pétain was incensed and wrote the publishers, complaining of inaccuracies in de Gaulle's dedication ("I never wanted the book published"), demanding that the publishers honor the agreement and that his own dedication be substituted. De Gaulle agreed to replace the dedication in the second edition, but the first one hadn't sold out when war was declared in 1939. Pétain went into a sour sulk, calling de Gaulle "that turkey-cock" and "a man without heart," and refused to speak to him when he next saw him at Metz in October 1938. The two men barely exchanged a word the rest of their lives. De Gaulle, with his formidable memory, could not have forgotten his agreement with the marshal. But he shrugged the whole thing off with the remark "The old man is losing his sense of proportion. Nothing and nobody will stop the marshal on the road to senile ambition. Old age is a shipwreck."

*

When Colonel de Gaulle completed his course at Centre de Hautes Études Militaires, he asked for posting to a tank unit and was promptly assigned to command the 507th Tank Regiment, stationed at Metz. The military authorities were happy to see him out of Paris: "You've given us enough trouble with your paper tanks—now go and see what you can do with metal ones." He took up his new command in October 1937. The commander of the Metz Region, a key defensive position in the Maginot Line, was another senior officer destined to cross paths with de Gaulle, General Henri Giraud.

Like all French tank units at that time, the 507th was part of an infantry division. Tanks operated, therefore, only under infantry commanders, in support of infantry and moving at the speed of infantry. Dogma had it that tanks would be knocked out if they got ahead of the infantry. The tragedy of the Battle of France in 1940 was not that the French did not have tanks, but that perfectly good tanks were kept locked up this way in infantry formations instead of in units organized, trained and commanded to do battle as tank divisions against the Panzers. This was the situation that de Gaulle had been fighting in Paris and which he now had to face as a regimental commander in Metz. It was his first experience with tanks in the field, and soon after he had settled in and conducted some field exercises with the 507th, he was writing Captain Nachin:

> I find myself more than ever convinced of the soundness of the ideas which I tried to spread and which, alas, have up till now been listened to far more willingly by the Germans than by my own compatriots. The possibility of maneuver and attack can no longer be demanded on land except from tanks. The age of infantry is finished except as a defensive arm. Artillery keeps its relative value, but from now on it is in support of tanks that it must be used before all else. It remains to recognize these facts and to organize the French Army accordingly—that is to say, an armored corps.

As de Gaulle drove his regiment in training and maneuvers, challenging existing tactical doctrine with his handling of his tanks in field exercises and arguing the results with his superiors, Europe teetered through the appeasement year of 1938 to the brink of war—and then pulled back when Britain and France abandoned Czechoslovakia to Adolf Hitler in the Munich Agreement of September 29. A few days before, de Gaulle wrote from Metz to Paul Reynaud, who by now was leading the antiappeasement forces in the National Assembly: "Events show with terrible clarity how right you have been. As for me, my regiment is ready. I see ahead without the slightest surprise the greatest events in the history of France, and I am sure you are marked to play a predominant role in them. Let me tell you that in any case I shall be—unless I am dead—resolved to serve you if it should please you."

With excruciating slowness, the High Command at last began to give ground on the tank question before the overwhelming evidence of what the Germans were up to, equipping and training their new Panzer formations. In December 1938, three months after Munich, when it was clear to de Gaulle and many other prominent Europeans (though unfortunately not to the men in charge) that war was inevitable, the French Higher War Council finally decided to create two armored divisions, each with four tank battalions. But even this recognition that something had to be done to meet the Panzer threat was hedged with delay. The divisions were authorized, but their creation would be deferred for further de-tailed study and preparation. Meanwhile Colonel de Gaulle was transferred from the 507th Regiment to command of tanks of the 5th Army, stationed along the Rhine in Alsace to support the Maginot Line.

War began on September 1, 1939, but all remained quiet on the western front. Panzer columns rolled across courageous but helpless Poland, which disappeared as a state for the next six years, divided up in three weeks between Hitler and Stalin. De Gaulle, despite his distance from the fighting, could clearly see the speed with which the Panzer-led Blitzkrieg had sliced through all defenses. In November 1939 he submitted to the General Staff a lengthy analytical memoran-dum on the vulnerability of France's long defense front against attack of this kind with armored spearheads. He was not alone. Two other similar analyses came in, unsolicited and unwelcome, from French Air Force General Armengaud, who was in Poland as an attaché and saw some of the fighting before escaping via Denmark, and from the head of the Deuxième Bureau Intelligence Section, Colonel Gauche. Ironically, the officer who received de Gaulle's report was none other than General Dufieux, who had been commandant of the École Supérieure at the time of de Gaulle's secondary passing grade in 1924. Now inspector general of infantry and tanks, he gave de Gaulle another secondary grade, noting on his memoran-dum: "These conclusions, in the present state of the question, are to be rejected."

So the 1939 winter of the Phony War gave way to the fateful spring of 1940. In mid-March, as Hitler prepared to launch the Nazi armies into Denmark and Norway, the government of Édouard Daladier fell and Paul Reynaud became premier of the ninety-eighth and next-to-last government of the Third Republic. He summoned de Gaulle to Paris immediately and asked him to draft his first statement of aims of the new government, which he then read to the National Assembly virtually without change. Next, Reynaud sought to include de Gaulle in a newly created Conseil de Guerre with the title of undersecretary of state, but Daladier and the Radicals objected and threatened to withdraw their support if this happened. Reynaud could not risk falling overnight, so de Gaulle took a train back to Wagenbourg, his headquarters in Alsace, to await events.

But first he stopped at Supreme Headquarters at the Château de Vincennes on the outskirts of Paris where General Gamelin, who had held up his promotion three years before, was ensconced in security, isolation and splendor. Gamelin offhandedly told de Gaulle that the High Command had decided to double the number of armored divisions—from two to four—and that he would be given command of one of the new formations beginning May 15. De Gaulle expressed his appreciation, but made a few gloomy comments about the military outlook. Gamelin told him: "I understand your satisfaction. But as for your worries, I do not believe them justified."

Back at his post with the 5th Army tanks, de Gaulle wrote another letter to Reynaud on May 3, 1940—an urgent, almost desperate appeal for action in the face of an attack that was only a week away, coupled with a rather unctuous appeal for a place in the government.

> The events in Norway, following those in Poland, demonstrate that today no military enterprise is possible except in the function and on the scale of available mechanized forces. The French military system is conceived, organized, armed and commanded on the opposite principle of this law of modern warfare. There is no necessity more absolute or more urgent than that of radically reforming this system. The military, because of its inherent conformity, will not reform itself on its own.
>
> This is above all an affair of state. A statesman is needed. . . . You alone . . . by reason of your situation, your personality, and the position you have taken in this matter—and taken alone during the past six years—can and must see the task through. I will take the liberty of adding that in making this question the major concern of your government, you would change the atmosphere within the government and in the country and would bring into play trump cards that have not yet been used. From now on, each day that passes, each event, helps our doctrine, but, alas, also aids the enemy, who is also putting it into practice.
>
> I hardly need say that I have no greater ambition than the honor of serving you in this capital undertaking as soon as you judge that the moment has arrived for it.

The moment was not far away. Destiny was in the making, and Colonel de Gaulle was not one to await its unfolding silently in the ranks.

II

COMBAT

FOUR

THE FALL OF FRANCE

On April 9, 1940, Denmark surrendered to Hitler before breakfast, barely five hours after the first Nazi troops crossed its land borders and disembarked in Copenhagen harbor in darkness, unopposed. Norway, invaded the same day, was far different terrain and a different people. The king, most of the government ministers and all but two members of the Parliament escaped from Oslo before the Nazis could take the city. They rejected Hitler's ultimatum to surrender and began a long withdrawal to the far north, with the little Norwegian Army fighting a series of weak but often heroic rearguard actions to delay and harass the advancing Germans. The end finally came with a military armistice on June 8, 1940, after King Haakon and his ministers had sailed in a British warship from Tromsø near the North Cape to England. There they constituted one of the first wartime governments-in-exile, and began the slow task of rallying a resistance movement at home and carrying on at the side of the British in fighting the war.

On May 10 the Nazi armies were unleashed against Holland, Belgium and Luxembourg, ignoring their neutrality, and France. The center of Rotterdam was pounded into ruins in history's first experiment in terror bombing. The Wehrmacht began a vast wheeling movement through Holland and Belgium to descend on France from the northeast, by way of those flat, open approaches that de Gaulle had written about in his 1925 study for Pétain on fortifications in French history. On May 13, as this advance got rolling in the north, the two top Panzer generals—Heinz Guderian and Erwin Rommel—opened a new front farther south with an attack straight into eastern France at the town of Sedan, below the Belgian border on the edge of the Ardennes Forest. It was at Sedan that Bismarck's armies attacked at the start of the Franco-Prussian War in 1870 and trapped and defeated the French under Napoleon III.

On May 11, as this fury burst, de Gaulle received orders to report to Paris immediately to take command of the new 4th Armored Division, as promised by General Gamelin a few weeks earlier. He first had to assemble a divisional staff at a temporary headquarters at Le Vésinet, in suburban Paris, because the division itself did not yet exist. It was being put together out of bits and pieces of units from various points in France, ordered to converge near the town of Laon to the northeast of Paris. On May 15, de Gaulle was summoned to GHQ and ordered to go into action with this nonexistent force as quickly as possible on the advancing flank of Guderian's Panzer columns, with the aim of checking any German turn southward in the direction of Paris until major reinforcements could arrive to hold a defense line on the Aisne.

De Gaulle sped to Laon on the sixteenth and began an immediate reconnaissance to determine where he would attack. By a small miracle of staff work in the midst of debacle, the units that were to make up his division did indeed begin to materialize late that day. Three tank battalions arrived, but only one of them had ever been on maneuvers. Many of the crews had been in a tank only four hours— the time it took to get to Laon. Officers who were to take command met their men for the first time on the battlefield. There were no tank radios, and de Gaulle had to rely on motorcycle dispatch riders to communicate with his company commanders. To build up his division, he preempted command of some scattered troops of a cavalry division permanently stationed in Laon, along with an independent artillery group that he found in the town, forgotten by GHQ and without orders. All around, as he reconnoitered the roads, there was sickening chaos— refugees streaming south from Belgium, French soldiers who had been routed by the Nazis and ordered contemptuously to throw away their weapons and head south, get out of the way, "No time to take you prisoner." Of this bitter scene, de Gaulle wrote in his Memoirs:

> At the sight of those bewildered people and of those routed soldiers, I felt myself carried away by a boundless fury. "Ah! It's too stupid! The war is beginning as badly as it possibly could. So it must go on. The world is wide. If I live, I will fight, wherever I must, as long as I must, until the enemy is defeated and the national stain is washed clean." All I have managed to do since was resolved upon that day.

On the morning of May 17, de Gaulle threw his newly arrived tank battalions, with minimal infantry support, into action in an attack to the northeast of Laon to the town of Montcornet, twenty miles away, a key road-junction on the south of Guderian's advance. As yet, the division had no artillery, no antiaircraft guns, no major infantry units, and it could not call for air support even if good communications had existed. But the day began well for de Gaulle, with his tanks sweeping scattered and surprised German infantry screening forces before them as they sped toward Montcornet. By midafternoon, the French had reached their objective.

Meanwhile, around midday, de Gaulle received his first infantry unit, a battalion of *chasseurs*, his old command in Germany in 1927. He rushed it immediately up the flank of the tank advance to deal with a pocket of German opposition that the tanks had bypassed at the village of Chèvres. By late afternoon another unit had reached the 4th Armored Division, a reconnaissance regiment of the 10th Cuirassiers, and de Gaulle ordered them all the way to Montcornet to reinforce his tanks, which were lodged in the town but beginning to come under German artillery fire. Throughout the day, this unexpected dash from the French had thrown the Germans into confusion and uncertainty as to how big a force was hitting their vulnerable flank. But de Gaulle, alas, had no artillery or weight or staying power to put behind his audacious advance and he knew it. His orders, moreover, were to limit his operations to delaying attacks and to keep his division intact. So, at the end of the day, his tanks were ordered back from Montcornet, with the Cuirassiers covering the withdrawal as night fell.

The 4th Armored Division was short on artillery, antiaircraft guns and radios, and its units had never even seen each other before, but they all knew they had a commander. Jean-Raymond Tournoux, journalist-biographer and indefatigable collector of de Gaulle anecdotes and minutiae, records this from an interview with a division officer:

> He was admired and feared, but no feeling of affection for him. But his prestige was overwhelming. He would dash to any point where things were going badly. If an attack was to be launched, he listened to no objections, even though they might be well founded. He never tired, and you saw him everywhere—that leather jacket, his casque and the inevitable cigarette. He was not an easy man to be with, was aloof and serious, didn't talk much, and if questioned would shake off the tiresome interlocutor with, "You don't ask a brigadier general questions" or "Whether captain or major, you have the same opinion as your brigadier." He was tough, ruthless, inhuman, letting nothing and nobody count except the battle.

The first action, according to de Gaulle, cost the Germans "several hundred dead and plenty of burnt-out trucks and vehicles on the field; we took 130 prisoners and lost fewer than 200 men." All the same, the action has been overblown in Gaullist legend, as in other instances in his life and career. The facts of his achievements should have been impressive enough without embellishment. Legend has it that de Gaulle's attack temporarily halted Guderian and delayed the drive of the German Army toward Paris. Guderian did indeed pause on May 17, but it was not because of de Gaulle. It was a direct order from Hitler, who had begun to worry that his army was getting too far out in front of the main advance and outrunning support columns and supplies. When Guderian received this order on the night of the sixteenth, he protested immediately to his commander, Paul von Kleist. Guderian got a revision of the order, permitting him to continue "reconnaissance in force" but not to move his Corps Headquarters. This was the situation when de Gaulle's armor hit him on the morning of the seventeenth. The attack did cause confusion enough among the Germans for most of the day, however.

Unknown to the French defenders, a German divisional command post had been established at the village of Lislet, barely a mile from Montcornet. Moreover, the German commander, General Kirchner, had been injured in a road accident and was running the division from a stretcher, refusing to relinquish command. This was the situation when de Gaulle's tanks suddenly cut into the German rear area that morning, heading for Montcornet. The German divisional staff reacted quickly. Newly arrived tanks heading west were swung around to the south to meet the French, and artillery was quickly recalled to the flank. De Gaulle had been audacious in mounting the attack with a tank force that had never even maneuvered together, and he was also certainly right to withdraw. One of his tank commanders, Captain Idée, kept a diary and recorded: "1900 hours. Petrol running low. The B tanks have just turned about. They are leaving Lislet. The infantry has not been able to follow them, and what can we do without them? There must be some infiltration at our rear. The enemy platoon commanders have a terribly enterprising air about them."

By the time the retreat got under way, Stuka dive bombers had also been brought into action against de Gaulle's column. So by nightfall on the seventeenth, the 4th Armored Division was back where it started, on the outskirts of Laon. But morale was high. As a scratch unit, it had mounted one of the very few successful armored attacks against the Germans during the entire Battle of France. On the nineteenth, after a day's rest and reconnaissance, as Guderian resumed his advance deeper into French territory, de Gaulle attacked for a second time on his southern flank—this time north of Laon toward the town of Crécy. Two more tank squadrons and an artillery regiment had reached the 4th Division, but the Germans of course were vastly stronger. They held de Gaulle at a river crossing, and in the early afternoon he received orders not to attempt any further advances. He broke off action slowly during the next twenty-four hours, still hoping he could delay any German turn toward the south and Paris.

All hope of a French defensive line on the Aisne had evaporated, and Guderian pushed to the Somme as well, seizing Amiens and Abbeville on May 20. Two days later, de Gaulle's division was ordered to shift from the southern flank all the way around to the west to try to contain the German thrust head-on outside Abbeville. It was a movement of some 150 miles for an untrained outfit under chaotic conditions of choked roads and delayed supplies. While the movement was under way, on May 25 de Gaulle received formal notification of his promotion to brigadier general. He had also picked up two more tank battalions, a heavy artillery group, an antiaircraft battery and two more infantry units. He now had about 140 tanks in all, and the 4th Armored was beginning to look like a real division.

Reaching position at Abbeville, de Gaulle decided on an immediate attack on the evening of May 27 in order to avoid being spotted by the relentless German reconnaissance aircraft, which had freedom of the skies. In the next three days, he drove the enemy back from a strip of territory about ten miles deep west of Abbeville. His division fought without reinforcements or relief while the Germans threw fresh troops into the line to stem the attack. Another 500 German prisoners were taken. Then, on May 30, the 4th Armored was relieved by the 51st Scottish Division, freshly arrived in France.

If none of de Gaulle's attacks had any effect on the outcome of the Battle of France, the fact remains that his division, conjured up out of bits and pieces in the midst of the greatest debacle of World War II, was the only one of France's four armored divisions to carry out any notable actions. Moreover, everything they accomplished was owing to the leadership and drive of its commanding officer. In two weeks, starting with a couple of staff officers and dispatch riders, de Gaulle had created an imposing fighting force out of units, officers and men who had never seen each other before.

> During those difficult hours [he wrote in his Memoirs], I could not help but imagine what the mechanized army of which I had so long dreamed could have done. If it had been there to debouch suddenly, the advance of the Panzer divisions would have been halted instantly, serious confusion caused in the rear areas, and the northern group of our armies enabled to join up once more with those of the center and the east.

But all was now dissolving in disaster when de Gaulle received a telegram on the night of June 5 instructing him to leave for Paris immediately. Paul Reynaud, reshuffling his government for the last time, had taken up de Gaulle's appeal to serve and was naming him undersecretary of state for national defense.

*

By the time de Gaulle reached Paris, King Leopold of Belgium had surrendered, as had Holland, but Queen Wilhelmina had escaped with a few ministers to London. Grand Duchess Charlotte of Luxembourg had also managed to flee her tiny realm, which was subsequently annexed by Hitler. With the Belgian surrender leaving a gaping hole between British and French forces on the northeastern front, the British Army fell back to Dunkirk. But Hitler again halted his Panzers, and during this respite, in the five days from May 29 to June 4, the British managed to evacuate 335,000 troops from Dunkirk, including 120,000 French.

Meanwhile Weygand had succeeded Gamelin as French supreme commander. Reynaud had also recalled Pétain from Madrid, where he was serving as ambassador, to become a vice premier. Before leaving Madrid, Pétain had a final meeting with Generalissimo Francisco Franco, and the Spanish leader urged him not to join a government facing a defeat for which he would not be responsible. Pétain replied: "I know, but my country is calling me and it is my duty to go. It will perhaps be the last service I can render."

On the morning of June 6 de Gaulle went to see Reynaud. "In my cantonment in Picardy I had no illusions," he wrote, "but I was determined not to abandon hope. If the situation could not be restored in the homeland, it must be re-established elsewhere. The Empire was there, the fleet to protect it." He pressed this view on Reynaud, pointing out that, logically, Reynaud's determination to fight on required a clear policy to fit, and this meant preparation for moving the government to North Africa. He proposed that he go to London to discuss the situation and this eventuality with the British. Reynaud agreed and gave him instructions to request again additional air squadrons from Britain.

While preparations for the trip were underway, de Gaulle met with Weygand at GHQ in Vincennes on June 7. Weygand was then a spry seventy-three-year-old, but in all his military career this was the first time he had commanded troops in battle. He made his reputation as chief of staff to Marshal Ferdinand Foch in the First World War and spent his Army life as a staff officer. He had been recalled from the Middle East supposedly to restore the shattered front and revitalize the troops, but he was totally defeatist. He greeted de Gaulle with the news that the Germans were now across the Somme in force, and de Gaulle replied:

"All right! They're crossing the Somme. And then?"

"Then? The Seine and the Marne."

"Yes—and then?"

"Then? But that's the end!"

"The end? What do you mean? And the world? And the Empire?"

"The Empire? But that's childish! As for the world, when I've been beaten here, England won't wait a week before negotiating with the Reich!"

*

For the next turbulent ten days, the future of France depended on a ceaseless battle between Weygand and de Gaulle to gain control of Reynaud and force him to make a decision, Weygand having made up his mind on an armistice, and de Gaulle having resolutely determined that France must fight on at all costs and that the government move to Algiers to carry on the war from its overseas territories. The Battle of France was effectively over, and Reynaud wavered, now ordering preparations for evacuation of the government, now asking the British what they might do if France decided to seek an armistice. But Weygand had the backing of Pétain, Paul Baudouin, who was now at the Quai d'Orsay, and a coterie of appeasement-minded ministers, while de Gaulle was fighting a lone battle. In seeking to construct a broad government to prosecute the war, Reynaud had put himself into a straitjacket laced up by defeatists. In the end he could procrastinate no longer, and fell. All of this has been examined at length by an endless procession of participants and historians from Winston Churchill to Weygand, but the prime source for de Gaulle's actions and attitudes remains his Memoirs.

He returned to Paris from his Vincennes meeting with Weygand and at once urged Reynaud to find a new commander in chief who would be committed to fighting on at the instructions of the government instead of trying to influence the government. He recommended General Charles Huntziger, and Reynaud, typically, approved in principle but said an actual decision would have to wait.

On June 9 de Gaulle arrived in London for the first time—"a look of tranquility, almost indifference; the streets and parks full of people peacefully out for a walk; the mass of the population with no idea of the gravity of events in France. It was plain that to English minds, the Channel was still wide."

He went at once to No. 10 Downing Street to meet Winston Churchill for the first time, and although no doubt he pondered that "first impression" for years before writing his Memoirs in 1953, it was a word picture and a judgment deeply felt and genuine:

The impression he gave me confirmed my conviction that Great Britain, led by such a fighter, would not flinch. Mr. Churchill seemed to me to be equal to the rudest task, provided it also had grandeur. The assurance of his judgment, his wide culture, the knowledge he had of most of the nations and men involved, and finally his passion for the problems proper to war, found in war their full scope. Above all, he was fitted by his character to act, to take risks, to play the part totally without scruple. In short, I found him well in the saddle as guide and chief. The harsh and painful incidents that often rose between us, because of the friction between our two characters, the opposition of some of the interests of our two countries, and the unfair advantage taken by England of wounded France, have influenced my attitude toward the prime minister, but not my judgment. Winston Churchill appeared to me, from one end of the drama to the other, as the great champion of a great enterprise and the great artist of a great History.

After the chaos of battle, the defeatism of Weygand, the waffling politics of Reynaud, in London de Gaulle found a man after his own heart. Churchill does not mention that first meeting in his War History—not surprisingly, since the brief visit of a brigadier general and junior French minister in the midst of a torrent of meetings, events and decisions could easily have been overlooked. In accordance with Reynaud's instructions, de Gaulle once again asked for the transfer of more Royal Air Force squadrons to France, this time to be flown all the way south of the Loire, far west of Paris, and again Churchill categorically refused. But he did promise to move a Canadian division to France and leave the 51st Scottish Division, which had relieved de Gaulle's division at Abbeville and had not retreated to Dunkirk, in line to fight on. He also promised to ship French troops evacuated from Dunkirk back to France as quickly as possible with such equipment as Britain could spare to rejoin the fight.

After a round of meetings with British ministers and senior staff chiefs, de Gaulle flew back to Paris that evening, taking a wide detour around the fighting front now approaching the Seine, and landing at Le Bourget just after it had been bombed. He reported to Reynaud at his apartment, there to be greeted with news from the French ambassador to Italy that Mussolini would be declaring war at any moment. Once again de Gaulle urged the only practical course—a maximum military effort and evacuation of the government to North Africa as soon as possible.

On June 10—"a day of agony" in de Gaulle's phrase, when the government quit Paris—he was closeted with Reynaud, preparing a statement that the premier was to broadcast, when General Weygand arrived. Weygand had not been summoned, nor had he asked for a meeting, and his arrival was a surprise to Reynaud, but Weygand plunged in at once. The situation, he said, was now hopeless and the government must ask for an armistice without delay. He had even brought with him a written document because, he said, "everyone's responsibilities must be clearly established and for that reason I am putting my opinion on paper and handing you this note." Weygand produced the text of this document in his Memoirs, pointing out that the document itself as yet made no mention of an armistice, but the thrust and intention was clear enough. Reynaud disputed Weygand's opinion, and de Gaulle interjected that "there are other possibilities"—to which Weygand responded somewhat sarcastically, "Have *you* something to suggest?"

De Gaulle drew himself up and replied: "The government has no suggestions to make, but orders to give. I am sure it will give them."

But alas, it did not. The only order of that day was to burn files and head south—first to Orléans and then to the town of Briare, where Weygand was setting up a new GHQ. Meanwhile, the High Command, acting on its own with government approval coming afterward, declared Paris an open city.

Toward midnight, de Gaulle and Reynaud left Paris together in a car for Orléans—the last time de Gaulle would see the capital for more than four years. It took all night over choked roads to make what is normally a drive of about two hours. On arrival at the Préfecture in Orléans, they learned to their surprise that Weygand, acting on his own in what clearly was a matter for the premier, had sent a message to London through military channels asking Churchill to come at once to France to confer on the situation. In the face of this breach of authority, de Gaulle again urged Reynaud to replace Weygand with Huntziger, and again Reynaud agreed and then immediately prevaricated.

"You go and see him alone and discuss it and I will prepare for the meeting with Churchill. We will meet at Briare," he told de Gaulle. Accordingly, de Gaulle spent the morning finding Huntziger at his headquarters southeast of Paris. He told him that with the Battle of France "virtually lost," it was the intention of the government to continue the war from Africa with all the resources that could be moved there, and that Weygand was "not the man to carry this out." Would he agree to take command? Huntziger said yes immediately. De Gaulle told him that he would be receiving the government's instructions. But by the time de Gaulle got back to Briare, all thought of a change of command had evaporated from Reynaud's mind.

There in the conference room, as they waited for Churchill and the British party to assemble, de Gaulle was face to face with Marshal Pétain for the first time since Pétain had refused to speak to him at Metz in 1938. De Gaulle saluted and Pétain simply said rather gruffly, "You are a general! I don't congratulate you. What good are ranks in defeat?"

The Briare conference began in the early evening of Tuesday, June 11, and centered on a long, pessimistic review of the military situation from General Weygand. There was no open mention of an armistice yet, although Reynaud told Churchill during the dinner which followed that Pétain had told him an armistice would be necessary and had written a paper on the subject "which he has not yet handed to me—he is still ashamed to do it." To the British, Reynaud no longer seemed in control either of events or of his government. De Gaulle sat at the conference table but did not intervene in the discussions, listening in frozen, expressionless immobility, according to Major General Sir Edward Spears, who was taking notes for the British side: "His bearing alone among his compatriots matched the calm, healthy phlegm of the British." At dinner, de Gaulle was seated next to Churchill. De Gaulle later wrote, in his elliptical style: "Our conversation fortified my confidence in his strength and purpose. He himself, no doubt, went away with the feeling that de Gaulle, though without means, was no less resolute."

The two sides met again next morning for another inconclusive discussion, this time centering on yet another appeal from the French for transfer of more British air squadrons. As Churchill noted dryly: "They ought to have been ashamed to support even tacitly Weygand's demand for our last twenty-five squadrons, when he had made up his mind that all was lost and France should give in." In midmorning, Churchill and his party took off for England. They could see the flames of battle below at Le Havre as they reached the Channel.

De Gaulle did not attend this second round of talks with the British. He was closeted with a French staff officer working on plans for the transportation of the government and whatever military supplies and forces could be gotten away from France to North Africa. He completed these standby operational orders at the end of the day and then sought out Reynaud—only to find him locked in an argument with his ministers over where the government should head next.

The choice now was either Bordeaux or Quimper, a small provincial capital on the Atlantic on the southern coast of the Brittany peninsula. Quimper was de Gaulle's choice simply because he reasoned that once the government removed there it would in the end be forced to evacuate and put out to sea, and once out to sea it could go only to North Africa. But those who were working for capitulation argued fiercely for Bordeaux. Reynaud decided to sleep on it and asked de Gaulle to report to him early on the morning of Thursday, June 13.

The two men then went over the arguments of Bordeaux or Quimper again, until Reynaud finally declared that he had to accept the view of the majority of his ministers. Next de Gaulle pleaded with him to sign the operational orders that he had prepared to set in motion organizing transportation and evacuation for North Africa. But all Reynaud was prepared to do was draft a formal letter to Weygand instructing him "to hold out as long as possible in the Massif Central and in Brittany," followed by a declaration that if this failed, the government would "install ourselves and organize the struggle in the Empire, making use of the freedom of the seas." A declaration of intent was not an operational order to act, and it was certainly not enough to stop Weygand in his determination to abandon the fight as quickly as possible.

Meanwhile, as Reynaud and de Gaulle were talking, a message from Reynaud had gone to London asking for another meeting with Churchill as quickly as possible. Churchill accepted at once and left London midmorning Thursday, arriving at Tours, where the meeting was to take place at lunchtime. De Gaulle was not told by Reynaud, who apparently did not want him present, but he was alerted by Reynaud's staff when word got out that Churchill had arrived. He sped immediately from the château where he had been working to Tours, and arrived at the Préfecture, site of the meeting, just as the conference was recessing to allow the British to discuss alone what they had heard.

Only Reynaud and Baudouin had been present on the French side, but Reynaud had informed Churchill that Weygand was now insisting on an armistice. He had called the meeting to ask what Britain's attitude in this case would be, in view of the solemn mutual pledge of the two countries at the outbreak of the war not to conclude a separate peace until victory. Churchill, replying in grave and measured tones, had said that no matter what course France chose, "England will not retire from the struggle," and that "in no case would Britain waste time and energy in reproaches and recriminations." But this, he said, was a very different matter from becoming a consenting party to a peace made in contravention of an agreement so recently concluded. He ended by declaring that "if England won the war, France would be restored in her dignity and in her greatness."

De Gaulle had missed all this, and when the meeting resumed, the British had decided to cut off further discussion quickly and return home. With de Gaulle now at the table, Churchill asked for a precise guarantee that the French Fleet would never be handed over to the Germans, whatever France sought in the way of an armistice. He also asked that some 400 German aviators who had been taken prisoner be handed over to the British immediately so they could not return to Germany to fly against England. The French, apparently a little relieved to be let off the hook so easily, immediately promised both.

De Gaulle was appalled, and in some agitation sought out Reynaud when the conference broke up to demand whether it was possible that he had really proposed an armistice. Reynaud, waffling in embarrassment, told him: "Certainly not, but we must give the British a shock to get more help out of them." De Gaulle says that "he could not take this as valid," and that he was also upset with Churchill for showing such sympathy as he did and thereby abetting the defeatists. All the same, de Gaulle had clearly made his mark on Churchill by now, who glided up to him, shook his hand goodbye, and murmured in French: *"L'homme du destin."* It was a sentiment that de Gaulle certainly shared.

*

That evening, after the departure of the British, de Gaulle decided to resign from the Reynaud Cabinet. He had failed to get Weygand replaced by Huntziger, he had failed to get a clear and unequivocal order out of Reynaud on evacuation orders for North Africa and now the premier was giving way on an armistice as well. He drafted a letter of resignation, but one of his staff alerted Georges Mandel, the minister of the interior, about his intention. Mandel, a Jew with a strong antiappeasement record, was one of the few in the Cabinet trying to stem the tide of defeat, but his post as interior minister left him outside the circle of decision-making and power. Within months after the surrender, he was arrested and imprisoned by the Vichy government, turned over to the Germans, then returned by the Germans to Vichy after more than two years in a concentration camp, and finally murdered by the Vichy police in 1944. Mandel sent for de Gaulle on the night of June 13 and begged him not to leave the government. Like de Gaulle, he was determined that the fight go on, and he argued that it was not yet final whether they could get the government to move to Algiers or not. "In any case," he argued, "we are only at the beginning of a world war. You will have great duties to fulfill, but with the advantage of being, in the midst of all of us, an untarnished man. Think only of what has to be done for France, and consider that, in certain circumstances, your present position may make things easier for you."

De Gaulle, who did not usually appreciate advice, was grateful on this occasion, for he changed his mind—which he usually did not do either, once he had taken a position. Mandel was right—it was only by remaining in the government for the next few vital days that he was able, in the end, to play the role he did. Had de Gaulle quit on the night of June 13, as he had intended, history would have passed him by.

He spent June 14, along with the rest of the government, making his way to Bordeaux, and when he reached the city late in the afternoon he found Reynaud installed at the headquarters of the local military command. At once, despite what had happened at Tours the day before, de Gaulle resumed his incessant theme, telling Reynaud first of all that he himself would refuse to submit to any armistice, and that "you must get to Algiers as quickly as possible" or be submerged by defeat.

At this eleventh hour, Reynaud again agreed—he would go to Algiers. In that case, de Gaulle said, transportation must be arranged and this meant British help. He proposed another trip to London. Again Reynaud agreed, with the parting works: "You will rejoin me in Algiers."

De Gaulle went off to the Hôtel Splendide for a hasty dinner with his aide, Geoffroy de Courcel, who was to remain close to him for the rest of his life. There they found Pétain dining also. As the meal ended, de Gaulle went over and saluted the marshal, who rose silently, shook his hand briefly and sat down without exchanging a word. It was the last time the two men saw each other. De Gaulle and Courcel drove through the night to the city of Rennes to meet the local military commanders and give instructions to prepare plans for a "Brittany redoubt" into which the government would withdraw and troops would be ordered to retreat, to be taken off from the Brittany ports for North Africa. He drove on to reach Brest on the afternoon of the fifteenth, and went aboard a French destroyer that was also taking a group of scientists and a precious shipment of heavy water, vital in atomic research, to England. They sailed for Plymouth, and de Gaulle was flown to London.

While de Gaulle was traveling across Brittany, the last act began to unfold in Bordeaux. Reynaud, still temporarily buoyed up by his pledge to de Gaulle to rejoin him in Algiers, held a Cabinet meeting and then summoned Weygand for a "final decision."

"The ministers," he informed Weygand, "are for the solution of a capitulation of the Army alone, and this capitulation should be requested by the commander in chief." This, he pointed out to Weygand, is what already had happened in Holland and Norway, where the armies had finally surrendered but governments were still carrying on the war, and it was his intention to leave for Algiers.

At this, Weygand went into a near apoplexy of indignation and protest. Having worked assiduously ever since taking command of the French forces to abandon the fight and engineer an armistice, he now indignantly asserted that "never would I inflict such shame on our flags" by asking for it himself as commander in chief. He told Reynaud that he was deceiving himself if he thought that in ordering him all the way back from the Middle East to take command he had someone ready to do any sort of job. No one, he said, could force him to commit a "dishonorable act." It was the government that had led France into the war and therefore cessation of hostilities was the business of the government. "So let the government make up its mind to shoulder all its responsibilities!" With that, he turned on his heel and walked out on the premier.

In 1918, as chief of staff to Foch, it had fallen to Weygand to dictate the armistice terms to the German High Command in the famous railway car in Compiègne Forest. For the rest of his life, he carried with him the briefcase in which those documents had rested. As the debacle unfolded in 1940, he would refer to the armistice, and as his own Memoirs show, he was subconsciously if not consciously obsessed by the specter of experiencing what he had done to the Germans on November 11, 1918. To avoid this, to save his obtuse sense of honor while sinking in dishonor, he would force the government to take responsibility for the catastrophe he had helped to bring about.

In the end, it fell to the unfortunate Huntziger, the officer de Gaulle tried to place in Supreme Command, to sign the armistice terms in the same railway car in Compiègne Forest in a replay of 1918 that was Hitler's ultimate revenge. Huntziger died in an air crash on a flight to North Africa in 1941. Weygand, meanwhile, left Bordeaux after his extraordinary scene with Reynaud and boarded his private train for an overnight trip to Vichy, where his new GHQ was already being installed.

*

Sunday, June 16, 1940—"a day of lost opportunities" in the words of Jean Monnet, another extraordinary Frenchman who was then in London, where he was chairman of a joint Anglo-French Coordinating Committee charged with economic direction of the war effort. Monnet had also served as head of a French purchasing mission and member of a joint transportation committee in London during the First World War and was a man of wide international experience whose impact on history across nearly fifty years of this century was out of all proportion to any job he ever held. He was not a man of power, but he was a man of ideas and decisive influence. As the extent of the catastrophe overtaking France became clear, Monnet had conceived of a political stroke of breathtaking boldness to retrieve the situation and pull France back from the abyss into which it was plunging—a joint British-French declaration of "indissoluble union," with joint citizenship, a joint parliament, and joint "organs of defense, foreign, financial and economic policies." With indefatigable energy and a rare knowledge of the British and how they work, Monnet had made remarkable progress behind the scenes in working out a draft of his proposal and getting it placed on Churchill's Cabinet agenda by the time de Gaulle arrived in London.

De Gaulle telephoned Monnet on reaching London from Plymouth, and then arrived at Monnet's apartment for a late dinner Saturday night. Monnet's wife greeted him, and the General lapsed into a deep and embarrassing silence, waiting for Monnet to arrive. Finally Madame Monnet inquired politely how long de Gaulle's mission to London would last, and he replied: "I am not here on a mission, Madame. I am here to save the honor of France."

Monnet arrived, and de Gaulle plunged in at once, telling him that although in London officially to organize transportation for a move by the government to North Africa, he had in fact concluded that nothing more could be done in France and had already decided to stay in Britain. Monnet then countered by disclosing how far he had gotten with his Anglo-French Unity plan, which had been put before the British Cabinet that same afternoon. But, Monnet said, what the plan clearly required next was the support of someone in the French government—and this de Gaulle could furnish in his capacity as one of Reynaud's ministers. Of the plan, de Gaulle wrote:

> It was clear to me at once that the grandeur of the thing in any case made its rapid realization impossible. It was obvious that one could not, by an exchange of notes, even in principle fuse England and France together, including their institutions, their interests and their Empires, supposing this were desirable. But the offer did involve a manifestation of solidarity which might take on real significance. Above all, I thought, like M. Monnet, that the proposal was of a nature to provide Paul Reynaud, in the supreme crisis in which he was plunged, with an element of comfort, and, vis-à-vis his ministers, an argument for tenacity. I consented, therefore, to do what I could with Mr. Churchill to get him to adopt it.

Sunday morning, de Gaulle first dealt quickly with some transport questions—diverting an enormous cargo of arms aboard the French vessel *Pasteur* from Bordeaux to a British port; finding the British Admiralty "sincerely anxious to strengthen our means of getting our troops away." He then joined Monnet and Sir Robert Vansittart from the Foreign Office for a final polishing of the text of the unity declaration. Meanwhile he telephoned Reynaud to alert him of "something important being prepared" and to urge him not to give in.

But during the night a telegram from Bordeaux had reached the Foreign Office in which Reynaud had formally asked the consent of the British government for release from France's pledge of "no separate peace" so that a request for an armistice could be made to the Germans. Weygand, after his overnight train ride to Vichy, had dealt with a few matters at his new GHQ and on Sunday morning had flown back to Bordeaux, where he immediately sought out Marshal Pétain. From Pétain he got full backing for "the unanimous opinion of the military commanders who rejected the idea of a capitulation and considered it indispensable that the government should ask for an armistice." Pétain told Weygand that Reynaud had fixed a Cabinet meeting for 5 P.M.—by which time he would expect to have a reply from the British on the armistice request. It was still not clear at that point whether Reynaud would insist that the armistice be requested by the military command or whether it would be a government capitulation.

In the midst of these climactic events, Churchill, with true British phlegm, invited General de Gaulle to have lunch with him at the Carlton Club, that citadel of the Conservative Party, while the translators and experts worked over a final agreed text of the Unity Declaration for submission to the British Cabinet. De Gaulle was accompanied by the French ambassador, Corbin, and Churchill had with him his private secretary, Desmond Morton. Just before leaving Downing Street, Churchill had sent off a rather stiff telegram to Bordeaux to be handed to Reynaud by the British ambassador, Sir Ronald Campbell, acceding reluctantly to France's armistice. But as the luncheon began, de Gaulle opened up with a rather strong attack on Churchill over his handling of the meeting at Tours, telling him that his attitude of sympathy and resignation "plays into the hands of those among us who favor capitulation" and expressing "unpleasant surprise that you appear to attach little value to our alliance." De Gaulle concluded that "What you have to do to encourage us in this frightful crisis is something quite different."

De Gaulle says that Churchill "seemed disturbed" by his remarks, and that Churchill held an aside conversation with his private secretary, which de Gaulle believed "was to modify a decision already taken." At this same time, a similar conversation was taking place at another lunch at Monnet's apartment, where Vansittart and René Pleven, Monnet's deputy, were dining. Vansittart disclosed that the telegram releasing France from its separate peace pledge had gone to Bordeaux, and Monnet was appalled: "What—this morning you send a telegram authorizing the French government to sound out terms for a separate armistice and this afternoon you plan to propose indissoluble union? It's crazy! I don't understand. It's got to be stopped!"

At this, Monnet says, they got on a direct line from his London apartment to the Cabinet Office in Downing Street. There are differing versions in Monnet's Memoirs, de Gaulle's Memoirs and Churchill's War History of the precise details of this episode, but the outcome was the same. At these remonstrations from the two Frenchmen, Ambassador Campbell was instructed urgently in Bordeaux to retrieve the telegram acceding to an armistice, which he in fact had already handed to Reynaud as the two luncheons were beginning in London. This Campbell did, not without embarrassment.

After lunch, Churchill and de Gaulle returned to Downing Street, where they were joined by Monnet, Pleven and Vansittart. Churchill went into a meeting of the full British Cabinet shortly before three o'clock to discuss the final draft of the Anglo-French Unity Declaration. His feelings about the document when he first saw it the day before were much as de Gaulle's had been:

> My first reaction was unfavorable [Churchill wrote]. I asked a number of questions of a critical character, and was by no means convinced. However, I was somewhat surprised to see the staid, stolid, experienced politicians of all parties engage themselves so passionately in an immense design whose implications and consequences were not in any way thought out. I did not resist, but yielded easily to these generous surges which carried our resolves to a very high level of unselfishness and undaunted action.

The Sunday Cabinet meeting lasted about an hour, when Churchill strode out with his cigar at a belligerent angle and announced to the French, "We are agreed." From Churchill's desk, de Gaulle got on the telephone immediately and got through to Bordeaux to talk to Reynaud. (How did the phones work in all that chaos?) He told Reynaud what had been agreed with the British and read to him in full the brief text of barely six hundred words. Churchill then got on the line and added: "Hello, Reynaud! De Gaulle is right. Our proposal can have great consequences. He's leaving now. He'll bring you the text. You must hold out. We must meet quickly, tomorrow morning at Concarneau. I'll bring Attlee [Clement Attlee, Labour Party leader and deputy prime minister]. Bring some good generals! Au revoir!"

On this note of excitement, de Gaulle left Downing Street immediately for Hendon Airport in the London suburbs, where Churchill had ordered an RAF liaison plane to be ready to fly him to Bordeaux. A special train was ordered to leave Waterloo Station to take the prime minister, Monnet and an official party to Portsmouth, where they would sail on a British warship for the meeting with Reynaud and the French at Concarneau, near Bordeaux, to seal the indissoluble union. But it was not to be.

Reynaud went into a Cabinet meeting as scheduled at 5 P.M., barely half an hour after his conversation with de Gaulle and Churchill. According to Major General Spears, who had been with him when he received the telephone call from London, Reynaud went to the Cabinet in an almost euphoric mood. He now had a proposal to defeat the defeatists and keep France in the war. Spears was optimistic, but when the Cabinet meeting lasted beyond one hour, his optimism began to fade. Finally, at 7:30 P.M., Campbell and Spears were summoned to the government headquarters. As they entered the building they were met by Reynaud's chef de cabinet, Roland de Margerie, who informed them: "He is going to tell you that he is going to resign." Marshal Pétain would form a new government.

Churchill, Monnet and the rest of the official party had boarded the special train at Waterloo Station for the journey to Portsmouth when a messenger rushed from Downing Street with the news that Reynaud had fallen and the trip was off. Churchill wrote that he returned to Downing Street "with a heavy heart."

De Gaulle, meanwhile, was airborne while all this was going on. He landed at Bordeaux airport at 9:30 P.M., to be met by two officers from his office with the same fateful news. He said nothing, but knew at once that he must return to London in the morning. He was certain that his arrest would be ordered once a Pétain government took over, and in any case everything that he had said and done for the past tumultuous weeks committed him to continuing the fight somewhere if France gave up.

As darkness settled over Bordeaux, he made his way to Reynaud's office, and was standing in the hallway when Spears and Campbell arrived for a last meeting with the fallen premier. They made hasty arrangement with de Gaulle to meet later at the hotel where the British embassy was functioning. After they left, de Gaulle then saw Reynaud for a last time—"the spectacle of that man's high value, ground down unjustly by too great a weight of events, was a tragic one," he wrote—more generously than he dealt with others more deserving. It was all over, and he informed Reynaud that he would return to London in the morning. Reynaud gave him all the secret funds that he still possessed in his government safe—100,000 francs, worth only about $500 after the collapse of France.

Next de Gaulle sought out de Margerie and asked him urgently to get passports to his wife and children at the town where they were living in Brittany so they could join him in London. There were three de Gaulle children now, Philippe, Elizabeth and Anne. Anne was mentally defective and a precious and poignant burden to her father. After the outbreak of the war, he had moved the family from the country home that he had bought in 1933 at Colombey-les-Deux-Églises in eastern France to the safer distance of Brittany, where his aging mother was also living.

Before the debacle, de Gaulle had confided to his wife his intention to go to London if the Germans overran France. She was to join him there with the children if that happened. The passports reached her forty-eight hours later, and she set out immediately for Brest. She just missed the next-to-last ship out of the harbor, which was fortunate because it was sunk. She got aboard the last ship to leave before the Germans marched in, and it arrived safely at Plymouth.

Late Sunday night de Gaulle met with Spears and Campbell, and Spears telephoned Churchill to ask permission to accompany de Gaulle back to London. Churchill was reluctant to allow Spears to abandon his post as military liaison officer with the French, but finally gave his grudging consent. De Gaulle and Spears then arranged to drive to the airport together in the morning in Spears' official car, as if de Gaulle would be seeing the British General off. Spears had an anxious wait until de Gaulle arrived shortly before 8 A.M. Monday with Courcel. The Bordeaux airport was jammed with small craft, but they found the little RAF plane and loaded up. The pilot went aboard and started engines as Spears stood chatting, pretended goodbyes with de Gaulle and Courcel. He then climbed into the plane, and as the pilot prepared to taxi out to the runway for takeoff, de Gaulle and his aide scrambled in as well.

> We flew over La Rochelle and Rochefort [de Gaulle wrote]. Ships set on fire by German aircraft were burning in these ports. We passed over Paimpont, where my mother lay very ill. The forest was all smoking from the munition dumps which were being destroyed there. After a stop at Jersey, we reached London in the early afternoon. While I was taking rooms and Courcel was telephoning to the Embassy and the missions, and finding them already reticent, I seemed to myself, alone as I was and deprived of everything, like a man on the shore of an ocean, proposing to swim across.

And Churchill wrote: "De Gaulle carried with him, in this small airplane, the honor of France."

FIVE

L'APPEL

Speaking in full knowledge of the facts, I ask you to believe me when I say that the cause of France is not lost. For remember this, France does not stand alone. . . . The outcome of the struggle has not been decided by the Battle of France. . . . The destiny of the world is at stake.

I, General de Gaulle, now in London, call on all French officers and men who are at present on British soil, or may be in the future, with or without their arms; I call on all engineers and skilled workmen from the armaments factories who are at present on British soil, or may be in the future, to get in touch with me. Whatever happens, the flame of French resistance must not and shall not die.

GENERAL DE GAULLE
BBC BROADCAST TO FRANCE
TUESDAY, JUNE 18, 1940

The little airplane landed at Heston Airdrome on the western outskirts of London shortly after noon on Monday, and General Spears telephoned No. 10 Downing Street to ask that Churchill be advised of their safe arrival. He then took de Gaulle and Courcel to lunch at the Royal Automobile Club on Pall Mall. As they finished lunch, word came that Churchill would see de Gaulle immediately, and when he arrived at Downing Street he was taken out into the garden, where the prime minister was working under the trees in brilliant warm soft London June weather. Neither man left any record of the conversation, but it was a brief meeting and very much to the point. Both men had one simple overriding objective: France must be kept in the fight. If France sought an armistice, as now seemed certain, then Churchill wanted someone from France at his side to rally resistance, as had already happened in the case of the Poles, the Norwegians, the Dutch and the Belgians. For his part, de Gaulle was already determined that "it would be the end of honor, unity and independence if it were to be admitted that, in this world war, only France had capitulated and that she let the matter rest there." But no time was wasted in the Downing Street garden philosophizing.

Indeed, there was little to discuss, for de Gaulle brought nothing with him but his own convictions about the honor of France and a determination to act. He was no longer a minister of the French government, and he was a general without any troops except his aide, Lieutenant Courcel. He outlined to Churchill what he wanted to do, but his only means of doing it lay in Churchill's hands—access to the BBC broadcast to France. "Washed up from a vast shipwreck upon the shores of England, what could I have done without his help?" de Gaulle wrote. Churchill agreed immediately that de Gaulle should broadcast, and they were in accord that he should wait until it was clear to all that the new government in Bordeaux had asked the Germans for an armistice. They did not have to wait long.

During the afternoon, the voice of eighty-four-year-old Marshal Pétain was heard on Bordeaux radio pronouncing the fate of his nation: "I give to France my person to assuage her misfortune. It is with a broken heart that I tell you today it is necessary to stop fighting." Whatever Pétain's intention, by this unfortunate choice of words he instructed French troops to lay down their arms before an armistice request had even been sent to the Germans, and without any advance warning to the still fairly sizable British forces fighting side by side with the French in Normandy and Brittany under General Sir Alan Brooke. But this was only one more ignoble episode in France's pell-mell rush to surrender. Needless to say, the Nazi armies pushed on as fast and as far as they could travel until the formal French request for an armistice brought orders to halt and cease fire.

After seeing Churchill, de Gaulle went to a small apartment just off Hyde Park belonging to a French banker who had served with a financial mission in London. There he wrote out in longhand a text of what he intended to say in his broadcast. Courcel got in touch with a family friend, Elisabeth de Miribel, who was working as a secretary for one of the French missions, and asked if she could come to the apartment and do some typing. She was the first Free French recruit.

The broadcast, which became a great deal more famous in history than it was at the time, took place at 6 P.M. on Tuesday, June 18, from Studio B-2 in Broadcasting House, the BBC headquarters. De Gaulle arrived, accompanied by General Spears and Courcel, and was greeted at the studio by Elizabeth Barker from the staff of what was then known as the BBC Foreign Broadcasting Service. She continued with the BBC long after the war, and remembered de Gaulle in that first encounter as "above all, icily contained within himself—not at all what one imagines a Frenchman to be. There was something different about him, different from other men. One could sense that straight away—I don't mean the 'man of destiny' business, but he was most remarkably self-possessed." The BBC had been told only about an hour before to put General de Gaulle on the air in what was then a prime-time news broadcast to France, and at that time regular news programs were not normally recorded. "Had we known sufficiently in advance that a very important statement was going to be made, we would certainly have laid on recording arrangements," Miss Barker related. But it was, to say the least, a time of fast-moving events and no recording was made. Nor, indeed, was de Gaulle very widely heard, for at that stage of the war there were few listeners in France who felt the need of tuning to the BBC. That dependence was to develop in the months ahead.

De Gaulle's first "Call to Honor" took barely four minutes to deliver, and was couched only in general terms—France was not alone; the war was not lost because the Battle of France had been lost; resistance must go on. Although he asked French officers "to get in touch with me," de Gaulle did not in that first broadcast proclaim himself the head of the French Resistance. Nor in that broadcast did he use the famous phrase "France has lost a battle, but it has not lost the war." This he wrote out in longhand several days later as the text for a poster General Spears asked him to prepare, which was then put up with a tricolor border all over London and elsewhere to recruit for the Free French.

Still, a die was cast, a Rubicon crossed. De Gaulle wrote in his Memoirs: "As the irrevocable words flew out upon their way, I felt within myself a life coming to an end—the life I had lived within the framework of a solid France and an indivisible army. At the age of forty-nine I was entering upon adventure, like a man thrown by fate outside all terms of reference."

Fifteen years before, de Gaulle had lectured officers at the École Supérieure de Guerre on the historic necessity of disobedience in certain circumstances as a mark of greatness and leadership. Now he was putting this into practice on a scope and scale unknown in French history. A marshal of France and head of government had ordered French soldiers to lay down their arms before the enemy. A brigadier general virtually unknown outside military circles was refusing to obey, and compounding this disobedience by calling upon others to join him and follow his example. De Gaulle remarked to his entourage that "I alone know what it cost me." He was asked in those days by Maurice Schumann, who became the first official spokesman of the Free French (and later a French foreign minister), if he had told himself in those first hours that duty was still duty even if all was lost, and that above all France must be in the camp of Allied victory. De Gaulle replied: "I told myself all of that and none of it. It was really more simple. I saw treason before my eyes, and my heart refused in disgust to recognize it as victorious."

To a British liaison officer, he brooded: "For those still over there, the younger men, the senior officers, it's a dreadful thing to decide, whether to obey orders, remain under Pétain and the armistice, or risk everything, defy the authorities, leave France, leave all in order perhaps to lose all. A terrible choice! It's not the same for me. My decision is taken. I have no hesitation, no doubts left—all that is finished."

But on Tuesday, June 18, 1940, General de Gaulle was not yet the last card that Churchill and the British sought to play with falling France. Britain still had full diplomatic relations with the government in Bordeaux. The Anglo-French Alliance had not yet been severed. On paper at least there were still mutual obligations, and the terms of an armistice that Germany would demand of France were not yet known. From Bordeaux, Sir Ronald Campbell reported that there were those in the government who were still determined on the possibility of a move to North Africa of some, if not all, the ministers, and he was also receiving brave assurances that if the armistice terms were too humiliating they would be refused. If all this seemed to be grasping at straws, nevertheless perhaps events still could be influenced, and Churchill was no man to sit idly by without giving it a maximum try.

That same Tuesday afternoon, Jean Monnet telephoned Downing Street to propose that he go to Bordeaux with a member of the British War Cabinet to make a last effort to get someone—some senior political figure of France—to remove to London and continue the fight. Churchill agreed.

Monnet got in touch with de Gaulle immediately and asked him if he would return to Bordeaux once more and join in the effort. But de Gaulle, already immersed in getting ready for his broadcast, with his mind made up both as to the course events were taking and what he proposed to do, simply said that from what he had seen of the situation in Bordeaux the mission would fail, and he would remain in London. Churchill made a large seaplane available, with plenty of range and room for thirty or more passengers, and on the morning of Wednesday, June 19, Monnet took off for Bordeaux accompanied by his deputy, René Pleven, and Lord Lloyd, colonial secretary in the Cabinet and one of Churchill's intimates. The men whom Monnet hoped to bring back were the president of the Repubic, Albert Lebrun; the deposed Paul Reynaud, Édouard Herriot, who was president of the Chamber of Deputies; Jules Jeanneney, president of the Senate; former premier Léon Blum; or the minister of interior, Georges Mandel. All were strong antiappeasers, all were committed to keeping France in the fighting. Any one of these political figures would or could have superseded the virtually unknown de Gaulle. But in the event, not one would leave, despite personal pleadings from Monnet, and a seaplane, empty and waiting, in the Gironde estuary off Bordeaux. Paul Baudouin, who was continuing as foreign minister under Pétain, told Monnet that it had been agreed in a Cabinet meeting to transport President Lebrun and the presidents of the Senate and Chamber of Deputies to North Africa by ship, along with a few Cabinet ministers. This then became both an excuse and a trap for their not departing on the British seaplane. Herriot told Monnet: "You don't need to convince me, but we shall leave under the flag of France—it cannot be otherwise. The *Messilia* is ready to sail." Meanwhile, Lord Lloyd was having an even bleaker and more hostile round of talks. By a stroke of good fortune Pleven ran into his wife and children on the street in Bordeaux. Together with a French diplomat, Henri Bonnet, and his wife they were the only new passengers when the seaplane flew back to Britain on Thursday morning.

Apart from the political aspect of trying to keep French resistance alive, of even greater immediate importance and urgency for Churchill was the question of what would happen to the French Fleet under the terms of an armistice with Germany. The naval balance was both precarious and vital for Britain. With Italy now in the war and France quitting, it was a balance that was already swinging against the Royal Navy. Were the Germans ever to lay hands on the French ships and add them to their strength by one device or another, Britain would face a peril unlike anything since the days of the Spanish Armada. Churchill had raised this question with the French at Briare on June 11, and again at his last meeting with Reynaud at Tours on June 13. At Briare he also had a personal exchange with Admiral François Darlan, who never forgot or allowed the British to forget that his great-grandfather was killed at Trafalgar by Nelson's forces. Darlan gave Churchill the first of a long series of pledges that the Fleet would never be allowed to fall into German hands. But Churchill wanted not just pledges, he wanted action to place the French ships beyond German reach. So, on the same plane that took Monnet to Bordeaux, Churchill also sent First Lord of the Admiralty A. V. Alexander and First Sea Lord and Admiral of the Fleet Sir Dudley Pound with the most weighty and determined final appeal to Darlan he could dispatch. They met Darlan, who under Pétain had now become both minister of marine and fleet commander, for a stiff and frigid conversation. Again there were "many solemn assurances," but as Churchill also noted, "no more French warships moved beyond reach of the swiftly approaching German power."

There was one last throw of the dice left with the French. On Friday, June 21, the *Massilia* was finally allowed by Darlan to clear Bordeaux and sail for North Africa with twenty-four Deputies, but only one government minister, Georges Mandel, aboard. Others avoided the sailing at the last moment, suspecting a trap. Still, former Premier Édouard Daladier was aboard, and it was a nucleus of *résistants.*

On Sunday, June 23, the Pétain government accepted and signed the German armistice terms. The men aboard the *Massilia,* who believed they were heading for North Africa to continue the fight, then tried to persuade the captain to alter course for England, but under strict orders from Darlan, he refused. The *Massilia* reached Casablanca on June 24. Despite the signing of the armistice, Mandel, with courage that was rare in those times, drafted a proclamation setting up a Resistance administration in North Africa and went ashore and made contact with the British consulate. A few days earier, the French governor-general, General Auguste Noguès, had procaimed himself ready to fight on, but with the armistice he swung back in line behind Pétain, Weygand and Darlan. When he heard of Mandel's planned proclamation, he stopped its publication and cabled Pétain for instructions. Back came orders to arrest Mandel, who was put back on the *Massilia,* which was moved to a mooring out in the harbor, all its passengers now in effect political prisoners.

At this point, aware from intelligence sources that the *Massilia* had reached Morocco with a contingent of *résistant* French politicians aboard, the War Cabinet in London decided to fly two senior figures to the scene to try to bolster any efforts the French might make to stay in the fight. Alfred Duff Cooper, who was minister of information, and Field Marshal Lord Gort, who had commanded British forces in the Battle of France, flew to Rabat, the capital, in a Sunderland flying boat, arriving late on June 25. But all attempts to get in touch with Mandel or anyone else aboard the *Massilia* were caustically refused by the French. General Noguès declined to see the British, and after twenty-four hours of useless palaver, they had no choice but to fly back to Britain. Churchill then gave orders to the Admiralty to try to intercept the *Massilia* when Darlan ordered it back to France, but this failed. Most of the politicians wound up in Vichy jails.

The last hope of organizing some other organ of resistance was now gone. It was General de Gaulle alone.

*

When Jean Monnet returned to London from Bordeaux on the morning of Thursday, June 20, General de Gaulle had already taken additional steps to stake out and consolidate his position as leader of the Resistance. First of all, he had delivered a second BBC broadcast on Wednesday evening while Monnet was in Bordeaux—more precise and clear in its call to resistance and above all much more of a declaration of the assumption of personal power:

> Faced by the bewilderment of my countrymen, by the disintegration of a government in thrall to the enemy, by the fact that the institutions of my country are incapable, at the moment, of functioning, I, General de Gaulle, a French soldier and military leader, realize that I now speak for France.
>
> In the name of France, I make the following solemn declaration: It is the bounden duty of all Frenchmen who still bear arms to continue the struggle. For them to lay down their arms, to evacuate any position of military importance, or agree to hand over any part of French territory, however small, to enemy control would be a crime against our country. . . . Soldiers of France, wherever you may be, arise!

Meanwhile, responding to General Noguès, who had shown brief stirrings of resistance, de Gaulle sent a cable to Rabat on June 19 stating: "Hold myself at your disposal, whether to fight under your orders, or for any step which might seem to you useful." But by the end of the week, Noguès went down like a cooling hot-air balloon and was ordering the arrest of Mandel in Casablanca. Then, on June 20, de Gaulle transmitted a letter to General Weygand through the French embassy military attaché in which he said: "I feel it is my duty to tell you quite simply that I wish, for the sake of France and for yours, *mon Général,* that you may be willing and able to escape disaster, reach overseas France and continue the war. There is at present no possible armistice with honor. I could be useful to you or to any other eminent Frenchman willing to place himself at the head of a continued French resistance." The letter was returned three months later with a typed note to "communicate with General Weygand through regular channels."

It may be argued, as critics and cynics about General de Gaulle have done, that he was simply engaged in a political ruse to outmaneuver any potential rivals and preempt the high ground of leadership and power at the outset, with the dispatch of these and other messages to French officers and colonial administrators and French community leaders in all parts of the world. Charles de Gaulle never deigned to discuss or explain. Whether his motives were pure or political, the fact remains that he *did* offer to serve alongside or under other potential leaders of a

French Resistance Movement, or a French government overseas committed to remaining in the fight, and no one else would move. French officers were immobilized by Vichy orders; French politicians were too stunned by events to act. France had descended into that depth of degradation that de Gaulle had been anticipating with a modicum of melancholy certitude since the days of his youth. At this darkest moment in French history, de Gaulle, but for the political accidents of the previous two weeks that had landed him in London, might again have been just another prisoner of war. But he was alone, free to act, uninhibited by anyone any longer able to give him orders. All his life he had studied, lectured and brooded with fascination on the subject of power, the exercise of power. He had watched the power of the Third Republic vanish in a kind of anarchy, compounded in the end by what he regarded as treason. Power lay at his feet, and no man came forward to challenge him or even to ask to share it.

One challenge did come, however, from Jean Monnet—but it was not a challenge for power. It was an intellectual challenge over methods and means. As soon as Monnet got back to London, he sought out de Gaulle to tell him: "You must stop sending off telegrams. Those to whom they are addressed cannot help but think that with the help of the British prime minister you, a young French general, are arrogating to yourself the right to represent France. Are they, your seniors in age and service, to take orders from you issued in London on foreign soil?"

Monnet was every bit as determined as de Gaulle to remain in the fight personally and to do everything possible to keep French Resistance alive at the side of the British. But there was a fundamental difference of approach that reflected not only the high intellect and character of these two great Frenchmen, but even the schism in France itself.

Monnet wanted to work side by side with the British while "the question of France's role in the war remained open." He felt that by hasty and precipitous action to declare himself head of the Resistance, de Gaulle was freezing a situation that was still fluid, and would make it more difficult, not less, to rally hesitant Frenchmen and parts of the Empire to continue the fight. He was deeply against General de Gaulle's equating himself, and the Resistance Movement he was determined to create, with France. Finally he contended forcefully to de Gaulle in a personal letter on June 23 that it was wrong "to try to set up in Britain an organization which would appear to the French as a movement under British protection, inspired by British interests and therefore condemned to a failure which would make further efforts at recovery all the more difficult." And in fact, this was precisely the difficulty that de Gaulle encountered, and why he felt that he had to feud and argue and fight so continuously across the next few years, first with the British and then with the Americans, constantly to prove to himself, to France, to the Alliance, to the world that he was not serving British interests but the interests of France.

There was a deeper element in this de Gaulle-Monnet debate, and that was their divergent philosophies. Monnet by experience and political outlook was an internationalist who devoted his life to getting nations to work together and blur the edges of sovereignty. De Gaulle was an intense nationalist to whom the sovereignty and greatness of France became life itself.

De Gaulle, in his Memoirs, makes no mention of this fundamental argument with Monnet, but he probably had it all in mind when he wrote:

> Many, even among those who approved of the undertaking, wanted it to be no more than aid given by a handful of Frenchmen to the British Empire, still standing and in the fight. I did not look at the enterprise in that way for a moment. For me, what had to be served and saved was the nation and the State. Whatever might be the outcome of the conflict—whether the country, after decisive defeat would one day be rid of the invader by foreign arms, or would remain enslaved—her self-disgust and the disgust she would inspire in others would poison her soul and her life for many generations. As for the immediate future, in the name of what were some of her sons to be led out to a fight no longer France's own? What was the good of supplying auxiliaries for the forces of another power? No! For the effort to be worthwhile, it was essential to bring back into the war not merely some Frenchmen, but France.

And so, as Monnet wrote, "we parted—or rather the separate paths we chose to reach the same ultimate goal soon gave us no further occasion to meet, at least in London. He respected my choice as I admired his determination." Monnet declined to join the Free French, and instead was appointed by Churchill to serve with the British Purchasing Mission in Washington, where he continued to render exceptional service to the war effort. Three years later, in Algiers, Monnet would play a decisive role in bringing about the unity of Frenchmen, which he foresaw at the outset in London would be deeply sundered by the course de Gaulle was taking. De Gaulle no doubt saw this as well, but he was determined that Frenchmen would have to choose: Pétain's France or de Gaulle's France.

To create de Gaulle's France in London, the General's next step was to form a "Provisional French National Committee," which was then duly recognized by the British government on the day France signed the armistice with Germany, June 23, as "fully representing independent French elements determined on prosecution of the war in fulfillment of the international obligations of France."

Next, to ensure the personal co-identity of himself and France, de Gaulle drew up an *acte d'engagement,* or enlistment form, for all those recruited into the Free French Forces, in which, as a substitute for the standard oath of allegiance to the French State, the engagement was to serve General de Gaulle, *commandant-en-chef,* with "honor, fidelity and discipline" for the duration of the war. For some, this oath-taking was inconsequential, a matter of indifference normal to any military enlistment, but to others it became a deep moral and political question of binding oneself personally to General de Gaulle instead of to the nation.

But de Gaulle never debated or argued these issues with Frenchmen, apart from that early private discussion with Monnet, which was more of a statement of each man's position and point of view than any effort at agreement. In a technique of power that he was to adopt consistently for the rest of his life, de Gaulle simply took a position—that he was France—and it was then up to Frenchmen to decide for themselves to join his cause on his terms or turn away as they wished.

In the event, not one member of the French embassy diplomatic staff in London joined de Gaulle—nor, indeed, for many months did any senior French diplomat anywhere. Ambassador Charles Corbin, devoted to the Anglo-French Alliance, resigned his post in bitter disgust when Pétain took power, lost his pension, but returned to France to sit out the war, telling de Gaulle, "You are right, but I'm an old civil servant. Outlawry is too much for me." Roland de Margerie, who had been at the center of all this as Reynaud's diplomatic adviser and knew more than most about the rotten weakness inside the Third Republic, wanted nothing to do with Vichy, so he arranged to distance himself as far as he possibly could with an assignment as consul general in Shanghai. Monnet, of course, went to Washington. But his deputy, Pleven, stayed on with de Gaulle, and for months was the only man with solid governmental and political experience sitting on the Free French Committee.

In those early days, it was not men of experience or leadership, it was not the intellectuals or politicians or administrators or serving officers who were the first Gaullists and rallied to the Cross of Lorraine. They did not come from the châteaux or the cathedrals, but from the parish churches and the synagogues, the French of the Paris Métro, the fishing villages, the factories, for whom all was clear and simple.

*

General Spears found a couple of vacant office rooms for General de Gaulle at St. Stephen's House, an old Victorian brick building across the street from the House of Commons. Courcel went to the Bank of England to change the 100,000 French francs that Reynaud had given them, and it produced barely £100, not much of a treasury on which to restore the honor of France. All was makeshift and haphazard, a handful of people rushing in and out, with de Gaulle, entirely by his own towering physique and massive presence and aloof style, creating a sense of institution, the beginnings of an organization. An early recruit to parade before him was Captain André Dewavrin, who had been in Norway with a contingent of Alpine Chasseurs, then evacuated from Narvik and left stranded in Britain during the Battle of France. He was given the standard de Gaulle glacial welcome: "Brief questions in a clear, incisive, rather brutal voice; a grey and piercing look in the eyes, his tenacious will still more apparent in word than in gesture; also perhaps a touch of pride and scorn, but it could just as well have been a form of shyness." De Gaulle elicited the fact that Dewavrin had a law degree and spoke fluent English, and at the end of this brief exchange abruptly appointed him to be chief of the Second and Third Bureaus of his embryo staff—Intelligence and Operations. Dewavrin, taking the code name of Passy after the Paris Métro stop, was an exceptional choice in an extremely difficult and tricky assignment involving the trust and confidence of the British, and he served with distinction to the end of the war.

A young civil servant with experience at the French Treasury, Pierre Dennis, found himself appointed just as abruptly by de Gaulle to take charge of Free French finances. He later wrote:

> I went down the corridor and opened a door on which the word *Caisse* was written in a sergeant major's round handwriting. I came into a small triangular room with a window facing the Thames. There I found an old man with a grave emaciated face, sitting at a rickety table. He and I held the first technical conversation concerning Free France's financial situation. It turned out that on the previous day, there had still been fourteen shillings in the till, but that this had run out during the day. He had had to put in ten shillings out of his own pocket to pay for two telegrams that the General, in his lack of consideration for our limited means of action, had thought it useful to send. We did not have an account anywhere, nor, as far as we knew, was there anyone who would give us credit. He himself had just come from France and felt out of his element. He had not yet had the opportunity to check if there were any banks in England.

The flag had been raised, the cry had gone out—but who would respond? At that time in Britain there were approximately 20,000 Frenchmen in uniform and another 30,000 civilians. The British promptly designated Olympia Hall, a large exhibition center in southwest London, as a Free French recruiting center. De Gaulle set out on a series of contact visits to such French units as there were, but it was a slow and discouraging start. Out of 2,000 French wounded who had been evacuated from Dunkirk and not yet repatriated, only 200 joined him. He traveled north to visit the Alpine Chasseurs, Dewarvin's unit, commanded by General Émile Béthouart, an intelligent and honorable man and a fine solider, who was the senior French Army officer then in Britain. Béthouart wanted to continue the fight, but he did not think Britain was the place to do it, nor was he ready to place himself under de Gaulle, his junior in rank. Instead he elected to make his way to North Africa where, consistent to his pledge to fight on, he played an instrumental role in preparing for the Allied landings in 1943 and then went on to serve in battle with distinction.

But he did arrange for de Gaulle to address all the units under his command. As a result, most of two battalions and a tank company, plus some headquarters staff, gunners and engineers, rallied to de Gaulle. They became the nucleus of the Free French Army.

Nor, in fact, were the British consistently helpful to de Gaulle in those early days. Of course he had the full backing and blessing from Churchill on high, and the energetic activity of General Spears, who scrounged for everything from office space and typewriters to secret funds to tide things over until a permanent arrangement of financial subsidy for the Free French was worked out some weeks later. But it was a time of maximum peril and preoccupation for the British, with Hitler's armies massing across the Channel and the Battle of Britain about to begin. Accordingly, the down-the-line enthusiasm and support for de Gaulle was rather minimal. As he commented dryly in his Memoirs:

> The British High Command, which from one day to another expected the German offensive and perhaps invasion, was too much absorbed by its preparations to busy itself with a task which in its eyes was secondary. Besides, it was inclined by professional decorum and habit to respect the normal order of things—that is to say, Vichy and its missions. Finally it looked with some mistrust upon those allies of yesterday humiliated by misfortune, dissatisfied with themselves and with others and loaded with complaints.

When de Gaulle finished his rallying speeches to the Alpine Chasseurs, and had departed, two British officers assembled the French units and told them that they were perfectly free to join General de Gaulle "but it is our duty to point out to you that if you so decide you will be rebels against your government." In Liverpool, when de Gaulle arrived to address an assembly of French sailors, the British admiral commanding the shore facilities firmly turned him away on the grounds that his visit would be prejudicial to order. Moreover, there were numerous pro-Vichy, anti–de Gaulle French officials still active at the French embassy and French consulates in England.

In those first weeks it was usually individuals rather than units of either the military or the French Empire that rallied to de Gaulle. A submarine cruising off the Norwegian coast elected to join the Free French and surfaced in a British port, while another in the Mediterranean sailed from Sfax in Tunisia and reported to the British in Malta. In England, a trawler captain and a couple of patrol boat captains came over. A little flotilla of fishing boats sailed to Cornwall from the island of Sein off the Brittany coast with forty men, almost the entire able-bodied population of the island, who were to serve daringly and dangerously as couriers, running Free French agents back into occupied France. The nucleus of the Free French Air Force formed around a few dozen airmen camped in South Wales, who were then joined by another hundred or so who made their way to Britain via Gibraltar, some from North Africa, some from France via Spain.

Finally, at the end of June, came a major "recruiting break" for de Gaulle. Admiral Émile Muselier, a Corsican character out of an Alexander Dumas novel, arrived in Britain from Gibraltar from the 11th Cruiser Squadron, which he was commanding in the Atlantic. Muselier, with a pirate's *visage* of sharp swarthy features, a swashbuckling fighting personality and temper and a proclaimed passion for women, was most things that General de Gaulle was not. For some reason he had run afoul of Admiral Darlan and had been abruptly placed on the retired list before the war. He was then recalled to action, and he arrived in Britain not out of any enthusiasm for de Gaulle—in fact, he had not even heard of de Gaulle—but out of distaste for Darlan and a determination to fight the Germans. He first went to the French embassy, having been at sea during the period in which the armistice was accepted, but it was quickly obvious that this was not the place for a fighting Frenchman. So he found his way to de Gaulle and wrote a vivid if not very flattering picture of the man he met.

> I was immediately struck by the physique of the man. His great height, with a small, rather ill-formed head and too low a forehead. His small grey eyes did not look squarely into one's own but always turned away when he was answering a precise question. The chin, of a very peculiar shape, did not suggest a strong will. The pronounciation was slow, as if he were listening to himself speaking; and his mouth, neither large nor small, sometimes opened in a complete circle over his irregular teeth. The nose was powerful, almost Bourbon. The ears, badly formed, stuck out widely.

All Muselier wanted to do was fight—he was not interested in politics and not in the least preoccupied with metaphysical considerations about whether or not Charles de Gaulle had a right to consider himself the embodiment of France. De Gaulle for his part badly needed a senior serving officer at his side, so Vice Admiral Muselier almost instantly became commander of all Free French naval forces. But it was a somewhat stormy relationship between two very disparate and strong characters that finally came to an end in 1942. In fact, the British nearly blew it out of the water in the first week.

*

Neither the terms of the French armistice with Germany nor the conduct of the Pétain government were at all reassuring to the British as far as the French Fleet was concerned. To begin with, the French at Bordeaux had already welshed on the pledge given by Reynaud at his last meeting with Churchill at Tours on June 13 to deliver all captured German pilots to Britain so they could not take to the skies again as the war continued. Instead, these airmen, some 400 in all, were released to the Germans under the armistice and soon were taking part in the Battle of Britain. At the same time, the armistice agreement specified in Article 8 that part of the French Feet would remain operational to safeguard French colonial interests, but the remaining vessels "shall be collected in ports to be specified and there demobilized and disarmed under German or Italian control." Orders were then under way for the bulk of the French ships to return to French ports.

But all the French ports on the Atlantic and Channel coasts were now under German occupation. Thus, any French vessels putting into Brest or Saint-Nazaire or Bordeaux or Le Havre would automatically fall under German control. The ports of Toulon and Marseilles were in unoccupied France, under Vichy control, but what was the worth of Darlan's pledges that he would never allow his ships to fall into enemy hands? Were the French naval vessels that had taken refuge in British ports in the tumult and confusion of the last ten days of June now to be allowed to sail away on Darlan's orders to French ports? Winston Churchill was far too much of a naval strategist, far too much of a warrior, to allow that to happen.

The number of French ships involved was considerable—in Plymouth and Portsmouth no fewer than two battleships, four light cruisers, several submarines, eight destroyers and some 200 small but valuable patrol boats, minesweepers and antisubmarine craft. On July 3, 1940, swiftly and without warning, British Marines and armed naval boarding parties carried out an early-morning seizure of all these vessels. French sailors were marched ashore under armed guard and interned. Fighting broke out between the British and the crew of the submarine *Surcouf,* in which two British officers and two seamen were wounded and a French sailor killed. Otherwise the operation was swift and bloodless, but it was scarcely designed to enhance the Entente Cordiale. All the same, as Churchill noted, "the whole transaction showed how easily the Germans could have taken possession of any French warships lying in ports which they controlled." Worse was still to come for the French.

At the French Mediterranean naval base of Mers el-Kébir near the Algerian city of Oran, more of the Fleet had assembled, including the modern battle cruisers *Dunkerque* and *Strasbourg* along with light cruisers, destroyers, submarines and support craft. They were vital to the naval balance in the Mediterranean and had to be kept out of German hands.

On Churchill's orders, a Royal Navy task force of battle cruisers, an aircraft carrier and light cruisers and destroyers sailed from Gibraltar under Admiral Sir James Somerville early on the morning of July 3, while French sailors were being interned in Britain. It arrived off Oran in midmorning with an ultimatum for the French vessels at Mers el-Kébir. The French were offered three choices—sail away from their base with the British to continue the fight, sail with reduced crews to British-controlled ports with the crews then to be repatriated to France, or sail under British escort to the West Indies and be demobilized at Martinique or elsewhere, far from German hands. Failing this, the ultimatum declared: "We must with profound regret require you to sink your ships within six hours or it is the orders of His Majesty's Government to use whatever force may be necessary to prevent your ships from falling into German or Italian hands."

A British destroyer was dispatched into the harbor with Naval Captain C. S. Holland, a former British naval attaché in Paris who was fluent in French and a deep Francophile, carrying the ultimatum to the French commander, Admiral Marcel Gensoul, a Darlan loyalist. Gensoul refused to see Holland, replying in writing to the ultimatum that in no case would French ships be allowed to fall into German or Italian hands and that force would be met with force.

Meanwhile, from Churchill a personal dispatch went to Somerville: "You are charged with one of the most disagreeable and difficult tasks that a British Admiral has ever been faced with, but we have complete confidence in you and rely on you to carry it out relentlessly." Further back-and-forth exchanges took place between Holland and Gensoul, but nothing altered. Finally Holland's destroyer was ordered to rejoin the British task force. Meanwhile, in London the British Naval Intelligence had picked up and decoded signals from Gensoul to Toulon and the French Naval Command asking that Italian submarines be notified of the location of the British ships to attack them offshore from the rear.

Shortly after 6 P.M., on the evening of July 3, a final signal went from the Admiralty in London to Somerville: "French ships must comply with our terms or sink themselves or be sunk by you before dark." But the admiral had already opened fire at 5:54 P.M. In an action that lasted only ten minutes, the battleship *Bretagne* was blown up, the *Dunkerque* run aground, the *Provence* beached. The *Strasbourg* escaped from the harbor but was damaged by torpedo aircraft, and although it made port in Toulon in southern France, the British were satisfied that it was out of the war. More than 1,200 French sailors died under British guns in the first such encounter since the days of Napoleon and the battle of Trafalgar.

This was one of the most ruthless decisions that Winston Churchill took in the entire war. It was done not merely to secure the naval balance of power in the Mediterranean, but probably more for the shock effect on Hitler, the Germans, and indeed on France, the United States and the entire world. As Churchill wrote: "Here was Britain, who so many had counted down and out, which strangers had supposed to be quivering on the brink of surrender to the mighty power arrayed against her, striking ruthlessly at her dearest friends of yesterday and securing for a while to herself the undisputed command of the sea. It was made plain that the British War Cabinet feared nothing and would stop at nothing."

All the same, the momentary effect on the two-weeks-old Free French movement was appalling. Muselier stormed to British officer-friends at the Admiralty that they were behaving like fools and criminals and threatened to throw over his new command under General de Gaulle and return to France or remove to Pondicherry in India, the French enclave that had refued to endorse the armistice and Vichy rule.

Still, Muselier found many British officers just as appalled as he was over the killing of French sailors by British guns. In the end, he acceded bitterly to the realities of war and stayed at his post. Meanwhile, when Churchill went to the House of Commons on July 4 to report on these events, he was given a rapturous welcome. He dealt with the affair soberly and somberly, but in the House and the nation, the Mers el-Kébir action roused a jingoistic, chauvinistic response. If regrettable, it was certainly understandable. There had been very little to cheer about in England for the past two months, and the behavior of France had not been valorous. All the same, the cheering and applause of the British press for this "victory" was an awful lot of salt in the wounds of Frenchmen like de Gaulle and Muselier who were trying to ignite some fighting flame in the cold ashes of defeat.

Next day, July 5, the French government, which had now removed to Vichy under Pétain, broke diplomatic relations with Britain. Thus, at least the Mers el-Kébir affair as far as General de Gaulle was concerned clarified in his favor the question of which France the British would deal with—Pétain's or de Gaulle's. But the affair had a devastating effect on Free French recruiting among the soldiers and sailors in Britain, and on popular support from the French community for de Gaulle. The anglophobia of Darlan, Weygand, Baudouin, Laval and others of the Vichy clique had been a leitmotif of their behavior and of the attitudes that led to their capitulation. With the jubilant assistance of the Nazi propaganda machine, the Vichy leaders now gave vent to their anti-British feelings in full, seeking to whip French public opinion along with them. Pressures mounted on Pétain to change sides completely and not just to break diplomatic relations but declare war on Britain. This he never seriously considered, but there were those in Vichy who tried.

General de Gaulle initially kept public silence as these shattering events unfolded. By its impact and nature, the Mers el-Kébir affair came pretty close to stopping the Gaullist movement in its tracks. Churchill, knowing full well what de Gaulle and other Frenchmen must be going through, invited the General to lunch at No. 10 Downing Street, together with Mrs. Churchill, who spoke fluent and precise French, much better than her husband. An unusual scene then took place at the luncheon table.

The conversation naturally centered on the French Fleet, and Mrs. Churchill remarked how she ardently hoped that ships and crews would rally to fight with the British. De Gaulle retorted to her rather curtly that he imagined what would give the French Fleet satisfaction at that time would be "to turn their guns on you," meaning, of course, the British. Mrs. Churchill then rounded on him, telling him in her rather formal but impeccable French that he was uttering words and sentiments that ill became either an ally or a guest in Britain. Her husband, listening to all this, then intervened to try to be conciliatory, telling de Gaulle: "You must forgive my wife. *Elle parle trop bien la* [sic] *français.*" (She speaks French too well.) But Mrs. Churchill, a strong-minded woman, then turned on her husband and continuing in French said: "No, Winston, it is because there are certain things that a woman can say to a man which a man cannot say, and I am saying them to you—General de Gaulle." After this, de Gaulle apologized, probably one of the few times in his life, and next day sent a large basket of flowers to Mrs. Churchill. In fact, he and Mrs. Churchill remained on good terms the rest of their lives, and she strongly supported the General behind the scenes with her husband.

The exchange at Downing Street may well have affected the manner in which de Gaulle now rose to the occasion. He brooded in pained silence for five days and then went on the BBC to broadcast again to France on July 8. He fully understood that the British action at Mers el-Kébir and against the French naval units in British ports was part of the price of surrender, and France was paying for the condition into which it had been delivered by Pétain and Darlan. The British government, he noted in his Memoirs, "was clever enough and elegant enough to let me use the BBC, however disagreeable for the British the terms of my statement may have been."

In fact, he showed vision, strength of character and skill in his response. After vigorously declaring that "there is not a single Frenchman who did not learn with grief and anger" of the shelling of the French Fleet, he went on to tell the British to "spare us as well as themselves any portrayal of this hateful tragedy as a direct naval success." He then continued resolutely to his countrymen:

> This being said, let me ask you to consider the whole affair fundamentally from the point of view that matters in the end—that is to say, the point of

view of ultimate victory and deliverance of our country. By virtue of an agreement contrary to all honor, the government then established in Bordeaux agreed to place our ships at the mercy of the enemy. There cannot be the slightest doubt that, on principle and of necessity, the enemy would have used them either against Britain or against our own Empire. I therefore have no hesitation in saying that they are better destroyed. I prefer to know that even our dear, magnificent and powerful *Dunkerque* is stranded off Mers el-Kébir rather than learn that one day she has been manned by Germans and used to shell British ports, or perhaps Algiers, Casablanca or Dakar.

By viewing the whole tragedy in its true light, but at the same time doing everything possible to prevent its resulting in mortal strife between French and British, all men of foresight on both sides of the Channel are also running true to form—the form of the patriot. Come what may, our two great peoples are still linked together. Either they will both succumb, or they will triumph side by side.

It was a courageous broadcast at an extremely difficult time, and it was eloquent proof of General de Gaulle's qualities of leadership. Churchill would hesitate at nothing, stop at nothing, to prosecute the war to victory. De Gaulle would give France the leadership to remain at his side.

S I X

ROOSEVELT'S VICHY GAMBLE

The town of Vichy lies 225 miles directly south of Paris on the river Allier in hilly wooded countryside at the edge of the Massif Central mountain range. Even today, Vichy is little changed since the 19th century—a typical spa consisting of hotels and rooming houses, a casino and concert bandstand clustered around an esplanade of trees and park with a *station thermale* as its centerpiece over a bubbling spring that has been bringing Vichy water to the surface since Roman times. Bottled water and liver trouble remain the town's biggest industry. But its reputation as a sedate, salubrious and fashionable place for restoration of health and spirits was rudely altered in 1940 when Vichy became synonymous with defeat, fascism, collaboration, anti-Semitism, a police state in servitude to France's ruthless enemy, and all that was malodorous and sick in the French body politic.

France in the person of Marshal Pétain and his government of defeatists and collaborationists arrived in Vichy at the end of June 1940. Pétain remained at Vichy for four ruinous and tragic years until the retreating Germans carted him off to a prison-castle in the Black Forest in August 1944. But at the outset in those June–July days, France was wallowing in an atmosphere of abject and total defeat and a false and momentary sense of relief that a losing struggle was over. The French people were more than ready at that moment to accord Pétain, along with his seven stars and his aging permanence, a halo of veneration and a patriotic embrace that he himself viewed as abundantly and historically justified. He changed the motto of France from *Liberté, Egalité, Fraternité* to the more suitably downtrodden *Travail, Famille, Patrie* and settled down at Vichy's Hôtel du Parc to seek a place in Hitler's New Order to restore the nation.

No thought clouded the minds of the Vichy leaders of what might have been had France remained in the war. Pétain, Pierre Laval, Paul Baudouin, Admiral Darlan, General Weygand were all convinced that Britain would follow them into defeat in a matter of weeks. More than that, they genuinely expected that the move to Vichy would be only temporary, and that they would soon be back in

Paris after negotiation of a peace treaty with Nazi Germany. They were resigned to the prospect that at a minimum this would again cost France the provinces of Alsace and Lorraine and were prepared to pay that price. Indeed, Laval was already proposing to the Germans as early as August 1940 that France could be compensated for such a loss by receiving parts of British Africa, where he foresaw chances of "beautiful Franco-German cooperation" after Britain's defeat.

Yet if France had remained in the war and carried on the fight from North Africa, what vast changes in grand strategy would have been open to the military commanders, what territory and lives and fighting could have been saved, what time gained in the final defeat of the Nazis. De Gaulle records that there were about half a million Frenchmen in uniform at training camps in the southern half of the country at the time of the Battle of France, and he had prepared orders under which they could have been marched to Marseilles and Toulon and crowded onto any kind of ships for the thirty six-hour crossing to Algiers. France's bomber force was largely intact and could have flown to North African fields without refueling. In 1939 Jean Monnet had placed an order in the United States for 600 fighter planes with another 1,600 on option for 1940. First deliveries had only begun when France fell. They could all have been delivered to the French in North Africa, but instead they were transferred to the British and began arriving in quantity during the Battle of Britain.

As for sea power, the French Fleet was formidable, more than enough to dominate the Mediterranean and protect the African coast from any German invasion threat. As Churchill wrote: "Admiral Darlan had but to sail in any one of his ships to any port outside France to become the master of all French interests beyond German control. He would not have come, like General de Gaulle, with only an unconquerable heart and a few kindred spirits. He would have carried with him outside the German reach the fourth Navy in the world, and would have become the chief of French resistance with a mighty weapon in his hand." If Morocco, Algeria and Tunisia had remained secure in French hands, fighting on at the side of the British, then French and British troops could have routed the Italians and met in Tripoli in 1940 instead of 1943. Rommel's menace to Egypt and the Suez Canal would never have materialized, and Italy could have been pounded from African airfields instead of by bombers flying all the way from Britain. France would have remained in the high councils of the war, first with the British and then with the Americans when they came in after Pearl Harbor. The Allied invasion of North Africa would never have been necessary. The subsequent invasions of Sicily, Italy and eventually into the south of France itself would have been carried out with France as the major contributor, probably even under French command. In France itself, collaboration with the enemy could never have been instigated as national policy, dividing the nation between honor and dishonor as it did. There would have been a painful and tragic division between Frenchmen suffering under German occupation and Frenchmen fighting overseas for France—but this happened anyway. Weygand gave as a *raison d'être* for Vichy that "the armistice saved liberties, lives, territories, and wealth, with an unoccupied France governed and administered by the French still preserving at least a degree of independence." This disappeared completely in November 1942, when the Nazi armies moved into unoccupied France and effectively obliterated the Vichy regime.

It is one of the great "might have beens" of history, not merely lost but in the end proven to have been completely within the grasp of Frenchmen who held the power and the choice. One of the excuses, totally wrong, was the contention of General Noguès that "my first impulse was to continue the struggle, but I soon realized that this would mean losing North Africa. I had reliable information that the Germans had prepared a substantial expeditionary force with a complete plan for its rapid transportation across Spain." The Germans in June of 1940 had done no such thing at all. They were fully extended by the Blitzkrieg successes in Denmark, Norway, the Low Countries and France, and were now trying to figure out what to do about crossing the Channel to get at Britain. To be sure, if a French government had evacuated with troops and aircraft and ships to North Africa, then all of France would have been occupied by the Nazis immediately, instead of waiting until 1942. But if they could not muster the invasion landing craft and sea power and air power to cross the Channel, how could they have mounted and sustained in the summer of 1940 a seaborne invasion across the Mediterranean to North Africa, or from the ports of southern Spain with a battle for Gilbraltar? It was Churchill's final judgment:

> Surveying the whole scene in the after-light, it seems unlikely that Hitler's main decision and the major events of the war, namely the Battle of Britain and the German surge to the East, would have been changed by the retirement of the French Government to North Africa. Once France was prostrate, he must if possible conquer or destroy Great Britain. His only other choice was Russia. A major operation through Spain into Northwest Africa would have prejudiced both these tremendous adventures, or at least have prevented his attack on the Balkans [in 1941]. I have no doubt that it would have been better for all the Allies if the French Government had gone to North Africa; and this would have remained true whether Hitler followed them thither or not.

Across the Atlantic, the rapid fall of Denmark, Norway, Holland, Belgium, Luxembourg and France shocked the United States out of all but the last vestiges of its isolationist torpor of the 1920s and 1930s. Months of bruising political battles still lay ahead for President Roosevelt, particularly when Charles A. Lindbergh entered the fray. But the Battle of France turned the tide in Roosevelt's favor behind a policy of preparedness and intervention short of war. Barely two months before the fury burst in Europe, the Senate that was dominated by veteran isolationists like William E. Borah, Gerald P. Nye and Burton K. Wheeler, had voted to cut an appropriation request from Roosevelt for more planes for the Army Air Corps (as the Air Force then was known). But with the fighting raging in France, and Paul Reynaud pleading for "clouds of airplanes," the president went back to the Hill in mid-May and astounded Congress with a request for a supplemental defense appropriation of one billion dollars to start America toward a goal of building 50,000 planes a year. In the months ahead, Roosevelt moved forcefully to gear up American readiness for war. In June he took Republicans Henry L. Stimson and Frank Knox into his Cabinet as secretaries of war and navy. He formed a Council of National Defense Advisory Commission, which was a forerunner of future war agencies and production boards. He pushed a selective service act through Congress in September. He initiated secret negotiations with Britain on the exchange of fifty old U.S. Navy destroyers, mothballed since the First World War, for British base facilities at strategic island points in the Western Hemisphere. At the end of the year came his sweeping proposal for Lend-Lease to make America "the arsenal of democracy." And in the meantime of course he ran for a third term and was re-elected over Wendell Willkie in November 1940.

Finally, Roosevelt slid into a relationship with Vichy France that began naturally enough and understandably enough, but was to become one of the major foreign policy controversies of his presidency and wartime leadership.

At the State Department in Washington in June of 1940, there was never any discussion or question of choices or alternatives when it came to recognition of the Vichy government. The United States was at war with no one, and at that time of course still had full diplomatic relations with Berlin and Rome. Its proclaimed policy was neutrality, to keep out of the war, but the primary concern of Roosevelt and Secretary of State Cordell Hull was to apply American pressure and influence wherever and however possible to deny victory to the Nazis and assure victory for democracy. French governments came and went, and American diplomatic relations with Vichy simply continued automatically when Reynaud fell and Pétain took over as a new but certainly legally constituted and fully legitimate government. There was never any question of withdrawing diplomatic relations from France simply because a French government had accepted defeat.

As for General de Gaulle, the blunt truth is that Washington had never heard of him. He may have been mentioned in some dispatch to the War Department in the mid-1930s by an alert or studious U.S. military attaché doing a report on armored warfare. But he was completely unknown to the American embassy in Paris. Nobody had a clue about his political activities and the role he had been playing, or trying to play, in defense policy, or how he had suddenly been transformed by Reynaud from a divisional commander into a Cabinet minister, or how he tried so desperately to get the government to move to North Africa. Robert D. Murphy, political counselor of the Paris embassy from 1930 to 1941, a man who played a key role in the period of U.S. relations with Vichy, relates with unabashed candor in his Memoirs:

> We who were at the American Embassy in German-occupied Paris on June 18 had listened to the French General's stirring appeal for continued resistance and had been moved by it. But we asked each other: How has this man suddenly become so important? Until that hour, I cannot remember ever having heard de Gaulle's name. It was not until we arrived at Vichy that I learned details of how he had been brought into the government by

Reynaud after the *blitzkrieg* started. It was understandable why many politicians distrusted him.

The American ambassador to France was William C. Bullitt, a scion of Philadelphia society and a close personal friend of Roosevelt's who had previously served as ambassador to Moscow when relations were re-established with the Soviet Union in 1933. Fluent in French and by nature a social and political activist, Bullitt had a wide circle of French friends and was influential and well informed (apart from the gap about General de Gaulle). Roosevelt had given him a special private code for direct communications with the White House, bypassing the State Department. He was a rather vain man, and as France's hour of disaster approached, he was determined to follow the examples of his predecessors, Ambassador Washburn, who remained in Paris during the siege of the Franco-Prussian War in 1870–71, and Ambassador Herrick, who had stayed in 1914 when the government removed temporarily to Bordeaux at the time of the Battle of the Marne. Bullitt had informed Roosevelt of his intention, but he had not informed Hull, and the president had raised no objection. It therefore came as a complete surprise to the secretary of state to discover at the last minute that the ambassador did not intend to accompany the Reynaud government when it departed from Paris on June 10. Hull objected immediately to Roosevelt, and the president signed a cable "strongly recommending" that Bullitt follow the government but leaving it to his discretion. Bullitt stuck to his decision to remain behind, and as a result the ambassador who was supposed to have such access and influence with the political uppercrust of the Third Republic was in the wrong place at the wrong time for the next crucial three weeks. Hull commented dryly in his Memoirs: "No one can say what would have been the precise effect of Bullitt's influence had he been able to exercise it personally on the government at Tours and Bordeaux. I feel that with Bullitt at Reynaud's side, we would have had a reasonable chance to induce the French Cabinet to continue the fight with the fleet and the colonies."

This was an opinion certainly shared by General de Gaulle, who in fact had a brief encounter with Bullitt on June 10, as the government was getting ready to leave Paris. De Gaulle recorded:

> I went to see Paul Reynaud, and I found Mr. William Bullitt there. I supposed that the United States Ambassador was bringing some encouragement for the future from Washington. But no! He had come to say goodbye. The Ambassador was remaining in Paris with the intention of intervening, if need be, to protect the capital. But praiseworthy as was the motive which inspired Mr. Bullitt, the fact remained that during the supreme days of crisis there would be no American Ambassador to the French Government. The presence of Mr. A. J. Drexel Biddle, responsible for relations with refugee governments, would not, whatever the qualities of this excellent diplomat, remove from our officials the impression that the United States no longer had much use for France.

And so it fell to Biddle to carry out various vital instructions in Bordeaux from Roosevelt and Hull, messages for Reynaud and Pétain primarily supporting Churchill with all the forceful language that could be diplomatically mustered on the question of the future of the French Fleet.

Meanwhile Bullitt and Murphy met the Germans on their arrival in Paris—to no great credit for the American image with the French and with no discernible result except some morale-building assistance for individuals who were caught and trying to get out. On June 30, ten days after the occupation began, they closed down the American embassy and headed by car for Vichy, having been completely out of touch with Washington during the most crucial period of the war thus far.

Bullitt then elected, probably wisely, not to present himself formally as ambassador in Vichy, but instead to return to Washington, where Roosevelt was promising him another job. So the embassy party stopped first at a country hotel at the village of La Bourboule, a few miles from Vichy. There Biddle joined them to bring them up to date on the cataclysmic events they had all missed in Bordeaux. After that Bullitt made final calls on both Pétain and Darlan and departed for Washington on July 3. Robert Murphy took over as chargé d'affaires of the American embassy to Vichy France.

*

As ministers and civil servants and parliamentarians of the defeated government trooped into Vichy to fill up its hotels and empty rooms and swell the population from a normal 30,000 to more than 100,000, Pierre Laval took charge of converting France into a Fascist state on the Hitler-Mussolini model. There was nothing in the terms of the armistice agreement that required France to dismantle the Third Republic, but in that rancorous atmosphere of defeatist self-flagellation, almost everyone joined in heaping condemnation on France's institutions rather than on the men who had insisted on surrender and had refused to consider how they might continue the fight. Laval at least had been consistent in his record, both in and out of government in the 1930s, as an out-and-out appeaser and advocate of cooperation with Fascist dictatorships. He now told the assembled parliamentarians of the doomed Third Republic:

> I have been among you since 1914, and I do not forget that I come from the people. But since parliamentary democracy insisted on taking up the struggle against Nazism and Fascism and since it has lost the fight, it must disappear. A new regime must follow, a regime which will be bold, authoritarian, social and national. . . . We have always followed in England's wake. Nothing was more humiliating than the sight of our politicians going to London to ask permission to be French ministers. . . . You can see where all this has led us. . . . We have no other road to follow than that of loyal collaboration with Germany and Italy. I experience no embarrassment in speaking thus, for even in peacetime I favored such collaboration.

A few honorable men like Blum, Herriot, Jeanneney and others in the National Assembly sought to stem the tide, but on July 10 the Deputies and Senators joined in a combined vote of 569 to 80 to abolish the constitution of the Third Republic and vest full powers in Marshal Pétain to promulgate his own draft of a new Basic Law. Pétain would become France's Hindenburg, and Laval its Hitler. Laval was quoted by Paul Baudouin as remarking, "Parliament vomited me up; now I shall vomit it up." It was certainly a remark in keeping with the character and atmosphere of what was happening to French democracy.

Bullitt, in his final telegram from France to the State Department after his last talks with Pétain and Darlan, summed up the mood and the intention rather more elegantly, but no less devastatingly:

> The impression which emerges from these conversations is the extraordinary one that the French leaders desire to cut loose from all that France has represented during the past two generations, and that their physical and moral defeat has been so absolute that they have accepted completely for France the fate of becoming a province of Nazi Germany. Moreover, in order that they may have as many companions in misery as possible, they hope that England will be rapidly and completely defeated by Germany and that the Italians will suffer the same fate. Their hope is that France may become Germany's favorite province—a new "Gau" [administrative district] which will develop into a new Gaul. . . .

Marshal Pétain went before the National Assembly as it voted itself out of existence to outline in blunt and unvarnished terms the kind of discipline and sacrifice and servitude he intended to impose on the nation. Léon Blum, Georges Mandel, Édouard Daladier, Paul Reynaud, Pierre Mendès-France and dozens of other leaders of the old regime were soon rounded up and jailed—some to stand trial the following year as scapegoats for France's defeat, some to be murdered by Vichy agents in prison, some to be turned over to the Germans. Mendès-France managed to escape and make his way to Britain to join de Gaulle and fly with the Free French Air Force.

Yet all this was accomplished by Pétain and Laval in those first six months at Vichy to the accompaniment of an extraordinary chorus of intellectual approval and praise. The poet Paul Claudel wrote an effulgent ode to Pétain, and the novelist François Mauriac gave his backing and blessing to the regime. André Gide, who had earlier flirted with communism, wrote in his Journals that Pétain's call for sacrifice had been "simply admirable" and went on to add: "I should rather gladly put up with restraints, and would accept a dictatorship, which is the only thing, I fear, which might save us from decomposition. Let me hasten to add that I am speaking here of a French dictatorship."

It was many months before de Gaulle's challenge to Pétain over the honor and survival of France began to penetrate the intellectual world of Vichy, and the record came back to haunt these writers, philosophers, political journalists and teachers who "evolved" into Gaullists. In 1948 a collection of awkward quotations from the past was published in Paris under the title *A New Dictionary of Weathervanes,* edited by a journalist who used the appropriate pseudonym of Jean Maze.

Under the terms of the armistice, the Germans took over about three-fifths of France in an occupied zone that included all of the Channel and Atlantic coasts. Vichy then ruled an unoccupied zone of the southern two-fifths of French territory, including all of the Mediterranean coast. At the outset, for the first few weeks at least, the atmosphere was relatively relaxed, and the Vichy leaders were preening themselves on what they believed to be the leniency of the armistice terms and the good graces with which they were being received and dealt with by the conquerors. It was at this stage that Pétain, Laval and Darlan genuinely believed that peace negotiations with Germany were just around the corner, after which they would return to Paris and settle down to governing the whole country again. So Laval in particular, with Pétain's indifference or acquiesence, began rapidly overhauling the laws and judicial procedures of France to bring it into line with Fascist principles and methods. This involved such refinements as stripping certain categories of Frenchmen, including several thousand Jews, of their French citizenship.

But the first great expectation of the Vichy regime—swift defeat of England and a quick peace treaty with Germany—was effectively smashed by British guns firing on the French Fleet at Mers el-Kébir on July 3. Of course on the one hand this was a godsend to the Anglophobes of Vichy—the ultimate act of *perfide Albion*. But it also signaled loud and clear Winston Churchill's message to the world that the war would go on.

The Germans drew the lesson more quickly than the Vichy leaders. The relatively easy days of the early occupation period quickly came to an end. On August 1 the head of the Armistice Commission in Wiesbaden, General Otto von Stulpnagel, told the French representative, General Charles Huntziger: "Germany would have thought even as recently as two weeks ago that negotiations with England would be possible. That hope has been disappointed, and the Reich has been obliged to take security measures which are dictated by the circumstances and by the need to continue the war." Stockpiles of military equipment from the defeated and demobilized French Army were seized despite the armistice terms and shipped to Germany. After weeks of fruitless negotiation, the Nazis imposed occupation costs of 20 million Reichsmarks per day on Vichy—the equivalent of 400 million francs. French prisoners of war in German hands began to be shifted in early August not to freedom and release in the unoccupied zone but to prison camps in Germany. The demarcation line between the two zones became a sealed frontier, with only 300 letters per day allowed to trickle through the postal services. Later a system of printed postcards with checkoff messages was authorized by the Germans as a humanitarian concession. But by September 1940, the separation of the occupied and unoccupied zones was complete, and it began to penetrate in Vichy that the war would be a long one, and the outcome therefore uncertain.

Laval, however, persisted in these months in seeking a silver lining of collaboration in these heavy clouds of defeat. Murphy tells of a meeting with Laval at which the French leader was showing supreme confidence in his ability to outsmart the Germans, when his chef de cabinet entered to say that the German embassy in

Paris was on the telephone, wanting to speak to the premier. Murphy rose to leave, but Laval instead motioned him to get on the extension phone and listen in on the conversation.

It seems that Laval had submitted to the German ambassador in Paris, Otto Abetz, a list of about ten concessions that he hoped would be made in armistice conditions and regulations, in order to bolster his own position politically in the Vichy regime. Among other things, he was asking for release of the 1.8 million French prisoners of war in German hands, larger shipments of food to the unoccupied zone, and German evacuation of Paris and the territory to the south to enlarge the unoccupied zone and allow the government to return to the capital. Murphy, who began his diplomatic career in Munich and was fluent in German as well as French, heard on the other end of the line to Laval the voice of Abetz's number two at the German embassy, a diplomat named Aschenbach, whom he knew and whose voice he immediately recognized. Murphy recounted:

> Aschenbach was very businesslike. He took up Laval's requests one by one in order, reading the Premier's own words and then replying either yes or no. Every major request was followed by No. Only two minor concessions were granted. After Aschenbach hung up, Laval turned to me with a satisfied air and said, "I just wanted you to see how well things are going between us and the Germans." At first I thought that he was being sarcastic, but he was quite in earnest. Adroit lawyer that he was, he had apparently sold himself on his case, and was determined to prosecute it to the limit—which he certainly did. The limit for him was ignominious death.

The American embassy established itself in Vichy in the Villa Ica, property of Mrs. Jay Gould, an American millionairess who used to take the waters regularly in the town in pleasanter times. Murphy's basic instructions were straightforward and simple: to see that the French Fleet was not used against the United States and kept out of German hands; to see that Germany and Italy did not get control of French bases in North or West Africa or the Western Hemisphere, and finally to see that the Vichy government did not go beyond the armistice terms on the path of collaboration.

Beyond these specific diplomatic tasks, there were broader American objectives as well. A first was simply to make the American presence felt among Vichy ministers and politicians and hammer home in this defeatist and collaborationist atmosphere the constant message of American determination that the war would end in the defeat of the Axis. Of course in June and July of 1940, eighteen months before America entered the war, this did not carry much weight in Vichy. But as American preparedness and American involvement in the conflict increased, the Vichy leaders had to take more seriously the prospect that they might wind up on the losing side.

The second American objective was to encourage political resistance and seek out those who might be prepared to work for Allied victory. There were any number of tragic figures in Vichy ready to cry on American shoulders and plead their abhorrence at what was happening. But brave men who would declare themselves unequivocally and then act on behalf of what they professed to believe were few in those days, and most of them wound up in Vichy jails. So the American search for French patriots in Vichy in the end netted mainly opportunists and second-raters and fence-sitters. The stalwart, the tough, the strong and the determined swung not behind the American effort to bolster resistance, but behind General de Gaulle.

The other major American objective was the gathering of both political and military information, and this broadened in an important direction in 1941 to include a major intelligence operation in North Africa. Roosevelt's Vichy policy at the outset, therefore, had clear advantages for the Allied cause that the British were more than ready to acknowledge. All British links with France were severed after the attack on Mers el-Kébir, so the American embassy acted in part as British eyes and ears as well. Of course a major effort got under way in London to beef up British secret Intelligence operations in France, although before long this began to run into an inevitable and at times damaging clash and competition with de Gaulle's Free French under Colonel Passy.

In the meantime, Roosevelt and Churchill had already embarked on their highly secret and completely personal exchange of private cabled correspondence between the White House and Downing Street direct, bypassing all other government departments, officials, Cabinet officers and military commanders on both sides of the Atlantic. The correspondence was drafted by the two men without reference to others, and therefore of a remarkably uninhibited and freewheeling character. In these exchanges, Churchill frequently asked Roosevelt to use American influence on specific matters in Vichy and sketched out various diplomatic tactics and moves on behalf of the Allied cause. Roosevelt was invariably receptive, although usually putting his own twist on the actions he took and seldom disclosing that he was acting in direct response to a British request.

Thus, in the beginning there was a certain logical division of labor—Churchill looked after the fighting French; Roosevelt looked after the defeated French. The trouble was that as the war went on, Churchill and the British inevitably became more and more committed to General de Gaulle while the United States dug itself deeper and deeper into coaxing, cosseting and cajoling Pétain and Vichy. Roosevelt's Vichy gamble was that America could save France from itself at this juncture of its fate—that the men of Vichy remained the men of France's future if they could ever be slipped out of Nazi handcuffs. He gambled that Frenchmen could be found in Vichy who would rise up out of this mess and rally to the Allied cause. He had loyal and enthusiastic and largely uncritical lieutenants in Murphy and Admiral William D. Leahy, who went to Vichy as ambassador in 1941. But neither Murphy nor Leahy nor Roosevelt nor Cordell Hull nor anyone else in the State Department would ever accept the fact that there could be another France besides Vichy France—that Frenchmen, however they might have embraced Pétain, in the end would not and could not leave it at that, and that France's future could never rest in the hands of those at Vichy who had accepted defeat and embarked on collaboration.

Of course this schism first and foremost divided France itself. But it then divided the Allies for four years of war and continued to color Franco-American relations for thirty years of General de Gaulle's life. From 1940 to 1943, Roosevelt rejected de Gaulle while the United States sought instead to elicit support or collaboration in Vichy and in North Africa, first with Marshal Pétain and then with General Weygand, Admiral Darlan, General Henri Giraud and with numerous Vichy lesser-lights such as Marcel Peyrouton, who was a minister of interior, and Pierre-Étienne Flandin, who was briefly Vichy foreign minister. It was a flawed policy because the men were flawed and the regime was flawed with defeat. Even when all the Vichy possibilities were exhausted in the middle of 1943 and there no longer could be any doubt about who was going to dominate the French scene, Roosevelt went on refusing to give recognition or wholehearted endorsement and support to de Gaulle. And of course the General did nothing to help, with his goading tactics of noncooperation, his petty displays of independence, his constant recourse to intransigence, his manner and his personality. Bitter at American dealings with those he considered traitors to France, de Gaulle was determined to prevail on his own terms and saw no reason to be accommodating with Roosevelt. On the contrary, his tactics and political strategy were deliberately designed to enhance his own power and prestige (at least in his own eyes) by forcing FDR to come to him—requiring the president to admit, one way or another, sooner or later, that this Vichy policy had been wrong, had failed, was abandoned and buried and that he had turned to de Gaulle. As 1943 turned into 1944, Vichy went steadily down and de Gaulle went up. The more de Gaulle went up, the less reason he saw to change his attitude to seek Roosevelt's accommodation. The haughtier de Gaulle got, the madder Roosevelt got and the more difficult it became for the president to back off and admit the failure of his Vichy gamble.

Had this not been a monumental and embittered temperamental clash of political wills as well as a fundamental divergence of each man's view of France, there were plenty of ways and means and plenty of opportunities when it could have been resolved. Initially there was nothing wrong with Roosevelt's Vichy policy, nothing wrong with setting out to use American influence to a maximum to thwart Nazi aims and nothing wrong with trying to cajole or blackmail cooperation out of men wallowing in defeat. It is debatable how much the American presence in Vichy really did influence events, but there is certainly little doubt that an American absence from Vichy (like Bullitt's absence from Bordeaux) would have been a mistake. The problem was that Roosevelt clung to the policy too long, made too many overtures and half-commitments to the wrong kind of French friends, pursued the policy with too much zeal instead of cynical detachment and finally invested too much presidential prestige in sending Admiral Leahy as his ambassador to hold hands with Marshal Pétain. Roosevelt's intention was to increase influence and pressure on Pétain, but instead it appeared that he was going beyond simply dealing with Vichy and tipping over to active support for the regime in preference to de Gaulle and the Free French, who were fighting while Vichy was collaborating. The dispatch of Leahy, de Gaulle remarked in his Memoirs, "was enough to cool the ardor of those personalities whose first impulse might have driven them toward the Cross of Lorraine." A more hardheaded and pragmatic course for Roosevelt would have been to leave the Vichy embassy permanently in the hands of a career diplomat *chargé d'affaires* to deliver the notes and issue the warnings and burrow away at contacts. The whole episode should then have been terminated, wiped clean and abruptly closed down once its purpose had been served and its usefulness to the Allied cause was finished. That moment surely came with the invasion of North Africa in November 1942. But instead the division festered on. Roosevelt continued to deal with Vichyites and never did break cleanly, and he declined to grasp de Gaulle by the hand wholeheartedly and unreservedly.

*

By the end of the summer of 1940, a first period of test had passed in Vichy as far as the United States was concerned. Murphy's initial diplomatic effort was to warn ceaselessly that France would forfeit American friendship if it went beyond the armistice agreement and signed a separate peace treaty with Germany, that the defeated government should not forget that America was behind Britain and committed to Nazi defeat. Vichy hopes for a peace treaty died quickly, not because of American pressure but simply because the British were fighting on and Hitler decided to wait until he had won the whole war before making peace with France. Meanwhile, the Nazis moved the German frontier west across the Rhine to include Alsace and Lorraine in the Third Reich. They then expelled from the territory some 100,000 Frenchmen who declined to be turned into Germans and insisted on keeping French citizenship. The Nazi occupation screws were tightening, while Pierre Laval continued his implacable and relentless search for Nazi goodwill through collaboration.

But General de Gaulle was registering his first fringe successes in distant parts of the French Empire. The French enclave of Pondicherry in India (surrounded by British India) refused to accept the armistice with Germany, and in the far Pacific the territory of the New Hebrides declared for de Gaulle. The first substantial break came on August 26, when Félix Éboué, black governor of Chad in the center of Africa, broke from Vichy and rallied to de Gaulle. Thus, Pétain faced harsh and conflicting strains and pressures in all directions.

As a first sign of this, Weygand left his Cabinet post of minister of defense to go to Africa as commissioner general of the African colonies. Having done everything he could to bring about the armistice with Germany, he was quickly soured by Laval's personality as well as his obsequious pursuit of collaboration, and he had tumbled to the fact that it was going to be a long war with the outcome in doubt. He had begun to turn like a weathervane.

On the one hand, Weygand's departure from Vichy removed from the government a critic and opponent of Laval and therefore left the premier less inhibited than before in his dealings with the Nazis. On the other hand, Weygand was now far away from Vichy with an important overseas command, a position of responsibility and a certain independence where he might be enticed or influenced from the outside. Weygand also realized full well that North Africa would become increasingly important to the grand strategy of the war, and by the same token to the future of France itself. Therefore he began operating in North Africa with three basic objectives in view. First, he seemed determined to keep the Germans out and resist any further encroachments or concessions under the armistice. Next, he was determined to keep General de Gaulle out and preserve French possessions under Vichy control. But finally, he was prepared to envisage an Allied victory and therefore was open to overtures that would enable him to wind up on the winning side.

A cat-and-mouse game thus began between the Allies and Weygand that went on for nearly two years. The opening move came unexpectedly with the arrival in London in late October 1940 of a secret emissary from Pétain. He was a history teacher at the University of Besançon, Professor Louis Rougier. Pétain was putting out feelers for an improvement of relations between Britain and Vichy, and Rougier was received by both Churchill and Lord Halifax, who was then still foreign secretary. Rougier subsequently wrote at length about his mission, and his account was produced in defense evidence at the trial of Pétain after the war. The British, however, declared that Rougier's account was exaggerated and the documents that he produced had no validity. It seems doubtful that the British took the overture seriously, but they did give it half a try to see what might happen. Nothing did, except to show that cracks were beginning to appear in Vichy.

The British told Rougier that they were prepared to consider some easing of the blockade against France if Vichy would stand aside and allow the French Colonial Empire to opt for General de Gaulle without a fight. They also sent through Rougier a message to Weygand that he could count on "wholehearted collaboration of the British Empire and on a share of assistance afforded by the United States" if he would raise the standard in North Africa and rejoin the fight.

But before Rougier even got back to Vichy, Pétain had moved in the opposite direction, closer to the Germans. His most steadfast quality seems to have been his infinite capacity for secrecy from everyone about what he was doing and thinking. While Rougier was in London, Pétain reshuffled his Cabinet and gave Laval the Foreign Ministry as well as the premiership, ousting Paul Baudouin. But of course he could not very well take Laval into his confidence and disclose his secret overtures to the British. So, as the British anticipated, the whole affair simply evaporated. Meanwhile, Laval proceeded playing his next card—he would arrange a meeting between Pétain and Hitler.

By now Hitler was frustrated in his hopes of invading England, and he decided to turn to North Africa. He arranged first to confer with Generalissimo Francisco Franco at the French–Spanish border town of Hendaye. His purpose was to pressure Franco into entering the war at Germany's side, allow German troops to transit Spain and seize Gibraltar, move across into French North Africa and thus secure the Mediterranean, cut the British Empire and force Britain out of the war. But Franco, to the Führer's disgust, put up endless arguments and excuses and refused to play ball.

Laval, meanwhile, apprised by the Germans of Hitler's plans for the Hendaye meeting, proposed a meeting with Pétain afterward. It was Laval's hope and expectation that a deal between Hitler and Franco would be followed by one between Hitler and Pétain to establish France's place in the Axis.

Pétain did not want the meeting, and apparently at first resisted going. But Laval, having persuaded the Germans to issue the invitation, now argued that Pétain could not decline without giving offense to Hitler and making things worse, whereas going could result in German concessions on behalf of collaboration. So Pétain dutifully boarded a special train from Vichy to meet Hitler's special train at the little town of Montoire in the Loire valley not far from the city of Tours on October 24, 1940. The meeting lasted only a few hours and was inconclusive. The Führer delivered his standard harangue about England and how it would soon be crushed and asked whether France was now prepared to help Germany in the war and thus gain a favored position in the ultimate peace. Pétain replied that he accepted the principle of collaboration but "could not define the limits," and Laval interjected to beg Hitler not to press France to declare war against England until public opinion was more prepared. A secret memorandum of understanding was then quickly put together in very general terms, including a pledge that Germany "undertake to see that at the conclusion of peace with England, France obtains territorial compensations and that in the final accounting she retains in Africa a colonial domain essentially equivalent to what she possesses today." The memorandum was found in the German archives after the war.

Pétain on his return to Vichy dismissed the meeting and the results with the remark that "It will take six months to discuss the program and another six months to forget it." The old marshal was satisfied that he hadn't given anything away. But of course he had, because the symbolic effect of Pétain being photographed in conference with Hitler was far more damaging than the agreement they reached. Whatever the fine print or the excuses and explanations, that photo put a final stamp of collaboration on France, while every other nation Hitler had overrun was rallying to resistance, even placid Denmark.

The French people, of course, had no means of showing their feelings publicly, but the disgust and resentment of France's recent allies was loud and clear. The British took the highly unusual course of involving King George VI in their response. Assuming, probably correctly, that Pétain would not be particularly happy with a letter from Churchill, a message was transmitted through American channels from King George to Pétain in which he assured the marshal of Britain's continued goodwill toward France and begged him not to harm a former ally by taking sides against her or making concessions beyond the terms of the armistice.

President Roosevelt was far tougher and more forceful. In a note handed over to the Vichy government the day after the Montoire conference, Roosevelt said:

> The fact that a government is a prisoner of war of another power does not justify such a prisoner in serving its conqueror in operations against a former ally. Any agreement entered into between France and Germany which partook of this character would most definitely wreck the traditional friendship between the French and American peoples, and would permanently remove any chance that this government would be disposed to give any

assistance to the French people in their distress, and would create a wave of bitter indignation against France on the part of American public opinion. If France pursued such a policy, the United States could make no effort when the appropriate time came to exercise its influence to insure to France the retention of her overseas possessions.

In unvarnished language, Roosevelt threatened to see France stripped of its colonial possessions if it entered the war against Britain. Vichy officials complained to the American mission that the message had been "painfully curt" and Pétain drafted a rather hurt reply contending that the French government had always preserved its "liberty of action." (It is remarkable how this theme of independence and liberty of action reverberates unceasingly from French leaders, whether Pétain, Laval and Darlan using it to justify collaboration or de Gaulle proclaiming independence from all and sundry.)

Pétain seems to have been shaken by Roosevelt's blast, for on November 16 he had a long conversation with H. Freeman Matthews from the American mission (in Murphy's absence) and said that collaboration would go no further than economic questions and that in no sense did it mean French military aid to Germany or cession of bases. After denouncing the British, as he regularly did, for their support of "the traitor de Gaulle," Pétain went on to say to Matthews: "But they are fighting a good fight now, and I do not believe they will ever yield. On the other hand, they cannot land on the continent and invade Germany. So I see a drawn peace after much tragic destruction. The sooner that can come, the better, for France will pay the price."

Thus, by the end of 1940, Pétain also had begun to take a different view on the course of the war. It followed from this that he began to entertain doubts about Laval taking France too far and too fast down the path of collaboration. He was also unhappy with Laval over being maneuvered into the Montoire meeting, which was rebounding badly against him. Others in his government were anxious to see Laval dumped, either because of his policies or because they simply detested him for his sinister reptilian character and personality.

In early December Laval had gone to Paris for a meeting with Abetz, the German ambassador. He returned to Vichy on December 13 beaming with pleasure at a new "concession." Hitler was going to move the ashes of Napoleon's son, the Duke of Reichstadt, from Vienna, where they had rested since 1832, to Paris and place them alongside Napoleon's tomb at the Invalides. The Germans wanted Marshal Pétain to attend the ceremony. Whether this was a last straw or not, Pétain suddenly called a full Cabinet meeting several hours after Laval's return and demanded the resignation of all his ministers. He then accepted the resignation of Laval and followed this by placing Laval under house arrest at his magnificent château at Châteldon, not far from Vichy. Admiral Darlan took Laval's place.

The Germans reacted furiously to Laval's dismissal, and at their insistence the house arrest was quickly lifted. Darlan rushed off first to see Joachim von Ribbentrop, the Nazi foreign minister, and later Hitler as well, to give assurances that the policy of collaboration would continue. There were brief hopes in London and

104 / CHARLES DE GAULLE

Washington that Pétain was stiffening, but in fact very little changed in Vichy behavior in the months ahead, and it was far from the end for Laval.

Meanwhile, Roosevelt had recalled Robert Murphy to Washington for fresh instructions and a new assignment. He was to make a tour of French Africa, report on conditions and attitudes and possibilities for American action. He was to establish himself at the consulate in Algiers and cultivate a close relationship with General Weygand as a prime objective. By making an "American presence" felt in North Africa, the aim was to try to rally Weygand to the Allies or at least make sure that the territory did not slip into German hands. Murphy then left Vichy on his new assignment the week after Laval's dismissal.

At this same time, Roosevelt picked Admiral Leahy to be ambassador to Vichy, upgrading American representation to the Pétain government. At first Roosevelt wanted General of the Armies John J. Pershing to take the assignment, but fortunately the old soldier was not well enough to go, so the world was spared the unhappy picture of the commander in chief of the victorious American Army in the First World War sitting down with the fallen Hero of Verdun. Leahy arrived in Vichy in January 1941 and remained until May 1942, well after Pearl Harbor and America's entry into the war against Germany.

After Marshal Pétain shook hands with Hitler at Montoire and pledged his collaboration, the tide began to turn for Frenchmen in the struggle between Pétain's France and de Gaulle's France. Nonetheless, Franklin Roosevelt continued to gamble on the losers.

SEVEN

1940: NADIR AT DAKAR

At the end of July 1940, General de Gaulle drove from London to a Royal Air Force station at Odiham in the Hampshire countryside southwest of the city to carry out an inspection and review of the first Free French Air Force squadron. In the wake of the sinking of French warships at Mers el-Kébir by the British, it had been a poor month for the Free French. Of the 18,000 French Navy men who had been forcibly removed from their ships in British ports and interned on the same day as the Mers el-Kébir action, only fifty officers and about 200 seamen had elected to stay in England and enlist under de Gaulle. The rest opted for repatriation to France and were on their way home. Remaining to fight alongside the British was not at that moment a popular cause with French sailors. The total Gaullist movement at the end of July had crept up to 7,000—less than one-sixth of all Frenchmen then on British soil. Still, the little ceremony that de Gaulle was to perform at Odiham was a moment of history.

A few days before, at General de Gaulle's special request, some of the more experienced of the French airmen among the handful in Britain had been included in Royal Air Force bomber crews after brief crash training and had flown on a night operation against the Ruhr. It had then been announced in an air communiqué that "units of the Free French Air Force" had struck the first French blow against the Germans since the armistice. All the French Air Force personnel who had rallied to de Gaulle had now been collected at Odiham to form a scratch outfit of about 300 men, with half a dozen serviceable French planes that had been collected from various airfields around Britain—a couple of Dewoitine fighters, a twin-engined Potez, a Caudron Simouns, the only planes the French knew how to fly. Flight training and equipping with British aircraft to enable the French to fight was still some months off. Still, this little band of brothers was immaculately uniformed, drilled and drawn up for de Gaulle's inspection.

De Gaulle trooped the line and then took his station to review a march-past. A French trumpeter sounded the colors and an airman tugged at the halyards of the flagpole in front of the squadron command hut. The Tricolor rose to the top, and when it unfurled in the light summer breeze, in the white field at its center had been added the two-armed Cross of Lorraine. It took de Gaulle by surprise, and he reacted with indignation. As soon as the march-past was concluded, he strode into the command hut and demanded to know who was responsible. *"Il n'y a qu'UN drapeau Français,"* he declared stiffly. (There is only ONE French flag.) But he was accompanied to the ceremony by Commandant Thierry d'Argenlieu of the French Navy, in peacetime a Carmelite monk who had temporarily relinquished his holy orders and his seclusion at the outbreak of the war to resume a Navy career and then had made his way across the Channel from Brittany in June to join de Gaulle. Listened to by de Gaulle probably more for the fact that he was a priest than a naval officer, d'Argenlieu argued that far from any disrespect to the French flag, the addition of the Cross of Lorraine made it the ideal emblem of resistance, recalling the banner under which Saint Joan of Arc fought to liberate France from an earlier occupation and a reminder as well for Frenchmen of the province of Lorraine, which had once again been annexed to Germany. No true Frenchman, he declared, could have it in his heart to despise such a banner under which France would find unity and resistance. De Gaulle probably did not need much convincing. Indeed, he had once lectured on the importance of symbols and appearances in the exercise of power and leadership, and the Tricolor emblazoned with the Cross of Lorraine forthwith became the flag of the Free French.

A few days later, on August 2, it was announced in Vichy that a military tribunal had tried General de Gaulle *in absentia* on charges of desertion and disobedience of orders and that he had been condemned to death.

De Gaulle records of this time that "it would be impossible to imagine the generous kindness which the English people everywhere showed." When the death sentence was announced, accompanied by an order confiscating all his property in France, he says that "quantities of jewels were left at Carlton Gardens [Free French headquarters] anonymously, and dozens of unknown widows sent their wedding rings in order that the gold might serve the work of General de Gaulle."

In the meantime more substantial British assistance was under way. For some weeks negotiations had been going on between de Gaulle's Provisional French National Committee and the British Foreign Office on a formal agreement of recognition and economic support for the Free French. Conducting the negotiation on behalf of de Gaulle was René Cassin, a distinguished constitutional jurist. Not for the last time the British were confronted with de Gaulle's extraordinary capacity for turning fine print into major issues of principle. General Spears, who followed the negotiations in his capacity as British liaison officer with the Free French, wrote: "The arguments over the text of the agreement between His Majesty's government and de Gaulle were conducted with exasperating acerbity on the latter's behalf by his tiresome bearded legal adviser, Professor Cassin, until even the best disposed of Foreign Office officials grew weary of trying to meet what appeared to be the manifestation of the overwrought nerves of our guests."

There were three basic points at issue, major objectives that de Gaulle sought at the very outset to achieve. First, he wanted a British guarantee in the agreement to restore not only the frontiers of Metropolitan France but also the French Empire—as he put it, "bearing in mind, on the one hand, the hypothesis that the fortunes of war might bring England to a compromise peace and considering, on the other, that the British might perhaps be tempted by this or that overseas possession of ours." It seems that *perfide Albion* was never far from his mind even then.

In the event, Churchill could not forecast the eventual conditions in which the world would emerge from the war any more than de Gaulle could, and he refused such a sweeping guarantee of return to the *status quo ante*. De Gaulle had to be satisfied, after much argument, with a formulation under which Britain undertook only to promise "the integral restoration of the independence and greatness of France" without any commitment to specifics about territories or empire. In a secret personal letter of interpretation and explanation, Churchill informed de Gaulle that Britain was unable to extend precise guarantees of restoration to any of the nations fighting at her side, although he added: "Of course we shall do our best." To which de Gaulle replied in secret that he took note of the prime minister's statement and hoped that the day might come when the British would "consider the question with less reserve."

The second basic objective for de Gaulle was the command structure and control over the Free French military forces he would be raising. Here the British chiefs of staff became involved, for clearly they did not want to endorse a situation in which Britain would equip a Free French military establishment only to find that it intended to fight its own war outside British control. De Gaulle was enough of a realist to know that he *had* to accept British supremacy, but he was determined to blur or minimize this as far as possible. In the end, a formula was agreed to under which the British recognized him as being in supreme command of French forces, while he accepted to place the forces under the general directives of the British High Command.

Finally there was the extremely tricky problem of the specter of Frenchmen fighting against Frenchmen under British orders. De Gaulle insisted on a clause specifying that volunteers who joined him would not be required "to bear arms against France."

Again Churchill got around this roadblock with a further secret personal letter to de Gaulle in which the prime minister stipulated that this must be interpreted as referring to "a France free to choose a road, and not subject to the direct or indirect constraint of Germany." Thus, if Pétain's government should declare war against Britain, the Free French would certainly be expected to fight Frenchmen of Vichy alongside the British. But in the meantime de Gaulle had made his points, and the agreement that was signed and announced on August 7, 1940, constituted the foundations of his accession to real power.

The agreement also provided for funding of the Free French by the British Treasury, which, according to Cabinet records, amounted to about £8 million in the first year, a bargain at less than $40 million, which France repaid to Britain before the end of the war. One final small point was decided personally by

Churchill in de Gaulle's favor. In the immediate period after the fall of France, the British services had accepted many French recruits who had put on British uniforms, and they were reluctant now to release them to General de Gaulle. But in the end Churchill ruled against his own services and decreed that as a matter of principle "new recruits should join their own national forces" in Britain, and General de Gaulle should be provided with lists of all Frenchmen serving in British uniform so they could be contacted and invited to transfer, at their own decision, to the Free French.

De Gaulle summarized:

> The August 7th agreement had a considerable importance for the Free French, not only because it got us out of immediate material difficulties, but also because the British authorities, having now an official basis for their relations with us, no longer hesitated to make things easier for us. Above all, the world knew that a new beginning of Franco-British solidarity had been made in spite of everything.

The first real stirrings of rejection of surrender in the French Empire now began to be felt, both in Vichy and at Free French headquarters in London. The territory of the New Hebredies had been the first to declare for General de Gaulle at the end of June, and Pondicherry had also rejected the armistice almost as soon as it was signed. Resistance to Vichy, it seemed, increased in direct ratio to distance from France. However gallant and welcome these changes of allegiance were, they were faraway places from which to rally the French to throw off the Nazi yoke. The key clearly lay in the possessions much nearer home—in Africa and the Middle East. If de Gaulle could not find support from some major French colony acknowledging his authority, he would simply languish as a stateless exile in London, to be used or discarded by the British.

Various messages of support had been reaching him in London from Africa and elsewhere, but the most promising had come from the governor of Chad, Félix Éboué—in de Gaulle's description, "This man of intelligence and heart, so ardently French, this humanist philosopher revolted with his whole being against the submission of France and the triumph of Nazi racial intolerance." On July 16 de Gaulle cabled Éboué from London: "I am aware of your attitude, which I approve entirely. Duty consists in holding every point of the Empire, for France, against the Germans and Italians. Please inform me of your situation as far as you think it opportune to do so. I am at your disposal for any help I can give."

Elsewhere there were resistance movements in embryo in the French Cameroons, with its capital at Duala; in the French Congo at Brazzaville; in French Guinea at Conakry; and in Ubangi-Shari, in the center of Africa on the upper reaches of the Congo. Moreover, British and French interests in Africa were continuously intertwined by geography, their colonies frequently bordering on each other. And there were memories of Germany in Africa as well, prior to the First World War.

Accordingly, there were many elements with which to work to bring French

Africa over to the Free French. De Gaulle received a positive response from Éboué in the Chadian capital of Fort Lamy before the end of July, supported by the local French commander, Colonel Marchand. But on both sides it was deemed necessary to proceed with prudence before declaring any break from Vichy. Viewed from Chad, it was quite possible for Vichy to mount a minimal military operation from a neighboring French African colony to remove the governor and block any defection to de Gaulle. And in fact, the Vichy government considered doing just that when Éboué finally did announce his transfer of allegiance at the end of August. From de Gaulle's standpoint, he—ever the strategist—wanted to fit the defection of Chad into a larger plan to obtain control over all of French Africa and not treat it simply as a one-shot isolated acquisition. Accordingly all was kept secret until de Gaulle could work out his moves to give greater security to those preparing to follow his lead.

With the groundwork being laid in Africa, de Gaulle clearly needed British help, and he turned to the colonial secretary, Lord Lloyd, who was aggressively pro-Gaullist and close to Churchill as well. Clearly British colonial interests, security interests and the war effort from its possessions of Nigeria, Sierra Leone, Gambia and the Gold Coast (now Ghana) would be well served if neighboring French colonies opted for de Gaulle. The problems of Vichy responding—both politically and militarily—would be both minimized and complicated if a number of colonies could be won over more or less simultaneously. De Gaulle believed that he could shake the tree in Fort Lamy, Duala and Brazzaville virtually without any military force. Lloyd readily agreed to cooperate with transport planes, communications and other aid to coordinate the operations from the security of Lagos, capital of British Nigeria.

In mid-August de Gaulle's "missionaries" began converging on West Africa. René Pleven, who had been with him from the first broadcast in London, was de Gaulle's choice to receive the allegiance of Chad. Assigned to handle the Brazzaville operation was Colonel de Larminat, who had defected to the Free French from French Somalia on the opposite side of the African continent. The takeover of Duala was entrusted to Captain Jacques de Hauteclocque, who adopted the *nom de guerre* of Leclerc and went on to command a Free French division all the way from Africa to the Danube.

All went like clockwork. Pleven flew from Lagos to Fort Lamy on August 25, and next day, as prearranged, Éboué announced that he was joining the Free French and de Gaulle broadcast news of the success over the BBC from London. On August 27 Leclerc, with a handful of soldiers, reached Duala by native canoes after a brief altercation with a local British commander in neighboring territory, who was fearful of failure and ordered the operation abandoned. Leclerc, with de Gaulle's full authority, pressed on regardless, arrived at Duala upriver by night, contacted local *résistants* and simply occupied government headquarters and raised the Cross of Lorraine. Finally, the next day, August 28, de Larminat, with a small party of soldiers, crossed the Congo River from the Belgian Congo capital of Léopoldville, where he had been warmly welcomed and supported, to the French Congo capital of Brazzaville. The Vichy governor protested, then surrendered meekly to the modest display of force and was shipped back across the river in the same boat to Léopoldville.

Thus, by the end of August three major pieces of the African jigsaw had been fitted into de Gaulle's map in lightning succession. Free France was no longer merely General de Gaulle's voice on the BBC: it had become a force to contend with. But then, on the heels of these August successes, came the nadir at Dakar.

*

The story of the Dakar episode deserves close study [wrote Winston Churchill in his War History] because it illustrates in a high degree not only the unforeseeable accidents of war, but the interplay of military and political forces, and the difficulties of combined operations, especially where allies are involved. To the world at large it seemed a glaring example of miscalculation, confusion, timidity and muddle. In the United States, where special interest was taken on account of the proximity of Dakar to the American continent, there was a storm of unfavorable criticism. At home there were many complaints of faulty war direction.

Jutting out into the South Atlantic on the westernmost point of the African continent just north of the equator, the fortified French port and naval base at Dakar was of major strategic importance, both militarily and politically, in that desperate autumn of 1940 when Britain was fighting alone. In the hands of Vichy France, Dakar was officially out of the war. But it was like one of those fortified castles in the Middle Ages that sat immobile in the landscape but dominated everything around it and had to be taken into account by all who wished to pass by. In the hands of the Germans, Dakar could have been turned into a major base for Atlantic submarine operations, vastly improving the range and efficiency of the U-boat fleets against British convoys moving around Africa and American shipping in the Caribbean and Latin America. But if Dakar could be delivered into the hands of the Free French, it would greatly alter the naval picture to the advantage of the British as well as providing a much-needed air staging post for the short 1,600-mile flight across the South Atlantic to Brazil. Above all, for the Free French it would constitute a major political prize, bringing all the vast hinterland of French West Africa with it. The Battle of Britain was approaching its climax, but with England's back to the wall, it was typical of Churchill to seek to strike back, however limited the means, in some bold stroke of war. Dakar offered such a possibility. The operation originated with Churchill, was his concept and drive. The failure—unfortunately and unfairly—came to rest primarily on Charles de Gaulle.

Originally, de Gaulle was against attempting a direct assault with Free French forces on Dakar. His resources were still quite small. He lacked infantry in numbers, the guns, the aircraft, the naval units to mount an attack with sufficient force to ensure success if opposed. And it was clear that Dakar would not drop into his hands like ripe fruit, as other African colonies were ready to do. In mid-July the Vichy authorities installed a strong and energetic Pétain loyalist as governor general of the colony, General Pierre Boisson. He had immediately imprisoned a number of officials and local French citizens who had expressed Free French sympathies and was clearly in firm control. The French battleship *Richelieu,* which lay in the harbor, had been damaged by a British torpedo attack in early July as part of the general action against the French Fleet everywhere. But its guns were still serviceable and its crew ready to obey orders to fight any invasion force.

De Gaulle therefore had to assume that Dakar would be a battle that at this early stage he should avoid. At the end of July he met with Churchill for a discussion of the whole picture and prospects in French Africa and explained his assessment of the Dakar problem. He proposed instead to land Free French forces on the "soft underbelly" to the south of Dakar at Conakry, the capital of French Guinea, where he knew that local defenses would be much lighter and the French population a great deal more receptive. Conakry was linked to Dakar by road and a railway line, up which de Gaulle proposed to advance, gathering defectors about him as he went. The one basic problem was that he would need support of the Royal Navy to get his forces ashore and then ensure that they were not subsequently cut off by some counteraction by Vichy forces. This was bound to be difficult if not impossible for the British to provide out of their stretched naval resources. Churchill listened and discussed all this with de Gaulle but made no immediate comments or commitments.

But afterward he gave immediate instructions to a Joint Planning Subcommittee of the chiefs of staff to draw up plans for landing Free French forces in West Africa, and an initial report came back to him on August 4. The planners estimated, in a fit of optimism, that de Gaulle's 2,500 soldiers could be loaded to sail for Africa by mid-August under British naval protection, but with no other British forces involved. They would be landed at either Dakar, Conakry or Duala, but only if it were certain there would be no effective opposition. The planners added a proviso that at this dangerous period of the war, there should be no action that might risk pushing the Vichy government into declaring war on Britain. Churchill brooded about the problem and then made up his own mind that the expedition should be beefed up with British forces as well, and that they should go for the big strategic target—Dakar itself. He sent for de Gaulle on August 6, and de Gaulle gives a vivid account of the scene in the Downing Street Cabinet room with maps spread out on the table and Churchill in full flight in one of his glowing monologues:

> Dakar wakes up one morning, sad and uncertain. But behold, by the light of the rising sun, its inhabitants perceive the sea, to a great distance, covered with ships. An immense fleet! A hundred war or transport vessels! These approach slowly, addressing by radio messages of friendship to the town, to the Navy, to the Garrison. Some of them are flying the Tricolor. Others are sailing under British, Dutch, Polish or Belgian colors. From this Allied force there breaks away an inoffensive small ship bearing the white flag of parley. It enters the harbor and disembarks the envoys of General de Gaulle. They are brought to the Governor. Their job is to convince him that if he lets you

land, the Allied fleet retires, and that nothing remains to be settled between him and you but the terms of his cooperation. On the contrary, if he wants a fight, he has every chance of being crushed. Perhaps he will wish, for honor's sake, to fire a few shots. But he will not go farther. And that evening he will dine with you and drink to final victory.

Two of the great dramatists of history were working on each other in that Cabinet room meeting. De Gaulle records that "stripping Mr. Churchill's idea of the seductive ornaments added to it by his eloquence, I recognized on reflection that it was based on certain solid data." He still had his doubts, but he decided to go along, largely, he says, because he reasoned that sooner or later the British were bound to "settle the question of Dakar" on their own, and it was therefore best that the Free French get there first whatever the risks. Once again those built-in historical French suspicions of Britain were never far below the surface in de Gaulle's mind.

Two days after this meeting, on August 8, with the Battle of Britain reaching its intensity in the skies over southern England, Churchill minuted firm instructions to the chiefs of staff to prepare orders for rapid mounting of the Dakar expedition, adding firmly that "the risk of a French declaration of war and whether it should be courted is reserved for the Cabinet." On August 12 Churchill went over the plans for the operation personally with the designated commanders, Vice Admiral John Cunningham and Major General N. M. S. Irwin. Final approval by the War Cabinet was taken on August 13. In Churchill's words: "I thus undertook in an exceptional degree the initiation and advocacy of the Dakar expedition, to which the code name 'Menace' was assigned." In a crash operation, the forces were assembled, the equipment loaded and the expedition sailed from Liverpool only eighteen days later, on August 31, with General de Gaulle flying the Cross of Lorraine in the Dutch ship *Westerland,* converted to a troop transport.

*

The prize was indeed glittering, for if Dakar could be seized it would bring all of French Africa south of the Sahara under the Free French, vastly damaging the strategic and political picture for Vichy and greatly strengthening Britain and her fighting allies. But before the expedition sailed, disquiet and uncertainties began.

The British in August of 1940 were in an understandably high state of security jitters, with the whole people, fearing invasion, geared up to watch for parachutists and listening for defeatist talk or indiscreet military gossiping. The Free French were still a miscellaneous collection of officers and men who had never worked together before and were motivated more by enthusiasm for a fight than by discipline. Soon word began filtering back through British counterespionage services that Dakar was becoming common talk among the French in London, and in Liverpool, where the troops were being concentrated. It was reported that French officers drank a toast to Dakar at a dinner in a Liverpool restaurant. Meanwhile British soldiers were turning up fitted out in tropical uniforms. Then Churchill received a specific minute from the Joint Intelligence Committee in the Foreign Office, the highest Intelligence body (then and today), of a definite leak of security information on Dakar, as opposed to mere loose talk. It was attributed to the wife of a Frenchman in Liverpool who was suspected of sympathies and contacts with one of the numerous pro-Vichy French in England. But the prime minister was less concerned simply because he reasoned that no one could be certain where a seabound force might turn up once it left England. Dakar, in other words, could merely be a cover for another destination.

Although there was too much loose talk, there was no leak or breach of security that in any way affected the outcome of the Dakar expedition. The convoy made its passage to its assembly point at Freetown, in the British colony of Sierre Leone, south of Dakar, without detection and without interference. The Germans knew nothing of the expedition and neither did Vichy. German naval archives captured by the British at the end of the war showed that on September 6, when the convoy had been under way for a week, Grand Admiral Erich Räder held a lengthy conference with Hitler without any mention whatsoever of a British convoy having sailed, or a suggestion or suspicion that any action against West Africa anywhere might be in the offing.

Moreover, the final date for the actual assault on Dakar was only fixed at Freetown, less than three days before the eventual H-hour, and at that point it was touch and go for twenty-four hours whether the attack might not be switched to another French African port. So there could not have been any valid leak by anyone in Britain in advance of either the timing or the target.

Nevertheless, a succession of those "accidents of war" of which Churchill wrote did combine to give the public impression that the whole thing was botched because the French talked too much. This was heightened by the fact that for perfectly sound reasons of security and Intelligence operations it was impossible at that time to explain publicly the succession of mishaps that derailed the Dakar expedition. Churchill declined on security grounds to make more than the barest statement to the House of Commons on what had happened, and the House respected his begging off further explanations. But this simply fired the impression that the prime minister was covering up for the French, which was not the case at all. It was his own services that had blundered.

Across the Atlantic, Churchill had secretly informed Roosevelt of the Dakar expedition in one of their private exchanges, and Roosevelt was sour about the whole affair. His pro-Vichy policy was in full swing, and he regarded it as a needless risk on the part of the British when he was doing everything he could to keep Pétain and Vichy from declaring war on Britain. And he had no sympathy whatsoever for furthering de Gaulle's cause in Africa at the expense of Vichy. So he grumpily replied to Churchill that he "better make sure it's a success," and when it failed he was more than ready to join in heaping all the blame on de Gaulle. Thus, the Dakar affair as one of its main aftereffects produced an in-eradicable conviction in Washington—bolstered by prejudice and policy—that General de Gaulle and the Free French could not be trusted with military secrets. This was to color everything for the next four years.

Immediately before de Gaulle sailed in the Dakar convoy, he had announced the change of allegiance to the Free French of the colonies of Chad, Cameroons and French Congo, and it was therefore to be expected that Vichy would react somehow to stop the rot in its empire. A first move came on September 5, when Pétain switched General Maxime Weygand from his post as minister of defense to Algiers to become resident general for the African possessions. His mission would be to ensure Vichy loyalty and control over the colonies against further defections to de Gaulle. At the same time plans were drawn up (although never put into effect) to send pro-Vichy forces into Chad to oust Félix Éboué and restore Vichy rule.

More important for the Dakar operation, on the evening of September 9 the British consul general in Tangier, the free city on the Moroccan coast of North Africa, received information that he immediately passed to the commander of the North Atlantic Station at Gibraltar, Admiral North, and to the Foreign Office Intelligence Branch in London that "French squadron may try to pass the Straits westward for unknown destination within next seventy-two hours." The information came from a French Navy intelligence officer who had secretly joined the Free French. But the telegram reached London in the early-morning hours of September 10, when air activity in the Battle of Britain was at its height and work continuously interrupted at the Foreign Office by raid warnings when everyone had to break off and head for shelters. As a result, the decoding branch was way behind on telegrams and the message from Tangier did not get processed for *four days*. Unfortunately, the consul general in Tangier had no way of knowing the potential importance of what he had been told, and he had failed to make it urgent. Nor had Admiral North in Gibraltar been told of the Dakar expedition, and he took no precautionary measures to receive, intercept or divert the French ships when the message was received. Accordingly, three Vichy cruisers and three destroyers passed Gibraltar at full speed on the morning of September 11 and turned south to Dakar. North was subsequently relieved of his command for this failure.

Frantic efforts by the British to lock the barn door after the French passed Gibraltar failed because the French ships were faster than anything the Royal Navy had available in the area and had a head start anyway. So, by September 14, the naval forces in Dakar had been substantially reinforced, and this was bound to mean a political as well as a military stiffening of pro-Vichy General Boisson to resist any further defections in the African Empire. Yet it seemed pretty clear that the Vichy French still had no foreknowledge of the Anglo–Free French expedition nearing Africa, for their ships spread awnings in Dakar against the tropical sun and crews were granted shore leave. Moreover, five days later, still innocent of the presence of the invasion force in the area that had now rendezvoused with naval reinforcements at Freetown, four French cruisers plus support ships abruptly put out from Dakar to try to reach Libreville in Gabon, well to the south, where Free French feeling was growing. In fact, the colony went over to de Gaulle a few weeks later. By now the Royal Navy was patrolling actively off Dakar, in advance of the planned assault, and two of the cruisers were intercepted and diverted to Casablanca while the other two eluded the British and made it back into Dakar.

News of the passage of the French ships through Gibraltar reached de Gaulle on

September 14, via the indispensable BBC, as his convoy chugged along in the South Atlantic at eight knots an hour, two weeks out of Liverpool. He immediately asked for an urgent conference with Admiral Cunningham, who meanwhile had received orders from the Admiralty to break off and attempt to intercept the French before they reached Dakar. De Gaulle's first opinion was that if the French ships could not be located, the convoy should turn back and scrub the operation. Meanwhile the convoy sailed on with reduced escort. So, on September 17, the little invasion force reached Freetown while the French sailors were relaxing under their awnings in Dakar.

It was by now a fairly impressive task force—two aging but powerful British battleships, three cruisers, the aircraft carrier *Ark Royal,* a flotilla of destroyers, three sloops and two armed trawlers of the embryo Free French Navy, and a collection of transports carrying Free French Army units totaling about 2,500 men, plus two battalions of Royal Marines. But when all was assembled on schedule at Freetown, a message arrived from London from Churchill informing Admiral Cunningham, General Irwin and General de Gaulle that "His Majesty's Government have decided that the presence of French cruisers at Dakar renders the execution of the operation impractical," and that "unless General de Gaulle has strong objections" his force should now be landed at Duala to consolidate the Free French gains in other parts of Africa.

De Gaulle immediately met with Cunningham and Irwin to consider a reply to London, and argued that since the whereabouts of the Vichy reinforcements were now known, the assault should go forward. He reasoned, correctly as it turned out in the next days, that the ships were probably only pausing en route to another African destination and that clearly the element of surprise had not been lost since Vichy was still not aware of the assault force in the area. Cunningham and Irwin were in complete agreement, and they cabled back to London asking that the assault go forward as planned on the grounds that "the presence of these cruisers has not sufficiently increased the risks, which were always accepted, to justify abandonment of the enterprise." Churchill, who was forever looking for audacity in his commanders, got War Cabinet agreement to reverse the cancellation and signaled on September 18 the authority to go ahead. This judgment was reinforced when the French vessels then sailed from Dakar, to be intercepted by the British on September 20. On that day in Freetown, de Gaulle got into an altercation with Admiral Cunningham, who wanted him to operate from the British flagship instead of among his own troops on the *Westerland,* but when this was settled on de Gaulle's terms the invasion force sailed for Dakar on September 21.

Just before they sailed, one of de Gaulle's trusted emissaries to Africa, Colonel Boislambert, arrived by air from Lagos with fresh intelligence from Dakar that colonial troops manning the coast artillery had been replaced by French sailors and that a police roundup of potential Free French supporters was under way. He urged a postponement to avoid a costly fight, arguing that with a little more time it would be possible to get Free French supporters back in place inside Dakar. But de Gaulle really had no choice. Having urged the go-ahead against Churchill's orders, he could not now reverse and ask that it be called off. So he dispatched

Boislambert with three volunteers to try to penetrate the city ahead of the arrival of the assault force—which they managed to do, only to be arrested and returned to a Vichy jail in France.

The expedition arrived off Dakar at 4 A.M. on September 23, sailing straight into the next of those "accidents of war" that sealed its fate. When the sun rose, a light morning mist began to thicken into a dense sea fog—not only unpredictable but almost totally unknown in that climate. Gone was Churchill's romantic vision of Dakar waking up one morning "sad and uncertain. But behold, by the light of the rising sun, its inhabitants perceive the sea, to a great distance, covered with ships. An immense fleet!" The inhabitants saw no such thing, and, far worse, the Royal Navy could not see its shore targets. This was still the era when targeting had to be visual or controlled by spotter aircraft. So the invasion flotilla sat in the sea fog, unable even to see each other.

Nevertheless, the opening phase of the operation got under way when two French airmen who had never flown before from a carrier deck got off the *Ark Royal* in a pair of French reconnaissance planes that had been found in England after the ill-fated Narvik expedition to fight the Nazi invasion of Norway. The planes were to land at the Dakar air base, and the commandant, it was hoped, would be persuaded to change sides.

With British aircraft patrolling and watching overhead, the two Free French planes landed and a few minutes later spread out special "success" signals on the airfield. At once the signal went to the *Ark Royal* to launch more aircraft to join the Free French on the ground and secure the field. But by the time reinforcements were airborne, everything abruptly changed. Vichy fighters began taking off, and antiaircraft fire opened up from the ground. The *Ark Royal* aircraft were immediately recalled.

Meanwhile General de Gaulle had broadcast to the people of Dakar from the *Westerland,* and two launches set out for the harbor, flying the Cross of Lorraine and a white flag of truce. The leading naval officer was Commandant Thierry d'Argenlieu, the Carmelite monk in uniform who had persuaded de Gaulle to adopt the Free French symbol. They reached the harbor and asked to deliver a letter to General Boisson. With some evident reluctance, the harbor officer, under orders, refused to accept the letter or permit them to land. They argued until armed harbor patrol craft arrived, and then had no choice but to pull away. As they moved back down the harbor, the Vichy forces opened up with machine-gun fire. D'Argenlieu was hit and wounded, and thus ironically became the first battle casualty under the Cross of Lorraine, which he had assured de Gaulle "no Frenchman could despise."

Cunningham now took his ships dangerously in toward shore to get out of the worst of the fog and, he hoped, to confront the Dakar garrison with that awesome picture which Churchill had envisaged. But shortly after 10 A.M., as the Royal Navy vessels began to emerge from the fog, coastal batteries opened up, and the cruiser *Cumberland* was hit in the engine room. Next, the battleship *Richelieu,* disabled in the harbor, was towed by tugs into firing position and brought its 15-inch guns to bear on the British. Cunningham had withheld British return fire during an exchange of radio messages with Boisson, who again rejected any parley. After returning some salvos, the British withdrew back into the fog at a report of submarines in the area.

Things were scarcely going according to plan, and at noon it was decided with de Gaulle that in the face of resistance an assault landing would be necessary. It was already planned that if this had to happen it would take place at a small fishing harbor three miles southeast of Dakar. But as the time to disembark the troops into landing craft approached, the fog grew so thick that it was impossible to see the surface of the water from the deck of the ships. No positions could be fixed, no rendezvous of landing craft was possible, no bearings could be given, and the danger of collision was constant. Unhappily the weather ashore was clear enough for the Vichy defenders to operate aircraft and fire on approaching targets.

Nevertheless, by 3 P.M. a Free French Navy escort ship, the *Commandant Duloc,* got clear of the fog and entered the fishing harbor as a surprised and excited crowd gathered and waved from the shore. Then firing opened up from a shore battery and the *Duloc* was hit. The landing craft with reinforcements from de Gaulle never even got away from the transports. At 4:30 P.M., after receiving a signal from Cunningham that two French cruisers had left Dakar harbor and were presumably heading for the invasion force, de Gaulle bowed to realities and withdrew his vulnerable transports out to sea behind the protection of the Royal Navy.

It had been a disastrous and totally depressing day, but as the invasion force withdrew seaward, the commanders received a message from Churchill in London: "Having begun, we must go on to the end. Stop at nothing." All agreed that evening to take a chance on another try on September 24, on the assumption that the incredible mishap of the sea fog would clear away. A surrender ultimatum was radioed that night to Boisson—who replied that he would defend to the last. Visibility improved slightly in the morning, and the *Ark Royal* got off some planes to spot for the Navy guns. But by midday the fog was again closing in, and the coastal batteries at Dakar and the guns of the *Richelieu* were still firing away at the British ships. Unable to return fire with accuracy, the British again withdrew out of range and broke off action.

On the night of the twenty-fourth, de Gaulle argued at length against the British commanders, who were convinced that the sun would at last shine on the expedition in the morning and wanted to resume with an intensive and remorse-less bombardment of the kind that hit the French Fleet at Mers el-Kébir and pound Dakar into submission. But de Gaulle wanted to break off. His argument was that if he had been able to get his own forces ashore he would have fought to the end. But he did not want the place destroyed by British guns in lieu of its surrendering to the Free French. No doubt spurred on by Churchill's exhortation to stop at nothing, Cunningham and Irwin rejected de Gaulle's position and prepared to fire away in the morning. But as the Fleet steamed into position soon after daybreak, in brilliant sunny weather at last, the final misfortune fell. A French submarine that had slipped out of Dakar put a torpedo into the battleship *Resolution.* She did not sink, but heeled over dead in the water and was taken in tow by the battleship *Barham*. This was enough for Cunningham, who knew that he had already been hanging around in one place for a dangerously long time, and it was also enough for Churchill and the Admiralty, poring over the hourly signals in London. All action was broken off and the naval vessels and the invasion force that never got out of its transports sailed dejectedly back to Freetown in the equatorial heat.

*

"In London, a tempest of anger, in Washington a hurricane of sarcasms were let loose against me," de Gaulle recorded in his Memoirs, almost with understatement. The London *Daily Mirror* unleashed a typical condemnation of "gross miscalculation, muddled dash, hasty withdrawal, wishful thinking and half-hearted measures," adding that "Dakar has claims to rank with the lowest depths of imbecility to which we have yet sunk." The brunt of the criticism was aimed full in the face of de Gaulle, for few knew or cared to understand what Churchill's role had been. Although Churchill stoutly defended de Gaulle in the House of Commons, this did not blunt condemnation in the United States at all.

As the flotilla limped back to Freetown, de Gaulle was in a mood of gloom and dejection bordering on despair. One of his French biographers, Jean-Raymond Tournoux, says that he "even confessed to one of his companions—'I went through a terrible time. I thought of blowing out my brains.'" Probably he said it, and maybe he did contemplate suicide, but it was not a course in keeping with his intellect, his character or his Catholicism. But his grim and deep depression were evident. On deck in the hot tropical night, dragging deeply on a cigaret, he turned to a British liaison officer and murmured in a rare moment of open emotion and anguish: *"Pour moi, ce qui est terrible c'est de me sentir seul. Toujours seul!"* (For me, what is terrible is to feel myself alone. Always alone!)

And indeed he was alone—for if he gave way, collapsed, disappeared, there was no Free French movement left. The colonies that had rallied to him, the men who had enlisted and sworn allegiance to him, all would simply be cast adrift and cut off as traitors to France, men without a country, patriots scorned and rejected. In that African heat, alone and thousands of miles from those who were watching him the most, he had reached his nadir. But he had to fight back. At Freetown on September 29 he received a message asking if he could get to Lagos in Nigeria urgently for a meeting with the British and one of his senior staff officers, Colonel Edgard de Larminat, who had been responsible for the takeover in Brazzaville a month earlier. By luck, a flying boat landed at Freetown that same day, heading south. So de Gaulle took off, after agreeing with Cunningham that his Free French forces should now be transported south to the Cameroons and landed at Duala, where he would rejoin them in a few days. The damaged French escort vessel *Commandant Duloc* would stop at Lagos en route to Duala to take him on the final leg of the journey.

By the time he reached Lagos on October 1, there was a mixture of good news and bad. Tahiti and the islands of French Oceania had deposed the pro-Vichy governor and declared allegiance to the Free French. This had been followed by the defection from Vichy of New Caledonia. A message also awaited de Gaulle from the two tiny islands of Saint-Pierre and Miquelon in the mouth of the St. Lawrence—France's last possessions in North America. In it, a veterans' group declared its confidence "in the final victory of General de Gaulle and his army." De Larminat also brought a fully positive assessment of how things were going politically in the African colonies that had already swung to de Gaulle, and proposed that they move next to secure Gabon, the last territory in French Equatorial Africa still holding out with Vichy. Even the Dakar debacle was now seen in retrospect to have produced some success, since ammunition stores in the fortress were now very low and so many additional French warships had been damaged by the British bombardment that it would be impossible for Vichy to reinforce the Gabon garrison at Libreville.

Finally, General de Gaulle had received his most important military recruit so far—General Georges Catroux, former high commissioner in French Indochina, who had first tried to bring the colony over to the Free French, and failing this had resigned and made his way to London. A respected senior five-star general, Catroux had been in prison with de Gaulle at Ingolstadt during World War I. He had arrived to place himself unreservedly at the orders of a one-star brigadier, much enhancing de Gaulle's own prestige and authority. But there were some uneasy shadows cast from London.

Before departing on the Dakar expedition, de Gaulle left behind in London a personal letter to be handed to Catroux on his arrival, asking him to proceed to Cairo to serve as his deputy in charge of Free French affairs in Africa and the Middle East. But Churchill then asked Catroux to come and see him at Downing Street to propose something very different.

Catroux, who promptly informed de Gaulle of the conversation, relates that Churchill talked "in the warmest and most grateful terms in praise of the force of character and sense of honor" of de Gaulle but then declared: "All in all, I believe it is in London that your presence would be most useful at the present time. The Free French movement needs to be led, and I believe you ought to assume its leadership." After that, Catroux saw the colonial secretary, Lord Lloyd, who added that Churchill was concerned that the Free French movement was so far commanding only modest support of Frenchmen, and that someone of Catroux's rank and stature in international circles might be more successful. Of course Churchill's use of the phrase "at the present time" apparently indicated that he had in mind only a limited period in which Catroux would act in London for de Gaulle instead of proceeding immediately to Cairo. In the event, nothing came of it because Catroux simply did not even consider acting as Churchill suggested. De Gaulle brushed the incident aside as "a classic objective of dividing in order to rule." More was to follow.

A telegram arrived in Lagos for de Gaulle from Churchill disclosing the first feelers from Vichy, via Madrid, on the possibility of improving relations and reaching a modus vivendi concerning the French colonies. It was this opening that subsequently led to the fruitless Rougier mission to London three weeks later. But Churchill's openness and correctness in informing de Gaulle of what was developing did not of course do much to allay the General's underlying suspicions of the

British, particularly coming on the heels of the Catroux conversation. Still, he replied to Churchill with a message of pointed comment about dealings with Vichy, and soon had a message back from London that "we are disagreeably impressed though not surprised" with Vichy's position but "since they do not wish to break with us, we should be glad to extract what we can from this situation."

At the end of a week in Lagos, de Gaulle had cast off the dejection and depression of Dakar and geared up for a response to all this by renewed action on his own in his own cause.

When he reached Duala in the *Commandant Duloc* on October 8, he was met at the quayside of the hot, humid, dusty little tropical town by Captain Leclerc and a guard of honor, with the streets hung with flags and practically the entire population turned out to cheer and applaud. It was four months since the fall of France, when he had been an unknown brigadier, and for the first time General de Gaulle was experiencing the spontaneous and genuine adulation and "crowd response" of ordinary people—local French and black colonial subjects—which would grow in intensity until the liberation of Paris four years later, and continue the rest of his life wherever he went, whatever the circumstances of his ups and downs. But he quickly got down to business at hand and prepared to push on.

He had 2,500 Foreign Legion troops in Duala, with supporting arms and equipment and a few aircraft that had been landed from the *Ark Royal*. With this force and the meager but sufficient naval units at his disposal, he decided on an attack on Libreville in Gabon. Prior to the Dakar affair, the Vichy governor of Gabon had first indicated that he was switching sides but then had swung back under pressure from General Boisson and Vichy. The failure at Dakar had no doubt stiffened things further in Libreville, so there was no avoiding a fight. But the Free French were smarting at the way their countrymen had fired on even the white flag of truce at Dakar, and the Foreign Legion was itching for action and rebellious at having been dumped in Duala. Leclerc was instructed to work out plans for a coordinate attack on Libreville to be mounted from Duala to the north and Brazzaville from the south.

De Gaulle then pushed on to Fort Lamy in Chad, where once again he was given a rapturous local reception when he arrived to confer with Félix Éboué, the first major figure of the Colonial Empire to rally to his side. Catroux joined him in Fort Lamy, reported in detail on his talk with Churchill, pledged again his decision to serve under and not alongside or above de Gaulle, and departed to take up his Cairo post.

De Gaulle next fixed an ambitious strategic military objective for his Free French forces. After the Gabon operation was concluded, troops were to be concentrated at Fort Lamy, hopefully with some new recruits, and trained and prepared for an audacious and risky overland advance of some 1,500 miles from the heart of Africa north across the vast and dangerous Sahara to attack the Italians in Libya and Tripolitania in the rear and link up with the British then fighting back and forth along the Mediterranean coast from Egypt. Leclerc would command the operation.

Finally de Gaulle flew on to Brazzaville, where he prepared to launch his next big political *coup de main*. On October 27, 1940—three days after Pétain had shaken hands with Hitler at Montoire—General de Gaulle issued a "Brazzaville Manifesto" in which he decreed the establishment of a "Defense Council of the Empire" for all of the colonial possessions that might flock to his banner, with all of the powers and attributes of a government. He declared that he would be accountable to the French people as soon as it was possible for them to decide on appointing him freely, and that the powers he was assuming would eventually transfer to a restored National Assembly. Meanwhile he was establishing his own personal authority amounting virtually to a dictatorship, with a decree in Article 3 of the Defense Council statute stating: "Decisions will be taken by the leader of the Free French, after consultation, *if the need arises,* with the Defense Council." De Gaulle followed this up ten days later with a second "organic declaration" in which he declared the creation of the Vichy State under Marshal Pétain and the dissolving of the Third Republic to be unconstitutional under a law of 1884 and therefore null and void, invalid and nonexistent. For the first time, now, he also adopted the royal style and wording of "We, General de Gaulle" in official decrees and ordinances.

De Gaulle, by this action, was going far beyond the powers of the French National Committee, which the British had recognized after such laborious negotiations with him only two months before. Now he was setting up his own government-in-exile—in his own eyes at least. He was doing this of course on French territory, and he was acting without any prior warning, discussions or consultations with the British or anyone else. In London the Foreign Office was shocked and stunned, for de Gaulle's manifesto could easily be read or interpreted as virtually a declaration of war on Vichy. If the Vichy authorities were to make this interpretation of what Britain's Free French protégé was doing, and the British were unable to disavow him or curb him, then all of the efforts to prevent Vichy from switching sides completely and joining the Germans in war on Britain were at risk and could collapse.

With remarkable insouciance, de Gaulle compounded what he was doing by calling in the United States consul at Léopoldville, across the Congo from Brazzaville, and handing him a formal communication for the State Department in which he coolly informed Washington that his Empire Defense Council now had at its disposal sufficient forces to ensure the protection of the French Antilles (Martinique and Guadeloupe), French Guiana on the Caribbean coast of South America, and the islands of Saint-Pierre and Miquelon. He proposed that if the Americans decided to occupy these possessions, he would assume responsibility for their administration and internal security through the Empire Defense Council and would cede air and naval base facilities to the United States after negotiation, similar to the agreement that Washington had concluded a month earlier with Britain in the destroyers-for-bases deal. But de Gaulle, as he later pointed out in one of his many needling comments at both London and Washington, wasn't asking for destroyers as part of his "offer."

There is no record of any American reply to this communication, which must have caused sputtering indignation in Washington. Certainly it can safely be assumed that Cordell Hull was not amused. Neither was the Foreign Office, for de Gaulle was now adding to his unpredictable brashness by attempting to enter into direct diplomatic government-to-government dealings with the United States, which wanted nothing to do with him. The status of head of a committee financed by the British government was not de Gaulle's idea of his France, and he would no longer be contained by it.

Meanwhile, another African possession was swiftly added to the roster of the Free French. On November 6 Leclerc's expedition embarked at Duala to take Libreville and complete the transfer of Gabon from Vichy to de Gaulle. Churchill, at de Gaulle's request, had instructed the Royal Navy to mount aggressive patrol action to protect the little French force from any possible intervention from sea by Vichy ships out of Dakar. Some military success was certainly needed to balance the accounts on the Dakar failure. One Vichy submarine was spotted trying to approach the Gabon coast, but after it had been depth-charged and forced to the surface and its crew taken off, it was scuttled by its captain, who went down with his ship rather than allow it to be taken over by the British. When the Free French landed at Libreville on November 9, sharp fighting broke out for possession of the airfield, and lasted most of the day before the local commander accepted a cease-fire. There were twenty-three casualties of Frenchmen fighting Frenchmen. De Gaulle arrived on a flying visit to the city on November 15 to confirm Free French rule and install a new governor.

But in London, tempers were simmering from Downing Street on down through the Foreign Office and the service ministries, and Churchill now sent a firm but courteous request to de Gaulle to return:

> I feel most anxious for consultation with you. Situation between France and Britain has changed remarkably since you left. . . . We have hopes of Weygand in Africa and no one must underrate advantage that would follow if he were to be rallied. We are trying to arrive at some *modus vivendi* with Vichy which would minimize the risk of incidents and will enable some favorable forces in France to develop. . . . You will see how important it is that you should be here. I hope you will be able to tidy up in Libreville and come home as soon as possible.

There were ample warning signals, real and implied, in this message. General de Gaulle had always to reckon with the possibility that he could be unceremoniously dumped by the British if they could find some valid Vichy figure to rejoin the fight against Hitler. With his own fortunes at a low ebb over Dakar, this was a time of danger of such an eventuality coming to pass. He had sensed this in Churchill's overture to Catroux and in the opening of secret talks between London and Vichy. He knew, of course, that Washington had no interest in him or in furthering his fortunes at all. But he had struck back against these moves and trends from a distance with his Brazzaville Manifesto and the formation of the Empire Defense Council. In two and a half months since his departure from London for Dakar, he had picked up all of France's island possessions in the far Pacific, the remainder of its enclaves in India, and consolidated his hold over all of French Equatorial Africa. He had two additional important senior military recruits in General Catroux and General Paul Legentilhomme, who had been governor of French Somalia on the African east coast. While this had been going on, Pétain had met with Hitler at Montoire and pledged a policy of collaboration. If Churchill and Roosevelt sought to blur the issue and image as far as Vichy was concerned, de Gaulle relentlessly determined to sharpen it. The more Free France advanced, the more impossible it would become to dump its leader. From the defeat at Dakar, it was a very different de Gaulle who returned to London on November 18, 1940.

EIGHT

1941: SYRIA, STALIN, SAINT-PIERRE AND MIQUELON

The decisive year 1941, when the Soviet Union, Japan and the United States all entered the war, began with a sour episode between the Free French and the British, and from then on things continued for the next four years in what at best was a perpetual state of wary and suspicious antagonism on the part of General de Gaulle toward the Allies. At worst, in events such as the clash over Syria and the affair of Saint-Pierre and Miquelon, de Gaulle pushed this antagonism deliberately all the way to the breaking point in order to assert himself and his unique view of French interests. At the height of the Syrian crisis, the Free French Committee in London sent a telegram to de Gaulle in Cairo warning in some alarm that his tactics had brought things near a rupture with Britain "that would mean the end of Free France, the disappearance of the last hope of saving our unfortunate country." De Gaulle sent back an imperious rebuke to his committee, which amounted to a basic declaration of his policy toward his allies to the end of the war.

> I am aware, better than anyone, of the grave national and international consequences which would be brought about by the rupture of Free France with England. It is just for that reason that I had to place England face to face with these consequences, if she should act towards us in an inadmissible way. I understand that the British should have been irritated, but this irritation has little weight in comparison with our duties towards France. I invite you to be firmer and not to give the impression that those who represent me do not follow my policy exactly. Our greatness and our strength consists solely in intransigence over what concerns the rights of France. *We shall have need of this intransigence as far as the Rhine, inclusive* [italics added].

In Cairo in this same period, de Gaulle had many angry exchanges with Major General Spears, his energetic British liaison officer who had been indispensable in getting him from Bordeaux to London and in organizing the initial logistic, financial and political support by the British government for the Free French. After a year of working closely together, early cordiality had given way to growing antipathy, and Spears was about to transfer to a new military assignment in Syria, which then produced a complete rupture between the two men. Spears, who spoke French, records that in one outburst de Gaulle declaimed to him: "I do not think I shall ever get on with *les Anglais*. You are all the same, exclusively concentrated on your own interests and business, quite insensitive to the requirements of others. You think I am interested in England winning the war? I am not! I am interested only in France's victory!"

When Spears replied in some astonishment that they were the same, de Gaulle retorted: *"Pas du tout!* Not at all in my view."

Apart from built-in prejudices and suspicions of the British, behind de Gaulle's incessantly embittered relationship with the Allies was the necessity that he felt to demonstrate constantly to the French that it was *he*—not the Vichy government—who was battling to preserve, protect and stand up for French interests in the world and restore France to the ranks of the victorious powers. In this, of course, he was fully justified, absolutely correct, as a political strategy. But the tactics he employed were appalling as far as the Allies were concerned, and scarcely enhanced or smoothed the conduct of the common war effort. Official records and personal memoirs of men who dealt with de Gaulle across the next four years—French as well as British and American—are replete with the kind of exchange he let loose on Spears, at all levels, in varying degrees of intensity and profanity, quite often petty, sometimes on a grand scale, always with the declared purpose of upholding "the interests of France" as determined by himself alone.

Of relations with the British, de Gaulle wrote in his Memoirs that "there was a cohesion among those in authority which I often envied and admired," and then he added sardonically: "But of which I also had to suffer the grip. For to resist the British machine when it set itself in motion to impose something was a severe test. Without having experienced it one's self, it is impossible to imagine what a concentration of effort, what a variety of procedures, what insistence, by turns gracious, pressing and threatening, the English were capable of deploying in order to obtain satisfaction."

Twenty years later, in the 1960s, the British were according President de Gaulle and his France of the Fifth Republic the same bitter admiration for the ruthless, single-minded way in which his machinery of government then operated to impose French policies on Europe and obtain satisfaction for French objectives. This is Europe's oldest antagonism, after all, going back to William the Conqueror in England and Richard the Lionhearted in France; to the Plantagenet kings and the Battle of Agincourt; the rivalry of the Crusades; to John Churchill, first Duke of Marlborough and his brilliant campaigning of the early eighteenth century against Louis XIV; to Wolfe against Montcalm on the heights of Quebec; to Napoleon versus Wellington and Nelson; to the nineteenth-century scramble for colonies in the Far East, the Indian subcontinent, the Middle East and Africa; the Fashoda incident of de Gaulle's boyhood, and then Mers el-Kébir in 1940, which Frenchmen still talk about today. Although Germany was France's military enemy, for the French this was recent history, contemporary and modern, naked and above board—while rivalry with the British was centuries old, historical and permanent, deep-seated and merely clothed in friendship forced on the two countries by a temporary common cause.

"England has no permanent friends, no permanent enemies—only permanent interests," Palmerston intoned back in the nineteenth century, and General de Gaulle was more than ready to take this as a permanent talisman, a warning and a watchword in his dealings with the British in the midst of the greatest conflict in history.

His apparent ingratitude toward England, to whom he owed much, generally struck Anglo-Saxons as all but incomprehensible. But as far as Charles de Gaulle was concerned, gratitude, sentimentality, accommodation and compromise were weaknesses that had no part in his character or personality or philosophy of power. For him, whatever he might owe Britain in gratitude would be repaid by rallying and restoring France. Knowing his weakness in those early days, he reasoned that he could not afford to give away anything and indeed had to fight to establish his power. Hence his conclusion that "Our greatness and our strength consists solely in intransigence over what concerns the rights of France."

When Anthony Eden once remonstrated to de Gaulle that he had more trouble dealing with him than any other ally, de Gaulle replied frostily that "France is a great power." It was an oddly negative way of measuring what constitutes being a great power, but he went on making intransigence and the creation of difficulties for others a basic tenet of power for the rest of his life.

It is easier to explain de Gaulle's attitude, even to understand it, than it is to excuse the extraordinary vindictiveness and outlandish suspicions that he proceeded to level remorselessly at the British and the Americans to the end of the war, to the end of his days. The British of course bore the brunt of this, for their dealings with him were far closer and more intertwined in every way. Not that they were entirely innocent or did not make mistakes. At times they were simply inept in dealings with de Gaulle. But this scarcely justified his across-the-board determination to see the hand of *perfide Albion* in practically every document the British handed him, in the most peripheral and pragmatic questions in the conduct of the war—even allocation of wartime shipping. De Gaulle had a genius for suspicion and an indifference to the consequences of any act of behavior of his own.

With Roosevelt he never had any meeting of minds or even any attempt at a meeting of minds. But with Churchill there were constant exchanges, written and personal, and some epic confrontations as the two men sparred with each other in vivid terms on the grand scale of men making history, sometimes together, sometimes in opposition to each other, but in the end whatever the quarrels, still with mutual respect. Churchill would rage about de Gaulle while Roosevelt merely sneered.

Harold Nicolson, the writer and historian who was at the Ministry of Information in London during the war, tells of listening to a Churchillian outburst over some incident with de Gaulle, and then venturing to remark that nevertheless de Gaulle was surely a great man. Churchill, he says, practically exploded: "A great man? Why, he's selfish, he's arrogant, he thinks he's the center of the universe . . . He . . . Yes, you're right, he's a great man!"

*

When General de Gaulle returned to London at the end of 1940, after the Dakar expedition and publication of the Brazzaville Manifesto, he had effectively transformed the Free French movement from a committee into an Allied Power, whether it was yet recognized as such or not. He now had a large and growing chunk of the French Empire under his flag to justify his claim to speak for France, and despite all the setbacks he had suffered, his military strength was growing in numbers, cohesion, quality and efficiency. In French territory he exercised sovereign power, free of any British interference or control. Indeed, when he next passed through Chad in 1941, he asked how many British there were in Fort Lamy and was told that there were only seventeen. "C'est trop," he remarked laconically, and from his next stop in Africa he telegraphed back to the governor instructing him to order all of them out of the colony. He had made up his mind that the war would be long, that Britain and the Allies would win, and that his priority therefore from then on would be to claw back everything he could for a victory for France.

During de Gaulle's absence of nearly three months, however, the Free French Committee had turned into something of a squabbling chicken house. Its members were an ill-assorted collection of strong-minded but largely inexperienced individuals who had joined in a common cause but had no common experience of working together. De Gaulle had to work with whoever turned up in London, and in the first six months there was not much from which to pick and choose. To run things during his absence on the Dakar expedition, he had, not surprisingly, avoided naming a deputy in charge and instead had divided up responsibilities under Vice Admiral Emile Muselier as "superior commander" of all Free French forces in Britain; civil departments under a somewhat shadowy French industrialist who had arrived in London barely two weeks before the Dakar expedition sailed, under the code name of Major Fontaine; and his all-important Intelligence Section under Colonel Passy, its chief through the war. The instructions in his absence then specified that "all promotions and appointments, both civil and military, are reserved for General de Gaulle himself."

It did not take long for strains and stresses and rivalries among the committee power-groups to surface and break out in the open. In particular, Admiral Muselier, by rank as well as personality, was not a man to subordinate himself readily, the more so since he felt that he should have been left in full charge in de Gaulle's absence anyway. Meanwhile, Passy, in order to strengthen his embryo Intelligence operation, had taken into his service two specialists who had been recommended to him by General Spears, the British liaison officer, to run internal security and the vetting of agents and granting of security clearances—a Captain Meffre, who took a *nom de guerre* of Howard (the French developed a passion for code names in those days), and a faceless young man named Colin, who was accompanied by a pretty young British secretary. They played a key role in the drama to come.

The details of the personality conflicts and internecine squabbling in de Gaulle's absence were obscure then and even more obscure today, but one exchange between de Gaulle and Muselier gives the flavor.

De Gaulle on October 20, 1940, from Brazzaville: "Your present attitude does not give me any satisfaction. For a month after my departure you gave proper service. This is no longer the case. I instruct you to deal only with military questions. I invite you not to make sudden appointments that cause disorder and discontent. I will not allow you to promote officers. I reserve such promotions entirely to myself."

Muselier replying to de Gaulle: "You will learn soon enough about the intrigues that have been conducted in your absence, in which the Navy has avoided taking part."

At any event, de Gaulle's return to London imposed a certain quiet, but then the lid blew off the steaming kettle suddenly on New Year's Day, 1941, as a result of a blunder by the British, of which the General wrote tartly : "I will not conceal that this lamentable incident, which revealed how precarious our situation still was vis-à-vis our allies, did not fail to influence my conceptions of what our relations with the British state really ought to be."

De Gaulle had spent New Year's Day with his wife and children at a country cottage they had rented in Shropshire when he received a call from the Foreign Office asking if he would return urgently to London for a meeting with Anthony Eden first thing next morning. He arrived at Eden's office to find the foreign secretary in a state of some agitation as he announced: "We have just had proof that Admiral Muselier is secretly in contact with Vichy, that he tried to transmit to Darlan the plan for the Dakar expedition at the time it was being prepared, and that he intends to hand over to Vichy the submarine *Surcouf.* The Prime Minister immediately ordered the Admiral's arrest, and he is incarcerated. It was impossible for us not to act without delay."

Whatever his own problems with Muselier, de Gaulle declared immediately that he believed there had been "a ghastly mistake." He did not, however, insist at once on Muselier's release—a fact which the admiral did not fail to hold against him subsequently. He took away the documents that Eden handed him as "proof" of Muselier's activities, and forty-eight hours later he returned to tell Eden that they were "highly suspect as to context and supposed source." By now de Gaulle was in high dudgeon over "the outrageous arrest of a French vice-admiral," and insisted that Muselier be allowed out of prison under conditions of house arrest until the matter was cleared up.

The documents consisted of a number of typed notes on paper bearing the official stamp of the French consulate in London, still in the charge of a pro-Vichy official. They purported to be information from Muselier passed via the Brazilian embassy. Yet there was one manifest mistake that quickly gave away the forgery to anyone in the know. A note concerning the Dakar expedition was dated August 5, which was *before* Churchill and de Gaulle had finally decided on the plan. De Gaulle next carpeted the two new internal security men appointed on British recommendation, Howard and Colin, and after relentlessly cross-examining them and finding their responses confusing, he concluded that the whole thing had been cooked up by British Intelligence.

On January 8 he summoned General Spears to declare that if Muselier were not released within twenty-four hours, "all relations would be broken between Free France and Britain." It was the first but by no means the last time he used such a threat. He cited to Spears his view that the documents were forgeries. A few hours later, Spears returned in an abject mood to acknowledge that the documents had been faked, and the admiral was being released. Churchill and Eden apologized personally to Muselier at Downing Street next afternoon, and Churchill invited him to a reconciliation luncheon. Howard and Colin were tried by the British. Colin was jailed for a year for forgery and Howard was interned on the Isle of Man for the duration of the war.

The Muselier affair was over, at least as far as events were concerned, but its damage lingered on. There never was and never has been any explanation of who initiated the whole idea of the forgeries and why. Howard and Colin certainly did not think it up on their own, but was it intrigue within the Free French, within Colonel Passy's Intelligence Section to get rid of Muselier? Was it, as de Gaulle was convinced, an operation by British Intelligence to smear the Free French? Or was it, as the British apparently came to believe, the work of Vichy through two agents whom they had unwittingly passed on to the Free French without vetting them closely enough themselves?

In the end, the main benefactor from the whole embroglio was certainly Vichy—for its effect was to sow further distrust of the Free French and add to the public impression that it was an organization riven by feuding and lacking in security. At the same time it heightened de Gaulle's visceral feelings about relations with his British hosts. He immediately ordered every British subject working for the Free French to be dismissed—even including the charwomen who cleaned at Carlton Gardens headquarters. It took a lot of Franco-British diplomacy behind the scenes to get the order rescinded. The year had started with a bang.

*

For Great Britain, 1941 was the most difficult and complex year of the war, even without the running problems with General de Gaulle. It was a heroic year, with Britain standing alone through the winter blitz against London, on the shipping lanes of the North Atlantic, in the Mediterranean, in Africa and the Middle East. It required an extraordinary sense of strategic direction on the part of Churchill and his chiefs of staff to deploy limited resources in the right place at the right time. They couldn't win everywhere, but they were right in their judgments more often than they were wrong.

The Italians had attacked Greece in October 1940, and although it meant a major strategic diversion of limited forces, British troops had been sent to Greece's aid and the Italian offensive had bogged down. General Sir Archibald Wavell, the commander in chief in the Middle East, still managed to launch a successful offensive against the Italians in Libya and Tripolitania in December 1940, in which good generalship made up for thin resources. By February 1941 the attack had carried the British all the way to El Aghleila, within striking distance of Tripoli itself. At that point, Hitler sent Field Marshal Erwin Rommel out to form the Afrika Korps and rescue the Italians. Wavell, meanwhile, also managed to put together still another offensive out of his limited forces with attacks against the Italians in Eritrea from the Red Sea and in Ethiopia from the Sudan, launched simultaneously in January. By April 1941 the Italians had been defeated and Emperor Haile Selassie was restored to his throne in Addis Ababa in the first liberation of the war.

But in early April the Nazis launched their Balkan campaign and Yugoslavia capitulated on April 17. Without a pause, they swept on south into Greece to do what Mussolini had failed to do and finish off the Greek Army. By this time Rommel was also driving Wavell's weakened British forces back across the Libyan coast. At the end of April Wavell was forced to withdraw British forces from Greece. By the end of May the British were besieged by Rommel at the Libyan coastal port of Tobruk, and the bulk of Wavell's desert forces were back inside Egypt holding defensive positions at El Alamein. It was a low point of the war for Britain, fighting alone.

In this swirl of events, Free French units had fought alongside the British in Eritrea and Ethiopia, and on de Gaulle's orders a column under Leclerc had pushed north from Chad to occupy a key Italian position in the southern Sahara. In March General de Gaulle decided to return to Africa via the Middle East.

After the Muselier affair, the Free French had been rapped back into order by de Gaulle, and he had completed some important organizational tasks at his London headquarters. A complex financial agreement was negotiated with the British to set up what amounted to a Free French Central Bank in everything but name, to issue a new unified French currency in the colonies that had rallied to de Gaulle's cause, and to conduct international financial and trade transactions with the independence of a government-in-exile. A Free French *Journal Officiel* was now being printed in London to carry decrees, orders, promotions and awards. De Gaulle had also established, in Napoleonic style, the Order of Liberation, with the Cross of Lorraine as its insignia and a distinctive dark green ribbon for its members, all of whom were chosen by him personally. But he was restless for action, as well as impatient at working so closely with the British in the confines of London.

> At the beginning of March 1941 [he wrote], I felt beyond doubt that the war was on the point of confronting us in the Middle East and Africa with great trials in the face of the enemy, obstinate opposition from Vichy and grave dissensions with our Allies. I would have to take the necessary decisions on the spot. I decided to go there. Towards the involved Orient, I flew with simple ideas. I knew that, in a welter of intricate factors, a vital game was being played there. We therefore had to be in it.

From the standpoint of French interests, the key to the Middle East lay in the Levant, where de Gaulle had served for two years with the French Army a decade before. But in both Syria and Lebanon, intensely loyal Vichy commanders held sway. A similar situation existed to the south in the key French possession of Djibouti, at the mouth of the Red Sea, and in French Somalia, farther south on the Horn of Africa. If Vichy could be dislodged from any of these territories, it would represent a major political success for de Gaulle and a considerable easing of the military and strategic problems facing General Wavell.

At that point, in the early spring of 1941, Wavell was probably one of the most hard-pressed military commanders in history—directing from Cairo simultaneous actions on fronts hundreds of miles apart in Greece, in Libya, in Eritrea, in Ethiopia, protecting his rear areas in Palestine, Iraq and Jordan, and cut off from his main source of supplies and equipment in England except by the long and slow and costly sea route around Capetown and the whole African continent. Then came signs of more trouble in his backyard. In February Free French Intelligence picked up word of the arrival in Damascus of two German agents named von Hintig and Roser, with a mission of contacting Syrian political leaders to prepare the way for some future arrival of Axis forces. German agents were also active in Iraq, where the British had treaty bases at Habbaniya, not far from Baghdad, and at Basara, in the south on the Persian Gulf. But the country had a pro-Axis premier named Rashid Ali.

When de Gaulle arrived in Cairo, he pressed Wavell with two proposals: first, to allow the Free French forces, then numbering about 6,000 in the Middle East, to assemble and launch an offensive to take over Syria and Lebanon, and secondly, at least to tighten up the naval blockade of the Levant ports as well as Djibouti to pressure the territories into changing sides. But Wavell refused any of these actions on the grounds that he had enough to handle already without courting more difficulties with Vichy France. In this he also had the tacit backing of the Foreign Office in London, which at that time was still following a mildly concilia- tory policy toward Vichy. Wavell felt, moreover, that de Gaulle was excessively optimistic about the prospects for getting any of the French territories to change sides. So in mid-April, de Gaulle quit Cairo in something of a huff to continue on to Brazzaville, convinced that the real aim of the British was to keep him out of Syria, Lebanon and Djibouti so they could eventually take them over for them- selves.

But the Germans, pouring down into Greece and about to launch a paratroop attack against the British holding the island of Crete, were not sitting still. Hitler was also preparing his invasion of the Soviet Union, and he had a new grand strategy for victory. Having failed to knock England out of the war, he now conceived of a vast flanking operation to reach the Suez Canal through the Middle East—thereby severing the British Empire and at the same time threatening the Soviet Union from the south as well as the north.

This began to unfold when trouble broke out for the British in Baghdad on May 2. Rashid Ali, amply fed by Nazi funds, forced the pro-British regent to flee the country, declared his support for Germany and ordered his troops to sieze the British base at Habbaniya. Fortunately the Iraqis were not very numerous, well equipped, brave or efficient. But German help was on the way, immediately. On May 3 Admiral Darlan was summoned from Vichy to Paris by the German ambassador, Otto Abetz, and informed that Hitler demanded an immediate agreement with Vichy for use of the Syrian air bases to facilitate a German airlift of reinforcements and war matériel into Iraq to support Rashid Ali. Three days later Darlan had signed—getting in return a cut in Vichy's occupation bill from the Germans from 400 million francs per day to 300 million and a promise of release of 83,000 French prisoners of war.

The Darlan agreement with the Germans clearly went beyond the original armistice terms and moved Vichy into open collaboration and support of the Nazi war effort against the Allies. By May 12 Darlan had gone on to Berchtesgaden for a personal meeting with Hitler in his mountain retreat and German transport planes were landing in Syria and flying on to Iraq.

In Brazzaville de Gaulle watched these events with anger and frustration against the British. But Churchill was no less agitated in London, and a series of Churchillian telegrams, mounting in impatience and peremptory tone, began bombarding Cairo to push Wavell into action.

Reinforcements were rushed from India by sea up the Persian Gulf to the British base at Basara, and a column started overland across the Jordanian desert to the relief of Habbaniya. Air reinforcements were flown in by the Royal Air Force to bomb and strafe Iraqi troops, who showed a marked reluctance to attack Habbaniya across open countryside anyway. All the same, it was not until the end of May that the British finally marched into Baghdad and restored the regent to power while Rashid Ali fled.

But while Wavell was concentrating on Iraq, de Gaulle from Brazzaville instructed his deputy in Cairo, the respected General Catroux, to press once again for a Free French offensive into Syria. He was furious to receive from General Spears a cable on May 9 telling him that "it will be impossible to provide transport for Free French forces for a month at least" in view of the Iraqi operation and adding that "General Wavell asks me to tell you that although personally always glad to see you, he sees no necessity for your coming to Cairo now or in the near future." At this, de Gaulle hit the ceiling and sent a telegram to Catroux on May 12 to withdraw from Cairo:

> Given the negative policy which our British allies have thought right to adopt in the Middle East as far as we are concerned, I consider that the presence in Cairo of a personality as considerable as yours to represent the Free French there is no longer justified. Please advise the British of this decision. There is no reason for you to conceal from them the reason for your departure. On the contrary, I ask you to make it plain to them.

But Churchill, just as impatient, had already cabled Wavell on May 9:

You will no doubt realize the grievous danger of Syria being captured by a few thousand Germans transported by air. In face of your evident feeling of lack of resources, we can see no other course open than to furnish General Catroux with the necessary transport and let him and his Free French do their best at the moment they deem suitable, the R.A.F. acting against German air landings. Any improvement you can make on this would be welcome.

When Churchill then heard of de Gaulle's instructions to Catroux to withdraw from Cairo, he immediately sent a mollifying message to Brazzaville asking that the order be rescinded and informing de Gaulle of the instructions he had sent to Wavell to provide transport for a Free French offensive against Syria, with the added information that the War Cabinet had also decided on a strict blockade of Djibouti. De Gaulle was so surprised and gratified by this sudden British about-face, entirely due to Churchill's drive, that he replied to Churchill for the first and only time in the war with a telegram *in English,* ending his personal message with a flourishing "You will win the war." But although things then began to move fairly quickly, this was only the beginning of a Syrian embroglio between de Gaulle and the British, which simmered and erupted continuously until 1945.

De Gaulle returned to Cairo on May 25—by which time the reluctant and hard-pressed Wavell had managed to put together a miscellaneous and ill-assorted force that he knew to be understrength for a Syrian campaign to face some 30,000 French troops under the Vichy loyalist General Fernand Dentz. The 6,000 Free French under General Legentilhomme were supported by a mere ten tanks, eight heavy artillery pieces and twenty-four aircraft. The British forces consisted of an Australian division less one brigade that was fighting at Tobruk, plus a cavalry brigade and a Palestinian brigade with a young Jewish soldier in the ranks, Moshe Dayan, who was to lose an eye in the campaign and then go on to become the most famous general in the postwar state of Israel.

But prospects for resistance by the French forces under Dentz had clearly stiffened, with German aircraft now landing regularly on Syrian fields. A French colonel defected from Syria to join the Free French on May 21, bringing the discouraging news that while allowing the Germans to land, orders were to fight the Allies, and defensive positions were already being mounted and manned inside the frontiers. Once again de Gaulle had to face the bleak tragedy of Frenchmen killing Frenchmen.

*

The Anglo-French campaign against Syria and Lebanon lumbered into action on June 8, 1941, under strict orders not to fire until fired upon. This did not take long. Initially the advance appeared to be going well until the Vichy French commanders realized how light the attacking forces really were. Resistance then began to stiffen, and the Free French were held up by particularly hard fighting on the road to Damascus, while the British were mauled by superior forces on the coast road north of the port of Aleppo. But with the Iraq situation now under control, Wavell moved three more brigades into Syria from the east, and on June 21 the Free French entered Damascus. General de Gaulle followed three days later.

This was also the weekend that Hitler launched the Nazi armies against the Soviet Union.

General Dentz, who had no reinforcements to call on, knew he could not go on fighting forever. On June 18 he asked the American consul in Beirut to obtain armistice terms from the British. But meanwhile the fighting continued, and it was not until July 10 that Dentz finally asked for a cease-fire and surrender negotiations. De Gaulle concluded that out of loyalty to Germany, Vichy was reluctant to allow the Syrian fighting to end just when Nazi troops were rolling into Russia. At any rate, total casualties on all sides—Free French, Vichy French, Australian, English, Indian and the Palestine Brigade—were in excess of 11,000 killed, wounded and missing, which was a pretty high price to pay for Darlan's Nazi collaboration.

De Gaulle, following the campaign in Cairo, was intensely unhappy with British generalship and the piecemeal fashion in which reinforcements were sent in. Wavell's problems were not his. His feelings of frustration were no doubt compounded by the unhappy fact that the Levant campaign, like the Dakar action before it, was scarcely turning out to be a political triumph for the Free French.

But his disappointment and irritation over the fighting was mild compared to the political blow-up that came with the Vichy surrender. Here the British bore a considerable responsibility for mistakes, misjudgments and plain ineptitude as far as the Free French were concerned that seemed to worsen at every turn of the way. Initially there was relative harmony over how to handle the surrender. General Wavell, de Gaulle, Catroux and the British ambassador to Cairo, Sir Miles Lampton, met jointly and agreed on recommendations for armistice terms that were transmitted to London on June 19. These specified that a representative of General de Gaulle would participate fully in the negotiations whenever they took place, and that the "representation of France in the Levant will be assured by the Free French."

These recommendations arrived in London almost simultaneously with the initial request from Dentz for an indication of armistice terms—sent via the American consul in Beirut and the State Department in Washington. Whether the Foreign Office then mislaid, ignored or disregarded the Cairo recommendations is not clear, but they certainly were not adopted. There has to be a suspicion that because the reply to the Vichy commander would be transmitted back through the State Department, it was tailored by the Foreign Office with an eye to Roosevelt's Vichy policy and the known feelings of Cordell Hull about de Gaulle. In any event, different instructions came back to Cairo. The negotiations would be conducted between the British and Vichy commanders, with no role for de Gaulle's representative, and there was no mention in the armistice terms eventually handed to the Vichy general of the Free French assuming authority in the Levant. De Gaulle wrote in his Memoirs: "The text of the agreement amounted to a pure and simple transference of Syria and the Lebanon to the British."

De Gaulle had returned to Brazzaville in early July and therefore was not present in Cairo when the Vichy commander finally asked for a cease-fire on July 10. Moreover, Churchill finally decided to relieve Wavell of his command on June 22, although this was kept secret for another week. But as a result there was no firm hand or clear control at the top in Cairo for almost a month, while General Sir Claude Auchinleck was in the process of transferring from India and taking over. De Gaulle had come to admire and trust Wavell, who, if he had been in charge, almost certainly would have kept closer control over General Sir Henry Maitland-Wilson, to whom the negotiation with the Vichy commander were entrusted. He also would have been more responsive to complaints about the conduct of British forces vis-à-vis the Free French. Auchinleck knew nothing of the political background or personality problems, and in any case he had plenty else to worry about simply assuming a new and complex military command.

When de Gaulle, simmering in Brazzaville, received the final text of the surrender agreement as negotiated by Maitland-Wilson, he announced publicly at once that the Free French repudiated the document, which he regarded as contrary to his original agreement with Wavell and Sir Miles Lampton. Worse news followed. De Gaulle quickly learned that Maitland-Wilson had also agreed in a secret protocol with the Vichy commander to deny the Free French all contacts with Vichy troops, and to repatriate both troops and civil servants to France *en masse* without giving any of them a chance to opt for Free France if they wished. The only possible excuse for this agreement, apparently made without consultation with Cairo or London, would have been that it offered the quickest and simplest way of getting rid of Vichy forces and civil servants from the Levant, removing them from the area to facilitate its rapid transfer out of Vichy's hands and over to the Allies. But it was a piece of stupidity on the part of the British and a monumental affront to General de Gaulle.

Moreover, a series of minor incidents with the British forces rapidly reinforced de Gaulle's conviction that the British were out to grab Syria from the French. In the town of Sweida, the British occupied a Maison de France administrative building. De Gaulle ordered a Free French unit to reoccupy the property by force if necessary. Shooting was barely averted. Then, Australian military police rudely refused General Catroux entrance to a British headquarters. Everywhere it was the British who were exercising authority to the exclusion of the Free French.

De Gaulle, receiving reports of all this in Brazzaville from Catroux, set out to return to Cairo on July 18, in mounting anger with the British and "explaining to British governors and military leaders at each stage of my journey how serious the matter was." He reached Cairo on July 20.

Meanwhile, as part of the reorganization following the removal of Wavell, Churchill had sent a senior political figure to Cairo to serve as minister of state for the Middle East to act for the War Cabinet in pulling together the whole problem of diplomatic and political policy coordination under the Military. His choice was Oliver Lyttleton, who had been a captain in the prewar Army and went on to a distinguished postwar career in Conservative Party politics and government. But it fell to Lyttleton to get his first blooding in political warfare from General de

Gaulle, who by the time he reached Cairo, had worked himself up to a towering rage over what the British were doing to France. Of their stormy meeting on July 21, de Gaulle wrote: "Captain Lyttleton, an amiable and thoughtful man with a lively and open mind, had manifestly no desire to begin his mission with a catastrophe. He welcomed me with some embarrassment. I tried to avoid explosions, casing myself in ice."

In a withering exchange lasting two hours and a half, de Gaulle denounced "unskillful and dilatory tactics" by the British in the conduct of the Syrian fighting and criticized the British government for trying to take control of the Levant away from France in contradiction to France's League of Nations mandate over the territories. He lashed the failure to abide by the original Cairo recommendations, and the incomprehensible decision to deny his officers any contact with the troops of Vichy France. He climaxed this by handing Lyttleton a written statement that he had prepared in advance ending with these words: "Free France, that is to say France, is no longer willing to entrust to the British military command the duty of exercising command over French troops in the Middle East. General de Gaulle and the French Empire Defense Council are resuming full and entire disposal of all Free French forces of the Levant as from July 24, 1941, at midday."

Lyttleton, reeling from this broadside, wrote subsequently that "from the remote recess of memory, the diplomatic phrase *non venue* came to the surface, and I said, 'General, I must regard this document as not received and I cannot accept it.'" He then proposed that they resume their discussion at 6 P.M. By evening, de Gaulle had cooled down somewhat and Lyttleton had figured out how he might make concessions—particularly in reaffirming Free French rights and interests and shelving General Wilson's secret agreement to deny Free French contacts with the Vichy troops.

In this, Lyttleton was considerably reinforced when the British suddenly learned that fifty-two British officers who had been captured by the French during the fighting had been put aboard the transports to be shipped to France as prisoners with the Vichy repatriates! At this, Lyttleton immediately ordered the arrest of General Dentz and other senior Vichy officers until the transports were ordered back and the British officers returned.

With a compromise "interpretation" of the armistice finally worked out by Lyttleton, de Gaulle's ultimatum about withdrawing French forces from British command was not renewed. Catroux established himself as French high commissioner for the Levant, but it was late for de Gaulle's officers to begin recruiting among the Vichy units, many already having left. He managed to detach only 127 officers from the Vichy forces. Still, de Gaulle's strength always lay with the ruled rather than the rulers, and some 6,000 soldiers and NCOs opted to stay in the Middle East and fight under the Cross of Lorraine. Some 25,000 sailed back to France.

For the moment, the crisis was over—but the Syrian problem went on festering between de Gaulle and the British right through the war, with the British continuously pushing him to make good on a pledge of independence for the two territories that he had given when the invasion was launched. Just as resolutely, de

Gaulle argued that the pledge could not be honored until the war was won.

Without any doubt, a spirit of common purpose and common cause was broken between de Gaulle and the British as a result of the Syrian affair, with mistakes on both sides. A new pattern of relationship had begun. Whatever errors the British made, on their part there were deep and bitter resentments—Churchill especially—at de Gaulle's handling of the situation, his tactics, his accusations and his mauling of a British minister of state.

It was at this point that de Gaulle received the warning telegram from the Free French Committee in London about the dangers of a rupture with the British—to which he made the memorable reply that "We shall have need of this intransigence as far as the Rhine, inclusive." He returned to Brazzaville after his confrontation with Lyttleton, and at the end of August, as he was about to leave for London, he let loose a public blast at the British that again took things to a breaking point. He gave an on-the-record newspaper interview to an American war correspondent, George Weller of the Chicago *Daily News*, which was like a dentist's drill on a bad tooth, without painkiller:

> England is afraid of the French Fleet. What in effect England is carrying on is a wartime deal with Hitler in which Vichy serves as a go-between. Vichy serves Hitler in keeping the French people in subjection, and selling the French Empire piecemeal to Germany. But do not forget that Vichy also serves England by keeping the French fleet from Hitler's hands. Britain is exploiting Vichy the same way as Germany, the only difference is in purpose. What happens is in effect an exchange of advantages between hostile powers which keeps the Vichy government alive as long as both Britain and Germany are agreed that it should exist.

This extraordinary exercise in French logic was then salted further when he continued to Weller: "I am not keeping facts secret any longer. I have offered the United States the use of the principal ports in Free French Africa as naval bases against Hitler. I have offered them upon the basis of a long-term lease analogous to the plan under which Britain offered her Atlantic bases to the United States. But I have not asked for any destroyers in return."

Two days later, as de Gaulle prepared to fly to London, Churchill dictated an instruction to all concerned: "No one is to see General de Gaulle. No English authority is to have any contact with him when he arrives. If the occasion demands, it may be conveyed to him that a most serious situation has arisen with which the Prime Minister is dealing in person."

*

Unruffled and certainly unrepentant, Charles de Gaulle returned to London on September 1, and it did not take long for him to sense the chilly atmosphere. Churchill had also minuted to Cabinet ministers that "in view of General de Gaulle's disturbing behavior in recent weeks, departments should for the time being adopt a cautious and dilatory attitude towards all requests by the Free French." As a start, de Gaulle was prevented from making a planned BBC broadcast on his return. He retaliated at once by suspending all Free French from broadcasting on BBC. But he did send a handwritten letter to Churchill saying that he would be happy to be received at No. 10 Downing Street, to which Churchill sent a chilly reply: "The evidences I have received of your unfriendly attitude towards the British nation have filled me with surprise and sorrow. Until I am in possession of any explanations you may do me the honor to offer, I am unable to judge whether any interviews between us would serve a useful purpose."

De Gaulle then saw Desmond Morton, of Churchill's personal staff, who frequently acted as a liaison with the Free French, and came about as close to an explanation and apology as he ever did. His one objective was to defeat Hitler at Britain's side, he told Morton, but if he honestly felt that the English were damaging French interests then he had to protest with all his might, because otherwise Frenchmen would regard him as "a mere English mercenary" and his value as a symbol of France would disappear. He was only a small man with a small following, he told Morton, and his protests had to be "louder and more frequent than if he were recognized as a head of a great nation," and he was sure that if roles were reversed and Churchill were in his position, then Churchill would do the same. Next he addressed a longer letter to Churchill, saying that he had returned to London to clarify things with the aim of complete harmony between two allied peoples, and finally a meeting was arranged at Downing Street for September 12.

A great human truth about Winston Churchill was that he was a poor hater. He was too full of warmth and humor, too knowledgeable about life's ups and downs, too generous and magnanimous in spirit to sustain animosity or feudings against those with whom fate decreed that he had to work. He could be ruthless and tough, but he could not hate.

For the great confrontation with General de Gaulle, he told his private secretary, John Colville, that when de Gaulle entered the Cabinet Room, "I will rise and bow slightly, but I will not shake hands with him and I will gesture him to the opposite side of the table." Colville, fluent in French, was to remain to interpret. De Gaulle arrived promptly at three o'clock and took this opening gesture of displeasure quite unabashed, settled in the chair indicated and gazed at Churchill, waiting for him to begin. Colville has written an amusing account of what happened next, although it was scarcely funny at the time.

Churchill began: "General de Gaulle, I have asked you to come here this afternoon," and paused and turned to Colville, who took over: *"Mon Général, je vous ai invité à venir cet après-midi . . ."* at which point Churchill interrupted fiercely and said, "I didn't say *Mon Général* and I didn't say I invited him." Colville managed to get through the opening, and then de Gaulle made his first response. But when Colville translated into English, de Gaulle, who understood English thoroughly although he almost never was heard using it, interrupted and said: *"Non, non. Ce n'est pas du tout le sens de ce que je disais."*

Churchill then dismissed the frustrated Colville and told him to send for another interpreter. From the Foreign Office, the most fluent French-speaker of the British diplomatic service came hotfooting across Downing Street while Churchill and de Gaulle sat in silence. But ten minutes later he came out of the Cabinet Room red-faced and muttered to Colville, "They must be mad!" From then on they continued alone with a bilingual British note-taker present.

An hour went by, and Colville recounts:

> I tried to eavesdrop, but double doors had recently been installed. I could hear nothing. I walked out into the hall and tried on General de Gaulle's *képi*, registering surprise at the remarkable smallness of his head. I did my best to concentrate on the papers on my desk. I decided it was my duty to burst in with a bogus message. Just then the bell rang, and I went in to find the two of them sitting side by side with amiable expressions on their faces. De Gaulle, no doubt for tactical purposes, was smoking one of the Prime Minister's cigars. They were talking French, an exercise Churchill could never resist and one which his audience invariably found fascinating.

The official British record discloses that the conversation began frostily enough, with Churchill registering his deep hurt at de Gaulle's anti-British outbursts, and de Gaulle assuring him that "it could not be seriously maintained that he was an enemy of Britain." They moved on to review the Syrian situation in detail, with explanations on both sides and assurances of future cooperation. Churchill then urged de Gaulle to broaden his Free French Committee to make it more representative, less authoritarian, more a coalition, and de Gaulle said he was in fact considering doing just that. By the end of the hour, each man clearly felt he had gained points from the other. Churchill then saw de Gaulle all the way to the door of Downing Street, where photographers were waiting, as a particular gesture of restored harmony between these two mercurial great men.

But it was an act of restoration and reconciliation that had to be repeated again and again and again throughout the war.

*

While the Syrian affair had been in the forefront for de Gaulle in the summer of 1941, the entry of the Soviet Union into the war had opened up new political possibilities for the French leader that he had been quick to exploit. Almost from the day the Nazis crossed the Soviet frontiers, "playing the Russian card" against his other allies became part of de Gaulle's political-diplomatic strategy, and continued almost to his last days in power in 1969.

General de Gaulle was in Cairo seeing Lyttleton when Hitler launched his attack on June 21, 1941. While waiting to enter Damascus after its capture by the Free French from the Vichy loyalists, he sent a telegram of instructions to his committee in London on June 24:

> Without consenting to discuss at present the vices and even the crimes of the Soviet regime, we must proclaim, like Churchill, that we are very frankly with the Russians since they are fighting the Germans. Make a discreet but

clear approach to Maisky [Ivan Maisky, the Soviet ambassador in London] yourselves, stating in my name that the French people are with Russia and that we desire to organize military relations with Moscow.

For de Gaulle and for France, there was an important political consideration in Russia's entry into the war that did not exist for Churchill and the British—and that was the effect it would have on the French Communist Party. In prewar elections at the time of the Popular Front in 1936, and again in 1938, the Communists had pushed up to nearly 15 percent of the vote. Of course they had then slavishly done all they could to sabotage the French war effort, politically at least, after the Hitler-Stalin pact of August 1939. The party leader, Maurice Thorez, deserted from his unit in the French Army before the Battle of France and had been spirited off to Moscow by Stalin's Comintern underground. But it was self-evident that the Communist apparatus in France, dormant while Vichy pursued its policy of collaboration with Germany, would now, with Germany butchering the Soviet Union, certainly be activated in resistance.

It was politically important to de Gaulle, therefore, that he gain Stalin's recognition as leader of French Resistance as promptly as possible. Not that he had any illusions about the ultimate loyalties and direction of the Communist underground network, but Stalin's recognition of the Free French movement would automatically reinforce and rally the entire left of French politics behind the Cross of Lorraine.

The first approach to Maisky in London was carried out by René Cassin, de Gaulle's principal adviser on legal affairs, who telegraphed Jerusalem that the interview had been cordial but noncommittal. But by a second meeting in early August after Maisky had consulted Moscow "he had stripped away the reserve which was still marked at our earlier visit" and agreed to take up the question of formal recognition of de Gaulle's movement. Meanwhile, Radio Moscow had switched on the praise for General de Gaulle and dropped its diatribes about "Gaullist mercenaries in the service of British imperialism."

The Soviet Union then accorded recognition to the Free French National Committee on the same terms as British recognition in an exchange of letters between Maisky and de Gaulle on September 26, 1941. De Gaulle somewhat grandly pledged that he would "lend the U.S.S.R. aid and assistance in this struggle by all the means available to me." He did not wait long to play his new card against the British.

Despite his reconciliation at the top with Churchill, he continued to feel only frustrations and antagonisms with the workings of the British command in the Middle East. In particular after his return to London de Gaulle kept pressing the British to provide equipment for two full Free French divisions, with more recruits coming in after the Syrian campaign. But on November 27 he was informed by Churchill's personal chief of staff, General Sir Hastings Ismay, that it would be impossible to assemble, equip and train the French units in the short time he was demanding.

De Gaulle replied immediately by canceling his request to the British to include Free French forces in any actions the High Command might be launching in the Middle East and North Africa—the same tactic he had used in his Cairo confrontation with Lyttleton. Next he called in Soviet Ambassador Alexander Bogomolov, who had been transferred from Vichy to London to represent Stalin with the Free French in a particular diplomatic gesture to underscore the switch in recognition that had been much appreciated by de Gaulle. To Bogomolov, he now made a surprising offer to transfer his two divisions in the Levant to the Russian front. How he expected to transport them or equip, train and support them in Russia is far from clear. In any event, a week later he received a soothing note from Churchill advising him that General Auchinleck was now anxious to make immediate use of a Free French brigade in operations under way in Cyrenaica (today Libya).

The "Russian card" had taken its first trick, at least in de Gaulle's view. Soviet recognition was reinforcing his status and independence as one of the Allied Powers, giving him more room for maneuver against the British and enhancing his political strength and following within France itself. Stalin's stance toward de Gaulle contrasted markedly with the coolness and hostility of Roosevelt and the United States—even though on this front also there were the first signs that the president was prepared to bow to realities.

De Gaulle had sent the faithful René Pleven to the United States on a special mission to lobby the Free French cause. He was there from June to October, but neither Hull nor Roosevelt would see him. Nevertheless, the United States had taken up de Gaulle's offer of base facilities in the African territories under his control. Using Pan American Airways as a cover, survey teams had been sent to negotiate local agreements to use airfields across French Africa to ferry aircraft to the British in the Middle East.

On October 4, 1941, Pleven was finally granted a meeting with Undersecretary of State Sumner Welles in Washington. He reported to de Gaulle in London that "Welles is always very cold—everyone here is aware that Welles and his school think they know better than our British allies and even than ourselves about France." As to a specific request that Free France be given US Lend-Lease assistance, Pleven recorded:

> I reminded him of the moral advantages which we would derive from such a measure. While avoiding giving me a negative reply, he declared to me that the problem was still under consideration, pointing out, however, that the way in which the law had been drafted specified that it could only apply to governments, and that the fact of giving us directly the advantages of Lend-Lease would imply recognition. I suggested that legal difficulties could usually be surmounted, but he replied that in this case he was doubtful.

But if logic and persuasion could not move Sumner Welles, the State Department and President Roosevelt, events soon did. In early September 1941 the

German ambassador to defeated France, Otto Abetz, handed Marshal Pétain a written demand for the recall of General Maxime Weygand from his post as commissioner general for Africa. Well aware of Weygand's close contacts with the American diplomat in Algiers, Robert Murphy, probably of overtures from the British as well, the Germans bluntly told Pétain that the general's continued presence in North Africa was "an act of hostility." Pétain had reported all this to the American embassy in Vichy, resolutely asserting that he would not give in. But in early November he finally gave way and ordered Weygand's recall. At this point even the American ambassador, Admiral William D. Leahy, began to have doubts as to the Vichy gamble. In a personal letter to Roosevelt, he now described Pétain as "a feeble, frightened old man" and said he saw no reason why under future pressure Pétain would not concede African bases, or even the French Fleet, to the Germans. He said he despaired of any further influence with Vichy and had given up hope of putting "some semblance of backbone in a jellyfish."

Against this background Roosevelt suddenly managed to resolve those legal difficulties over Lend-Lease aid for the Free French that Welles had cited to Pleven a month before. On November 11, 1941—Armistice Day, hallowed in French memories and history—the president wrote to his Lend-Lease administrator, Edward R. Stettinius: "In order for you to arrange for Lend-Lease aid to the French Volunteer Forces (Free French) by way of re-transfer from His Majesty's Government. . . . I hereby find that the defense of any French territory under control of the Free French is vital for the defense of the United States."

This formulation of course avoided actual recognition of the Free French, but nevertheless, with his Vichy policy increasingly frayed by the feebleness of Pétain and the mendacious evil of the men surrounding the marshal, Roosevelt was having to turn to General de Gaulle and accord him at least tacit recognition whether he liked him or not. Grudgingly it was done, but had de Gaulle been a more flexible, subtle and intuitive political leader, he could certainly have responded with diplomatic finesse and courtesy to push the door open and create a little goodwill in Washington for himself and his cause. He did not even bother to send any message of appreciation or thanks for the Lend-Lease decision to Roosevelt—at least none is mentioned in his Memoirs or appears in his published wartime documents. General de Gaulle was no man to concern himself with the sensibilities, foibles or susceptibilities of others.

*

"On December 7th, the attack on Pearl Harbor hurled America into the war," de Gaulle wrote in his Memoirs. "One might have thought that, from that moment, American policy would treat the Free French who were fighting its own enemies, as allies. Nothing of that sort happened, however. Before Washington finally made up its mind to do so, many painful ups and downs would have to be endured."

One might also have thought that the General would have realized this was no time to give offense to Roosevelt. From de Gaulle's standpoint, looked at pragmatically and coolly, everything was now moving his way at last in Washington. America's entry into the war meant that the issue of collaboration and support for

Vichy could no longer be blurred or long supported. Therefore the sensible course for de Gaulle was the obvious—whatever the cost to his *amour propre,* to go out of his way to seek directly Roosevelt's confidence and understanding, as smoothly and promptly as possible, and make it easy for the president to abandon his Vichy policy and switch to full recognition of the Free French with as little loss of face as possible.

Instead, de Gaulle siezed the first opportunity handed him, barely two weeks after Pearl Harbor, to stage a wholly unnecessary confrontation with Roosevelt and Hull over the tiny French islands in Canadian waters off the coast of Newfoundland: Saint-Pierre and Miquelon. He could have used the somewhat complex situation surrounding the islands to show a little diplomacy and the ability to deal in accommodation and trust with Washington. As it was, his handling of the Saint-Pierre and Miquelon affair cost him all hopes of early diplomatic recognition by Roosevelt and sealed his complete exclusion from the higher political and military councils of the war all the way to the Potsdam Conference in the summer of 1945. He seized the islands for the Free French in a *coup de main* that was unnecessary, a Pyrrhic victory that only reinforced all the deepest prejudices in Washington against him.

It had long been clear that the population of the islands—some 5,000 fishermen and their families—was overwhelmingly Free French in its sentiments. Technically, the islands were under the command of a pro-Vichy naval officer, Admiral Georges Robert, headquartered in Martinique, three thousand miles away. A pro-Vichy local administrator was in charge of the islands, but the local veterans' association had even sent a telegram of support to de Gaulle at the time of Dakar.

Still, the fishermen could not oust the local governor, and de Gaulle in 1940–41 was in no position to do much but send back messages of thanks to the population for its sentiments of support. Meanwhile the United States had entered into a complex negotiation with Admiral Robert in Martinique aimed at "neutralizing" all French possessions in the Western Hemisphere. By a combination of diplomatic carrots and the stick of economic blockade, the Americans had reached agreement with Robert to recognize the status quo of Vichy control of the islands, while Robert immobilized all French Navy vessels under his control except a few small patrol craft. There was also a considerable sum of Bank of France gold stashed away in Martinique.

But then, as the Battle of the Atlantic intensified during 1941, with the United States edging closer and closer to war by taking over naval convoy stations in the Western Atlantic, a Vichy radio transmitter on Saint-Pierre and Miquelon began to assume great importance. Washington did not mind very much its pro-Vichy, anti-de Gaulle propaganda broadcasts. But when it instituted daily weather reports back to France, this clearly had no purpose other than help for the German submarines in their attacks on Allied shipping. By the time of Pearl Harbor, therefore, the Americans were considering action to silence the island transmitter.

This, of course, was unknown to de Gaulle in London. But he reasoned quite logically that with the United States now in the war, the time would be ripe to

"rally" French possessions in the Western Hemisphere to the Free French—
Saint-Pierre and Miquelon first. Accordingly, immediately after Pearl Harbor, de
Gaulle asked Churchill if there would be any British objection to a small Free
French naval operation under Admiral Muselier, involving no more than a brief
diversion by a couple of warships, to take over the islands and hoist the banner of
the Cross of Lorraine.

On December 15, as Churchill was about to depart for Washington for his first
great wartime conference with Roosevelt, he replied to de Gaulle with the
welcome word that he and the British chiefs of staff had no objection to "unmuz-
zling Muselier," but he asked for a brief postponement of a final decision until he
could ascertain "whether the action would in any way be considered embarrassing
by the United States government." Muselier, meanwhile, had already sailed for
Canada to carry out an inspection of Free French Naval Forces, with secret orders
for the Saint-Pierre and Miquelon operation.

But Roosevelt, when informed of the plan by Churchill, immediately declared
himself "strongly opposed" to a de Gaulle takeover. Instead he said he wanted the
Canadians to go in and silence the transmitter, leaving the Vichy administrator on
the job in accordance with the agreement with Admiral Robert. Accordingly, de
Gaulle was then asked in London on December 17 to shelve the operation at the
request of the Americans. This he initially agreed to do.

But when he then learned of the American plan to have the Canadians go in, he
brooded for twenty-four hours, and without consulting anyone or asking any
further questions about the operation, he sent top secret instructions to Admiral
Muselier in Halifax:

> We have, as you asked, consulted the British and American governments.
> We know from a source beyond doubt that the Canadians intend to carry
> out the destruction of the Saint-Pierre radio station themselves. In these
> conditions, I order you to proceed to the rallying of Saint-Pierre and Mi-
> quelon by your own means and without saying anything to the foreigners. I
> take full responsibility for this operation, which has become indispensable in
> order to keep these French possessions for France.

In fact, if de Gaulle had troubled to try to find out, the Canadians had by that
time decided *not* to go along with Roosevelt's request because of the intensively
pro-de Gaulle feelings not only on the two little islands but among French-
speaking Canadians generally. With a little restraint, therefore, de Gaulle could
have had what he wanted without kicking the Americans in the teeth.

A violent snowstorm prevented Muselier from sailing until December 22. But
on Christmas Eve he dispatched a message to de Gaulle in London that the islands
had rallied "enthusiastically" and the Vichy administrator was under house arrest.
On Christmas Day de Gaulle cabled back: "My keen congratulations on the way in
which you have carried out this rallying with order and with dignity."

For de Gaulle it was a simple, even trifling affair. But his action in secret, out of
the blue and above all in contradiction to the assurances he had given the Foreign

Office to call off the operation, stunned the British and infuriated Roosevelt, but most of all Cordell Hull. The crusty old Tennessean, who believed above all else that a man's word ought to be sacred, called de Gaulle a "marplot." He went to the State Department on Christmas Day—while Roosevelt and Churchill were attending a special Washington church service—and issued a blistering statement: "Our preliminary reports show that the action taken by the so-called Free French ships at Saint-Pierre and Miquelon was an arbitrary action contrary to prior knowledge or consent in any sense of the United States Government. The United States Government has inquired of the Canadian Government as to what steps that government is prepared to take to restore the status quo in these islands."

De Gaulle's little coup de main now became a major and time-consuming issue for Roosevelt and Churchill at precisely the time when they were trying to devote all their energies and attention to outlining grand strategy and organizing the management of the war effort, with the profound and far-reaching decisions of that first Washington conference. Cordell Hull certainly over-reacted with his gratuitous statement about "the so-called Free French" and was promptly bombarded with telegrams from Americans addressed to "the so-called Secretary of State" and the "so-called State Department." But this did not improve either his temper or his judgment of de Gaulle.

Hull now insisted, beyond reason, that de Gaulle be forced to back down, withdraw from the islands and allow the Canadians and the Americans to take over supervision of the transmitter. Roosevelt, with bigger problems on his mind, was prepared to allow the affair to die away, but Hull refused to desist. De Gaulle, impervious to the consequences of what he had done, then messaged Churchill about "the harm to the fighting spirit in France and elsewhere" caused by the Hull statement, and urged the prime minister to make a public response "because you are the only man capable of saying it as it should be said." For Churchill, despite his troubles with de Gaulle, this was irresistible, and he used the occasion of a side trip to Ottawa in the midst of his Washington visit to deliver a speech of rousing support for the Free French before the Canadian Parliament. This only made Hull all the madder. Meanwhile, Churchill messaged de Gaulle in London:

> I pleaded your case strongly to our friends in the United States. Your having broken away from the agreement about Saint-Pierre and Miquelon raised a storm which might have been serious had I not been on the spot to speak to the President. Undoubtedly the result of your activities has been to make things more difficult with the United States and has in fact prevented some favorable developments from occurring. I am always doing my best in our interests.

But all that mattered to de Gaulle was that he was winning. He now gave Hull another taste of his total indifference to Great Power pressures over what he deemed to be the interests of France. As a final act in this French comédie, Anthony Eden summoned de Gaulle to the Foreign Office on January 14, 1942, to try to pressure him (though not, apparently, very hard) to accept yet another Hull formula for "neutralizing" the islands under the Free French but with joint Allied control. De Gaulle having predictably refused, Eden then asked what would happen if the Americans sent warships to the islands to enforce their wishes, as they were apparently prepared to do.

"The Allied ships will stop at the limit of French territorial waters and the American admiral will have lunch with Muselier, who will certainly be delighted," de Gaulle replied loftily.

"But what if their cruiser goes beyond the limit?" Eden asked.

"Our people will issue the customary challenge."

"And if the cruiser still continues?"

"That would be a great shame," said de Gaulle, "for in that event our people would have to open fire."

De Gaulle wrote that he then concluded his remarks "with a smile" at Eden's evident alarm by adding: "But I have confidence in the democracies."

On that note the curtain came down on the affair of Saint-Pierre and Miquelon, but not its consequences. One of these was immediate. Roosevelt and Churchill, among the other historic results of their Washington meeting, had drawn up their United Nations Declaration, which they then jointly signed on January 1, 1942, inviting a long list of other Allied Powers to follow. But when Churchill proposed that de Gaulle be asked to sign on behalf of Free France, Hull refused and Roosevelt declined to overrule him. Thus de Gaulle lost at once a chance to gain an important step toward that diplomatic recognition he was so insistently demanding. It was not until January 1945 that de Gaulle was finally invited to add his signature to the United Nations Declaration so France could take part in the San Francisco conference to draft the UN Charter.

But in the meantime he was self-satisfied and content, even giving the impression of elation with yet another victory over his allies. Throughout his life this extraordinary but determinedly lonely man always seemed to seek strength in isolation rather than working with others, in being alone and acting alone, which was the only form of "independence" he could recognize.

NINE

1942: NORTH AFRICA

The entry into the war of the United States, and in particular President Franklin D. Roosevelt, abruptly shifted the power center of the Alliance from London to Washington. Winston Churchill—astute and intellectually superior, older and more experienced, gallant and far-seeing—became by his own choice and definition "the President's loyal lieutenant." He accepted the reality of American power and the ascendancy that went with it, which Roosevelt was quick to assert. Through loyalty he would maintain his influence in the central direction of the war. But it was not a totally happy relationship. Roosevelt's American liberalism was at odds with Churchill's British conservatism, and Churchill's buoyant personality and boundless ideas were frequently met with a shallowness of intellectual response and understanding, and even occasional meanness, on the part of Roosevelt. Free France was the most difficult and divisive issue between them. Nevertheless, from the outset Churchill put agreement with the president above all other considerations in the prosecution of the war, and he put up with a lot and gave constantly and generously to achieve it. If his role was thereby diminished, his greatness was not.

General de Gaulle of course quickly saw this new pattern of relationships emerge in the affair of Saint-Pierre and Miquelon, when Churchill first gave his approval to the proposed operation by the Free French and then two days later at Roosevelt's insistence asked that it be called off. From then on the ups and downs of the de Gaulle-Churchill relationship intensified as the prime minister found himself caught and even torn between his proclaimed first loyalty to Roosevelt and loyalty to his first ally, de Gaulle. The relationship was scarcely helped by the fact that de Gaulle did not hesitate to berate the prime minister frequently and openly for giving way to the Americans and acceding to a secondary role. The idea of playing loyal lieutenant to anyone was totally alien to Charles de Gaulle.

In his War Memoirs he records a conversation with Churchill at No. 10 Downing Street in November 1942, after the Anglo-American landings in North

Africa, when Churchill counseled him not to go on confronting the Americans head-on—"be patient, they will come to you, for there is no alternative." To this de Gaulle says he replied:

> Perhaps—but how much crockery will be broken in the meantime! And I fail to understand your own position. You have been fighting this war since the first day. In a manner of speaking, you personally *are* this war. Your army is advancing in Libya. There would be no Americans in Africa if, on your side, you were not in the process of defeating Rommel. Up to this very moment, not a single one of Roosevelt's soldiers has yet met a single one of Hitler's soldiers, while for three years your men have been fighting in every latitude of the globe. Besides, in this African campaign it is Europe that is at stake, and England belongs to Europe. Yet you let America take charge of the conflict, though it is up to you to control it, at least ethically. Do so! All of European public opinion will follow you!

De Gaulle says that "this sally struck Churchill; I watched him waver," and that "we parted after having agreed that we must not permit the present crisis to crack Franco-British solidarity, which was ever more in accord with the natural order of things when the United States intervened in the affairs of the Old World." Maybe Churchill did waver as de Gaulle says. But if so, it was probably not because he had been struck or wounded by some powerful challenge of the General's argument and logic. De Gaulle persistently refused to see the world and the war through any focus but his own one-eye telescope. America must come to the rescue of Europe, but not "intervene in the affairs of the Old World." This same view and same logic led de Gaulle straight to his veto of British entry into the European Common Market twenty years later, convinced as he became at that time that the British were simply putting their nose under the European tent in order to bring an American camel inside.

*

De Gaulle remained in London continuously for eleven months, from September 1941 until August 1942—scarcely by his own choice, however. Twice Churchill flatly refused to allow him out of the country when he wanted to leave for the Middle East and Africa. The Syrian problem continued to fester between Britain and the Free French, and Churchill was still smarting over Saint-Pierre and Miquelon. He was also on the receiving end of constant complaints and snide condemnation of de Gaulle from Roosevelt. When de Gaulle first proposed leaving London in early April, Churchill minuted Anthony Eden at the Foreign Office: "I think it would be most dangerous to let this man begin again his campaign of Anglophobia in which he indulged when in Central Africa, and which he is now more than ever attracted to." De Gaulle then raised the matter again in late May, and Eden sent a note to Churchill saying that "a further attempt to get him to postpone would merely increase his suspicions of us, and we would find him even more difficult to deal with than he normally is—he has been rather better lately." But Churchill would have none of it: "I cannot agree. There is nothing hostile to

England that this man may not do once he gets off the chain." Wearily, Eden set about diplomatically persuading de Gaulle that certain matters were under consideration on which the British might need to consult him, and could he not delay for another six weeks?

De Gaulle accepted this veto over his travel with an outward display of phlegm, as though it weren't actually happening, but it scarcely improved his frame of mind or, as Eden forecast, his suspicions. When he finally did get "off the chain" and arrived back in Syria in August, his pent-up resentments against *perfide Albion* burst out in full, as Churchill predicted. Meanwhile, tethered in London though he was, he continued to consolidate his own organization, his power and authority, and in particular he forged ahead in France itself, where the Resistance Movement was at last beginning to gain both organization and momentum over the lethargy of defeatism and two years of German occupation and Vichy rule.

Across this period, General de Gaulle lived during the week in London at the Connaught Hotel—small, elegant, quiet and discreet, near Grosvenor Square, where the American military presence was burgeoning under General Dwight D. Eisenhower. When not away on inspection tours of French forces, he spent his working days at Carlton Gardens, where Free French Headquarters was established across The Mall from St. James's Park, The Admiralty, Horse Guards Parade and Downing Street. On weekends he would retire to a country home near London to be alone with Madame de Gaulle and their mentally retarded third child, Anne. At first in 1940 they lived at Ellesmere in Shropshire, and in 1941 they moved closer to London to the town of Berkhampsted. Eventually they took a house in London with a large garden at Hampstead Heath. His son, Philippe, was serving as an officer in the Free French Navy, first on convoy duty in the Atlantic on a corvette and later as second-in-command of a motor torpedo boat on hazardous patrol in the English Channel. His daughter Elisabeth was at a Catholic boarding school for girls before later going on to Oxford University. A family *femme de ménage* left France with Madame de Gaulle and the children when they escaped on the last boat out of Brest. All their lives, whatever the setting, they lived a very simple private family life. Madame de Gaulle did all the shopping, a petite dark-haired plain little Frenchwoman queuing up with her ration books with the English housewives. Whatever de Gaulle's difficulties with the British State, they both formed a deep respect and appreciation of the English.

> The ordinary people round about us observed a sympathetic discretion [he wrote]. The attitude of the English when they saw me with my family passing along a street, taking a walk in a park, or going into a cinema, was as kindly reserved as the demonstrations were fervent when I appeared in public. So I was able, to my advantage, to verify that, among this great people, each one respects the liberty of the others.

At three o'clock in the morning of May 5, 1942, General de Gaulle was awakened at the Connaught by a telephone call from Reuters News Agency informing him that British troops had landed at the port of Diégo-Suarez on the northeastern tip of the huge French island of Madagascar in the Indian Ocean off the coast of Africa. Over the phone, he confined himself to little more than a curt *"Merci,"* but he boiled with anger at the British for acting without him and keeping him completely in the dark. All the more so because he had been urging such an operation for months. On December 16, 1941, immediately after Pearl Harbor, he wrote Churchill proposing a Free French invasion to bring the island over to the Allies from Vichy control. He pressed again on February 19, 1942, pointing to the danger that Madagascar might suddenly be abjectly surrendered by Vichy to a Japanese force arriving secretly, the way Vichy had surrendered French Indochina. He followed this up with a third appeal for action to Eden on April 9. Now the response had come, and he was out of it.

Churchill at first gave Madagascar low strategic priority, but after the sinking of the two magnificent British battleships *Repulse* and *Prince of Wales* in the Far East by Japanese bombers, the fall of Singapore, the overrunning of Malaysia, Siam and Burma and the threat to Ceylon, he changed his mind. Madagascar had to be secured. But as he wrote: "With memories of Dakar in our mind, we could not complicate the operation by admitting the Free French." He had also consulted the Americans about his plans, and of course Roosevelt had urged that de Gaulle be kept out of it. The theory had taken hold that representatives of the Vichy government would be more ready to surrender or make accommodation with the Anglo-Americans than with General de Gaulle. Later in the day on May 5 a communiqué was issued in Washington stating, rather gratuitously, since no American forces were involved, that "the United States and Great Britain are agreed that Madagascar should be restored to France as soon as occupation of the island should cease to be necessary for the common cause."

This infuriated de Gaulle all the more—the very idea that (as in the case of Saint-Pierre and Miquelon) France could thus be deprived of rule over one of its possessions by the Anglo-American allies. From Carlton Gardens, a frosty silence greeted the news of the Madagascar invasion, and for six days de Gaulle refused an invitation to confer with Eden at the Foreign Office. On May 11 he finally went to see Eden, only to emerge madder than ever at being told that the British intended to try and seek a *modus vivendi* with the Vichy governor of the island, similar to the American arrangement with Admiral Robert over Martinique. Vichy, in other words, was to be left in nominal control over Madagascar provided it was "neutralized."

But by this time Pierre Laval had returned to power in Vichy, stiffening the local governor in Madagascar, who brusquely refused to negotiate. The island is a thousand miles long, so the British were left in embarrassing control of nothing but the port of Diégo-Suarez, while Vichy continued to rule everything else from the capital of Tananarive in the south. This stalemate persisted for another four months.

Meanwhile de Gaulle convened the Free French Committee and informed it that he intended to denounce the British publicly, break off all relations with London and withdraw permanently to Africa. Only with great argument was he dissuaded. So he now set about again playing the Russian card. Soviet Foreign

Minister Vyacheslav M. Molotov arrived in London in mid-May en route to Washington. De Gaulle conferred with him at length, made no secret of his irritation with the British and then issued a strong statement of support for Soviet demands for the opening of a second front in Europe in 1942—a sore point of major political and military concern at that time. Then, after Churchill blocked his second request to leave London at the end of May, de Gaulle called in Soviet Ambassador Bogomolov, told him he was considering breaking with the British and asked him to inquire of Stalin whether the Soviet government would accept him, and Free French military forces, to transfer to Soviet territory.

Either de Gaulle was bluffing, which was not generally the case, or he had lost his head. If he did not like the way the British were treating him, how could he have reasoned rationally that he would be better off in Stalin's clutches? Did he expect to be able to move about more freely or communicate more freely from Moscow? How could he have believed for one moment that he could rally Free France or the French people over Radio Moscow? How could he not have realized that Stalin would consign him to oblivion the moment he lost his usefulness or failed to do his bidding? His commissioner for foreign affairs, Maurice Dejean, was so appalled that he subsequently resigned and was moved to a different post. But in the meantime Bogomolov transmitted de Gaulle's request as a serious proposition to Moscow. It did not improve British trust or confidence in the General.

But at this juncture the fortunes of the Free French suddenly changed as a result of one of those accidents of war—the Battle of Bir-Hakeim (for which a bridge over the Seine was subsequently renamed after the war). During April and May, Rommel launched the most hard-driving and effective of his Afrika Korps offenses against the British 8th Army in Libya. With superior tanks and superior firepower from the famous 88-millimeter guns, he maneuvered and attacked to hurl the British back across the desert into Egypt. A Free French light division of 5,500 men under General Pierre Koenig held a key height on the southern flank of the retreating British in the open desert at a desolate juncture of trails nobody ever heard of before, called Bir-Hakeim. Rommel hit the French first with an Italian mechanized division, on May 27. The British commander, General Sir Neil Ritchie, appealed to Koenig to hold out while British forces retreated to establish new defensive positions around El Alamein. The Italians failed to dent the French, and on June 2 Rommel gave one of his Panzer units the task of cleaning up Bir-Hakeim. For the first time in two years, Frenchmen were now again fighting Germans.

With the British Army in retreat, headlines of the French stand at Bir-Hakeim began filling the London papers. On June 3 Rommel sent a surrender demand in his own handwriting, which Koenig refused. By June 7 the Free French were completely surrounded, and fighting on. The battle raged for another four days in the cruel desert heat, with Koenig's soldiers down to a ration of two quarts of water per day per man. On June 10 the British told Koenig to withdraw when he could, and on the evening of June 11 in London a War Office messenger took a dispatch to General de Gaulle at Carlton Gardens informing him that the bulk of the light division had successfully pulled back out of reach of the enemy. In fourteen days of fighting, the French had lost more than 1,500 killed, wounded, missing and prisoner. De Gaulle wrote: "I thanked the messenger, told him he could go, shut the door. I was alone. O heart throbbing with emotion, sobs of pride, tears of joy!"

There was a footnote to the battle. On June 12 the German radio announced that "Frenchmen made prisoner at Bir-Hakeim, since they do not belong to a regular army, will be subject to the laws of war and will be executed." Within an hour, de Gaulle says, the BBC was broadcasting his response in all languages beamed to Europe: "If the German Army were to dishonour itself so far as to kill French soldiers taken prisoner when fighting for their country, General de Gaulle announces that to his profound regret he would find himself obliged to inflict the same fate on the German prisoners who have fallen into the hands of his troops." By that evening, the German radio responded with an announcement "so there will be no misunderstanding" that "General de Gaulle's soldiers will be treated as soldiers." There it rested.

Bir-Hakeim, meanwhile, provided the atmosphere for another meeting of reconciliation between de Gaulle and Churchill, who only the week before had instructed Eden again to block de Gaulle from leaving London. At Eden's urging, de Gaulle was invited to Downing Street on June 10, as the battle reached its climax.

Churchill began by declaring the Free French stand to be "one of the finest feats of arms in this war," and then took up the subject of Madagascar, hoping to reassure, explain and soothe de Gaulle. "We have no designs on the French Empire," he said. "I am a friend of France! I have always wanted, and I want, a great France with a great army. It is necessary for the peace, order and security of Europe. I have no other policy." To which de Gaulle wrote that he replied:

> That is true. You even had the merit, after Vichy's armistice, of continuing to play the card of France. That card is called de Gaulle: don't lose it now! It would be all the more absurd since you have reached the moment when your policy is succeeding and when Free France has become the soul and frame of French resistance. On these bases I too am faithful to you. But I have very few resources with which to bear the responsibility for the interests of France. This involves great difficulties for me. I ask you to help me to overcome them. I agree that, on the whole, you are not ill-disposed towards us. But there are grave exceptions. Also American policy toward us is atrocious. It aims at our destruction. Do you know that, for Memorial Day, the American government invited Vichy military attachés and did not invite our officers? For the Americans, the Frenchmen of Bir-Hakeim are not belligerents.

But Churchill, after a limp explanation of American policy, responded grandly that "what is big and important is the war—we shall be in France perhaps next year, in any case we shall be there together. We still have great obstacles to overcome but I am sure that we will win." As the interview ended, Churchill pointed out that he had intentionally spoken in the House of Commons of the "Fighting French," which he said he thought "sounds much better than Free French," and he suggested that de Gaulle consider with the Foreign Office changing to this designation. Once again he saw de Gaulle to the door of Downing Street and parted with a warm handshake of reconciliation.

A few days later, Soviet Ambassador Bogomolov was told by Dejean that de Gaulle had unwittingly exaggerated his differences with the British and had unnecessarily raised the question of moving the Free French to the Soviet Union.

*

Bir-Hakeim also had an effect in Washington. Great strategic decisions of the war were impending between Roosevelt and Churchill, and although General de Gaulle could be kept out of this process he could not be ignored. Soon after the Downing Street meeting, Churchill departed for Washington in the second half of June for his second big wartime conference with the president. The prime topic was the question of a second front—whether the Allies would land in Europe during 1942, as the Russians were demanding and General George C. Marshall wanted to do, and if not a landing in Europe, then where would they take the offensive before the end of the year, as Roosevelt insisted?

Meanwhile, a small olive branch had been extended to de Gaulle from Washington. Late in May he had a long conversation with the American ambassador to London, John Winant, whose personal relationship with Roosevelt was close. After a second talk at the time of Bir-Hakeim, Winant urged Roosevelt to invite de Gaulle to Washington. Next, the War Department accepted a Free French liaison mission, and in London, Admiral Harold R. Stark, the senior American officer in Britain, was designated formally to handle contacts with de Gaulle "on all questions relating to the conduct of the war." In Washington, in the afterglow of Bir-Hakeim, Churchill then pressed Roosevelt on the question of recognition of what was now the Fighting French National Committee. Roosevelt inched forward. A joint Anglo-American communiqué on July 9, 1942, announced that the French National Committee was to be given "all possible assistance as a symbol of French resistance in general against the Axis powers." This of course still fell short of recognition, and the communiqué added that "the political future of France could only be decided in freedom and without coercion." Still, this was also accompanied by an American decision to make Lend-Lease aid available directly to the Fighting French instead of going through the British, and de Gaulle was pleased enough with the results to write his representative in Washington telling him so—but he did not go public with any expression of satisfaction.

When Churchill returned from Washington, he finally agreed to let de Gaulle "off the chain" to depart for Cairo on August 5. They had a somewhat testy talk when de Gaulle went to Downing Street to take his leave—a foretaste of the storm brewing up again. Churchill commented that the people of French Levant did not yet see independence as a reality and were dissatisfied. De Gaulle retorted that "they are at least as satisfied in Syria and the Lebanon as in Iraq, Palestine or Egypt" (all British controlled). He again protested against not being allowed to use Free French troops to go into the south of Madagascar, take Tananarive and clean up the Vichy regime. He also complained about the British resident in Syria, Major General Sir Edward Spears "causing us trouble," to which Churchill replied: "Spears has a lot of enemies, but he has one friend—the Prime Minister." They managed to part on equitable terms, but it did not last long.

De Gaulle reached Cairo and after a stormy first meeting with the new British minister of state for the Middle East, Richard Casey, an Australian, he went on to Damascus to take up a month-long residence. The political-military situation was indeed a witches' brew of Anglo-French hostility and troubles, which de Gaulle deliberately set about stirring and stoking to assert his authority and strike back at the British for Madagascar and all the other slights and pent-up frustrations he had endured in London. Since the British were by far the dominant military power on this French territory, they wanted to have their say in all administrative matters such as security, public order and communications, even, to de Gaulle's particular irritation, membership on a wheat-export board for the Levant. Moreover, whether de Gaulle would admit it or not, there was considerable "native unrest" against the French. This he was inclined to dismiss as British-inspired rather than anti-French. So he proceeded to block, oppose, challenge the British over every issue and incident he could find or invent, with "appalingly rude behavior" that was repeatedly reported back to London by British representatives at all levels.

Finally, on August 31, an exasperated Churchill cabled him asking him to return for a thorough discussion of the situation. Now it was de Gaulle's turn to administer a snub. He replied thanking the prime minister "for the invitation you were so kind as to extend" but said he had other business to complete in the French African possessions before he could return. He had another reason as well. He had either deduced or gotten some intelligence leak about the Anglo-American decision to invade North Africa, and he had cabled the Fighting French Committee in London on August 27:

> The United States has now decided to land troops in French North Africa. The operation will be launched in conjunction with a forthcoming British offensive in Egypt. The Americans have arranged for local cooperation by making use of the goodwill of our partisans and giving the impression that they are acting in agreement with us. Should the occasion arise, Marshal Pétain will certainly give orders to fight against the Allies in North Africa. The Germans will make the affair a pretext to rush in. The Americans thought at first that they would be able to open a second front in France this year. That is why, having need of us, they took the position indicated by their memorandum of July 9th [the Washington statement of half-recognition]. Now their plans have changed.

This was a prescient statement of what was to come, and since de Gaulle also realized that he would again certainly be cut out of all advance notice, consultation or participation in a North African landing, he now deliberately elected to make himself as difficult as possible to the Allies and the British in particular. If he was not to be treated with confidence and consideration, he was not about to make things easy for the Anglo-Americans. In his War Memoirs he states quite candidly that "I was stirring up controversy" and that "I had been able to change the atmosphere and put the helm over hard, permitting us to gain time." The Allies were not cooperating with him, so he would not cooperate with them.

On September 12, as de Gaulle tarried in the Middle East, the British finally launched a new assault in Madagascar in the south to clean up the long stall with the Vichy governor. Again the Free French were left out, increasing de Gaulle's irritation and mood of defiance and instransigence. Three days later he left Damascus on a swing to Fort Lamy, Brazzaville, Duala and other way-stops. He arrived back in London on September 25, primed for one of the most acrimonious meetings with Churchill of the war.

Accompanied by René Pleven, de Gaulle went to Downing Street on September 28. Eden was present with Churchill. From the outset it was bitter and unyielding on both sides, with Churchill telling de Gaulle that "in view of the state of affairs at Damascus and Beirut, we are not at all eager to install a Gaullist command" in Madagascar. For the first time in their relationship, he also attacked de Gaulle personally, telling him furiously, "You claim to be France—you are not France—I do not recognize you as France!" To which de Gaulle says he retorted: "If in your eyes I am not the representative of France, why and with what right are you dealing with me concerning her worldwide interests?" Eden got mad, Pleven was indignant, until finally, as de Gaulle wrote, "it was futile to continue."

There was no goodbye handshake at the door of Downing Street this time, and the British immediately applied the usual pressures. For ten days the French were cut off from all dispatch of telegrams to Africa and elsewhere. De Gaulle was denied the use of the BBC, cold-shouldered in all contacts, and delaying tactics were applied to all French requests and inquiries of the British government.

But with the North African landings less than a month away, the British could not keep up the charade of ostracization for long, and de Gaulle knew it or sensed it. In any case, he was always ready to outsulk an adversary.

Churchill concluded that "as a consolation prize—proof that we do not think of throwing over the Free French," the British should turn over control of Madagascar to de Gaulle just before the landings. Accordingly, by mid-October London began to ease up in the feud with the General, and on November 6 he was invited to confer with Eden at the Foreign Office—"all sugar and honey" in de Gaulle's account. At the end of the meeting they issued a joint communiqué announcing the appointment of General Legentilhomme as governor general of Madagascar, extinguishing Vichy rule and transferring the island to the Free French. De Gaulle added dryly: "I realized that events in North Africa were coming to a head." Thirty-six hours later, American and British forces began landing at Casablanca, Oran and Algiers.

*

The North African landings, coupled with General Sir Bernard L. Montgomery's great victory over Rommel the week before at El Alamein at the opposite end of the Mediterranean littoral, marked the turning point of the war from defensive to offensive. As Churchill wrote: "Before Alamein we never had a victory. After Alamein we never had a defeat."

The controversial decision to land in Morocco and Algeria was made only three months before, on July 23, 1942, at a special conference in London of the British and American combined chiefs of staff. General George C. Marshall was against going into North Africa, and argued long and hard for a direct immediate cross-Channel attack into France as the quickest way, the only way, to win the war. Strategically, Marshall was right. But the British countered with convincing analyses that it was impossible, even with surging American war production, to equip and train enough divisions, provide the landing craft and airplanes in sufficient strength to be able to mount such an operation with certainty of success against the Wehrmacht during 1942. Roosevelt, as commander in chief, was adamant that the American Army had to go into action in the European Theater before the end of the year.

Roosevelt always deferred far more to Marshall and intervened far less in the military conduct of the war than Churchill with his generals. But in this case he clearly had a North African campaign in the back of his mind even before the United States entered the war. A principal rationale or *raison d'être* of his Vichy policy had been to keep North Africa out of German hands. To this end he had moved Robert Murphy from the American embassy at Vichy to Algiers in December 1940 with the specific assignment of setting up an intelligence operation, fostering pro-Allied resistance cells and trying to play the Vichy resident-general, General Maxime Weygand, into changing sides at the right moment. Of course Churchill and the British chiefs of staff, apart from their technical arguments about capabilities for a cross-Channel attack in 1942, always favored a "Mediterranean first" strategy anyway. Therefore, when Marshall found himself dead-ended at the London meeting in his efforts to get the British to agree to invading France, the president turned at once to North Africa, and Churchill instantly followed with relief and enthusiasm.

Prior to Pearl Harbor, Murphy had concluded an agreement with Weygand to allow a modest amount of food, petroleum and other essentials into North Africa through the British naval blockade, and in return about a dozen US consular Intelligence posts had been established in Morocco and Algeria, ostensibly to "supervize" the supplies and see they were not diverted to the German war effort. But Weygand's recall to Vichy under German pressure in November 1941 was a marked setback for Roosevelt's gamble. Nevertheless, when Churchill came to Washington for their first post–Pearl Harbor conference, Roosevelt proposed a fresh joint approach to try to bring Weygand over. At this crucial juncture de Gaulle's highhandedness over Saint-Pierre and Miquelon had made Roosevelt all the more determined to find some alternative French leader, and Churchill went along.

The new approach to Weygand was carried out on January 20, 1942, by Douglas MacArthur II, a nephew of General MacArthur's, who was a young career diplomat then assigned to the Vichy embassy under Admiral Leahy. To maintain secrecy, only oral instructions were transmitted. A State Department man was briefed personally by Roosevelt and flew to Lisbon to brief another diplomat who then traveled to Vichy. MacArthur met Weygand secretly at a hotel near Nice, asking on behalf of the president whether "in the event of possible contingencies he would assume leadership of the French colonies." North Africa was not mentioned specifically, but with the Middle East and most of Africa already in de Gaulle's hands, what else could this have meant? At any rate, Weygand gave a dusty answer. Not only did he declare his "complete loyalty" to Pétain, but he told MacArthur he would have to inform the marshal of the American approach, although he would ask him to keep it a secret from the rest of his entourage. Finding a substitute for de Gaulle in the Vichy crowd was not going to be easy for Roosevelt.

The return of Pierre Laval to power as Pétain's prime minister on April 15, 1942, was effectively the end of the road for the United States with Vichy, although Roosevelt continued to try to "baby things along" right up to the North African landings. Admiral Leahy, who had told Roosevelt that his usefulness in Vichy was already at an end when Weygand was pulled out of Algiers in November, was now finally recalled by the president to Washington, to a newly created key post as chief of staff to the commander in chief. Leahy had a final interview with Laval on April 27, and reported to Washington:

> He said he was prepared to defend France and her Empire against all comers and he stated specifically that if the British or the Americans were to attempt to effect a landing either on the soil of Metropolitan France or on French North African territory, he would resist them to the best of his ability. His government, he maintained, would take no steps to provide military assistance to the Germans. He tried to convey the impression of being fanatically devoted to the interests of France, with a conviction that they are bound together irrevocably with the interests of Germany.

About this same time, on April 17, 1942, General Henri Giraud, who had been de Gaulle's old corps commander at Metz in 1938, escaped from a prison-fortress in Germany at the town of Koenigstein, near Frankfurt. A full general, he was the most senior escapee of the war. He was sixty-three years old and had also escaped from a German prison in the First World War. In Jean Monnet's incisive description, "he was tall, with a clear blank gaze, conscious of his own prestige, inflexible on military matters, hesitant on everything else." He made his way to Vichy, where Laval promptly tried to pressure him to returning to a German prison. To get out of this, Giraud appealed to Marshal Pétain with a declaration of loyalty that was to prove rather embarrassing to the Allies a few months later: "I want to express my sentiments of perfect loyalty toward you [he wrote Pétain]. I give you my word as an officer that I shall do nothing that might embarrass in any way your relations with the German government or impede the task with which you have charged Admiral Darlan and Prime Minister Pierre Laval to carry out under your authority. My past is the guarantee of my loyalty."

This was the French general to whom Roosevelt now turned, on the recommendation of Murphy, as an alternative leader to General de Gaulle. But Murphy in fact knew no more about Giraud personally at that time than he had known about de Gaulle at the time of the fall of France. He worked through two intermediaries. The first was a shady operator named Jacques Lemaigre-Dubreuil, a prewar, pro-Fascist businessman with the Banque Worms who was enlisted and trusted by Murphy in Algiers and was able to travel freely between Paris, Vichy and North Africa, playing both sides. By this time he apparently was genuinely working for an Allied victory; many French were changing sides. He was the principal political contact with Giraud and shared Giraud's ultraconservative views. On military matters, the intermediary was General Charles Mast, who had also escaped from Koenigstein ahead of Giraud in 1941 and had been given a corps command in the city of Algiers. With Roosevelt's knowledge, these contacts had begun well before the final decision to invade North Africa.

As military planning and clandestine preparations for the North African landings moved into high gear, Roosevelt from the outset was of course adamant against giving any information, advance warning or share in the operation to the Free French. He also became convinced early on—backed up by Leahy, newly arrived back from Vichy—that the French in North Africa would oppose any British landing in their territory, with French warships sunk by British guns lying in the waters of Mers el-Kébir. Murphy, in fact, felt that this supposed anti-British feeling was exaggerated and largely fostered by Nazi propaganda and would quickly evaporate. He was proven more right than Roosevelt and Leahy, but on August 30 Roosevelt cabled a somewhat wounding message to Churchill in London:

> I feel very strongly that the initial attacks must be made by an exclusively American ground force, supported by your naval and transport and air units. The operation should be undertaken on the assumption that the French will offer less resistance to us than they will to the British. I would even go as far as to say that I am reasonably sure that a simultaneous landing by the British and Americans would result in full resistance by all French in Africa, whereas an initial American landing without British ground forces offers a real chance that there would be no French resistance or only a token resistance.

Churchill replied on September 1 that "we could not contest your wish if you so desire it to take upon the United States the whole burden of the landings," but he added at least an implied dissent: "I do not know what information you have of the mood and temper of Vichy and North Africa, but of course if you can get ashore at the necessary points without fighting or only token resistance, that is best of all. We cannot tell what are the chances of this."

Churchill clearly did not like shrinking before the French in this fashion and did not agree with Roosevelt's assessment, but he remained the loyal lieutenant. Roosevelt replied that on the basis of "our latest and best information" it was "vital that sole responsibility be placed with Americans for relations with French military and civil authorities in Africa." This of course held strong future implications for de Gaulle as well.

In the event, there were not enough American troops and transport available to make all three landings purely American operations. The most important of all, to capture Algiers, had to be entrusted to the British. But to meet Roosevelt's insistence and preserve the "American character" of the operation, the British were placed under the temporary command of an American general with a façade of American staff officers to go ashore in the first wave. The French paid almost no attention at all to this nicety, and American troops landing in Morocco ran into heavier fighting than the British encountered at Algiers.

*

General de Gaulle, back in London at the end of September and convinced, correctly, that the Americans and the British were preparing once again to invade French territory and leave him out of it, now received a boost from his flirtation with the Soviet Union. Stalin, of course, had been told in early August by Churchill on a special trip to Moscow of the decision to invade North Africa. With this prior knowledge, he announced from Moscow to de Gaulle's enormous satisfaction on September 28—the same day de Gaulle met Churchill at Downing Street for their major confrontation over Syria—that the Soviet Union was recognizing the French National Committee as "the executive body of Fighting France, alone qualified to organize the participation of French citizens and territories in the war." This formulation went much further than Roosevelt had gone in the Anglo-American communiqué from Washington on July 9, and put Stalin firmly behind de Gaulle just at the time when the United States was moving secretly to throw its backing to General Giraud. Exalting over Stalin's move, de Gaulle commented in his Memoirs: "It must be said that if America, the new star of world history, believed herself in a position to direct the French nation, the European states, after centuries of experience, had no such illusion. Now France had made her choice."

Nevertheless, with his relations with Churchill at a low ebb after their acrimonious meeting at Downing Street, de Gaulle now decided to make a direct approach to Roosevelt for understanding and recognition. He realized full well that the stakes for him were high in North Africa—not only was it the most important of all France's overseas territories, but it contained approximately 150,000 French troops already in uniform and needing only new equipment and a change of loyalties to be thrown into battle against the Axis. So, on October 26, 1942, he sent a long personal letter to Roosevelt through a French National Committee representative in Washington, André Philip, a French union leader. If it was not entirely couched in terms that would appeal to Roosevelt, it was nevertheless a clear and straightforward declaration of de Gaulle's position. Its key passages read:

> I did what seemed necessary to keep France from abandoning the struggle and to appeal to all Frenchmen inside and outside of France to continue the fight. Is this to say that my companions and I posed at any moment as the

government of France? By no means. On the contrary, we have considered ourselves and proclaimed ourselves to be an essentially provisional authority, responsible to a future national representative body. . . .

We are told that we should not play politics. We do not recoil from the world "political" if it concerns rallying not simply a few troops but the whole French nation in the war; or if it means discussing French interests with our allies at the same time we defend them for France against the enemy. After all, who besides ourselves can represent these interests? . . .

Without asking to be recognized as the Government of France, we believe we should be approached each time there is a question of France's general interests; or of French participation in the war; or of the administration of French territories which the war's progress gradually brings into a position to rejoin the fight. . . .

I am told that members of your entourage fear that in recognizing our existence you will compromise the possibility that certain elements, mostly military, who are now attached to the Vichy Government, may soon re-enter the war. But, do you believe that you should ignore the French who do fight, letting them become discouraged in isolation, so that you can draw others into the struggle? On the other hand, what danger for France could compare to the fact that the Allies might provoke her own divisions by favoring the formation of several rival groups, the one neutralized by an agreement of the Allies themselves, the others fighting separately for the same Fatherland? . . .

All this is why I ask you to accept the idea of a general and direct examination of relations between the United States and Fighting France.

De Gaulle never received an answer from Roosevelt—or rather the answer came in the form of American backing for Giraud and then the cease-fire deal with Darlan after the North African landings.

Meanwhile, a few days after this letter from de Gaulle, Roosevelt received a cable from Churchill to the effect that "it will be necessary for me to explain Torch [code-name for the landings] to de Gaulle sometime during D-minus-1." But even this was too much for Roosevelt, who replied immediately:

I am very apprehensive in regard to the adverse effect that any introduction of de Gaulle into the Torch situation would have on our promising efforts to attach a large part of the French African forces to our expedition. Therefore I consider it inadvisable for you to give de Gaulle any information until subsequent to a successful landing. You would then inform him that the American commander of an American expedition with my approval insisted on complete secrecy as a necessary safety precaution.

Churchill bowed to the president's wishes, and instead of briefing de Gaulle in advance of the operations, he saw the General at Downing Street at noon on November 8, 1942, twelve hours after the landings had begun. But at least

Churchill got Roosevelt to tone down a "much too kind" message that he had drafted to "My dear old friend" Marshal Pétain to be sent the morning of the landings.

*

Meanwhile, in advance of the landings, General Giraud was proving to be every bit as much of a prima donna as General de Gaulle, with none of de Gaulle's qualities of intelligence, acumen or leadership. With little claim to importance except his uniform, Giraud was obtuse, intransigent, narrow-minded, ultraconservative, self-centered and obsessed with personal prestige, honor and rank. Preliminary soundings with him had been carried out during the summer of 1942 at his home near Lyons on behalf of Murphy by Lemaigre-Dubreuil. He was then sent a formal message from Eisenhower in London on September 22, extending "cordial greetings" and informing him that "in the near future concrete proposals will be sent you in which you will be contemplated as leader of the French effort which will be fully supported by the Allies." But there ensued much haggling in secret about the operation and Giraud's role, which Murphy in the end managed to plaster over with a letter of evasions and half-commitments. Giraud then even gave trouble about the date of his departure, with the Allied expedition already under way. He was finally prevailed upon to make a secret rendezvous with a British submarine which, to assuage his obtuse sense of French honor, had been placed under the nominal command of an American Navy captain. The extent to which Roosevelt and the Americans went to ostracize de Gaulle while soliciting in Vichy bordered on the absurd.

When Giraud was then put ashore at Gibraltar, the Allied convoys were nearing the North African coast. He proceeded to argue for *seven hours* with General Eisenhower and his chief of staff, General Mark W. Clark, demanding that he be made commander in chief over all the Allied forces and that the Allies under his command leap immediately from North Africa to an invasion of southern France. Whatever problems the Allies had with Charles de Gaulle, he was not dense or stupid. Finally, late at night, with the landings under way, Giraud consented that he would command only French troops but would also be named governor general for North Africa and would "do all in his power to stop all French resistance and organize French forces for use against the Axis."

Then, as the troops went ashore, this laboriously contrived Franco-American house of cards was suddenly blown down by a message from Murphy that Admiral François Darlan was not in Vichy—but in Algiers. He arrived two days before the landings to visit a son hospitalized with infantile paralysis. Despite obvious suspicions to the contrary at the time, there never was any evidence that this was anything but an accident of war. Darlan was certainly surprised to be wakened with news of the landings early in the morning of November 8. In any event, the presence in Algiers of Pétain's loyal deputy and commander in chief of all Vichy sea, air and land forces abruptly altered everything as far as the Americans and Giraud were concerned. Whatever Darlan's record, he was indubitably the most powerful Frenchman on the scene, whose presence and orders were bound to supersede those of any other Frenchman in uniform.

A wild night ensued. Shortly before midnight Murphy passed the signal to small but well-primed Resistance groups in the French Army to seize certain government buildings as planned—police headquarters and the post office, the radio station, the airport. He then drove to the home of General Alphonse Juin, French Army commander in North Africa and de Gaulle's old classmate at Saint-Cyr, who had shown pro-Allied leanings but had not been taken into the pre-invasion plotting. Informed that the Allied armada had arrived and was landing, Juin at once telephoned Darlan, who arrived posthaste. There then followed a long, early-morning palaver, with Murphy issuing a virtual ultimatum to Darlan that "it is your responsibility that no French blood will be shed in face of the massive landing of American forces now taking place," and Darlan wrestling with his flexible conscience and honor and pledges of loyalty to Pétain.

But, unknown to Murphy, the main landing force to seize Algiers had come ashore nearly four miles down the coast from its target, due to offshore winds and unexpected force of tides. Instead of arriving in the city at 2 A.M. as they were supposed to have done, the British troops with their American commanders did not begin trickling in until after daylight. During this interval, while Darlan, Murphy and Juin argued and debated, Vichy French opposition began to form, and gendarmes even turned up at Juin's residence to place Murphy briefly under house arrest. Finally, in the early morning, Darlan agreed to send a message to Pétain asking for authorization to surrender.

In Vichy, Pétain also received a message from Roosevelt in the early hours of November 8, shorn of an original address to "My dear old friend," but telling him: "My clear purpose is to support and aid the French authorities and their administration. I need not tell you that the ultimate and greater aim is the liberation of France and its Empire from the Axis."

To which Marshal Pétain replied immediately: "You knew that we would defend the Empire against any aggressor. You knew that I would keep my word. We have been attacked and we will defend ourselves. That is the order I am issuing."

By midafternoon in Algiers on November 8, with the full scale of the landings now clear to the French, Juin asked Murphy to inform the American commander, Major General Charles W. Ryder, that he wished to stop fighting. Darlan gave his approval to this local cease-fire and fighting ended in the city at 7 P.M. But there was no cease-fire at either Oran or Casablanca, where the ultra-Vichy loyalist General Noguès was in full control and fighting against US forces under the legendary Major General George S. Patton, Jr.

The next day, November 9, General Clark flew in from Gibraltar, empowered to act on behalf of Eisenhower. He also brought Giraud, but as soon as they landed it quickly became apparent that Giraud would be no use at all. Other French officers would not even acknowledge him, whatever grand plans the Allies had for him. So Clark and Murphy got down to cases with Darlan at once on a cease-fire for all North Africa. Pétain's proclaimed instructions were to resist, but German reaction had begun to change things completely. Although taken by surprise by the landings, the Germans acted swiftly. They immediately demanded landing rights from Vichy in French Tunisia to fly out reinforcements for the retreating Rommel. And on November 9 Hitler gave orders to the Nazi armies to move the next day into unoccupied France and take over the whole country.

After a day of argument, hesitancy and threat of house arrest, Darlan agreed on the morning of the tenth to issue a cease-fire order and communicated this decision to Vichy. But his message was intercepted by the Germans, who immediately descended on Pierre Laval with dire threats. Laval in a panic threatened to resign if Pétain acceded. Pétain then sent two messages to Darlan—a first one in code, the second more or less open for German interception. In the secret message, he accepted what Darlan was doing. In the other message he disapproved. But the secret first message took longer to transmit. The message of disapproval arrived first and Darlan at once tried to rescind the cease-fire order. "Damned if you do," Clark brusquely told him, whereupon Darlan announced that he considered himself under house arrest. But finally, when the Nazis began rolling into unoccupied France and the earlier message had been received and decoded, Darlan at last decided he could act because the marshal was now a prisoner.

On that day, in Gibraltar, Eisenhower says that he "went off alone for an hour or so" to brood about this welter of complex and emotive events and then assembled his British and American staff officers and told them:

> The military advantages of a cease-fire are so overwhelming that I will go promptly to Algiers and if the proposals of the French are as definite as I understand, I shall immediately recognize Darlan as the highest French authority in the region. None of you should be under any misapprehension as to what the consequences of this action may be. In both our nations, Darlan is a deep-dyed villain. When public opinion raises the outcry, our two governments will be embarrassed. Because of this, we'll act so quickly that reports to our governments will be on the basis of *action taken*. I'll do my best to convince our governments that the decision is right. If they find it necessary to take action against this headquarters, I'll make it clear that I alone am responsible.

And so the Darlan deal was closed. The North African landings were not much of a test of Eisenhower's military abilities, but the Darlan episode was certainly a test of his readiness to take command decisions. He had not underestimated the political furor that his decision would arouse, and he was perfectly clear and aware of what he was doing. He got his cease-fire, and the Allied armies headed east for Tunis. But it took far longer to clear up the political consequences that were left behind.

*

General de Gaulle was awakened at six o'clock on the morning of November 8 by his chief of staff, Colonel Pierre Billotte, with the news of the landings, and although the General was not particularly surprised, he thundered to Billotte: "Well, I hope the people of Vichy throw them into the sea. You can't break into

France and get away with it." But he also received a personal message from the chief of the Imperial General Staff, Field Marshal Sir Alan Brooke, explaining why the French had been kept out of the whole operation and admonishing in soldierly fashion, "I can understand your bitterness—now overcome it." Then a message arrived asking him to come to Downing Street at noon for a meeting with Churchill. By this time he had cooled down and was prepared to accept what was happening in a perfectly reasonable and constructive frame of mind.

Churchill summarized for de Gaulle everything that had so far taken place— the landings, the role planned for Giraud, the unexpected advent of Darlan on the scene. De Gaulle commented with restraint that "General Giraud is a great soldier and I wish him well in his undertaking." As to Darlan, he said that no agreement with him would be possible but added: "At any rate, nothing is more important for the time being than to bring the battle to a halt." He was critical of the military plan because the Allies were not also landing in Tunisia at the same time (a move the British had in fact urged but the Americans had refused) and he complained that the whole operation was under American control, telling Churchill: "I cannot understand how you British can stand aside so completely in an undertaking of such primary concern to Europe."

But it was a great deal less stormy than Churchill and the British anticipated, and that evening de Gaulle broadcast to France over the BBC:

> France's allies have undertaken to associate French North Africa with the war of liberation. They are beginning to land enormous numbers of troops there. Our Algeria, our Morocco, our Tunisia are to serve as a starting point for the liberation of France. This undertaking is led by our American allies. French leaders, soldiers, sailors, airmen, civil servants, French settlers in North Africa, arise! Help our Allies. Join them without reservations. Fighting France adjures you to do so. Don't worry about names or formulas. Only one thing counts. The salvation of the Motherland! This is a time for common sense and courage.

If American arrangements with Darlan had then stopped with the cease-fire agreement, this would have been acceptable to British and American public opinion and to General de Gaulle himself. But in overweening enthusiasm at the opportunity of Darlan's presence, with little or no thought or consideration of wider political consequences, Clark and Murphy pressed on to negotiate a full-scale agreement recognizing Darlan as the supreme French authority in North Africa, in return for Allied control over facilities such as airports, harbors, communications, and defense installations, and the naming of Giraud as military commander.

The Darlan–Clark agreement on control over civil affairs in North Africa meant that "the Vichy crowd" remained intact under Darlan—local governors such as Noguès, who had fought against Patton, and Boisson in Dakar, who had fought against de Gaulle. Moreover it meant that all the infamous fascism of Vichy remained untouched—its anti-Semitic laws, its justice system, its antidemocratic machinery of dictatorship which the Allies were supposed to be in North Africa to wipe clean. The storm of British and American public opinion was not long in building up, and Charles de Gaulle was certainly not one to suffer in silence this insult to France and himself. When the full scope and implications of the Darlan-Clark deal became known in London, de Gaulle sent a vicious letter to his American military contact, Admiral Stark, in which he said: "I understand that the United States buys the treachery of traitors, if it appears profitable, but payment must not be made against the honor of France." Stark returned the letter to de Gaulle with a suggestion that he might wish to reconsider what he had said.

On November 17, with British public opinion in an outcry, Churchill messaged Roosevelt:

> I ought to let you know that very deep currents of feeling are stirred by the arrangement with Darlan. The more I reflect upon it, the more convinced I become that it can only be a temporary expedient, justifiable solely by the stress of battle. We must not overlook the serious political injury which may be done to our cause, not only in France but throughout Europe, by the feeling that we are ready to deal with local quislings. Darlan has an odious record.

Even Cordell Hull and the State Department had become alarmed at the anti-Darlan, anti-Vichy backlash that was developing, if for no other reason than this would clearly play into the hands of de Gaulle and the Fighting French. So the State Department, too, was urging some presidential statement of clarification. With Churchill's message, Roosevelt moved promptly and adopted Churchill's language. He told a press conference in a formal statement on November 18:

> The present temporary arrangement in North and West Africa is only a temporary expedient, justified solely by the stress of battle. The present temporary arrangement has accomplished two military objectives. The first was to save American and British lives, and French lives on the other hand. The second was a vital factor of time . . . to avoid a mopping-up period in Algiers which might have taken a month or two to consummate. Temporary arrangements with Admiral Darlan apply, without exception, to the current local situation only.

Roosevelt used the word "temporary" five times and the phrase "for the time being" twice in the full text of his statement. He also adopted one of his favorite devices of recalling or devising "an old proverb" to explain a policy—in this case "an old Bulgarian proverb": "You can walk with the devil until you get to the other side of the bridge." As the Darlan affair wound on through the next five weeks, FDR told this one to various persons in various forms as an old Roumanian proverb, an old Orthodox proverb of the Balkans, and a Serbian proverb. But in fact, the president's bridge with Darlan seemed to get longer and longer.

De Gaulle, through Admiral Stark, now asked if Roosevelt would receive representatives of the French National Committee in Washington to try to dissipate some of the misunderstandings that North Africa was creating. Roosevelt agreed at once, no doubt reasoning that it would help damp the political furor that the Darlan deal was causing. De Gaulle assigned this first contact with the president to André Philip and Adrien Tixier, his representatives in Washington— and the interview was a total disaster. It took place at the White House on November 20, 1942. But instead of approaching Roosevelt with diplomacy and some deference, the two Frenchmen proceeded to launch into a tirade of attack, condemnation and criticism. Even a French account of the meeting, by Raoul de Roussy de Sales, of the Free French mission in the United States, recorded that "they made an absolutely deplorable impression on the President, who found them filled with personal ambition and totally incomprehensible, characterized by stupidity and rudeness." Roosevelt cabled Stark: "Why did you insist I receive that man Philip? He had not a word of appreciation."

Two days after this White House interview, Churchill, to please Roosevelt, stopped de Gaulle from making a BBC broadcast to occupied France and North Africa. The proposed broadcast was in fact a fairly anodyne text of vague and visionary declarations that French national will could not long be stifled in North Africa—but its implied criticism of Allied policy was too much for Churchill. Out of total loyalty to Roosevelt, Churchill was working up into another heavy anti–de Gaulle mood—no doubt spurred on by de Gaulle's taunts over his surrender of leadership to the Americans. But word of the BBC veto leaked to a member of the House of Commons, and the inevitable parliamentary question was tabled. From both Labour and Conservatives the prime minister was needled with comments over standards of free speech and dealings with the Vichy crowd.

Churchill got all the madder, and he hit back in a secret war speech to the Commons on December 10, 1942. Although the speech was subsequently published in a collection in 1946, Churchill's remarks about de Gaulle were omitted and came to light only with release of the full War Cabinet papers under the thirty years' rule in 1972:

> I have lived myself for the last thirty-five years or more in a mental relationship and to a large extent in sympathy with an abstraction called France. I cannot feel that de Gaulle is France, still less that Darlan and Vichy are France. France is something greater, more complex, more formidable than any of these sectional manifestations.
>
> I consider that we have been in every respect faithful in the discharge of our obligations to de Gaulle, and we shall so continue to the end. However, you must not be led to believe that General de Gaulle is an unfaltering friend of Britain. On the contrary, I think he is one of those good Frenchmen who have a traditional antagonism ingrained in French hearts by centuries of war against the English. . . . I continue to maintain friendly personal relations with General de Gaulle and I help him as much as I possibly can. I feel bound to do this because he stood up against the men of Bordeaux and their base surrender at a time when all resisting will-power had quitted France. All the same, I could not recommend you to base all your hopes and confidence

upon him, and still less to assume that it is our duty to place the destiny of France in his hands.

Nevertheless, whatever Roosevelt and Churchill felt personally about de Gaulle, the tide of public opinion, as well as editorial and press comment on both sides of the Atlantic, was now running at a flood in his favor. The Darlan deal, paradoxically, was strenghening the de Gaulle appeal everywhere. The British Special Operations Executive, charged with running the secret war of resistance, sent an alarmed report to the Cabinet: "The deal with Darlan has produced violent reactions on all of our subterranean organizations in enemy-occupied countries, particularly in France, where it has had a blasting and withering effect."

Roosevelt's feelings about de Gaulle were if anything more acrimonious than ever, but the president was far too much of a politician to allow American public opinion to run loose or unheeded and unchecked for very long on anything. So he now told Sumner Welles, on December 18, that he could arrange to see the General in early January. But in one of those protocol touches that de Gaulle himself so loved to employ, Roosevelt specified that he would not invite de Gaulle although he would fix an appointment if one were requested. Accordingly, plans were completed for de Gaulle and a party to include the diplomatic and experienced General Georges Catroux to fly to the United States via Accra in Ghana for a first meeting with Roosevelt, departing from Britain on December 26.

But on Christmas Eve in Algiers, as Admiral Darlan was mounting the steps of the government office building where he was headquartered, a young Frenchman named Fernand Bonnier de la Chapelle stepped out of the shadows, pulled a gun and fired. The admiral died an hour later.

On December 26 de Gaulle had already left for the airport for his flight to Washington when a message reached him from Churchill informing him that Roosevelt had asked that their meeting be canceled. With Darlan dead, Roosevelt probably concluded that he no longer need bother going through the motions of a gesture to General de Gaulle.

*

The death of Admiral Darlan removed a noxious embarrassment to the Allies from the Algerian scene, and little sorrow was wasted over his timely and probably inevitable demise. But the full circumstances of the assassination remain a mystery to this day. The gunman professed to be a *résistant* and a Royalist who wanted to restore the French monarchy. The comte de Paris, pretender to the throne, was certainly present and politically active in Algiers across this seamy period of intrigue. But a confession that Bonnier de la Chapelle made in writing and signed on Christmas morning was promptly burned by the police commissioner who received it, a man named Garinacci. A military tribunal was hastily convened that same day, and in a matter of hours the death penalty had been pronounced. General Giraud, as French commander in chief in North Africa, refused to commute the sentence, and Bonnier de la Chapelle was shot by a firing squad in secrecy at dawn on December 26. His name was not even mentioned in the communiqué on the execution. The court-martial records remain sealed today under France's fifty-year rule governing release of official documents, and may stay sealed forever.

Much circumstantial evidence pointed to involvement of the Gaullists, and this was certainly what American authorities were ready to believe at the time. But there is no proof about anything, apart from the identity of the assassin, who apparently believed up to the moment he was led before the firing squad that he would be reprieved by someone high up. He made a last confession to a fanatical Gaullist priest, the Abbé Cordier, who had earlier provided him with a false identity card that apparently had given him access through the security cordon around Darlan's headquarters. Another piece of circumstantial evidence had been the arrival in Algiers less than a week before of a special emissary from General de Gaulle in London, General François d'Astier de la Vigerie.

He was one of an intriguing trio of aristocratic brothers, all of them active in the Resistance but each operating in a different faction or political orbit, from crypto-Communist left to Monarchist right. He arrived in Algiers on December 20 to discuss with Eisenhower on behalf of de Gaulle possible moves toward French unity. He also brought with him about $35,000 to finance Gaullist activities in Algiers, and he made contact with his Monarchist brother, who was then in the city, Henri d'Astier de la Vigerie. But when Darlan heard of his arrival, he demanded that the Americans order him out of North Africa, and he left to return to London on the day of the assassination.

As a final footnote, about that time in London, the American writer Virginia Cowles, then a young and glamorous war correspondent, attended a dinner party at which a number of senior British Intelligence operatives were present along with a prominent member of General de Gaulle's Intelligence staff. After listening to the Frenchman inveigh against Darlan and the stupidity of the Americans, Miss Cowles interjected rather tartly that "Darlan is a Frenchman, and the French ought to be able to deal with him themselves." A few days later she received a telephone call from a Frenchman who refused to identify himself but said that he had been told of her dinner-table remark, and if she watched the papers she would soon see that her advice had been taken. Two days later Darlan was shot.

Whatever the mystery, events swept on. On Christmas Day General de Gaulle, still expecting to depart for Washington next day, sent a telegram from London to Giraud in Algiers, calling the assassination "a symbol and a warning" that made French unity more necessary than ever: "I propose [de Gaulle said] that we meet as soon as possible on French territory either in Algeria or in Chad. We will study ways to enable us to concentrate under a provisional central power all the forces of both metropolitan France and her overseas territories, which are capable of joining the struggle for the liberation and welfare of France."

On that same busy Christmas, from Washington Admiral Leahy sent a peremptory instruction to Eisenhower to "appoint Giraud" as Darlan's successor. Leahy consulted no one but the president, but it was beyond Eisenhower's power to "appoint" Giraud to anything. This was up to an Imperial Council of the French, composed of the governors of the territories involved. In the event, a council was hastily convened on December 26, American wishes were clearly known, and

Giraud was unanimously chosen. The Leahy cable was a fair indication of the prevailing American attitude toward management of French affairs. But Giraud and de Gaulle were still cut from the same French military cloth. Eisenhower says in his Memoirs: "General Giraud then visited my headquarters, and his first request was that I 'cease treating North Africa as conquered territory and treat it more as an ally which it was trying to become.' This attitude on the part of one who, I thought, understood our motives so well, was something of a shock to me."

Giraud sent "a dilatory reply" to de Gaulle in London on December 29, saying that the postassassination atmosphere in Algiers was unfavorable for a meeting. There never had been any love lost between the five-star general and the upstart brigadier, and whatever Giraud's glaring shortcomings as a leader and an administrator, he was never in any doubt about matters of rank, prestige and personal pride. In London de Gaulle decided to increase the pressure by going public, and despite Churchill's efforts to get him to delay, he issued a formal statement on January 2, 1943:

> Internal confusion continues to grow in North Africa. The reason is that French authority has no solid base there since the collapse of Vichy, as Fighting France is kept away from these French possessions. The way to remedy this is to establish in North Africa, as in all other French overseas territories, an enlarged provisional central authority. I suggested to General Giraud that we meet at once in French territory to discuss means of achieving this end. I believe, in fact, that France's position and the course of the war in general will brook no delay.

He did not know that the Casablanca conference was only two weeks away.

TEN

1943: UNITY

The Casablanca conference in January 1943 was the only one of the great high-level political-military grand-strategy meetings of the war that General de Gaulle attended. He deliberately delayed his arrival until the last moment, when the conference was nearly over, made a grand entrance totally exasperating to the prime minister of Great Britain and the president of the United States, and stole the show.

In the words of Robert Murphy, who played a key role on the American side at Casablanca, a cool diplomatic observer and scarcely a de Gaulle partisan:

> This professional soldier, who never had participated even in national politics before the war, put on such a sparkling performance in international power politics that he took the star role away from the two greatest English-speaking politicians. Within five months, the political ascendancy of de Gaulle in French Africa was absolute, although Roosevelt never did formally recognize it. The unproclaimed victory which he won at the Casablanca Conference was a great step forward in his plan to assure France the largest possible share in Allied conquests including full restoration of the French Empire.

But when Roosevelt and Churchill were preparing for the Casablanca meeting, there was no thought at all that de Gaulle should be invited, and not even any intention—at least on the part of the president—that French affairs would form any focal point of the conference or be discussed very much except in general terms in the informal conversations. To emphasize the military and strategic focus of the meeting, Roosevelt informed Churchill that he would not be bringing Secretary of State Cordell Hull. This meant that Churchill reluctantly had to leave Anthony Eden behind in London as well—to the irritation of both men.

Events then propelled the French question onto the Anglo-American agenda, whether the leaders were ready for it or wanted it or not.

The first of these was the fact that Charles de Gaulle had taken the political offensive with his immediate, unambiguous public proposal to Giraud that they meet on French territory and talk about French unity. In Britain, where public opinion was consistently out in front of the United States in support of de Gaulle, this proposal made eminent common sense and was greeted by strong public endorsement that the British government could scarcely ignore. Not so in Washington. On January 4 Undersecretary of State Sumner Welles summoned the French National Committee representative, Adrien Tixier, to the State Department and informed him that the American government disapproved of General de Gaulle's invitation to General Giraud on the grounds that this introduced unnecessary and diversionary "political" questions into what was primarily a military situation. De Gaulle, in his Memoirs, confined himself to the comment: "As if the agreement proposed by de Gaulle threatened Eisenhower's communications in North Africa!"

But it was quite clear from this that the United States was content with the situation that now existed in Algiers under Giraud and was not at all inclined to see de Gaulle come swooping down on the scene in the name of French unity. Nevertheless, from an ethical and moral standpoint, the United States had saddled itself with support for a pretty unsavory crowd of Vichy collaborationists, who had become unctuously ingratiating with their erstwhile invaders. In Morocco, General Patton, who never made any claims to political sophistication, by now was practically a bosom buddy of the Vichy loyalist General Noguès, who organized falcon hunts and gave lavish Arabian Nights banquets with manly entertainment for American officers. In Dakar, General Boisson, who had defended the fortress so resolutely against de Gaulle and the British, and imprisoned British merchant seamen, was now the soul of hospitality and cooperation to the United States Navy.

For General de Gaulle and the Fighting French, this simply stank, and it was smelling pretty bad in British and American nostrils as well. The purely military justification for the Darlan deal had long since been fulfilled, but rule by Vichyites went on virtually undisturbed. The Americans then suddenly made things much worse for themselves, on the eve of the Casablanca conference, by openly sponsoring the appointment of a former Vichy minister of the interior, Marcel Peyrouton, to be the new governor general of Algeria under Giraud. This was the work of Murphy, who usually did not make mistakes. He had known Peyrouton back in the early days in Vichy, and regarded him as "clean" because he had been instrumental in a government cabal that overthrew Pierre Laval in December 1940. But many laws and much infamous work had been done while he was interior minister. Soon after Laval's departure, Peyrouton himself had been pushed out of the Pétain government and had gotten himself made Vichy ambassador to Argentina. At Murphy's specific proposal, he was then wafted to Algiers on American travel orders to be installed at the top of civil administration for the whole territory.

Franklin Roosevelt was on his way to Casablanca in easy stages, with overnight stops along the way when this happened. The immediate public outcry at American resurrection of a former Vichy interior minister to a high post working with the Allies brought the president around to realizing that he would have to do something about French Africa while he was there. Even Wendell Willkie, the Republican leader whom he had defeated in 1940, was beginning to roar about continued American support of Vichy, and when any issue became *political,* Roosevelt's antennae would light up. From Casablanca, he sent an early message to Cordell Hull: "It had been my hope that we could avoid political discussions at this time, but I found on my arrival that American and British newspapers had made such a mountain out of a rather small hill that I should not return to Washington without having achieved settlement of this matter."

Churchill and Eden, in the meantime, had jointly concluded that the only sensible and logical course was to work for French unity—in other words, back de Gaulle in his proposal for talks with Giraud on formation of a new central French authority to replace the French National Committee. They were in no doubt about opposition to this course from Welles and Hull. But Churchill had made a solemn pledge of support to de Gaulle in 1940 that had been repeated on numerous occasions ever since, and no matter how difficult the General might be, he could not in honor or common sense be dumped simply because the United States preferred Giraud. So in order to steer things in the only direction in which they could sensibly go, Churchill made one of his shrewdest political-diplomatic appoints of the war.

He picked Harold Macmillan to be his special political representative at Eisenhower's headquarters in Algiers, to work alongside Robert Murphy on French affairs. Macmillan at that time had been a member of the House of Commons for twenty years and had finally made it into the wartime government as a junior minister. He went on up after the war to become a very successful prime minister from 1957 to 1963. He was a politician to his fingertips, urbane, intelligent, witty, efficient, and fluent in French. Soon after he had settled in at Algiers, he told a new British recruit to his staff, fresh from London: "My dear fellow, we are the Greeks in this American empire. You will find the Americans much as the Greeks found the Romans—great big vulgar bustling people, more vigorous than we are and also more idle, with more unspoiled virtues but also more corrupt. We must run Allied Force Headquarters as the Greek slaves ran the operations of the Emperor Claudius!"

All the same, Macmillan got on with Americans extremely well. He arrived in Algiers on January 2, with general instructions and wide latitude to work for French unity and keep in touch with Churchill personally. It was not long before he was making a considerable influence skillfully felt.

Roosevelt, preparing to depart for Casablanca, had no more interest in promoting French unity than did the State Department, but he did see a growing political problem. He now bypassed the State Department as he frequently did, with a personal message to Murphy in Algiers instructing him to work up a proposal to include de Gaulle in the North African administration in a subordinate capacity to Giraud! Anyone with even a passing knowledge of de Gaulle's record of the past three years could have told the president that this would be a total nonstarter. But at least the instruction enabled Murphy and Macmillan to draft a set of recommendations on French unity before the conference opened. There was still no thought or suggestion at this point of bringing the French leaders to Casablanca.

Roosevelt left Washington on January 9, accompanied by Harry Hopkins and others, first making a train journey to Miami. There he boarded a Pan American Airways Clipper flying boat for what was the first air journey by an American president. The last time Roosevelt had been in an airplane was when he flew to Chicago in 1932 to accept the Democratic nomination. The flying boat took him leisurely across the South Atlantic with overnight stops in Trinidad, Belem in Brazil and Bathurst in West Africa before finally reaching Casablanca on January 14. Churchill had arrived the day before with a full retinue and a special British support ship with a map room, war library, Intelligence files and cipher and communications equipment that was the instant envy of the Americans. To house the conference, an entire suburb of Casablanca, called Anfa, had been requisitioned by the American Army. It included a small hotel, and owners and residents of all the villas had been evacuated and the area surrounded by barbed wire and immersed in ultramilitary security. The biggest worry of the military was a sudden sneak air attack by Nazi planes, so the countryside was alive with antiaircraft gun emplacements.

*

President Roosevelt was in a buoyant mood at Casablanca—wonderful winter climate; an exotic setting yet near to the battlefront; stimulating discussions and decisions to be taken; a mixture of leadership, glamour and drama to be indulged; a sense of power being continuously exercised; probably the president's most enjoyable time in the whole war. On the first evening, Thursday, January 14, he and Churchill got down to work at once with a dinner party at which French problems were talked about in general terms.

On Friday morning Roosevelt first saw both Eisenhower and Murphy. Each gave the president a somewhat regretful report on the shortcomings of General Giraud, notably his declared and determined lack of interest in or grasp of matters of political decision-making and civil administration. All that Giraud knew about or was interested in was military organization—not the area in which Eisenhower and the Allies needed French advice or help. Then Macmillan joined Murphy and the president for a brief discussion of the "unity paper" on the French situation which they had prepared.

During the day, in the course of further discussions with Churchill about the French, Roosevelt, in what seemed to be a lighthearted fashion, suddenly threw out a proposal that altered the course of the conference and the future of French affairs.

"I'll tell you what," the president said. "We'll call Giraud the bridegroom and I'll produce him from Algiers, and you get the bride, de Gaulle, down from London and we'll have a shotgun wedding."

Most probably FDR had been toying with the idea for some days. It was a typical Roosevelt ploy, the kind of maneuver he had used repeatedly in American politics and running his New Deal government—get two men with the same interest or objective but opposing views about how to get there, put them in a room together and let them sort it out. But, what would work in American politics or government might not be the best way of handling two French generals.

Churchill, who knew the French situation and above all the personalities involved far better than Roosevelt, was taken aback. It was not a problem to be solved by window-dressing gestures, and the image of General de Gaulle as a bride at a shotgun wedding was not an entirely felicitous one for Churchill. He knew that he risked a rebuff at de Gaulle's hands, but what could he do? So on January 16 he cabled Eden with a message to be handed de Gaulle next morning at the Foreign Office: "I should be glad if you would come to join me here by first available plane which we shall provide, as it is in my power to bring about a meeting between you and General Giraud under conditions of complete secrecy and with the best prospects. . . . The conversations would proceed between the two French principals unless otherwise convenient. . . ."

De Gaulle's immediate reaction, to Eden's consternation though perhaps not his surprise, was negative and hostile. There could be no invitation to him from the Allies to meet anyone on French soil, he told Eden, and when Eden stressed it would also be an opportunity to meet the president of the United States, he replied that he could go to Washington anytime the president wished to see him. After a frosty discussion, de Gaulle said he would deliver a formal answer to the Foreign Office later in the day. Without even consulting his National Committee, he came back at 5 P.M. to hand Eden a note for Churchill:

> I value most highly the sentiments which inspire your message and thank you heartily for them. Allow me to say, however, that the atmosphere of an exalted Allied forum around the Giraud–de Gaulle conversations, as well as the suddenness with which those conversations have been proposed to me, do not seem to me to be the best for an effective agreement. Simple and direct talks between the French leaders would, in my opinion, be the best design to bring about a useful arrangement. I am telegraphing again to General Giraud to repeat once more my proposal for an immediate meeting. . . .

This was, to say the least, a mortifying rebuff to Churchill, made much worse by Roosevelt's manifest glee over the prime minister's embarrassment and discomfort. No one on the American delegation was inclined to sympathize, much less attempt to understand, what the British were up against in dealings with de Gaulle. Roosevelt set the tone rather like a picador teasing a bull when he said to Churchill: "Why don't you stop his food—maybe then he will come."

On the evening of the eighteenth, Churchill drafted a blistering message to de Gaulle, to be delivered by Eden, although he added the instruction that "I leave you latitude to make any alterations which you may think desirable, so long as its seriousness is not impaired." Churchill's language and threats were so unequivocal that when he got the message Eden convened the War Cabinet to consider exactly what should be done to tone it down. One of the sentences in the original draft read: "If, with your eyes open, you reject this unique opportunity, we shall endeavor to get on as well as we can without you. The door is still open." The War Cabinet thought it more prudent simply to say: "The consequences of the future of the Free French movement cannot but be grave in the extreme."

Eden then asked de Gaulle to come to the Foreign Office at 6 P.M. on January 19. Instead, the durable, loyal and diplomatic René Pleven arrived, explaining quite frankly that de Gaulle had sent him rather than coming himself because he anticipated that the message from the prime minister would be sharp and he couldn't trust himself not to burst out with something he might regret afterward! De Gaulle did not always show such prudence in dealings with friends and allies.

Churchill's toned-down message was now placed before the entire French National Committee. De Gaulle continued to show no enthusiasm for going to Casablanca, but even his own account of events reads as though he were ready to be forced off his own hook. In part, a way out was offered because Roosevelt's name had been added to Churchill's summons.

"We purposely took some time over our deliberations, and afterwards I made no particular haste to begin my trip," de Gaulle wrote. At 5 P.M. on January 20, he arrived at the Foreign Office to hand Eden about as ungracious an acceptance of the invitation of the prime minister and the president as he could contrive:

> President Roosevelt and you are asking me presently to take part, without warning, in discussions of which I know neither the program nor the conditions, and during which I will be led to discuss matters concerning the whole future of the French Empire and of France itself. I recognize, however, despite these questions of form, grave though they may be, that the general situation of the war and the position in which France is temporarily placed cannot allow me to refuse.

Time was running out. The Casablanca meeting was due to end on the weekend. Weather then delayed de Gaulle's departure even longer. As a particular touch, probably lost on the Americans but certainly not on Giraud and the French, de Gaulle included in his party Colonel Hertier de Boislambert, who had entered Dakar on a secret mission on his behalf just before that abortive operation began, but had been caught by the pro-Vichy police and had been shipped back to prison in France by the governor general, Boisson, whom the Americans were keeping in power. He had escaped and rejoined de Gaulle in London.

On Friday, January 22, at 11 A.M., General de Gaulle's Royal Air Force plane landed at Casablanca Airport. The welcoming committee consisted solely of low-level personal representatives of Churchill, Roosevelt and General Giraud, and de Gaulle noted that "no troops presented arms, though American sentries cleared a wide area around us." One of history's great actors had arrived at the center of the stage.

*

General Giraud, summoned out of the blue from Algiers at the same time as de

Gaulle, had arrived promptly in Casablanca on January 17. He brought with him an extraordinary military shopping list for the Americans to provide him with equipment for some fifteen French divisions totaling 300,000 men. But he did not seem to have a clue as to how French colonial troops recruited in Senegal and Algeria were to be trained in up-to-date weaponry when they could barely read. "Give us the arms and the tanks. . . . There are plenty of officers under my command. . . . It constitutes no problem. . . . Only give us the arms. . . ." This was the extent of his training program. He met Roosevelt, together with Murphy and General Mark Clark, soon after his arrival. The president's son, Elliott, an Air Corps captain who was also present, says that "he was a vast disappointment to Father." He quotes the president as saying to him later: "I'm afraid we're leaning on a very slender reed. This is the man Bob Murphy said the French would rally around! He's a dud as an administrator, and he'll be a dud as a leader."

But whatever Roosevelt's feelings about Giraud, they certainly did not incline him to shift United States policy in the direction of General de Gaulle. The president gave Giraud assurances that he would seriously consider his shopping list—and on Giraud's part, this presidential support plus all of the cosseting and cooperation he was getting from Murphy and Eisenhower's staff in Algiers certainly did not incline him to show any accommodation for de Gaulle.

Giraud invited de Gaulle to lunch immediately on his arrival, and the leader of the Fighting French arrived in a mood of deliberate arrogant anger at what he conceived to be "a flagrant insult to French sovereignty" all around him. Taking the offensive at once, he records that his first words to Giraud were: "What is this? I ask you for an interview four times over, and we have to meet in a barbed-wire encampment among foreign powers? Don't you realize how distasteful this is from a purely national point of view?"

Apart from some pleasantries when Giraud recounted at de Gaulle's request the story of his escape from the German prison fortress at Koenigstein, the two generals quickly deadlocked over French affairs in North Africa. De Gaulle says that Giraud insisted over and over that he gave his attention solely to military questions, did not concern himself with politics and that he "never listened to anyone who tried to interest him in a theory or a program, that he never read a newspaper or turned on the radio." Unfortunately, this was all too true. Giraud also went on to declare his full backing for the Vichy proconsuls—Noguès, Boisson and Peyrouton—"and did not conceal the fact that apart from his determination, unquestionably resolute, to join battle with the Germans, he had nothing against the Vichy regime" according to de Gaulle.

After this damp opener, de Gaulle retired to his villa "with calculated reserve" to leave it up to his hosts to make the next move. Late in the afternoon Harold Macmillan arrived to unveil for de Gaulle the "unity blueprint" which he and Murphy had drawn up. Basically it called for the establishment of a new French Committee with de Gaulle and Giraud as joint presidents. But Giraud would remain supreme military commander of all French forces, including the Free French, and the three Vichy proconsuls also would be retained, at American insistence, in Algiers, Dakar and Morocco. To Macmillan, de Gaulle simply said that agreement between himself and Giraud could be realized only by negotiations between themselves and not by any outside Allied intervention. They then went together for a meeting with Churchill, which the prime minister described with understatement as "a very stony interview."

De Gaulle kicked things off by declaring that "I would never have come here had I known that I would be surrounded on French soil by American bayonets," to which Churchill retorted, "This is an occupied country."

Churchill then turned to the unity plan. De Gaulle listened impatiently and brusquely swept it all aside.

> I replied to Mr. Churchill that the solution might seem adequate at the quite respectable level of American sergeant majors, but that I did not believe that he himself could take it seriously. As for me, I was obliged to take into account what remained of French sovereignty. The Allies had, without me, and indeed against me, set up the system now functioning in Algiers. Apparently finding it only half satisfactory, they now proposed to submerge Fighting France in it. But Fighting France would have none of it; if it must disappear it preferred to do so with honor.

To Churchill's pleas for political flexibility, de Gaulle retorted that "I am not a politician trying to set up a cabinet and find a majority in Parliament." Churchill then interjected in his inimitable fractured French: *"Si vous m'obstaclerez, je vous liquiderai!"* (If you "obstacle" me, I will liquidate you!—These verbs do not exist in French.) But as de Gaulle stalked out to return to his own quarters, Churchill remarked to his doctor, Lord Moran, as they watched him stride away: "Look at him! Just look at him. I was pretty rough with him, but he might be Stalin with two hundred divisions behind his words."

Next Robert Murphy called on the General to discuss arrangements for the meeting with Roosevelt and to offer some carefully thought-out diplomatic advice that probably would have appealed to any leader but de Gaulle:

> I said to him that while I would not presume to advise him about French and North African politics, I felt that I should say that it would be very helpful to everybody concerned if he could come to Algiers without making legalistic conditions. I said that I was certain that if he did, he would have complete control of the French political situation within three months, because General Giraud was interested solely in his military command and had no political ambitions. De Gaulle smiled thinly and replied: "Political ambitions can develop rapidly—for example, look at me!"

Murphy says that he was encouraged "by this unexpected expression of wry humor." But the common sense of his message had no appeal to de Gaulle. He would go to Algiers and join Giraud only on his own terms—not on Anglo-American terms; it was as simple as that. An hour or two later, Charles de Gaulle arrived at the Casablanca White House for his first meeting with Franklin D. Roosevelt.

After all the political wrangling over French affairs, and the highhanded performance of de Gaulle in first snubbing the invitation to come to Casablanca, that first encounter with Roosevelt was low-key, almost anticlimactic. If intransigence and obstruction were basic tenets of the General's policies and exercise of power, he was nevertheless a flexible tactician when he wanted to be or sensed that he needed to be. He would argue with Churchill fiercely, slugging away point by point over history and detail. But these were not his tactics with the president of the United States. In his laconic comment, "by mutual agreement, we maintained a certain vagueness on the question of France."

Harry Hopkins and Elliott Roosevelt were present when de Gaulle arrived, "giving us the impression that thunder clouds were billowing around his narrow skull," in Hopkins' description. Elliott recorded that "Father, all charm, began by saying 'I am sure that we will be able to assist your great country in re-establishing her destiny, and I assure you that it will be an honor for my country to participate in the undertaking.'" These were not sentiments to appeal to de Gaulle, who believed above all else that only France herself could restore French destiny. He grunted to Roosevelt stiffly: "It is nice of you to say so."

After that, on the president's instructions, Hopkins and Elliott withdrew. Roosevelt wanted to talk to de Gaulle alone without an interpreter. But, to Hopkins' amusement and de Gaulle's silent irritation the Secret Service had insisted on posting armed men not very discreetly behind the window curtains and in a gallery overlooking the room. An aide, Captain McCrea, was also listening behind a door slightly ajar, and taking notes. But he recorded that he had "a relatively poor vantage point" and that de Gaulle spoke in such a low voice he could scarcely be heard at all.

At any rate, McCrea noted that the president began by saying that he and Churchill were in Casablanca "to get on with the war," and that as far as the exercise of French sovereignty in North Africa was concerned, "none of the contenders for power has the right to say that he, and only he, represented the sovereignty of France—the Allied nations were fighting for the liberation of France and they should hold the political situation in trusteeship for the French people." Roosevelt went on to picture France, rather condescendingly, as "a little child unable to look out and fend for itself, and in such a condition a court appoints a trustee to do the necessary." He concluded this little homily by telling de Gaulle: "The only course of action that could save France was for her loyal sons to unite and defeat the enemy, and when the war was ended, victorious France could once again assert the political sovereignty which was hers over her homeland and the Empire."

McCrea could not hear de Gaulle clearly enough to make any notes, but de Gaulle records:

> I pointed out, just as delicately, that the national will had already made its choice, and that sooner or later the authority established in the Empire and ultimately in metropolitan France would be the one France chose for herself.

Nevertheless, we took care not to meet head-on, realising that the clash would lead to nothing and that for the sake of the future we each had much to gain by getting along together.

So ended a first encounter, which lasted only a little over half an hour. But if a head-on clash was mutually avoided, the conversation did nothing to clear the air and only stiffened mutual suspicions and underlying antipathies. "Beneath his patrician mask of courtesy, Roosevelt looked at me without goodwill," de Gaulle wrote, and in this he was certainly right.

Next morning, Saturday, General Giraud and his officers came to de Gaulle's villa for a long and detailed conference, and lunch. Giraud, with no ideas of his own, took up the Anglo-American unity plan as the basis for an agreement. De Gaulle again rejected this approach out of hand and assailed Giraud with near savagery for his political and administrative inadequacies and his "dependence on the Anglo-American authorities." Witheringly, he threw back in Giraud's face the letter he had written pledging total loyalty to Marshal Pétain:

> At the moment, what are your triumphs? Are you really skilled in the business of legislation and administration? Furthermore, you cannot fail to know that in France public opinion will from now on condemn Vichy, yet it is primarily from Darlan, and then from Noguès and Boisson that you derive your powers. It is in the Marshal's name that you have assumed them. Everyone knows of your letter to Pétain in which you gave your word that you would never act against his policies. Do you think that under these conditions you can gain even an elementary support from the French people, without which a government is either an illusion or indeed the target of a revolution?

After this contemptuous broadside, de Gaulle offered what he considered "the common-sense solution"—he would go to Algiers and form a wartime French provisional government that would make Giraud the commander of an army of liberation. But at the outset the Vichy proconsuls would have to be replaced, the armistice of 1940 declared null and void, and the provisional government "must identify itself with the Republic and, in the eyes of the world, with the independence of France." Eventually, this was precisely what de Gaulle achieved.

The only agreement which they then reached—although an important one from the standpoint of future developments—was that they should exchange liaison missions. De Gaulle immediately said that he would send General Catroux to Algiers. Catroux was an officer whose rank and credentials were certainly on a par with those of Giraud, and his political intellect was considerably superior. This being all they could agree on, the French officers then had what de Gaulle described as a gloomy lunch together.

The Casablanca conference was due to end the next day, and no shotgun wedding had been consummated. For the rest of Saturday, the General kept to his villa, visited once more by Harold Macmillan, who resumed the arguments about what would happen to his movement in London if he did not come to an agreement with Giraud under Allied auspices. After that, an American officer, Major General William H. Wilbur, came to see him. They had been in the same class at the École Supérieure de Guerre ten years before. Wilbur was fluent in French, and it was the most sympathetic hearing that de Gaulle got from an American in Casablanca. The American general then wrote a long report that went to Harry Hopkins and quite probably influenced Hopkins in the direction in which he subsequently steered Roosevelt.

On Sunday, January 24, with the conference ending, Murphy and Macmillan arrived at de Gaulle's villa in the morning with the draft text of a communiqué on the French discussions, which they wanted him to accept. Given what had transpired, it was somewhat audacious of them even to try, but it was a last throw to salvage something from the diplomatic debacle. The draft sought to plaster over the Giraud–de Gaulle differences by stating that they were agreed on "forming a joint committee to administer the French Empire during the war." In a sense this was true, but it was not yet a fact, and de Gaulle simply sent Murphy and Macmillan away, telling them that French affairs could not be settled by foreign intervention "no matter how high and how friendly."

De Gaulle had now forced the Casablanca conference to the brink of failure and a public relations disaster as far as French affairs were concerned, and it was time for him to make farewell calls on the prime minister of Great Britain and the president of the United States. He went first to Churchill's villa, where, he says, "we had an extremely bitter interview—the roughest of all our wartime encounters."

> He declared that on his return to London he would publicly accuse me of having obstructed the agreement, would rouse public opinion in his country against me personally and would appeal to the people of France. I confined myself to replying that my friendship for him and my attachment to our alliance with Britain caused me to deplore such an attitude on his part. In order to satisfy America at any cost, he was espousing a cause unacceptable to France, disquieting to Europe and regrettable for England.

This version, from de Gaulle's Memoirs, was rough enough, but Jacques Soustelle, who was then the Free French information chief in London, wrote that de Gaulle went further and told the prime minister that he was "free to dishonor himself" if he chose. Churchill in his Memoirs does not mention the interview at all. At any rate, de Gaulle walked out, to go and see Roosevelt.

Meanwhile, Murphy brought the news to Hopkins of de Gaulle's refusal to accept the proposed communiqué—leaving things high and dry with a flock of war correspondents now flown in from Algiers and waiting for a planned press conference. Hopkins, in his papers, tells what happened next:

> I left Murphy and Macmillan in my room and went to see the President to tell him the news. He was none too happy about it, but I urged him not to

disavow de Gaulle even though he was acting badly. Believing as I did and still do that Giraud and de Gaulle want to work together, I urged the President to be conciliatory and not beat de Gaulle too hard. If there is any beating to be done, let Churchill do it, because the whole Free French Movement is financed by them. I told the President I thought we would get an agreement on a joint statement issued by de Gaulle and Giraud—and a picture of the two of them.

At 11:30 A.M. General Giraud arrived for a final meeting with Roosevelt—asking once more for confirmation that he would get the arms for his fifteen divisions, to be told by the president to take it up with Eisenhower. But Giraud did say that he was prepared to sign a communiqué with de Gaulle—as he had been prepared to sign the Anglo-American draft. Giraud then left the president, but Hopkins alerted his staff not to let him leave the area.

General de Gaulle now arrived for his farewell talk, and Hopkins says that "the President expressed his point of view in pretty powerful terms and made an urgent plea to de Gaulle to come to terms with Giraud to win the war and liberate France."

This is de Gaulle's version:

> My reception at his hands was a skillful one—that is, kind and sorrowful. The President expressed his disappointment that French support should remain uncertain and that he had not been able to prevail upon me to accept even the text of a communiqué. "In human affairs," he said, "the public must be offered a drama. The news of your meeting with General Giraud in the midst of a conference in which both Churchill and I were taking part, if this news were to be accompanied by a joint declaration by the French leaders—even if it concerned only a theoretical agreement—would pro-duce the dramatic effect we need." I replied, "Let me handle it—there will be a communiqué, even though it cannot be yours."

At this point Churchill arrived to join the president, and Hopkins then had Giraud brought back into the room. Churchill, in a fury over de Gaulle's conduct, strode up to him, shook a finger in his face and all but shouted at him in his inimitable French: *"Mon Général, il ne faut pas obstacler* [sic] *la guerre!"* (General, you must not "obstacle" the war!)

De Gaulle's version continues:

> The President afforded to pay no attention [to Churchill], adopting instead the kindest manner in order to make me a last request on which he had set his heart. Would I at least agree to being photographed beside him and the British Prime Minister, along with General Giraud? "Of course," I answered, "for I have the highest regard for this great soldier." And would I go as far as to shake General Giraud's hand before the camera? My answer in English was, "I shall do that for you."

And so, Franklin D. Roosevelt was carried out into the sunny garden, where four chairs had been hastily arranged in front of a horde of photographers and war correspondents, to photograph and witness the shotgun handshake. Apart from the smiling president, it was a pretty solemn quartet—Churchill still scowling belligerently after dressing down de Gaulle, the two generals extending their arms stiffly as if they were touching sabers instead of shaking hands. But Roosevelt got his picture for worldwide distribution—and for the moment that was enough.

De Gaulle and Giraud left immediately after being photographed, and in a matter of half an hour or so they had agreed on a brief joint statement that de Gaulle of course drafted. "Let me handle it," he had told the president, and he did. Meanwhile, Churchill and Roosevelt continued with the press conference, summarizing what they could say about the far-reaching military decisions of their ten-day meeting. It was on this occasion that FDR made his famous and unexpected declaration about "unconditional surrender of Nazi Germany" being the ultimate war aim of the Allies.

The French statement, after announcing the minuscule face-saving decision to exchange liaison missions between the Fighting French in London and the Algerian French, simply said: "We have met, we have talked. We have registered our entire agreement on the end to be achieved, which is the liberation of France and the triumph of human liberties by the total defeat of the enemy. This end will be attained by the union in war of all Frenchmen, fighting side by side with their Allies."

*

From a position of weakness, face-to-face with the two most powerful men in the democratic world, General de Gaulle had staged an extraordinary demonstration of the power of intransigence—the power on which he would base his dealings with his allies "all the way to the Rhine, inclusive." He had stood like granite on his own principles and demands, and when these had not accorded with those of his allies, he refused to compromise or even to be accommodating—except for the photographers. He refused to blur the edges or the choice between himself and Giraud, between the Fighting French and the French of Vichy, who were now so ready to change sides. He refused to countenance any Anglo-American intervention or mediation or formulas for settling French affairs. He walked out of Casablanca with nothing but his integrity and his intransigence, but there was no doubt as to who was the dominant leader of France.

In the short term he paid a price, and in some ways the ensuing four months immediately after Casablanca, before he finally arrived in Algiers to begin the final consolidation of his power, were the most difficult and even precarious of the war years. Winston Churchill—deeply wounded, angered, embittered and embarrassed by his tactics and performance—moved to open hostility and a readiness to "dump de Gaulle" at the first opportunity. Roosevelt simply took the view that de Gaulle was a British problem, and since the General had refused to compromise or cooperate with the United States, all the eggs were in the Giraud basket.

But de Gaulle had picked up an important hidden ally—Harry Hopkins, the president's intuitive, intelligent and totally self-effacing personal adviser. Hopkins proposed that the astute and experienced Jean Monnet, then in Washington working on supply problems, be sent to Algiers and installed in Giraud's entourage to give it some badly needed political expertise. Over Cordell Hull's objections this was done, and Monnet almost at once moved into a pivotal role in negotiating unity between the two French camps.

Churchill made his attitude felt immediately. After Casablanca, de Gaulle wanted to visit Free French troops in Libya and then go on to Syria. But he was abruptly told on Churchill's orders that the only transport available for him was a flight back to London. As de Gaulle commented, "the weeks that followed were painful—but if the Allies pelted us with abuse, in French Africa the evidence of approval kept multiplying."

Moreover, Churchill's attitude of extreme hostility toward de Gaulle was by no means shared in the War Cabinet. Time and again across these months and into 1944, Eden led a very effective rear-guard action in the secrecy of the Cabinet to restrain Churchill, tone down some of his proposed *démarches,* as was done with his message to de Gaulle from Casablanca, and on one or two occasions impose what amounted to a veto over extreme actions he was proposing that would have brought a break with the General. In this, Eden was consistently supported by the two key Labour members of the wartime coalition, Deputy Prime Minister Clement Attlee and Labour Minister Ernest Bevin, the weighty trade union leader who became a very considerable foreign secretary in the postwar Labour government. There was even surprising though totally secret restraining support from King George VI, whose private diaries, made public long after his death in 1952, carried this entry for February 9, 1943, immediately after Casablanca: "Prime Minister to lunch. He is furious with de Gaulle over his refusal to accept FDR's invitation to meet him and Giraud. . . . I warned Winston not to be too hasty with de Gaulle and the Free French National Committee. . . . I told Winston I could well understand de Gaulle's attitude and that of our own people here, who do not like the idea of making friends of those Frenchmen who have collaborated with the Germans."

Churchill appeared so all-powerful in those days that it was difficult for Roosevelt and the Americans to believe that he was *not* entirely his own boss, that he could *not* dump de Gaulle anytime he wanted to. But the War Cabinet records give a far different picture.

The British could keep de Gaulle in London, but they certainly could not keep him quiet or inactive. He held a press conference on February 9 to give his version of what happened at Casablanca, which did not exactly pour oil on troubled waters. Then, on February 23, he formally transmitted to General Giraud a memorandum from the Free French National Committee on "conditions indispensable to unity." These followed the lines of what de Gaulle had told Giraud in their meeting at Casablanca: the 1940 armistice to be declared null and void, dismissal of the Vichy proconsuls still in office in Africa, creation of a French "central power having all the prerogatives of government" with a "consultative assembly of the Resistance," and re-establishment of Republican law in place of Vichy law in North Africa. Two weeks later, Giraud still not having responded, de Gaulle made these conditions public in London.

A response of sorts did come, however on March 14 in Algiers, in the form of a speech delivered by Giraud but drafted by Jean Monnet. In it, Giraud suddenly turned over a new leaf, although given the circumstances under which the speech came about and Giraud's determined opaqueness about political matters, he may not have been entirely aware of the full import of what he was reading. At any rate it was full of new liberalism and dedication to democracy and was accompanied, at last, by a series of ordinances wiping a sheaf of Vichy statutes off the books—anti-Semitic regulations among them. De Gaulle responded from London with a statement congratulating Giraud for "great progress toward the doctrine of Fighting France as it has been upheld since June 1940, again expressed in its memorandum of February 23."

With this "new look," Giraud now sent de Gaulle new proposals for unity, in which he would play the top role, and de Gaulle again came under heavy pressure from the British and Americans to throw in his lot. This he refused, but to the consternation of the Allies he countered by announcing that he planned to fly to Algiers "without accepting any conditions beforehand."

The British hastily moved to block this by producing a message for de Gaulle from Eisenhower (initiated and drafted by Macmillan in Algiers) asking him to postpone because "a very great battle is impending and it would be undesirable to have a protracted political crisis at the same time." This was in early April, and it was the third time since February that the British blocked de Gaulle from leaving London. On April 6 he then had his first meeting with Churchill since Casablanca, and if the opening was devoid of pleasantries, at least it showed Churchill's irrepressible and ever-ready wit.

"Enfin," de Gaulle began, "je suis prisonnier, bientôt vous m'enverrez à l'Ile de Man." —So, I am a prisoner, next you'll send me to the Isle of Man. (A British wartime internment center for refugees.)

"Non, non, mon Général," Churchill replied. "Pour vous, très très distingué, tourjour la Tower of London."—No, General, for a distinguished man like yourself, the Tower of London.

It was always difficult for the two men to stay mad at each other for very long, and their conversation was frank and difficult that day but ended amicably enough.

Throughout the rest of April, with Jean Monnet as the indispensable middleman in Algiers, messages and formulas went back and forth between the Giraud and de Gaulle camps, always revolving around the same central issue of the powers and composition of a new French National Committee and the subordination of the French military commander in chief to this new authority.

But in the meantime something else very basic was happening as well—and that was the rapid erosion of popular support or popular acceptance in North Africa for the Giraud regime. Gaullist political cells were springing up everywhere and the Cross of Lorraine was everywhere. Free French forces, fighting with the

British, had by now reached Tunisia, and there were heavy desertions from Giraud's units to join Leclerc, Koenig and Lariminat. The political sands were running out for Giraud—and Murphy, Macmillan and Eisenhower all knew it and were reporting it to London and Washington.

On April 20 de Gaulle met Giraud's liaison officer in London, General Bouscat, and told him:

> If there is no agreement, that will be too bad! All France is with me. My resistance and combat groups are everywhere growing stronger every day. France is Gaullist, fiercely Gaullist. She cannot change. We must not forget that we are alone among foreigners, for the Allies are foreigners. They may become our enemies tomorrow. Giraud is subordinating himself to the United States. He is preparing France's servitude and will be gravely disappointed.

In the wake of Casablanca, and in the face of Anglo-American, or more specifically American, handling of the situation in North Africa, de Gaulle's choler at his allies was rising. This, indeed, had become his war—not the war against Germany, which was the affair of Roosevelt and Churchill. Nor did the General particularly try to conceal these feelings, which by now were flooding back to the State Department to fuel the anti-de Gaulle bias of Hull and Roosevelt.

On April 27 Giraud, in a message from Algiers with Monnet's guiding hand, inched backward, saying that he would no longer insist on his own "preponderance" in a new National Committee. De Gaulle responded with an unyielding restatement of his terms, and then in a public address in London on May 4 declared that "There must be an end to delay." Finally, on May 17, Giraud caved in, with an invitation to de Gaulle to come to Algiers "at once" to form a French central power with him. All preconditions disappeared. They would start out as co-presidents of a small committee. Everything else was to be decided.

De Gaulle did not rush to reply—that was not his style. After a week he cabled Giraud that "I shall be delighted to work directly with you in the service of France." He took another week of formal goodbyes in London. He arrived in Algiers at long last at about as inauspicious an hour as could be devised—at midnight on May 30, 1943, at a remote military airfield, at Boufarik, far from public gaze. News of his arrival was censored for twenty-four hours. It scarcely mattered. His London days were behind him now. He was back on French soil to stay, and power was within his grasp.

*

As these exchanges between de Gaulle and Giraud approached their decisive final stage, Churchill sailed for the United States aboard the *Queen Elizabeth* on May 4 for another meeting with Roosevelt. En route he received a memorandum from the president on French affairs that said in part:

> I am more and more disturbed by the machinations of de Gaulle. . . . All in all, I think you and I should thrash out this disagreeable problem and establish a common policy. I think we might talk over the formation of an

entirely new French committee subject in its membership to the approval of you and me. I do not think it should in any way act as a provisional government, but could be called advisory in its functions. Giraud should be made the Commander-in-Chief of the French army and navy and of course would sit on the advisory national committee. . . . I do not know what to do with de Gaulle. Possibly you would like to make him Governor of Madagascar!

Under heavy pressure from Roosevelt and the Americans after his arrival in Washington, Churchill sent a decisive cable to London for consideration by the War Cabinet on May 22—just as de Gaulle was preparing to accept Giraud's invitation to come to Algiers. After saying that "hardly a day passes that the President does not mention de Gaulle to me," Churchill summarized at length a list of American grievances against the French leader and then laid it on the line:

> I must ask my colleagues to consider urgently whether we should not now eliminate de Gaulle as a political force and face Parliament and France upon the issues. The French National Committee would in this case be told that we will have no further relations' with them or give them any money whatever as long as de Gaulle is connected with their body. . . . I beg that you will bring this before the Cabinet at the earliest moment. Meanwhile and pending my return, the strictest control of de Gaulle's movements and of Free French propaganda by radio and in the press should be maintained. . . .

At this point de Gaulle's fate hung in the balance. If the War Cabinet had endorsed Churchill's wishes, it would have plunged French affairs into utter chaos. But the reply to Churchill on May 23 was a model of sober historical judgment.

After acknowledging that "we are fully conscious of the difficulties which de Gaulle has created for us, and of your position under heavy pressure from the Americans," the War Cabinet unanimously rejected Churchill's call for a break, telling the prime minister:

> The latest phase of the Giraud–de Gaulle negotiations indicates that union is nearer than it has been at any time. De Gaulle has been invited by Giraud to Algiers, and it seems probable that he will accept. We anticipate an early application from de Gaulle for transport facilities. It has been the policy of HMG and the U.S. government for the past four months to bring the two generals together, blessed by yourself and the President at Casablanca. If, as we believe, it was the right policy then, it is our view even more that it is the right policy now.
>
> We are advised that there is no likelihood of any of the present members of the French National Committee continuing to function if General de Gaulle were removed by us. Is there not a real danger that if we drove de Gaulle out of public life at this moment when a union between the two French movements seems on the point of being achieved we would not only

make him a national martyr, but we would find ourselves accused by both Gaullists and Giraudists of interfering improperly in French internal affairs with a view to treating France as an Anglo-American protectorate? If so, our relations with France would be more dangerously affected than by a continuance of the present unsatisfactory situation.

Somewhat humbled, Churchill replied from Washington on May 24 that "it is a new fact to me that de Gaulle is about to meet Giraud," but he added grumpily that "I should be very sorry to become responsible for breaking up harmony [with the United States] for the sake of a Frenchman who is a bitter foe of Britain and may well bring civil war upon France."

That day, General de Gaulle, unaware how close things had come to a decision by the Allies to put out his light, cabled Giraud with his message that he would be arriving on May 30.

*

Three days after de Gaulle's arrival in Algiers, he and Giraud formally proclaimed a new French Committee of National Liberation, themselves as copresidents with five other committee members. From that moment on, General de Gaulle mounted a single-minded, relentless and utterly ruthless campaign to strip Henri Giraud of power and consolidate his own sole control over the affairs of the committee that eventually would become the nucleus of the government of France itself. It was a sustained performance of power politics that left those who witnessed it, or tried to impede it or check it, gasping on the sidelines—Murphy, Macmillan and Eisenhower among them. The hapless Giraud was caught up in a wholly unequal struggle, and he hadn't a clue how to play the game. As an example, he made a major tactical error in absenting himself from the Algerian scene for three weeks beginning in early July, to accept an invitation from Roosevelt to visit the United States. By the time he got back, after basking in American and British honors and hospitality and assurances of full confidence and support, the skids had been greased, his power and authority undermined and his demise only a question of time and circumstances of de Gaulle's making.

Barely two weeks after de Gaulle's arrival in Algiers, Roosevelt could see in the making the collapse of the American-backed edifice in North Africa, and on June 17 he sent a somewhat frantic cable to Churchill:

> I am fed up with de Gaulle and the secret personal and political machinations of that committee in the last few days indicates that there is no possibility of our working with him. I am absolutely convinced that he has been and is now injuring our war effort, and that he is a very dangerous threat to us. The time has arrived when we must break with him. It is an intolerable situation. We must have someone whom we can completely and wholly trust.

But Churchill, who had already lost this battle once in the War Cabinet, cabled back to Roosevelt almost immediately, referring to the decision of a month before and adding: "I agree with you that no confidence can be placed in de Gaulle's friendship for the Allies . . . but I am not in favor at this moment of breaking up the French Committee or forbidding it to meet."

De Gaulle, meanwhile, was clearly in a mood of exhilaration, wielding power on his own from French territory, free of London, free to move about within his own domains without seeking Anglo-Saxon permission, free to communicate with Moscow and the entire French Empire, free to mold French affairs to his own will at last.

On de Gaulle's arrival, Peyrouton immediately submitted his resignation as governor general of Algeria to the co-presidents of the new Committee of National Liberation. De Gaulle then took the first trick from Giraud by accepting the resignation instantly, by return letter. Giraud instead debated overnight and then decided to refuse it. Immediately he discovered, not for the last time, that he was confronted with a de Gaulle *fait accompli.* Giraud had been outmaneuvered, and so had the Americans. Then, at de Gaulle's instigation, the full committee (then seven members) outvoted Giraud to remove both Noguès from Morocco and Boisson from Dakar. American support and protection of the Vichyites was crumbling fast. After that, on de Gaulle's proposal, the committee voted to double its size, and when this was effected, Giraud no longer had a chance of prevailing in committee votes. The power balance had swung fully behind de Gaulle.

It was at the height of this infighting that Giraud mistakenly departed for the United States, thinking naïvely that this show of American backing would secure his position in Algiers. But while he was away, the enlarged Committee of National Liberation agreed on de Gaulle's proposal to dismiss from service a list of 400 pro-Vichy military and naval officers.

On Giraud's return, the committee voted that only de Gaulle should preside at future meetings. This effectively stripped Giraud of any role in the proceedings. But he still was military commander in chief and he still retained control over the established Military Intelligence Service, in rivalry with de Gaulle's Resistance and Intelligence aparat under Colonel Passy. To breach this final Giraud defensive position, de Gaulle adroitly proposed that the Committee of National Liberation approve an order placing all Free French forces under Giraud's unified command. This of course was unanimously carried and Giraud was then asked to sign the decree of the committee in accepting the Free French under his command. He did so with delight—only gradually realizing that by doing so he had acknowledged what de Gaulle had always insisted upon: that the military commander in chief was subordinate to the power and authority of the Committee of National Liberation. What the committee giveth it could also taketh away—which it next proceeded to do by consolidating the Intelligence Services under de Gaulle's leadership.

While all this French infighting was taking place, the war moved on. The North African campaign had long since ended with complete victory in Tunisia in May. Next the Allies landed in Sicily and completed their conquest of the island in August. After that they crossed the Messina Straits to the toe of the Italian boot. Then came the landings at Salerno, south of Naples, on September 9, 1943.

Meanwhile, Mussolini had been overthrown in Rome and the Italian government under Marshal Pietro Badoglio signed an armistice with the Allies on September 3, which had been kept secret until the Salerno operation was under way.

General Giraud enjoyed a last brief moment of military glory for France. With the Americans and British fully occupied in precarious combat on the Salerno beach, the French on their own mounted a shoestring operation against Corsica— their own men transported in their own ships, landing of necessity in small numbers but ably commanded. Italian forces on the island quickly took the opportunity under the armistice to lay down their arms, while the Germans fought a rearguard action and with superior air cover managed to embark and get away. The first territory of the French homeland was liberated, and on October 8, 1943, de Gaulle arrived in Ajaccio to congratulate Giraud and proclaim that "a tide of national enthusiasm today bears us all onwards."

In November General de Gaulle put in place the last part of the structure of a provisional government, ready to return to France. A Consultative Assembly was formed in Algiers. To be sure, its members were appointed and it had only advisory debating powers. Under the wartime circumstances it could scarcely be otherwise. Nevertheless it was undeniably a democratic voice behind the Committee of National Liberation. Moreover, by the end of 1943, the tide had turned decisively and the rallying of France of the Resistance began to surge with hope and resolution after the dark degenerate despondent years of 1940, 1941 and 1942.

By now, men of ability and strength and talent were coming out of occupied France in a flood, emerging from the shadows of Vichy to join General de Gaulle—military men, career diplomats, civil servants, politicians, bankers, industrialists, labor leaders, the whole panoply of French society, in particular the upper echelons of the nation, those who had lowered their gaze and retired in defeat three years before. Now victory was in the air, and there was only one French leader to whom they could turn, around whom they could rally. He welcomed them with open arms, but not without cynical regard.

ELEVEN

1944: INVASION

General de Gaulle had won the battle of unity, but his war with Franklin Roosevelt went on. Indeed, after the Casablanca conference Roosevelt's opposition and antipathy to de Gaulle seemed to harden and deepen as he was forced to watch with mounting anger while the General repeatedly turned intransigence and obstruction into personal victory and power in Algiers. Far from welcoming French unity under de Gaulle, Roosevelt fell back on intransigence of his own. He held out alone to the bitter end to deny de Gaulle the one prize within his power ultimately to bestow: full governmental diplomatic recognition.

Every other government-in-exile from Nazi-occupied Europe had long been recognized by Britain and the United States, beginning as far back as 1940: Poland, Czechoslovakia, Holland, Belgium, Luxembourg, Norway, Yugoslavia, Greece. But it was not until October 25, 1944—nearly five months after the invasion of France and two months after the liberation of Paris—that Roosevelt at last relented, permitting his irritated British and Soviet allies to do the same. De Gaulle waited two days before welcoming the action with the sardonic comment: "The French Government is satisfied to be called by its name."

This stubborn and prolonged snubbing of de Gaulle by Roosevelt, which in de Gaulle's definition of course constituted a snub of France itself, certainly fueled the General's not-very-latent prejudices against the United States as a power insensitive and inimical to Europe, which had been late twice in history in coming to France's aid and now sought to frustrate France's return to greatness and to impose its own new domination and will on Europe and the world. These themes became part of the litany and *leitmotiv* of de Gaulle's thinking, his policies, pronouncements and attitude toward the United States in the war years, and then broke out with vengeance when he was at the height of his power in France in the 1960s.

Moreover, there was plenty of open evidence in Roosevelt's remarks and conversations about France and de Gaulle, and in his handling of French affairs from 1940 to his death in 1945, to reinforce and justify the General's visceral feelings. France "is a little child unable to look out and fend for itself, and in such conditions a court appoints a trustee to do the necessary," Roosevelt had told de Gaulle at their first meeting at Casablanca. This scarcely constituted a very generous or valid approach toward a country much older than the United States, or even much of a reading of the ups and downs of French history. But it was typical of the superficiality in Roosevelt and of the way he often shaped his policies. Under Roosevelt, American power was cresting in the world at last, and his attitude toward France was largely one of ill-concealed condescension—a nation incapable of producing strong government, no longer in control of its destiny, and therefore deserving of only marginal consideration and a minor role in the emerging new alignment of the postwar world. The Vichy regime fitted this view of France; General de Gaulle did not. The president had committed himself to Vichy not only as the legitimate France of 1940, but also the real France, the true France. He had little interest, let alone belief, in Charles de Gaulle's vision of the France in those ashes, and seemed, therefore, to be doing everything he could to impede its realization.

Robert Murphy records Roosevelt telling him at Casablanca:

> "You overdid things a bit in one of those letters you wrote to General Giraud before the landings, pledging the United States to guarantee to return to France every part of her empire. Your letter may make trouble for me after the war." That was the first indication to me that Roosevelt planned extensive reductions in the French Empire, but it was apparent at Casablanca that this project was much on his mind. He discussed with several people, including Eisenhower and me, the transfer or control of Dakar, Indochina and other French possessions and he did not seem fully aware how abhorrent his attitude would be to all the imperialist-minded Frenchmen, including de Gaulle, and those with whom I had negotiated.

To his son, Elliott, at Casablanca, Roosevelt said:

> Elliott, de Gaulle is out to achieve one-man government in France. I can't imagine a man I would distrust more. His whole Free French movement is honeycombed with police spies, he has agents spying on his own people. To him, freedom of speech means freedom from criticism. Why should anybody trust completely the forces backing de Gaulle? He makes it quite clear he expects the Allies to return all French colonies to French control imme-diately after their liberation. You know, apart from the fact that the Allies will have to maintain military control of French colonies here in North Africa for months, maybe years, I'm by no means sure in my own mind that we'd be right to return to France her colonies at all, ever, without first obtaining in each case some sort of pledge, some sort of statement of just exactly what was planned. Anything must be better than to live under French colonial rule! Should a land belong to France? By what logic, by what rule?

Along with this readiness to dispose of the possessions of other nations (Great Britain was by no means immune either from presidential needling and pressures about the postwar future of its Empire), Roosevelt was also often maddeningly and sometimes dangerously glib in his pronouncements on the future of Europe itself. Anthony Eden recorded with some dismay one of Roosevelt's flights of postwar fantasy in a dinner conversation at the White House in March 1943, when FDR spoke in a throwback to Woodrow Wilson redrawing the map of Europe at Versailles in 1919:

> He said he thought the three powers (Britain, the United States and the Soviet Union; not France) should police Europe in general after the war. I pointed out that the occupied countries, as they then were, would want to put their own houses in order, and I thought we should encourage them to do so. We should have our hands quite full enough with Germany. Roosevelt next showed anxiety over the future of Belgium, and described a project for a new state called Wallonia. This would include the Walloon parts of Belgium with Luxembourg, Alsace-Lorraine and part of northern France. I poured water over this, I hope politely, and the President did not revert to the subject.

This sort of offhanded, ill-informed, half-serious try-on approach to French affairs, affairs of state and the conduct of international relations that surfaced regularly from Roosevelt was of course anathema to de Gaulle and not much appreciated by Churchill and the Foreign Office. Churchill was caught in the middle of this stormy triangle—doubly so because while suppressing his frustrations to play the role of Loyal Lieutenant to Roosevelt, he found his own Foreign Office battling constantly behind the scenes on behalf of de Gaulle, and the two Labour members of the War Cabinet, Clement Attlee and Ernest Bevin, consistently throwing their weight also behind recognition and support for the Free French and against Roosevelt's foot-dragging. But de Gaulle would regularly worsen the atmosphere with his own bitter clashes with Churchill and his open condemnation of the prime minister for siding with the United States "against the interests of France and of Europe."

In later years, President John F. Kennedy asked de Gaulle at their one and only meeting in Paris in May 1961 about this wartime relationship, and the General replied that although he quarreled violently and bitterly with Churchill, he always felt a basic accord with him. But with Roosevelt, he said, although he never quarreled openly with him, neither had he ever felt a moment of rapport.

He also told an American historian, Arthur Layton Funk, in 1954:

> My personal relations with Roosevelt were extremely cordial, but our policies were entirely different. Roosevelt was a star—*une vedette*—and he disliked sharing the spotlight. He had difficulties in getting along with anyone, like Churchill for example, who was also a star, but whom Roosevelt did not like although both made great pretense of friendship. With his

physical handicap to overcome, Roosevelt was obsessed with a psychological requirement of rising above his difficulties, of being the principal in the show.

But General de Gaulle was scarcely content to be relegated to the role of a satellite in this stars war. His first battle was the revival and reassertion of France as an Allied and victorious power, not the defeated and rescued power that the Vichy regime would have conveniently been for Roosevelt. For the stubborn president of the United States, it was enough that Frenchmen had been over-whelmingly behind Marshal Pétain in 1940. For General de Gaulle, this was dishonor and treason, and he was determined to wipe the record clean.

"To the President," wrote Roosevelt's experienced and respected secretary of war, Henry L. Stimson, "de Gaulle was a narrow-minded zealot with too much ambition for his own good and some rather dubious views on democracy." Of course de Gaulle was autocratic and authoritarian. He was a general, he was a national leader, and there was a war on. But to translate that into accusations of dictatorship or neofascism, as Roosevelt offhandedly and regularly would do, was scarcely justified—especially in view of the dubious character and records of the Vichy admirals, generals and political turncoats with whom the United States was consorting. De Gaulle did indeed have "agents spying on his own people"— security agents, counterintelligence agents, political informers. How could he have operated otherwise? The war, above all the secret underground war of resistance, was no parlor game. The Free French were fighting not only the Germans but more often Vichy French as well. They had more than their share of double agents and security problems. In screening their own flotsam and jetsam, the methods of interrogation used at their London Intelligence headquarters on Duke Street were not always those of friendly village policemen. The Free French were the butt of constant accusations from their allies over slack security—and then equally blamed for the methods they used in policing their movement.

If Roosevelt did not trust General de Gaulle, neither did de Gaulle have much reason to trust the president to support the interests of France. Mutual trust was indeed the root of the problem. At the outset, after Pearl Harbor, trust was aborted in the affair of Saint-Pierre and Miquelon. In a downward spiral, de Gaulle went on to pile on one action after another that he would justify as "defending the interests of France," often petty in the extreme. For this he paid the price of increasing mistrust on the part of his principal allies. Yet to this he seemed impervious, not even to care.

No man to make understanding easier, he declined to plead or bend, to solicit or explain, to compromise and keep quiet, to substitute friendly, intimate, infor-mal conversation for hard national positions or the determination of fixed policies of state. He was a French general to whom these Anglo-Saxon attitudes and tactics and political advice bore little relevance to his problems and his concepts of the exercise of power in war. It was epitomized on one occasion, at the height of the crisis that de Gaulle precipitated at the time of the D-Day landings in France, when Anthony Eden told him: "It is a fatal mistake in national policy to have too much pride. 'She stoops to conquer' is an action each of us can find useful to observe at times." Only there was then a long pause at the dinner table where this took place, while the British linguists present tried to figure out how to translate "She stoops to conquer" into some French idiom that would be clear to the unbending General de Gaulle.

Nevertheless, the logic of fighting a war is to line up the strongest possible leadership and forces to defeat the enemy. Hence the wartime alliance with Stalin, not the most trustworthy of men. Hence the Allied switch to support of Marshal Tito in Yugoslavia. But Roosevelt refused this logic in the case of France. He had backed Pétain in 1940, and he had backed Giraud in 1942–43, and he had backed Darlan, Noguès, Peyrouton and Boisson. No doubt these failures made him all the more stubborn in resisting all the evidence, all the intelligence and all the political advice and pressures from the British and others about France and General de Gaulle—even after the liberation of Paris, when de Gaulle had walked down the avenue des Champs-Élysées in one of history's great moments of emotional triumph on August 26, 1944.

If at any one of a number of opportune and logical times after Pearl Harbor, in 1942, in 1943, early in 1944, Roosevelt had brought himself to accept the French reality, wholeheartedly acknowledge France's strongest leader, cut his Vichy entanglements and deal with General de Gaulle unambiguously despite all of the problems he embodied, much would have been different. But he would not. Yet de Gaulle prevailed.

Franklin D. Roosevelt and Charles de Gaulle were forces of history—of vastly different power and perspectives, of course, but each a force in his own right. There is not much point in speculating about what history might have been if each had acted differently and they had not been the men they were. In the end, fundamental differences of outlook and temperament, of personality and background, of intelligence and method, and above all their clashing precepts of what constituted national interests were simply unbridgeable. They readily maintained their superficial cordialities by instinctive mutual consent on the only two occasions when they met, but there never was a time or an atmosphere between Roosevelt and de Gaulle, or any real effort, to establish a mutual basis for Franco-American trust and understanding. It remained this way between de Gaulle and five more American presidents—Truman, Eisenhower, Kennedy, Johnson and Nixon. From the war years, it became an impossible divide.

*

The recognition issue stared the Allies in the face as soon as the French Committee of National Liberation was established in Algiers in June 1943 under de Gaulle and Giraud as co-presidents. French unity had been the declared aim of the Allies at the Casablanca conference, and once it was achieved there was no logical reason why diplomatic recognition of the committee should not follow. But in the face of de Gaulle's inexorable cutting down of the rather hapless General Giraud to bring the committee under his sole domination, Roosevelt devised a new logic for refusing recognition, which he clung to stubbornly until October

1944. It was summarized in the British record of discussions at the Anglo-American strategy conference at Quebec in August 1943:

> Mr. Churchill said that all liberal elements in the world, including the governments-in-exile and the Soviet government, were demanding an immediate decision granting full recognition of the committee. The President took the view that we had to think of the future of France herself. He said this would in no way be advanced by turning over the whole control of the French liberation movement to the present group comprising the French committee. The President said he did not want to give de Gaulle a white horse on which he could ride into France and make himself the master of a government there. He was willing to deal with the committee on all French territories over which it exercised control, but no further.

On this specious and untenable position, Roosevelt rested his case against recognition and would not budge. Churchill again found himself in the middle, determined to keep in line with Roosevelt, but under very heavy pressure from Eden and the Foreign Office, the War Cabinet, and the evidence and advice of his own Intelligence Services as to sentiments and conditions inside France—evidence that Roosevelt either never bothered to examine or determinedly ignored and rejected if it ever was laid before him.

On the eve of the Quebec conference, Churchill received a blunt memorandum from Lord Selborne, his minister in charge of the Special Operations Executive (SOE) responsible for direction of the resistance movements throughout occupied Europe. Selborne wrote:

> Organized resistance in France is now almost solidly in favor of de Gaulle as the symbol of resistance to the enemy and of democracy. This certainly confers power on de Gaulle, but it also exerts democratic influence upon him. He is well aware that the resistance groups will follow him only so long as he pursues a policy acceptable to them. The name of Giraud counts for very little indeed in France. The name of Georges [General Alphonse Georges, an old personal friend of Churchill's] is mud. The name of anyone else in power in 1940 is manure. The French have their own attitude in the matter and will not accept leadership from Britain or America.

Moreover, by July 1943, both Eisenhower and Murphy in Algiers had become convinced that it was time to stop fiddling around with the French, and for *military* reasons it was time to recognize the committee. Both were so urging in cables to the State Department and to General Marshall, the Army chief of staff. The British soon knew of this through Harold Macmillan in Algiers, but when Churchill then saw this as an opportunity to open the matter with Roosevelt, the immediate response of the president was a peremptory cable to Eisenhower with a repeat to Churchill: "You are not to recognize the committee under any condition without full consultation and approval of the President."

Meanwhile, de Gaulle had again played the "Russian card." He instructed the

Free French representative in Moscow to request Soviet recognition of the Committee of National Liberation, and Foreign Minister Molotov had responded favorably. When the British got wind of this, Churchill went into action immediately.

He sent a minute to Eden that "it would be most unfortunate" if the Russians acted independently of the British and Americans, adding, "pray let me know what you are doing about this." But he then cabled Stalin himself. Stalin replied testily that he thought the British government supported de Gaulle, and that in the Soviet view "French opinion would be unable to understand any refusal to recognize." But he said if the British wanted recognition postponed, then the Soviet Union "would meet their wish."

Against this background, the British took their case to Quebec, where Cordell Hull was also present with Roosevelt. While Churchill and Roosevelt concentrated on grand strategy, Eden took on Hull for hours on the French question, recording in his diary at the end of the first day of the meeting, August 20, 1943:

> Talk for more than two hours with old Hull. Most of it was about recognition of French committee. I failed to make any impression and we both got quite heated at one time when I told him we had to live twenty miles from France and I wanted to rebuild her so far as I could. This was a first though small step. He retorted by accusing us of financing de Gaulle with the implication that our money had been used to attack him, Hull, personally for a long time past.

Hull would not give an inch, and Roosevelt refused Churchill's entreaties that "however justly founded one's misgivings may be, there is no use making a gesture of this kind in a grudging form." Eden insisted, with War Cabinet backing, that the British had to go further than the Americans were prepared to go, and Churchill finally, reluctantly, agreed. Each government then issued its own formula. The time-consuming arguments and emotions on both sides far overshadowed the diplomatic delicacy of the words finally chosen.

The British statement said:

> His Majesty's government recognize forthwith the French committee of National Liberation as administering those French overseas territories which acknowledge its authority . . . also as the body qualified to ensure the conduct of the French effort in the war within the framework of inter-allied cooperation.

The Americans said:

> The government of the United States takes note with sympathy of the desire of the committee to be regarded as the body qualified to ensure the administration and defense of French interests. The extent to which it may be possible to give effect to this desire must be reserved in each case as it arises. On these understandings, the government of the United States recognizes

the French committee. This statement does not constitute recognition of a government of France or the French Empire by the government of the United States.

Hull and Roosevelt had brought themselves to swallow the word "recognize," but there was a very important essential practical difference between the British and American statements, as the events of the next months soon disclosed. The qualifications and hedges of the American statement adopted were there to enable Roosevelt to continue to deny de Gaulle and the French Committee any role or recognition in the administration of France itself, once the invasion began and liberation got under way. This he proceeded to do with a long series of stonewalling instructions to Eisenhower and arguments with Churchill and the British, until eventually he was overtaken by de Gaulle and the inexorable force of events.

Meanwhile, Stalin, not unexpectedly, jumped in with the warmest formulation of all, declaring the Soviet Union's "recognition of the French committee as representing the state interests of the French Republic and as the sole representative of all French patriots in the struggle against Hitlerism." De Gaulle responded just as warmly by declaring to the irritation of London and Washington that "France must be with Russia in the future."

Hull and Roosevelt had succeeded in making the United States out to be France's most reluctant ally.

But when the president traveled to Tehran at the end of November 1943 for his first meeting with Stalin, he satisfied himself that Stalin's attitude toward de Gaulle and the French was largely negative and indifferent. Stalin, the power realist, characteristically wanted first of all to know how many French divisions the Americans intended to equip. Roosevelt gave him the figure of nine. After that they had a discussion that seemed at least to Roosevelt to produce a meeting of minds about how the collaborationism of Vichy came closer to representing the real France than the spirit of resistance of de Gaulle.

Because of Stalin's seeming indifference, Roosevelt came away from the Tehran conference convinced that de Gaulle did not really have any Russian card to play against the Western Allies. But whatever the president's conclusion, this scarcely prevented de Gaulle throughout the war, and then in his later years in power, from making regular overtures to Moscow, which the Soviets were invariably ready to welcome to see what they could get out of it. This repeated tactic may have served the interests of France as de Gaulle defined them, but it was not a diplomatic game that improved mutual trust with his Western Allies.

On the way home from Tehran in December 1943, Roosevelt stopped off to confer with Eisenhower in Tunisia. This was French territory, and de Gaulle was not informed of the stopover, nor asked or invited to see the president, and he did not forget. Roosevelt's main purpose was to inform Eisenhower that he would be the Supreme Allied Commander for the invasion of France. A new phase of the French drama was beginning.

*

General de Gaulle's relations with General Eisenhower were one of the few bright spots in the Franco-American tangle. In his Memoirs de Gaulle was invariably sparing, precise, careful and critical in bestowing praise on anyone, and his tribute to Eisenhower, thought out and written well after the war, was one of his most generous:

> It was a piece of luck for the Allies that Dwight Eisenhower discovered in himself not only the necessary prudence to deal with thorny problems, but also an attraction toward the wider horizons that history opened up before his career. He knew how to be adroit and flexible, but if he used skill he was also capable of audacity. By choosing reasonable plans, by sticking firmly to them, by respecting logistics, General Eisenhower led to victory the complicated and prejudicial machinery of the armies of the free world.
>
> It will never be forgotten that in this capacity he had the distinction of leading them in the liberation of France. But since a great people's needs are on the scale of its misfortunes, it will doubtless be thought too that the Commander-in-Chief might have been able to serve our country still better. . . . In my own relations with him, I often had the feeling that this generous hearted man inclined toward these points of view. . . . Actually the policies of Washington dictated his behavior and necessitated his reserve.
>
> Nevertheless, if occasionally he went so far as to support the schemes to keep us in obscurity, I can affirm that he did so without conviction. I even saw him allow my intervention in his own strategy whenever national interest led me to do so. At heart this great soldier felt, in his turn, that mysterious sympathy which for almost two centuries has brought his country and mine together in the world's great dramas. It was not his doing that this time the United States cared less for our distress than for the appeal of domination.

Eisenhower called on de Gaulle in Algiers on December 30, 1943, before departing for Washington prior to taking up his new command in London. De Gaulle had just infuriated Roosevelt by ordering the arrest of three Vichyites—Boisson, Peyrouton, and Pierre Flandin, a prewar French foreign minister who also served briefly under Pétain. In that last exchange with de Gaulle on Algerian soil, Eisenhower showed his adroit political feel.

He had received another peremptory instruction from Roosevelt: "Please inform the French Committee as follows: In view of the assistance given the Allied armies during the campaign in Africa by Boisson, Peyrouton and Flandin, you are directed to take no action against these individuals at the present time."

But Eisenhower had stopped delivery of the message to the French, realizing that de Gaulle would certainly reject it out of hand and might even respond by speeding up the trials and sentencing of the three men, making matters much worse. He then went to see the French leader for their final talk. Not surprisingly, de Gaulle wanted to discuss the thorny question of cooperation for the invasion of France. A tacit deal was struck. De Gaulle gave Eisenhower assurances that the three Vichyites would receive preferential treatment in detention and would not be tried until there was a properly constituted National Assembly in France. This was subsequently accepted by Roosevelt on Eisenhower's "earnest recommendation" sent via General Marshall, and another minor de Gaulle crisis was overcome. But de Gaulle also records Eisenhower as telling him in that final talk:

> "I can assure you that, as far as I am concerned and whatever apparent attitudes are imposed upon me, I will recognize no other French power in France than your own in the political sphere." I pointed out that we should probably have an opportunity to manifest our mutual understanding in regard to the way Paris would be liberated. "It must be French troops," I told him, "that take possession of the capital. In view of this operation, a French division must soon be sent to England as the French have requested." Eisenhower acquiesced.

In his war memoirs, *Crusade in Europe,* Eisenhower makes no mention of such a pledge to de Gaulle or even of this meeting. But in fact this was precisely the way he subsequently acted. On the other hand, de Gaulle makes no mention in his Memoirs of any promise in his handling of the three former Vichy officials.

Protocol was always of high importance to General de Gaulle, and full diplomatic recognition by his allies was vital. But in the meantime, what counted most was the *reality* of his power in the face of Roosevelt's intransigence. This he was consolidating in Algiers day by day in the runup to the invasion of France, in the Empire and inside France itself. In his actions and conduct of French affairs, he remained utterly impervious as to whether he had been formally and officially recognized as the leader of France or not. Naturally, he was extremely touchy about anything that smacked of interference in French internal affairs. If Roosevelt insisted on being the last to recognize the reality, well, *tant pis*—too bad!

To Eisenhower, and those close to the French scene in Algiers, the transformation in the whole tone and direction of French war effort with the ascendancy of de Gaulle had been extraordinary. In place of the political and moral weaknesses and confusions and the internecine squabbling of the Darlan-Giraud period, there was now firmness and clarity, efficiency and growing strength. Whatever difficulties there were in dealing with de Gaulle, there was a single French leader from whom real power, as well as symbolic resistance, now flowed. No longer could Vichy collaborationists count on a free ride on the turning French political merry-go-round. Autocratic this leadership certainly was, but democratic as well in the broad support the Gaullist movement was summoning from the depth of France and the width of the Empire.

The maneuverings by which de Gaulle had slowly eliminated Giraud from any power sharing during 1943 were followed by a new political phase. The Consultative Assembly had been established in Algiers, and de Gaulle's next objective was to give the French Committee of National Liberation both the attributes and legal authority of a provisional government—recognized or not.

In particular, this meant imposing his own austere, orderly, authoritarian style of governing, in Algiers first but much the same in later years as well. Here is his own description:

> In my office, I kneaded heavy dough. There were papers to be read, though my immediate colleagues brought me, on my orders, only the most essential. There were decisions to make, even if it was only a question of determining principles. . . . The government met in the Summer Palace twice a week. With the assistance of Louis Joxe (later to play an important role in the Fifth Republic), I had drawn up the agenda. On each item, the committee heard the report of the minister concerned and a debate followed. Each member gave his opinion. If necessary, I called on him to do so. Then I offered my own, generally at the end of the discussion. Then I formulated the council's resolutions, and if necessary settled their disputes. The decisions were subsequently reported to the ministries. Often they were handed down in the form of decrees, published in the *Journal Officiel de la République Française* in Algiers in its traditional format.
>
> My own nature warned me and my experience had taught me that, at the summit, one can preserve time and strength only by remaining on the remotest heights. By taste and expediency, my private life was very simple.

General de Gaulle's wife and their mentally retarded daughter, Anne, had arrived from London in the summer of 1943, and his daughter Elizabeth left Oxford University to work in an Algiers office of the French Committee, which monitored the foreign press. Meanwhile, Philippe de Gaulle continued his sea duties with the Free French Navy in the North Atlantic and the English Channel. The de Gaulles lived in a villa, called Les Oliviers, overlooking the city. In his private life, as in running the government, he established a rigid order, the same routines he had followed in all of his military postings and would continue to follow to the end of his days. On weekends he would regularly drive with his wife and daughter to a cottage in the Kabylia mountains behind Algiers, the region from which the Algerian civil war erupted ten years later. It always required a major event, after much trepidation on the part of his staff, to interrupt the General on a weekend, even in wartime.

He disliked the telephone all his life. "On principle, I used the telephone only rarely, and no one was ever permitted to ring me up," he recorded. If someone wanted to talk to de Gaulle by phone, he would be told that the General would decide whether to call back. Entertainment, too, was minimal, "dinners extremely simple, for rationing necessarily applied to everyone." There were no cronies or personal friends with whom de Gaulle would relax over a drink, as there were around Churchill and Roosevelt. He was rigid in sifting those whom he would receive personally in his office, using this access as a means of exercising power and establishing a de facto recognition of his governmental authority, whether it had been recognized de jure or not. Only top people had access, and this included his "national commissioners" or Cabinet ministers, the heads of foreign diplomatic missions in Algiers, top Allied commanders and French military leaders, and Resistance couriers and leaders from France.

In this atmosphere, under systematic governmental routine and unchallenged authority, it became more and more academic whether Roosevelt chose to recognize who was running France or not. Moreover, the patchwork quality of de Gaulle's original Free French Committee of the early London days had given way in Algiers to a body of strong and experienced ministerial talent, men of ability who would play important roles in French affairs for the next quarter of a century.

A number of Algerian commissioners went on to become premiers of the Fourth Republic—Henri Queuille, Pierre Mendès-France, René Mayer, René Pleven. Others became top diplomats of the postwar period—Hervé Alphand, René Massigli, Henri Bonnet, Maurice Couve de Murville. Jean Monnet returned to Washington to the vital task of negotiating Lend-Lease arrangements and economic support for the French Committee, and then went on to his extraordinary work in directing French economic planning and creating the European Coal and Steel Community, forerunner of the Common Market, in the postwar period.

In Algiers under de Gaulle, a new era began for France, the new generation of national leadership emerged to take over. Vichy was but a husk, an empty spent shell.

But personal news from France for de Gaulle was grievous and painful, as it was for many thousands of Frenchmen. The Gestapo hunted down his relatives and family. His mother had died at her country home in Brittany in August 1940 and thus was spared the misery of the Nazi occupation. His sister, Mary Agnès, was arrested by the Germans and first imprisoned for a year in Fresnes and then transferred to Germany. Her husband, Alfred Cailliau, was sent to Buchenwald at the age of sixty-seven. De Gaulle's older brother, Xavier, with whom he had played war games in his childhood, managed to escape the Gestapo's clutches and was living an underground existence in the town of Nyons in southwest France. But Xavier's daughter, Geneviève, had been seized and sent to Ravensbruck concentration camp. Another brother, Pierre, was under close police surveillance for three years and in 1943 was picked up and sent to a concentration camp at Eisenberg. Pierre's wife and their five children then managed to escape across the Pyrenees and make their way to Morocco. The fourth of the de Gaulle brothers, Jacques, a paralytic polio victim, was first sheltered by a priest and then smuggled to safety over the Swiss frontier. Meanwhile, sons of Jacques, Xavier and Mary Agnès had all gotten out of France and were serving with the Free French forces, as were Madame de Gaulle's brother and sister.

But miraculously, all of de Gaulle's relatives survived the concentration camps and the war.

*

In the run-up to the invasion, one of the most difficult and complex problems for the General was the direction and organization of the Resistance inside France itself. It was a twofold problem. First and foremost, of course, was its effectiveness: supply, discipline and leadership in fighting and harassing the German enemy and in providing effective intelligence for the Allies.

But de Gaulle had a second and perhaps more important preoccupation with the Resistance, and that was political—his determination to bring its disparate, secretive, competing groups under his own control and direction. When he returned to France, he wanted the Resistance behind him—not competing for power against him, not challenging his political authority and rule. It was therefore essential from his point of view that he designate from outside France the supreme leader or leaders of the Resistance, loyal to him personally, and that the various Resistance groups then fall into line behind this leadership. He could not afford, or at least did not want to take a chance, on the movement throwing up its own leader, who might become a political threat or challenge to his authority when he returned to France.

In particular, this meant either bringing the Communists into line with the rest of the Resistance organization, or at least neutralizing them so they could not on their own seize control of the whole apparat. If the Communists could grab control of the Resistance, they would indeed present de Gaulle with precisely the political challenge he was maneuvering to avoid. Hence, on the one hand his overtures and flirtations with Stalin and the Russians were designed to try to ensure that the French Communists would be told by Moscow to accept his leadership. But at the same time he was constantly aware of the dual allegiance of the Communists and the permanent risk of a double-cross if an opportunity for them to seize power ever presented itself.

Finally, running through the whole complex history of the Resistance in France—about which many volumes have been written—was the feud between the Free French and the British, who not only had their own network of agents in France, but who were basically responsible for secret communications, supplies and the movements of all agents in and out of France, particularly in the early stages in 1940, 1941 and 1942. In time the Free French developed their own networks and logistics, but the operational history of the Resistance was overloaded with competition and mistrust between the British SOE and Colonel Passy's Free French Intelligence. It was here that British misgivings about French security were deepest and therefore most damaging to relations. But at the same time, de Gaulle was suspicious and resentful of anything going on in France that was directed by foreigners outside his control. This "secret war" between de Gaulle and the British lurched from one crisis to the next and never was resolved by any full trust and understanding. But at least in the final crunch of the invasion, it was submerged in common battle. The Resistance, British-controlled and French-controlled, rose to do its job, after which the feuding no longer mattered.

De Gaulle's first choice as his designated leader inside France was a remarkable young civil servant who had been the prefect, or departmental administrator, in Chartres at the time of the fall of France. His name was Jean Moulin. Of exceptional intellect, strong personality and organizing ability, he made his way to London via Lisbon at the end of 1941. The British also recognized his potential, and much to de Gaulle's irritation they kept Moulin in Lisbon for several months, trying to recruit him for their own secret SOE. But he determinedly rejected their overtures and would serve only the Free French. De Gaulle then sent him back to France in 1942 with the mission of organizing a "National Council of the Resistance," to which all the groups forming in France, or at least the principal ones, would pledge their loyalty.

In late May 1943 Moulin passed a triumphant secret message to London that his mission had been completed and the Resistance Council had held its first clandestine meeting in Paris. A declaration of "total adherence" was sent to de Gaulle as "the sole leader of French resistance whatever the result of the negotiation" that was then going on with General Giraud. This message, which arrived just as de Gaulle was about to leave for Algiers, was of importance in the power struggle that ensued. It was proof that de Gaulle had the Resistance behind him while Giraud had nothing but a decimated French Army Intelligence Service and the Americans.

Jean Moulin had scored an extraordinary success in moving about the whole country secretly from one group to the next, getting representatives from each to a rendezvous in Paris and finally inducing them to agree on a joint political declaration. But it was tragically short-lived. Less than a month later, on June 21, 1943, Moulin fell into the hands of the Gestapo under circumstances that seemed almost certain to have been the work of a double agent. He had convened a second meeting of the Resistance Council at a doctor's home in a suburb of Lyon, in central France. The Gestapo pounced as the meeting assembled. Moulin possessed extraordinary secrets about the whole Resistance network, but he remained silent and died under appalling Nazi torture.

His death left de Gaulle with a major problem of naming, or indeed finding, a successor with all of the extraordinary qualifications that were demanded. It was quickly followed by other Gestapo strikes that decimated the leadership. In September he chose Émile Bollaert as his leader in France, but Bollaert was picked up on the Breton coast as he was about to embark secretly for London and Algiers and sent to Buchenwald. Next Pierre Brossolette was caught, but managed to jump out of a window at Gestapo headquarters in Paris to die before he could be tortured.

Finally, in March 1944, de Gaulle selected Alexandre Parodi, a senior civil servant who had refused to serve the Vichy government, as his Resistance representative. But unlike Moulin, Parodi was only a member of the Resistance Council, which then decided to elect its own president. Of fifteen council members, at least five were open or secret members of the Communist Party. The presidency went to Georges Bidault, a young and ambitious politician of the center-left Catholic Christian Democrats. Next, under Communist manipulation and the not unreasonable excuse of the danger of holding frequent meetings of the full council, it was agreed to delegate leadership powers to a small "action committee" of only four members, two of whom were Communists.

Thus the Resistance movement seemed to be turning into precisely the kind of power base and power threat to de Gaulle that he had striven to prevent by bringing it under his own control. Bidault was a brave, active and effective choice as head of the National Council of Resistance in those decisive six months of 1944 across the invasion and liberation, but was he in control or was he being controlled? Of course as the hour of liberation neared, the National Council of the Resistance remained fervently loyal to de Gaulle in its declarations, actions and acceptance of his directions. But de Gaulle simply had a delegate on a council whose power levers were precariously divided between Bidault and the Communists. The Resistance was the embodiment of French heroism, but it was becoming something of a genie for de Gaulle that threatened his power at the climactic moment and had to be thrust back into a bottle. Ruthlessly, this is what he prepared to do.

*

When General Eisenhower returned to Washington on January 1, 1944, to prepare for his new Supreme Command in London and take a brief leave, he did his best with Roosevelt to plead the case that a close understanding with de Gaulle and the Committee of National Liberation was the only practical and logical way of dealing with the myriad of military and civil problems inherent in the invasion of France. He got strong support from Secretary of War Stimson and also from John J. McCloy, the astute and efficient lawyer who was the assistant secretary in the War Department in charge of civil affairs and civil administration in liberated territories. Moreover, under the urgings of Stimson and McCloy and the inexorable pressure of the realities, even Hull began to move, if somewhat glacially, in the direction of allowing Eisenhower to work with de Gaulle and the committee with less ambiguity. Roosevelt, however, continued to receive pseudo-intelligence through Admiral Leahy's old Vichy contacts to the effect that de Gaulle was not really strong in France, that civil war would break out unless the way were kept open to create some broadly based postliberation coalition. So the president stonewalled against his senior Cabinet officers and military commander.

In mid-February 1944 there was a brief flurry of anticipation that Roosevelt might be ready to move on the de Gaulle issue when he was scheduled to hand over a new destroyer escort to the French at the Washington Navy Yard. There were hints and expectations that he would use the occasion to say something positive about de Gaulle, and French officials gathered for the ceremony anxious and waiting. But, from microphones in front of him in an open limousine on the quayside, Roosevelt merely said: "On behalf of the American people, I transfer to the Navy of France this warship. . . ." He did not even mention General de Gaulle, the French Committee of National Liberation, or the Fighting French.

When Eisenhower took up his command in London, he had to deal with the realities of the problem whether he had any final directive or not. He began cautiously trying to lay the groundwork for cooperation with the French without authorization, in initial contacts with General Pierre Koenig, hero of Bir-Hakeim, an able officer whom de Gaulle had named as his military representative to Supreme Allied Headquarters and commander designate of the French Forces of the Interior—the Resistance.

In early March Roosevelt finally dictated a draft of a directive to Eisenhower on relations with the French. But Stimson found it so restrictive and sharp in its wording and tone that he felt forced to take the risk of confronting Roosevelt with a rewrite. He recorded that the president "was very nice about it" and said it was only a draft. But he then sat on Stimson's version for another two weeks before finally sending it off to London for British approval.

Its key paragraphs (italics added) read:

> In order to secure the setting up of any civilian administration locally in any part of France *you may consult* with the French Committee of National Liberation and *you may authorize* them in your discretion to select and install the personnel necessary for such administration. You are, however, not limited to dealing exclusively with the said committee for such purposes in case at any time in your best judgment you determine that some other course or conferee is preferable.
>
> Nothing that you do under the powers conferred in the preceding paragraph in connection with the French Committee or with any other group or organization shall constitute a recognition of said committee or group as the government of France *even on a provisional basis.*

There now ensued an extraordinary series of exchanges between London and Washington, with the Foreign Office trying to get the State Department to change the wording of the Eisenhower directive from "may consult" to "should consult" or even "will consult."

Roosevelt, meanwhile, was again laid low by one of his recurring bouts of bronchial trouble and fatigue, and had gone off for three weeks' complete rest at Hobcaw Barony, a private estate in South Carolina owned by Bernard Baruch. At long last the argument over "should" and "may" was referred all the way to the top, and in mid-April, with D-Day barely six weeks away, Churchill finally received a message from Roosevelt himself refusing any retreat from his draft.

This argument was petty enough at this climactic period of war history, but something even more puerile was going on in secret in Washington. Without informing the French, the Americans had decided to issue their own "occupation currency" French francs when they arrived in Normandy. This of course was another affront to de Gaulle, who had long since established a Central Bank that was issuing currency throughout the territories he already controlled. He had therefore expected and prepared to introduce the committee's notes into liberated France as soon as he could get to the banks.

It was bad enough that another clash with the French was thus building up— but Roosevelt was even arguing with his secretary of the treasury, Henry Morgenthau, over the design and wording on the bills. The Treasury had prepared a design that carried on one side the traditional French motto *Liberté, Égalité, Fraternité* and on the other side a French flag with the words *La République Française.* But when Morgenthau and McCloy showed the design to the president, to their astonishment Roosevelt crossed out *La République Française* and insisted that he wanted the notes to carry only *La France*. McCloy and Morgenthau listened incredulously to the president argue: "How do you know what kind of a government you will have when the war is over? Maybe it will be an Empire."

When Morgenthau interjected that putting *La République Française* on currency "isn't going to tie your hands at all," Roosevelt shot back: "Henry, you talk just like the British Foreign Office." Morgenthau replied that he "had never been so insulted in ten years," and in his diary he went on to record:

> The answer always came back that he [FDR] didn't want anything on the money which would indicate what kind of a government it was going to be. I argued and McCloy argued and while the President was in a grand humor he had his "Dutch up" and you couldn't budge him at all. He said, "I've heard all these arguments. De Gaulle is on the wane. . . ." We got off the *"Liberté, Égalité, Fraternité";* he said we couldn't have that. He also asked for "La France" off. So it got back to the flag and nothing else.

About this time, Eisenhower sent the president a message from London in which he suggested in careful and deferential language that his intelligence information from inside France now indicated that there were only two groups—the Gaullists and the Vichyites. But Roosevelt tossed the message aside, telling General Marshall that Eisenhower "evidently believes the newspaper stories that I am anti-de Gaulle, that I hate him and all that. . . . It's utter nonsense; I am perfectly willing to have de Gaulle made President or Emperor or King or anything else so long as the action comes in an untrammeled unforced way from the French people themselves." He went on to question how Eisenhower could know there were only two groups in France and said to Marshall:

> It's awfully easy to be for de Gaulle and to cheer the thought of recognizing that Committee as the provisional government of France, but I have a moral duty that transcends an easy way. It is to see that the people of France have nothing foisted on them by outside powers. It must be a French choice— and that means as far as possible, forty million people. Self-determination is not a word of expediency. It carries with it a very deep principle in human affairs.

And again, to Marshall, the President said he was convinced that General de Gaulle was on the wane.

Meanwhile, in line with FDR's refusal to permit Eisenhower automatically to turn over control of liberated France to de Gaulle and the committee, the War Department began to assemble and train special civil affairs teams for France under its organization known by the dreadful acronym AMGOT—Allied Military Government in Occupied Territories. In other words, liberated France was to be treated the same as Mussolini's Italy and Sicily. American military officers, preferably with a smattering of French, were assembled at Charlottesville, Virginia, and in sixty days they were supposed to master the language and the art and technique of acting like French *préfets*. They were supposed to be prepared to move in behind the Allied armies and take over rear-area civil administration. Fortunately this ultimate insult to Charles de Gaulle, and to the French people, was never carried out. Events and realities after D-Day far outraced Roosevelt's policies and directives.

General de Gaulle, kept largely in the dark in Algiers by the Allies on both the military planning and political preparations for the invasion of Europe, as well as all these extraordinary behind-the-scenes British–American arguments about the French Committee and its role, had already made his own proposals to the Allies for administration in liberated France. They were never even acknowledged.

In a formal memorandum sent from Algiers to London and Washington in September 1943, General de Gaulle had proposed a straightforward arrangement under which his representatives of the French Committee would take over local civilian administration from the Vichy officials in liberated areas, step-by-step behind the advancing armies as battle conditions permitted. Acting on this basis, even though his proposals had not been answered, he then assigned 170 French officers to London to form an "administrative liaison corps." His intention and expectation was that these officers would accompany various divisional and corps headquarters with the Allies to give orders on behalf of the commanders to the local authorities installed by the committee.

This was a logical and clear-cut approach to the problem—but it was blocked by Roosevelt's directive to Eisenhower, since it meant recognizing the committee's governmental powers over French territory. Eisenhower's directive also specified among other provisions that if he made any use of the committee, he should first ensure that "it has no intention of exercising indefinitely in France any powers of government, provisional or otherwise, except to assist in the establishment by democratic methods a government of France according to the free choice of the French people." Eisenhower was manfully struggling to stretch the interpretation of his directive as far as he could in his negotiations on military arrangements with General Koenig, but everything was up in the air and tempers and frustrations were rising.

Moreover, de Gaulle in Algiers had by now learned of the American plan to issue occupation currency (*faux billets* he contemptuously called it, counterfeit or phony notes), and he also learned that the War Department was training AMGOT teams to take over civil administration, as though the French were incapable of looking after their own affairs. Things were heading for a blow-up.

On top of all this, on April 17, 1944, the British abruptly imposed a total security ban on *all* diplomatic cipher communications out of London except their own, American and Russian to protect against any leak of D-Day secrets. De Gaulle was thus cut off from communicating in code with London from Algiers, and he was outraged. He retaliated at once by ordering General Koenig to break off his negotiations with Eisenhower on the logical grounds that Koenig was no longer able to receive instructions and communicate with his superiors.

Churchill, in the second half of April, began frantically trying to arrange a quick meeting in Washington between Roosevelt and de Gaulle in the hope of sorting out the recognition issue, but neither man was ready to play. Numerous back-and-forth Alphonse-and-Gaston messages were passed over whether, if de Gaulle asked for a meeting, the president would invite him, but it came to nothing. Next Churchill considered asking the General to come to London in early May, but de Gaulle would travel only if he could communicate with Algiers, and if he was assured that it would be to settle things with both the Americans and the British. Roosevelt declined to empower anyone to act on his behalf and insisted that once de Gaulle got to London he would be kept there until after D-Day. So this Churchill initiative collapsed also.

By now—mid-May—the prime minister was under extremely heavy pressure from public opinion, the Foreign Office, the War Cabinet, the House of Commons and above all the appalling growing muddle to cut loose from the Americans, force a recognition of de Gaulle's French, or take some action to break the deadlock.

Eden minuted the prime minister on May 8:

> We have to make up our minds whether we are prepared to work out plans with the French Committee on the basis that we would deal with them as the authority in France. There is no other authority with whom we could deal. If the President continues to refuse an agreement, there would be a real estrangement between us and the French Committee. No one except the Russians would gain from this, and the position of our friends in relation to General de Gaulle would be weakened.

Within the War Cabinet, Clement Attlee, the Labour leader, sent a note on the subject to Eden:

> We have a much bigger stake in France than the USA. The French are always difficult and never more so when they owe gratitude to others for their deliverance, as we saw after the last war. I do not think that the President has any real understanding of the French temperament. Nor do I think that his attitude is dictated from a zeal for democracy. This did not prevent him from running Darlan and afterwards Giraud. I am very sensible how much we owe to the President, but this should not lead us to agree to a mistaken policy. We are the only people in this set-up who can speak as Europeans concerned with the future of Europe.

Finally, after a particularly difficult House of Commons debate in which it was plainly clear that the weight of Parliament was heavily against him on the French question, Churchill wearily made one last effort to persuade Roosevelt. On May 27, 1944, he sent an appeal:

> I would earnestly ask you to send over someone of the rank of Stettinius [Edward R. Stettinius, then undersecretary of state] to express your point of view. I see the growth of opinion very powerful here and the feeling that the French should be with us when we liberate France. Naturally there is a great

wave of sentiment for France on account of the bravery and success of French troops in our Italian battle. There is also the sense that they should share in the work which we have in hand. No one will understand them being cold-shouldered.

De Gaulle was about to be invited to come to London on the eve of D-Day, but Roosevelt replied with airy indifference to the explosive problem that his obstinacy was creating: "I am hopeful that your conversation with General de Gaulle will result in inducing him actually to assist in the liberation of France without being imposed by us on the French people as their government. Self-determination really means absence of coercion."

To a last appeal by Churchill three days later that someone from Washington be present, Roosevelt simply sent a curt and irritated reply: "I think I can only repeat the simple fact that I cannot send anyone to represent me at the de Gaulle conversation with you."

On May 27, the French Consultative Assembly in Algiers voted overwhelmingly that the Committee of National Liberation immediately change its status and name in anticipation of the invasion of France, and should henceforth be known as the Provisional Government of the French Republic. The General then sent a long dispatch by courier from Algiers (since he could not use radio code transmission) to his able ambassador in London, Pierre Viénot:

> The forms of recognition of the French government by London and Washington now interest us very little. The moment has passed when agreeable formulas might have been useful. The essential point is our recognition by the French people, and that is now a *fait accompli*. As to the functions and the exercise of French administration in the liberated territory of France, there is no question either. We are the French administration. . . . There is us, or chaos. If the Western Allies bring about chaos in France, it will be their responsibility, and we believe that they will be the losers in the end.

On May 31, 1944, in this tense and difficult atmosphere, with one week to go before the greatest military amphibious operation in all history, Winston Churchill dispatched through his ambassador in Algiers, Duff Cooper, an invitation to de Gaulle to come to London "at the earliest possible moment and in the deepest secrecy." In an effort to improve the atmosphere, he told the General that he would be the guest of His Majesty's Government while in London, and sent his own personal York transport to Algiers for him to make the air journey.

But even Churchill, with all of his experience of confrontation with de Gaulle, could not dream how explosive this climax would be.

> June 2nd: I went to see General de Gaulle in the morning [Duff Cooper wrote in his diary] with an urgent personal appeal from the Prime Minister to come to London, and argued with him for nearly an hour. He said it would be useless for him to go if conversations were not to be tripartite, and

he was merely being sent for because it now happened to suit the convenience of the Allies to put him up to make a speech which would give the French people the false impression that he was in agreement with the British and the Americans which was not the case. . . . I looked in on Massigli [René Massigli, de Gaulle's foreign minister at the time and later ambassador to London] to tell him of my conversation with de Gaulle. He was as usual sensible and also very firm. He said that if de Gaulle refused to go to London, he would resign.

The storm signals were clearly hoisted. Late that night, Cooper saw de Gaulle a second time, to tell him that "as a soldier it is your duty to help the battle which is about to take place," but de Gaulle resumed his arguments about conditions for going to London and demanded the ambassador's word of honor that he would be allowed to communicate with Algiers by radio cipher. Finally, next morning, he sent a formal letter agreeing to go. The party hastily organized and took off in Churchill's York from Algiers that afternoon. They stopped in Rabat for dinner and refueling and flew through the night to land at Northolt Airfield on the outskirts of London at 6 A.M. on June 4, a Sunday. Despite intense security precautions in force everywhere on the eve of D-Day, the British, anxious not to wound General de Gaulle's sensitivities any further, turned out an RAF honor guard and a band to play *La Marseillaise*. A personal letter from Churchill was handed to de Gaulle asking him to come as soon as convenient "to see me in my train, which is close to General Eisenhower's headquarters" and have lunch.

That train, where Churchill had been lodged for several days in wooded countryside north of Southampton, was regarded by his entourage as an unnecessary nuisance. There was one bath and one telephone, and in Anthony Eden's account "Mr. Churchill seemed to be always in the bath and General Ismay always on the telephone." But it appealed to Churchill's sense of romance and drama, and as General de Gaulle drove up to the siding and got out of his car, Churchill walked down along the tracks with his arms outstretched in an expansive mood of a moment of history to be savored and shared. But there was nothing romantic or warm about Charles de Gaulle, who had not come for conversation and hospitality, but to uphold the interests of France. He offered Churchill a stiff handshake in return. They repaired to the train to get down to cases. On the British side with Churchill were Eden, Duff Cooper and Ernest Bevin. General de Gaulle had deliberately left his government ministers in Algiers, and was supported by General Émile Béthouart, his able defense chief of staff, and an aide, Colonel Billote. The South African leader, Field Marshal Jan Christiaan Smuts, and Churchill's personal chief of staff, Sir Hastings Lionel Ismay, were also present.

The discussions began with a certain tense amiability. While de Gaulle had been flying north from Morocco, Eisenhower had taken the decision to postpone D-Day by twenty-four hours because of worsening weather conditions. Churchill opened the talks with one of his sweeping and vivid discourses on impending events, the scope of the D-Day operations, targets and organization. He said he hoped that de Gaulle would be prepared to broadcast to France when the operation got under way, and the General replied that "he would be very glad to do this." So far so good—but not for long.

The table was then prepared for lunch, and the conversation continued in an equitable mood, with de Gaulle offering his praise that "after so many ordeals so valiantly endured, thanks to which she had saved Europe, Great Britain should today be the base for the attack on the continent." All this was gratifying. Then, as they neared desert, Churchill suggested they turn to political matters. De Gaulle said coldly and bluntly: "Political matters? Why?" Churchill replied that he had of course been in touch with Roosevelt, and he knew that although the president did not want to issue a formal invitation, he nevertheless would welcome a visit from General de Gaulle. Just as coldly, de Gaulle said he was in no hurry and that it was better that he be where he was than in Washington. Churchill, with growing impatience, insisted that he was "strongly advising" de Gaulle to seek a meeting with Roosevelt and that he "could live agreeably" with FDR. Eden intervened to remark that if de Gaulle would agree to making arrangements for a visit to Washington, they could begin preliminary talks about political matters at once in London to reach some Anglo-French proposals that he could take with him. Bevin interjected at this point that if de Gaulle did not agree to begin political discussions while he was in London "the Labour Party would resent it."

With that, the fat was in the fire, and de Gaulle turned on Bevin and let loose with all of the pent-up anger and resentments he had been harboring. According to the British official record, he said:

> It is all very well to talk like that. On more than one occasion I have tried to initiate discussions. I have made proposals as long ago as last September but have received no reply. It therefore does not mean anything to say that the British Labour Party would be offended. The battle is about to begin, and I will speak on the wireless. That is all right. But as regards discussing the question of administration, it is clear that the President never wanted to see me, and now suddenly I am being told that I must go and talk to the President. . . .

In his own account of this stormy scene, de Gaulle, whose memory was both formidable and selective, says that he told the British:

> Why do you seem to think that I need to submit my candidacy for the authority of France to Roosevelt? The French Government exists. I have nothing to ask in this respect of the United States of America nor of Great Britain. Once this is recognized, it is still essential for all the Allies that we organize relations between the French administration and the military command. I understand your haste to see the question settled. We ourselves are ready to do so. But where is the American representative? Without him, as you well know, we can decide nothing. Furthermore I notice that Washington and the London Government have made arrangements to do without

such an agreement. I have learned, for example, that despite our warnings, the troops for the landing are provided with so-called French currency issued by foreign powers which the government of the Republic refuses to recognize. . . . I expect that tomorrow General Eisenhower, acting on instructions of the President of United States, and in agreement with you, will proclaim that he is taking France under his own authority. How do you expect us to come to terms on this basis?

After this blast, Churchill went over to the attack, according to the British record:

Mr. Churchill said that whether or not General de Gaulle visited the President was a matter for the General himself to decide. But he must tell him bluntly that if, after every effort had been exhausted, the President was on one side and the French National Committee of Liberation on the other, then he, Mr. Churchill, would almost certainly side with the President and that anyhow no quarrel would ever arise between Britain and the United States on account of France. As regards the civil affairs agreement, he would sum up the view of His Majesty's government as follows: If General de Gaulle wanted us to ask the President to agree to give him the title deeds of France, the answer was "No." If he wanted to ask the President to agree that the Committee of National Liberation was the principal factor with whom we should deal in France, the answer was "Yes." To which de Gaulle replied icily that he quite understood that in case of a disagreement between the United States and France, Great Britain would side with the United States.

De Gaulle's version of this passage with Churchill is rather more colorful than the British record. He quotes Churchill as declaiming:

How do you expect that the British should take a position separate from that of the United States. We are going to liberate Europe, but it is because the Americans are in agreement with us that we do so. There is something you ought to know: Each time we have to choose between Europe and the open sea, we shall always choose the open sea. Each time I have to choose between you and Roosevelt, I shall always choose Roosevelt.

Whatever the detail, the thrust of the two accounts is the same. Moreover, this exchange burned itself into Gaullist litany and legend, and became part of General de Gaulle's political dossier for his eventual veto of British entry into the European Common Market nearly twenty years later, when he deemed that Britain still was not ready to choose Europe in preference to the open sea, an association with a French-led continent as opposed to her links with America.

De Gaulle wrote that "I sensed that this was destined more for his British colleagues than for myself," and that he noted Eden shaking his head in disbelief at Churchill's outburst. Moreover, he says that Bevin then came up to him as the meeting broke up "and declared loudly enough for everyone to hear: 'The Prime Minister has told you that in every case he would side with the President of the United States; I want you to know that he is speaking on his own initiative and not in the name of the British Cabinet.'"

In this charged atmosphere, Churchill nevertheless raised his glass as they got up from the table with a toast "To General de Gaulle, who never accepted defeat." De Gaulle responded: "To England, to Victory, to Europe."

They then descended from the train, and Eden and Churchill drove with de Gaulle and the French officers to Eisenhower's operational headquarters deep in a forest behind Southampton. Eisenhower and his chief of staff, Lieutenant General Walter Bedell Smith, were waiting to take de Gaulle into their map tent for a detailed briefing on the military operation, which at that hour was still hanging in abeyance, awaiting the supreme commander's final orders to move. After going over the weather problem, which had already forced one twenty-four-hour postponement, Eisenhower asked de Gaulle what he thought. De Gaulle says he replied: "I will only tell you that in your place I should not delay. The atmospheric dangers seem to me less than the disadvantages of a delay of several weeks, which would prolong the moral tension of the executants and compromise secrecy."

Next, as de Gaulle prepared to go, Eisenhower handed him a copy of the proclamation he would issue to the people of occupied Europe, the French in particular. De Gaulle says Eisenhower acted "with evident embarrassment" and said that "It's only a draft; I am ready to alter it at your suggestion." De Gaulle, after a quick glance, declared the text "not satisfactory" and said he would let him know what changes he wanted made.

Churchill had expected that de Gaulle would remain with him for the afternoon, touring the invasion camps, but de Gaulle instead offered his thanks, made his farewells and drove back to London with his officers. He returned to the Connaught Hotel and his London headquarters at Carlton Gardens. While Eisenhower worried about the weather, Charles de Gaulle was blowing up another storm. His first concern was the Eisenhower proclamation. Its key passage, offensive to de Gaulle, read:

> Prompt and willing obedience to the orders that I shall issue is essential. Effective civil administration of France must be provided by Frenchmen. All persons must continue in their present duties unless otherwise instructed. Those who have common cause with the enemy and so betrayed their country will be removed. As France is liberated from her oppressors, you yourselves will choose your representatives and the government under which you wish to live.

To General de Gaulle this was "unacceptable" because, as he wrote:

> In short, General Eisenhower appeared to be taking control of our country even though he was merely an Allied general entitled to command troops but not qualified to intervene in the country's government and, moreover,

quite incapable of doing so. In this declaration, not a word was said of the French authority which for years had aroused and directed the war effort of our people and which had done Eisenhower the honor of placing under his command a great part of the French Army.

De Gaulle overreacted in criticizing Eisenhower for demanding in his proclamation "prompt and willing obedience to the orders I shall issue." This, after all, was no more than a statement of the exigencies of military operations, which he was fully entitled to make. More to the point was the fact that the proclamation, tailored to Roosevelt's directive, made no mention whatsoever of what was now the provisional government of the French Republic, and indeed was worded as if no such French authority even existed.

At the Connaught that evening, de Gaulle drafted a memorandum of his objections and amendments to the proclamation, which was sent to Eisenhower next morning, June 5. De Gaulle says that "as I expected, I was told that it was too late, for the proclamation was already printed." In fact, General Béthouart, who was present at the meeting with Eisenhower, wrote that Eisenhower had told de Gaulle at the outset that the document "had been approved by his government and could not be altered." De Gaulle was probably determined to make a record of his disapproval in any case.

Meanwhile, during the night of June 4–5, Eisenhower gave the order to launch the invasion. In the evening, his senior commanders assembled at the naval headquarters near Portsmouth—Admiral Sir Bertram Ramsay, General Sir Bernard L. Montgomery, Air Marshal Sir Arthur Tedder, General Bedell Smith and others. They went over the state of readiness and the latest weather reports, and Ramsay told Eisenhower that Admiral Alan G. Kirk, the American task force commander "must be told within the next half hour" if he was to sail or not; otherwise it would mean a forty-eight-hour postponement. At 9:45 P.M. on Sunday night, Eisenhower told Ramsay and the other officers: "I am quite positive that the order must be given." Ramsay left at once and the code word to sail flashed to the Allied fleets. Then, after midnight, the weather worsened and Eisenhower woke in his trailer at 3:30 A.M. Monday with rain pelting and a wind of near hurricane force. He dressed and drove back to the naval headquarters for a last meeting. Once more they went over the weather reports, up to the minute. There was still time to call the fleet back. But after brief discussion, it was up to Ike. Quietly but clearly he said: "OK. Let's go." The Allies would land in Normandy at dawn Tuesday morning.

At five o'clock that Monday afternoon, Charles Peake, the Foreign Office liaison diplomat with the French, arrived at the Connaught to see de Gaulle. Fortunately his personal relations with de Gaulle had withstood many extremely difficult problems and encounters. Peake was a diplomat of cool nerves, great intelligence and professional ability, and de Gaulle showed unusual admiration for the way in which he withstood the traumas of their troubled affairs. They were about to have their worst twenty-four hours.

Peake informed de Gaulle that the invasion was now under way, and that it had been arranged for heads of state to address their peoples over the BBC next morning after the troops had gotten ashore. First the king of Norway would speak, then the queen of the Netherlands, the grand duchess of Luxembourg and the prime minister of Belgium. After that, Eisenhower's voice would be heard reading the proclamation, and then General de Gaulle would address the French people.

To Peake's consternation, de Gaulle flatly refused to participate in this order of battle. After outlining the "unacceptable" aspects of Eisenhower's proclamation, he told Peake: "I would appear to sanction what he said, and I would be assuming an unsuitable rank in the series of speeches. If I broadcast, it can only be at a different hour outside the series."

Meanwhile, Churchill had returned from the south coast, where he had been seeing troops off for the invasion, and the War Cabinet had gathered in Downing Street. Peake hurried back to the Foreign Office and word was passed to the prime minister that de Gaulle was refusing to broadcast. Unfortunately this was not entirely accurate. Churchill flew into a rage at what he saw as another de Gaulle double-cross, bursting out in fury to the Cabinet about "this obstructionist saboteur."

Then, while the meeting was in progress, further word came that de Gaulle had issued orders to his 170 French liaison officers in Britain that they were not to embark with the Allied forces for France. At this the prime minister became almost speechless with anger. Moreover, he had also by now—understandably and not unreasonably—reinforced himself for the long invasion night with a number of whiskies.

Indeed, sympathy at this moment must be with the great Churchill. For nearly five years his inexhaustible energy had fired the crucible of war. At this moment 23,000 airborne troops were beginning to take off from bases in southern England, and 75,215 British and Canadian soldiers and another 57,000 Americans were crammed into transports, seaborne for the invasion beaches. The memory of the awful slaughter of the First World War—in which he had commanded a front-line infantry regiment at Passchendale—was never far from Churchill's thoughts. He had brought General de Gaulle to London in 1940, and it was not his fault now that there was no agreement with the French on political and military cooperation on the eve of the liberation. Whatever the logic of de Gaulle's position in defending the interests of France, here he was, arguing about broadcasting time and refusing to allow 170 French officers to assist the Allies. To Churchill this was a monstrous and inexcusable betrayal of loyalty among allies. But Charles de Gaulle knew only one loyalty—and that was to his idea of France.

When the Cabinet broke up, de Gaulle's ambassador to London, Pierre Viénot, was summoned to the Foreign Office by Eden at 10 P.M. to be told of the heated discussion and Churchill's anger. Viénot cleared up the question of the broadcast—de Gaulle was not refusing, but was insisting on his own air time separate from the others. But he confirmed that the French liaison officers had been ordered to stay in Britain. Eden requested that the ambassador see his chief at once to do all he could to get the decision reversed.

Viénot then drove to the Connaught at 11:30 P.M. to see de Gaulle. When he recounted his discussion with Eden, de Gaulle let loose with a violent diatribe against Churchill and the British, and turned on his poor ambassador as well with what Viénot said was "the worst dressing-down in my whole life." He utterly refused to change his orders to his liaison officers. Without political recognition, they would not participate.

At 1 A.M. Viénot returned to report this to Eden, and found Churchill also sitting in Eden's office. He then had to go through a second dressing-down as Churchill "exploded, roared, bellowed in incoherent rage." When that was finally over, the unfortunate Frenchman made his way back to the Connaught at 3 A.M., and to his great relief found that de Gaulle had calmed down and regained his habitual icy cool.

Meanwhile, Churchill strode back across to No. 10 Downing Street from the Foreign Office and in his furious mood sent for Desmond Morton, who had frequently dealt with the Free French in the past. He told Morton: "Go and tell Bedell Smith to put de Gaulle in a plane and send him back to Algiers—in chains if necessary. He must not be allowed to re-enter France." The prime minister then dictated a brutal letter to de Gaulle ordering him to leave England immediately, which Morton was instructed to deliver in person.

Morton, however, prudently contacted Eden to tell him what the prime minister was doing. So around four-thirty in the morning, Eden got Churchill on the telephone in one of the most bizarre secret episodes of the war. By what means the foreign secretary managed to calm down the prime minister at that hour, no one knows. But as the invasion force arrived off the Normandy beaches, Churchill's order to transport General de Gaulle back to Algiers "in chains if necessary" was forgotten, and the letter in Desmond Morton's possession was retrieved by Eden and burned.

"We've had a crazy night," Eden remarked with understatement a few hours later when he saw Robert Bruce Lockhart, who supervised BBC propaganda operations. And it was far from over with General de Gaulle.

At 9 A.M., after it was clear that the first lodgings on the beaches had been successful, the scheduled broadcasts to occupied Europe began, and General Eisenhower's voice was heard with that "unsatisfactory" proclamation to the French people. The Allies had achieved total surprise and were well on their way to a striking military success. At a cost of about 7,000 casualties, more than 156,000 Allied soldiers had breached Hitler's Atlantic Wall by the time the first D-Day phase was over.

But where, the French were no doubt wondering, was General de Gaulle?

The tireless Charles Peake arrived at the Connaught on Tuesday morning and de Gaulle said that he would record a broadcast to France at noon. After the stormy night, neither Peake nor Viénot dared ask him if he would submit a script in advance—yet the Foreign Office was naturally worried that he might burst out with some denunciation of Britain and America in the hour of the start of liberation. All they could do was await the recording and then kill it if de Gaulle

said something unacceptable. In the event, de Gaulle rose to the occasion eloquently, as he almost always did when he knew he had to. But his message was
skillfully worded to supersede what Eisenhower said in his proclamation (italics
added):

> The decisive battle has begun. . . . For the sons of France, whoever they may
> be, wherever they may be, the simple and sacred duty is to fight the enemy
> with all available means. The directives *issued by the French Government and by
> the French leaders who have been delegated to issue them* must be followed to the
> letter. . . . Behind the heavy clouds of our blood and our tears, the sunshine
> of our greatness is presently reappearing. . . .

The broadcast went out over the BBC at six o'clock on D-Day evening.
Meanwhile, Duff Cooper was instructed by the Foreign Office to try his persuasion on de Gaulle over the question of the liaison officers.

> I saw de Gaulle at 3 o'clock [he wrote in his diary]. I pointed out to him that
> in his own interest he ought to agree to the officers going, as otherwise it
> would be said of him that he had refused to help us in the battle itself. He
> would not accept the logic of this argument, but eventually said that to
> please *me* he would agree to send at least some of the officers, if not all.

That D-Day night, Eden had another long argument with Churchill lasting
several hours, telling the prime minister *ad infinitum:* "We must either break with
de Gaulle—which means breaking with France—or conclude an agreement with
him. There is no middle course. We must tell the President that de Gaulle must be
supported."

*

Despite de Gaulle's obstinate political tactics and behavior with his Allies on
the eve of D-Day, there was little doubt where feelings at the Foreign Office lay in
the crisis. Eden and the career diplomats who backed him up and advised him—
the permanent undersecretary, Sir Alexander Cadogan, Sir Oliver Harvey, Charles
Peake, Duff Cooper—all had been struggling for months to get recognition and
an agreement with de Gaulle's French Committee, and if this simple diplomatic
decision had been taken then, the D-Day crisis would have been averted. They
had argued fruitlessly with the State Department about the political reading of the
French situation, and Eden had spent endless hours trying to pry Churchill away
from his attitude of blind unity behind FDR, against de Gaulle. The British
diplomats had seen the crisis building up, and as far as they were concerned it was
not the obstinacy of de Gaulle but the obstinacy of Roosevelt and Hull that had
landed everyone in this D-Day mess. De Gaulle's behavior, unfortunately, was no
help at all to his best friends in Britain, but seldom if ever did the General concern
himself about the reactions of others when he had determined on a course of
action. Nevertheless, Eden and his team were in no doubt that their first diplomatic task was to pick up the pieces and sort out a solution and an agreement with

de Gaulle as rapidly as they possibly could. Moreover, since the Americans were at that point deliberately boycotting the political crisis, Eden had the field temporarily to himself, along with the stimulating certainty that he was right and the Americans wrong. His first move was to turn Churchill's wrath of the moment to his favor. He persuaded the prime minister to let him handle de Gaulle for the next few weeks and transfer to the Foreign Office the sole responsibility for trying to work out an agreement with the French. Churchill was certainly in no mood for such a negotiation.

Meanwhile, Roosevelt, in a post D-Day mood of generosity that success often brings, and in response to all those urgings from Churchill, suddenly sent an unambiguous invitation to de Gaulle to visit Washington either later in June or between July 6 and July 14. This sudden invitation, however, did not in the least reflect any basic change of attitude on the part of Roosevelt on the issue of recognition and dealings with the provisional government on administrative arrangements in France, as soon became clear. The invitation was primarily a reflection of the fact that Roosevelt, like Churchill, was feeling the heat of public opinion in opposition to his attitude toward de Gaulle and the French. Nevertheless, the invitation had finally come and it did give Eden and the British some additional room for maneuver with de Gaulle.

At a dinner on June 7, Eden, accompanied by Cooper and Peake, had a long and at times heated discussion with de Gaulle and his advisers as they sought to persuade the General to enter into negotiations with them alone on a civil affairs arrangement in France. De Gaulle stonily argued that "it was a waste of time and would be a humiliation for both our countries to be obliged after coming to an agreement to go and ask the United States for their kind approval." Eden countered that "we are asking you to work with us so that the civil administration of France can be set up." In the end, de Gaulle rather grudgingly authorized Ambassador Viénot to start talks with the British, which put things at a lower diplomatic level but at least was a start.

The fact was that de Gaulle had already decided in his own mind to resolve the matter of civil administration in France on his own terms, and until that was achieved, he was less interested in seeking a negotiated arrangement with Britain and the United States. He was stalling for time. Meanwhile, much of the time at the dinner was taken up with de Gaulle condemning the Allies for introducing *faux billets* occupation currency into France.

In fact, the *faux billets* were already creating problems between Britain and the United States. Who would back the currency? Roosevelt had painted himself into a corner. If de Gaulle's provisional government were asked to back the currency, this inevitably would mean at least a de facto recognition, but as Churchill cabled the President: "The only alternative is to guarantee the money ourselves." Roosevelt once more airily refused to be forced or maneuvered into any gesture toward de Gaulle, and cabled back to Churchill on June 12:

> I suggest we tell de Gaulle that if the French people will not accept the
> invasion currency, Eisenhower be authorized to use UK Military Authority

money and yellow-seal dollars [a special issue for wartime use overseas]. Thus, if de Gaulle encourages the French to refuse invasion money, he will be responsible for the certain depreciation of the franc which will follow. I do not favor any effort to press de Gaulle for a statement in support of the new currency, but if he wants to issue something on his own individual responsibility, he can put his signature on any currency statement he desires, even to that of the King of Siam.

But de Gaulle had no intention of giving any support whatsoever to the *faux billets,* and, as in the case of establishing his civil affairs authority in France, he already had his own plans and tactics for imposing his power.

On June 10 in London, he "went public" with a press conference at which he confirmed that he was refusing to allow most of his French liaison officers to proceed to various Allied headquarters in France because there was no Allied recognition of the provisional government and "we do not intend to contribute to the usurpation" of civil authority in France by anyone else. He also announced that he would be happy to accept the invitation he had received from the president of the United States to visit Washington.

General Marshall and Admiral King arrived in London three days after D-Day to get a firsthand view of how the invasion was going. From Eisenhower's political advisers—William Phillips of the State Department and Brigadier General Julius Holmes—they got a forceful briefing about the mess that was rapidly developing with the French as a result of the directive under which they were having to operate. These conclusions were put in memorandum form, which Marshall cabled back to Stimson and the president. When Stimson and McCloy read Marshall's message, they decided that they had to persuade the president to grant de Gaulle some degree of recognition, as Stimson recounted in his diary for June 14, 1944:

> I telephoned the President. He had already received the telegram from Marshall but gave it scant attention. He was adamant in his refusal to depart from his position. I patiently went over the different steps in a talk which lasted nearly an hour, but I made very little advance. . . . The President believes that de Gaulle will crumble and that the British supporters of de Gaulle will be confounded by the progress of events. This is contrary to everything I hear. I think de Gaulle is gaining strength daily as the invasion goes on, and that is to be expected. He has become the symbol of deliverance to the French people. The President thinks that other parties will spring up as the liberation goes on, and that de Gaulle will become a very little figure. He said that he already knew of some such parties. . . .

It is all but unbelievable that on the day General de Gaulle landed in Normandy, the president of the United States was clinging to this view of the French situation, against all of the secret intelligence and all of the public evidence and political advice of the men to whom he had entrusted responsibility for the conduct and fighting of the war. There can be no rationale or explanation of what amounted to a personal obsession.

In London, as de Gaulle awaited the moment of his return at last to French soil in the second week of June, he was personally lobbying his case with growing success. The myriad of other European governments-in-exile lodged in London were themselves both bewildered and fed up with the incomprehensible mish-mash being made of relations with the French. De Gaulle saw many of these leaders personally, and one after another they began announcing their official formal recognition of the provisional government of the French Republic, despite British urgings that they "not break ranks with us and the United States." Between June 8 and June 20, the French government was recognized by Czecho-slovakia, Poland, Belgium, Luxembourg, Yugoslavia and Norway. The Dutch gave their full recognition to the Committee of National Liberation—a step ahead of Roosevelt, but held back from governmental recognition in the apparent hope that this would get them American support for the return of Indonesia to Dutch colonial rule.

It was now agreed with the British and Supreme Allied Command that General de Gaulle would cross the Channel on June 14. (De Gaulle in his Memoirs gives the date incorrectly as June 13.) On the evening of the thirteenth, Anthony Eden gave a dinner in de Gaulle's honor at the Foreign Office. Churchill had not seen de Gaulle since their stormy luncheon on the train, and refused to attend. But Eden, striving ceaselessly to ease the tensions and resolve problems still ahead, took General Béthouart aside to suggest that "if General de Gaulle were to send a telegram of greetings and thanks to the Prime Minister tomorrow during his visit to France it would dispel the present misunderstandings." Béthouart said that it was more than a matter of misunderstanding—"it was a question of capital importance"—but he would try. The long-suffering Viénot was then enlisted to put it up to de Gaulle. The two retired to a corner of the room, and after a brief exchange everybody heard de Gaulle utter a loud, harsh *"Non!"*

As the dinner progressed, a letter was delivered to Eden. According to de Gaulle's account, it was from Churchill, "raising last-minute objections to my plan" to visit the beaches next day. But, he says, "Mr. Eden, having consulted his colleagues around the table, particularly Clement Attlee, informed me that the whole Cabinet was standing by the arrangements."

At 5 A.M. on the morning of June 14, General de Gaulle left the Connaught by car with a party of officers and civilian aides to drive to Portsmouth harbor. There the French destroyer *La Combattante* was waiting. He was piped aboard with Navy honors, and shortly before 10 A.M. they sailed for a high-speed dash across the Channel to the beaches of Normandy.

TWELVE

LIBERATION

There was a chill wind and a choppy sea in the English Channel as *La Combattante* passed the Isle of Wight and headed for open water. General de Gaulle wore his dark-brown Army greatcoat with the two stars of his rank on the sleeves. The crossing took four hours at a high-speed zigzag, as RAF and US fighter planes swept the skies above on covering patrol. De Gaulle spent the entire voyage on deck, scanning the horizon with his binoculars for his first glimpse of France, wrapped in deep silence, keeping his emotions and thoughts to himself. That silence engulfed all the others of his party too, until at one point Ambassador Viénot approached him to remark that they were returning to France on the fourth anniversary of the entry of the German Army into Paris, June 14, 1940. De Gaulle grunted curtly without taking his eyes off the horizon: "Well, they were wrong, it was an error. . . ." And the silence resumed.

Accompanying de Gaulle were Béthouart, his defense chief of staff; General Pierre Koenig, commander of the French Forces of the Interior; Admiral Thierry d'Argenlieu, who had fought with de Gaulle at Dakar; Colonel Henri de Boislambert, who had been captured at Dakar and escaped from a French prison to rejoin the Free French; Commandant Pierre Laroque; the faithful Geoffroy de Courcel, now an infantry captain; and three civilians, Chef de Cabinet Gaston Palewski; Ambassador Viénot; and last but not least, François Coulet. The day before, Coulet had been summoned by de Gaulle to be told that he would be left behind in France to become the first Gaullist administrative official to take over a liberated region of metropolitan France. Whatever Roosevelt's directive to Eisenhower, whatever the diddling of the Allies over recognition and political agreement, Charles de Gaulle was not going to wait or falter at this turning point in French history.

Detailed administrative plans for the liberation had long been worked out in Algiers by the full Committee of National Liberation. There were two key elements. First, France was divided up into ten regions, and as each of these regions was freed, a Gaullist *commissaire régional de la République* would be named with sweeping powers of law and order and the purging of the civil administration. These all-powerful commissioners would be responsible directly to General de Gaulle. The second element in the takeover plan was a secret list of Gaullist loyalists inside France who would be the replacements for the Vichy *préfets, sous-préfets,* police chiefs, judges, mayors, teachers, etc. The list had been drawn up by Michel Debré, who was a Gaullist agent while working for the Vichy regime in a key civil service position on the Conseil d'État. From this vantage point he had been able to assess the collaborationist leanings of the upper-bracket civil servants and establish who would be loyal and worthy of Gaullist trust. Later, Debré would also play a decisive role in the birth of de Gaulle's Fifth Republic. It was remarkable that he survived the Nazi occupation, for not only was he a Gaullist secret agent; his father was a rabbi, although he himself had given up the Jewish religion.

Coulet had already received several months "on-the-job training" in the liberation of Corsica, where he had been installed as secretary general at the Préfecture of the island soon after it fell to the Free French in October 1943. He thus knew firsthand the kind of problems he would face in dealing with law and order, purging collaborationists and organizing food supplies and all the other challenges and dangers when one army was in retreat, another advancing, and no central government was yet in charge.

Of course de Gaulle had said nothing to the British or anyone else in London about his plans when he landed in France. This was strictly a French internal matter, no business of the Allies in his view. Also loaded on the deck of *La Combattante* was a trunk containing 25 million French francs issued under the authority of the provisional government of France—General de Gaulle's answer to the *faux billets* that the Americans had printed and were already issuing in the liberated beachhead towns. Coulet sat on the trunk most of the voyage across the Channel.

The destroyer dropped anchor a few hundred yards from the shore at about 2 P.M., with a moderate sea-swell running. They rolled at anchor, waiting for a small landing craft to pull alongside, and then in two trips the French party (and the money trunk) put ashore at the village of Courseulles, where the Canadian 3rd Division had landed on D-Day with the British forces under Montgomery. An honor guard was drawn up for de Gaulle's brief inspection, and a Canadian major and a British naval commander were there to welcome the General to France. There was an invitation from Montgomery to lunch at his trailer headquarters a few miles away, but de Gaulle said that a visit would be enough—"We have not come to France to have lunch with Montgomery." With the Canadian major at the wheel of a jeep, he then drove off to see Montgomery with General Béthouart and Ambassador Viénot. They arrived shortly before two thirty in the afternoon.

Meanwhile, the Royal Navy commander took Admiral d'Argenlieu, General Koenig and Colonel Boislambert to the town of Bayeux, about three miles inland to the south, one of the ancient cradles of French civilization with its medieval cathedral and its famous tapestry of the Norman invasion of England in 1066 and the Battle of Hastings, victory of William the Conqueror. Bayeux was now the

seat of a sous-préfecture, a town of about 8,000 inhabitants, the largest community yet liberated by the Allied armies on June 14, 1944.

General Montgomery, full of his bouncy self-confidence, greeted de Gaulle and
took him into his famous trailer with Rommel's picture on the wall next to one of
Eisenhower. Then he gave a rapid staccato briefing on the military situation on the
British front, where he had run into heavy German opposition south of Bayeux on
the approaches to the city of Caen. Next he asked if de Gaulle would say a few
words to his staff, which the General did with evident pleasure. But he kept his
remarks minimal, anxious to be off for his first contact with the French people.

Shaking hands and making his farewell to Montgomery, he said with almost
offhanded casualness: "I have brought with me Commandant Coulet, who will be
concerned with the administration in Bayeux." (Although Coulet was a civilian, he
also held military rank.)

Montgomery, with other things far more pressing on his mind, merely nodded,
paying scant attention to de Gaulle's remark. Either the significance of what de
Gaulle was about to do escaped Montgomery or he did not care. He refused to
concern himself with politics—that was Eisenhower's business—and it was probably a matter of indifference to Montgomery who was in charge of civil affairs in
Bayeux as long as he cooperated with the Allies. But what de Gaulle was about to
do ran completely counter to Roosevelt's directive to Eisenhower. Civil administrators in liberated France were supposed to be named by the supreme commander. General de Gaulle was to be consulted if it was felt to be necessary.
Whether Monty was aware of it or not, de Gaulle was going to plant his own large
Trojan horse in the Allied camp. De Gaulle also had not forgotten Eisenhower's
secret pledge at their last meeting in Algiers that "whatever apparent attitudes are
imposed upon me, I will recognize no other French power in France than your
own in the political sphere." Nevertheless, how would Eisenhower react to
another surprise de Gaulle *fait accompli?*

De Gaulle's jeep now headed for Bayeux. A remarkable photo taken of him at
that hour caught him with a cigaret sticking straight out of the corner of his
mouth, his jaw thrust forward defiantly, but his eyes staring out from deep dark
circles of fatigue, with a distant searching look of pain and sadness, no joy or
happiness or excitement in his face at all.

On the outskirts of Bayeux, his jeep overtook two gendarmes on bicycles, and
de Gaulle stopped and called them over. The two policemen saluted smartly, not
having a clue who the French officer was.

"I am General de Gaulle," he began, at which the policemen almost dropped
their bicycles. "My friends, I am going to ask you to do me a service. I am on my
way to Bayeux. Would you be kind enough to go there and tell them I'm coming,
so that I take no one unawares? We shall not move from here for a quarter of an
hour."

The policemen saluted again and hastily pedaled away. General de Gaulle had
betrayed a certain apprehension at his reception in Bayeux, but his advance party
was at work. D'Argenlieu, Koenig and the others had now been joined by Coulet
with his trunk of money and also by Maurice Schumann, the Free French spokes-

man in London and BBC broadcaster to France who had been sent over by the British as a war correspondent. Armed with a bullhorn, Schumann had toured the town to announce that General de Gaulle would soon appear in the main square, the Place du Château, and practically the whole town flocked in that direction. Accordingly, when de Gaulle's jeep drove into Bayeux, it looked as if his fears for his reception might be realized, for the streets were practically deserted. He had told his officers that he would meet them at the *Préfecture* and they were waiting as his jeep drove up, while the people waited in the Place du Château.

As always with General de Gaulle, first the affairs of state, then the people.

He strode through the gates and on the steps waiting to greet him was the *sous-préfet*, Pierre Rochat, who had been appointed by the Vichy government and had served in the post for nearly four years. De Gaulle nevertheless shook him by the hand and they mounted the steps into a large reception room. But a *champagne d'honneur* offered by the *sous-préfet* was declined. It was scarcely a moment to exchange toasts. Instead, in a meeting lasting about a quarter of an hour, Rochat was questioned by de Gaulle with distant courtesy about matters such as bomb damage, food stocks, currency reserves and civilian morale. Under these tense and awkward circumstances, Rochet came out of it well. He was one of those unfortunate "soft collaborationists" in which France abounded, a civil servant who had followed orders, gotten on well enough with the Germans, and was now getting on with the Allies. But as the party left the room, Boislambert noticed a portrait of Marshal Pétain on the wall. He gestured imperiously to Rochat, who summoned the doorkeeper, and with General de Gaulle watching, the two of them climbed up on chairs to pull the frame from the wall. The transition had begun.

In the meantime, a number of local notables had been hastily summoned to the Préfecture to be introduced to de Gaulle and receive perfunctory handshakes. It was a ceremony that was to be repeated endlessly, countless times across France for the next twenty-five years to the end of de Gaulle's life. This over, he then headed for the Place du Château.

Now at last the enthusiasm burst, cheers mingled with tears, flowers thrown, mothers holding out their children, Frenchmen straining to touch him. De Gaulle circled through the little square, containing his emotions simply by mumbling repeatedly, *"Bonjour . . . comment ça va. . . . Bonjour . . . comment ça va. . . ."* Finally he mounted an improvised platform with American, French and British flags as a backdrop and the flag of the Cross of Lorraine hanging from tree branches overhead.

He had discarded his greatcoat in the warming afternoon sunshine and he put down his *képi* and faced the crowd bareheaded. His first address to Frenchmen on French soil was brief, almost perfunctory:

> We are all moved to find ourselves together again in one of the first Metropolitan French towns to be liberated; but it is no moment to talk of emotion. What the country expects of you, here behind the front, is to continue the fight today as you have never ceased from fighting since the beginning of the war, and since June 1940. Our cry now, as always, is a war-

cry, because the path of war is also the road to liberty and honor. This is the voice of the Mother Country. I promise you that we shall continue to fight till sovereignty is re-established over every inch of our soil. No one shall prevent our doing that. We shall fight beside the Allies, with the Allies, as an ally. And the victory we shall win will be the victory of liberty and the victory of France.

He then stretched his arms above his head in an enormous V-sign and broke into a loud, croaking rendition of *La Marseillaise* with uncertain pitch but high emotion, in which the whole town joined. To have asserted to these placid Norman *citoyens* that "you have never ceased from fighting since the beginning of the war" would, under other circumstances, have provoked guffaws of laughter. But General de Gaulle was in the process of creating a national legend, the legend of heroic resistance of all the people, to be a kind of cloak of honor for the French to put on to cover up, particularly from themselves, the bitter truth with which they had been living for four years of occupation. And by adopting the legend, endorsing the legend, coming to believe in the legend, Frenchmen whatever their records thus rallied perforce to General de Gaulle.

When he descended from the little platform, the crowd broke and thronged around the jeeps, reaching to grasp his hand, until finally he stood up and said a few words more. Then at last the police cleared the way for the vehicles to head back to the beaches.

On the way, Maurice Schumann had preceded him to pass the news of his coming in the coastal villages of Isigny and Grandchamp, where the scene was then repeated—the brief address, the praise for ceaseless fighting, the singing of *La Marseillaise*. By about 6:30 P.M. de Gaulle was at the beach waiting for a landing craft to ferry him out to *La Combattante*. In a final handshake with François Coulet, he said: "You're staying—don't act on a political basis, the population doesn't want it." He had spent only a little over four hours on French soil, but he was satisfied that the tide was now running to carry him all the way to Paris.

*

Next morning, as de Gaulle began tidying up affairs at his London headquarters for a prompt return to Algiers, Coulet arrived at the Bayeux Préfecture to find Pierre Rochat also there and working as if nothing had happened. He had appointed one of the townspeople to requisition beds and bedding for a supplementary hospital, and a butcher to supply meat to a village near Bayeux and someone else to look into the problem of batteries and tires for whatever trucks there were left in the town. But Coulet, meanwhile ordered the immediate printing and distribution of the first poster proclamation of the provisional government of General de Gaulle:

> *To the Liberated Population:* The Provisional Government of the French Republic has placed upon me the duty of representing it and exercising the rights of French sovereignty in the liberated territories of the Rouen region. . . . The war continues. The Battle of France is being fought among us.

Behind the lines, the combatants of the interior are harassing the enemy without cease and with an ardor and courage that are the admiration of the world. . . . To our British and American friends you owe every assistance you can render, fraternally united as we are in the same battle and for the same ideals. All this General de Gaulle told you yesterday as he passed through our liberated towns and villages. As one man we shall go forward along the path he has traced for us.

That afternoon Coulet summoned a young landowner who farmed near Bayeux, Raymond Triboulet, and appointed him to be *sous-préfet* replacing Rochat. Triboulet's credentials as a *résistant* had been fully established as a result of his contacts with two of the senior civil servants who were on the "secret list" prepared by Michel Debré. This process of transfer of power from Vichy to de Gaulle that began in Bayeux was then repeated in town after town across France as the Allied armies rolled eastward. Meanwhile, Rochat simply retired to his country home, his name in the history books only because he was the first *préfet* greeted and the first to be ousted by de Gaulle in France.

Four days later, however, word filtered up to the senior echelons of the civil affairs section of the British Army that a new *sous-préfet* had taken over in Bayeux on the authority of someone calling himself a regional commissioner for the provisional government. No one seemed to know how either one of them had got there. Coulet was told to prepare for a visit from General Lewis and several other officers of the British Civil Affairs staff.

When they arrived, Lewis got down to cases in an abrupt no-nonsense tone, declaring that he wanted order maintained and did not intend to have to deal with French civil administration, but "we know you are here without the agreement of our government and we are prepared to accept your presence only on a provisional basis." To this, Coulet replied that "this war is ours too," and under his authority, order was being maintained and a service thus rendered to the Allied cause. He then rose behind his desk, banged his fist and said in English: "As for my presence here, it has nothing to do with you. I have received the order to be here from General de Gaulle's government, and I shall leave only on his orders."

That ended it, and as the British officers left, one was heard to remark that he was glad the regional commissioner spoke good English.

When the Allies landed in Normandy, contrary to expectations they found a land quite literally overflowing with milk and honey. The dairy farmers, the beekeepers, the cheesemakers of the region—one of the richest agricultural areas of France—had gone right on producing among the German bivouaks and gun emplacements and tank traps. But the abundance of their farms had been bottled up, so to speak, right in Normandy because of the total disruption of the French railway system and the absence of any trucks or gasoline to cart the surpluses away to their ration-starved countrymen. There was no problem of food in Normandy—only a problem of distribution. It had been this way in the region pretty much throughout the occupation.

By circumstance and by local temperament, Normandy had not exactly been seething with trouble for the German occupiers. Indeed, one of Coulet's early problems was the demand from the French in London and the French in Algiers to produce more evidence of popular resistance and to produce a more spectacular purge of collaborationists. The Normans almost to a man seemed to fall between the two stools, in the mushy category of nonresistant soft collaborationists, deserving of neither medals nor punishment. Every farm now broke out its secret cache of Calvados to celebrate the departure of the Germans and drink with the British and Americans, and life went on.

Coulet's first problem with the Allies involved those *faux billets* occupation francs that the American and the British brought with them. On June 16, as soon as he had proclaimed his powers, he had blocked all bank accounts in Bayeux and other towns under his nominal control. But his "war chest" of 25 million French francs of the provisional government took time to issue, and meanwhile the *faux billets* were circulating in increasing numbers and being gobbled up by the canny Normans.

Having lived under one occupation for four years and now under the temporary changeover of another, they sensed pretty quickly that those franc notes they were being handed, designed by President Roosevelt and not even bearing the *"La République Française"* let alone *"Liberté, Égalité, Fraternité,"* were not likely to be worth their face value or last very long. Accordingly, they were accepting them as they were told to by the Allies—but they were then rushing straight to the tax office to use the *faux billets* to pay their taxes *in advance!* Flabbergasted tax officials confronted Coulet with the question, what do we do with this money, who is backing it anyway? Coulet at once sought a meeting between Allied Civil Affairs officers and French finance agents, which took place on June 25. After much acrimonious discussion, a compromise was finally agreed on, under which Coulet would instruct his tax collectors to go on accepting the *faux billets,* but the Allies would then exchange them at equal value for real French francs issued by the French National Committee's embryo Central Bank, of which the Allies held a reserve in London. In other words, it was the beginning of the phasing-out of Roosevelt's occupation currency and its replacement by the notes backed by the provisional government—another clear victory for recognition for General de Gaulle.

Meanwhile, on June 24, the port of Cherbourg was taken by the Americans, the largest city to be liberated so far, and Coulet at once transferred his headquarters there from Bayeux. This time he was officially welcomed on his arrival by an American Army colonel, head of the Civil Affairs Section. He was escorted by the Americans around the city as a demonstration of their backing and given formal assurances that "the Allies have no intention of interfering in French affairs and will make official contact with the population only through the intermediary of the French administration."

Less than two weeks after landing in France with General de Gaulle, Coulet had thus consolidated Gaullist civil administration throughout the liberated areas of Normandy and the Cotentin Peninsula. He proceeded vigorously to dissolve municipal councils, find new mayors, purge officials of the Préfectures, replace

magistrates, arrest collaborationists, install new company managers where necessary in private industry and organize public services and logistic support to assist
the Allies. Finally, he used the extraordinary powers conferred on him by Gaullist
authority to promulgate a decree suspending a long list of laws of the Vichy
government, including in particular "the constitutional law of July 10, 1940, and
all other constitutional acts and decrees showing discrimination against Jews and
all decrees relating to secret societies [the Masonic Order was one] and all laws
giving jurisdiction to special courts. . . ." In contrast to the long political fumbling
that went on in North Africa in the Darlan–Giraud period over wiping the Vichy
statute books clean, this time action came promptly and decisively. Recognized or
not, the provisional government of General de Gaulle had arrived in France and
was firmly in control.

*

On June 26, the same day that François Coulet established himself as regional
commissioner in Cherbourg, de Gaulle telegraphed an acceptance of Roosevelt's
invitation to visit Washington.

> The indications of French unity were now too clear for anyone to ignore [de
> Gaulle wrote in his Memoirs]. The President of the United States at last
> acknowledged as much. I had no favors to ask and I would undertake no
> negotiations. The conversations would have no other object than inquiry
> into world-wide problems of interest to both countries. If, afterwards, the
> American Government wanted to open negotiations with the French Gov-
> ernment about relations between the Allied armies and our administration,
> it could do so, like the British government, through normal diplomatic
> channels. . . .

Roosevelt sent a special plane to Algiers for de Gaulle's flight to Washington on
July 6. The timing of the visit, as far as de Gaulle was concerned, was governed
primarily by the military outlook. He was fully aware that August would be the
climactic month of the campaign in France, and was therefore anxious to get the
visit out of the way rather than invent any further delays, which he certainly was
capable of doing. American and British forces were massing for the breakout from
Normandy, and Allied landings in southern France were due to take place in mid-
August. These were of great importance to de Gaulle because it would bring the
French Army back to France from the Italian front. It was vital for him from every
standpoint—military, political, strategic, internal security—to have as many
French divisions as possible on French soil under his ultimate orders and control.
Since the weeks ahead would be crucial, he needed to get the inevitable visit to
Roosevelt behind him.

From Roosevelt's standpoint, there was a different consideration in the timing,
and that was political. The Democratic Party would be holding its nominating
convention for the 1944 presidential election the last week of July. Roosevelt was
again playing one of those adroit charades that make him the most fascinating
political president in American history, but it was abundantly clear that he was not

about to abandon the role of commander in chief in the middle of the war, and that he would be a candidate for a fourth presidential term. The major criticism he was encountering at this time over his war leadership was his handling of French affairs and General de Gaulle. Almost across the board—Democrats and Republicans, editorial writers, columnists and front-line reporting from liberated France—he was under heavy fire for his stubborn refusal to recognize the realities of the French situation. By inviting de Gaulle to Washington, Roosevelt intended to defuse this criticism *politically,* but he was not about to change his policies or change his mind about de Gaulle.

For the trip to Washington, de Gaulle adopted an attitude and personal approach that was the reverse of his stormy trip to London on the eve of D-Day. There would be no confrontation with Roosevelt as there had been with Churchill. In Washington, he would treat the matter of diplomatic recognition with aloofness and not get into any high-level arguments. He would ask for nothing, except to place more French divisions in the Allied front lines, which would mean more American arms and equipment. This matched Roosevelt's mood and approach to their meetings, since he did not want to be pressed and forced again to rebuff de Gaulle openly. All that Roosevelt wanted out of the visit was to be able to say, as he did in a White House toast to General de Gaulle:

> There are all kinds of problems, most of them what might be called technical, or detailed, or local, which can be resolved by the meeting of the leaders—the old idea that if you get around the table with a man you can solve anything. There are no great problems between the French and the Americans, or between General de Gaulle and myself. They are going to work out all right, if they will just leave a few of us alone to sit around the table.

This, to put it mildly, was soft-soap for Roosevelt's critics, and certainly no reflection of the realities of the meeting. Things went well, superficially, because the two men avoided problems and issues, not because they sat down around a table and discussed them with the aim of coming to understandings. Nevertheless, de Gaulle performed with such impressive intelligence and evident qualities of leadership that even crusty old Admiral Leahy, protagonist of Vichy, admitted that he was "more agreeable in manner and appearance than I had expected," while Cordell Hull wrote: "He went out of his way to make himself agreeable to the President, to me and to other members of the government, and to assure us emphatically and repeatedly that he had no intention of forcing himself or his committee upon France as her future government."

By now, with all of France rallying to the Gaullist banner, this was a meaningless, face-saving assurance for Hull to have asked, and an easy one for General de Gaulle to give.

As for the substance of their discussions, the president raised with de Gaulle his recurring theme of America's postwar security objectives and the need for strategic bases for US forces on a global scale—Dakar and French Indochina in particular. De Gaulle was not unresponsive; after all, here was the president of the United States asking something of France, whose government he was still declining to recognize. But all was left vague.

The inescapable core problem between the two leaders came when de Gaulle raised the question of France's role in the eventual occupation of Germany, and Roosevelt sketched his ideas about the new World Order he intended to build. At this time, not only was France still not recognized, but there was as yet no firm agreement either on the partitioning of Germany into occupation zones or the assignment of a zone to the French. As for Roosevelt's broader concepts of the postwar world, the most detailed account comes from de Gaulle's Memoirs:

> He avoided any reference to immediate issues, but allowed me glimpses of the political objectives he hoped to achieve through victory. His conception seemed to me an imposing one, although disquieting for Europe and for France. It was true that the isolationism of the United States was, according to the President, a great error now ended. But passing from one extreme to the other, it was a permanent system of intervention that he intended to institute by international law. In his opinion, a four-power directorate— America, Soviet Russia, China and Great Britain—should settle the world's problems. . . . Roosevelt thus intended to lure the Soviets into a group that would contain their ambitions and in which America could unite its dependents. Among the "four," he knew that Chiang Kai-shek's China needed his cooperation, and that the British, in danger of losing their dominions, would yield to his policy. As for the horde of small and medium size states, he would be in a position to impose upon them by virtue of the help he could provide.

In this sweeping Rooseveltian concept, there was nothing very reassuring or even acceptable for General de Gaulle and his France. Indeed, France was not assigned any role at all except as a spectator. The president, de Gaulle wrote, "sketched in his notions with light touches, so skillfully that it was difficult to contradict this artist, this seducer, on any particular point." But de Gaulle countered with some historical sketching of his own, telling FDR that "by considering Western Europe as a secondary matter, he was going to weaken the very cause he meant to serve—that of civilization."

De Gaulle focused at once on the great flaw he perceived in Roosevelt's logic and concept. In order to get Soviet approval and cooperation, he pointed out, "he would have to yield to them the Danubian and Balkan states, to the detriment of Poland and the Baltic, and certain other advantages that would threaten the general equilibrium." Moreover, de Gaulle told Roosevelt, there was no guarantee that China would remain the same ally under the same system. While agreeing with the president that colonialism must undergo postwar evolution and change, de Gaulle argued that to force such change too hastily "would risk unleashing a xenophobia and an anarchy which would be dangerous for the entire world."

Above all, he argued, Western Europe must be restored in order to re-establish a secure balance for peace in the world, and in particular this meant a restoration of France. De Gaulle says that Roosevelt "was open to these arguments" and "felt a genuine affection for France, or at least the notion of it he had once had." But this being said, there was no meeting of minds. De Gaulle concluded:

> The American President's remarks ultimately proved to me that, in foreign affairs, logic and sentiment do not weigh heavily in comparison with the realities of power. What matters is what one takes and what one can hold. To regain her place, France must count only on herself. I told him this. He smiled and concluded: "We shall do what we can. But it is true that in helping France, no one can replace the French people."

And so, on this much Roosevelt and de Gaulle were in agreement—it was up to France herself. De Gaulle left Washington to return to the battlefront more convinced and determined than ever that only by his own constant clawing and cutting, by intransigence and unyielding interventions and initiatives against his allies, could he regain for France a place in the galaxy of nations that Roosevelt, in his grand design, did not foresee. In particular this meant also to de Gaulle the restoration everywhere of the French Empire, which only France herself could dispose of or set free.

Before leaving Washington, de Gaulle paid a call on General of the Armies John J. Pershing, then eighty-four years old, at Walter Reed Hospital. From the dim recesses of his memory of World War I, the old soldier asked: "And tell me, how is Marshal Pétain?" General de Gaulle replied with grave courtesy: "It is a long time since I have seen him."

Meanwhile, an Anglo-French draft of an agreement on civil administration in liberated France arrived in Washington from London. It was not discussed with de Gaulle in Washington, but it worked its way up to Admiral Leahy for submission to the president while de Gaulle was still there. On July 11, while de Gaulle was traveling to Ottawa, Montreal, Rome and back to Algiers, Roosevelt held a press conference and announced that the United States was granting de facto recognition to the French Committee of National Liberation as "qualified to exercise the administration of France." This had already been going on for nearly a month and was expanding day by day. Roosevelt had grudgingly edged another step toward the inevitable, but full diplomatic recognition of de Gaulle's provisional government was still many weeks down the road.

*

The atmosphere of the Washington visit had been positive, on the whole, even though basic differences and the underlying sense of mistrust between Roosevelt and de Gaulle remained largely unchanged. But the public and private reception accorded the General had been cordial and enthusiastic everywhere, and at the end of the visit there had been forward movement from Roosevelt on the vital central problem of the moment, which was recognition.

In short, it seemed that with the liberation of France now dramatically unfolding, there was an atmosphere and an opportunity in which some fresh spirit of accord and common purpose could, and certainly should, take hold among the three Western Allies as the war approached its climax. Had Anglo-Saxon logic now applied, de Gaulle would have sensed at this moment that events were moving satisfactorily in his favor, and would have speeded the process by going out of his way to show harmony, cooperation and understanding. But this was not de Gaulle's French logic. He worked by his own rules, as he proceeded to demonstrate at the first opportunity.

On August 11, 1944, a few days before the landings were due to begin in southern France on the Riviera coast near Nice and Saint-Raphaël, Churchill flew into Algiers at the start of a visit to the battlefronts of the Mediterranean. Through Duff Cooper, he sent word in advance to de Gaulle of his coming, with a message that he would be glad to have an informal talk during a stopover of eight hours or so, while his plane would be refueling for a flight on to Italy. But, as Cooper commented, "there are men whose instinct is to say No whenever ordinary people would say Yes." In his diary, he recorded:

> I went to see de Gaulle with the Prime Minister's message. He said he thought nothing would be gained by an interview at the present time. I did my best to persuade him to change his mind, reminding him of the extremely warm terms in which the Prime Minister had referred to him in the House of Commons, and saying that it was only common civility to pay a call on so distinguished a traveller passing through French territory. I spent three quarters of an hour with him, but did not succeed in convincing him. . . . It is incredibly stupid on his part, one of the most foolish things he has yet done.

Instead, when Churchill landed, he was handed a personal letter from de Gaulle, which said in rather cold terms: "All things considered, I think it is preferable that I should not see you this time, so that you may take some rest between two flights. . . ." Churchill commented in his War Memoirs: "I thought this needlessly haughty, considering all the business we had in hand, and what I could have told him, but he was still offended by what happened at OVERLORD (D-Day) and thought this was a good chance of marking his displeasure." To Eden at the time, however, Churchill was a great deal more indignant, in a message from Algiers: "This is certainly a good indication of the relations we shall have with this man as he, through our exertions, gains supreme power in France. Certainly it was a great mistake to give de Gaulle the opportunity of putting this marked affront on the head of a government which has three-quarters of a million soldiers fighting with heavy losses to liberate France."

De Gaulle was to repeat this tactic and snub against Roosevelt six months later. Meanwhile, Churchill flew on from Algiers to Italy, where he embarked on a British warship to watch the naval support of the first day's landings of French and

United States forces on the French coast—an operation, incidentally, which he had strongly opposed for his own strategic reasons. He stopped briefly to visit Corsica, and this occasioned another explosion from de Gaulle, as Cooper recorded:

> August 15. I saw René Massigli [commissioner for foreign affairs] in the afternoon. It appears that de Gaulle is now in a violent rage because the Prime Minister has gone to Corsica without warning the French authorities. I said I thought it quite absurd to make a fuss about such a small matter at a moment like this. We are now in the middle of a battle, and the Prime Minister had a perfect right to visit any part of the battlefield he chose. Massigli really agreed with me, but I gathered that he had found the General in so violent a mood that he had not been able to make any protest.

This needless, insensitive and indeed absurd behavior toward Churchill may have served in some way to satisfy de Gaulle's *amour propre*, but it scarcely furthered mutual trust and confidence among allies at the top. The closer de Gaulle got to returning to Paris, the greater his inflated suspicions and mistrust of Britain and the United States seemed to become. Indeed, going back over the multiple and many-faceted records and accounts of those hectic, action-filled, dramatic times, it seems that at times some of de Gaulle's actions, judgments and convictions bordered on paranoia. He could, and regularly did, twist and interpret the most inconsequential and accidental happenings into what he conceived to be an inexhaustible and unceasing web or pattern of Anglo-Saxon plotting against France.

The unlucky sequence of events surrounding his return to France on the eve of the liberation of Paris was a case in point. It goes without saying that all movements in and out of the war zone at that time, from the lowest private to the highest chief of state, had to be cleared and controlled by Supreme Headquarters Allied Expeditionary Forces. When de Gaulle's request for clearance to return to France reached SHAEF in London, Eisenhower's brilliant but short-tempered chief of staff, Walter Bedell Smith, insisted that he travel from Algiers in an American Flying Fortress. De Gaulle had indicated that he intended to fly in his personal transport, an American-built twin-engine Lockheed Lodestar supplied to the French under Lend-Lease. But as far as Smith was concerned, this was out of the question. A Flying Fortress would be armed, it would have plenty of range, it would have a battle-experienced crew and it would be readily identifiable when it came in over the antiaircraft batteries close to the battlefront in France. Smith wrote a formal memorandum on the subject to General Pierre Koenig, the senior French officer attached to SHAEF, informing him that if de Gaulle insisted in coming in his own plane, "it would be at his own risk and the supreme commander will not be responsible for the consequences."

Faced with this edict, de Gaulle demanded that the Flying Fortress in which he would travel be repainted with French markings and the Cross of Lorraine, and that a French crew back up the American crew. The Americans were not too dumbfounded to refuse, informing de Gaulle's staff that this was against their regulations and pointing out that it was ridiculous to put a French backup crew on a Flying Fortress they would not know how to fly. Fuming, de Gaulle had no choice but to accede. Things then went from bad to worse.

On August 17 a Flying Fortress was flown into Algiers to pick up the General, but it overshot the runway on landing, ground-looped and was out of action. De Gaulle immediately formed a suspicion that this was not entirely accidental. Never mind, the Americans said, we will fly in another Fortress to pick up the General in Casablanca. So de Gaulle took off from Algiers in his personal Lodestar with his French crew for the Moroccan coast. At Casablanca, in a black mood, he transferred to the American plane to fly to Gibraltar, where the British insisted that they had to land in order to refuel to the limit and clear a flight plan under British military control. But the Fortress then burst a tire on landing and the pilot informed General de Gaulle that it would be twenty-four hours before a replacement could be flown in.

By now de Gaulle was convinced of an Anglo-Saxon plot to delay his return to France at this crucial hour or even keep him out of the country entirely, by some contrived way or another. His Lodestar had also flown into Gibraltar with others of the French party aboard, including General Alphonse Juin. De Gaulle summoned his own pilot to Government House, where he was being entertained at dinner by the Gibraltar governor. They had a brief discussion of the probable flying time, the conditions for the flight, and the plane's maximum range, and de Gaulle announced that whatever General Smith's warnings and whatever the British thought about it, he intended to take of for France in his Lodestar immediately after dinner, as soon as the plane was refueled and ready.

Accordingly, on the night of August 19, the unarmed, unescorted Lodestar lifted off heavily from the Gibraltar runway with Colonel Lionel de Marmier at the controls, and a grave risk that adverse winds or bad weather could abort the flight before they ever landed.

De Gaulle disliked flying anyway, and he sat silent and chain-smoking in the dark throughout the night, as the weather worsened the farther north they flew. They were supposed to pick up an RAF fighter escort when they reached the English coast before turning toward France, but in cloudy, squally weather they could make no contact. The last fuel tank was now running out, and Marmier sent word back to the General that he would have to land in England to refuel. De Gaulle's response was a furious *"Non!"* He absolutely refused to touch ground in England because he was convinced the British would find some excuse to keep him there. In something of a cold sweat, Marmier turned on a blind course, heading for France, with the fuel gauge bouncing near zero. His engineer got set to hand-pump the last drops from the tank. They came down out of thick cloud, but when they sighted land and crossed the coast, Marmier was uncertain of his position and sent the map back to General de Gaulle. Putting on his glasses and peering out of the window, without hesitation de Gaulle said they were just east of Cherbourg, not far from their intended destination, an airfield near the town of Maupertuis. But with the fuel gauge now on empty, Colonel Marmier glided in to land on the first fighter strip he could find.

It was the morning of August 20, 1944. General de Gaulle, certain that he had again foiled his allies, was back in France to stay, and his entry into Paris was only five days away.

*

The French 2nd Armored Division, under Brigadier Jacques Leclerc, had arrived in Normandy from Britain in the early days of August. It was a first-rate, battle-hardened force, some of whose veterans had been with the division all the way from Chad in Central Africa. Its commander had captured the Cameroons capital of Libreville for de Gaulle in 1940. He was slight of build but hard-bitten and hard-driving, "a magnificent tank commander" in the words of General Omar Bradley, under whom he fought.

In the breakout from Normandy, which began on August 7, the French division was first attached to George S. Patton's 3rd Army and then transferred to Courtney Hodges' US 1st Army. When de Gaulle arrived back in France, the division had reached the town of Argentan, in the heart of Normandy, about 100 miles from Paris and approximately midway in the long north-south front of the Allied line moving eastward across France. Leclerc had been held back from the slugging engagements in Normandy before the breakout so the division would be fresh and in good shape for the advance on Paris, which it had been earmarked to lead ever since de Gaulle's discussion on the subject with Eisenhower in Algiers eight months earlier.

At the airstrip where Marmier landed on his last drop of fuel, de Gaulle's aide, Captain Claude Guy, managed to commandeer a vehicle from the surprised field commander to drive into Cherbourg. They headed straight for the Préfecture, where François Coulet was installed as regional commissioner. General Koenig arrived quickly and greeted de Gaulle with the dramatic but not entirely welcome news: "There has been an uprising in Paris."

It is true that de Gaulle himself, from the start of the D-Day landings, had proclaimed to Frenchmen everywhere that "it is your simple and sacred duty to fight the enemy with all available means." But the eruption of fighting in Paris was premature for two reasons. As far as de Gaulle was concerned, first and foremost it was not under his control and he had not specifically ordered it. It had been triggered by the Paris leader of the Communist Party against the advice and instructions of the Gaullist Resistance leaders, who were under orders to wait until the General and the French division were close at hand. De Gaulle saw the uprising instantly for what it was—a threat to his own authority by the Communists and a potential civil war.

The uprising was equally unwelcome to Eisenhower, who had decided to bypass Paris in his advance to the east. He did not want to have to divert either infantry divisions or supplies into a potential streetfight for the city that would be costly, destructive and time-consuming. Therefore he planned to go around Paris to the north and south and push his advance eastward toward Germany as far and as fast as possible, leaving the Germans in Paris to surrender to Leclerc's division later on. But an uprising by Resistance forces would quickly lead to impassioned calls for help, which would force a change in the supreme commander's strategic plan.

There was then a third element in this turbulent and fast-breaking situation, and that was the last political machinations of Pierre Laval. The Vichy premier had embarked on one final extraordinary maneuver to try to save his skin and block de Gaulle. On August 12 he suddenly appeared at a lunatic asylum near the city of Nancy in eastern France, where the Vichy authorities had locked up Édouard Herriot, last president of the 1940 National Assembly. Laval ordered Herriot's immediate release, and together they drove back to Paris while the premier unfolded his plot. He proposed that Herriot announce a recall of the old National Assembly, to reconvene in Paris before the Allies entered the city and legitimize some kind of a new "national government" to prevent de Gaulle from installing himself in power. Given the fact that Pétain and Laval had dissolved the National Assembly in July 1940 and then imprisoned its most independent-minded members such as Herriot, Laval's proposal was one of desperate idiocy. But he apparently had the momentary blessing of both Pétain and the German ambassador to France, Otto Abetz, with whom Laval and Herriot dined on their arrival back in Paris. Herriot was glad enough to be out of the asylum and played along, at least until he had seen his tailor to order a new suit of clothes. It was not long before the harebrained idea collapsed anyway.

But de Gaulle had learned of Laval's scheme from his own Intelligence Service before he left Algiers to return to France, and he convinced himself that it had American backing and would be welcomed by Roosevelt and the United States if it ever got off the ground. The scheme indeed was also known to the Americans, through at least three lines of contact operating between Washington and Vichy.

It is true also that Roosevelt had voiced to a number of persons before the invasion his off-the-cuff conviction that "new parties will emerge" in France once the liberation got under way and that "de Gaulle is on the wane." He never bothered to substantiate these assertions, which were totally at odds with all other Intelligence evidence and seemed mainly to be inventing an excuse for continuing to deny recognition to de Gaulle. But he could have been basing his remarks on secret information reaching him through Leahy on the plots and activities of Laval and the Vichyites as the ring closed in.

Thus, given de Gaulle's mania about Roosevelt and the Americans, there was enough circumstantial evidence kicking around for him to piece together in his own mind a conviction that Washington was mounting a concerted plot first to delay or prevent his return to France, and now to delay his entering Paris in order to further the chances of the Vichyites against him.

De Gaulle even convinced himself that Roosevelt was intervening for this purpose directly in Eisenhower's battle decisions—something Churchill did repeatedly throughout the war with his generals, but never Roosevelt. Yet de Gaulle wrote in his Memoirs, after more than a decade of reflection on these events:

> Eisenhower's uncertainty [about moving directly against Paris] suggested to me that the military command found itself somewhat hampered by the political project pursued by Laval, *favored by Roosevelt* [italics added] and requiring that Paris be protected from all upheavals. The resistance had doubtless put an end to this scheme by engaging in battle, but it took some time for Washington to admit as much. This impression was confirmed when I learned that the Leclerc division, hitherto quite logically assigned to Patton's army, had been re-attached to Hodges' army and placed under the close supervision of General Gerow [a US corps commander] and kept in the area of Argentan as if someone feared it might make off toward the Eiffel Tower. . . . At the moment of the most striking success of the Allied armies, and while the American troops were giving evidence of courage deserving every praise, I found this apparent stubbornness of Washington's policy most depressing.

This de Gaulle logic is badly flawed and totally unfair. There is not a shred of evidence, except de Gaulle's own deduction, that the Laval project was "favored by Roosevelt." Simply because de Gaulle assumed that the Americans also knew about the plot was no reason at all for him to leap to the conviction that they were backing it. Moreover, if he had any reading at all of the American political scene, he would have known that it would have been political suicide for FDR, then embarking on his fourth-term election campaign, suddenly to attempt to make a deal with Laval at the very moment of the liberation of Paris. The furor over the Darlan deal in 1942 would have been nothing to the political storm which any deal with the Vichyites in 1944 would have raised.

In any case, by the time de Gaulle arrived back in France, the Laval plot had collapsed anyway, and it was not the uprising of the Resistance in Paris that "put an end to this scheme." It was the Germans who abruptly decided to cut the nonsense. On August 17 they took Laval into custody, and Pétain three days later, transporting them first to the city of Belfort in eastern France and then to an old Hohenzollern castle at Sigmaringen, near the Black Forest. Herriot was also re-arrested and considered himself lucky to be sent back to the asylum near Nancy.

Thus, the Laval plot could not and did not have the slightest effect on either Roosevelt's political decisions or Eisenhower's battle decisions. It was a nonstarter from the outset and a dead duck by the time de Gaulle reached the scene. But the affair remains a measure of how far de Gaulle could go in concocting deliberate mistrust of his allies when he chose to do so.

*

At the Cherbourg Préfecture, General de Gaulle spent about an hour with Koenig discussing the situation in Paris, as well as reports from the Resistance all over the country and the situation of the Leclerc division. They then set out for Eisenhower's advanced headquarters in the town of Granville, south of Cherbourg on the western coast of the Cotentin Peninsula, looking across the water to the famous island of Mont-Saint-Michel. Eisenhower of course also had full knowledge of the uprising in Paris, and later he related that he was "damned mad about it—just the kind of situation I didn't want, a situation that wasn't under our control and might force us to change our plans before we were ready for it." He knew that when de Gaulle arrived, his first demand would be the dispatch of Leclerc's division immediately to Paris, and he was determined to refuse.

As far as Eisenhower was concerned, the liberation of Paris was not a military but a *political* objective. He had a West Point fetish about not mixing politics and war, and he felt very deeply that one of his successes as supreme commander had rested on his refusal to countenance for political considerations or pressures any alteration or adjustment in his *military* plans. It was on this basis that he had adamantly refused Churchill's long importunings to cancel the invasion of southern France, so those troops could stay in Italy and fight their way up the Po Valley toward Vienna and Budapest. Eisenhower's approach was of course the antithesis of de Gaulle's thinking, in which the *political* objectives of the war were always the prime consideration. Thus, Eisenhower's very soldierly refusal to advance on Paris on *military* grounds was instantly seen by de Gaulle as a political act of string-pulling of some kind by Roosevelt. He wrote of his conference with Eisenhower on the twentieth: "Eisenhower did not conceal his embarrassment from me; I had an idea that fundamentally he shared my point of view, that he was eager to send Leclerc to Paris, but that for reasons not entirely of a strategic nature he could not yet do so. Ultimately he assured me that he would shortly give orders to march on Paris and that it would be the Leclerc Division that he would assign to the operation."

First, Eisenhower gave de Gaulle a full and detailed map-briefing on the disposition of his forces moving across France and his plans to push Patton's 3rd Army around south of Paris while Hodges' 1st Army crossed the Seine north of Paris. De Gaulle says he told Eisenhower: "Paris is a communications center which will later be essential and which it will be to your advantage to re-establish as soon as possible. If any place except the capital of France were in question, my advice would not commit you to any action, for normally of course the conduct of operations is your responsibility. But the fate of Paris is of fundamental concern to the French government."

Eisenhower recalled the conversation more simply: "He made no bones about it; he said there was a serious menace from the Communists in the city, and that if we delayed moving in we would risk finding a disastrous political situation, one that might be disruptive to the Allied war effort."

Next day, on August 21 de Gaulle sent a formal letter to Eisenhower in which he politely declared that if the Leclerc division were not ordered soon to advance on Paris, he would issue the orders himself, and that Leclerc would certainly follow the orders of his government. By this time Eisenhower was beginning to find military reasons for changing his mind about Paris. Various couriers and messengers from the Resistance, as well as Allied Intelligence sources in the capital, were now bombarding the advancing Allied commanders with situation reports indicating that the city would fall like a ripe fruit if help arrived quickly, but the Germans would probably make a desperate last stand if they were bypassed. This was something of the reverse of what Eisenhower had originally calculated. In particular, General Bradley, the soldier whose judgment Eisenhower probably respected the most of all his commanders, was now pushing to move on Paris.

Eisenhower wrote in hand across the top of de Gaulle's letter a note to his chief of staff, Bedell Smith: "I talked verbally to Koenig on this. It looks now as if we'd be compelled to go into Paris. Bradley and his G-2 [Intelligence] think we can and *must* walk in."

In Paris itself, events were indeed moving rapidly and somewhat chaotically in one of the great dramatic climaxes of the war. Much of the drama centered on a new German commander who had been assigned to Paris in early August with Hitler's personal instructions to hold and if necessary destroy the city, General Dietrich von Choltitz.

Choltitz had commanded the destruction and capture of Rotterdam at the outset of the war in 1940, and he was also in command of the forces that reduced the Crimean fortress of Sebastopol in the Soviet Union in 1942. He had the reputation of a ruthless disciplinarian, but hidden beneath his Nazi uniform was a humane streak and even a certain sense of humor. Before taking up his Paris command he had been summoned to the Führer's headquarters in East Prussia, and found Hitler a human wreck after the July 20, 1944, bomb plot against his life. His mouth drooled, his eyes wandered and watered, and he was given regular jabs of stimulants as he issued virtually incoherent orders in a running rambling monologue. Choltitz decided then and there that the war was lost and Hitler was to be ignored.

Alexandre Parodi was acting for de Gaulle in Paris as his political delegate to the National Council of Resistance, with Jacques Chaban-Delmas, a prewar Wimbledon tennis player and later a frequent Cabinet minister and prime minister in the Fifth Republic, who was the chief Gaullist military delegate on the NCR. They took their instructions from Koenig in London, as chief of the French Forces of the Interior. Orders had been firm and clear—to hold off on any insurrection until word from London, so that an uprising would be coordinated with the arrival of the Leclerc division.

But on August 15, while de Gaulle was still waiting impatiently in Algiers for the Allies to clear his return to France, the Communists in Paris forced the Gaullist hand. The key figure was a Breton metalworker who had won his spurs as a party organizer and loyalist in the Spanish Civil War, Henry Tanguy, who went by the *nom de guerre* of Colonel Rol. "Paris is worth 200,000 dead," he had declared to his Communist lieutenants—and what's more he meant it. Ignoring Gaullist orders, Rol-Tanguy managed to trigger a strike by the entire Paris police force, and without any police on duty the way seemed clear for a popular uprising that could no longer be held in check.

But at this crucial juncture the first of the key appointees who were to take over the administration of Paris on behalf of de Gaulle managed to slip into the city through the battle lines. He was Charles Luizet, who had been serving as *préfet* of liberated Corsica and had been selected by de Gaulle to take over as *préfet* of the Paris police. When the police went out on strike at Rol-Tanguy's call, the Germans had occupied the central Paris police headquarters on the Île de la Cité.

On August 18 Parodi decided on his own that it was too dangerous to allow the Communists to go on forcing a Resistance uprising, and that in order to get the situation back under Gaullist control it was necessary to break the orders from London. He therefore sent his own Resistance courier network into motion with a call to the Gaullist cells in the police force to assemble and storm the police headquarters the next day. The building was only lightly held by the Germans. On the morning of the nineteenth it was swiftly retaken by the French police. Luizet then promptly installed himself in the office of the *préfet*. The Communists were furious at being outmaneuvered, but Parodi's action was vital to retaining Gaullist control of both the situation and the city. It had also pushed things toward a premature general uprising.

The National Resistance Council met on the nineteenth after the police head-quarters had been retaken, and a sharp exchange ensued between Parodi and Chaban-Delmas who, as a brigadier general, insisted on adhering to orders from Koenig. But with the Communists on the NRC howling for an uprising, it was impossible to hold back any longer. Thus it was that the Resistance burst into open street-warfare against the Germans on August 20, when General de Gaulle landed near Cherbourg.

Everything now depended on what action Choltitz would order to crush the Resistance. He hesitated. He had a city garrison of about 22,000 second-class troops, enough to hold out for a while in siege positions but not enough to secure the city against a general uprising. Choltitz knew that the High Command was preparing to withdraw eastward with such reserves and fighting units he would need if it came to a showdown defense.

Nevertheless, a special demolition squad had been sent into the city and was at work with demoniacal skill, systematically preparing to blow up just about every-thing sacred to the Parisians. All forty-five bridges across the Seine in the Paris area had been chambered and mined with explosives, and so were the cast-iron legs of the mighty Eiffel Tower. Some 200 factories, power stations and telephone exchanges were ready to be blown, along with public buildings such as the Luxembourg Palace. Everything was ready to go when Choltitz gave the order.

But on August 20 there was a totally unexpected intervention from an unlikely outsider—the Swedish consul general in Paris, Raoul Nordling. Hearing that the Germans were preparing an attack to retake the police headquarters, Nordling managed to get through to see Choltitz at his city command headquarters in the Hôtel Meurice on the rue de Rivoli, overlooking the Tuileries Gardens, to plead for a cease-fire and a truce.

Choltitz, who was looking for an out, agreed, and Nordling at once made contact with Parodi, who accepted a cease-fire on behalf of the Resistance. Accordingly, the German attack to retake police headquarters was stayed, but

Rol-Tanguy was out for blood and on August 21 he countermanded Parodi's order and instructed the Communists to take to the streets in earnest. Moreover, that morning, Parodi fell into the hands of a German street patrol. With German efficiency, the officer in charge of the patrol telephoned Choltitz to ask permission to carry out a summary execution. Instead, Choltitz ordered Parodi brought to the Meurice for questioning. At that point Nordling again fortuitously appeared to plead for a second cease-fire to spare destruction of the city.

Choltitz had already been telephoned once by Hitler's Wehrmacht Oberkommander, General Alfred Jodl, demanding to know whether the demolitions in the city had yet begun. He had temporized by replying that his orders were first to defend Paris, which he was doing, and he would order the destruction when defense became impossible. But Choltitz had also learned that German divisions to the south of Paris, in the path of Patton's advance, had now been withdrawn to the east, leaving the city approaches open. He was therefore now desperately anxious that the Allies arrive promptly so that he could surrender. He did not have enough troops to put up any real fight, but if the Resistance forced his hand and there was no Allied force to surrender to, then in the end he would give the orders for demolition.

If there had been a different German commander in Paris, it would be a far different Paris today. But Choltitz told Nordling and Parodi that he would hold off for forty-eight hours. Another cease-fire was declared (though not very fully observed) and Parodi was released. And, as part of the secret deal struck with Choltitz, a Resistance courier was allowed to slip through the lines around the city to contact Bradley's Army Group headquarters, the highest command of the advancing Allies.

Nordling also got out an urgent message to Stockholm for relay to Supreme Allied Headquarters in London, urging a swift advance to accept a surrender. The Resistance messenger, appropriately named Major Gallois, got through to Bradley's headquarters near Chartres on August 22 and quickly convinced Bradley that he must advance on Paris promptly. Meanwhile, Eisenhower had received de Gaulle's letter insisting on prompt orders to the Leclerc division, and also Nordling's cabled message relayed from Stockholm via London. There was, therefore, now a clear *military* necessity for Eisenhower to change his plans, as he had written across de Gaulle's letter: "Bradley and his G-2 think we can and *must* walk in."

*

Late on the afternoon of August 22, a Tuesday, Eisenhower issued orders to the impatient Leclerc to advance on Paris. But he specified that "no advance must be made into Paris until the expiration of the armistice [agreed between Choltitz, Parodi and Nordling for forty-eight hours] and Paris is to be entered only in case the degree of fighting is such as could be overcome by light forces." Eisenhower told Leclerc that he did not want a severe fight for Paris, nor did he want any "bombing or artillery fire on the city if it can possibly be avoided." Leclerc was to advance into the city from the south, while the American 4th Infantry Division would operate around the edge of Paris to the north. The whole operation would be under Major General Leonard Gerow, commander of the US 5th Corps. The armistice in Paris would expire the next day, August 23, but Leclerc had to advance nearly 100 miles from Argenten, where the bulk of his division was waiting to go.

With the endorsement of de Gaulle, Leclerc had already undertaken "aggressive patrolling" in the direction of Paris on August 21 and had been rebuked for this by Gerow, yet another sore point between allies. But Leclerc now wasted no time getting his advance parties on the road to Paris, via the towns of Dreux and Rambouillet to the outskirts of Versailles, where the Germans were holding light defensive positions. The division moved rapidly all day on the twenty-third, and by nightfall the bulk of Leclerc's force was in position for a breach of the German defenses and the move into Paris next day.

General de Gaulle had spent his first night back in France, on August 20, at the Préfecture in the Normandy capital of Rennes. He moved on to the town of Laval on the twenty-first and then to Le Mans on the night of the twenty-second, when Leclerc received Eisenhower's green light to advance. Everywhere the scene at Bayeux was repeated—the meeting with the Préfecture authorities, the interrogation on local conditions, the brief speech to assembled townspeople, the singing of La Marseillaise, and the jeeps speeding off to the next town or village.

On the night of the twenty-second, de Gaulle sent word to Leclerc to meet the next afternoon at the vast seventeenth-century presidential château at Rambouillet, to receive final orders on the liberation of Paris. They would also be joined at Rambouillet by General Koenig and General Alphonse Juin, who was now the defense chief of staff. From Le Mans next morning, de Gaulle drove through Chartres, with its famous cathedral that had barely escaped artillery shelling, and then he overtook the advancing columns of the French armor as he reached Rambouillet. Soon after he arrived, a courier from the Paris Resistance, a Dr. Favreau, also reached Rambouillet with a report from Luizet, installed in the Préfecture de Police. The Resistance was in full control of the streets, with the Germans holed up in various strongpoints and barracks around the city on the defensive, venturing out only sporadically in armored vehicles. But would Choltitz order the demolitions?

Leclerc arrived with his battle plans. One of his regiments would cover the flank of the advance along the roads leading into Versailles, while the other two regiments would hook farther south to enter the city from the southwest at the Porte d'Orléans. The discussion was brief, with de Gaulle simply instructing Leclerc that when he entered Paris he should establish his command post at the Gare Montparnasse. They shook hands, and General de Gaulle murmured a rare personal comment: "How lucky you are."

Then, with memories of the War of 1870 and the bloody aftermath of the siege of Paris, he added: "Go quickly. We cannot afford another Commune."

The Château de Rambouillet had been occupied by the Germans for four years, and even now there were still patrols harassing Leclerc's advance only a few miles away. The building at least was undamaged and most of its furniture was intact, but electricity was a problem.

The commissary chief of de Gaulle's personal staff, Commandant Lignières, had arrived at the château to take charge of arrangements, and discovered a mobile generator in the cellar, abandoned by the Germans. He found the town electrician, who tinkered a while and finally got it to cough into action to put a faint charge of electricity into the old lamps of the Third Republic. He then ordered the presidential suite, where French heads of state had slept for a century and a half, prepared for General de Gaulle. But when de Gaulle arrived and was ushered upstairs, he froze the poor Lignières with icy disapproval. Ever a sticker for protocol, he was only the head of a provisional government.

"Do you mean to say you have made ready for me the Presidential bedroom? You don't really imagine, do you, that I'm going to sleep in the President of the Republic's bed?"

Another bed in a less exalted chamber was hastily prepared.

Leclerc's division began the attack at dawn on August 24. Throughout the day it was a series of slow but steady platoon actions to reduce German strongpoints and pockets of resistance by flanking maneuvers and tank attacks. For the most part these engagements were short and sharp, as the Germans fell back before the three French columns pushing relentlessly toward the capital. By evening one regiment was holding a bridge into the city across the Seine at Sèvres, while another regiment had taken the suburban town of Fresnes, where one of the major Paris prisons is located. The American 4th Infantry had worked its way around the suburbs to the north to encounter heavy German units, including armor being held in reserve, in the vicinity of Le Bourget airfield on the northeast of the city. During the night, all was prepared and poised for the glorious final push to the Place de la Concorde and Notre-Dame.

At Rambouillet throughout the day, General de Gaulle paced the gravelled terraces, receiving hourly reports of the advance of Leclerc's forces and also a stream of visitors and messages from the city. Among these were Rolf Nordling, brother of the Swedish consul general, and Baron Poch-Pastor, an Austrian officer in the German Army on Choltitz's staff, who in fact was an Allied secret agent throughout the war. During the afternoon, de Gaulle sent Dr. Fevreau back into Paris with a personal message for Charles Luizet at police headquarters. Luizet and Parodi had both urged that on entering Paris he should go straight to the Hôtel de Ville, where they would assemble the National Council of the Resistance, the Paris Committee of Liberation, and the population of the city to greet him. Instead, de Gaulle informed Luizet in his message that he would first stop at Leclerc's command post at the Gare Montparnasse and then proceed directly to the center of power—the Ministry of War on the rue Saint-Dominique, not far from the Invalides. The Hôtel de Ville would have to wait.

Late in the day, with Leclerc now poised to enter the city but still mopping up in the suburbs, de Gaulle received a telegram of congratulations on the liberation of the French capital from King George VI in London. Shortly after, the message was released and broadcast over the BBC. It was premature by some hours, but even this simple gesture of friendly comradeship fed de Gaulle's remorseless feelings of mistrust of his Allies: "No doubt the telegram was intended [he wrote in his Memoirs] to force the Americans to renounce their ulterior motives, which the English did not approve. The contrast between the warm satisfaction expressed by the BBC with regard to events in Paris and the reserved, even bitter tone of the Voice of America led me to realize that this time London and Washington were not in agreement about France."

At first light on Friday, August 25, a day of hot and cloudless brilliance, Leclerc's tanks and infantry platoons began their final advance into the heart of the city. Their objective: the Grösser Paris Kommandantur [headquarters] of General Choltitz at the Hôtel Meurice. The regiment that had captured the bridge at Sèvres the night before moved across the river and through Boulogne and Passy toward the Arc de Triomphe, to descend the avenue des Champs-Élysées to the Place de la Concorde and the rue de Rivoli. Leclerc entered Paris with another regiment through the Porte d'Orléans to the southwest, first establishing his command post on de Gaulle's instructions at the Montparnasse railway station. The troops and tanks pressed on through delirious hordes of Parisians jamming the streets and not making the military movement any easier, through the Latin Quarter and then across the Seine in the center of the city by the Châtelet bridge, to begin working their way along the rue de Rivoli from the opposite end. The Germans were concentrated in strongpoints along the way—public buildings where they were holed up, sandbag machine-gun posts, artillery positions and armored vehicles at each end of the rue de Rivoli and in the Tuileries Gardens, protecting the approaches to the Meurice.

Choltitz ate a last impassive meal at lunchtime with his officers as the gunfire of the approaching enemy came closer and closer from either side of the hotel. He gave instructions that if uniformed troops of the French Army took the hotel, his officers were to surrender, but if it was the *maquis* forces of the Paris Resistance, they were to fight on. He then went back upstairs to his office, where Nazi military governors had held life-and-death power over the Parisians for more than four years, to await capture or death.

A platoon section of Leclerc's infantry dodging machine-gun fire behind the pillars of the rue de Rivoli colonnade, reached the hotel soon after Choltitz had finished his lunch, and Lieutenant Henri Karcher led the dash through the door. He first fired an instinctive blast from his automatic rifle at a portrait of Hitler in the lobby, and then tossed a phosphorous grenade into the ornate and spacious public lounge beyond. Almost at once, German officers came streaming down the stairs with their hands above their heads, and Karcher dashed up to take Choltitz prisoner in his office.

The German commander was marched out into the rue de Rivoli through a jeering, screaming, spitting mob of Paris citizens until an armored car was found to drive him to the Préfecture de Police building on the Île de la Cité, where Leclerc was waiting with the surrender documents. It was midafternoon.

Meanwhile, General de Gaulle had left Rambouillet three hours earlier in a convoy of cars and escorting armed jeeps, recording these thoughts in his Memoirs:

I myself had already determined what I must do in the liberated capital. I would mold all minds into a single national impulse, but also cause the figure and the authority of the state to appear at once. Walking up and down the terrace at Rambouillet . . . considering the causes of the impotence which had deprived us in the past—that is, the bankruptcy of governmental power—I resolved more firmly not to let my own be infringed. The mission with which I was invested seemed as clear as it could be. Getting into the car to drive to Paris, I felt myself simultaneously gripped by emotion and filled with serenity.

In this mood, as rapidly as the convoy could travel, which was not very fast, General de Gaulle passed through mobs of cheering villagers and finally the dense throngs at the Porte d'Orléans and the avenue de Maine to the Gare Montparnasse, where he arrived at 4 P.M. Leclerc was waiting proudly with Choltitz's signature on the surrender document.

But the proceedings with Choltitz at the Préfecture de Police had suddenly been interrupted by the arrival of the belligerent Communist activist, Rol-Tanguy, who had insisted that the surrender document be reworded to include the Paris Resistance as well as the French Army and that he should sign the document side by side with Leclerc. Exasperated and not wanting to prolong a French argument at this moment in front of the defeated German commander, Leclerc agreed. Soon he would wish he hadn't.

Rol-Tanguy was then waiting with Leclerc to greet de Gaulle, who descended from his car—impassive, grave, and distantly preoccupied in the midst of all the delirious excitement around him. He exchanged salutes and handshakes of congratulations with Rol-Tanguy and with Leclerc ("What a stage on his road to glory!" he wrote in his Memoirs. "With all my heart I embraced this noble colleague.") and others of the command post staff. Then he caught a glimpse of his son, Lieutenant Philippe de Gaulle, who had transferred from sea duty to the Naval Infantry and had arrived in Paris with the Leclerc division. It was a brief, even terse greeting, as young de Gaulle sped off with another officer and a platoon of soldiers to accept the surrender of one of the German garrisons on the other side of the city.

General de Gaulle next turned to the surrender document which Leclerc handed him, and at once the congratulatory atmosphere changed. When he discovered that it had been amended, and that Rol-Tanguy had been permitted to sign it, he rebuked Leclerc: "You were the highest-ranking officer present, and therefore the only person responsible. But above all, the insistence which has led you to accept this formula proceeds from an unacceptable tendency."

De Gaulle then went on to point out to Leclerc, and others listening, that only that morning the National Council of the Resistance had published its own proclamation in Paris which spoke of the "French nation" without mentioning either the provisional government or General de Gaulle. This action, coupled with the signature of Rol-Tanguy, a Communist, on the surrender document, constituted in de Gaulle's view an immediate challenge to his authority and power, which he had resolved on the terrace of Rambouillet was his first duty to protect and preserve and expand. At this tumultuous, emotional, historic hour, de Gaulle never for an instant relaxed in imposing discipline, the basis of power.

Resistance leaders and Parisians by the tens of thousands had by now gathered at the Hôtel de Ville—the splendid city hall and traditional place of welcome. No one knew of de Gaulle's plans except his immediate entourage and the *préfet de police,* Luizet, who had been informed by the courier from Rambouillet the day before. Paris was waiting to greet and acclaim him, but instead, after barely half an hour at the Gare Montparnasse, de Gaulle's convoy set off, not for the Hôtel de Ville, but the Ministry of War. A burst of machine-gun fire on the boulevard des Invalides forced them to turn off the main route and dodge through almost empty backstreets to the rue Saint-Dominique, where he arrived at five o'clock.

General de Gaulle, with a handful of aides and General Alphonse Juin, strode through the doors and up the familiar staircase and corridor. He recorded in one of the most memorable passages of his Memoirs:

> I was immediately struck by the impression that nothing had changed inside these venerable halls. Gigantic events had overturned the world. Our army was annihilated. France had virtually collapsed. But at the Ministry of War, the look of things remained immutable. In the courtyard, a unit of the Garde Républicaine presented arms, as in the past. The vestibule, the staircase, the arms hanging on the walls—all were as they had been. Here, in person, were the same stewards and ushers. I entered the "minister's office," which M. Paul Reynaud and I had left together on the night of June 10th, 1940. Not a piece of furniture, not a rug, not a curtain had been disturbed. On the desk, the telephone was in the same place, and exactly the same names on the call buttons. Soon I was to learn that this was the case in all the other buildings in which the Republic housed itself. Nothing was missing except the state. It was my duty to restore it: I installed my staff at once and got down to work.

THIRTEEN

DE GAULLE'S OTHER WARS

Commandant de Lignières, in charge of logistics at Rambouillet, had been ordered to go directly to the War Ministry and prepare billeting arrangements and dinner for fifty officers and members of General de Gaulle's staff that evening. He arrived to find Resistance fighters and underground leaders milling about all over the place, and not ready to show much cooperation or respect for a lowly supply officer, even if he was working for the General. Finally, with the help of a colonel of the gendarmerie, Lignières managed to clear the main offices of the building and the grand staircase for de Gaulle's historic entry and installation of his staff. There remained the problem of dinner for fifty. He asked a cleaning woman in the corridors if she knew anyone available to cook, and she told him there was a chef hanging around without a job. He was located and brought before Lignières, who asked where he had worked before.

"At Vichy," he replied. And what was he doing in Paris? "I was sent to the kitchens of the Élysée Palace to await the return of Marshal Pétain," he told the surprised commandant. He had been chef to the presidents of the Republic, moved to Vichy, and had come back to Paris for Pétain's last visit at the end of April 1944, when there had been a brief flurry about a possible permanent return of the marshal to the city. After four years cooking for Pétain, he set to work at once in the War Ministry kitchens to prepare the first meal in Paris for General de Gaulle—fresh chickens that Lignières had scrounged, with army rations to round out the menu.

Soon after de Gaulle reached the War Ministry at 5 P.M., Alexandre Parodi arrived, exhausted from the strain of the last five days but jubilant. It was his first meeting with de Gaulle, and his immediate task, which he thought was simple, was to ask the General to come at once to the Hôtel de Ville to meet the Resistance leaders, who were all gathered there, and greet the people of Paris.

But de Gaulle's response was a flat refusal. Coldly, he reminded Parodi that he was the head of the French government, that he represented the State, and he would not go calling at a municipal building to be received by local leaders. It was up to them to visit him at the seat of government. Parodi pleaded on behalf of the great crowd that had been waiting already for several hours in front of the Hôtel de Ville. But he got nowhere. Perhaps because it was a first meeting, he was unable to shape his arguments in a manner best calculated to get de Gaulle's support. But an assistant who accompanied Parodi, and had known de Gaulle in London, thought to telephone Charles Luizet at police headquarters and ask him to come to the ministry at once. Luizet had been on de Gaulle's top team for several years, and had served the General effectively and well as *préfet* of Corsica. He was able to back up Parodi's plea with more force and confidence, and finally de Gaulle relented—but he decreed that he would visit the Hôtel de Ville only briefly, and only after first stopping at the Préfecture de Police, in order to emphasize his control of the government centers of power. A police honor guard was then hastily turned out in the Préfecture courtyard, with a band to play *La Marseillaise.* After de Gaulle completed his inspection, he elected to walk the half-mile or so across the Seine from the Île de la Cité to the Hôtel de Ville, in the company of Luizet, Parodi, Juin, and a small party of aides and security troops.

Meanwhile, Georges Bidault, head of the Council of National Resistance, and the other leaders were fuming at the Hôtel de Ville. "This is where the people of Paris are, not at the *maison des flics* [the stationhouse], Bidault kept muttering, while another *résistant* swore: "Those *salauds* [sons-of-bitches] have been arresting us for four years and now de Gaulle goes and pays tribute to them." But the police were part of the power apparat of the State, and the people could wait.

While they were waiting, an officer of the Paris *maquis* got a tip that two armed men had managed to enter the Hôtel de Ville with intent to assassinate de Gaulle when he arrived. He contacted the military command at the Hôtel de Ville, and the building was immediately sealed off. Identity checks were run on everyone inside, and those who were not known to be members of the French Forces of the Interior were searched. Two men were found armed with pistols, and they confessed. One of them had been a Vichy secret policeman who carried out the murder of Georges Mandel, a Jewish former minister of the Third Republic, in jail. The two were locked up under close guard in the Hôtel de Ville and summarily executed next morning.

At long last, by now nearly eight o'clock in the evening, General de Gaulle came walking across the Pont d'Arcole to the massive ornate pile of the Hôtel de Ville. Resistance fighters lined the great stairway, presenting arms in an honor guard. Members of both the Council of National Resistance and the Paris Liberation Committee were waiting in the office of the Paris *préfet,* and their impatience and irritation now dissolved in emotion and tears as they greeted the man they had followed for months if not years, but few had ever seen.

There was a brief and warm speech from one of the Communist leaders, Georges Marrane, and a brief and flowery speech from Bidault. But it was an atmosphere of mixed emotions, and if the *résistants* expected words of praise or thanks from General de Gaulle, they got a dash of cold water instead:

The French people has decided by instinct and by reason to satisfy two conditions without which nothing great can be done, which are order and ardor. A Republican order under the only valid authority, that of the State; the concentrated ardor that will allow the legal and fraternal building of the edifices of renewal. That is the meaning of the manly acclamations of our towns and villages, purged at last of the enemy. That is what the great voice of liberated Paris is saying.

The battle was over, in Paris at least, and the Resistance must now submit to Republican order and the authority of the State. When Bidault then asked de Gaulle to go out on the balcony and "proclaim the Republic," de Gaulle curtly replied: "No. The Republic has never ceased to exist. Vichy was and still remains null and void. I am president of the government of the Republic. Why should I proclaim it now?" From de Gaulle's point of view, to do as Bidault asked would have been a recognition of the legitimacy of the Vichy regime, as well as a role of special authority for the Council of National Resistance. It would therefore be an act that would detract from his power, not enhance it. And at this supreme moment of the liberation, Charles de Gaulle's total concern was the clear establishment of power.

He then stepped over the sill of the window of the office of the *préfet* and out onto a small ornamental balcony, to the frenzied cheers of a crowd of tens of thousands massed in the big square in front of the Hôtel de Ville. As he stood with his arms outstretched above his head, fists clenched defiantly, an aide reached to grip his Sam Browne military belt from behind to prevent him falling over the balcony in case he was hit by a sniper's bullet. After a few minutes before the cheering crowd, de Gaulle climbed back inside.

Champagne and glasses had been produced to celebrate this supreme moment. But de Gaulle stunned the Resistance leaders by simply nodding, waving a curt goodbye, turning his back and walking out of the building, without any presentations or even the customary French handshake all around for those who had greeted him.

The liberation of Paris was to be General de Gaulle's apotheosis, and not that of the French Resistance and its leaders.

Already he had given instructions to Leclerc to organize a great procession down the Champs-Élysées the next day, Saturday, August 26. He did not even inform Bidault and the Council of National Resistance of his plan or invite them to join him in the parade. But of course it was not a secret, and Bidault and the Communist leaders and all the others turned up uninvited at the Arc de Triomphe.

Leclerc's division was still operating, however, under the American 5th Corps, commanded by Gerow. To the northeast of the city, the US 4th Infantry Division was hitting pockets of stiff German opposition, and Gerow wanted the 2nd French Armored Division back in the line of advance as quickly as possible to push the retreating Germans. When Gerow heard of de Gaulle's planned parade, he sent

Leclerc a written order on the morning of the twenty-sixth: "Operating as you are under my direct command, you will accept no orders from any other source. . . . The troops under your command will take no part in the parade, either this afternoon or at any other time, except on orders personally signed by me."

Gerow then sent a liaison officer to de Gaulle to inform him of his orders to Leclerc. De Gaulle stiffly informed the officer that Gerow was showing "remarkable incomprehension," and that Leclerc was taking his orders from the head of the French government. He had a perfect right, he said, to use one of his own divisions to enter his own capital.

In the meantime de Gaulle and Leclerc had taken reasonable military precautions. A unit of the division was moved eastward out to Le Bourget, along with a group of Resistance fighters, to engage and hold the enemy, and Leclerc throughout the parade was in constant radio contact with his unit commanders. De Gaulle commented that "it seemed to me highly unlikely that the German rear-guard would suddenly transform itself into an advance guard and march toward the center of Paris." It did not. But the affair fed his bitterness about his allies.

Promptly at 3 P.M. General de Gaulle arrived at the Arc de Triomphe, where his generals, admirals, *préfets* and the Resistance leaders were waiting. The eternal flame on the tomb of France's unknown warrior of the First World War was relit and de Gaulle laid a huge Cross of Lorraine wreath in rose gladioli on the grave. He then turned to look down the broad avenue des Champs-Élysées, jammed by the greatest throng in the history of Paris—well over a million people who had made their way since early morning on foot and by bicycle, for there was no public transport and fighting was still going on here and there around the capital.

The Resistance leaders were firmly told to remain several paces behind General de Gaulle, who with his great sense of occasion, elected to walk to the Place de la Concorde.

> I went on, touched and yet tranquil [he wrote in his Memoirs] amid the inexpressible exultation of the crowd, beneath the storm of voices echoing my name, trying, as I advanced, to look at every person in all that multitude in order that every eye might register my presence, raising and lowering my arms to reply to the cheers. This was one of those miracles of national consciousness, one of those gestures which sometimes in the course of centuries light up the history of France. The children—so pale but dancing and screaming for joy; the women—bearing so many sorrows but now smiling and cheering; the men—flooded with long forgotten pride, shouting their gratitude; the old—doing me the honor of their tears; how like one another they were! And at the center of this outburst, I felt I was fulfilling a function which far transcended my personality, for I was serving as an instrument of destiny.

At the Place de la Concorde, the General got into a military staff car for a slow drive down the long colonnade of the rue de Rivoli, past the Hôtel Meurice, scarred with the gunfire of only yesterday when General Choltitz gave up. All the way to the Hôtel de Ville, the crowd was jam-packed but restrained; wet with tears of emotion but orderly. Another brief stop at the Hôtel de Ville, where the band of the Garde Républicaine was drawn up in full dress, and then across the Seine to the Cathedral of Notre-Dame.

As de Gaulle got out of his staff car in front of the cathedral, two Alsatian girls stepped forward to present a bouquet of flowers, and at this moment there was a sudden burst of gunfire in the square. In an instant the scene turned to panic as spectators flattened on the pavement or dashed to the protection of the cathedral. Resistance fighters in the crowd then began shooting wildly, and de Gaulle, although remaining calm, was pinned by the rushing mob to a column at the cathedral door. A colonel in charge of the security detail forced his way through the crowd, and de Gaulle then entered the cathedral, unruffled and impassive. But he had advanced only a few steps down the great nave when more firing rang out—apparently coming from the galleries above the choir. The General walked calmly on to a place of honor at the front of the congregation, and by his own demeanor he managed to instil a tense order in the scene. More shots were heard as the congregation began singing the *Magnificat*. The service was cut short and a planned *Te Deum* was omitted. Just as impassively, de Gaulle left the cathedral to return to affairs of state.

Although security men swarmed all over Notre-Dame, it was never established how the shooting began or who was responsible, whether it was an assassination attempt in the making or a deliberate provocation by Resistance elements in order to justify reprisals. De Gaulle dismissed it as "a vulgar piece of showing off" in a private letter which he wrote the next day. "Many are walking about with arms, excited by the fighting of these last days, always ready to fire at the roofs. The first shot starts a wild fusillade. We shall fix this too."

*

The next day, Sunday, August 27, General Eisenhower drove into Paris with General Bradley from Bradley's Army Group headquarters, then at Chartres. It was Eisenhower's first visit to the city since he had served in France on the War Graves Commission in the 1920s, but he was not there for sightseeing.

"I went to call on General de Gaulle promptly, and I did this very deliberately as a kind of de facto recognition of him as the provisional President of France," Eisenhower told an interviewer after the war. "He was very grateful—he never forgot that. After all, I was commanding everything on the continent, all the troops, all that de Gaulle could count on, everything supplied by America was under my orders. So he looked upon it as what it was, and that was a very definite recognition of his high political position and his place. That was of course what he wanted and what Roosevelt had never given him."

But Eisenhower found Charles de Gaulle a very worried man. He wanted the Allies to facilitate movement of food and supplies to Paris, and then he asked in particular for Eisenhower to give him "thousands of uniforms" that he would issue to the motley Resistance units in order to incorporate them rapidly into the

French Army, under his own discipline and orders. He needed the uniforms first, but he also wanted military equipment—always more military equipment—to put more units in the front line.

Above all he asked for the immediate loan of two American Army divisions as a temporary show of force in the city, to establish his own position firmly in control. Eisenhower, in *Crusade in Europe,* says that when de Gaulle made this request his mind flashed back, across the past two years in North Africa, when never once had any French official ever asked for Allied troops to support his local authority. He goes on to comment: "Here there seemed a touch of the sardonic in the picture of France's symbol of liberation having to ask for Allied forces to establish and maintain a similar position in the heart of the freed capital." But he added, "I understood de Gaulle's problem," and he responded as best he could.

Pursuit of the retreating Germans across France was Eisenhower's first task— not the security of the city of Paris. But he told de Gaulle he would immediately order two American divisions routed through the capital and would have them paraded down the Champs-Élysées on their way to the front in a show of Allied strength that he said he hoped would serve the purpose. This was done in the next forty-eight hours, with Bradley and de Gaulle on the reviewing platform. Eisenhower says that this was "possibly the only instance in history of troops marching in parade through the capital of a great country to participate in pitched battle on the same day."

However grateful de Gaulle may have been to Eisenhower, he makes no mention of any of this in his Memoirs. This is not surprising, for it scarcely accords with the splendid word-picture that de Gaulle drew of his own parade down the Champs-Élysées, and how "around me rose extraordinary testimonials of unity." Instead, he relates only that he complained to Eisenhower of Gerow's orders to Leclerc and says that he "informed the commander-in-chief" that he would be keeping the Leclerc division in Paris for a few more days. His account leaves the impression that about the only business transacted was de Gaulle telling off Eisenhower, although he does add: "I expressed to this great and good leader the esteem, confidence and gratitude of the French Government."

Some weeks later, after de Gaulle had completed a whirlwind tour of France in postliberation unrest, he told his Intelligence chief, Colonel Passy: "The Communists had grabbed all the sources of production. I couldn't smash them, for to do that I should have had to bring back from the front several of our five divisions. But it was indispensable to keep them at the front so that France could take her place with honor among the victors."

It was, as Wellington said of the Battle of Waterloo, "a damn close-run thing."

The day after Eisenhower's visit, before the parade of the American troops took place, de Gaulle had his showdown with the Resistance leaders. He summoned the Council of National Resistance and the Paris Liberation Committee to his "center of power" at the Ministry of War, and after first warmly and elegantly congratulating them for their heroic past services to France and their part in the liberation of the capital, he dropped the guillotine. Their role was now over, he announced.

The Resistance organization in the liberated areas of France would immediately be disbanded. Some members of the council would be included in the new government, which he would shortly announce. Others from the council and the Paris Committee would be invited to join the enlarged National Consultative Assembly as soon as that body transferred from Algiers to Paris. As for the men of the Resistance forces, they would now join the French Army (in those uniforms Eisenhower would provide) to continue the fight against the Germans. Whatever the feelings of the leaders present at this cold douche, there were no expressions of dissent, which would have been quite useless anyway. When they left de Gaulle's office, the Resistance Movement had ceased to be an organization.

But declaring the disbandonment of the Resistance organization and asserting Gaullist control and authority over the seething cauldron of liberated France were quite different problems. In the early days of the liberation in Normandy in June and July, and even in Paris in August, this had been relatively simple for General de Gaulle—first because the Allied armies were sitting there in massive force waiting for the breakout, and second because he himself was present to take charge. But by the end of August, after the important landings of French and American forces on the Riviera, whole new areas of the country had been liberated, and the armies had swept on to the north and east. There was neither a military presence nor the presence of General de Gaulle.

Marseilles, with its vital port; Toulouse and the southwest; Grenoble, which was the key to the Alpine region; Lyons, with its industry and rail hub on the banks of the Rhône; Clermont-Ferrand and the Massif Central; Bordeaux and the Atlantic coast—in each of these regional centers a kind of hidden civil war was going on. Old scores were being settled with a vengeance between the *résistants* and the collaborationists, and many personal vendettas as well. But at the bottom line, it was a struggle for local power between the Communists and the Gaullists. General de Gaulle could declare the Resistance organization dissolved, but he could not dissolve the Communist apparat and he knew it. He had appointed his own regional commissioners of the Republic everywhere (in several cases he had even accepted Communist nominees), but these men had practically nothing to rely on in the way of instruments of power in those chaotic days of August, September, October and November except their own initiative, courage and decisiveness.

De Gaulle was well aware of this precarious and dangerous situation and anxious to come to grips with it. If the Communists had been able to gain decisive control of even one region of France, independent of de Gaulle, there is no telling what might have happened to the nation, how this might have spread. But de Gaulle first had to secure his power base in Paris, and hence his anxieties to Eisenhower.

On September 9, two weeks after his return to Paris, he announced the formation of his new provisional government. Georges Bidault became foreign minister, and Pierre Mendès-France was given the Finance Ministry. De Gaulle then took in two prominent Communists—Charles Tillon, a leader of the Paris

Resistance, as minister for air, and François Billoux, a trade unionist, as minister of health. It was a gamble to engage the Communist Party in "national unity" so he could subdue their bid for power in the provinces.

Next, on September 12, de Gaulle outlined the aims of his new government at a political mass meeting at the Palais de Chaillot, an invited audience of several thousand drawn from a wide spectrum of the unions, industry and commerce, universities, the bar association, the civil service and of course the Resistance. His speech was decidedly leftist in its internal political program, in line with earlier political discussions he had held in London and Algiers with leaders of the Socialist Party, and also reflecting a declaration that had been produced by the Council of National Resistance. De Gaulle promised

> to raise the workers' standard of living as the rate of production rises; to requisition or sequester certain public services and enterprises for the direct use of the state; to appropriate for the nation the illegal profits made by those who collaborated with the enemy; to fix commodity prices and regulate commerce as long as what is produced and transportable is not equivalent to consumer demand; to subordinate private interest to public advantage; to exploit the natural resources of the nation and administer them to the general advantages; finally to permit each of France's sons and daughters to live, work and to raise their children in security and dignity.

He was now ready to turn to the chaos and uncertainty in the provinces, to make his presence and authority felt, and stiffen the machinery of public order, which was there in form but without a firm grip. On September 14 he left Paris on the first of a series of lightning tours which in the next six weeks took him to every part of liberated France to be seen in person by at least 10 million Frenchmen, one-quarter of the country's population at the time. It was a starving and shabby nation that he toured, run down, exhausted, depleted and all but inert but for the personal enthusiasm that greeted him and the sense of freedom at last that prevailed after five years of war and occupation.

France did not remotely suffer the scale of sheer physical destruction visited on the cities and towns of Germany by Allied bombings and subsequently the artillery and streetfighting of the advance into the heart of the country against die-hard Nazi opposition. In France there was localized damage but not general destruction except of the railway system. Out of 12,000 prewar locomotives, only 2,800 were left. Upwards of 3,000 road and rail bridges were down, blown up either by the retreating Germans or bombed by the Allies to cut off retreat. It was estimated that 90 percent of the country's prewar automobiles and trucks had either broken down, disappeared or been destroyed. Transportation was the key to everything, from food supplies to factory output. But in the early months of the liberation, no trains ran anywhere on the long-distance services out of Paris, and only sporadic short-haul services operated. Moreover, good communications were also essential to strong government from the center in Paris, for without this unifying force, the tendency was even stronger for the regions to take things into their own hands.

De Gaulle's first trip took him to Lyons, Marseilles and Toulouse—cities where the situation was particularly precarious and complex, indeed almost a microcosm of the postliberation chaos of France as a whole.

In Toulouse for the previous three weeks, a remarkable young Frenchmen named Pierre Bertaux had been struggling as regional commissioner of the Republic for the southwest to maintain law and order and his own position as authority of the central government against a highly organized local Communist movement with several thousand Resistance activists under its control. The local Communist commander was a young officer of the French Army, Second Lieutenant Claude Asher, who had joined the Communist underground after the fall of France and had adopted the rank and *nom de guerre* of Colonel Ravanel.

To add to the local complexities, a British officer named Colonel Hilaire had been parachuted into the region by the Special Operations Executive two years earlier, and he had organized under his command and control a well-equipped *maquis* force of about 700 men. Finally there was a contingent of several thousand Spanish Republicans in the region who wanted to seize the opportunity of the German retreat from the southwest to cross the Spanish border and march on Barcelona to overthrow Generalissimo Franco.

Bertaux, a professor of German at Toulouse University, had joined the underground in November 1940. He had been caught by the Vichy police and imprisoned, but escaped with the help of the Resistance. His Resistance credentials were high, and he was a political moderate. The Gaullist coordinators of the Resistance in London and Paris then selected him to be deputy regional commissioner for the southwest when Toulouse was liberated. The commissioner was to have been a Communist supporter, Jean Cassou, who later broke with the party after the war.

On August 19, as the Free French Army began advancing from the Mediterranean up the Rhône Valley, German forces in Toulouse were ordered to withdraw north to avoid being cut off. Cassou that night attended a Communist underground meeting to make preparations for taking over the next day, but as he was returning to Toulouse by car he was challenged at a German roadblock, shot, beaten up and left for dead. Companions got him to a hospital in a coma and he eventually survived.

When word of this reached Bertaux, he realized at once that if he did not move fast to assert his authority as Cassou's deputy and replacement, the Communists under Ravanel would install themselves in power and confront Paris with a *fait accompli*. He rushed immediately to the Toulouse Préfecture and informed the Vichy-appointed *préfet:* "I am the commissioner of the Republic."

With punctilious politeness, the two men then briefly discussed the local electricity-supply situation, reserves of gasoline, water and flour; where the worst German damage had occurred; and the most immediately urgent problems of the city. Bertaux next informed the outgoing *préfet* that he was under arrest and was not to leave his private quarters.

Bertaux was now sitting behind the *préfet*'s desk, but what power did he have and how long would he stay there? Within an hour members of the Communist-dominated local Committee of Liberation charged into the building, followed shortly after by Ravanel. Bertaux imperiously informed them that "I am replacing Cassou on orders of General de Gaulle."

The Communists, meanwhile, had seized the local newspaper office and radio station, but at the Préfecture it was a stalemate. Bertaux slept that night, and for the next few weeks, in his office, "a pistol with me, and before I locked the door for the night I informed people outside that if anybody tried to open the door during the night I would shoot."

There was no communication with Paris for the next crucial two weeks, and Bertaux was on his own with only about 800 policemen under his direct orders to control eight *départements* (counties) of the southwest. Little by little, he first simply had to make it known who he was, and then have his authority recognized, and finally his orders and instructions carried out. This was the situation when de Gaulle reached Toulouse on September 16 and met Regional Commissioner Bertaux for the first time.

Whatever the scenes of destruction and the plight of the French people that de Gaulle had encountered on the journey from Paris, it had not stirred his sense of compassion. Rather he seems to have been infuriated by the breakdown of authority that he found, for he was in a mean mood and a foul temper every stop he made.

All the same, restoring order and authority was his purpose and he had done his homework. When "Colonel Ravanel" was introduced to him, he looked the young man up and down coldly and snapped: "Second Lieutenant Asher." Soon after de Gaulle returned to Paris, written orders arrived returning Asher to duty with the Army—and that was the end of his independent Communist force in Bertaux's domain.

Bertaux then told de Gaulle about Colonel Hilaire and related how, earlier on, the British officer called at the Préfecture to declare that "order must be maintained here, and if there is any trouble I will simply bang my fist and take over command." When de Gaulle heard this, he demanded of Bertaux, "Didn't you have him arrested?" Bertaux said that Hillaire had 700 armed men with him, and anyway it was all smoothed over. De Gaulle grunted that at least he hoped Bertaux had not invited Hilaire to the official luncheon he was giving.

"Of course I have," Bertaux replied. "He fought for nearly two years in the *maquis* under your name and Churchill's."

De Gaulle flew into a temper and said he absolutely refused to eat with the British officer. Hilaire then arrived at the Préfecture to be presented to de Gaulle, and a stormy scene took place behind closed doors. Finally the door burst open and Hilaire stalked out in a rage while de Gaulle followed to order Bertaux: "You will give him twenty-four hours to leave French soil. If he stays, you will have him arrested." The expulsion order was carried out—though not quite as brusquely or promptly as de Gaulle wanted.

As for the Spaniards who wanted to march on Barcelona, regular French troops were moved in to secure the frontier under Bertaux's control. The Spaniards were told they could join the Army or be disbanded or arrested. By the time de Gaulle left Toulouse, there was no longer any doubt where supreme authority in France lay and who was to exercise it locally.

Pierre Bertaux, who was then thirty-four years old, rose after the war to head the Sûreté Nationale, the national police force. Despite the tensions of the Toulouse visit, he seems to have hit it off with de Gaulle. He related later that at the luncheon after the Hilaire incident, he asked the General about his intentions for the future, and de Gaulle replied with great gravity: "As for me, I shall withdraw. . . . I have a mission, and it is coming to an end. I must disappear. France may again one day have need of a pure image. That image must be left with her. Had Joan of Arc been married, she would no longer have been Joan of Arc. I must disappear."

*

No one knows for certain how many Frenchmen died in World War II as a result of the fighting, of deportation or executions during the occupation, or above all in the turmoil of the purging and killings and legal executions that followed the liberation. It is a question that has never been answered with authority or accuracy. Official statements by responsible ministers have differed widely, and over the years several commissions of the National Assembly have sifted the evidence and come up with various estimates and conclusions.

General de Gaulle's attitude toward the whole problem of dealing with Vichy collaborators and French traitors was that justice should be rigorous and above all swift, but on the whole he wanted it to be confined to clear and obvious cases— minimal numbers rather than any wholesale settling of scores. His attitude was not so much one of generosity, but was based on reasons of authority and integrity of the State. Summary executions, private vendettas, were a defiance of authority. "In spite of everything [de Gaulle wrote] no individual had the right to punish the guilty; it was the State's concern. Therefore the State must provide, and without delay, that its courts investigate cases and give verdicts. Not to do so was to risk being swamped by the fury of groups or individuals."

But "the fury of groups or individuals" did indeed swamp justice. De Gaulle's hopes for a quick-purge-and-over were clear. When he walked into the Hôtel de Ville the evening of his return to Paris, his first words to the *préfet* of Paris whom he had appointed, Flouret, as they started up the stairs, were: "How far have you got with the purge? The important thing is that it be done quickly. The whole business must be finished within a few weeks." But the French being French, the machinery of French justice being what it is, and passions being what they were, neither order nor speed nor justice prevailed. Trials of Vichy collaborators went on until 1949.

As for the summary executions, without trial and without records, Adrien Tixier, who was minister of the interior at the time of the liberation, gave the Intelligence chief, Colonel Passy, a figure of 105,000 in late 1944 or early 1945, and this figure tended to become fixed in much reporting and writing about these events in the postwar years. But in 1953, Henri Queuille, who was then premier and minister of the interior, gave a parliamentary committee a figure of only 9,675 summary executions.

The most careful sifting of the facts and evidence was carried out by the historian Robert Aron in his three volumes of liberation history, in which he drew on masses of day-to-day documents, region-by-region of the country. Aron comments that "Tixier was an impulsive man, given in speech at least to exaggeration," and points out that 105,000 deaths by summary execution would have meant an average of 1,000 for every *département* of France, and "no private witness, however emotional, ever suggested a figure of this sort." On the other hand, he totally dismisses the lower figure given by Queuille. But when Aron tried through the highest levels to gain access to detailed reports by the *préfets,* and those of other ministries and departments such as War and Justice, he ran into a stone wall. So did a Judicial Action Committee of the Resistance, which tried to get the facts in 1955 and was turned down.

Aron's main source, therefore, was local police records in various towns, which were mountainous. He records cases of wives taking the opportunity of the liberation to kill mistresses of their husbands as "collaborationists," of criminals on the rampage looting and killing, of the police themselves settling personal scores with lawyers who had opposed them in courts. There were endless cases of women who had served as prostitutes for the German occupiers. And finally there were the politically motivated killings. A few years after the war, I vacationed at the little village of Saint-Maxime, on the Riviera, not far from where one of the major landings of the invasion of southern France took place. I was shown a site near the town where the Communist *résistants* shot and killed sixteen men from a rival non-Communist Resistance group. In this general area, Aron estimates the summary executions to have been "something like 800" as opposed to the official figure in the 1953 summary given by Queuille of 310.

All in all, Aron estimates that between thirty and forty thousand men and women were "shot and massacred" in France between June 1944 and May 1945 without any process of law, and he leans to the higher figure. There were 779 legal executions carried out after trial and sentence for collaboration. Aron then fixes the total French wartime dead from August 1939 to May 1945 at 628,000—of whom, he says, 200,000 were political, racial and labor deportees to Germany. He gives a figure of 133,000 civilian casualties as a result of military operations. The remaining deaths took place on the battlefield in 1940 and later stages, in the Resistance, executions by the Germans and deaths in prisoner of war camps.

If these figures are approximately accurate—and they have not been basically disputed since Aron published them in the late 1950s—then France's total dead in World War II was far higher than that of either Great Britain or the United States, which carried the main burden of the fighting.

Battlefield and naval deaths of British forces in six years of war from August 1939 to the Japanese surrender in September 1945 were 357,000 men. The figure for the United States was 291,000. These do not include merchant marine deaths or civilian deaths due to the war, bombings, and similar causes. But these would not raise the American or British totals appreciably higher, and certainly nowhere near a French toll of combined war-related deaths, military and civilian, of 628,000.

*

As General de Gaulle made his rounds of the French cities, struggling to reimpose law and order and bolster his regional commissioners, Eisenhower in October again resumed efforts to get Roosevelt to finally recognize the newly formed and clearly established French government. Roosevelt and Churchill had met again in Quebec in mid-September 1944, as the president headed into his fourth-term election campaign. Once again they had hashed over the same old arguments about de Gaulle, and once again Churchill had agreed with FDR's refusal to recognize, despite urgings from Anthony Eden. Churchill was still smarting over de Gaulle's ridiculous refusal to meet him in Algiers the month before, and was not overly inclined to buck Roosevelt on the recognition question at this point anyway.

Meanwhile, Jefferson Caffery, a US Foreign Service career diplomat, had arrived in Paris in early October with the designation of American ambassador to France. But his status was anomalous, to say the least. Roosevelt had named him ambassador to a government that he did not recognize, without even going through the age-old diplomatic practice of asking the French in advance for their permission to receive Caffery in Paris.

Accordingly, de Gaulle had flatly refused to see Caffery—and had administered the same diplomatic snub to Duff Cooper, the British ambassador who had transferred from Algiers to Paris on September 13, even though he knew Cooper well and respected his professionalism and his weight with the British government. So the two Allied ambassadors were confined to doing diplomatic business with Foreign Minister Georges Bidault at the Quai d'Orsay. Without full diplomatic recognition of the French government, de Gaulle's door was closed. If this was judged in Washington or London to be petty, it was certainly understandable.

Eisenhower took up the cudgels for de Gaulle in a long conversation with Caffery, which was transmitted to the State Department and Roosevelt. Eisenhower urged that the United States realize that if the forces of disorder that General de Gaulle was battling ever got the upper hand, and if there were a breakdown of governmental authority, it would create an intolerable situation behind the battle lines for the Supreme Allied Command. Whatever might be said about de Gaulle, Eisenhower told Caffery, there was no opposition leader in sight with the slightest chance of taking over. But if by some miracle de Gaulle were overthrown, chaos would follow. Eisenhower pleaded that difficulties could be avoided and the French government strengthened if it were promptly recognized and if Washington began working with it fully and unambiguously. He commented to Caffery that it was going to be a long hard winter, and the Allies would probably be able to assure the French only one-third as much coal as they had been getting during the occupation. "Better a French government be blamed for this than SHAEF," he commented.

Meanwhile, Churchill, back in London after Quebec and a quick visit to Stalin in Moscow, was under very heavy pressure in the House of Commons and from public opinion on the French recognition situation, which was plainly becoming ridiculous.

On October 14 Churchill wearily cabled FDR again: "I have been reflecting on the question of recognition. . . . There is no doubt that the French have been cooperating with Supreme Headquarters and their provisional government has the support of the majority of French people. I suggest, therefore, that we can now safely recognize General de Gaulle's administration."

Still Roosevelt would not budge. He replied that nothing should be done until there was a real "zone of the interior" in France, recognized by Eisenhower as free of fighting, and until the Consultative Assembly, moving from Algiers, had been enlarged along with the formation of the new government. Roosevelt added sourly that "I would not be satisfied with de Gaulle merely saying that he was going to do it."

One of de Gaulle's private secretaries, Claude Mauriac, son of the great French author François Mauriac, recorded in a secret diary that he kept and later published that at about this time de Gaulle also received a personal letter from Roosevelt "advising him" to include General Giraud in his government, and that "the General's reply was extremely impertinent."

But on October 20, Eisenhower changed everything with a cable to the joint chiefs of staff in Washington that he had now reached a firm agreement with the French on boundaries of a zone of the interior to be turned over completely to French administration and control. SHAEF was as anxious to be rid of its internal responsibilities (even though they were largely nominal) as the French were to end the anomaly.

Eisenhower's action cut the last ground from under Roosevelt. After months and years, the stubborn president now reversed himself overnight, without any warning or advance notice to Churchill—another of those small snubs, hurts and affronts that the prime minister suffered from Roosevelt in their one-sided relationship. Churchill heard about it from the Foreign Office, which got word of it from the United States embassy in Paris. The Americans intended to recognize on October 23, 1944, when Eisenhower would also be signing the agreement with the French on the zone of the interior.

And so it was done at last, the United States, Great Britain and the Soviet Union acting in parallel on the same afternoon, long after all the other European allies had recognized both reality and virtue. General de Gaulle treated the move with total silence for two days and then held a news conference with the Allied press at which he simply made the sardonic comment: "The French Government is satisfied to be called by its name." On the evening of the twenty-third, he saw Ambassador Duff Cooper for the first time in Paris and invited him to dinner. Cooper recorded in his diary: "It was an extremely frigid and dreary party, worse than his entertainments usually are. He made no reference when I arrived to the fact that his government had been recognized by the three Great Powers that afternoon, and when I said that I hoped he was glad it was finished, he shrugged his shoulders and said it would never be finished."

*

Winston Churchill flew to Paris on November 10, 1944, at the invitation of de Gaulle—a visit that was organized with some trepidation on the British side and not without some fussy protocol problems raised by de Gaulle. The two men had not met since their stormy session in Churchill's train on the eve of D-Day. Churchill remained in a sour mood about de Gaulle right up to the time he took off for Paris, and there were justifiable worries that the visit was likely to do more harm than good.

In the event, it was an occasion almost as great and memorable for the people of Paris as de Gaulle's return to the city four months earlier—who could not have been misty-eyed at the sight of the indomitable Churchill side by side with General de Gaulle, laying a wreath at the Arc de Triomphe on Armistice Day, 1944? De Gaulle had turned over an entire floor of the private reception rooms and apartments of the Quai d'Orsay for Churchill and his party, and the prime minister took special pleasure lolling in a gold bathtub that had been installed for Hermann Goering.

Immersed in the atmosphere of how far they had advanced together toward victory in four years, despite all the bitterness through which they had fought, their discussions were largely prudent and philosophical, gentle probing and side-digs but no confrontation or recrimination. De Gaulle pressed hard for more and more arms, and Churchill resoundingly affirmed his desire to see France restored as a great military power. He promised to do what Britain could do with military aid, but sighed that only America could supply real weight, and the Americans, he told de Gaulle, now judged that the war would be over within six months before they could divert any major amounts of equipment to France.

This was already rapidly becoming another paranoid sore point with de Gaulle—an inner conviction that Roosevelt was holding out on him to keep France in a subordinate military condition and deny his nation the power position in Europe which was hers. Whatever the realities of the Allied supply problem, they were never accepted or even examined by de Gaulle. As far as he was concerned, arms were being withheld from France because of politics, not because of logistics.

At any rate, on the last day of Churchill's stay in Paris, the prime minister proposed to de Gaulle that the two governments begin discussions on an Anglo-French Treaty of Alliance—something that had never before existed, formally, despite two world wars. But Churchill got a dusty answer. De Gaulle was still at loggerheads with the British over the Middle East, and he deeply resented Churchill's continual siding with Roosevelt and the Americans against what he considered to be the interests of France and Europe.

Unless Great Britain were in agreement to act with France "in mutual resolve," the General told Churchill, "why sign a document that would be ambiguous?" In an important passage of his Memoirs, de Gaulle elaborated his reasons for this rebuff, which continued to echo in the history of the next twenty-five years:

> England was in favor of France's political reappearance. She would be increasingly so for reasons of equilibrium, tradition and security. She desired a formal alliance with us, but she would not consent to link her policy with ours, in the belief that she could play her own game between Moscow and Washington, limit their demands, but also take advantage of them. . . . In fact, they were pursuing certain precise goals in areas where the position of states and the status quo were not yet firmly established, and offered to British ambitions numerous opportunities of manipulation and expansion. This was especially true in the Mediterranean. According to London's plans, Athens, Belgrade, Beirut, Damascus and Tripoli under various forms of association would tomorrow supplement British influence previously dependent on Gibraltar, Malta, Cyprus, Cairo, Amman and Baghdad. Thus the concessions which Great Britain could not avoid making to Russian voracity and American capitalist ideology would find their counterpart. No ordeal changes the nature of man; no crisis that of states.

Perfide Albion! Certainly no ordeal had changed the nature of General Charles de Gaulle, nor his extraordinary capacity for arranging a chessboard to his own vision of history and plotting his moves accordingly.

*

Whatever reasoning or arguments he voiced to Churchill in rebuffing the offer of an Anglo-French Alliance, de Gaulle had already decided first to approach the Soviet Union for such a treaty. Already, as early as November 6, he had discussed with the Soviet ambassador to France, Alexander Bogomolov, his desire to visit the Soviet Union and meet Marshal Stalin. Of course de Gaulle revealed none of this to Churchill during the Paris visit. The Allies never informed him when they were going to hold meetings—why should he inform them? Churchill and Roosevelt learned of the Moscow visit, then, in messages from Stalin on November 22.

In his Memoirs, de Gaulle says that Bogomolov "took every opportunity of urging me to visit Moscow," but this effort to make it appear that the Russians took the initiative in inviting him to see Stalin does not accord with the facts. Soviet documents, researched by Alexander Werth for his monumental book *Russia at War,* disclosed that Bogomolov relayed a request to Moscow from de Gaulle on November 8, and the Russians then replied on November 18 with an invitation "in view of the desire General de Gaulle has expressed in his recent conversation with A. E. Bogomolov to visit the Soviet Union." But it was a basic tenet of de Gaulle's exercise of power, or a fetish of his character, never to appear to be the *demandeur* who asks, always the one who is asked. Of course he never ceased to ask his allies for arms, but that was a matter of military necessity, not diplomacy. At any rate, there is no doubt that he initiated the Moscow visit, not the Russians.

Immediately before setting out for the Soviet Union, on November 24, de Gaulle suddenly announced a "free pardon" for the leader of the French Communist Party, Maurice Thorez, who had deserted from his Army unit in 1940 at the start of the Battle of France and had been spirited by the Comintern network to Moscow, where he had spent the entire war. At de Gaulle's announcement, the Russians acted with remarkable swiftness to get Thorez back to France. Despite all the exigencies of wartime transport, he arrived in Paris on November 27, while de Gaulle was en route to Moscow.

Did de Gaulle make a deal with Stalin on the Thorez pardon? It is unlikely, but there is no doubt that he made the move in order to improve the atmosphere for his Moscow visit, and above all to continue to mollify the Communist Party and keep it generally in line behind his authority. To have pardoned Thorez *after* he saw Stalin would clearly have looked like a deal under Soviet pressure, so if he was going to do it he had to act before he left Paris.

De Gaulle records that Stalin brought up the subject of Thorez in their Moscow talks and said: "Let me only say that I know Thorez and that in my opinion he is a good Frenchman. If I were in your place, I would not put him in prison—at least not right away!" De Gaulle says that he replied: "The French Government treats the French according to the services it expects of them."

De Gaulle's gamble in allowing Thorez to return to France—if that's what it was—certainly paid off, in the short term at least, through 1945 until after the war was won and the Cold War began to set in. While Thorez spent a rather inglorious war in Moscow, the party leadership under fire in France itself had rested with Jacques Duclos. Having fought the battles of the Resistance, the Communists came out of the liberation in a militant mood—anxious at the cadre levels in particular to crash on ahead to proletarian victory, revolution and the overthrow of the Vichy regime in favor of a Socialist Republic. This had been blocked almost entirely through the presence of General de Gaulle. After de Gaulle pronounced the Resistance movement to be at an end and disbanded, Duclos, in October, had suddenly announced the formation of a Communist "patriotic militia." De Gaulle immediately cracked down by declaring it illegal, to a chorus of leftist protests and a series of bombings in Paris and elsewhere.

This seesaw struggle between the Communists and Gaullist authority continued not very far below the surface through the remainder of 1944. But in January— two months after Thorez returned to France and one month after de Gaulle got back from Moscow—Thorez convened the French Politbureau for a decisive session. He pronounced that patriotic armed groups had now served their purpose and were to be wound up. The direct Communist threat to de Gaulle abruptly receded. Thorez was Stalin's man in Paris, and perhaps Thorez had eliminated a threat to his own power within the party as well. At any rate, he continued to control the party with slavish loyalty to Moscow for the next twenty years.

Meanwhile, de Gaulle left Paris by air, first for Cairo and then Tehran. With King Farouk of Egypt and the young Shah Reza Pahlavi of Iran, he exchanged mutual antipathies and animosities about British designs or ambitions in the area, real or imagined. To the shah, de Gaulle said, "Your Majesty must be independence personified." He then advised him that "if one of the three occupying powers [Britain, the United States and the Soviet Union all had forces in Iran at the time] attempts to obtain your cooperation to his advantage, let him find you inaccessible, even when this attitude involves considerable discomfort for yourself." De Gaulle says the shah was "comforted by the advice I had given him." It was not the kind of advice he would have wanted the British giving the rulers of Syria or Lebanon, but *tant pis* for loyalty to allies.

De Gaulle's party arrived at Baku in the Soviet Union on November 26 and found that the Russians were in no apparent hurry to speed their way to Moscow. They declined to allow the General to proceed in his own plane and told him that in any case the weather was too bad for any flying at all. He was kept waiting in Baku for two days for a special train that hauled the Grand Duke Nicholas around during the First World War. It then took four days to reach Moscow, where he arrived on December 2.

*

De Gaulle's stay in Moscow lasted one week, and he spent about fifteen hours in all in direct talks with Marshal Stalin—"all strategy, suspicion and stubbornness, used to disguising his features as well as his inmost soul, to dispensing with illusions, pity or sincerity, and to see in each man an obstacle or a threat." The visit climaxed with one of the most extraordinary diplomatic banquet scenes ever staged in the Kremlin.

De Gaulle badly wanted a treaty with the Soviet Union to wave at his Western allies as evidence of his admission to the ranks of the Great Powers. Stalin deemed it useful to conclude a treaty with France if he could get something out of it. From the moment de Gaulle set foot in the Kremlin, therefore, an intricate diplomatic duel was played out over who would pay a price for the treaty and what that price would be. De Gaulle won, virtually hands down.

While de Gaulle was making his slow journey to Moscow, Stalin had cabled both Churchill and Roosevelt that there was "every evidence" he would want a Franco-Soviet pact and "I would like to know your view." Churchill, having been rebuffed by de Gaulle over an Anglo-French pact in Paris barely three weeks before, replied to Stalin that of course the British had no objection, but why not make it a three-way, Anglo-Soviet-French treaty of friendship and alliance? This became a joker in Stalin's hand when the play began in the Kremlin.

De Gaulle opened at once at their first meeting by going to what he considered the heart of the matter, which was Germany. Rather audaciously he proposed that "Moscow and Paris establish a settlement which they would jointly propose to the other Allies." He wanted Soviet agreement on a dismemberment of Germany that would, in effect, advance France's eastern frontier to the Rhine by permanently detaching the Rhineland from any central German authority and also placing the industrial Ruhr under permanent international control.

Stalin's reply was that the German question must first be studied with Britain and the United States. But, he said, Germany's eastern frontier would have to rest on the Oder and Neisse rivers, and East Prussia, Pomerania and Silesia would all disappear and become part of Poland. De Gaulle retorted that "apparently the Rhine cannot be broached at present, but the Oder-Neisse has been discussed."

Nevertheless, Georges Bidault and the Soviet foreign minister, V. M. Molotov, now began putting together a treaty draft. Meanwhile the Russians turned on the hospitality while haggling remorselessly behind the scenes over what seemed to de Gaulle to be trivial detail. Finally, in a meeting on December 6, Stalin showed his hand, his real objective. He launched into a long and bitter discourse, or diatribe, on the Polish problem—at the end of which he proposed that the treaty include French recognition of the Soviet-backed Lublin Polish Committee. This would have meant French abandonment of the Polish government-in-exile in London, which had been one of the first to recognize de Gaulle's Free French back in 1940. Moreover, the Polish question touched de Gaulle particularly, since he had spent nearly two years in the country and fought with the Polish Army against the Bolsheviks in 1919.

At once he demurred that "the future Government of Poland is the business of the Polish people, who must be able to express themselves by universal suffrage." After this, the discussion more or less circled the Balkans, and the more Stalin talked about his Balkan plans, the more de Gaulle realized that "he was going to try to sell us the pact in exchange for our public approbation of his Polish operation."

But Stalin next played his "Churchill card," disclosing to de Gaulle that the prime minister had cabled a proposal that they conclude a tripartite pact and indicating that the Soviet Union was disposed to go along with this approach. De Gaulle was incensed at this move. Albion was being *perfide* again! He replied to Stalin with a vigorous argument about how only France and the Soviet Union on the continent could act to intervene promptly against any renewal of a German threat and asked, "Must we wait to act until London is ready to do so?" De Gaulle was probably content when Stalin finally abandoned the tripartite proposal with the remark, "Churchill will be offended, of course, once more, but he's offended me often enough."

Meanwhile, Averell Harriman, then the United States ambassador to Moscow, held a long talk with de Gaulle at the French embassy at which the question of the Lublin Poles was predominant. De Gaulle told Harriman that "Soviet policy will make for great fear among the small nations of Europe," which, he said, would have to rally round France because Britain was an island with imperial entanglements and the United States was far away with interests of her own. Harriman was not much impressed by this Gaullist vision, but he was reassured by de Gaulle that "he had made it plain to Stalin that he would take no action on Poland without consulting us and the British."

Next the Soviets sent a delegation from the Lublin Committee to call on de Gaulle at the French embassy. Since they had been seen by both Churchill and Eden on their earlier visit to Moscow, de Gaulle saw them on the afternoon of December 9, his last day in Moscow. Although most of the treaty draft had by now been laboriously ironed out, the Soviets were still insisting on a parallel statement of recognition, which de Gaulle was just as resolutely refusing. He told the committee representatives, "obliged to speak lines prepared for them in advance," that he would go no further than sending a French Army captain to Lublin on a liaison mission to handle freed French prisoners of war.

So, with negotiations deadlocked on the final night, the entire French delegation arrived at the Kremlin, where Stalin presided at "an overpowering banquet, the table sparkling with inconceivable luxury." In the early stages of the banquet, de Gaulle says, the deadlocked negotiation was not even mentioned, apart from Stalin asking him about his meeting with the Lublin Poles, to which he replied that "they were certainly not independent Poland." De Gaulle's account of the banquet is one of sardonic disgust.

The toasts began—first to France and de Gaulle, then the United States and England, then the French Army, Foreign Minister Bidault, General Alphonse Juin, on and on. After that, de Gaulle counted more than thirty Stalin toasts to individual Russians present, praise mingled with threats, as when he raised his glass to Alexander Novikov, chief of the Air Staff: "You are the one who uses our planes. If you use them badly, you should know what's in store for you!" Having witnessed this "tragicomic scene," de Gaulle wrote, "I was still less inclined to support the sacrifice of Poland."

De Gaulle got in his digs too. Harriman records that after the toasts were over and coffee and brandy were being served, de Gaulle, sitting next to him, suddenly pointed across the room to Marshal Nikolai Bulganin and said in a loud voice: "Isn't that the man who killed so many Russian generals?" It was loud enough for an interpreter to hear, and moments later, this having been repeated to Stalin, he called out to Bulganin: "Bring the machine guns. Let's liquidate the diplomats." General de Gaulle was not amused.

Molotov and Bidault, meanwhile, had settled down at another table for another argument about the deadlocked treaty negotiations, and Stalin then swept everyone else into his private theater to see a film, "extremely conformist and quite naïve." Before the film began, de Gaulle had a brief word with Bidault, who reported that everything still depended on French acceptance of a declaration recognizing the Polish Committee. He told Bidault that further negotiation would be useless and disadvantageous, and he would bring it to an end.

When the lights then came on after the propaganda film, General de Gaulle rose and said to Stalin, "I am making my farewells." With elaborate courtesy he said his train would be leaving early in the morning, that France and Russia would continue side by side to victory, and that "I cannot thank you enough for the way in which you have received me."

Stalin did not quite comprehend—this certainly had never happened to him before. He mumbled something about staying for another film, but de Gaulle merely held out his hand, shook Stalin's hand and walked slowly but purposefully from the room, nodding goodbyes to the other guests "paralyzed with astonishment" as he went. Molotov, pale with confusion and fear, rushed with him to his car and de Gaulle drove off to the French embassy.

He says that "fundamentally, I had few doubts as to what would happen next." Stalin and Molotov went into a huddle, and about 2 A.M. one of the French delegation who had stayed behind, Maurice Dejean, came hurrying to the embassy with word that the Russians were proposing compromise language on the Polish question.

Instead of a declaration of recognition, they now suggested wording that "by agreement between the French Government and the Polish Committee of National Liberation," a French liaison officer was being sent to Lublin. De Gaulle sent Dejean back with a refusal. The wording implied French recognition, and he would agree only to a simple unilateral announcement that France was sending a liaison officer to Lublin.

At about four in the morning, the Soviets gave way. A new treaty text and modified draft statement on Poland were sent to de Gaulle at the embassy. He returned to the Kremlin for a signing ceremony. Harriman then records, although de Gaulle does not:

> When de Gaulle arrived, Stalin handed him the original draft of the treaty to sign. He appealed for French support of the Lublin Committee. France as a continental ally should understand the requirement more clearly than Britain or the United States, Stalin argued. De Gaulle was furious at having been called from his bed to listen to the same argument all over again. "France has been insulted," he said, and started to stalk out of the room. Stalin then calmly asked Molotov for the new draft, oblivious to his own crude last-minute effort to break down de Gaulle's resistance.

De Gaulle carefully satisfied himself as to the texts he was approving, and the documents were signed at 6 A.M. on December 10, 1944. He had held out as well against even a simultaneous announcement of the assignment of a French liaison officer to Lublin, which was only released a week later, after Captain Christian Fouchet had reached the Polish town. Meanwhile, in the Kremlin room a newly laden table again appeared and Stalin prepared to start another round of eating and toasting. De Gaulle cut it as short as courtesy would allow. He records a sinister finale: "Suddenly, calling over Podzerov, the Russian interpreter who had attended every meeting and translated every exchange, the Marshal said to him, his expression grim, his voice harsh: 'You know too much! I'd better send you to Siberia.' I left the room with my ministers. Turning back at the door, I saw Stalin, sitting, alone, at the table. He had started eating again."

*

Stalin had gambled de Gaulle wanted or needed a treaty with the Soviet Union so badly that he would pay a Soviet price—and he lost. He went as far as to grumble congratulations to de Gaulle ("You played your hand well—well done— I like dealing with someone who knows what he wants, even if he doesn't share my views," according to de Gaulle), but he did not like losing. This became clear in his attitude toward the French at the Yalta conference a few weeks later.

De Gaulle's train left Moscow a few hours after the treaty signing, and after again stopping in Tehran and Cairo and a brief visit in Tunis he reached Paris on December 16, 1944—one of the momentous days of the war.

That morning, Field Marshal Karl von Rundstedt launched his massive surprise counteroffensive against thinly held American lines in the Ardennes Forest at the juncture of the Belgian-Luxembourg-French frontier in what became known as the Battle of the Bulge—Hitler's last strategic gamble.

A total of twenty-three Nazi divisions crashed through the American positions and drove relentlessly forward for the next eight days, aided by a freezing fog that hung over the battle area, nullifying Allied air operations against them on the ground. In the midst of the advance, a United States Airborne division, cut off and surrounded, held out heroically at the town of Bastogne, a crucial junction of mountain roads. As the German advance gradually slowed down or was contained, Eisenhower prepared to counterattack on the flanks of the bulge from the south and the north, to cut off the salient and trap the enemy forces.

This meant consolidating and shifting in the long Allied front, which extended almost the length of the Rhine from Holland in the north to the Swiss frontier in the south. The French held the southern end of this line—its 1st Army under General Jean-Marie de Lattre de Tassigny now numbering seven divisions. On the French northern flank, Leclerc's 2nd Armored division had fought a swift and brilliant action just one month before to liberate the ancient Alsatian capital of Strasbourg on November 23, in a victory that ranked next to the liberation of Paris in French emotion and pride.

But to the south of Strasbourg, the French were bogged down in difficult mountain terrain and winter weather around the valley towns of Colmar and Belfort, strongly held by the Nazis, all the more obstinately after the loss of Strasbourg. Thus, the French in Strasbourg were well out in front to the east of the rest of the French 1st Army and therefore exposed to counterattack at a time when the Allies had their hands full with the Battle of the Bulge.

To minimize this risk and shorten lines to provide reserves needed for the counterattack in the north, Eisenhower decided to order the French to fall back from Strasbourg and the flat country of the Rhine to defensive positions, with the Vosges mountains at their backs.

Eisenhower reached his decisions on December 26—as it happened, the day after de Gaulle had elected to make a morale-boosting visit to Strasbourg and the 1st Army. By December 30 orders to prepare for withdrawal to new defensive positions had reached de Lattre. De Gaulle, appalled and incensed, swung into action.

First he telegraphed direct to de Lattre de Tassigny: "In case Allied forces retire from their present positions north of the French 1st Army, I order you to take matters into your own hands to guarantee the defense of Strasbourg." Next, to Eisenhower he wrote: "The French Government, for its part, can obviously not let Strasbourg fall into enemy hands again. Whatever happens the French will defend Strasbourg." Finally he telegraphed both Roosevelt and Churchill, for the first time on a military decision by the High Command, of the "extremely serious consequences which would result for France" from Eisenhower's decision, and his resolute objections. Roosevelt, predictably, declined to intervene in a military matter, but Churchill, predictably, got into his airplane and flew to Eisenhower's headquarters at Versailles with his Army chief of staff, Field Marshal Sir Alan Brooke, on January 2.

The British party lunched with Eisenhower and his staff, and Brooke recorded in his diaries that "Ike had already decided to alter his dispositions so as to leave the divisions practically where they were" in the Alsace. General de Gaulle, with General Juin, his defense chief of staff, then arrived for a joint conference with Eisenhower, Churchill and Brooke. If Eisenhower had already decided to alter plans, he did not make this known to de Gaulle, and a tense and heavy discussion took place.

Eisenhower—as in his earlier argument with de Gaulle about the liberation of Paris—defended his action on purely military grounds, to which de Gaulle curtly replied that "If this were a *Kriegsspiel* [war game], I would agree."

But he then went on to lecture Eisenhower that it would be "a national disaster" for France to retreat from Alsatian territory, with all that it symbolically implied, and allow the Nazis back into Strasbourg to wreak a new round of vengeance on the city. Armies, he told Eisenhower, "are created to serve the policy of states," and if Strasbourg were evacuated it would risk a rupture of the Allied command as well as "the risk of seeing the outraged French people forbid him the use of its railways and communications indispensable to operations."

Churchill added his agreement: "All my life I have known what significance Alsace had for the French, and I support General de Gaulle that this fact must be taken into consideration."

Eisenhower says that "when I found that execution of the original plan would have such grave consequences in France that all my lines of communication and my vast rear areas might become badly involved through loss of service troops and unrest," he told de Gaulle he would hold Strasbourg. As in the case of ordering the advance on Paris, he was now satisfied that he had to act for military, not political reasons. Eisenhower was a West Pointer to the end. Orders were telephoned immediately to General Jacob Devers, the US Army group commander on the southern sector of the long front, to cancel the planned withdrawal.

When it was over, Churchill said he would like to have a talk with de Gaulle. De Gaulle beckoned Juin to accompany him and the three settled down in a small room adjoining Eisenhower's office. Juin recorded this footnote to the affair:

> Churchill began by saying that Eisenhower was not always aware of the political consequences of his decisions, yet for all that he was an excellent supreme commander and he had a heart—as he had just shown. But de Gaulle remained obstinately silent, so that in the end Churchill did not know what to say. Presently de Gaulle began to speak, asking Churchill about his trip to Greece. The later was much relieved to hear de Gaulle speak at last. His face lit up and he exclaimed: "Oh yes, very interesting, it was good sport indeed. The most extraordinary thing is that they shot at me with the weapons I had given them." "It's the kind of thing that happens," de Gaulle concluded, and thereupon we parted. On the way back, I could not help

telling de Gaulle that he should at least have expressed his thanks to Churchill. "Bah," he answered, and with a gloomy expression he went back to his thoughts.

That was the last time that these two great allies and indomitable adversaries met and talked during the war.

FOURTEEN

1945: VICTORY AND EXIT

In mid-January it was announced that President Roosevelt, Prime Minister Churchill and Marshal Stalin would shortly meet at the Black Sea resort of Yalta, summer playground of the czars and their Communist heirs. "Naturally I was offended that we were not invited, but I was not at all surprised," General de Gaulle wrote. He lost no time in turning his absence from Yalta to maximum political and diplomatic advantage, which he never would have enjoyed if he had been a participant. To the end of his life de Gaulle seized and invented every opportunity to decry what happened at Yalta, to denounce an Anglo-Saxon sellout of Europe's interests to the Russians, to rejoice in the fact that France took no part in it, and to imply that the outcome would have been different if he had been at the table. There is little point in speculating on what the results of Yalta might have been had de Gaulle and France been present. Quite probably Europe today would look about the same, for in the end it was the military realities of 1945 that decided its fate, not the political decisions taken by the Big Three. There is no doubt, therefore, that for de Gaulle's historical purposes it was far better that he was absent.

He acknowledged that "Marshal Stalin, who knew my position with regard to Poland, and Mr. Churchill, who expected to obtain carte blanche in the Middle East from his partners" did not want him at Yalta, but he blames the "explicit refusal" of an invitation on Roosevelt. This was probably more or less correct. In December, while arrangements for the meeting were under discussion, FDR messaged Churchill that "I still adhere to my position that any attempts to include de Gaulle in the meeting of the three of us would merely introduce a complicating and undesirable factor."

But Eden and the Foreign Office tirelessly continued to argue for the French being present—not so much on behalf of de Gaulle, certainly, but because important decisions on the occupation of Germany and other postwar arrangements were to be made, and it was essential for Europe's long-term security and stability that France play its role. In Eden's phrase, Britain should not be left "to share the cage with the bear." But Churchill replied to these arguments by letter to his foreign secretary in mid-January:

> I fear we shall have the greatest trouble with de Gaulle, who will be forever intriguing and playing off two against the third. I quite agree that France should come in as a Fourth Power, and certainly at any moment when it is proposed to bring in China. I cannot think of anything more unpleasant and impossible than having this menacing and hostile man in our midst, always trying to make himself a reputation in France by claiming a position far above what France occupies, and making faces at the Allies who are doing the work.

After the brief mellow mood of his Armistice Day visit to de Gaulle in Paris, the prime minister was now back on the other tack. But in the meantime Roosevelt decided to dispatch Harry Hopkins to London and Paris for some preparatory diplomatic spadework in advance of Yalta. Ever since the Casablanca conference, Hopkins had been consistently disposed to accept the French reality as embodied by de Gaulle and to recognize that long-term relations with France would suffer otherwise. He had not been very successful in moving Roosevelt, but he had tried, and besides he had his own ups and downs with the president. Now, like FDR, in precarious health, he came to Europe on his last mission for Roosevelt, who would be dead in barely three months. As a placating gesture to de Gaulle, Hopkins was authorized to extend an invitation to meet Roosevelt after Yalta for a discussion of its results, and even to explore the possibility of having de Gaulle come to Yalta to join in talks on European political matters of interest to France. But de Gaulle was not interested in placating gestures.

Hopkins saw de Gaulle on January 27. He had been warned earlier by Foreign Minister Georges Bidault: "The General believes that Frenchmen are always trying to please the man to whom they are talking. He thinks they overdo it and he adopts a different attitude. He makes no effort to please." The talk certainly lived up to Bidault's advance billing. From de Gaulle's account of what he said, it was little more than a long-pondered, pent-up, one-way remorseless historical lecture on the failures, iniquities and tergiversations of United States policy toward France during the twentieth century. Hopkins, expecting to have a dialogue, opened with a candid acknowledgment of past mistakes, hoping that in this way they could examine the future. De Gaulle retorted that "If you really mean that you believe that relations between the United States and France are not all that they should be, why don't you do something about it?" De Gaulle says he told Hopkins:

> For us, this is the crux of the matter: In the mortal dangers we French have survived since the beginning of the century, the United States does not give the impression that it regards its own destiny as linked with that of France, that it wishes France to be great and strong, that it is doing all it can to help

her to remain or become so once again. Perhaps, in fact, we are not worth the trouble. In that case, you are right. But perhaps we shall rise again. Then you will have been wrong. In either case, your behavior tends to alienate us.

He lectured Hopkins on America's long delay in entering the First World War "after attempting to make a compromise peace on the terms of which France would not even have recovered Alsace and Lorraine," and then abandoning the Treaty of Versailles. He declared that "a mere promise of help" from Roosevelt to Reynaud in 1940 "would have been enough to persuade the government to continue the war," which America entered only "when you were obliged to by the Japanese attack." Now, he said, France was excluded from Yalta and treated as a subordinate, denied the arms it needed. Remorselessly de Gaulle went on:

> I cannot understand how America can undertake to settle Europe's future in France's absence. Especially since after pretending to ignore her in the forthcoming discussions, she must ask Paris to agree to whatever has been decided. You have come on behalf of the president to discuss profound problems of Franco-American relations. I think that we have done so. The French have the impression that you no longer consider the greatness of France necessary to the world and to yourselves. This is responsible for the coolness you feel in our country and even in this office. If you want relations between our countries established on a different footing, it is up to you to do what must be done. Until you reach a decision, I send President Roosevelt a salute of friendship on the eve of the conference that will bring him to Europe.

So it was entirely up to America to put things right; the situation was no responsibility of de Gaulle's. Hopkins, experienced in intellectual and political sparring with Churchill and Stalin as well as generals and admirals every bit as imperious and high-handed as Charles de Gaulle, took this in stride and returned to Bidault to talk about practicalities. He had not raised the question of any invitations with de Gaulle directly. Bidault promised to consider both the proposal for de Gaulle to attend Yalta for the political discussions about Europe, and also putting before him the president's invitation to meet on French territory after Yalta in a stopover en route home.

After Hopkins then reached Yalta in the company of the president on February 4, he received two messages from Bidault. The first was to the effect that on reflection, Bidault had decided not to propose the idea of partial participation in the deliberations to de Gaulle because he was certain it would be turned down, and raising it might only make feelings worse. However, in the second message, somewhat to Hopkins' surprise but to his gratification, Bidault said that de Gaulle would be happy to meet with FDR "at any point on French soil." Bidault himself also expressed surprise at this.

Meanwhile, as the conference began, General de Gaulle made a special radio broadcast to disavow and disassociate France in advance from anything that happened there:

> We have informed our Allies that France will of course be committed to absolutely nothing she has not been in a position to discuss and approve in the same way as the others. I specify that the presence of French forces from one end of the Rhine to the other, the separation of the territories on the left bank of the Rhine and of the Ruhr Basin from what will be the German state, the independence of the Polish, Czech, Austrian and Balkan nations, are conditions which France judges to be essential in the future peace settlement.

In the event, the results of Yalta for France itself were quite favorable and positive, even without de Gaulle at the conference table to bang his fist and stonewall. France was assigned an occupation zone in Germany that in location and area more or less conformed to the General's wishes. It was decided to include France as a full fourth member of the Allied Control Council, which would administer postwar Germany, and to give France a sector of divided Berlin. She was asked to become one of the sponsoring powers of the conference to draw up the charter for the United Nations, which would meet in San Francisco in a few months, and was assured a permanent seat on the projected UN Security Council along with the other Great Powers. Most of these concessions—or recognition of France's rights—were agreed at Yalta as the result of Winston Churchill and Anthony Eden battling on behalf of France against Roosevelt and Stalin.

The attitude of these two leaders toward France was clear from the very outset, when the president met Stalin alone for a cozy chat before the full deliberations began. Roosevelt made a fetish at both Tehran and Yalta of wanting to avoid any appearance of ganging up with Churchill and the British, and of seeking to show that he could handle Stalin and get results that Churchill could not. The American record of this first talk, published in the official Yalta papers, is revealing of this Roosevelt attitude and state of mind.

He began by asking Stalin how he had gotten along with de Gaulle at their Moscow meeting two months earlier.

> Marshal Stalin replied that he had not found de Gaulle a very complicated person, but he felt he was unrealistic in the sense that France had not done very much fighting in this war and de Gaulle demanded full rights with the Americans, British and Russians who had done the burden of the fighting. . . . Marshal Stalin said that de Gaulle did not seem to understand the situation in France, and that in actual fact the French contribution at the present time to military operations on the Western Front was very small and that in 1940 they had not fought at all. [Neither, of course, had the Russians in 1940.]
>
> The President said he would tell the Marshal something indiscreet, since

he would not wish to say it in front of the Prime Minister, namely that the British for two years have had the idea of artificially building up France into a strong power which would have 200,000 troops on the eastern border of France to hold the line for the period required to assemble a strong British army. He said the British were a peculiar people and wished to have their cake and eat it too. The President then said that he understood the tripartite zones in regard to the occupation of Germany were already agreed upon, to which Marshal Stalin appeared to agree, but he went on to say that the outstanding question was that of a French zone of occupation. The President said he had a good deal of trouble with the British in regard to zones of occupation.

Marshal Stalin inquired whether the President thought France should have a zone of occupation, and for what reason. The President said he thought it was a bad idea, but he added that it was only out of kindness. Both Marshal Stalin and Mr. Molotov spoke up vigorously and said that would be the only reason to give a zone to France, and the question would have to be considered further at Yalta.

Against the background of this "meeting of minds" between Stalin and Roosevelt about France, Churchill and Eden fought hard, with intelligence and eloquence, to obtain for France what was obtained. If de Gaulle ever knew or realized how much he was in Churchill's debt, he never acknowledged it—but he never would have acknowledged anyway a debt to anyone for mere recognition of what he considered to be France's rights.

When the formal Big Three discussions opened on February 5, Churchill and the British were disturbed by Roosevelt's not only siding with Stalin against them over France, but also his sudden offhanded disclosure that he expected United States forces to remain in occupation of Germany "only about two years." This of course hardened the British resolve not to be left "to share the cage with the bear." Summing up a brisk argument against Stalin and Roosevelt, Churchill said:

> I was very much against General de Gaulle's coming here and the President's view was very much the same. Apparently Marshal Stalin feels the same. But the fact remains that France must take her place. We will need her defense against Germany. We have suffered badly from German robot guns and should Germany again get near to the Channel coast we would suffer again. After the Americans have gone home, I must think seriously of the future. I propose to offer the French a zone of occupation out of present British and American zones, and that technical studies be made of the French position in the control machinery.

Stalin again objected, and Roosevelt said he was prepared to let the French have a zone but not share in control machinery. As usual in Big Three deadlocks, it was referred back to foreign ministers for further discussions. Churchill and Eden dug in. At the fourth Yalta session on February 7, Churchill declared with some heat: "All this argument seems to me futile—I feel sure that the French will take no zone unless they are given participation in the control council, and I must say I think they would be right." Meanwhile, Harry Hopkins and Charles E. Bohlen had gone to work on Roosevelt on France's behalf, and finally, at last, as the eighth formal meeting of the conference was nearing its end, Roosevelt switched his position to support the British. At this, Stalin raised his arms above his head and said, *"Sdaiyu."* (I surrender.)

Bohlen, who was interpreter and Soviet adviser to the president, says this reinforced Roosevelt's idea that he had great personal influence over Stalin. But Bohlen concluded that Stalin played this "concession" to maneuver Western support for his positions on Poland and German reparations.

The Yalta decisions, and an invitation to France to join in Great Power sponsorship of the United Nations Charter conference in San Francisco, were formally transmitted to General de Gaulle in Paris by the American ambassador, Jefferson Caffery, on February 12, the day the meeting ended. "The steps that were taken on our behalf were in no way offensive," de Gaulle commented, but soon after he announced that France was declining to be an "inviting power" for the UN conference because she had not taken part in the preparatory drafting work that had been carried out at Dumbarton Oaks in Washington by the United States, Britain, the Soviet Union and China.

*

This was not the only invitation de Gaulle declined. From Yalta, Roosevelt now sent via Caffery what Bohlen described as "a warm message welcoming a meeting and expressing appreciation that the General would take time out from his duties to travel to the Mediterranean, and proposing that they meet at Algiers, at that time an integral part of France, that de Gaulle join him for lunch where he would be given a detailed account of exactly what happened at Yalta." The president acted in every confidence that this would be accepted, on the basis of the earlier response Bidault had sent from Paris.

De Gaulle's account is very different. He contends that when Hopkins raised the possibility of a meeting during his discussions in Paris, "Bidault had made it clear that it would be better not to extend an invitation at all." Yet this does not accord with the facts, for Bidault certainly subsequently informed the Americans that an invitation would be accepted. In any event all hell now broke loose.

De Gaulle summoned Caffery on February 13, and in his most imperious manner he personally informed the ambassador that

> It was impossible for me to come to Algiers at this time and without warning and that, consequently, I could not, to my regret, receive the President there. The French Government had invited him, last November, to come to Paris and greatly regretted that he could not do so at that time, but would be happy to welcome him in the capital should he wish to make a visit at any time whatsoever. If he wished, during his trip, to make Algiers a port of call in spite of this, would he be so kind as to inform us of the fact, in order that

we might give the necessary instructions to the Governor General of Algeria for everything to be done in accordance with his wishes.

In his Memoirs de Gaulle rants on about "why should the American President invite the French President to visit him in France," and says that maybe Roosevelt didn't know that Algiers was part of France "but all the more reason to remind him of that fact." He berated Roosevelt for receiving aboard his cruiser the presidents of Syria and Lebanon, Ibn Saud of Saudi Arabia and Haile Selassie of Ethiopia and then "offering to receive General de Gaulle on the same ship under the same conditions." He concludes: "The sovereignty, the dignity of a great nation must be inviolable. I was responsible for those of France."

De Gaulle thus managed to snub the president of the United States in the most highhanded and offensive manner he could contrive. Caffery's report reached Roosevelt aboard the cruiser *Quincy* in Alexandria Harbor in Egypt. Roosevelt at once summoned his press secretary, Stephen Early, and dictated what Bohlen describes as "a terse and insulting statement" in reply to de Gaulle. Even Early was taken aback, and he showed it to Harry Hopkins, who sent word from his sickbed in a cabin on the *Quincy* that it should be toned down as it would antagonize not only de Gaulle but the French people. But the president sent word back that he insisted it be released as written.

Hopkins then turned to Bohlen, who later became ambassador to France when de Gaulle was at the height of his postwar power, and said: "Chip, go and see what you can do with the President." Bohlen relates:

> The President was sitting in his cabin working on his stamp collection. I offered the same arguments that Hopkins had about the difficulty of hitting at de Gaulle without at the same time hitting at France. "No, no," the President said, "what you don't seem to realize is that the United States has been insulted through its President and this requires an appropriate answer." We kept talking, and eventually I said, "We can all admit that de Gaulle is being one of the biggest sons-of-bitches who ever straddled a pot." For some reason that remark tickled the President. His tired eyes suddenly twinkled and his face broke into his famous smile. He threw back his head in his characteristic manner, laughed and said, "Oh, go ahead, you and Harry try your hand at a draft." I went back to Hopkins, and we worked out a statement that did no more than express the regret of the President at the inability of de Gaulle to join him.

It was sound advice on the part of Hopkins and Bohlen, for the soft answer which they produced turned away the wrath of the French people from the American president to their own president. A storm of press and public criticism broke around de Gaulle's head—the first real outburst of democratic public condemnation he had experienced from the French since his return to Paris. Had Roosevelt issued the statement he originally planned, the French almost certainly would have been rallying to the defense of the General. As it was, even de Gaulle acknowledged that "I must confess that I was profoundly affected by this initial dissension, which with increasing effect compromised all my future efforts." Thus, ironically, his snub of Roosevelt marked a clear turning point in his own political fortunes and standing with his own people, leading directly to his abrupt withdrawal from office one year later. But as usual, he blamed it all on the inability of the French to comprehend greatness, not that he might have been wrong to snub the president of the United States:

> Prominent citizens are generally inclined [he wrote] to favor the foreigner, provided he is rich and strong, and to criticize any French action which seems to indicate a policy. Furthermore, all these groups had begun to withdraw their support from me as they foresaw the possibility of returning to the pleasant tactics of illusion and denigration. I was therefore forced to recognize that the notion I had formed of France's status and rights was shared by few of those who shaped public opinion. To support my policy, that of national ambition, I could count less and less on their voices, their pens and their influence.

Charles de Gaulle refused to accept that the French did not necessarily regard impoliteness and deliberate rudeness, whatever the excuse or rationale, as a concomitant of national dignity and greatness.

President Roosevelt sailed through the Mediterranean on a sad journey home. Hopkins left the *Quincy* to be flown home for urgent hospitalization and Bohlen left for other diplomatic duties. Then the president's faithful doctor for twelve years, Major General "Pa" Watson, died during the voyage and was buried at sea. On his return to Washington at the end of February, Roosevelt went before Congress almost immediately to report on the Yalta meeting and to remark in passing that excuses of a "prima donna" had prevented him holding further valuable discussions during his travels. It was FDR's last major speech and public appearance. A few weeks later he set off for Warm Springs, Georgia, to rest and try to regain his fast-failing strength.

De Gaulle was not without gall. The last week of March, a detailed request from the French government reached the president for military assistance to equip *fifty* French divisions. Roosevelt simply minuted across it that this "would interfere with the prosecution of the war." It was his last decision with regard to France. He died two weeks later, on April 12, 1945.

*

The political decision by the Big Three at Yalta to assign an occupation zone in defeated Germany to the French was not of itself enough for de Gaulle. This was merely a declaration, or a piece of paper, and he was determined to preempt the situation and reinforce France's claims on the ground by relentlessly pushing the Army as deep into Germany as he possibly could, without regard any longer for the operational directives of the Supreme Command. In the first instance, this involved crossing the Rhine. Eisenhower had already determined that the major thrusts across the Rhine would be in the north, by the British and Americans, first to encircle the Ruhr Valley and second to push into the center of Germany through Frankfurt and along the Main. There were neither orders nor plans on the part of SHAEF for any French crossing of the Rhine at the southern end of the long Allied front, except in supporting operations once the northern crossings had been secured.

De Gaulle's view was otherwise, and he summoned General de Lattre de Tassigny to Paris in early March and told him that "for reasons of national interest his army must cross the Rhine." De Lattre was an outstanding military commander, respected, popular and loyal to his allies. But he had been through the command crisis with de Gaulle over Strasbourg, and as a French officer there could be no question about ultimate authority. He pointed out to de Gaulle, however, that at the moment his army was merely looking across the Rhine at the Black Forest. If he were going to force a crossing, the only place that would make any military sense would be farther to the north, where there would be good roads to advance around the edge of the Black Forest when he got to the other side. Using the confidence and good relations he enjoyed with the American Army Group commander, General Jacob Devers, de Lattre first got approval to work his army north along the Rhine to a new operational boundary at the town of Speyer, just below the ancient city of Worms.

Meanwhile, to the north, on March 7 the American 9th Armored Division had seized a railroad bridge across the Rhine that the Germans had been slow to destroy, at the town of Remagen, not far from Bonn. General Patton then got his 3rd Army across at Mainz on March 22, and Montgomery made his crossings with his Army Group at the northern end of the river on March 23. By the end of that week de Lattre had cleared the Germans in the path of his advance to Speyer and had a choice of crossing points himself. On March 29 he received a stiff order from de Gaulle: "You must cross the Rhine even if the Americans do not help you, and you are obliged to use boats. Karlsruhe and Stuttgart expect, even if they do not desire you." De Lattre needed no urging. Using boats and light bridging equipment that the French had built themselves, he got his first units across on March 30. By April 4 he had approximately 125,000 men on the eastern bank, and on April 7 he entered Karlsruhe. De Gaulle also crossed the Rhine that day to congratulate de Lattre and urge him on.

The French had taken Supreme Allied Headquarters by surprise, but certainly they had done no harm to the Allied effort. But de Lattre was now instructed by Devers to avoid any "premature advance" and to concentrate toward the south to clean up the German 19th Army in the Black Forest. De Gaulle ruled otherwise, and ordered de Lattre to advance rapidly to the east to Stuttgart, capital of the state of Württemberg, a major industrial city and a road and rail hub astride the main route into Bavaria. Devers, however, had assigned the capture of Stuttgart to General Alexander Patch's US 7th Army. De Lattre and the French got there first, on April 23.

Patch's forces arrived at the city next day on the heels of the French, but de Lattre, on orders from de Gaulle, refused both Patch's request and Devers' direct order to leave.

De Gaulle told de Lattre: "I require you to maintain a French garrison at Stuttgart and to institute immediately a military government." De Lattre informed Patch that his orders from his government were "to hold the territory conquered by our troops until the French zone of occupation has been fixed between the interested governments." Devers then appealed to Eisenhower over this flouting of his authority by an army commander supposedly under his orders.

Eisenhower immediately dispatched a formal letter of protest to de Gaulle, but it was carefully couched more in sorrow than in anger. After pointing out that the question of a French zone of occupation was entirely outside his scope, which was the military defeat of Germany, Eisenhower told de Gaulle: "I can do nothing else than fully inform the Combined Chiefs of Staff of this development, and point out that I can no longer count with certainty upon the operational use of any French forces they may contemplate equipping in the future." De Gaulle at once replied that the situation was not Eisenhower's fault but "lack of agreement between France and the Allied governments on war policy in general and in particular the occupation of German territory." He even added a complaint that the United States was not fulfilling its commitments to rearm the French Army. But he did not budge from Stuttgart.

In Washington the impasse was quickly referred to the new American commander in chief, President Harry S Truman, barely three weeks in office after the death of Roosevelt. Truman, an artillery battery commander in the First World War, promptly fired off a terse personal letter to de Gaulle backing up Eisenhower's veiled threat of a cutoff of aid and supplies for the French forces. With victory in Europe only days away, a face-saving end was found. The French reduced their forces in Stuttgart to a symbolic presence. The Americans moved in to take over in force (and remain there to this day).

In the closing week of the war, then, the French under de Lattre, cooperating fully with Patch on their northern flank, made a magnificent dash that carried them south into the Austrian Alps, Innsbruck and the Arlberg Valley and at the same time east, where they crossed the Danube, with Leclerc's 2nd Armored Division hoisting the Tricolor on the last day of the war over Adolf Hitler's retreat at Berchtesgaden. Leclerc had come a long way from Lake Chad in 1940.

Meanwhile, however, on top of the Stuttgart affair, de Gaulle was playing the same game with his allies in northern Italy. Immediately after the crossing of the Rhine, he launched French troops based near Nice in the Alpes-Maritimes *département* across the Italian frontier to repair the indignity France had suffered at Mussolini's hands in the collapse of 1940. All this was done of course without any warning or discussion or planning coordination with the Supreme Allied Command in Italy, headed by Field Marshal Sir Harold Alexander. Relentlessly the French pushed on into northern Italy, taking the Lombardy passes, the Alpine ski resort of Val d'Aosta, and moving along the Ligurian coast and inland to capture the major Italian city of Turin. All this was accomplished by the first days of May, while Alexander's forces were occupied to the south and east pushing the Germans up the Po Valley, taking Milan, Venice and heading for Trieste.

Now the same act that took place over Stuttgart was repeated. Alexander asked the French to withdraw to establish an Allied military government in the north under plans already agreed by the British and American governments. The French commander, General Paul-André Doyen, not only refused but told Alexander in writing that "if need be" he would extend his refusal to extreme consequences, "in accord with General de Gaulle's order." In other words, he was threatening to fire on his allies. At this, both Truman and Churchill rumbled into action again.

After an exchange of messages with Churchill ("Is it not very disagreeable for us to be addressed in these terms by General de Gaulle," the prime minister cabled), Truman came down hard. In a cable to de Gaulle he protested Doyen's threat to his allies and demanded the evacuation of French forces "until the settlement of the claims which the French government wishes to formulate with regard to the frontier can be effected normally and rationally." Unless this was done, Truman said firmly, "I will be obliged to suspend the distribution of equipment and munitions allocated to the French Army by the American services." De Gaulle now made a tactical but not a strategic retreat. He told Truman that he was sending General Juin to Alexander's headquarters to work out details, and the French then gradually pulled back from Turin and other points, but they continued to hold frontier territory that Italy subsequently ceded in the peace settlement.

Into this situation, entirely of his own making, de Gaulle assumed the most extraordinary portents and Machiavellian motives on the part of his Anglo-Saxon allies. In his Memoirs he wrote:

> To a certain extent, the source of this affair was the United States' desire for hegemony, which they readily manifested and which I had not failed to discern on every occasion. But above all, I saw in their demand the effect of British influence. For at that same moment, England was preparing her decisive maneuver in the Levant. For London to inspire Washington to find a source of friction with Paris was a strategic move. Various facts indicated that this was the case.

It was the case that events in the Levant were also being propelled by de Gaulle to a crisis, but only he had an imagination that would stretch as far as to connect the action Britain took in the Middle East with the crisis he had created in northern Italy. It was also certainly the case that Winston Churchill was about at the end of a five-year tether in dealings with General de Gaulle. At the height of the Italian affair, he messaged Truman:

> I consider General de Gaulle one of the greatest dangers to European peace. No one has more need than Britain of France's friendship, but I am sure that in the long run no understanding will be reached with General de Gaulle. Between us and France, there can be no bridge via de Gaulle, ever. . . . De Gaulle's present program of defiance and scorn to Britain and the U.S. leads only to unimaginable misery and misfortune.

Churchill's sharpest—and last—showdown with de Gaulle now began to unfold, in the very place where the first troubles of their long and stormy wartime relationship began—over Syria and Lebanon. From the outset of this permanent running crisis with the British in 1941, de Gaulle remained utterly convinced that Britain's sole aim was to oust the French from these territories she held under League of Nations mandate and take them over for the British Empire. Never once did de Gaulle admit to the depth of anti-French feelings of the local populations—even this he regarded as the work of British agents. Nevertheless, under both internal pressures and British pressure he had given way slowly during the war years, with pledges of full independence for Syria and Lebanon and an end to the French-held mandate once the war had ended. Internal administration had been progressively transferred to Syrian and Lebanese hands, and at France's instigation Syria had even been invited to attend the United Nations Charter conference in San Francisco. But the French were still in occupation of the two countries, and undeniably were wielding arbitrary powers over and against the two governments, increasingly eager for the complete independence they had been promised. The French, in short, were extremely unpopular in their Middle East stamping grounds, and it did not require British agents to feed the flames. Churchill, on the contrary, commented in one of his dispatches on the Middle East: "All the arguments and means of pressure used by the Levant people against the French might one day be turned against us; we should discourage the throwing of stones since we have greenhouses of our own, acres and acres of them. It should be our endeavor to damp things down."

But with the war in Europe now over, the situation in Damascus and Beirut began deteriorating rapidly, in street demonstrations for immediate full independence and complete French withdrawal. The British urged de Gaulle to negotiate promptly on treaties with the two States that would retain French interests while recognizing their independence. De Gaulle's response was to propose arrangements that in effect would have perpetuated French military dominance—and to order troop reinforcements to Beirut as if to back up his demands with force. Next the British tried to have this French reinforcement diverted, but de Gaulle pressed on, and when the soldiers arrived in late May, troubles broke out on a scale approaching full insurrection and civil war.

As French tanks and troops took to the streets to crush the demonstrations, the British kept urging that they cool it and avoid escalating the fighting. Meanwhile they began preparations to intervene themselves with their far greater forces in Palestine and Transjordan. On the evening of May 30 Churchill called in French Ambassador René Massigli and demanded that the French government immediately order a cease-fire in Syria, warning that if fighting went on, "His Majesty's forces in the region cannot remain inactive." Next afternoon in the House of Commons, Churchill made a very grave announcement:

> In view of the situation which has arisen between French troops and the Levant states, and the severe fighting which has broken out, we have with profound regret ordered the Commander-in-Chief Middle East to intervene

to prevent further effusion of blood in the interests of the security of the whole Middle East. In order to avoid collision between British and French forces, we have requested an immediate order to the French troops to cease fire and withdraw to their barracks.

The British rolled into Damascus, with a real risk of war, or at least shooting, with the French. As a result of a mixup in communications, the formal text of the announcement was not handed to de Gaulle in Paris until one hour after Churchill had read it to the House of Commons—adding to de Gaulle's utter fury with Churchill and Britain.

For Charles de Gaulle, this was the Fashoda incident all over again—France being forced to back down before the might of Britain. To Ambassador Duff Cooper he declared in a cold rage: "I admit that we are not in a position to wage war against you at the present time. But you have insulted France and betrayed the West. This cannot be forgotten."

Nevertheless, a good many French in Damascus owed their lives to the swift arrival of the British forces. De Gaulle claims he had already ordered a cease-fire and that the situation was under control when Churchill acted, but this is not in accordance with the historical facts. In any case, the Syrians had begun to turn on French civilians, looting shops and private property and assassinating isolated Frenchmen. Then native Syrian troops under the control and command of the French, independent of the Syrian government, mutinied and turned against their officers, who had to be escorted to safety from their bases by British forces. But with the French confined to barracks and the British moving through the streets in force, order was fairly quickly restored. After several weeks the British then began pulling out—many of their troops to be shipped to the Far East. The French presence was quietly dismantled, and when the United Nations came into being, the old League of Nations mandate was formally dissolved. The French disappeared from the Levant entirely—except for the French language, which has held out in Beirut and Damascus longer against England than General de Gaulle was able to do.

De Gaulle's account of these events in his Memoirs is perhaps the most one-sided, misleading and tendentious historical summary of the many in which the book abounds. In writing about the affair, his feelings probably were exacerbated by his knowledge that his own ministers were against him, and the failure—indeed the indifference—of French public opinion to rise up and support him and "France's honor" against the British. Bitterly, de Gaulle says:

> If Prime Minister Churchill counted on the crisis to isolate de Gaulle from leading French circles, he was quite justified in doing so. As in the case of Roosevelt's summons to me immediately after the Yalta conference, the Levant incident left me with no effective support among the majority of men who held public office. It was either distress or downright disapproval which my action provoked among almost all influential men and articulate public figures.

Foreign Minister Georges Bidault, in his dealings with the British and others, left no doubt of his disagreement with de Gaulle over the handling of the crisis. Basically, the problem was that the General saw it entirely in terms of French interests in competition with Britain in the Middle East, instead of addressing himself to the real problem—which was Syrian and Lebanese interests. It was an imperial and colonial approach that continued to cost France dearly until the end of the Algerian War in 1961.

General de Gaulle could recognize when he had lost public support, when public opinion was no longer behind him—but never could he or would he recognize that he might have been wrong, that he might have made a mistake. In upholding the dignity and honor of France, in fighting to restore France to greatness and insisting that France receive her just dues from the rest of the world, there could be no de Gaulle mistakes—only the faintheartedness and lack of will and understanding on the part of others.

*

And so the war in Europe came to an end amid public jubilation and above all enormous emotional relief—but with relations at the top between France's leader and his Western Allies more rancorous and mistrustful than they had ever been. On the streets in every Allied capital, in the front lines where armies mixed, among commanders, it was a time of intense comradeship and elation, a sharing of a common language and common emotions that would never happen again in the lives of those who experienced those heady days of victory.

None of this elation was shared by General de Gaulle, enmeshed as he was in antagonisms and isolation, where he always seemed to prefer to dwell. Was it necessary for him to have snubbed Roosevelt over a meeting in Algiers—and what had he gained? What was achieved by steering the French Army into a collision course with the American Army in the last days of the war at Stuttgart? What did he have to show for his commander in northern Italy threatening to fire on his allies if they tried to interfere with French seizure of Italian territory? Was the dispatch of French reinforcements to the Levant the only solution France had to offer Syria and Lebanon after more than a quarter of a century of neocolonial French rule?

The Big Three were about to meet again, for their last conference, in Potsdam in mid-July, and there was less disposition than ever on the part of Churchill, Truman and Stalin to include General de Gaulle in the deliberations. He had little trouble consoling himself that (as he wrote) it was "preferable not to be introduced into discussions which could be nothing but supererogatory." Nor was there in fact much point in France's presence at Potsdam. The occupation zones had already been agreed upon at the diplomatic level by the European Advisory Commission, which France had joined eight months earlier, sitting permanently in London until the war was over. At Potsdam, on European questions it was largely detail—vital and controversial though this often was—about implementation of arrangements generally agreed at Yalta.

For the French, the main result of Potsdam was an invitation to join the Council of Foreign Ministers, henceforth the Big Four, who for the next fifteen years would meet periodically to wrestle, usually fruitlessly, over aspects of a permanent peace that has never been achieved. This set the final seal on France's full return to the ranks of the major powers in the postwar world.

Potsdam was punctuated, however, with the news that stunned the world of the election defeat of Winston Churchill and his ouster from office after six of the most turbulent and decisive years of Britain's history. De Gaulle's reflections on his going, written more than a decade after the event, bore a typically mordant quality:

> In some respects, Churchill's departure facilitated the conduct of French affairs; in others it did not. In any case, I saw it with melancholy. In general, he had supported me for as long as he took me for the head of a French minority which favored him and which he could put to good use. But when he saw France represented by me as an ambitious state, apparently eager to recover her power in Europe and the world, Churchill quite naturally felt something of Pitt's spirit in his soul. In spite of everything, by lending me a strong and willing hand when he did, Churchill had vitally aided the cause of France. Having seen a great deal of him, I had greatly admired though quite as often envied him. Learning that England had asked her captain to leave the command to which she had called him when the tempest rose, I foresaw the moment when I would relinquish the helm of France, of my own accord, as I had taken it.

Already, General de Gaulle was feeling the shifting winds of French public opinion and feelings about his wartime stewardship. Now, in the British dismissal of Churchill, he could see a portent for his own future—except that, typically, he was determined that he would go at a time of his own choosing, not the people's choosing. In the meantime, France's restoration to her place in the councils of the mighty must be proclaimed, pressed and consolidated.

After the Potsdam conference, when sufficient time had elapsed so he could not possibly be accused of any association with anything that was done there, de Gaulle accepted an invitation to visit Truman in Washington at the end of August. "It was natural for the President to lose no time in consulting France; despite the ordeals she had just survived, the only nation on the European continent on which Western policy could count," de Gaulle wrote modestly.

In all, he spent seven hours with Truman—"for all his simplicity of manner, an extremely positive man." Gone were the cloudy, abstract and irritating approaches to France and the world he had listened to from Roosevelt. The account of this visit is one-sided, however, for Truman does not even mention it in his Memoirs, while de Gaulle gives it eight pages. He was gratified to get Truman's assurance that the United States was ready to consider French proposals on a permanent dismemberment of Germany at the next Big Four foreign ministers meeting. He was particularly pleased with a Truman promise that the United States "did not oppose the return of the French Army and French authority to Indochina," which de Gaulle took as a reversal of the earlier American attitude under Roosevelt. A loan agreement for $650 million was signed, and at the end of the stay in Washington, Truman presented General de Gaulle with a brand-new DC-4 four-motor Skymaster transport for his personal use and his trip back to France.

After that, for all the rancor he had caused below the surface, de Gaulle basked in a genuine outpouring of American affection for France and victory spirit in visits to New York, West Point, Hyde Park and Chicago. Of official relations with Truman from then on, which in fact was only another five months, de Gaulle said that "no hard words ever passed between us." He returned to Paris from his second American visit satisfied, or at least mollified, but in fact only the atmospherics had changed and no real problems or big issues had been addressed. A French journalist reported to his Paris newspaper from Washington that when he was introduced to Truman at a reception during the de Gaulle visit and asked for comment, the president snapped at him: "I hope you will in future be more loyal to the United States. I have nothing to add."

*

On April 26, 1945, Marshal Pétain, with his wife and a last loyal staff officer, drove across the French frontier from the Swiss town of Vallorbe. On de Gaulle's orders, General Pierre Koenig, who had been condemned to death by the Vichy government, was waiting at the frontier to take Pétain into custody and transport him by train to Paris, where he was imprisoned in the Fort Montrouge. His trial then opened at the Palais de Justice on the Île de la Cité on July 23.

General de Gaulle would have preferred that Pétain live out his life in exile in Switzerland, not burden the French State with trying him, and had so secretly informed the Swiss government. Pétain had been taken by the Nazis to Germany in August 1944 and lodged in a castle in the Black Forest at Sigmaringen. In early April, with Germany's defeat clearly only a matter of days or at the most weeks, Pétain wrote Hitler petitioning for release: "I can answer for my actions only in France. At my age the only thing one fears is not to have done one's full duty; I wish to do mine." Whether this was instrumental in his release is not known, but in any case he was granted his liberty and driven to the Swiss border only a short distance from his place of detention. To the Swiss, he firmly insisted on returning to France.

The Pétain trial, which lasted until August 15, was scarcely a model of judicial integrity and decorum, but it had reasonable dignity compared to the display of vicious venom with which the French dispatched Pierre Laval to a firing squad two months later. De Gaulle had created a special High Court to try the leaders of Vichy, and it was both ironic and somewhat degrading to the process of justice that the presiding judge and the chief prosecuting attorney had earlier sworn allegiance to Vichy and the marshal they were now trying. They had even participated in the infamous Riom trial of leaders of the Third Republic in 1942. The prosecutor, Mornet, had also prosecuted Mata Hari in 1917, perhaps the most famous spy trial of the First World War.

Pétain, eighty-nine years old, spoke only once, at the outset, refused to answer any questions, refused any participation in his own defense. French judicial procedure does not lend itself very readily to precision and order, since almost everyone is able to interrupt everyone else. Jurors can ask questions of witnesses, and witnesses who have testified can leap up to question other witnesses. Judges can put questions, and, of course, opposing attorneys can question and debate each other. The trial, therefore, was one of constant cacophony, and the prosecution case was poorly prepared and poorly presented. It was if the prosecuting lawyers knew the outcome and didn't bother to do their homework on all of the mass of available evidence from Vichy archives that would have made a case clear and convincing.

De Gaulle had hoped Pétain would be convicted for accepting an armistice and then dissolving the Third Republic and replacing it with his own regime. Such a verdict would have vindicated de Gaulle's own claim to legitimacy. But this proved too slippery a legal problem for the court—particularly since its presiding officer had once sworn allegiance to the regime that he was now expected to declare illegitimate. So the focus switched instead to the iniquities and crimes of Vichy against the French people, in the name of and with the condonation of the Marshal.

At the end, the presiding judge first proposed to the jury, when it began its deliberations, that a minimum penalty of banishment for five years and loss of civil rights be considered. But after hours of argument the jury voted fourteen to thirteen for the death penalty—immediately adding a recommendation that it never be carried out.

De Gaulle signed the reprieve and never in any way commented on the outcome. For him, the Marshal Pétain whom he knew had long ceased to exist—a "drama of senility." But this husk lived on in a nineteenth-century fortress-prison on a little island off France's Atlantic coast until 1951, when he died at the age of ninety-five.

Laval, on the other hand, with the aid of the Nazis had managed to escape Allied capture and flee in a German airplane to Spain, where he counted on Franco's hospitality. But in July, shortly after the Pétain trial opened, the Spanish shipped him back to Germany, where he was taken into custody by the Americans and handed over to the French. He then made a brief and dramatic appearance as a witness at the Pétain trial. His own trial began in early October and was, to put it mildly, grotesque. Laval, himself a lawyer as well as an experienced parliamentary debater, fought back skillfully and eloquently, provoking the magistrates, the lawyers, the jurors, with stinging counteraccusations of his own. But the trial was a sordid circus out for blood, and the death sentence was returned on October 9. De Gaulle refused a petition for a retrial and confirmed the death sentence. The end was sickening and revolting. When prison guards arrived to take Laval before a firing squad, he bit and swallowed a cyanide capsule that he had managed to hide in a coat pocket. But the capsule was faulty and the poison had lost its lethal fatal impact. He was thereupon rushed to a hospital where his stomach was pumped, and then back to the prison where he was frog-marched to the execution post, a last cigaret dangling from his mouth, to die shouting *"Vive la France!"*

In all, there were 2,071 death sentences handed down by French courts in

Vichy purge trials, with some 40,000 sentences of detention. It fell to de Gaulle as head of state to pass personally on all the death sentences that reached him before he stepped down in January 1946. He pondered each and every one with great care and in total isolation, never asking advice or explaining a final decision. He searched constantly for any extenuating circumstances, and reprieved all women. He signed 768 execution orders.

*

In October 1945 France prepared to go to the polls in its first postliberation national election, to choose a new Constituent Assembly that would have as a prime duty, along with legislative functions, the drawing up of a new constitution for a Fourth Republic. Municipal elections had been held six months earlier, and not unnaturally after years of Vichy dictatorship, political activity was growing steadily more complex and intense. France was rapidly returning to what de Gaulle contemptuously called "the game of the parties," and there was little he could do to stem it.

He had formed a postliberation provisional government from a wide political spectrum of Communists, Socialists, Radical Socialists, Mouvement Républicain Populaire (MRP) Christian Democrats, independents, interlarded with his own loyal Gaullists, who were generally on the political right. But presiding over a coalition scarcely suited Charles de Gaulle's authoritarian temperament, style or ideas about how government should operate. In any case, the coalition at the top in no way curbed the ferment of politics going on among members of the Constituent Assembly and in the country. De Gaulle also made various efforts with senior and respected men of the Third Republic, untainted by Vichy, to enlist their support as a means of containing the political situation and reinforcing the image of national unity under his leadership. He proposed a post to the veteran Socialist leader Léon Blum, after he came out of a German prison (following a Vichy prison), but Blum was old and tired and preferred freedom of activity. De Gaulle sent his own aircraft to Beirut to fly Édouard Herriot back to France when he was liberated by the Russians, but Herriot elected to return to politics rather than serve in a government. Others who had rallied strongly behind de Gaulle in the apolitical days of the liberation were now staking out their own turf for a democratic future. Pierre Mendès-France resigned from the Finance Ministry in a showdown over anti-inflation policies, which he lost, and went back to Radical Socialist politics.

Inevitably there was a feeling of letdown following the liberation, when it became clear that the country's problems were simply far too great to permit any quick fulfillment of social dreams. Hence there was great political agitation, particularly on the left, demanding that the politicians deliver faster on the things the Resistance and France had fought for in the way of revolutionary reforms of the French economy and society. De Gaulle compounded these political tensions by his rough handling of the Resistance and its leadership in those first days after the liberation of Paris, and by addressing himself so completely to the restoration of France's grandeur rather than the domestic political ferment. As both the

Roosevelt affair and the Levant affair showed, he was increasingly out of touch with the French people.

His dominance of the French scene was to all appearances as great as ever. He had only to rise in the Constituent Assembly for it to come to attention like an unruly schoolroom. The trouble was that when the teacher left, the class began throwing spitballs at each other all over again instead of completing its lessons for the day. Although de Gaulle could be a master of any parliamentary debate he chose to enter, he was never cut out for the maneuvers and cut-and-thrust of parliamentary democracy, the infighting over votes, the risks and the rewards. It was not his idea of how to run a government. He was all for parliamentary debates, but not parliamentary sapping of the roots and trunk of power. This was what was now rapidly overtaking the lone supremacy he had enjoyed when he walked down the avenue des Champs-Élyseés the year before.

Given the enormity of the postwar problems, France's recovery under de Gaulle was in fact going remarkably well. Food aid, and above all transport aid in the form of locomotives and railway equipment, trucks and bridging materials from the United States, helped enormously.

France got through the difficult winter of 1944–45 without a major food or fuel crisis, despite the fact that harvesting and food distribution had been almost totally disrupted by the armies sweeping across the country in the summer of liberation. In 1945 the country began to get back to work, and by the end of the year the French had made the extraordinary economic achievement of restoring general output and activity back to the levels of 1939.

Meanwhile the government and the Constituent Assembly were moving ahead on implementation of the social program that de Gaulle had outlined in his initial policy speech at the Palais de Chaillot on September 12, 1944. The electricity industry was taken over by the State, and so was the privately owned gas industry. The Banque de France was nationalized along with the "big four" private banks—Banque Nationale de Paris, Crédit Lyonnais, Crédit Commercial and Société Générale. The coal fields were nationalized, and groundwork was laid for a State takeover of the Renault and Berliet automobile and truck manufacturers, whose owners had collaborated far too enthusiastically with the German war machine. The government also began overhauling and improving the social security system and its benefits of family allowances, medical care, retirement pay and unemployment pay. Peasant farmers were granted under the law life tenure of their land and first rights to buy from the big landowners. In short, there was a great deal of liberal, Socialist reform under de Gaulle in the liberation period. But the politicians craved for something much more—and that was power.

In the end, the crux of the matter was the form of the new constitution, to replace the Third Republic constitution of 1875. There was even a strong movement simply to go back to the Third Republic constitution, and although this never became a serious possibility, it nevertheless was symptomatic of the difficulties that lay in the path of getting a new Constituent Assembly to agree on any kind of a constitution that might satisfy de Gaulle.

During the summer of 1945, the five major political parties, or groups, all held conferences, and the consensus that began to emerge over a new constitution was not at all to de Gaulle's liking. The parties favored a system in which sovereignty would rest with a single-chamber, popularly elected National Assembly that would approve—or reject—premiers and their governments. De Gaulle, with all of the experience of the Third Republic, wanted power to reside in a strong presidency of the Republic, one that could not be overturned by parliament.

His first move to try to gain control over this political unraveling was to turn the forthcoming election into a national plebescite—the device of going over the heads of the parties and the politicians to the people themselves, which became a hallmark of de Gaulle's postwar reign of power. In addition to electing Deputies to the new Constituent Assembly, the voters were also to be asked in a yes-or-no referendum to limit the life of the Assembly to seven months, and to approve a requirement that the constitution it was to draw up within that time then also be submitted to national referendum. But the political parties wanted an assembly of indefinite life. De Gaulle was determined to limit its mandate in order to be able to pressure it into the decisions he wanted taken. The outgoing Constituent Assembly next voted to reject de Gaulle's election-and-referendum plan when it was submitted for approval. De Gaulle calmly went ahead and promulgated it into law anyway on his own authority as president of the provisional government.

The election, on October 21, was a firm plebiscite victory for de Gaulle as far as limiting the life of the new Assembly. But it saddled him with a fragmented legislature that became the parliamentary mold in which France would flounder for the next thirteen years.

The Communist Party emerged as the strongest single party in France, with 26 percent of the vote, trailed by the Socialists with 24 percent, the MRP Christian Democrats just under 24 percent, the moderate Rightists 15 percent, the Radicals 6 percent and the remainder of the votes for minor splinter groups and independents. It was scarcely an Assembly to de Gaulle's political taste. When it met in early November, it debated a whole week (de Gaulle took no part in the proceedings) before unanimously electing the General as interim president of the Republic to form a government pending the adoption of the new constitution.

At that point the Communists flexed their muscles by demanding a major Cabinet post—the Foreign Ministry, the Defense Ministry or the Ministry of the Interior. De Gaulle at once rejected this, telling the French people in a radio address that he refused to allow the Communists to dominate the policy of France in "the diplomacy which expresses it, the army which supports it, or the police which protects it." He was "returning his mandate" to the new Assembly. In haste, the Assembly unanimously re-elected him and the Communists backed down in their demands. A new government was finally formed on November 21, a full month after the election. But the whole process had the smell and feel of a weakening political structure—a situation in which General de Gaulle would increasingly look like a figurehead on a French pedestal, with parliament chipping away at his power base. This quickly showed in a major budget debate barely three weeks after the new government took office. Although there were Socialists in the Cabinet, on the floor of the Assembly the Socialist Party voted for a 20 percent cut in military spending. It was then the Communists who came to de Gaulle's support, voting on the instructions of Thorez to have the cut restored. For de Gaulle this was intolerable, to have the defense budget of France decided one way or the other by Communist votes. He began to number his days.

*

As Charles de Gaulle neared what was already seen as an inevitable end of his wartime power, two developments emerged that were to have major impact on the future of France after he was gone. The first was in overseas policy and the second in the management and direction of the French economy.

With the defeat of Japan, de Gaulle had dispatched a French military force to the Far East under Leclerc to reoccupy French Indochina. With the help of British and American forces already fighting on the scene, and plenty else on their platter and no wish to remain, French imperial control of the three Indochina States was uneasily re-established by the end of 1945, with Leclerc as military commander and the Gaullist loyalist, Admiral Thierry d'Argenlieu as high commissioner. But in the north of the country, a young French-educated Communist revolutionary, Ho Chi Minh, had been operating underground against the Japanese during the war and had formed a Vietnamese People's Liberation Committee. Moreover, he had "persuaded" by some means the emperor of the Annamite Kingdom, Bao Dai, who had been supported by the French before the war, to give the committee his backing. Bao Dai then wrote an eloquent appeal to General de Gaulle for Vietnamese independence: "You have suffered too much during four deadly years not to understand that the Vietnamese people, who have a history of twenty centuries and an often glorious past, no longer wish, can no longer support, any foreign domination."

But General de Gaulle was in no mood to dispose of the French Empire—at least not yet; that was to come much later. He had made a general policy statement of readiness to offer "freedom" and "economic autonomy" within the French Union to the States of Indochina. But he did not even answer Bao Dai's letter, and what he had in mind in the way of freedom was not that of Ho Chi Minh.

Leclerc, on the scene in Indochina, was convinced that the French could and should come to terms with the postwar revolutionary force in the country, but D'Argenlieu, his superior as high commissioner, took a hard line, proclaiming quite correctly that he was acting in complete accord with General de Gaulle. Accordingly, the French military, together with returning French bankers and colonial traders and civil administrators, pressed on to turn the clock back to 1939, with the full blessing of de Gaulle from Paris. Ho Chi Minh, meanwhile, converted his People's Liberation Committee into a provisional government. Thus, as de Gaulle prepared to leave power, the path was set for the inevitable confrontation in Vietnam that flamed into open war barely a year later, first enveloping France and then the United States until the last foreign troops left the territory about the time of Ho Chi Minh's death almost a quarter of a century later.

De Gaulle's final decisions on the economic front were more fortunate. When he went to Washington in August 1945, he had a long talk with the ubiquitous Jean Monnet, who was handling Lend-Lease matters with the United States and had negotiated the $650 million credit with the Export-Import Bank that was concluded during the visit. Monnet had been brooding about the crushing problems of economic recovery and modernization that France was facing, and he tackled General de Gaulle in terms couched to elicit his response.

> You speak of greatness [Monnet told de Gaulle] but today the French are small. There will be greatness only when the French are of a stature to warrant it. That is how they are. For this purpose, they must modernize themselves—because at the moment they are not modern. They need more production and greater productivity. Materially the country needs to be transformed.

Three months later Monnet returned to Paris, charged specifically by de Gaulle with tackling the problem of modernization of France.

Jean Monnet was one of the most fruitful minds and influential men of this century, even though he never held elective office or even served in a Cabinet in his life. His great forte and talent was getting his ideas and concepts into the hands and heads of men of power and happily allowing them to take all the credit they wished in carrying them out.

Working with three or four close assistants of high intellectual quality and economic expertise, Monnet decided that the horse that had to go before the cart to pull French industry and the French economy into the postwar half of the twentieth century was, very simply, public understanding and support for doing what would be necessary. He therefore devised a proposal for establishing an entirely new form of economic-planning machinery for France that was as simple as it was far-reaching. It was based on the creation of a series of study commissions to look at specific economic areas such as raw material needs, energy, steel, transport, agriculture, capital, foreign currency, manpower. But each of these commissions would be manned by a combination of industrial leaders in the field, trade unionists or labor representatives, independent economic specialists and civil service staff experts under the chairmanship of his own planning organization to fit all this into government policy decisions. The final key element of the structure rested in the power of decision. Once adopted by the planners and endorsed by the government, the economic targets and policy decisions were to be firm and fixed, and in no way subject to parliamentary approval or change.

Monnet had completed his proposals and submitted them to de Gaulle in early December 1945. It was all much to de Gaulle's taste and liking. First of all, Monnet had dealt with a complex subject in a short, concise and precise manner. Second, it was a plan to produce action and decision in a vital area and avoid the vagaries of parliamentary interference. It was in essence a plan for "a government within the government."

On January 3, 1946, General de Gaulle, with full approval of his mixed Cabinet of Communists, Socialists, Christian Democrats and Gaullists, issued a decree establishing a "Commissariat-General of the French Modernization and Investment Plan." Monnet became France's first planning commissioner, remaining in the post until his departure for Luxembourg seven years later to establish the High Authority of the European Coal and Steel Community, forerunner of the Common Market of today.

Across the vicissitudes of the Fourth Republic, Monnet's planning commission gave France a surprising stability and continuity of economic policy. Governments came and went, but the planning machinery profited, in a curiously inverse way, from the political disarray going on outside its bastion. Governments were too weak and changed too rapidly to tinker very much with the recommendations the planners produced. Allocation of Marshall Plan funds, priority targets for State investment, interest rates and the money supply, allocation of raw materials, approval of major construction projects such as port facilities and generating stations, production targets for tractors for farms—all these matters and much more fell within the purview of Monnet's Commissariat du Plan with its unique and undiluted powers of decision. To ensure this power and independence within the government, Monnet had insisted that the planning organization be attached directly to the premier's office so its direction and its recommendations would not be suffocated by control of the Cabinet or responsibility to any other element of the government.

The creation of the Monnet Planning Commission by de Gaulle closed out an unusual cycle in the lives of these two great Frenchmen. It had begun in London in June 1940, when Monnet proposed—and de Gaulle briefly bought—the plan for Anglo-French union to try to save the Reynaud government from accepting defeat. Then they separated, but as a last act in office, de Gaulle invested Monnet with unique powers and opportunity that he did not fail to use.

By the time de Gaulle signed the decree creating the Commissariat du Plan, the constitutional drafting committee of the Constituent Assembly had reached agreement on proposals that would again subordinate government in the new Fourth Republic to the will of parliament. It is a system that has worked for the British for centuries, but has never worked for the French. General de Gaulle lashed out with a vigorous public warning in a New Year's Day address to the parliamentarians over the consequences of the path they were embarking on, and more than just a hint that his tenure was coming to an end.

> The issue that separates us [he told the Assembly] is a general conception of government and its relations with the national representation. We have begun to rebulid the Republic. After me, you will continue to do so. I must tell you in conscience—and doubtless this is the last time I shall speak in this enclosure—that if you do so in misunderstanding of our political

history of the past fifty years, if you take no account of the absolute necessities of authority, of dignity, of the responsibility of government, you will head toward a situation such that, one day or another, I predict, you will bitterly regret you have taken the path you now follow.

The nation now waited, so to speak, for the other shoe to drop. Instead, de Gaulle left Paris for the Côte d'Azur at the end of the first week of January to brood and to rest. This was as surprising as it was sudden, for, as he records, it was "the first time for seven years I took a few days' rest." He went to Eden Roc on the Cap d'Antibes, and on January 14 he returned to Paris, his mind made up. He arrived back by train and was met at the station by Jules Moch, his Socialist minister of transport. As they drove away, the General confided his decision to go, telling Moch: "Really, one can scarcely imagine Joan of Arc, married, the mother of a family and—who knows—with a husband unfaithful to her." It was a comparison he had used talking to Pierre Bertaux in Toulouse fifteen months earlier.

During the rest of the week, de Gaulle continued to sign decrees and legislation, held a Cabinet meeting and even went to the Constituent Assembly although he did not speak, except one intervention in a debate in which he flattened Édouard Herriot, who had been president of the last Assembly of the Third Republic before the events of June 1940. Herriot had the temerity to call on General de Gaulle to cancel medals and citations that had been awarded three years earlier by General Giraud to French servicemen who had lost their lives or been wounded in opposing the Allied landings in North Africa under Vichy orders. De Gaulle had approved the awards in the *Journal Officiel* simply on the grounds that they were for Frenchmen who had become casualties while obeying orders. He turned on Herriot, whose political support he had solicited without much result, and retorted: "I myself am the best judge of the validity of these awards since I never had anything to do with Vichy or the enemy, except by cannon fire." This was an allusion that Herriot clearly understood to his luncheon in Paris with Pierre Laval and the German ambassador, Otto Abetz, when Laval was plotting his last move to block de Gaulle's path to Paris and power.

At the end of the week he summoned a Cabinet meeting for January 20, 1946, a Sunday. This fact alone signaled that the end was at hand, for never except in emergencies did the French Cabinet meet on Sundays. His ministers gathered, then, in his office at the War Ministry on the rue Saint-Dominique, where he had continued to exercise power ever since his return to Paris sixteen months before. The end was brief and sharp as a guillotine. After the ministers had assembled, General de Gaulle entered the room. He shook hands all around but did not invite anyone to be seated. He then informed them:

> The exclusive regime of the parties has come back. I disapprove of it. But short of establishing by force a dictatorship, which I don't want and which would probably turn out badly, I lack the means to prevent this experiment. I must therefore retire. This day, I shall address to the president of the

National Assembly a letter informing him of the government's resignation. I thank each of you very sincerely for the help you have given me and I ask you to stay at your posts to ensure the despatch of business until your successors are appointed.

That said, he nodded a farewell to all and walked out.

POWER

F I F T E E N

THE DESERT YEARS, 1946–57

General de Gaulle had exercised supreme autocratic power on behalf of France, and over France, for nearly six years, but it was power that was never consolidated politically. He had tried to achieve a consolidation by moving swiftly as soon as he returned to Paris to liquidate the organizational machinery of the Resistance, which he clearly saw as a political rival for power. But he could not suppress the Communist apparat, and his autocratic methods and style and attitude toward all politicians simply added to discontentment with his leadership. He himself, of course, always insisted on resting his power not on any political machinery, but on the elevated role of symbol and embodiment of national unity. When he abruptly resigned that role on January 20, 1946, his name all but disappeared from the pages of the Paris press within a week, and, it seemed, from the political conscience of the French people as well.

Whether de Gaulle really believed, as some biographers have contended, that his resignation would produce public demonstrations and an immediate popular demand for his return must be doubted. He was too much of a historian, too steeped in the processes of power not to know that he could scarcely step down from the heights and pull up those roots on one day and expect the French people to invite him to plant them all over again the next. But of course he quit utterly convinced that the constitutional system on which the politicians were determined to embark would not work, and that its collapse one day was inevitable. For that day he must wait, and meanwhile keep clear of politics and politicians, to remain as pure as Joan of Arc. It took a great deal longer than he expected, to a point where he had practically given up hope before it finally came.

Meanwhile, in the depth of that first postwar winter of 1946, the French people had enough to worry about without taking to the streets to demonstrate for the return of Charles de Gaulle. Nevertheless, there was a certain apprehension as to what the General might do. Vincent Auriol, the Socialist leader who was minister of state in the Cabinet (and later first president of the Fourth Republic) was away in London on the day of the resignation, and he came hurrying back to Paris to write de Gaulle a personal letter appealing to him not to go on the air with a broadcast that "would divide the country to the advantage and satisfaction of the enemies of democracy." De Gaulle says tartly that if he had wanted to make a broadcast, he certainly would have gone ahead and done so, "but I considered that my silence would weigh more heavily than anything else, that thoughtful minds would understand why I had left, and that the rest would sooner or later be informed by events themselves."

To Jean-Raymond Tournoux, the General said in 1952:

> I had the material means to establish a dictatorship. Of course I could have called in Leclerc and expelled the Assembly. I must confess, without requesting absolution, that events forced me to exercise a dictatorship during nearly six years. But France was gagged at the time and was in mortal peril. Should I have maintained that dictatorship? My answer to my own question was No. Dictatorship always ends badly in France if it is maintained when circumstances have returned to normal.

Still, de Gaulle was clearly disappointed that public response and reaction to his departure was so meager, that the people's interest in him seemed to fade so fast. At one point he even sent one of his aides out from the suburban Paris *pavillon* where he had gone to live after he left office to make sure that there were no police cordons on the approach roads keeping visitors or sightseers away.

When he returned to Paris at the time of the liberation, de Gaulle had refused to take up residence in the Élysée Palace since he was not a fully invested president of the Republic, only the head of a provisional government. Instead he had settled in a comfortable villa in Neuilly, which of course was paid for by the State. His own country home, 120 miles east of Paris at Colombey-les-Deux-Églises, the only property de Gaulle ever owned, had been damaged by the retreating Germans, but while in office he had studiously avoided arranging any priority building permit for its repair. Now, however, the work got under way, but it was not until May 1946 that the de Gaulles could return to the home they had left in 1939.

In the meantime the authorities offered him the choice of a number of State-owned mansions, and he elected to move into an old Louis XIV hunting lodge on the edge of the Marly Forest, near Versailles to the west of Paris, for which he paid a modest rent to the Service des Beaux-Arts, the State owner. But the place was run down, needing paint, plumbing, electricity repairs and a decent heating system after years of wartime neglect, and it was with relief that he finally returned to Colombey. A tower had been added to the end of the very simple narrow stone country house, to de Gaulle's own architectural design, to provide a study where he could work with a panoramic view of the rolling woods and countryside.

The DC-4 Skymaster that had been Truman's personal gift was turned over to the French Air Force with a proviso that it be made available for any overseas traveling the General might decide to undertake. He got rid of a large American car and acquired a small French car, and Madame de Gaulle took driving lessons. For all the grandeur with which de Gaulle invested the exercise of high office, in personal living habits and tastes his life was utterly simple to a point of dullness. He was not even all that well off financially, and had to live prudently on the retired pay of a brigadier general plus some small supporting emoluments from the State.

Soon after he stepped down, the government proposed raising him in rank to full general, increasing his pension accordingly. But he wrote back a disapproving brushoff, saying that since no one had "apparently" thought of promoting him "during an epic struggle" it would be "strange and even ridiculous" to do it now that he was in retirement.

Meanwhile, his daughter Elizabeth married an officer, Captain Alain de Boissieu, who later became an *aide de camp* to his father-in-law. His son Philippe, making his career in the Navy, married Henriette de Montalembert, and a first grandson, Charles de Gaulle, was born. Family life enlarged, and was practically the only activity at La Boisserie, the three-acre wooded estate at Colombey, where the gates, like de Gaulle's life, otherwise remained firmly closed to outsiders. Personal visits from old associates grew more infrequent, the visitors inevitably wondering at the paucity of de Gaulle's table. Was it money or taste? Probably both. He liked cheap and simple food, such as *tripes à la mode de Caen* or *blanquette de veau*, with even *boeuf bourguignon* something of a luxury. For guests there would be a bottle of *vin ordinaire*, but sometimes only water would be served.

De Gaulle's mentally retarded daughter, Anne, remained his deepest personal concern—indeed the deepest human concern of his life. In 1948 Anne died of pneumonia, shortly before her twentieth birthday. She was buried in the little churchyard at Colombey, where her father and mother now also lie. As the service ended, with only the family gathered, de Gaulle took his wife's hand to lead her home, saying gently: "Come. . . . Now she is like all the rest."

*

For the politicians, de Gaulle's departure was like the rolling away of a great stone, even though something resembling a political nest of maggots was exposed. When the Constituent Assembly got down to electing a successor to form a new government, three votes were still forlornly cast for the General, but the choice went to Félix Gouin, the Socialist president of the Assembly, described by the Socialist newspaper *Le Combat* as "a man of goodwill rather than will." It was a description that fitted most of the seventeen men who followed him to form twenty-four different governments in the ensuing twelve years. Gouin lasted until June. Meanwhile, a February public opinion poll showed that a majority of the French people were glad that General de Gaulle had gone, and very few of them expected him ever to return to power.

By April the Assembly's drafting committee had clobbered together a new constitution of exactly the system de Gaulle warned against and would have rejected. There was to be a one-chamber legislature in which sovereign power would reside, with a president of the Republic whose functions would be limited and largely ceremonial and a premier to be chosen, or dismissed, by the parliamentarians. The constitution was then submitted to a national referendum on May 5. General de Gaulle took no active part in the campaign. But to the surprise of the politicians, and de Gaulle as well, the constitution was rejected by nearly a million votes. In part this was because the Socialists and Communists had joined forces to eliminate from the draft any guarantee of State support for Catholic schools—an issue going all the way back to the early days of the Third Republic and de Gaulle's boyhood. Along with the "Catholic issue" there was also the sudden realization that the new constitution might well result in bringing the Communists to power, since they were indisputably the strongest party in the country with the greatest number of Assembly seats.

With the first attempt at a constitution voted down, the mandate of the Constituent Assembly also expired, and elections for a new Assembly to make another try were set for June. De Gaulle decided to break his political silence with a major speech at the town of Bayeux on June 16, 1946, to mark the second anniversary of his landing in France after D-Day at the place where he first addressed the French on their own native soil. The speech was a broadside at the constitutional problem, warning that only under a system based on a strong chief of state could France achieve stability, cope with the problems and dangers she was facing and indeed avoid the threat of dictatorship. What had been the fate, de Gaulle asked, of the First, Second and Third French Republics, of the Weimar Republic, of Italy's democratic experiment and of the Spanish Republic? All had ended in dictatorships because the parliamentary systems on which they were based were too weak to govern. But dictatorship was not the answer.

The system de Gaulle outlined at Bayeux in that speech was almost identical to the one he eventually ensured was written into a constitution when he returned to power to establish the Fifth Republic: A president of the Republic, chosen by a "grand council" of electors, with the power to appoint prime ministers, preside over the government, dissolve parliament, make treaties and conduct foreign policy, and command the armed forces. Parliament would have purely a legislative role, and the president could take great national questions direct to the voters by referendum.

But it was a speech for the future that had little immediate effect. In the Assembly elections, however, the Catholic MRP passed the Communists to emerge as the nation's strongest single party, even though the Communists gained votes at the expense of the Socialists. A new constitution was now completed fairly quickly, establishing a legislature of two chambers but still leaving the basic life-or-death powers over future French governments in the hands of the National Assembly.

De Gaulle campaigned openly against the second version of a Fourth Republic constitution, with the clear political possibility of forcing the country into a deadlock or stalemate that he might then be called upon to resolve. Perhaps because of this possibility, the Communists pulled out all the stops to have the constitution approved. The referendum result, in October, was a minimal majority. Roughly one-third of the voters abstained, just under one-third voted no, and a little more than one-third voted yes, to assure a narrow adoption. In November the French had to troop back to the polls for the fifth time in 1946 to elect a new National Assembly under the new constitution. This time, ominously, the Communists swung back on top over the MRP as the country's strongest party with the most Assembly seats once again.

The constitutional struggle was over and the Fourth Republic had been born, but France's troubles were multiplying rapidly. In November 1946, on the other side of the world, the man de Gaulle had installed as high commissioner in Indochina, Admiral d'Argenlieu, suddenly, without reference to Paris, ordered a naval bombardment of Haiphong, killing or wounding many thousands of Vietnamese. He acted on the excuse of quelling resistance to the reimposition of French rule, while the government in Paris had its mind on other things. Three weeks later, in mid-December, Ho Chi Minh's followers retaliated by massacring forty French civilians in Hanoi. From that moment, the die was cast toward war. If there had been strong, clearsighted liberal French leadership on the spot in Indochina and within the government in Paris, there would still have been time and opportunity to turn back and negotiate an agreement or a settlement with Ho Chi Minh and avoid conflict. There were men who could have and would have (Leclerc was one), but the government was too weak, and de Gaulle bears a large share of the responsibility because of the intransigent attitude he took as the confrontation grew, whenever he commented.

As France headed into war in Indochina, the country's economic plight grew more and more grim in the terrible winter of 1946–47, the worst winter in Europe in this century. The initial burst of basic postwar repair work slowed down in the face of overwhelming problems of raw materials with which to produce, factories where there was production, and coal to produce the energy to run the factories. Another loan had been negotiated in Washington, and the money was fast running out with little to show how it had been spent. It was the same story all over Western Europe, with Communists then in almost every one of its governments, rapidly sliding into chaos and collapse.

Stalin meanwhile was ruthlessly pressing the consolidation of Soviet control over Eastern Europe. Communist regimes had already been imposed on Bulgaria and Roumania, and Tito had emerged as the victorious leader of Yugoslavia. Poland's turn came in January 1947, when a rigged election closely watched by the Red Army snuffed out the last struggling vestige of a "democratic coalition" that was supposed to have been guaranteed by the Yalta and Potsdam agreements.

In the growing East-West split, French policy toward defeated Germany as laid down by de Gaulle was running into trouble and causing trouble as far as the Western Allies were concerned. It was based first of all on cooperation with the Soviet Union, in line with de Gaulle's constant wartime game of balancing—or playing off—between East and West. And the French were determined to achieve a permanent dismemberment of Germany into separate states under some kind of weak confederated central authority that would never be able to raise an army or contemplate waging war again. But Soviet intransigence and the growing Soviet menace were wrecking this French approach. The Americans were insisting that the Western occupation zones had to be combined to put Germany on a sound economic and political footing to create an anti-Communist barrier against what was happening in East Germany and the rest of Eastern Europe.

Georges Bidault continued at the Foreign Ministry after de Gaulle's departure (with a brief spell as premier also) and continued a rear-guard action on the German policy, mainly fighting his own allies as de Gaulle had done so often before him. In early 1947 the British and American occupation zones were merged into one for economic purposes, but the French held out, keeping their zone intact and separate. They also stepped up the economic separation of the contentious Saar Valley from Germany and its de facto incorporation into France.

On March 12, 1947, President Harry S Truman threw down the gauntlet to the Soviet Union with an address to the United States Congress that was one of the turning points of history—the Truman Doctrine speech in which he launched the American rescue operation for Turkey and Greece, then in the throes of a savage civil war with the Communists. "I believe that it *must* be the policy of the United States to support free peoples who are resisting attempted subjugation by armed minorities or by outside pressures," Truman said in a speech that has shaped— and misshaped—American foreign policy every since.

General de Gaulle, brooding at Colombey-les-Deux-Églises over these gathering domestic and foreign storm clouds, was also preparing a major move. The first sign of this had come in mid-February, when he made an unusually extended visit to Paris lasting several days, conferring at length with an inner-circle coterie of old loyalists from the London days and the Resistance—Jacques Soustelle, who had been his spokesman and later an Intelligence director; Michel Debré, who had been his key agent inside the Vichy regime; André Malraux, who conceived of himself as the in-house Gaullist intellectual; Colonel Rémy of the Resistance organization in France; Olivier Guichard, Léon Mazeaud; Pasteur Valéry-Radot; and others. They had been summoned to make preparations for General de Gaulle to enter the political arena.

*

De Gaulle's decision to launch his own political movement was not only controversial but unsuccessful—without much doubt the biggest mistake of his life (at least in French domestic affairs). After an ephemeral and deceptive initial success, the movement went into a political tailspin. Moreover, it quickly took on a disturbing neo-Fascist coloration through its stage-managed mass rallies, for which Malraux was responsible; its strongarm Service d'Ordre, which Colonel Rémy enthusiastically organized from old Resistance fighters; and the right-wing following that the movement attracted, including many an old Vichy loyalist who now saw an opportunity to climb safely aboard the Gaullist bandwagon with money and patriotism. By the time de Gaulle abandoned his political effort five years later, the movement he had founded was more fractured than most French parties, his own nonpolitical image was tarnished and his standing with the French people weakened. He retreated, more bitter than ever, into isolation greater than ever, writing off his own future—as well as the future of France.

But after the February 1947 meeting of the "Gaullist barons," the work of creating a new Gaullist political apparat got under way through the old-boy network of veterans of the Resistance whose first loyalty was to de Gaulle. Soustelle and Rémy took charge of organizing a political underground out of the remains of the Resistance underground, and Malraux took charge of preparations for a propaganda blitz when the movement was unveiled. On March 30, 1947, less than three weeks after the Truman Doctrine had been proclaimed, General de Gaulle addressed a mass audience in a Resistance setting on the cliffs at Bruneval, near le Havre, overlooking the English Channel. Here the British in cooperation with the Resistance had carried out a spectacular and successful commando raid in February 1942, seizing a piece of German radar equipment that was of vital importance in devising the countermeasures by which the British won the "radar war."

In somewhat delphic terms, after evoking a fanciful retrospective picture of how France had been "one and indivisible" in those Resistance days, de Gaulle ended with his audience crying *"De Gaulle au pouvoir!"* as he spoke these words: "The day will come when, rejecting the sterile games, and re-forming the ill-constructed framework in which the nation is losing its way and the state disqualifying itself, the immense mass of French people will rally round France!"

Was he calling for a *coup d'état*—what did he have in mind? The hint of things to come was enough to send the current premier, Paul Ramadier, a Socialist, hurrying out to Colombey-les-Deux-Églises two days later for an extraordinary secret midnight meeting. Ramadier, in an account of this conversation to Jean-Raymond Tournoux, says that he acted "to put an end to equivocation" and to warn the General that while no one could forget the debt the country owed him, it would be impossible to overlook a distinction between de Gaulle the liberator and de Gaulle as a politician. The discussion between the two men, lasting well over an hour, was conducted in terms of careful courtesy, even a certain cordiality. De Gaulle responded that "the resistance was not only a national phenomenon—it was also political, and I am maintaining my role, that is all." Having restored the Republic, he said, "Do you think I now want to overthrow it?", but he insisted that "I shall remain the nation's guide."

Ramadier then informed de Gaulle that if he launched himself into political life and put himself at the head of a movement, the government with regret would have to treat him like any other political leader, and he would no longer be entitled to a special police bodyguard and escort or the honor guard that regularly turned out for his public appearances. Nor, most of all, would he any longer get automatic air time over the State-controlled radio facilities for his public speeches.

De Gaulle took this news with seeming indifference, and politely escorted the premier to his automobile in the early-morning hours for his drive back to Paris, with the parting words: "You may reassure the worriers—I'm not going to be a Boulanger" (a reference to General Georges Boulanger, who staged an abortive comic opera coup attempt in Paris in 1886). When this remark was subsequently relayed to President Vincent Auriol by Ramadier, Auriol replied: "Let him take note that I'm not going to be a Hindenburg" (the German field marshal-president who called Adolf Hitler to come to power in 1933).

Meanwhile, Malraux was at work on the stage setting for a huge meeting on April 7 in Strasbourg, a permanent Gaullist stronghold. To wild cheers, de Gaulle declared in the climax of his speech: "The time has come to form and organize the rally of the French people which, within the framework of the law, will promote and lead to triumph, above differences of opinion, the great effort of common salvation and the profound reform of the State. And so, tomorrow, in line with the common actions and will, the French Republic shall build the new France!"

So, typically for de Gaulle, it was not to be a new political "party" that he was creating, but the Rassemblement du Peuple Français, the Rally of the People of France (RPF). One week later, on April 14, 1947, a formal announcement of the launching of the new movement was issued from the office which de Gaulle had maintained in Paris since his retirement. Jacques Soustelle became the secretary and organizational chief of the movement.

In one sense de Gaulle had chosen his timing well. Fear was rising all over Western Europe, and the Truman speech had galvanized the anti-Communist mood in the democracies. De Gaulle now proceeded to play on fear and anti-Communism to maximum political advantage.

De Gaulle had never hesitated to use the Communists when he felt it necessary and could do so to his advantage. His "free pardon" for Thorez, enabling the Communist leader to return to France from his wartime refuge in Moscow, was evidence of that. But de Gaulle certainly never trusted the Communists, and he was outraged that the Communist presence in the government, which he had initiated back in Algiers, had now spread from relatively minor peripheral ministerial posts to a Communist minister of defense. This was also becoming intolerable to Ramadier, and even in a way to the Communists themselves.

Presumably on Stalin's orders, Thorez and the other Communist ministers had stayed on in the government even though France was now engaged in almost open hostilities against Ho Chi Minh, and even though foreign policy was now ipso facto swinging completely away from any more wistful attempts at bridge-building with the Soviet Union and firmly with the United States and Great Britain in the growing East-West split. It was no longer a question of whether to expel the Communists from the government, but when and how they would go.

The breaking point came at the end of April 1947, two weeks after de Gaulle launched his RPF movement, when workers at the newly nationalized Renault automobile works went on strike for higher pay, against a government wage-freeze policy that had been instituted by the Socialist Léon Blum during his brief tenure as premier. The Communist ministers were again caught in a bind. Did they support the workers or did they support the policy of the government of which they were members? They elected to support the workers, and they were at once dismissed by Ramadier. They remained outside French governments for the next thirty-four years, until they were taken back in by Socialist François Mitterrand when he was elected fourth president of the Fifth Republic in 1981.

The Communists, no longer inhibited by participation in the government, at once unleashed a violent wave of strikes throughout France in 1947—clearly designed to intimidate the authorities and harass the nation in its economic weakness and political confusion, in parallel with the pressures that Stalin was mounting in the East. But the government held on, thanks largely to the tough-minded and intelligent Socialist interior minister, Jules Moch. The strike wave was contained because Moch was prepared to be ruthless in sending in his newly formed antiriot shock battalions of the Compagnies Républicaines de Sécurité (CRS) to break heads and arms without questions asked.

Meanwhile de Gaulle's new movement took off in a blaze of patriotism and propaganda, with a large propulsion of fear. Within twenty-four hours of the April 14 announcement, more than 12,000 Parisians had joined the RPF, and by May 1 an astounding 800,000 French men and women had written to its Paris headquarters from all over France asking how, what and where to join. But a neo-Fascist style of rallies with floodlights, backdrops and music, and the bodyguards, the lurking sense of both intimidation and power that were the work of Malraux's stage-managing, were disturbing. Malraux throughout his erratic and not always honorable intellectual life had a fascination with power, without much regard for its human results. He had flirted with Communism in his youth and in his old age sat spellbound before Mao Tse-tung. He had watched the rise of Hitler with fascination and had gone to fight on the Republican side in the Spanish Civil War. He attached himself to General de Gaulle as the first Frenchman of the century to be a true man of power, like other Malraux heroes. So he set out to provide de Gaulle with the gaudy trappings that had worked so well for Hitler at Nuremberg. For a while it seemed to succeed, but in the long run it did not go down well with the French people.

The high point of this ugly period came in September 1948, when a three-way pitched battle was fought in Grenoble at the end of a rally addressed by de Gaulle. Communists locked with Gaullist strongarm squads, with the police in the middle. One Communist was shot and killed and fourteen persons seriously injured. Moch ordered a Ministry of the Interior investigation and subsequently reported to the National Assembly that no arms had been found on any of the Communists taken into custody and that no shots had been fired by the police. The shots, therefore, were presumed to have come from the Gaullists. Moch's report went on to state that investigation showed that de Gaulle's Service d'Ordre commanded by Colonel Rémy consisted of six thousand trained men in Paris and another ten thousand in the provinces. They were not armed (gun control was and is extremely strict in France), but they had the makings of a shadow army. In addition, however, Moch told the Assembly that there were "shock formations" that followed the General on his tours, and these men were armed and on occasion had driven jeeps into crowds of demonstrators. It was "inadmissible," Moch said, to have such a private motorized police force in a democracy. He also deplored the fact that the State had expended more than one million francs in the first eight months of 1948 to provide security arrangements against the demonstrations and violence that General de Gaulle's rallies were producing.

*

If there had been a general election for a new National Assembly in the offing when de Gaulle launched the RPF, the postwar history of France would almost certainly have been far different. Instead, there were only municipal elections coming up in October 1947. But in this demagogic atmosphere, de Gaulle's Rally of the People of France rode to a stunning success.

The Gaullists captured an astounding 40 percent of the total votes cast. Gaullist mayors were installed in fifty-two out of the ninety-two major cities and towns of France, including Paris, where the RPF took more than half the seats in the municipal council and elected de Gaulle's brother, Pierre, as mayor. Without much doubt, if it had been an election for the National Assembly, the Gaullists would have emerged as the strongest single party in Assembly seats and possibly even a majority party on its own. But it was a municipal election, and therefore although things had changed politically, constitutionally they remained the same. *Plus ça change, plus c'est la même chose.*

In the wake of this victory, de Gaulle issued an immediate call for the government to dissolve the Assembly and call national elections. "An immense power has risen in France and the regime of division and confusion has been condemned," he declared. If the government would not act, then the Assembly could dissolve itself by a two-thirds majority, he pointed out, and this would also clear the way for drastic reform of the constitution.

But the effect of this call, treated by the government as an arrogant threat if not an ultimatum, was to stiffen the Socialists, the Catholic MRP and the other political parties and leaders—including of course the Communists, who still could count on more than 5 million French votes—to close ranks to bar de Gaulle's path to power.

Meanwhile the international situation was deteriorating rapidly into the Cold War. General George C. Marshall had delivered his famous speech at Harvard in June 1947, with its offer of aid for Europe that would turn the tide of history. Soviet Foreign Minister Molotov then walked out of a conference in Paris with Georges Bidault and Britain's Ernest Bevin to discuss Europe's response to the Americans, leaving the Western Europeans, to their relief, to get on with a joint recovery effort on their own with Europe now totally cut in half.

In February of 1948 the Communists snuffed out the last flicker of democracy in Czechoslovakia. Berlin was to be next, and at 11 P.M. on the night of Wednesday, June 23, 1948, the Soviet blockade of the city began.

General de Gaulle was in action continuously across these months with speeches and rallies up and down the country—but in fact his movement had peaked in the municipal elections and was already declining. The government somehow was coping, and the parties were at least united in being anti–de Gaulle. The Marshall Plan had already brought hope and first emergency shipments of grain and food to get through the winter of 1947–48, and the essentials for genuine economic recovery would soon follow. De Gaulle therefore began to look less and less necessary to the French for their salvation.

He continued to demand a dissolution of the National Assembly and new national elections, but this was the last thing the government or the party leaders were going to give him. So he had to battle on in mounting frustration, with political speeches that became more and more right-wing and less and less democratic as time went on. At one point he told an audience that under the constitutional reform which he would carry out "it would not be necessary to recognize the trade unions. The trade union organization will have to be subjected to a profound evolution. If we establish a Capital–Labor association, the very nature and appearance of the trade unions will be changed, for there will be no class struggle inside the association of capital and labor."

This kind of concept of the future of France, with the Malraux backdrop of spotlights and banners and strongarm squads, was beginning to worry a lot of Frenchmen.

In March 1949 cantonal elections were held in France for the regional assemblies that are part of its system. Again it was an election with no bearing on the central government except to disclose the current relative standing of the political parties. Only half of the cantons elect at any one time, and on this occasion those of the Paris region, where the Gaullists might have expected to do well, were not voting. The election therefore was a limited, not a conclusive, test. Nevertheless, the RPF vote skidded from 40 percent of the ballots cast at the time of the municipal elections seventeen months earlier to only 25.3 percent, barely ahead of the Communists, who polled 23.5 percent. The psychological shock to the movement was worse than the results themselves. General de Gaulle was no longer on the upswing, but in a downswing. The start of a period of recovery and relative stability under the premiership of Henri Queuille, a Radical who lasted thirteen months, did not offer the General much opportunity to reverse the trend.

Moreover, de Gaulle in his public statements and private comments across this volatile period of postwar history continued to criticize or condemn outright many of the key decisions being taken by the French government and the United States and Britain to create the security and strength that France and the Atlantic Community enjoy today.

On the eve of the Berlin airlift in June 1948, for example, Georges Bidault finally agreed at a meeting with Marshall and Bevin in London to merge the French occupation zone of West Germany with the British and American zones in order to facilitate Marshall Plan aid and economic recovery for Germany, and at the same time to allow the Germans to proceed with drafting a constitution for a Federal Republic. De Gaulle came down on Bidault with a rancorous denunciation about "creating a Reich in Frankfurt" and selling out France's interests, and as a result of this intervention the National Assembly came within five votes of killing the agreement.

Had de Gaulle had his way, Germany would have remained divided into Western occupation zones, the Saar would have been permanently ceded to France, the Ruhr would have been administered by an international high authority, and the emergence of the Bonn government would have been slowed down indefinitely—regardless of the Soviet blockade of Berlin and what the Soviets were doing in their zone of East Germany to convert it into a Stalinist satellite.

When the North Atlantic Treaty was signed in Washington in April 1949, he issued a short statement of welcome in principle, with an added warning that

France must reserve final judgment "until she knows under what conditions she will be getting the arms she needs . . . and what her commitments would be, should she have to send help to others." Then, as the NATO organization and a new Supreme Headquarters, Allied Powers Europe (SHAPE) began to emerge again on French soil, the sniping over France's loss of independence and surrender to American domination quickly resumed: "Preparing for world war, America deploys great efforts to arm all countries liable to combat man to man with the Communist armies, and she takes care to take over the command of their forces, but she herself has chosen a peripheral strategy which would commit the smallest possible number of her own children."

If de Gaulle had returned to power in 1947 or 1948, it is difficult not to conclude that he would have opposed any integrated command structure such as was created under NATO by Eisenhower, and might well have opposed even putting an Allied headquarters on French soil. Most certainly he would have fought with maximum obstruction and intransigence to block the rearming of Germany—as he fought to defeat the European Defense Community treaty and the European Army in 1953 and 1954.

Above all, France under de Gaulle would never have proposed the creation of the European Coal and Steel Community as she did in May of 1950—the most imaginative act of French foreign policy in this century. A product of the fertile and far-reaching mind of Jean Monnet, who sold the plan to a politically skillful foreign minister, Robert Schuman, this formed the basis not only for Franco-German reconciliation but the creation of the European Common Market of today. But as far as de Gaulle was concerned, the mere idea in 1950 of France giving up sovereign control over its own heavy industry as a means of seeking accommodation with defeated Germany was totally ridiculous. He opposed the Schuman Plan in its passage through the National Assembly, leading to a break with a number of his otherwise loyal followers, among them General Georges Catroux.

For the security and economic stability of Western Europe, and indeed the world, it is well that these important basic treaties and institutions were all created and firmly established during de Gaulle's desert years, well before his return to power. Europe would have been a very barren and dangerous place in the 1950s and today without a NATO military command, without a Bonn government, without German rearmament, without the Schuman Plan.

*

At last it was time to elect a new National Assembly in June 1951, a crucial test as to whether de Gaulle and his movement was a spent force or not. This time the RPF vote dropped again by another four points to 21.5 percent. The Gaullists trailed the Communists, who moved up slightly to 25.6 percent. Even though, with 121 seats, the RPF was the largest party in the new National Assembly, thanks to the way district boundaries were drawn, it was still a failure for de Gaulle. The other parties could still patch together a coalition majority, and de Gaulle wanted no part of the "party games" anyway.

De Gaulle was furious when the RPF general secretary and party leader in the

National Assembly, Jacques Soustelle, called on President Auriol at the Élysée Palace to discuss the postelection political situation and a possible government solution. Yet it was impossible for de Gaulle to hold 121 Deputies in line with a policy of aloofness and isolation and indifference. The breakup quickly began when twenty-seven RPF deputies voted for the investiture of Antoine Pinay as premier. An attempt by Soustelle to impose disciplinary rules brought the resignation of nearly a quarter of the Gaullists to form a new Assembly group. Then, in the municipal elections in April 1953, the movement that had gotten off to such a spectacular start in the towns and cities five years before was virtually annihilated—losing two-thirds of its municipal council seats.

Three days later General de Gaulle called it quits.

> The efforts I have made since the war, seconded by resolute Frenchmen, to enable our country to find its unity at last and to put at its head a government which really would be a government, have so far been without results. I acknowledge this without equivocation. The Rassemblement du Peuple Français must regroup against the day when the influence of a restless dissatisfaction could lead the French people to unite and the regime to transform itself.

Henceforth the Gaullist deputies in the National Assembly could act as they pleased. De Gaulle did not admit defeat to the extent of dissolving his movement, but he never addressed another rally and its activities were at an end.

The gates now closed at La Boisserie, and the visits to Paris became less and less frequent. Loyalists who visited were treated to bursts of angry barracks-room invective about the French people—"cattle" or "slackers"—and worse for the politicians: eunuchs of the Fourth Republic, vinegar-pissers, imbeciles, cheats, vomit, whiners and other things less translatable.

For the next four years de Gaulle immersed himself in the writing of his War Memoirs—a magnificent literary work whatever its shortcomings as history. He was a slow writer, working entirely with pen and ink in a sloping script difficult to decipher, writing and rewriting, scratching out and correcting remorselessly. His handwritten pages were then typed by his daughter Elisabeth. In contrast to Churchill, who worked by dictation and loved to ramble and wander and expand, de Gaulle's Memoirs are a masterpiece of condensation and swift telling of complex events. Often, of course, this was a useful way of leaving out details that might alter the picture he was determined to present. Certainly there is no pretense of impartiality. The word pictures are lapidary and vivid, the judgments often caustic and biting, the narrative flow lucid and concise, the recognition of the accomplishments of others minimal rather than generous. It is exactly what it was intended to be—a monument to de Gaulle, by de Gaulle.

Meanwhile the Fourth Republic got a new lease on life in 1954 when Pierre Mendès-France managed in a spectacular eight months as premier to end the draining war in Indochina before it tore the nation apart completely, to set Tunisia on the road to autonomous self-government and a promise of independence before it broke into rebellion against French rule, and to settle the question of French acquiescence in the rearmament of West Germany and the entry of the Bonn Republic into the NATO alliance. Mendès-France was the only really historic figure among the premiers of the Fourth Republic—but of course he was too good to last.

Moreover, as his hold on office was running out, war against French rule broke out in the mountains of Algeria. After making peace and withdrawing the French Army from Indochina, there could be only one answer in Algeria—repression and force.

From de Gaulle's standpoint, the greatest service that Mendès-France rendered to the nation was to stand aside and allow the National Assembly to kill the European Army treaty. This he hailed with the comment: "The nation has roused itself. This healthy reaction will soon bring others in its train." But all it brought was another Fourth Republic government, and the shadows lengthened.

In July 1955 de Gaulle called a press conference in Paris and first went through a familiar litany. He deplored the fact that France had agreed to the rearmament of Germany. He said that a solution for the Tunisian and Moroccan parts of the Empire might lie in an "association" with France, but in the case of Algeria he called for "integration, provided it can be sincere."

He ended with a note of finality: "Everything suggests that it will be a long time before we meet again. It is my intention not to intervene any longer in what is called 'public affairs.' I will take no interest at all in elections. It may be that I would intervene again, but it would take a rather unusual shock for this, and in the meantime I say good-bye to you, perhaps for a long time."

De Gaulle was nearing sixty-five, and there was no reason not to take him at his word. He was retiring from public life. He completed his War Memoirs in 1957, making no mention of his ill-fated Rassemblement du Peuple Français. This was perhaps the final record of his life and he drew a veil across a political failure.

The concluding passages of the Memoirs read like poetry, a mood of resignation toward the lengthening shadows and the winter of life:

> Old Earth, worn by the ages, racked by rain and storm, exhausted yet ever ready to produce what life must have to go on!
>
> Old France, weighed down with history, prostrated by wars and revolution, endlessly vacillating from greatness to decline, but revived, century after century, by the genius of renewal!
>
> Old man, exhausted by ordeal, detached from human deeds, feeling the approach of the eternal cold, but always watching in the shadows for the gleam of hope!

SIXTEEN

THE DE GAULLE REVOLUTION, 1958

The de Gaulle revolution of May 1958 ranks with the storming of the Bastille in 1789 and the cataclysmic events of the Paris Commune in 1871 as one of the decisive turning-point dramas of France that produced a complete change in its system of government and the way the country is run. To be sure, the fall of France in 1940 scarred the lives and memories of the French people far more, with its years of German occupation and 628,000 casualties of war. But when the tragic interregnum of the war years was over, the Fourth Republic largely took up where the Third Republic had left off. This "return to normalcy" perpetuated a political system inadequate to cope with the enormous forces of economic, social and political change that the war had produced in France and the world. It took another war, in Algeria, to lance the boil.

The French Army stood in mounting intimidation over successive governments of the Fourth Republic. It had been defeated in 1940 and it had been defeated at Dien-Bien-Phu and withdrawn from Indochina in 1954. Since then it had been fighting continuously against the Algerian insurrection, and it was not going to accept another defeat or another negotiated political settlement. For French governments, moreover, there was the political complication that Algeria was supposed to be "French," because it had been constitutionally incorporated into the French Republic for more than a century. In theory it was another *département* of France like all the rest. But in fact, of course, a French governor general exercised total colonial rule over a territory larger than France itself, and only the French *pied-noir* settlers and a handful of wealthy Algerians enjoyed the benefits of French citizenship. There was not even a pretense that the Algerian Moslem masses were entitled to French rights or had any democratic voice in how their country was run.

For the harassed and ever-changing governments of the Fourth Republic, neither a military nor a political retreat in Algeria was possible. The Army was determined to crush the Front de Libération Nationale (FLN) rebellion and fight to victory. Any tampering with the constitutional status of Algeria was out of the question. Any moves in the direction of liberalization to win support of the Moslem population was treated as a sign of weakness. The solution of "full integration" with France was regularly propounded, but always floundered at the prospect of granting full French citizenship to all those Moslems. At the first sign of any change or fresh political initiative even being contemplated in Paris, the Army, backed by a powerful Algerian lobby, was able to bring a government down. Jacques Soustelle, the leading Gaullist in the National Assembly, was known as the wrecker. The Algerian War was thus tearing apart the political stability of France itself.

There is a precise date when the government in Paris finally lost its political control over events in Algeria—February 6, 1956. Guy Mollet, leader of the Socialist Party, had just taken over as the nineteenth premier of the Fourth Republic and was expected to bring a ray of Socialist liberalism to the problem. He decided to send the respected General Georges Catroux to Algiers with a new and more elevated political title of minister resident and a broad brief to work for reconciliation. It would have been a shrewd appointment, for Catroux was one of de Gaulle's earliest supporters in 1940, and he had great experience in colonial administration and the reputation of a moderate and a liberal. This was too much for the *pieds-noirs,* who, with the tacit blessing of the Army, which stood idly by, immediately took to the streets in angry demonstrations in Algiers to protest the appointment.

Mollet bravely decided to go to Algiers himself to explain and impose his decision, but he was greeted by a mob attack on his limousine with a hail of stones, eggs, tomatoes and even manure. White and shaken by the time his car made it to the official residence, it was with relief that he accepted a telephone call from Catroux in Paris offering to withdraw from the post he had not yet assumed. A Socialist named Robert Lacoste was named instead, with the sole policy of supporting the Army in repression and ruthless prosecution of the war. A French mob in Algeria had successfully dictated to a premier of France, and from that moment on the Fourth Republic was on its way to dissolution.

General de Gaulle, in retirement at Colombey-les-Deux-Églises, deliberately remained aloof and enigmatic on the Algerian question. This master of hard clarity, of challenges and choices, retreated into adroit ambiguity when visitors questioned him on the major problem facing the nation. Everyone seemed to come away with a different idea or impression of what the General had in mind, where he stood and what he might do. Mendès-France believed him to be firmly committed to *Algérie française*—keeping Algeria French. But Maurice Schumann, who had been with de Gaulle in London, was convinced after a visit that the General was ready to make a deal with the FLN. To others he spoke of a solution of "integration, provided it is genuine." But an Austrian journalist, granted an interview on the eve of the events that brought de Gaulle back to power, was astounded to record him remarking that "certainly Algeria will be independent." To Jean-Raymond Tournoux he said he always hoped he could talk the Algerian Moslems out of wanting to secede from France. Louis Joxe, who had been secretary general of the provisional government in Algiers and who conducted the final cease-fire and peace negotiations in 1961–62, said that the General "always seemed to be groping" toward a solution.

One Frenchman said that de Gaulle reminded him of Molière's stage character Don Juan, who "promised marriage to five or six women and absolutely had to avoid being pinned down by any one of them." Along with all his delphic and confusing utterances, de Gaulle at one point issued a formal public warning against anyone believing anything attributed to him in a private conversation. "When General de Gaulle thinks it useful to make known the opinion he holds, he will do it himself and do it publicly," the statement said.

Nevertheless, if it seemed madness that France's great leader and guide could not or would not pronounce a clear view on the Algerian War, this was not without method. De Gaulle simply did not want to be committed. His attitude toward the French Empire and the problem of policing colonies had always been ambivalent, from his earliest days at Saint-Cyr. He was never of the romantic school of French Army officers who sought a career in subduing natives and leading a life of proconsular luxury with the Tricolor fluttering over a tropical villa. Fundamentally General de Gaulle had always believed that the Empire was a diversion and a weakening drain on the Army's main function and priority, which was the security of France itself. On the other hand, when France lay defeated under Nazi occupation, the rallying of the Empire and the establishment of full colonial control by Free French forces under his own command and control was of paramount importance to General de Gaulle. No one was to be permitted to grab part of the Empire (Britain in the Middle East) or dispose of any part of the Empire (Roosevelt in Indochina). The future of the Empire was the business of France alone. But in January 1944 he had also proclaimed in a far-reaching speech at the African city of Brazzaville that it would be postwar French policy "to lead each of the colonial peoples to a development that will permit them to administer themselves and, later, to govern themselves." All these competing themes of de Gaulle's thinking and policies were caught up in the Algerian War, and it is not surprising that he took refuge in ambiguity to retain his ultimate freedom of action.

The more intractible the Algerian problem became, the more the war bogged down in military and political quicksand, the greater the probability that the nation would again turn to de Gaulle. Why, therefore, should he say anything or take any position that would tie his hands? Moreover, by ambiguity he was hastening the day of his return.

Of the active political plotting and maneuvering by his loyal adherents to speed the day, he dismisses it all rather loftily in the volume of Postwar Memoirs that he completed before his death:

> I played no part whatsoever either in the local agitation, or the military movements, or the political schemes which provoked it, and I had no connection with any elements on the spot or any minister in Paris. It is true that two or three enterprising individuals, who had participated in my public

activity at the time when I was still engaged in it, spent their time in Algeria spreading the idea that one day the fate of the country would have to be entrusted to me. But they did so without my endorsement and without having even consulted me.

This disavowal is, to say the least, somewhat disingenuous. No doubt in the narrow sense de Gaulle "played no part whatsoever" in stirring up local agitation and was not "consulted" and did not endorse the specifics of what was going on. Of course he kept his distance—why should he get mixed up in the grubby details? Suppose it were to backfire? He kept his freedom of action in this, too. But he was certainly continuously *informed* about what was going on. His supporters were not staging Hamlet without the prince. Jacques Soustelle, Jacques Chaban-Delmas, Michel Debré, Olivier Guichard, Jacques Foccart, Georges Pompidou were all working openly as well as clandestinely for the return of de Gaulle, and were in continuous contact with Colombey-les-Deux-Églises. But in the end, the "plotters" were only bit players in a much wider, more complex open-stage political drama that General de Gaulle alone controlled from first to last with prodigious skill and sense of timing.

*

On April 15, 1958, the government of Félix Gaillard fell to the votes of the Algerian lobby, and President René Coty began the search for the last premier of the Fourth Republic. The interregnum lasted four weeks, which was a godsend to the Gaullist agitators and other miscellaneous plotters. There were enough plots going on, either real or imagined, to provide a racy title for one of the first French books to be written on the de Gaulle revolution: *Les 13 Complots du 13 Mai.*

A key figure among the Gaullists was Jacques Chaban-Delmas, who served as minister of defense in the Gaillard government. His credentials in the Resistance and as a loyal Gaullist were well known. As soon as he took over the Defense Ministry late in 1957 he had picked a man named Léon Delbecque for a secret assignment in Algeria. Delbecque was a businessman, a reserve officer who had been active in the Rassemblement du Peuple Français. Now Chaban-Delmas sent him to Algeria under the cover of a specialist in psychological warfare, to lecture officers and troops. But in fact his real mission was to organize Gaullist political cells in the Army.

Meanwhile, Soustelle and Debré, who was a member of the upper chamber of the legislature, were reactivating the RPF political machinery in secret, including its Service d'Ordre, and lobbying and lining up all the members of the legislature they could find, regardless of party, to support the return of Charles de Gaulle. Guichard ran de Gaulle's private office in Paris, Foccart undertook personal intelligence work for de Gaulle, and Pompidou was a close personal financial adviser who, as a director of the Rothschild Bank, had wide contacts in the business world.

But there was no certainty at all that the Army wanted to see a return of General de Gaulle. In fact, the evidence was largely to the contrary as far as the senior officers were concerned, in particular the Algerian commander in chief, General Raoul Salan.

De Gaulle's delphic utterances and contradictory statements on the Algerian question were well short of unequivocal backing for total prosecution of the war, which was all the *ultras* of the Army wanted to hear from Paris. This simply compounded the fact that de Gaulle had never been popular with the older French military, and they had no great reason to want him back. They wanted a government they could control—not a strong leader who would most certainly control them. The Army, therefore, dealing its own blows to the tottering Fourth Republic, was also plotting its own solution. Supported by civilian extremists among the *pieds noirs* in Algeria and the *Algérie française* lobby in Paris, with Salan certainly informed if not directly in the leadership, a group of senior officers prepared plans for a military coup. Key commanders of four of the nine regional military districts of metropolitan France were supporting the plot to seize public buildings, depose the National Assembly and install a "government of public safety," in effect a military dictatorship.

However, word of the plot had reached Chief of the Defense Staff General Paul Ely, an upright man who was loyal both to the Republic and to General de Gaulle. He had passed this secretly both to President Coty and to de Gaulle, warning of the grave threat of civil war if the political crisis were not quickly resolved.

On April 26 Coty picked as his first choice to form a government the old reliable René Pleven—decent, solid, colorless—who had been in and out of governments ever since the very first Free French Committee in London in 1940. On that same day in Algiers, Delbecque moved into action by proclaiming a "Committee of Vigilance" and calling for a great public demonstration. The committee he had formed was a mix of civilians and military commanders, and it was his hope or intention at the climax of the rally to get the committee to declare publicly for the return of General de Gaulle—and thus preempt the support of the Army and the reluctant General Salan.

The Delbecque rally was a popular success, but the Committee of Vigilance leaders held back from being carried along in a call for de Gaulle. Meanwhile, as Pleven began the usual consultations to see if he could put together enough support to form a government, Coty—in response to the warning from General Ely—made a first secret contact with de Gaulle. On May 5 he sent his personal military staff officer, General Ganeval, to meet with Guichard, Foccart, and de Gaulle's aide-de-camp, Colonel Gaston de Bonneval, at a private apartment in Paris, to ask on what conditions the General might consider an invitation to form a government. By telephone from Colombey, de Gaulle sent a chilling reply. He informed Coty that he declined to present himself to the National Assembly in person to ask for a vote of investiture, although he would accept power if it was voted to him. But he thought it was too soon to make his detailed conditions known, even to the president of the Republic.

Pleven labored until May 8 when, at 3 A.M., he thought he had formed a government and so informed Coty, but at 1 P.M. the Radical Party withdrew the support it had tentatively promised and Pleven gave up. Next day, May 9, Coty called in Pierre Pflimlin, an Alsatian from Strasbourg who had supplanted Bidault as the leader of the MRP Catholics, telling him: "You are my last card. If you fail there will be only one way out—to call on General de Gaulle."

At the same time the four top military commanders in Algeria—Salan and the subordinate commanders of the Army, Navy and Air Force—sent a telegram to Ely, warning him that "the French Army would unanimously feel a sense of outrage at any abandonment of our national patrimony," and asking the chief of the defense staff "to draw the attention of the President of the Republic to our anguish, which only a government determined to maintain our flag in Algeria can efface." It was a direct shot at Pflimlin, who had once had the temerity to write an article in a local Alsatian newspaper suggesting the possibility of negotiations with the FLN.

So far the political maneuvering and backing-and-filling had not been very different from the fall of other governments of the Fourth Republic. The rising tensions were largely confined to government and political leaders behind the scenes, as the French people went about their routines relatively oblivious that the country might be on the brink of a civil war. They had heard menacing noises from the military leaders in Algeria before, and the name of Charles de Gaulle had cropped up before, and it seemed to be a crisis like all the rest. No one knew anything at all about the military plot or President Coty's secret approach to de Gaulle, and so far the General had maintained a complete silence behind the walls of his country home.

But on May 13 the pace suddenly quickened. Pflimlin, moving rapidly in his political consultations against the now open threat from the military in Algiers and the prospect of a "de Gaulle solution" if he failed, suddenly found all the panic support he needed for an investiture vote from the National Assembly. But as the Assembly debate began, Delbecque turned out the Algiers mob again to demonstrate behind his Committee of Vigilance. While the Army looked on, the mob broke through the gates protecting the Government-General building and sacked its offices and files. Yet Delbecque once again failed to turn the demonstration into a call for General de Gaulle. As news of the violence in Algiers reached Paris, the Deputies of the National Assembly hastily gave Pflimlin one of the largest investiture votes in the history of the Fourth Republic, which was rapidly coming to an end.

Thus, on May 14, France again had a legally constituted government, but the threat to the existence of the Republic itself from the mob and the military in Algiers was growing more menacing by the hour. De Gaulle was under increasing pressure from events and from his own "plotters" to break his silence and declare his readiness to come to France's rescue. Still he waited for two more days, and it probably was the most difficult and anxious two days of his life since Dakar.

He knew very well from Ely and from his own followers and intelligence sources that the military plot against the Paris government was ready to go, awaiting only a final order from Salan and other key leaders. Whether it would succeed was another question, but it certainly would preempt the situation against de Gaulle and probably would trigger civil war. On the other hand, if de Gaulle moved out in front too quickly with a declaration of readiness to return to power, he could have the Army openly against him, and he would not be much better off than Pflimlin.

All France was now waiting for him to break silence. On May 15 Delbecque called yet another Committee of Vigilance demonstration in Algiers. This time he had arranged for a "unity appearance" by Salan and the senior commanders on the balcony of the sacked Government-General building. Salan addressed the mob with an adroit statement that he had "assumed full military and civil powers"—a kind of personal declaration of martial law—but he didn't say exactly what this meant. He ended with the traditional cry: *"Vive l'Algérie française, vive la France!"* and stepped back from the microphone to wave triumphantly to the cheering throng. But Delbecque, at his elbow, playing a kind of Iago to Othello, hissed, *"et vive de Gaulle"*—whereupon Salan hesitated visibly and then stepped back to the microphone and pronounced the decisive words: *"Vive de Gaulle!"* At once a mighty roar went up from the crowd. When he drove home from the rally, his wife berated him angrily for what he had done.

This indeed was the moment or the opportunity de Gaulle had been waiting for, and at five o'clock that afternoon a statement was issued in Paris, dictated from his home in Colombey: "Once before, from the depths of the abyss, the country gave me its confidence to lead it back to salvation. Today, with new trials crowding in upon it, it is right that it should know that I am ready to assume the powers of the Republic."

*

Still, the drama had another excruciating two weeks to run. Pflimlin was an honorable man heading the legally constituted government of France, backed by a large National Assembly majority, and he was not about to be pushed out of power by a military insurrection. The first thought of the parliamentarians now was to "save the Republic"—by which they meant saving their own skins, not only from the military but also from General de Gaulle. The political leaders quickly pointed out that de Gaulle had said absolutely nothing to condemn the insurrection in the Army, from which they concluded that he must be in cahoots with the military to overthrow the government. They were largely unaware that the Army had its own plot and that some of its extremists were already in action. The military plotters had decided to install Georges Bidault as the head of their "Government of Public Safety," and several of the key officers had left Algiers and flown to France to prepare for the order for final action. Tensions behind the scenes were becoming unbearable.

On May 19 de Gaulle drove to Paris to hold a news conference—probably the most masterful and dramatic of his long life. It was his first meeting with the press, indeed his first public remarks of any kind, in three years since his July 1955 "farewell, and perhaps for a long time to come." Now sixty-seven years old, he was a much changed man from the image that Frenchmen carried of the leader of the war years. The black hair was wispy gray and the mustache almost invisible against the gray of his skin. Still toweringly tall and straight-shouldered, there was a paunch of age under his double-breasted suit. His ears seemed to jug out more, his eyes looked out from deepening circles, and there was a kind of elephantine fold and sagging to his face and bearing, aged, but to be sure still powerful. He had given up smoking and also undergone an operation for cataracts. Aged he was, but not old, and his presence and voice—at once rasping and resonant—instantly dominated the vast ballroom of the Hôtel d'Orsay, where 1,300 journalists had assembled.

"I addressed the press in the tones of the master of the moment," de Gaulle wrote in his Postwar Memoirs, "and indeed, to judge from the questions that were put to me, all of them relating to what I would do in power, no one had the slightest doubt that I would soon be there." He began with a brief review of the "extremely grave national crisis" which he declared "may also be the beginning of a sort of resurrection." He had deliberately stayed aloof for six years and said nothing at all politically for three years, and therefore remained "a man who belongs to no one and who belongs to everyone." He adroitly turned the Algerian situation upside down by blaming both the FLN insurrection and the behavior of the French Army "on the present system in Paris that cannot solve its problems." But, he said:

In case I should be asked by the French people to arbitrate, that would be all the more reason for me not to specify at the present time what the conclusions of my arbitration would be; indeed, the parties concerned must be heard, a decision must be rendered and we must be in a position to carry it out—all these are factors that do not at present exist. I know of no judge who hands down his decision before hearing the case.

When, at the end, a questioner asked him what his attitude would be toward basic public liberties, his voice rose in rasping scorn and anger:

Did I ever make any attempt on basic public liberties? On the contrary, I restored them. Why should I, at 67, begin a career as a dictator? It is not possible to solve the serious national crisis of the present time within the limits of everyday routine. These cards which we hold may lead in the near future to the resurgence of France, to great prosperity in which all Frenchmen must share, and in which the people who need and ask for our assistance must also be associated.

He concluded magisterially: "I thought it would be useful for the country to say what I have said. Now I shall return to my village and I shall remain there at the disposal of the country."

Not surprisingly, public reaction to the press conference both in France and Algeria was overwhelmingly pro–de Gaulle. After all, was Pflimlin going to see France out of its turmoil or would Salan save the Republic? There really was no one else. Nevertheless, both the government in Paris and the military in Algiers held out—the military leaders with the intention of pushing their own *coup d'état* forward, and the politicians out of *immobilisme*. On the military side, Lieutenant

Philippe LaGaillarde, one of the *ultras* of the Algerian scene, arrived secretly in France on May 21 to take final charge and push the button. Meanwhile, despite the outward show of standing firm, the Pflimlin Cabinet was beginning to crack. Old Antoine Pinay, the finance minister, made a secret trip to Colombey to pledge his support, and outside the government even Socialist Guy Mollet began throwing out hints in the National Assembly that he might be ready to back de Gaulle under proper constitutional circumstances.

In Algiers the struggle between the Gaullists and the *ultras* of the military sharpened with the arrival of Jacques Soustelle to join Delbecque. Soustelle had served for two years as governor general of Algeria in the early stages of the war, and his return to the city occasioned rapturous demonstrations that were both *Algérie française* and pro–de Gaulle. Together, Soustelle and Delbecque next put heavy pressure on Salan to hold off on final orders for the military uprising in metropolitan France, and instead simply seize power on the island of Corsica as a first step. It was a shrewd move that appealed to Salan, not known to his associates as "the Chinese general" for nothing. He could show action without sticking his neck out too far. But this would give time for de Gaulle to act.

On May 25 a handful of paratroopers from Algeria landed at Ajaccio airport to establish a "Committee of Public Safety" takeover without firing a shot. As proof of the impotence of Paris, even a company of the CRS riot police stationed on the island went over to the insurrection.

General de Gaulle had waited with extraordinary control and sense of timing for events to come to him, but now, a week after his news conference, with Corsica in the hands of the military, he decided to act. On the morning of May 26 he sent a personal letter to Premier Pflimlin proposing that they meet in complete secrecy late that very night, at the Château de Saint-Cloud, one of the former imperial residences on the outskirts of Paris, whose conservator was a friend of de Gaulle's. Arriving from different directions at midnight, the two men talked for two hours, calmly and carefully reviewing the situation each from his own perspective, and each sticking to his own position. They agreed that the meeting remain a secret. On the morning of the twenty-seventh, however, news reached both de Gaulle, who had returned to Colombey, and the minister of the interior, Jules Moch, that the Army was preparing to jump off from its Corsican success and stage its planned coup against Paris that night.

De Gaulle at once decided to preempt the situation by taking a public initiative, and at 12:30 P.M. his office in Paris issued a statement of decisive importance and masterly politics:

> I began yesterday the regular process needed to establish a Republican government capable of ensuring the unity and independence of the country. I believe this process will be continued and that the country will show, by its calm and its dignity, that it wishes it to succeed. Under these conditions, any action endangering public order, from whatever side it originates, could have grave consequences. Even though I understand the circumstances, I could not give my approval. I expect the land, sea and air forces in Algeria to maintain exemplary behavior.

This warning almost certainly stopped the *putsch* in its tracks. Salan and all the others realized at once that if they moved against a warning from de Gaulle they were unlikely to succeed, and if they did not succeed they would wind up court-martialed for rebellion against the State.

Pflimlin, on the other hand, was incensed at what he regarded as a de Gaulle double-cross. The unexplained reference to starting "the regular process needed to establish a Republican government" could only mean their midnight meeting, which both had agreed should remain secret. Under the worst pressures a democratic leader could possibly face, Pflimlin had been upright and honorable, but with the situation crumbling all around him, his irritation at de Gaulle's move rapidly turned to despair, and on May 28 he handed his resignation to President Coty. It was as well that he did, for Coty had already made up his mind on the de Gaulle solution as the only way to save the Republic.

With Pflimlin's resignation, Coty immediately asked de Gaulle to meet with the presiding officers of the two houses of the legislature—André le Trocquer, from the National Assembly, and Gaston Monnerville, of the upper house—to discuss terms and arrangements for an investiture. The evening of May 28, de Gaulle again drove from Colombey to the Château de Saint-Cloud, but the meeting was close to a disaster. Le Trocquer accused him of having "the soul of a dictator" with his demand for complete emergency powers, while Monnerville appealed to him to at least follow constitutional practice by appearing before the National Assembly to ask for investiture, and to accept a limit of six months on emergency powers as prescribed in the constitution. In the end, de Gaulle stalked out, telling the two leaders he would leave them "to sort things out with the paratroops and go back to my retreat and nurse my sorrow."

Monnerville and Le Trocquer drove directly from Saint-Cloud to the Élysée Palace in the early-morning hours to report to Coty, who was in his pajamas, on the breakdown of their talks. Coty knew full well that it was either de Gaulle or the paratroops from Algeria. The situation was perilous, and the president of the Republic could allow for no more constitutional shilly-shallying. After they had gone, he wrote out a statement that was an ultimatum to the National Assembly.

General de Gaulle had returned to Colombey-les-Deux-Églises around 5 A.M., and in the late morning he was awakened by a call from the Élysée Palace. Coty read him the text of the message he was sending to the National Assembly. The two men then arranged that de Gaulle would make a formal call on the president at 7:30 P.M. that evening. At three o'clock on the afternoon of May 29, in the Palais-Bourbon, across from the Place de la Concorde, Le Trocquer rapped his gavel on the podium of the National Assembly to hear the reading of a message from the president of the Republic. In definitive terms to bring the government crisis to an end after six weeks, Coty first declared that the nation faced a danger of civil war, and then said: "I have called on the most illustrious of Frenchmen, who, during the darkest years of our history, was our leader for the conquest of liberty and who, having achieved national unanimity around his person, spurned dictatorship, to establish the Republic."

The message was heard in complete silence.

*

Ultimate political power, which had eluded General de Gaulle after the liberation of Paris, was about to be handed to him in full measure. The desert years of
bitter exile were over. Thanks largely to his own skill, his sense of timing, and his
pervasive authority and control over events while 120 miles away in the country, a
revolution had taken place without bloodshed, unlike 1789 or 1871. Legitimacy,
so dear to Frenchmen in the midst of political trauma, would be fully preserved.
Power would be transferred and the nation transformed by a vote of the National
Assembly, the elected representatives of the people—just as an earlier National
Assembly had voted for Pétain.

General de Gaulle's meeting with President Coty that evening was fervent but
brief and to the point. Driving from Colombey for the third time in forty-eight
hours, he entered the Élysée Palace by a side gate on the avenue Marigny, hoping
to avoid photographers, who nevertheless had every entrance staked out. De
Gaulle's terms for forming a government were devastatingly simple. He would ask
the National Assembly for full powers for an emergency period during which it
would go into recess and he would govern by decree. The government he would
form must also be given a mandate to draw up a new constitution for a Fifth
Republic that would then be submitted for approval by national referendum.

Knowing that he had won hands down, de Gaulle made two concessions to ease
his own path and the consciences of the legislators. First, he relented about
appearing in person before the National Assembly to present himself for an
investiture vote as premier of the Fourth Republic, like all those who had gone
before. Next, taking Monnerville's advice, he did not ask for an unlimited period
of emergency powers or any permanent recess of the National Assembly. Instead,
he smoothed the Assembly's departure by proposing that it simply recess until its
scheduled autumn session, which was supposed to begin on October 7, while
granting the government six months' emergency powers in the meantime. This
was enough time for de Gaulle's purposes, to get an entirely new constitution
quickly in place, and in fact the Fourth Republic National Assembly never convened again.

De Gaulle spent the next two days receiving various parliamentary leaders,
including especially the Socialists Vincent Auriol and Guy Mollet, at the Hôtel
Lapérouse, near the Étoile, where he regularly stayed when he came to Paris from
his country home. He also assembled a personal staff to take over power once
again and drew up his list of Cabinet assignments. On June 1 he took the rostrum
at the Palais-Bourbon.

After the tensions and turmoil of the previous weeks, it was an anticlimactic
moment, and de Gaulle did not in any way attempt to stage another drama over
what was about to happen. He had agreed to appear in person to ask for an
investiture but not to take part in any debate on his qualifications or his request,
and his statement was naturally quite brief. He summarized the crisis into which
the State had plunged, and the need for reform—themes that France had been

hearing from him for a dozen years. He asked for a vote of full powers and left the rostrum. The debate, too, was relatively brief, and the vote to invest him as premier was 329 to 224, with 32 abstentions. The Communists, many Socialists and a mixed list of other party members and independents voted against de Gaulle—including Pierre Mendès-France and François Mitterrand. The next day bills were formally introduced to confer special powers on the government for six months, and on June 3 at 9:15 P.M. the National Assembly rose and the curtain came down on the Fourth Republic.

De Gaulle's first government was swiftly formed. Maurice Couve de Murville, who had served the provisional government in Algiers, was summoned from a golf course near Bonn, where he was ambassador to West Germany, to return to Paris immediately to take over as foreign minister. He remained in the job for a decade, to outlast even Tallyrand's record. The faithful, mordant Michel Debré was given the Ministry of Justice, and more importantly the chairmanship of the special committee of lawyers and constitutional experts that would draft the new Fifth Republic constitution. The inclusion of Socialist Guy Mollet, MRP Catholic Pierre Pflimlin and Conservative Antoine Pinay gave the new Cabinet a cosmetic coloration of a political coalition. Malraux became minister of culture, prepared to show that a new renaissance had begun for the whole world.

These formalities over, General de Gaulle took off to grasp the Algerian nettle.

De Gaulle's arrival in the city of Algiers on June 4, 1958, bore an unusual resemblance to his entry into Paris on August 25, 1944, in an important particular—his brusque treatment of the local Committee of Public Safety to assert his own power and authority over what was still a near-revolutionary situation. In Paris in 1944, de Gaulle had made the leaders of the Council of National Resistance and the Paris Committee of Liberation cool their heels at the Hôtel de Ville while he first called at the Préfecture de Police, and when he did finally appear before them they did not even get a handshake. In Algiers, citizens (mainly French) turned out as if it were the liberation all over again, but de Gaulle kept the Committee of Public Safety *ultras* waiting while he first received members of the local diplomatic corps (many countries, including the United States, maintained consulates in Algiers) followed by Catholic and Moslem leaders, town councilors, directors of the university and other notables. By the time this was concluded, the impatient members of the Committee of Public Safety were feeling about like the Resistance leaders in Paris had felt. Moreover, when de Gaulle did appear before them, he replied frigidly to their appeals to declare at once for a policy of "integration" for Algeria, and to regard them as the "most reliable supporters" in the revolution that was taking place. Acknowledging nothing, conceding nothing, offering no thanks for anything, de Gaulle informed the committee that he would speak to the people himself to avoid any misunderstandings.

By the end of the afternoon a crowd of some 200,000—almost entirely European—had massed in the open square, the Forum, in front of the Government-General building to greet General de Gaulle with a mighty roar when at last he stepped out on a balcony, arms outstretched and fists clenched in the defiant gesture of exhortation that was his permanent hallmark. But he responded to the cheers with one of the most famous and most elusive utterances of his life: *"Je vous ai compris"*—I have understood you.

In the political, emotional and Mediterranean alchemy of the occasion, that vast audience never bothered to grasp the essential *meaninglessness* of de Gaulle's words, which were greeted with a delirium of cheers of response. Nor did they note, apparently, that not once did he use the words *"Algérie française,"* the battle cry of the *ultras*. Instead he spoke of renewal, fraternity, reconciliation, and all French-men voting together in a few months for a new constitution, after which "we shall see what to do about the rest."

As in Paris in August 1944, everything de Gaulle said and did, every move he made on his arrival in Algiers, was calculated to impose his power, his discipline, on the Army and on local leaders, over whom the Fourth Republic had long since lost control. Without re-establishment of discipline, no solution was possible. He went on to visit the cities of Constantine and Oran, where he exploded vehe-mently and deliberately at a meeting with the local Committee of Public Safety: "You gentlemen will *not* continue to make a revolution. Your job is to win over people's minds to national unity, to reform of France, and to support for General de Gaulle, without trying to force his hand, and within the framework which I shall set down."

There was not much concession or satisfaction for the *ultras* in these words, and on only one occasion was de Gaulle heard to utter *"Algérie française."* That was at the very end of the visit in remarks to a gathering at the town of Mostaganem. When, later, a member of his staff told him that he had indeed heard him use the words, de Gaulle in some irritation said that it must have escaped him and was meaningless anyway—"After all, one refers to French Canada, French Switzer-land . . ."

But, having traversed Algeria in a cloud of ambiguity as far as the political solution he might choose to pursue, de Gaulle tossed a bone of reassurance to the dogs of war in the French Army. On his return to Paris, he confirmed Salan as commander in chief with the elevated title of "delegate general" of Algiers. But the trumpets had sounded for the end of Salan's career.

*

In domestic affairs, the advent of a de Gaulle government with powers to rule by decree was rather like putting air into the bellows of an unused pipe organ. The keyboard was there, in the form of the French bureaucracy and all of the dossiers and decisions that had piled up, awaiting a government that could turn up the pressure and start to play. The mere sense of *order* worked wonders in the French scene.

The drafting of the new constitution under Michel Debré moved rapidly ahead, and at the end of August, de Gaulle set out on a journey to the African colonies. Each was being offered a choice: to vote in the forthcoming constitutional referen-dum to remain in a new French Community or to reject the constitution and vote for independence. There was a choice, but no halfway house. Eventually those

African colonies that elected to remain French all became fully self-governing, but today are still tied to the purse strings of the French Treasury through economic assistance, trade preferences and currency links with the franc.

De Gaulle swept through seven of the thirteen African possessions in nine days, but in only two was the outcome much in doubt—Senegal and Guinea. His visit quelled the independence-separatist ferment in Senegal, but not so in Guinea, where he delivered a brutal warning to the country's nationalistic leader, Sékou Touré (who remains in power twenty-five years later).

> Don't get things wrong! The French Republic you are dealing with now is no longer the one you have known, and which used cunning instead of decision. France is quite prepared to cut her losses. She has lived a very long time without Guinea and she will go on living a very long time if the two are separated. If your answer is No, we shall withdraw immediately, and you must not doubt that our relations will lose the character of friendship and preference among the states of the world.

Charles de Gaulle certainly was not kidding. When Guinea voted for independence and rejected the new French constitution in the referendum at the end of September, the country was given independence with a vengeance. All French civil servants, teachers, doctors, military personnel, all Frenchmen on the government payroll, were ordered back to France immediately, and all their files and archives went with them from government offices. Even the telephones were ripped out from the official buildings, and a shipment of grain en route from France was diverted as all aid ceased. But in teaching Sékou Touré a lesson, de Gaulle may also have helped ensure Touré's survival as black Africa's longest-lasting ruler.

In any case, the constitution rapidly clobbered together by Debré and his committee contained no surprises for anyone who had read de Gaulle's speech at Bayeux on June 16, 1946. France would be governed by a president in whom supreme powers would be vested. He would have the power to appoint and dismiss prime ministers, who would be charged with running the government, but the president would preside over Cabinet meetings, would be responsible for the direction of foreign policy, and would control and direct the armed forces. The role of the National Assembly would be strictly that of passing legislation. It could pass a vote of no confidence in a prime minister, but this would not bring a government down. The president, elected for seven years, could not be turned out of office, and could take major national questions direct to the people, over the heads of the legislators, for decision by referendum. About the only concession de Gaulle made in the original Fifth Republic constitution was to allow the election of the president by the then traditional method of a "grand council of electors" (parliamentarians, mayors, city councilors). But even this he changed by national referendum in 1962 providing for direct election of the president of the Republic by universal suffrage.

The new constitution was overwhelmingly approved in a referendum on September 28, 1958. In metropolitan France, the turnout was the highest since 1936, nearly 85 percent of the registered electorate, with a yes vote close to 80 percent. In the overseas possessions, approval averaged 95 percent—except in Guinea, the only place that had the temerity to vote against de Gaulle. The constitution of the Fifth Republic was formally promulgated on October 5, 1958.

Next came elections for the new National Assembly, in two rounds of voting at the end of November. De Gaulle had personally intervened in the argument over the election system to impose the two-stage runoff which, he correctly calculated, would be to his benefit by eliminating minority candidates on the first round and requiring the voters to make a clear choice on the second round, generally between candidates of the left and right. It worked, the Gaullist Union pour la Nouvelle République (UNR) gaining just over 200 out of the 465 Assembly seats. With plenty of miscellaneous support from other factions, this was more than enough to ensure almost monolithic political power for the de Gaulle regime for the next five years at least.

Finally, the last act in installing the new Republic came on December 21, 1958, when notables of the grand council of electors gathered for the counting of some 80,000 ballot papers for election of the president. De Gaulle received about 78 percent of the votes, to become first president of the Fifth Republic and eighteenth president of France. A Communist, Georges Marrane, who had made one of the welcoming speeches to de Gaulle at the Hôtel de Ville in August 1944, drew 13 percent of the ballots, and a candidate for the democratic left, Albert Châtelet, got the remaining 9 percent.

On January 8, 1959, President Coty and President-elect de Gaulle rode together to the Arc de Triomphe to mark the transition to the Fifth Republic by paying homage together at the tomb of France's unknown warrior. When the ceremony ended, de Gaulle abruptly turned his back on Coty and did not do the courtesy of accompanying the last president of the Fourth Republic back to his car. Instead he strode to the waiting presidential limousine, and with Georges Pompidou at his side and a mounted escort of the Garde Républicaine he rode back down the avenue des Champs-Élysées and through the gates of the Élysée Palace to take up residence at last.

*

France had a new constitution, a new Republic, and a government that could not possibly be overturned or ousted for at least seven years, when President de Gaulle's first term of office would end. But the nation remained mired in the Algerian War, and until this could be resolved, the de Gaulle revolution was incomplete. General de Gaulle realized full well that whatever aspirations of grandeur he might hold for France, it would come to nothing as long as the nation remained locked in the draining and divisive Algerian struggle. As his long-time aide, Geoffroy de Courcel, put it: "General de Gaulle did not want to give up Algeria, but he knew that he had to." It took him three years from his return to power to bring the conflict to an end—and even then it rattled on with Secret Army Organization (OAS) terrorism for another six months. But of all the services de Gaulle rendered to France, extraction from the Algerian War was the most difficult and decisive. It was his masterpiece in the skilled exercise of political power, and if he had failed, history would have been far different and his stature diminished to the level of other French leaders defeated by the Algerian War.

Moreover, across this period de Gaulle was not only maneuvering through the minefield of military, political and constitutional complexities of the Algerian problem. He was the target of at least nine assassination attempts mounted by the *Algérie française* extremists and the fanatics of the OAS. Two of these came within millimeters of succeeding. In one case an explosive charge had been placed on a stretch of open country road on his route to Colombey-les-Deux-Églises, and was blown by remote control only seconds after his car sped past. In the other case, his limousine was machine-gunned in a Paris suburb in an ambush by the OAS as he was on his way to a military airfield with his wife to helicopter to his country home. Bullets smashed into the rear seat, barely missing both the General and Madame de Gaulle. A tire was hit, but its inner safety-tire held up as the driver jammed down the accelerator to get away.

It was after this attempt that de Gaulle abruptly called a national referendum in September 1962 to alter the new Fifth Republic constitution to provide for immediate direct election of French presidents whenever the office might become vacant. A president elected by the people directly had long been one of de Gaulle's political goals, and it was typical of him to turn the near-miss of an assassination attempt into yet another political achievement.

The Algerian War was a triple problem for him. First it was necessary to bring the Army under firm control. Long used to dictating to the politicians of Paris, the Army—at least many of its senior officers—was convinced it could win the war and was determined to keep Algeria French. De Gaulle's second problem was the constitutional fiction that Algeria was indeed an integral part of France. Finally there was the diplomatic-political problem of arranging a negotiation with the FLN Algerian enemy and neutralizing the domestic opposition of right-wing political factions, of which Gaullist Jacques Soustelle was a prime mover.

Senior generals of the Army of course had been suspicious of de Gaulle and scarcely enthusiastic about his return to power. It did not take long before these suspicions were justified. In the initial euphoria of the de Gaulle revolution, General Salan had been confirmed by de Gaulle as commander in chief in Algeria. But barely six months later he was abruptly ordered back to France to the ceremonial post of military governor of Paris. Meanwhile, across this same period, General Paul Ely, the chief of the defense staff and a true loyalist to de Gaulle, began systematically transferring officers known to be activists or extremists on the Algerian question to new postings in Metz or Toulouse or with the occupation forces in Germany, where they would be politically neutralized.

Yet while all this was going on, de Gaulle lulled the Army's political suspicions by encouraging it to step up the military campaign in 1958 and 1959. General Maurice Challe, a first-rate commander with imagination and drive, replaced Salan, who in any case had been much more of a political general. Challe adopted new tactics of harassment and aggressive patrolling that seemed to breath life into the campaign. All the same, the very successes of the Army in 1959 and the spring of 1960 really served to demonstrate the ultimate impossibility of ever achieving anything like total victory or complete subjugation of the Algerian nation. It was an experience the Americans were to repeat in Vietnam only five years later.

By 1960, therefore, de Gaulle had achieved his first major objective in the zigzag advance to a negotiated peace. He had the Army under tight disciplinary control from Paris once again, and he had demonstrated that a negotiated settlement was the only way in which the conflict could be ended. In June of 1960 he issued a public invitation to the leaders of the FLN to send emissaries to France "to seek an honorable end" to hostilities.

This broke the ice politically toward a negotiated settlement—despite the fact that those first talks, held at the town of Melun, east of Paris, ended in deadlock after only four days. But as de Gaulle moved to the negotiating table, civil violence in Paris reached a new pitch as the FLN Algerian underground, the *ultras* of the *Algérie française,* and the renegades of the OAS all wildly tried to force de Gaulle to their own ends. Every Paris police station sprouted a brick bunker around its entrance and wire netting over its windows against bomb attacks or machine-gun bursts from one terrorist faction or another. Scarcely a day went by in Paris in those days without some *plastique* explosion—bombs in cars, bombs hurled through apartment windows, planted in doorways, tossed into crowded cafés. Spontaneous street demonstrations by *Algérie française* backers turned into constant clashes with the hardened shock troops of the CRS Republican Security Companies.

None of this, of course, had the slightest effect on de Gaulle, who responded in the summer of 1960 by announcing the first withdrawal of French forces from Algeria. With the Army disciplined and moves toward a negotiated settlement under way, he then turned to the constitutional problem. In November 1960 he announced that he was going directly to the people with a referendum in both France and Algeria in which the nation would pronounce on whether or not self-determination should be offered to the Algerians.

It had long been assumed, and correctly so, that the people of metropolitan France were fed up with the Algerian War and would be perfectly content to see Algeria go the way of the other French colonies that de Gaulle had already set on the road to independence. In France itself, 76 percent voted to allow Algeria its self-determination, and in Algeria, despite strong opposition from the French settlers and attempts at intimidation, the vote was 70 percent yes.

Thus, by the end of 1960, de Gaulle had gotten a firm grip on all of the elements necessary for an Algerian settlement. The ambiguities had fallen away and there could no longer be any doubt about his ultimate intentions. Self-determination could only mean an independent Algeria. The people of France were strongly behind de Gaulle, ready to see Algeria go free and independent, but the *ultras* of the Army had one more shot at imposing their will on Paris.

General Salan had retired completely in 1960, and late that year he slipped across the border into Spain and took up residence in Madrid. There he began to agitate openly against de Gaulle's Algerian policy and quickly made himself the center of a net of OAS extremists preparing a counterblow to keep Algeria under

330 / CHARLES DE GAULLE

the French flag. Meanwhile, General Challe had been brought back from his command in Algeria and given a high NATO post, but he then took retirement partly out of disagreement with de Gaulle's growing anti-NATO policies but more especially over his Algerian policies. In March of 1961 Challe agreed to a secret overture from Salan in Madrid to join in a coup attempt to seize power in Algiers. Two other senior commanders on the spot in Algiers were then also drawn into the plot—General Edmond Jouhaud, an Air Force officer, and General André Zeller, a high Army commander. Both had served with distinction with the Free French forces in the Italian and French campaigns in World War II.

On the night of April 21, 1961, Challe arrived secretly in Algiers in the private aircraft of one of the French Air Force commanders. Salan slipped out of Spain and into Algeria. In the early-morning hours, a veteran regiment of Foreign Legion paratroops moved out of its barracks, seized the main government buildings and locked up both the Army commander in chief, General Gambiez, a Gaullist loyalist, and the civilian delegate-general who ran the government, Jean Morin.

With the seat of government power in Algeria in their hands, the four generals made a triumphant balcony appearance together before yet another of those frenzied throngs of *pied noir* colonists. But appearances were far from the reality of the situation, and it was a short-lived triumph. The subordinate commanders of the Army and Air Force units scattered across the country showed a marked reluctance to join the revolt. Their loyalty lay with Gambiez, not Salan or Challe, and they knew full well the kind of retribution de Gaulle was capable of imposing on those who disobeyed his orders or challenged his power.

Nevertheless, the specter of civil war hung over Paris once again. All airports in metropolitan France were closed, and trucks placed on the runways to prevent any airborne landings anywhere. All communications with Algeria were cut except official military channels. Gasoline issue was stopped at all Army bases so there could be no unauthorized movement by tanks or troops toward Paris. In order to ensure de Gaulle's personal security against any plot or assassination attempt, the guard units around the Élysée Palace were reinforced, but changed every hour on a spot-rotation schedule during the next three days. Jacques Foccart, de Gaulle's personal Intelligence chief, slept in the corridor outside de Gaulle's bedroom.

De Gaulle himself was awakened for the first and only time in his eleven years at the Élysée Palace with the news of the revolt on the night of April 21 by Geoffroy de Courcel, then his secretary-general. But, de Courcel recalls, de Gaulle simply commented, "Well, this is serious," and then asked what steps the government, under Prime Minister Debré, were ordering. He then simply grunted *"Bien"* and went back to sleep.

On April 22 de Gaulle maintained a public silence, leaving it to Debré to make a somewhat hysterical broadcast warning of the dangers of a paratroop invasion of Metropolitan France, while loyal Army units were moved to the outskirts of Paris. After reviewing the situation throughout the day, de Gaulle then ordered the chief of the defense staff, General Olié, to Algiers to assume local command over all French forces, together with Minister of State for Algerian Affairs Louis Joxe, a loyalist from the London days, to take civilian control. They were to leave very early on the morning of April 23, and Joxe was surprised to receive a call from de Courcel telling him that de Gaulle wanted him to stop by the Élysée Palace at 5:30 A.M. on his way to the airport.

Joxe later related that he arrived in the dark forecourt of the presidential residence and a military aide was waiting behind the glass doors to greet him. He was immediately escorted to de Gaulle's office. There he found de Gaulle dressed in his brigadier general's uniform. He rose from behind his desk, extended his hand, and said: *"Au revoir, Joxe, et bon voyage!"*—and that was all.

That evening, still in his brigadier's uniform, de Gaulle went on television to address the nation in a mood and demeanor of bull-like anger that seemed to shake the television screens. He delivered a verbal *coup de grace* to the dying revolt: "The State is flouted, the nation defied, our power shaken, our international prestige reduced, our place and our role in Africa compromised. And by whom? Alas! Alas! By men whose duty, honor and *raison d'être* are to serve and to obey. In the name of France, I order that all means—I repeat *all means*—be used to bar the way elsewhere to these men until they are brought down."

This was no less than an order by the French chief of state to French soldiers not only to refuse to follow the revolt, but to shoot its leaders. On April 25 General Challe called it off and gave himself up to be flown back to a French prison.

The *ultras* had shot their last bolt. Zeller surrendered a few days later, and Jouhaud and Salan went underground but were eventually caught. All served prison terms until released by de Gaulle in 1968, on the eve of the general election following the student uprising that shook the regime to its foundations. In the cleanup in Algeria that followed the revolt, the Foreign Legion paratroop regiment was disbanded and its personnel scattered among other units. More than 200 officers and 160 civilians were arrested or interned and another 140 civilian officials in Algeria fired for having supported the coup attempt.

Meanwhile, under Louis Joxe, the efforts to reach a negotiated settlement were speeded up—a process that proved to be every bit as complex a game as the American negotiation for a cease-fire in Vietnam would turn out to be a decade later.

Eleven months after the revolt of the generals, a cease-fire agreement was signed at the town of Évian-les-Bains, on the shores of Lake Geneva, on March 18, 1962. It provided that following the cease-fire a referendum would be held on self-determination and independence. In April the French people voted overwhelmingly to endorse the Évian agreement, and in June the Algerians voted 99.7 percent for independence. Algeria then emerged as an independent state on July 3, 1962, after 132 years of French rule.

When the cease-fire took effect, French soldiers had been engaged in war continuously, somewhere in the world, for nearly twenty-three years. They have carried out a number of intervention missions since then, but France has probably fought its last war. Without an Algerian peace settlement, all else for General de Gaulle would have been failure. The de Gaulle revolution was complete.

SEVENTEEN

OLD ALLIES, OLD SCORES, 1959–62

General de Gaulle's return to power re-established a unique wartime triumvirate of Allied leadership, with President Dwight D. Eisenhower in Washington and Prime Minister Harold Macmillan in London. The three men, all about the same age, had been in Algiers together for seven months in 1943, working under difficult political circumstances engendered largely by Roosevelt's anti–de Gaulle complex and rigid refusal to bend or give way on recognition of the Free French. Despite the endless troubles this caused, de Gaulle was well aware that both Eisenhower and Macmillan had basically supported him, arguing on his behalf with Washington and London and modifying their instructions in his favor as best they could. At the same time, they had become thoroughly aware that in dealing with de Gaulle, personal relationships, friendship or sentiment counted for nothing when he was pursuing or defending what he conceived to be the interests of France. Nevertheless, both had wholeheartedly welcomed and supported de Gaulle's return to power. The Central Intelligence Agency, through its Paris operatives, had even been making regular secret cash contributions to support the Gaullist political movement during the "desert years" of the 1950s, although it is probable that de Gaulle himself was unaware of this. Eisenhower and Macmillan knew full well that de Gaulle, back in power, would not be the easiest of men to deal with, but a strong France was preferable to a weak France, whatever difficulties de Gaulle might bring. Having shared a common wartime experience, the three men could approach one another openly and realistically, with respect and resilience, with insight and without illusions. But in the end, neither Eisenhower nor Macmillan fully realized or anticipated how harsh and deep de Gaulle's Anglo-Saxon prejudices, suspicions and resentments would prove to be.

Neither twelve years of brooding exile nor the total change in the world balance of power had in any way softened or diminished this obsession, which underlay much that was basic in his foreign policy of the next eleven years. Massive Soviet forces were barely four days' march from Paris. West Germany, under Konrad Adenauer, had rearmed and taken its place firmly among the Western democracies. The whole postwar movement toward unity in Western Europe had become a political reality while de Gaulle had been writing his Memoirs in Colombey-les-Deux-Églises. The North Atlantic Treaty Organization was proof of a permanent reversal of the American isolationism that de Gaulle had so bitterly condemned in the past. Yet in his vision, all of this—even Marshall Plan aid—simply added up to a new form of Anglo-Saxon dominance, not a new era of European peace and security, not the base for a revival of Europe's economic strength and influence in the world.

In his Postwar Memoirs he lashed out bitterly at all that had taken place in his absence from 1946 to 1958:

> Everything I had accomplished by dint of arduous efforts, as regards the independence, the status and the interests of France, was immediately jeopardized. Lacking the drive and the energy thanks to which we were on our feet, the regime was to all intents and purposes concerned with pleasing others. Naturally enough it found the required ideologies to camouflage this self-effacement: the one in the name of European unity, liquidating the advantages which victory had gained us; the other on the pretext of Atlantic solidarity, subjecting France to the hegemony of the Anglo-Saxons. The re-establishment of a central German administration in the three Western zones had been accepted, in spite of the absence of genuine guarantees. Once the declaration of principle known as the Atlantic Alliance had been adopted in Washington, the North Atlantic Treaty Organization had been set up, under the terms of which our defense and hence our foreign policy disappeared in a system directed from abroad, while an American generalissimo with headquarters near Versailles exercised over the old world the military authority of the new.

As Tallyrand said of the Bourbon kings: "They have forgotten nothing and they have learned nothing." General de Gaulle certainly had forgotten nothing of his wartime dealings with the United States and Great Britain, the subsidiary role he had been forced to play and the exclusion of France from all of the central decision-making by the Allies. But he had learned plenty about the tactics of intransigence and noncooperation as a means of demonstrating from a position of weakness that France had a will of its own and would act independently whatever the rest of the world did or said. When he returned to power, de Gaulle seldom left his allies in any doubt about what he was *against*. It was more difficult to figure out what he was for. Everything revolved around the endless allusions and justifications embodied in "independence"—a sacred word in Gaullist liturgy that applied equally to a refusal of a presidential handshake or the veto of British entry into the European Common Market. An official of the Quai d'Orsay once told the author how, on one occasion, he had drafted a policy memorandum recommending that France "cooperate" with the United States on some relatively minor project in Africa that Washington had submitted in advance to the French for comments. His memorandum came back with a rejection written in de Gaulle's own hand: "Non. To cooperate is to lose one's independence." De Gaulle had neither considered nor examined the project on its merits. It involved cooperation with the Americans, and he would have none of it. Moreover, this was not an isolated case, but a fundamental attitude, as de Gaulle demonstrated again and again with NATO, the European Common Market, in the United Nations, over disarmament talks, in actions great and small against almost every nation with which France had active dealings. The independence of France and the breaking of Anglo-Saxon hegemony—these obsessions dominated his foreign policy to the very end, although he often seemed to be some vainglorious Don Quixote inventing his own windmills at which to tilt.

Insofar as there was some "grand design" to Charles de Gaulle's foreign policy on his return to power, these were the objectives:

• Demonstration of France's complete independence in all military, defense and political policymaking and decisions;

• Creation of France's own nuclear capability and *force de frappe* (strike force) to give her equal standing with the United States, Britain and the Soviet Union as a nuclear power;

• Withdrawal of France from NATO and the disappearance of the NATO military command structure in Europe, but continuance of the twenty-year American security guarantee to Western Europe embodied in the North Atlantic Treaty that had been signed in 1949;

• Establishment under French leadership of a purely continental system of loose military, political and economic cooperation around the European Common Market, in which France would wield veto power against any excessive integration and control its policies;

• Exclusion of Great Britain from this continental system, as long as her "special relationship" with the United States remained a British first interest;

• Finally, in de Gaulle's words: "To make this European organization one of three world powers and, if need be one day, the arbiter between the two camps, the Soviet and the Anglo-Saxon."

Around these themes or objectives, General de Gaulle's foreign policy evolved, fluctuated, rotated and reverberated in one way or another across the ensuing years. In essence, he wanted to do away with the postwar Euratlantic economic and security system that had been built during his years of exile and replace it with some vaguely nineteenth-century or eighteenth-century *Europe des patries*, with France as its epicenter in the West. This was never quite spelled out in any one Gaullist doctrine or declaration, but it is the summation of his concept and strategic aims.

This was a foreign policy of *la nostalgie*, a resumption of his 1940 struggle for recognition and national vindication, as if he were now bearing the Cross of Lorraine up some new Anglo-Saxon Mount Calvary yet again. To achieve the aim of making France the controlling force in continental Europe under some new political-security arrangement, de Gaulle first had to convince the rest of the Europeans of the iniquities of supposed Anglo-Saxon hegemony and persuade them to share his phobias about NATO and the dominant role that the United States was playing in European defense. The only aspects of his "grand design" that he could put into effect on his own were those relating to France itself. He could withdraw France from NATO, create a French *force de frappe* and impose a French veto on Britain's entering Europe. But to achieve any wider European goals beyond this, he needed the cooperation of the other Europeans—their belief in the wisdom of his leadership and judgment and the validity and soundness of his goals and his political strategy. Above all he had to convince them that they would be just as secure under French leadership as they already were under "Anglo-Saxon hegemony." This was simply beyond France's means.

About the last thing de Gaulle inspired in other governments was a sense of trust. Not only did his "Third Force" concept seem to be flirting dangerously with neutralism—it also ran up against hard realities such as the Berlin Wall and the crushing of the Dubcek regime in Prague. At the bottom line, when it came to a choice between putting trust in de Gaulle's concepts of how continental Europe should group itself politically and defend itself, as against the existing structure of the Atlantic Alliance with the Anglo-Saxons and a broadening of European unity under this security umbrella, the rest of Europe chose to play it safe, and General de Gaulle continued as he had all his life to walk alone.

*

Charles de Gaulle's principal *bête noire* was NATO and its integrated military command structure under Supreme Headquarters, Allied Powers Europe (SHAPE), organized and established by Eisenhower in 1951 and commanded ever since by an American general with a British deputy commander in chief. Under SHAPE, a French general held command of the European Central Front at that time, including all of the Allied forces stationed in West Germany. But as far as de Gaulle was concerned, NATO and SHAPE were the embodiment of the same subjugation of the French military establishment to Anglo-Saxon dominance and command that he had lived with during the war. The removal of France from this NATO military structure was therefore his first priority when he returned to power. This was basic to his entire foreign policy and was not negotiable. But he was enough of a realist and political tactician to know that he had to move gradually. His ultimate determination was thus apparently obscure or uncertain—yet the wonder really is that the other Allies were so taken by surprise when de Gaulle struck the final blow of disengagement from NATO in April of 1966.

Prime Minister Macmillan was one of the first leaders to visit de Gaulle on his return to power, flying over from London for a quick meeting at the end of June 1958. It was an "old comrades" reunion, but de Gaulle told Macmillan in their wide-ranging general conversation that "France will be in NATO less and less." John Foster Dulles then got a frosty lecture from de Gaulle about NATO when he followed Macmillan to Paris in July. The Anglo-Saxons had been alerted, and there could have been no great surprise when the General made his first major move against NATO in personal letters to Macmillan and Eisenhower dated September 17, 1958.

The letters were accompanied by a formal French government memorandum drafted by de Gaulle of proposals for a sweeping reorganization of global strategic policymaking machinery by the three Western Allies. After first asserting "the worldwide character of France's responsibilities and security concerns," de Gaulle told the president and the prime minister that NATO "no longer answers the essential security requirements of the free world as a whole." He proposed that it be supplanted or replaced: "Political and strategic questions of world importance should be entrusted to a new body, consisting of the United States, Great Britain and France. This body should have the responsibility of taking joint decisions on all political matters affecting world security, and of drawing up, and if necessary putting into action, strategic plans, especially those involving the use of nuclear weapons."

De Gaulle asked for "the earliest possible consultations" on his proposal and added the not very veiled threat: "The French government regards such an organization for security as indispensable. Henceforth the whole development of its present participation in NATO is predicated on this."

He had presented the Anglo-Saxons with a demand that was politically shrewd and impossible of practical fulfillment. It was shrewd because it did indeed go to the heart of the wider problems of global security arrangements among the powers of the free world, which continue to bedevil the NATO alliance to this day. But it was impossible for the United States to accept de Gaulle's demands for one reason alone (and there were many), which was that in effect he was asking for a say, even veto power, over the use of American nuclear weapons on a global basis. In fact, his memorandum was a political move that he assumed would probably be rejected. This would provide him with the excuse and justification for going ahead with his real policy—which was to get out of NATO. He affirms this himself in his Memoirs:

> My aim was to disengage France, not from the Atlantic Alliance, which I intended to maintain by way of ultimate precaution, but from the integration realized by NATO under American command. But I was anxious to proceed gradually, linking each stage with overall developments and continuing to cultivate France's traditional friendships. As I expected, the two recipients of my memorandum replied evasively. So there was nothing to prevent us from taking action.

If Eisenhower and Macmillan expressed themselves "evasively" in their replies, which reached de Gaulle about a month later, at least they were candid, and they were also open to trying to accommodate his wishes for consultation machinery that would operate in secret without any decision-making powers and without replacing the existing NATO structure or creating new institutions that would offend other members of the alliance, West Germany in particular. Eisenhower in his reply told de Gaulle that he wished "to avoid anything that would prevent or destroy the growing trust in consultation among all the members of NATO," and that it would be wrong to give the other Allies the impression that "basic decisions affecting their own vital interests were being made without their participation." Eisenhower and Macmillan did agree to de Gaulle's request for a discussion of his memorandum, although not all that urgently. These meetings, at ambassadorial level, took place in Washington in mid-December 1958 and ended inconclusively after four days.

This was the beginning of a long and fruitless effort by the Americans and the British to work out something that would satisfy de Gaulle. But he had quite deliberately posed an irreconcilable problem. The three men exchanged more personal letters, their foreign ministers held diplomatic discussions, and they themselves argued and wrestled with the problem in summit meetings—right through to a final effort by President Kennedy to see if he could square this circle on his visit to Paris to meet President de Gaulle in May 1961.

But it was all to no avail, as Eisenhower summarized to an interviewer after he left office:

> De Gaulle knew where I stood on this question of being a loyal ally and good friend, so he did not doubt my motives when I disagreed with him on the big pitch he made for a three-power directorate. It was part of his obsession about the Anglo-Saxons. He had this fixed misconception and he would never forget it. I would say to him—I'll consult you as you request, I'll promise to make no move and neither will the British unless we've all agreed that we'll do this thing by study, but let's don't proclaim it publicly as a three-power directorate. You can't have just two or three pals acting as a self-contained unit in the diplomatic and strategic world, and that's all there is to it.
>
> Why, he said we shouldn't use our nuclear weapons anywhere in the world without consulting him, and his sharing in the policy decisions. Well, the British haven't got any such kind of a deal. But just short of delivering our initiatives over to him and submitting ourselves to his judgments, short of that I really did try to meet his desire and the need for some kind of world position and prestige. I offered him everything it was possible to offer, very far toward his requests. But he wouldn't have it. It was all or nothing for him.

Soon after the first round of diplomatic talks in Washington had ended inconclusively, as de Gaulle expected, and even intended, he struck his first blow directly at the NATO military structure. In March 1959 he abruptly announced on the eve of a planned NATO naval exercise in the Mediterranean that the French Fleet was being withdrawn from NATO assignment on the grounds that its primary task was to serve French interests in the Algerian War and to be free to move as directed by the French government to African waters, or to the Red Sea or the Indian Ocean or the Caribbean, wherever France required it.

He followed this a few months later by decreeing that no nuclear weapons or warheads could be stationed on French territory unless they were under the complete and sole control, lock and key, of the French government.

This move by de Gaulle came as the United States was beginning to introduce its new generation of smaller tactical nuclear weapons in Europe. After some weeks studying the effect of the de Gaulle decree, Washington began its first withdrawal of military forces from France. US Air Force fighter-bomber squadrons stationed at seven NATO-built air bases in France were transferred either to West Germany or to Great Britain. The fields remained in American hands on a standby basis for another seven years, and American transport squadrons continued to operate in France. But the fighter-bombers had to go where the new nuclear warheads could be stored. De Gaulle's military disengagement from NATO was under way.

*

At the time de Gaulle launched his triumvirate proposal on his Anglo-Saxon allies, he also began the groundwork for his purely continental European policy with a first meeting with Chancellor Konrad Adenauer. The dates directly and no doubt deliberately coincided. He met Adenauer for their first private talk on September 14, 1958, and it was only three days later that he sent off to Eisenhower and Macmillan his first formal communication about NATO. In order to give that first meeting with the West German chancellor special character, de Gaulle took the unusual step of inviting him to be his house guest overnight at Colombey-les-Deux-Églises. Adenauer arrived in the afternoon and left the next afternoon after lunch to drive back to Bonn, recording rather flatly in his Memoirs later: "I was glad to have met a totally different person from what I had expected. I was convinced that de Gaulle and I would have a good and mutually trusting relationship."

But all had not been smooth sailing. In general the meeting itself had appeared to go well, as the two men ranged over Franco-German relations, the need to stand firm in Berlin with Nikita Khrushchev beginning to build up to a new crisis confrontation, and a mutual skepticism they shared about Britain entering Europe. But as far as Adenauer was concerned, much of this initial atmosphere of confidence was vitiated by the fact that de Gaulle did not say one word to him about his intention to propose to the United States and Britain only three days later a tripartite global strategic directorate, from which West Germany would be excluded, to supplant NATO. Adenauer did not learn of this until September 24, when the Quai d'Orsay was authorized by de Gaulle to give the West German ambassador a summary, but not the text, of the French memorandum. The chancellor was infuriated, not only by the proposal but more especially by de Gaulle's duplicity in leaving him deliberately in the dark about this intention during his visit to Colombey. He was still sputtering with anger about it when Macmillan arrived in Bonn to see him two weeks later, on October 8. Macmillan sought to cool things by recounting some of his own de Gaulle stories from the wartime days in Algiers.

Nevertheless Adenauer was utterly devoted to the cause of Franco-German reconciliation and determined to do all he could to make this one of the permanent historic achievements of his life. At this point, moreover, he realized fully that with his own age—he was then eighty-two—his last chance had to be an understanding with General de Gaulle, France's hero of the century. Therefore, angered and offended as he was over the way de Gaulle had played their first encounter, he was unable to hit back. In the larger interests of cementing relations with France, he had to swallow his wrath and sit and take it. It was not the last time by any means that he was affronted and hurt by some act of duplicity or chicanery, or by a deliberate snub on the part of de Gaulle.

Meanwhile, Macmillan was the next to feel the back of de Gaulle's hand in the assertion of France's new continental political strategy. The Treaty of Rome, creating the European Common Market, was virtually the last foreign policy act of the old Fourth Republic. It had been signed on March 25, 1957, by the same six continental powers joined in the original Schuman Plan treaty for the European Coal and Steel Community—France, West Germany, Italy, Holland, Belgium and Luxembourg. The ratification process also had been completed before de Gaulle's return to power. Yet the question hung over Europe—would de Gaulle proceed with the treaty or would he find some way of sabotaging it, relegating it to the shelf? Would he demand a renegotiation to satisfy his own views of French interests? His hostility to the original Schuman Plan was well known, as well as his hostility to "integration" of any kind, whether under NATO or under a European label.

Great Britain, meanwhile, was finally rousing itself after having twice missed the European boat. She had elected to stay out of the Schuman Plan when it was masterminded by Jean Monnet in May 1950 and then stayed out a second time when negotiations on the Common Market treaty were launched at Messina, Sicily, in 1955. The British calculation that this historic development of supranationalism and European integration would end in failure was one of the biggest foreign policy and political misjudgments of that nation's history. But with the Common Market about to turn into a reality, London embarked on a major maneuver to submerge all of this into a much wider "European Free Trade Area." They were proposing that all of Western Europe, under the existing Organization for European Economic Cooperation (OEEC) that had been created in the Marshall Plan days, join in one big free-trade area by eliminating all customs duties and tariffs on one another's industrial products.

Thus, the British were trying to gain the economic advantages of the wider European market for their manufactured goods without any of the political sacrifices or commitments of supranationalism and integration that the Common Market involved, and in particular without any common market or free trade in agricultural products. Under the British plan, the Common Market was supposed to go ahead and build its own integrated structure within the free-trade area if it wished, but clearly the overall effect would be to submerge it economically in the larger European arrangements. There was momentary hope in London when de Gaulle returned to power that this might appeal to him as a convenient way of ditching the supranationalism of the Common Market. But de Gaulle's prejudices against the Anglo-Saxons were a great deal stronger and deeper than those about European integration.

Macmillan had sought indirectly to elicit de Gaulle's support for the free-trade area by showing more sympathy than Eisenhower for de Gaulle's ambitions to set up a global strategic triumvirate. But de Gaulle was even less interested in seeing Britain in Europe than he was in the fate of his triumvirate plan. During the summer of 1958 the British plodded around Europe to lobby support for their free-trade-area scheme, in preparation for a decision at a ministerial meeting of the OEEC countries in mid-November, five months after de Gaulle's return to power. By November de Gaulle had received the "evasively" worded response of the Anglo-Saxons on his NATO memorandum and was set to counterattack.

On the eve of the OEEC meeting, he lowered his first veto on Britain joining Europe. He simply had his minister of information announce to the press, not even to the OEEC ministers, that "it has become clear to France that it is not possible to set up the free-trade area as wished by the British."

The continent of Europe was to be Charles de Gaulle's sphere of influence, and it was an exclusion that would take the British fifteen years to overcome.

Vetoed by de Gaulle, the British retired wounded and indignant to the European sidelines. But that first rebuff was not the political disaster or humiliation they were to feel from de Gaulle in later years. The Common Market was not yet a going entity, and therefore its economic and political impact on Europe was yet to be fully realized by the British. In the meantime they were able to assuage their wounded pride by going ahead and setting up a separate free-trade area with the "outer seven" European States outside the Common Market—Britain plus Norway, Sweden, Denmark, Austria, Portugal and Switzerland.

De Gaulle's "grand design" was still obscured in the atmosphere of Algerian old comradeships, and Prime Minister Macmillan was much more absorbed at this point in the diplomacy of the Berlin crisis than he was in entering Europe. Berlin was to dominate East-West relations and the international diplomatic scene throughout 1959, 1960, and 1961, when the Berlin Wall was built, and then up to the Cuban missile crisis in October of 1962—after which the Berlin crisis also abruptly receded, rather like a pop-music radio station going off the air at midnight.

*

The long-running Berlin crisis was useful to de Gaulle in several ways. First of all, while Macmillan rushed off to Moscow at the outset in February of 1959 to seek a Big Four foreign ministers meeting on Berlin later that year, de Gaulle adopted an utterly rigid hardline stance. He took the firm position that there was nothing to negotiate about—that Allied rights in Berlin could not be given up, nor could the Allies be forced out. Khrushchev had proclaimed that he intended to sign a peace treaty with East Germany and transfer to the East Germans all Soviet rights, duties and controls with regard to Berlin, which he said should be made a "free city."

Throughout all of the diplomatic maneuverings and endless summit meetings and military brinksmanship of the three years of Berlin crisis, de Gaulle's position remained clear and hard as crystal. To Khrushchev himself, when the Soviet leader visited Paris in March of 1960, de Gaulle laid it on the line in simple, blunt terms:

> No one can prevent you from signing what you call a treaty with Pankow [the East Berlin capital of East Germany] that would merely be a document

drawn up among Communists and which you would be addressing to yourselves. But when you have done so, the German problem will still remain unresolved. Moreover, everyone would know that the difficulties created by your initiative for the French, American and British occupation forces in Berlin stemmed from you. The three Western powers will never allow their troops to be insulted. If it leads to war, it will be entirely your fault. And yet you never stop talking about peaceful co-existence. If you do not want war, do not take the road that leads to war. The question at issue is not how to stir up conflict but how to organize peace.

Thus, de Gaulle was able to perform as the NATO strongman ready to go all the way to the brink of war in resisting Khrushchev's threats over Berlin, while at the same time pursuing his anti-NATO campaign and beginning his moves toward ultimate withdrawal from military participation in the Alliance. Moreover, with Adenauer and the robust and intelligent mayor of Berlin, Willy Brandt, he constantly sought to capitalize on this hardline stance to undercut his Anglo-Saxon allies. Scarcely a meeting with Adenauer or Brandt went by during those years without some kind of drip-treatment by de Gaulle against the Americans and the British—as in one talk that Brandt records in which de Gaulle told him that "with the Americans there is always a risk they will accept sham compromises" over Berlin while "France will continue to support a firm stance." In furtherance of his European policy, he used the Berlin crisis to proffer the Germans his leadership in place of the Anglo-Saxons.

Adenauer was more susceptible to this than Brandt—particularly after the death of John Foster Dulles, the American secretary of state who had been Adenauer's Cold War soulmate. The very fact that Macmillan and Eisenhower were prepared to sit down and talk with the Soviet Union about Berlin was enough for de Gaulle and Adenauer to work over with doubts and suspicions. It mattered little that in all of the talking and negotiating, nothing of substance, no basic Allied rights were given away by the Americans and the British. The talking always ended in deadlock and failure until the status quo in Berlin was finally inscribed in a four-power agreement negotiated and signed in 1972, after de Gaulle's death. In the meantime, his hardline stance gave him another cherished dividend—and that was the display of independence, distancing himself from his Anglo-Saxon allies.

Thanks largely to the tireless and peripatetic Harold Macmillan, summitry became a remorseless, wearisome and tedious fixation of the international scene during the Berlin crisis. Summitry began, of course, of necessity during the war, between Roosevelt and Churchill. But Truman scarcely stirred outside the United States except to go to Potsdam, and it had taken much maneuvering to get President Eisenhower to a summit meeting with the British, French and Russian leaders in Geneva in 1955. But with Macmillan's visit to Moscow in February 1959, a frenetic round of summit meetings began—not one of which produced anything decisive or memorable for the history books except photographs. All the same, Macmillan satisfied himself that by keeping Khrushchev traveling and talk-

342 / CHARLES DE GAULLE

ing, he was keeping him from shooting. De Gaulle, on the other hand, adopted his posture of lofty indifference to the Berlin crisis, engendered in part, no doubt, because Macmillan was temporarily upstaging him on the world scene.

The top-level travel in 1959 and the first six months of 1960 was little short of staggering, although de Gaulle himself for the most part stayed at home while managing to make Paris the diplomatic focal point of the comings and goings. After Macmillan got back to London from his February meeting with Khrushchev, he took off promptly in March 1959 to talk things over with Eisenhower and then visited de Gaulle and Adenauer. In May a Big Four foreign ministers meeting on Berlin opened in Geneva and lasted nearly two months, totally without result. At the end of August Eisenhower set off on a swing through Europe with visits to Macmillan in London, Adenauer in Bonn, and an elaborate state visit to de Gaulle in France that was staged with particular Gallic flair and enthusiasm. Then Khrushchev flew to the United States in the second half of September for a meeting with Eisenhower at Camp David and a wild inspection of American capitalism from Wall Street through the farm belt to Hollywood. In December Eisenhower set out again on a long trip including India and Afghanistan that ended with a four-power meeting in Paris with de Gaulle, Macmillan and Adenauer. There it was agreed in principle to arrange a Big Four summit meeting on the Berlin question with Khrushchev in Paris in the new year—but de Gaulle insisted on a round of his own bilateral visiting first. He began with Khrushchev, inviting him to Paris. The ebullient Russian leader arrived in France at the end of March 1960 for talks that were marked by his usual mixture of hard bluster and high humor. Then, in early April, de Gaulle made a state visit to Britain, full of warmth, pageantry and sentiment. After that, in the second half of the month, he took off for Canada and the United States—addressing Congress, visiting New York, San Francisco and New Orleans, and telling Eisenhower that "while believing America to be indispensable to the world, I did not wish to see her setting herself up as a universal judge and policeman."

At last the Big Four summit conference, Paris, May 1960—but, alas, one of the fiascos of postwar diplomatic history. The four principals gathered in Paris, but their meeting never took place. Nor has there ever been a suggestion since that a Big Four meeting might be a good idea to try again.

Two weeks before the conference was due to take place, an American U-2 reconnaissance spy plane was shot down by Soviet antiaircraft at an altitude of about 70,000 feet over the Siberian city of Sverdlovsk, and its pilot, Francis Gary Powers, was captured when he ejected from the plane and parachuted to earth. At first the United States put out a cover story about a missing weather reconnaissance aircraft, assuming that the plane had crashed in the Siberian wilds and the pilot was dead. But on May 5 the truth came out, in a bombastic speech before the Supreme Soviet in Moscow by Nikita Khrushchev. Powers was in a KGB prison, and parts of the aircraft were photographed and displayed. With the Paris summit only ten days away, Khrushchev demanded an apology by the president of the United States, punishment for those responsible, assurances that this would never be repeated, etc., etc. President Eisenhower did accept full public responsibility and announced suspension of further flights, which would have happened anyway since the operation, which had been going on for several years, was now blown. But that was as far as the president would go. He left for Paris as scheduled, commenting in his White House Memoirs that "it might prove to be unpleasant, but I had no intention of evading it—indeed I welcomed the opportunity to uncover more Soviet hypocrisy."

The president reached Paris on the morning of May 15, a Sunday, and learned that while he was traveling, Khrushchev had sent personal messages to both President de Gaulle and Prime Minister Macmillan that unless he received a full public apology "I cannot be among the participants in negotiations when one of them has made perfidy the basis of its policy toward the Soviet Union." Meeting that afternoon with de Gaulle and Macmillan, Eisenhower said that in no way would he apologize for decisions he had taken in the security interests of the United States, nor would he in any way tie the hands of American governments with pledges about the future, as Khrushchev was also demanding. De Gaulle's response to this was understanding, calm and matter-of-fact. But Macmillan had invested an enormous amount of time, energy, hope and diplomatic prestige in working for a summit conference, and he agonized over the prospects of its collapse. He wanted to play for time, keep talking, find a formula. De Gaulle loftily summed up how he intended to handle the meeting next day as host and chairman:

> I refuse to allow the conference to degenerate into an exchange of invective between the Russians and the Americans. I intend to put matters on the only basis which is both dignified and may possibly be fruitful. Are we all prepared to tackle the great questions which are the object of the meeting: disarmament, Germany, aid to the underdeveloped countries? If so, the debate can begin. If not, the conference has no immediate purpose and is adjourned *sine die*.

At 11 A.M. Monday the four arrived at the Élysée Palace as scheduled and settled around a square table, Eisenhower opposite Khrushchev. De Gaulle opened impassively with brief welcoming remarks, and Khrushchev impatiently asked to speak. Reading from a long, prepared text, he began a diatribe against the United States. When he concluded, Eisenhower replied in restrained terms that he was there to talk about problems of peace. De Gaulle then told Khrushchev:

> At this very moment a Soviet satellite is passing over France eighteen times in every twenty-four hours. How do we know that it is not taking photographs? How can we be sure that all the machines of every sort now flitting across the skies may not suddenly rain down terrible projectiles on any country in the world? The only possible guarantee would be a peaceful détente backed up by adequate measures of disarmament. That is the object of our conference. I therefore propose that the debate be opened.

Macmillan pleaded, but Khrushchev would have none of it and ranted on with his demand for an apology from Eisenhower, who was rigidly controlling his anger. They argued for three hours (with translations) until de Gaulle brought the useless and unseemly farce to a close by adjourning the meeting and announcing that he would keep in touch with each of the delegations to see if there was any point in meeting again. The three Western leaders reconvened after lunch, but Macmillan next embarked on extraordinary maneuvering to try to save the conference, resulting in what he himself acknowledged was "a rather unpleasant scene" with de Gaulle and Eisenhower, who wanted to issue a formal declaration on the circumstances of the collapse. But at Macmillan's behest they met again on Tuesday morning to await Khrushchev, who instead held a street press conference outside the Soviet embassy and thumbed his nose at the meeting by going for a drive in the country. Yet Macmillan continued to block a formal declaration of demise until ten o'clock that night, after making a last personal call on Khrushchev to plead with him to come to a meeting. This was scarcely robust or enhancing for Macmillan, in contrast to de Gaulle, who remained a figure of icy calm and dignity, of aloof imperturbability. Those four traumatic days in Paris ended Wednesday, when Khrushchev went before a press conference of some 1,200 journalists who had come from all over the world. Full of profanity, he stormed on about the U-2 incident and proclaimed once again his intention to sign a peace treaty with East Germany and liquidate Allied rights in West Berlin.

The fiasco was over and the world waited—but nothing happened. Khrushchev flew back to Moscow, stopping in East Berlin on the way, but he never signed his peace treaty. Instead, East German refugees streamed out from their Communist domain into West Berlin while they could still get away relatively easily, and the crisis simmered on.

For Harold Macmillan, the collapse of the Paris summit had been not merely a diplomatic failure but a personal disaster. But de Gaulle shrugged it off, and the firmness, clarity and dignity that he had displayed in all the turbulence had greatly enhanced his image and international prestige as a statesman unruffled by bombast and threats.

*

By this time, moreover, de Gaulle's position and that of France had been reinforced by one of the decisive events of French postwar history. On February 13, 1960, France's first atomic device was successfully tested in the Sahara, an oasis site near Reggane. The decision to take France into the ranks of the nuclear powers had been made four years earlier during the Fourth Republic by Socialist Premier Guy Mollet in the wake of the Suez War in 1956. De Gaulle, of course, sezied upon this as a major goal of the Fifth Republic, spurred it on as a matter of national priority and poured the funds necessary into simultaneous development of the whole range of military delivery vehicles for the force de frappe when the nuclear warheads were ready—a medium-range bombing force, medium-range ballistic missiles with a trajectory sufficient to reach Moscow from France, and nuclear-powered submarines for French-built sea-launched ballistic missiles. In no way did de Gaulle ever pretend that France was tipping the balance-of-power scales. His purpose, indeed, was much more political than military—the enhancing of French independence.

For this reason, France's nuclear policy was another non-negotiable subject with de Gaulle. All dialogue and discussion with him about nuclear questions was like talking into a telephone when the other party has long since hung up. He had not the slightest interest in the question of control of nuclear weapons, in nuclear disarmament, in a test-ban treaty, in the nuclear nonproliferation treaty, or in any of the treaties that were spawned in Geneva on keeping nuclear weapons out of Antarctica or the seabeds or outer space. He had no interest in think-tank theories about the use of nuclear weapons or the risks of one country triggering another into holocaust. He had only one theory and that was nuclear retaliation. There was no point in even discussing any cooperation with the United States, since the price of such cooperation was certain to be a loss of his own independence. In the end there was quite simply nothing to discuss or negotiate with him on the nuclear subject—a fact that took a long time to be fully realized in the United States.

President Eisenhower gave it an old soldier's try when he visited de Gaulle in Paris in September 1959 and hinted that America could relieve France of an expensive and largely unnecessary burden if they could agree on nuclear cooperation in return for joint control over weapons. But he got from de Gaulle virtually the same lecture and the same reasoning that the General would repeat more than four years later in rejecting a similar offer from Kennedy:

> If Russia attacks us, we are your allies and you are ours. But in this eventuality, and in any other for that matter, we want to hold our fate in our hands, and that fate would depend above all upon whether or not we were the victims of a nuclear attack. We must, therefore, have the means to deter any potential aggressor from striking at us directly, which means we must be capable of striking back at him and that he must know that we would do so without waiting for permission from outside. How can we French be sure that unless were bombed directly on your own soil, you would invite your own destruction?

When Eisenhower asked, "How can you doubt that the United States identifies her fate with that of Europe?" de Gaulle rolled on:

> In the course of two world wars, America was France's ally, and France has not forgotten what she owes to American help. But neither has she forgotten that during the First World War that help came only after three long years of struggle which nearly proved mortal for her, and that during the Second she had already been crushed before you intervened. In saying this, I intend not the slightest reproach. I know, as you yourself know, what a nation is. It can help another but it cannot identify itself with another. That is why, although remaining faithful to our alliance, I cannot accept France's integration into NATO. As for harmonizing the possible use of our nuclear bombs and yours insofar as this might be feasible, we could do so within the

framework of direct cooperation of the three atomic powers, which I have already proposed to you. Until you accept this, we shall, like you, retain complete freedom of action.

Somewhat wearily, Eisenhower says of this conversation that "I tried to convince him of my desire to coordinate our respective policies and actions around the globe, the substance and benefits of coordination, not the façade of self-assumed authority among three great nations; although this was not what de Gaulle had in mind, he accepted my views in good grace and did not push further the matter of a formal tripartite organization."

Did General de Gaulle *really* want a tripartite organization to control strategic decision-making on a global basis? Was he *really* ready to submit to the same veto power over France's emerging *force de frappe* that he was asking over the American strategic nuclear deterrent? In the light of his passion for independence, his abhorrence of integration, his reluctance to cooperate on anything unless on his own terms, the logical and realistic answer, the cynical answer, has to be that from the outset the tripartite proposal was a political sham, a red herring to confuse and divert his allies, unworkable and unacceptable by his own standards, but a convenient maneuver to "retain complete freedom of action," with its inevitable rejection. De Gaulle was his own Machiavelli.

But there was one more try on tripartitism during the final days of Eisenhower's presidency. After the breakdown of the Paris summit, de Gaulle, Eisenhower and Macmillan held a last meeting to discuss how they would respond to the Berlin situation in the event Khrushchev did go through with his threat to sign a peace treaty with East Germany. Eisenhower remarked that without disturbing existing structures (meaning NATO), it was obviously important that the three keep in closer touch. De Gaulle complained that "little attention had been given" to his memorandum on tripartite machinery and said he would be sending another. But when Macmillan got back to London, he jumped in first with a memorandum at the end of May in which he proposed that the three foreign ministers get together privately on a regular basis three or four times yearly, under the cover of meetings at the United Nations, NATO, or other organizations. Heads of government should then meet once or twice yearly. Then de Gaulle's memorandum of June 10, 1960, asked for something more precise on military and strategic questions, apart from political matters.

Eisenhower's reply in July ingeniously said that he was prepared to have "military representatives" engage in talks on strategic problems outside the NATO area, but at the same time he wanted "a close military cooperation in NATO"— which of course was exactly what de Gaulle was trying to ditch. De Gaulle came back on August 9 with a surprise proposal for a Big Three summit meeting in Bermuda in mid-September to discuss, as he put it, "the need for close tripartite cooperation" based on an extension of NATO's geographical area and doing away with military integration in the Alliance. He mentioned in passing the need for coordinating their policies on the question of the breakdown of law and order taking place in the Belgian Congo, newly independent, where France was rigorously opposing an American-backed intervention by the United Nations.

Eisenhower by now was beginning to get a little fed up with chasing the problem around in circles. He wrote de Gaulle firmly that a summit in September would not be possible. The 1960 presidential election campaign would just be getting under way, but Eisenhower did say that "in principle" they might arrange a meeting for December. He warned de Gaulle, however, that he could not accept any military and political tripartite cooperation at the expense of American relations with the other Allies. He enclosed a full list of dates and participants in meetings already held between the French and the Americans on the touchy subject of the former Belgian Congo, noting dryly that since their positions still remained "somewhat apart" it was difficult to see that higher-level tripartite discussions would have made much difference. He concluded that he found it difficult to understand "the basic philosophy of France today" in rejecting cooperation within NATO but at the same time trying to set up tripartite machinery with a veto over other members of the Alliance.

De Gaulle made his reply, in effect, at a press conference on September 5, 1960, in which he once again attacked integration in NATO and denounced the failure of the three Western Powers to coordinate their policies toward the Congo through tripartite machinery such as he had proposed. Subsequently, in a brief formal letter to Eisenhower, he did not even mention the president's tentative acceptance of a summit meeting in December.

That virtually ended the long hassle over tripartitism and the global triumvirate, although de Gaulle's 1958 proposal was continually cited to the end of his era in power as some great opportunity that the United States and Great Britain had failed to grasp.

*

By the time Kennedy was inaugurated in January 1961, de Gaulle had been in power for two and a half years, and in Washington the problem of "understanding de Gaulle" or "what to do about the French" had become a major preoccupation. What did de Gaulle want, what was he trying to achieve, what was the point or the object of his dissension? In American eyes there was no logic in preaching firmness against Khrushchev in Berlin and then pulling NATO apart. There was no logic in France building an expensive tiny independent nuclear force and at the same time asking for a veto over American weapons. There was no logic in de Gaulle repeatedly protesting about America having been late in coming to France's assistance in two world wars, and then wanting to do away with the American command in Europe that made it impossible for that ever to happen again. Americans who thought they were in Europe to support France's independence and freedom were baffled, and even hurt, by the accusation that they were exercising some sinister "Anglo-Saxon hegemony" over an ally of the American Revolution. So Eisenhower searched for two years for some way to give satisfaction to de Gaulle over the triumvirate proposal, and Kennedy searched for another two years for some accommodation with de Gaulle in nuclear cooperation and control. But the real problem was that both presidents sought to find understanding with General de Gaulle, to accept, encompass and accommodate his ambitions and assertions of French independence *within* the framework of the existing Euratlantic system, while it was de Gaulle's objective to break the mold and get out.

The Eisenhower presidency had been an era of national restraint rather than challenges, adventure or aggressive foreign policy. Kennedy arrived on the scene determined to reassert American leadership (like all newly elected presidents) and to resume the momentum of "the American Century" as proclaimed by its journalistic godfathers, Walter Lippmann and Henry R. Luce.

In the Eisenhower days, de Gaulle's challenge to the NATO Alliance and his deep anti-American antipathy had still remained relatively muted and abstract—in part at least because of the personal relationship between the two presidents. But with the arrival of Kennedy, an inexorable collision was in the making between the new president's intention to demonstrate American ascendancy and de Gaulle's intention to reassert France's European prominence and seek some kind of third force role. All the same, Kennedy was certainly genuine in his desire at the very outset to come to some understanding and working relationship with de Gaulle. As an earnest of this, he made Paris his first European port of call four months after taking office.

The state visit to France in May 1961 was a glittering social and public success in which the actors triumphed repeatedly before packed houses—in particular the leading lady, Jacqueline Kennedy. In dazzling sets—the Hall of Mirrors at Versailles, the lavish official guest apartments at the Quai d'Orsay, the *grands salons* of the Élysée Palace—the visit unfolded as a pageant of elegance and taste. The thrusting youth, good looks and virility of Kennedy harmonized with the vigorous age and grand style of Europe's last great man of the century.

De Gaulle wrote of Kennedy in his one volume of Postwar Memoirs:

> Chosen to get things done, enjoying the advantages of youth, but suffering the drawbacks of a novice—in spite of so many obstacles the new President was determined to devote himself to the cause of freedom, justice and progress. It is true that, persuaded that it was the duty of the United States to redress wrongs, he was to be drawn into ill-advised interventions. But the experience of the statesman would no doubt have gradually restrained the impulsiveness of the idealist. John Kennedy had the ability, and had it not been for the crime which killed him, might have had the time to leave his mark on our age. . . . I had been dealing with a man whose ability, whose age and whose justifiable ambition inspired immense hopes. He seemed to me to be on the point of taking off into the heights, like some great bird that beats its wings as it approaches the mountain tops.

But, for Charles de Gaulle, personal respect, social cordiality and public welcome and acclaim were never any substitute for the interests of the State. The formal talks between the two men were cordial and searching, and successful in the sense that Kennedy from the outset won de Gaulle's confidence and liking despite his "suffering the drawbacks of a novice." Indeed, as they ended one of their sessions, de Gaulle told Kennedy: "I have more confidence in your country now." But for all Kennedy's satisfaction at having quickly established a certain rapport with de Gaulle, they remained apart on almost every substantive problem that they discussed, as de Gaulle summarized in his Memoirs:

> Now the Americans acknowledged our independence and dealt with us directly. But for all that, they could not conceive of their policy ceasing to be predominant, or of ours diverging from it. What Kennedy offered me in every case was a share in his projects. What he heard from me in reply was that Paris was by all means disposed to collaborate closely with Washington, but that whatever France did, she did of her own accord. . . . Kennedy listened to me. But events were to prove that I had failed to convince him.

They opened their discussions on May 31, 1961, with a review of the situation in Berlin. From Paris, Kennedy would be traveling on to Vienna to meet Khrushchev, and once again the Soviet leader was cranking up his threats to sign a separate peace treaty with East Germany, turn control of Berlin over to the Communist puppet regime and force the Western Allies out of West Berlin. But when Kennedy broached with de Gaulle the tactic of "an appearance of negotiations with the Soviets by opening the future status of Berlin as a subject for discussion," he got a stony response. Khrushchev had been blustering about a peace treaty for two and a half years, de Gaulle replied, and the last thing he wanted was war. There was nothing to negotiate about. It was simply a matter of the Allies standing united, firm and immovable.

At their next session they turned to the situation in Southeast Asia, and Kennedy said that military intervention by the West might be necessary to bring the Communists to some agreement in Laos or Vietnam. This elicited a broadside from de Gaulle, who says that "instead of giving him the approval he wanted," he lectured Kennedy as follows:

> You will find that intervention in this area will be an endless enganglement. Once a nation has been aroused, no foreign power, however strong, can impose its will upon it. You will discover this for yourselves. For even if you find local leaders who in their own interests are prepared to obey you, the people will not agree to it, and indeed do not want it. The ideology which you invoke will make no difference. Indeed, in the eyes of the masses, it will become identified with your will to power. That is why the more you become involved out there against Communists, the more the Communists will appear as the champions of national independence, and the more support they will receive, if only from despair. We French have had experience of it. You Americans want to take our place. I predict that you will sink step by step into a bottomless military and political quagmire, however much you spend in men and money.

At that time de Gaulle was still bogged down in the military and political quagmire of the Algerian War, from which he was in the process of skillful disengagement. Kennedy, in May of 1961, had not yet fully made up his mind as to the extent to which he could, would or should get involved militarily in Southeast Asia. His reaction to this "de Gaulle warning" is not recorded. The exchange passed off more as a conversational discussion of a future possibility than any direct debate or argument about a policy that Kennedy was then proposing. But in any case, de Gaulle's early warning was on the record to the president of the United States, and his opposition to American involvement in Vietnam soon became one of his major anti-American rallying points in his efforts to project French leadership of the Third World.

The third major area that the two presidents covered, and of course did not agree upon, concerned NATO and nuclear weapons. Kennedy heard the standard de Gaulle case that France had to have her own nuclear weapons because she could not be certain that the United States would risk its own destruction in the defense of Europe. This was argued by de Gaulle with even more force and agitation because Kennedy and his defense secretary, Robert S. McNamara, were in the process of developing a new American strategic doctrine—the substitution of "graduated nuclear response" for the "massive retaliation" of John Foster Dulles' days. This, as far as de Gaulle was concerned, represented a weakening of the American nuclear guarantee. Kennedy's hints about providing France with nuclear weapons in return for a voice in their use were simply brushed aside. Nevertheless, Kennedy was still resolved to keep on trying.

In his last session alone with de Gaulle at the end of a three-day visit, Kennedy reopened the possibility of an understanding on the triumvirate proposal. He told de Gaulle he was prepared to examine the establishment of such machinery, and apparently attached no hedges or preconditions. But de Gaulle, curiously, said they should hold off further discussions "until after the German elections," which were to be held in August. It was an odd excuse for a delay, since Germany was in no way involved. But by this time de Gaulle had gotten all the diplomatic mileage out of his triumvirate proposal that he needed, and was no longer interested in its possible success, if he had ever been interested in it. His goal now was to line up his continental leadership with Germany in his wake.

"I am the man who accompanied Jacqueline Kennedy to Paris, and I have enjoyed it," the president said when he rose to address a vast press luncheon at the Palais de Chaillot. It had indeed been Jackie Kennedy's Paris triumph, as she drove to the old haunts of her student days on the Left Bank, shimmered in a Givenchy gown in the Hall of Mirrors, viewed the Impressionist paintings in the Jeu de Paume in the illustrious and imperious company of André Malraux, and chatted away in French with Charles de Gaulle about French history, art, education and her French ancestors.

The *son et lumière* success of the Paris visit faded as the Kennedys flew on to Vienna. In the meeting with Khrushchev, there were few surprises. The Soviet leader renewed face to face the threat to sign an East German peace treaty, declare

Berlin a "free city" and force the Allies out. It is your choice—not mine, Khrushchev told Kennedy, whether there will be war or peace.

"It looks like a cold winter," Kennedy remarked to Charles E. Bohlen, his Soviet adviser, on the steps of the American embassy residence after they said goodbye to Khrushchev.

De Gaulle's assessment of Kennedy's performance at the Vienna meeting was rather like a teacher marking down an examination paper of a prize young student. He wrote: "The American president did not allow himself to be pushed into endorsing the Soviet plan for a so-called free city then and there, but he was visibly overawed by the aggressive assurance of his interlocutor. . . . He wrote me month after month telling me that in order to avoid disaster we should have to agree to negotiate with the Soviets about Germany."

*

When Kennedy returned to Washington, he went on television to deliver a restrained and sober but forceful account of his meeting with Khrushchev. He announced an increase in US defense spending and the dispatch of American reinforcements to the NATO command, including more troops on the US supply lines across France. Next, he decided to have Secretary of State Dean Rusk conduct what was called a "diplomatic probe" with the Russians to see if there were some basis for a negotiation on Berlin. This was the tactic he had discussed with de Gaulle in Paris. Now, when he sought de Gaulle's backing, the response was a harsh *non*. In a personal letter to Kennedy, followed by a television address to the French people, de Gaulle bluntly disapproved of the American move and said France would have nothing to do with the initiative or its possible findings. To Kennedy he wrote: "In the event of a crisis provoked by the Soviets, only an attitude of firmness and solidarity, adopted and affirmed in good time by America, Britain and France, will prevent unpleasant consequences. . . . Only after a long period of international *détente*—which depends entirely on Moscow—can we enter into negotiations with Russia on the German problem as a whole."

De Gaulle records with relish that his firm stand brought a response from Adenauer in Bonn that he was "overwhelmed with confidence and joy by such unqualified support for Germany in her hour of danger." But Kennedy could not afford the luxury of standing at the helm of a ship apparently heading straight for the rocks. So, with the fervent support of Macmillan and the British, the diplomatic probe by Rusk went ahead anyway. It produced nothing and gained nothing except, perhaps, diplomatic marking-time. But the breach between Washington and Paris was again opening up.

In June and July 1961, after Khrushchev delivered a couple of hair-raising diatribes on the German question, the flow of refugees into West Berlin from East Germany became a hemorrhage—more than 30,000 crossed over during July, and a peak of more than 4,000 in one day was reached in early August. Then, suddenly, on the night of August 12–13, barbed wire was uncoiled across the center of Berlin and the building of the infamous Berlin Wall got under way.

The joint response of the Western Powers to this climactic event in Berlin's postwar history was pretty pusilanimous after all the heat and emotion and attention the crisis had been getting. It was a Sunday morning, and de Gaulle was at Colombey-les-Deux-Églises, Kennedy was sailing off Hyannisport, and Macmillan was at Chequers, the country home of British prime ministers. The Western military commandants in the city, waiting for instructions from their capitals, could not even order military police patrols to back up the West Berlin police, who were coping with near-hysterical Berliners watching in rage and disbelief at what was happening in the heart of their city. It was twenty hours before Allied MPs established patrols along the sector line, forty-two hours before an Allied protest was delivered to the Soviet commandant in East Berlin, and seventy-two hours before a protest was delivered to Moscow. Even if it was a clear fact that, short of some act of war such as running tanks into East Berlin, the Allies could do nothing to stop the East Germans building a wall on their own territory, it was a sorry Allied performance. When de Gaulle's foreign minister, Maurice Couve de Murville, got the news, his immediate, laconic, dismissive comment was: "Well, that settles the Berlin problem." De Gaulle wrote more elaborately: "The edifice provided physical proof of the fact that the Kremlin had given up hope of frightening the Americans, the British and the French into allowing them to lay hands on the city."

However true this was, the crisis did not end that abruptly by any means. From behind the wall, the Communist forces continued to bluster and threaten, and the immediate economic blow to the city was severe. But the Soviets did not go as far as imposing another blockade of the road, rail and canal links between West Berlin and West Germany, or interfere with the air traffic, even though there was a lot of dangerous buzzing of aircraft in the air corridors. Kennedy sent additional reinforcements into the city for the American garrison, and General Lucius D. Clay returned to the scene of his 1948–49 airlift triumph to act as a sort of "resistance coordinator." Throughout the winter of 1961 and the spring and summer of 1962, Berlin was constantly in the headlines with heroic escape stories and repeated confrontations with the Soviets and the East Germans that seemed to teeter permanently close to a spark that could explode into war.

De Gaulle had given early assurances to Eisenhower that he would do nothing to disrupt the Atlantic Alliance as long as the Berlin crisis remained unresolved, and continued to be as good as his word, on this at least. The triumvirate proposal was dead, but in the meantime de Gaulle found other ways to take his distance from Kennedy and Washington. He refused to have anything to do with Kennedy's initiative in 1961 to try to resolve the problem of neutrality for Laos through negotiations. He rejected even suggestions that France might join in the American-British-Soviet negotiations that were going on in Geneva on a nuclear test ban treaty. In March 1962, after the Berlin Wall, de Gaulle abruptly pulled the French out of the United Nations disarmament talks in Geneva just as the Kennedy administration was about to launch a new (if futile) round of negotiations in agreement with the Soviet Union.

Meanwhile de Gaulle was assiduously pursuing his policy of rapprochement with West Germany and cultivating his personal ties with Adenauer—cemented by their mutual concern over what the Americans and the British might surrender in Berlin. The two leaders exchanged state visits, and de Gaulle made a particular impact in his tour of West Germany in September 1962, even though he deliberately avoided including West Berlin on his itinerary. At the working levels of diplomacy, de Gaulle took more and more care to make West Germany his favorite ally.

Berlin simmered on, but the real crisis was now building up far away on the other side of the Atlantic. In October 1962 the Cuban missile crisis suddenly brought the United States and the Soviet Union face to face with possible nuclear war. Europe was caught in between, its fate and its possible annihilation resting with Moscow and Washington. Kennedy secretly dispatched former Secretary of State Dean Acheson on a personal mission to Europe, first to brief de Gaulle, and later the ambassadors of the North Atlantic Treaty Organization, which then still had its headquarters in Paris. Accompanied by a senior Central Intelligence Agency man in Paris, Acheson met de Gaulle alone at the Élysée Palace, with only a French interpreter present. Acheson reviewed the situation and spread out a batch of air reconnaissance photos establishing the evidence of the installation of Soviet medium-range nuclear missiles in Cuba. He told de Gaulle that the next move would probably be a United States naval blockade of Cuba, and that this carried with it the risk of an engagement with Soviet ships, naval action—and possible war.

De Gaulle wasted no time.

"You may tell the President," he said to Acheson, "that if there is a war, France will be with you. But there will be no war."

He paused and then added, typically: "I must note that I have been advised, but not consulted."

De Gaulle was convinced from the earliest stages of the Berlin crisis that Khrushchev was bluffing, and he saw the missile crisis as the other side of the same coin. When the Berlin Wall went up, in de Gaulle's view, Khrushchev's bluff had finally been called by Allied firmness and refusal to be forced out of the city. Now the bluff would have to be called in Cuba. De Gaulle had not the slightest hesitation in perceiving the Cuban crisis this way, and no hesitation in acting on that conviction and backing the United States. In London, on the other hand, Macmillan was more cautious. Instead of an Acheson briefing, he got several telephone calls from Kennedy himself, and the president sensed "a certain reserve" in Macmillan's responses. Even *The Economist* in London warned at one point against forcing a nuclear showdown over a mere shipment of arms to Cuba. In the end, Macmillan's hesitations gave way to wholehearted support for Kennedy, and Britain's own nuclear force of American-built Jupiter missiles under a two-key control was put on alert on the launch pads as the crisis neared its climax—a risk and a contribution that de Gaulle was not called upon to take. Still, the contrast between de Gaulle's instant and unequivocal firmness and Macmillan's more cautious initial attitude was much the same as Eisenhower had experienced in their confrontation with Khrushchev at the 1960 Paris summit conference.

There was a final footnote from de Gaulle. As the Soviet ships neared the American naval blockade perimeter around Cuba, the Soviet ambassador to France, Serge Vinogradov, received an urgent instruction from Khrushchev to seek an immediate meeting with the French president to warn him of the consequences for France of a possible nuclear war, and France's inevitable responsibility for this if she continued to side with the United States.

The appointment was quickly arranged, and Vinogradov was ushered into de Gaulle's office at the Élysée Palace. It was de Gaulle's invariable custom to open such meetings merely by saying, "Well, Mr. Ambassador, I am listening." Vinogradov, referring to his telegram of instructions, launched into his warning of the nuclear destruction that France was risking. De Gaulle sat immobile, expressionless and silent, not responding at all. Vinogradov kept going, but de Gaulle's silence was crushing. At last the Soviet ambassador ran out of things to say.

De Gaulle then rose from behind his desk with heavy and ponderous motion, stretched out his hand in farewell to Vinogradov and said:

"Hélas, Monsieur l'Ambassadeur, nous mourrons ensemble! Au revoir, Monsieur l'Ambassadeur." (Alas, Mr. Ambassador, we'll die together! Goodbye, Mr. Ambassador.)

EIGHTEEN

THE ATLANTIC TO
THE URALS, 1963–65

President Kennedy drew one set of conclusions from the outcome of the Cuban missile crisis. President de Gaulle drew another, almost diametrically opposite.

For the president of the United States, the crisis dramatically enhanced American power and leadership and was a victory of the solidarity of the Atlantic Alliance. In standing down the Soviet threats posed in Cuba and Berlin, the clear fact of United States military superiority in both conventional and nuclear weapons was convincingly re-established for the world to see and to know. Finally, in the Kennedy view, the crisis demonstrated the vital importance of the close, single and absolute American control over nuclear weapons in any confrontation with the Soviet Union. Peace and security lay in a consolidation of this demonstrated strength.

For the president of the French Republic, the Cuban missile crisis first and foremost marked the end of the postwar era of the Cold War. Having been forced to retreat before American power, in de Gaulle's view the Soviet Union would be unlikely and unable to risk any such confrontation again for a long time to come. Therefore, for him the crisis opened up a new period of diplomatic opportunity in Europe, the era of *détente* and cooperation with the Soviet Union that he had regularly sought and that he saw as the only alternative to confrontation. Moreover, for de Gaulle the crisis demonstrated the extreme risk that Europe's fate could be abruptly determined by a superpower conflict that had nothing whatever to do with Europe itself. He had been loyal to the United States, but when it was all over, the lesson he drew was that Europe must never be put at risk in such a manner again. It therefore must find its own place and role between the superpowers, and France would take the lead with its independent foreign policy backed by its own nuclear deterrent.

In the summer of 1962, before the Cuban crisis, Kennedy had delivered a major foreign policy speech in Philadelphia in which his theme was the interdependence of the United States and a united Europe and the need to strengthen the Atlantic partnership. In part the speech was designed to prod the British into backing Macmillan's bid, at long last, to join the European Common Market. Kennedy then sought to give fresh impetus and vitality to "interdependence" and "partnership" after the Cuban experience by opening up the question of how decision-making power over the use of nuclear weapons might be shared within the Alliance under ultimate American control. He proposed the creation of a "multilateral nuclear force" for NATO, naval vessels or submarines carrying nuclear weapons with mixed-manned crews from the various NATO navies, so there would not be an American finger alone on the nuclear button. At the same time, while seeking to capitalize on this new momentum with his allies, Kennedy set about after the Cuban crisis to dispell any atmosphere of continuing confrontation with the Soviet Union. He quickly offered to conclude a treaty with the Soviets banning nuclear testing above ground—an offer Khrushchev promptly grasped with evident relief. The treaty was signed in August 1963.

None of these post-Cuban initiatives from Kennedy had any appeal whatsoever to de Gaulle. All he could see was a Kennedy effort to strengthen Anglo-Saxon hegemony over Europe and to decide things alone with the Soviet Union in a superpower relationship over the heads of the Europeans—Yalta all over again. His policy therefore was the opposite of Kennedy's. With the Cuban crisis over, the Berlin problem resolved and the danger of confrontation receding, now was his moment to step up the process of withdrawal from NATO, break out of the Euratlantic system and press forward with his vague goal of "cooperation within the framework of our continent, between Europeans from the Atlantic to the Urals."

Throughout his life Charles de Gaulle's concept of Europe remained stubbornly rooted in the turn-of-the-century perspective in which he grew up, and the history books of that era from which he studied. It was the Europe of the nineteenth century, long before the Russian Revolution—the Europe of nation-states legitimized by the Congress of Vienna in which nationalism was the only true and lasting historical force, far stronger than any ideology or passing phase of a country's rulers or leadership. He always spoke of "Russia," never of the Soviet Union. Willy Brandt records with amusement de Gaulle's asking him about "the situation in Prussia and Saxony," meaning Communist East Germany. De Gaulle was openly contemptuous of Belgium because it was a clobbered-together country of French-speaking Walloons and Flemish-speaking Flemings and therefore not in his view a true nation-state. He regarded Italy as an artificial creation, not a nation, and took more interest in the Vatican than he did in Rome. Social systems, the development of political power blocs, meant little to him. Nations, homogeneous peoples, the traditions and cohesions of the nation-state, these were permanent, these were everything.

De Gaulle therefore regarded communism in Eastern Europe as only a phase of history whose passing he would seek to speed up by "dissolving the power blocs." His goal, he said in a television broadcast on October 1961, was "a Europe balanced between the Atlantic and the Urals, once totalitarian imperialism has ceased to deploy its ambitions." Of communism, he said contemptuously in July 1963:

> Since I was born, Communist ideology has been personified by many people. There was the period of Lenin, Trotsky, Stalin whom I knew personally, of Beria, Malenkov, Khrushchev, Tito, Nagy and of Mao Tse-tung. I know as many trustees of Communist ideology as there are fathers of Europe, and that makes quite a number. Each one of these trustees in his turn condemns, excommunicates, crushes and sometimes kills the others. In any case he firmly combats the cult of others' personalities. The standard of ideology in reality does no more than cover ambitions.

De Gaulle's perspective on communism and Europe's past and future was all very grand, romantic and desirable. But whatever truths and hope it contained, it was not a particularly realistic or valid approach to the real world of the twentieth century. It presupposed, first of all, that the present-day rulers in the Kremlin would be as weak in controlling their empire and satellites as the czars had proven to be, and as benign in their relations with a Europe of nation-states as Alexander I had been on his visit to Paris in 1815. Of course Poland wants to be Poland, Hungary wants to be Hungary, and Czechoslovakia would even like to be Czecho-slovakia—and perhaps one day they all will be. In the meantime de Gaulle was unable to achieve much more of his pan-European vision than demonstrating that it is much easier to break out of the NATO bloc than it is to break out of the Soviet bloc.

*

Prime Minister Macmillan had applied to join de Gaulle's Europe in July 1961, but the very form of the application had some self-defeating aspects. First of all Macmillan made a great deal of the fact that he had "cleared it with Kennedy" and that the president of the United States had given his blessing. This may have been useful and necessary as a reassurance to British Conservatives, as Macmillan seemed to think it was, but it was scarcely any demonstration to de Gaulle that Britain was now going to put its European interests ahead of its special relation-ship with Washington. Moreover, Macmillan did not make a direct application to join the Common Market, but simply asked for negotiations with the Six to see if he could get terms on which he would then decide to join. It was all hedged and tentative, trying to back into Europe instead of marching in. The very form of the negotiation greatly complicated things and eventually facilitated de Gaulle's ulti-mate veto against the British bid.

Harold Macmillan was certainly sincere in his conviction that Great Britain had to join Europe. He was one of the most skillful politicians ever to sit in No. 10 Downing Street, and taking Britain into Europe would have been a crowning act of a very successful career. But as a politician, he always preferred to "have things happen" instead of "get things done." Joining Europe was deeply divisive within his own party as well as with the Labour opposition. So he chose to tiptoe cautiously around the problem. Ideally, Macmillan simply wanted Britain to wake up one morning and find it had joined Europe undisturbed, rather the way Disraeli acquired the Suez Canal or Clive moved into India. But in order to slide into Europe this way, with a maximum list of concessions from the Europeans with which to lull the opponents, Macmillan needed de Gaulle to play the game with him, to sympathize with his political difficulties and smooth things in the complex negotiation when the going got rough.

Macmillan certainly recognized that sentiment was not a notable quality in General de Gaulle. But he did enjoy a good conversational and personal relationship with de Gaulle, and he believed that ultimately the General would support Britain out of logic and persuasion, without sentiment. Macmillan did not realize or did not accept the real depth of de Gaulle's anti-British feelings and his basic determination to keep Europe as a kind of French preserve. Nor did he perceive that the French might not be negotiating completely in good faith—that is to say, in order to achieve success. It was only late in the game that it became clear to the British that de Gaulle was using the negotiations to show how impossible it was to let the British in. Moreover, the British unwittingly played into French hands with endless demands for special deals and nitpicking concessions and petty adjustments during the fifteen months of frustrating negotiations in Brussels.

After it was all over, de Gaulle contended in various remarks and conversations that he had been genuinely ready to see Britain enter Europe when Macmillan applied. Perhaps he was. But at any rate he said that as the talks wore on, and with each of his summit meetings with Macmillan, it became more and more clear to him that Britain was unwilling or unready to make the European adjustment that membership in the Common Market demanded. It would be more realistic and candid to assume that de Gaulle was simply waiting for the excuse and opportunity that he was sure would come for him to slam down his veto.

He and Macmillan conferred three times during the Common Market negotiations—a private weekend at Macmillan's home at Birch Grove in Sussex in November 1961; at the Château des Champs outside Paris in June 1962; and a final decisive meeting at the presidential château at Rambouillet in December of that year. The final exchange between the two leaders at Rambouillet—indeed, the final conversation of their lives—was marked by a summing up on the part of de Gaulle that revealed what his true feelings about Britain's entering Europe must have been all along.

Macmillan records in his Memoirs:

> De Gaulle said that for France it was important that the Common Market should remain unchanged for the present—there was no need to hurry. Britain was on the right road, but she should be patient. In the Six, France could say "no" against even the Germans; she could stop policies with which she disagreed, because of the strength of her position. Once Britain and all the rest joined the organization, things would be different. Moreover, the rest of the world would no doubt demand special arrangements, and the enlarged Common Market would not be strong enough to stand them. A

sort of world free trade area might be desirable—but it would not be European. Collecting my thoughts, I said with indignation that what President de Gaulle had now put forward was a fundamental objection in principle to Britain's application. If that was really the French view, it ought to have been made clear at the start. It was not fair to have more than a year's negotiation and then bring forward an objection in principle. De Gaulle seemed rather shaken, and said that I had misunderstood him.

But there had been no misunderstanding at all on Macmillan's part—as de Gaulle would make devastatingly clear only four weeks later. Moreover, there was a second important element in the Rambouillet conversation that played into de Gaulle's hands in his predilection to find reasons to keep Britain out of Europe.

The prime minister was scheduled to fly almost directly from Rambouillet to Nassau in the Bahamas for a meeting with Kennedy, where he intended to discuss a deal to obtain American Polaris nuclear missiles for a new British strategic deterrent force. He explained what he was about to do, and even says that "de Gaulle said he was glad to hear my opinion about an independent nuclear force." But in the discussion, de Gaulle wafted a vague suggestion to Macmillan that perhaps Britain and France might consider jointly developing their own nuclear missile. He was so offhanded that the remark did not even appear in the French notes on the conversation when the British and French exchanged their records, as is customary in such discussions. Nevertheless, it soon became part of Gaullist legend that he proposed nuclear cooperation to Macmillan at Rambouillet, but the prime minister decided to cooperate with the United States instead.

From this gloomy meeting, in chill, damp December weather, Macmillan flew to the sunshine of Nassau to meet Kennedy from December 18 to 21, 1962. Kennedy was not entirely happy to be faced with the British request for Polaris missiles. But the Americans had already let the British down by canceling an earlier joint project to build an airborne missile called Skybolt. The president may also have reasoned that if the United States did not replace Skybolt with Polaris, then the British might indeed decide to get together with de Gaulle on an Anglo-French nuclear program.

So Kennedy extracted a price. He agreed to sell Polaris to the British, who would design and build their own nuclear warheads and their own submarines, provided that the submarines be assigned to NATO command and provided also the British join in the new American pet project of a NATO multilateral nuclear force (MLF). Macmillan agreed to these conditions without much enthusiasm and with some fine-print loopholes. In any event the MLF project eventually sank without a trace.

While at Nassau, Macmillan sent personal reports each evening on his discussions with Kennedy to de Gaulle via the British embassy in Paris. With his bid to join the Common Market clearly hanging in the balance, he sought to keep on intimate terms with de Gaulle in the hope that personal relationships would prevail.

Kennedy then added a further effort to accommodate de Gaulle. When the deal with the British was finally wrapped up, he decided to make the same offer to the French—American Polaris missiles for French submarines provided France would also join the MLF and assign its units to NATO command. Kennedy's biographer, Arthur M. Schlesinger, Jr., says, "this was an entirely genuine proposal, though made public without the ceremony the General might have expected, but the President himself and others—McGeorge Bundy (security adviser) and William Tyler (political adviser) especially—hoped that it might throw the French a bridge back into NATO."

Next Kennedy summoned Ambassador Charles E. Bohlen to Palm Beach to brief him personally on a message for de Gaulle. He was to tell de Gaulle that acceptance of the American offer could well open the way for much closer cooperation in the nuclear field. Bohlen returned to Paris and saw de Gaulle on January 5, 1963. With a certain Machiavellian malevolence, de Gaulle gave the impression that he would think seriously about the proposal, giving the Kennedy advisers a modicum of hope.

But de Gaulle's mind was already made up. He was deliberately lulling his allies until he was ready to act. He had no interest in "a bridge back into NATO." On the contrary, he had at last found his moment, the circumstances and the excuses, for a smashing double-blow at the Anglo-Saxons.

*

A few days after the meeting with Bohlen, it was announced that de Gaulle would hold a news conference at the Élysée Palace on January 14, 1963. Orderly in everything, he had established from the time he returned to power the routine of two major news conferences every year, about six months apart, plus four set-piece television speeches to the nation. He might then add other appearances as the need arose on special issues, during elections, or on ceremonial occasions. His news conferences were stage-managed, with planted questions that he would call for at the outset and then would group and summarize in his own words to set up the subjects on which he wished to lecture France and the world. Almost never was there any quick give and take. The conferences usually lasted about an hour and a half, during which he covered perhaps four to six major topics. He always carefully thought out what he wanted to say, and often he would discourse in great factual detail and precision, always of course without notes. When it was over, what he had said would read in print with the clarity of an essayist who had put thought to paper.

The news conference of January 14, 1963, was probably the most important General de Gaulle ever held, a historic and decisive watershed in the development of his policies. It marked the open and undisguised breach with the Anglo-Saxons; the point at which he moved from ruminations about his major allies into action to implant his own policies for Europe in place of the Atlanticists' policies he had inherited.

Up to the time of the de Gaulle press conference the United States and the nations of Western Europe had worked broadly together for more than a quarter of a century in common purpose and common aims of building and solidifying the

Atlantic Community. When de Gaulle came to power, he left no one in doubt that he did not like a lot of these arrangements, particularly its features of integration, but still the system remained intact and the sense of common purpose seemed to hold. It was in this framework that Macmillan still expected to take Britain into the Common Market and Kennedy thought that his new offer of nuclear assistance to France would stabilize and revitalize the unity of NATO. When the press conference was over, what may have seemed merely dubious and sour rhetoric from de Gaulle had been turned into hard and clear action. There were two policies and two approaches in the Western camp where there had been one before.

De Gaulle first dealt with Britain's bid to join Europe, in much the same language he had rehearsed with Macmillan at Rambouillet:

> Sentiments, as favorable as they might be and as they are, cannot be put forward in opposition to the real factors of the problem. . . . England is insular, maritime, linked through its trade, markets and food supplies to very diverse and often distant countries. Its activities are essentially industrial and commercial and only slightly agricultural. . . . In short, the nature and structure and economic context of England differ profoundly from those of other states of the continent.
>
> It must be agreed that the entry first of Great Britain and then of other states will completely change the series of adjustments, agreements, compensations and regulations already established between the Six. This community, growing in that way, would be confronted with all the problems of its economic relations in a crowd of other states, and first of all with the United States. It is foreseeable that the cohesion of all its members would not hold for long, and that in the end there would appear a colossal Atlantic Community under American dependence and leadership which would soon completely swallow up the European Community.
>
> This is an assumption that can be perfectly justified in the eyes of some, but it is not at all what France wanted to do and what France is doing, which is a strictly European construction. It is possible that Britain one day would come around to transforming itself enough to belong to the European community without restrictions and without reservation, and placing it ahead of everything else. In that case the Six would open the door to it and France would place no obstacle in its path. It is also possible that England is not yet prepared to do this, and that indeed appears to be the outcome of the long, long Brussels talks.

De Gaulle went on to try to apply some soothing balm for the British by saying that "respect due that great state and that great people will not be altered in the least" by the end of the Brussels negotiation, and that "nothing would prevent the conclusion of an agreement of association between the Common Market and Great Britain." And he added rather condescendingly that "it will in any case be a great honor for my friend Harold Macmillan" to have perceived so early of the need to join Europe and to have taken "the first steps along the path that one day perhaps will bring his country to make fast to the continent."

So much for Britain joining Europe. Next he turned to the question of the Nassau agreements and the American offer to supply France with Polaris missiles. He rolled relentlessly on:

> It remains the fact in the light of the Cuban affair that the American nuclear power does not necessarily and immediately meet all the eventualities concerning Europe and France. Principles and realities combine to lead France to equip herself with an atomic force of her own. It is completely understandable that this French undertaking does not appear to be highly satisfactory to certain American circles. In politics and in strategy, as in the economy, monopoly quite naturally appears to the person who holds it to be the best possible system.
>
> It is quite true that the number of nuclear weapons with which we can equip ourselves will not equal, far from it, the mass of those of the two giants of today. But since when has it been proved that a people should remain deprived of the most effective weapon for the reason that its chief possible adversary and its chief friend have means far superior to its own? I can only say that the French atomic force from the very beginning of its establishment will have the somber and terrible capability of destroying in a few seconds millions and millions of men. This fact cannot fail to have at least some bearing on the interests of any possible aggressor.
>
> Undoubtedly no one will be surprised that we cannot subscribe to the Anglo-American Nassau agreement. It does not meet the principle of disposing of our own right of our own deterrent force. To turn over our weapons to a multilateral force under a foreign command would be to act contrary to that principle of our defense policy. This multilateral force necessarily entails a web of liaisons, transmissions and interferences within itself, and on the outside a ring of obligations such that there would be a strong risk of paralyzing it just at the moment, perhaps, when it should act.
>
> In sum, we will adhere to the determination we have made: to construct and, if necessary, to employ out atomic force ourselves. And that without refusing, of course, cooperation, be it technological or strategic, if this cooperation is desired by our allies.

And so it was all over for Kennedy's efforts to come to a nuclear understanding with de Gaulle. Under the US Macmahon atomic secrets act, there was no legal way in which Kennedy could enter into the only kind of "no-strings-attached" nuclear cooperation that de Gaulle was prepared to envisage. By coincidence, the president had also scheduled a press conference in Washington that same Monday, and barely controlling his anger, he struck back:

> President de Gaulle may not believe that the United States' commitments to Europe are good, but Chairman Khrushchev does and Chairman Khrushchev

is right. There may be reasons for a country to wish a nuclear force of its own, and France has put forward its reasons, but in my judgment it is inaccurate and not really in the interests of the Alliance to justify itself on the grounds that the United States would fail to defend Europe with whatever means necessary.

As for the British, they were not going to be fobbed off with an "association agreement" in lieu of Common Market membership. The end came in Brussels two weeks later, when de Gaulle's foreign minister, Couve de Murville, forced the permanent suspension of the negotiations by pronouncing that France no longer saw any hope of their succeeding or any point in going on. Macmillan recorded in his diary in some anguish: "All our policies at home and abroad are in ruins. Our defense plans have been radically changed, from air to sea. European unity is no more; French domination of Europe is the new and alarming feature; our popularity as a government is rapidly declining. We have lost everything except our courage and determination."

Then he went on the air in a television broadcast to the British people in which he had some pretty outspoken things to say about his Old Comrade of Algiers:

> Europe's great conflicts of the past fifty years have generally been brought about by the attempt of one nation, even of one man, to dominate the whole of Europe, to create a sort of sham united Europe, not by agreement or partnership, but by power. We want to stop this happening again. . . . What has happened has revealed a division. France and her government are looking backwards. They seem to think that one nation can dominate Europe, and, equally wrong, that Europe can stand alone. But Europe cannot stand alone. She must cooperate with the rest of the free world, and with the United States in an equal and honourable partnership. That is why we in Britain mean to stand by the Atlantic Alliance.

De Gaulle had struck at his Anglo-Saxon allies decisively and hard, even with a certain evident relish. He had freed himself at last of any pretense of cooperation or keeping in step with allies, any loyalty to or interest in the Atlantic Community. In the wake of his press conference, he rapidly escalated his campaign against NATO and against the policies and supposed hegemony of the United States worldwide. At the same time he deliberately sought to move closer and closer to the Soviet Union, just as he had sought to play with Stalin against Churchill and Roosevelt during the war.

*

One week after the de Gaulle double-veto, Chancellor Konrad Adenauer arrived in Paris for what he rightly intended to be a crowning achievement of his sagacious and skillful fourteen-year rule of the Bonn Republic—the signing of a Franco-German Treaty of Friendship and Cooperation. But the de Gaulle press conference had abuptly altered the whole political context and circumstances in which the signing would take place, as well as the meaning and interpretation that the rest of the NATO Allies would place on what was about to happen. This certainly was what de Gaulle intended. It was a classic example of how men can control events.

De Gaulle, on his state visit to West Germany in September 1962, had first proposed to Adenauer that they institutionalize the working relationship between the two nations with a formal agreement on cooperation. This had been fervently welcomed by Adenauer, not only as a culmination of his own hopes to reach a permanent, historic Franco-German rapprochement. Such an agreement, in Adenauer's view, would also fit logically in the context of the Atlantic Community. It would buttress cohesion and strength both within NATO and within an enlarged European Common Market after Britain joined. But de Gaulle saw it entirely differently. It was his intention that a Franco-German agreement be the instrument of a purely European political cooperation grouping and construction under French hegemony and leadership. The negotiation between Paris and Bonn had been conducted in the closest secrecy. But, equally, de Gaulle had given Adenauer no hint or warning of his intention to veto British entry into Europe and veto the Americans over their MFL nuclear proposal for NATO.

Moreover, de Gaulle's hand was strengthened at the last moment when Adenauer, only ten days before he was due to arrive in Paris, proposed that for German constitutional reasons the agreement they were about to sign be made a full-fledged treaty. De Gaulle agreed at once, to spring another surprise on the Anglo-Saxons.

This was still a closely held Franco-German secret when Adenauer landed in Paris. London and Washington, moreover, were still reeling under the impact of the de Gaulle press conference and worrying about the response they should make. A first priority was to ensure the cohesion and strength of collective purpose of the rest of the NATO Alliance in the face of de Gaulle's double-veto. Therefore it came as another shock, particularly in Washington, that Adenauer was about to sign a bilateral treaty of cooperation with de Gaulle.

When Jean Monnet learned what was afoot, he hurried at once to the Hôtel Crillon, where Adenauer was staying. Monnet knew Adenauer well from the earliest days of the Schuman Plan proposal for the Coal and Steel Community. Now he pleaded with Adenauer to refuse to sign the Franco-German treaty unless de Gaulle lifted his veto over British entry into the Common Market and allowed the negotiation in Brussels to continue, and succeed. But the eighty-seven-year-old chancellor had never been an enthusiast or champion of the British, who were paying yet again the price for their postwar European attitudes. As far as Adenauer was concerned, he was not prepared to put Franco-German rapprochement at risk at this eleventh hour simply to support Britain.

The Franco-German Treaty was therefore signed by Adenauer and de Gaulle on January 22, 1963, in the climax of an extraordinary ten days of postwar European history. In that brief period, de Gaulle had ruthlessly rejected further cooperation with his Anglo-Saxon allies and embraced the chancellor of West Germany to launch a new political alignment on the continent of Europe.

But the appearances soon turned out to be stronger than the reality. When

Adenauer returned to Bonn, the questioning pressures built up from the other NATO Allies—the United States in particular—about which now came first, his loyalty to the Alliance or his new treaty with France and de Gaulle.

This reached a climax when Adlai E. Stevenson, who was then Kennedy's envoy to the United Nations, arrived in Bonn in April and publicly declared that the United States would welcome some clarification of the treaty. This was a direct and open intervention in internal German affairs, but it certainly produced results. A bipartisan group of Bundestag leaders hastily drafted a preamble stating that nothing in the treaty superseded West Germany's commitments and obligations under the NATO treaty, and in this form the treaty was ratified. Adenauer, nearing retirement after his long tenure in office and no longer wielding his old political clout, went along with the preamble although he was not happy about it. De Gaulle was furious with the Germans. The Americans had asserted their "hegemony" and the Germans had put NATO ahead of their treaty with him.

Next, Kennedy himself made a quick trip to Europe in June 1963, to confer with Adenauer and Macmillan and to visit Berlin, where he made his famous and emotional *"Ich bin ein Berliner"* speech. His main purpose was to rally Allied support behind the MLF mixed-manned nuclear ship project in NATO. He would have liked to see de Gaulle, and he sent discreet word to Paris that he would come if invited. But no invitation came. Instead, the Élysée Palace put it out that it was Kennedy's turn to invite de Gaulle to Washington.

De Gaulle had no interest in any appearances of closing ranks with the United States. His response to the Kennedy visit came in the form of an announcement on June 21, 1963, that all units of the French Fleet were being withdrawn immediately from assignment to NATO. Previously, only Mediterranean Fleet units had been pulled out. One month later, in the NATO Council, the French vetoed a proposal put forward by the then secretary-general of the Alliance, Dirk U. Stikker, to set up a special long-range study of NATO's strategy and military requirements.

At a news conference in July, de Gaulle showed some concern about what he called "journalistic ill will" in Franco-American relations, proclaiming: "If there are divergencies between Washington and Paris on the functioning of the organization of the Alliance, the fact that in the event of a general war, France, with the means it has, would be at the side of the United States—and this I believe is mutual—is not in question except in the wanderings of those who make it their profession to alarm good people by depicting each scratch as an incurable wound." But having said that, he went on to elaborate his refusal to have anything to do with the American-British-Soviet nuclear test ban treaty that had just been concluded, and warned sourly: "All the separate negotiations between the Anglo-Saxons and the Soviets, starting with the limited agreement on nuclear testing, seem likely to be extended to other questions, notably European ones, until now in the absence of the Europeans, and this clearly goes against the views of France." Shades of Yalta!

At the end of the summer de Gaulle was scheduled to visit Adenauer in Bonn for the first of the twice-yearly Franco-German summit conferences called for under the new friendship treaty. But his irritation with the Germans over their loyalty to NATO was by now so great that he was already running his own treaty down. To a group of French parliamentarians on the eve of his trip, he remarked: "Treaties are like young ladies and roses. They last while they last." And he went on to quote a line of poetry from Victor Hugo: "Alas, how many young ladies I have seen die."

But when this was relayed to Adenauer in Bonn, the old chancellor adroitly turned the metaphor back around.

"I know quite a lot about roses, for I have raised them all my life," he said. "And the plants which have lots of thorns are the most resistant ones."

*

A few weeks before the assassination in Dallas, Kennedy had a talk at the White House with one of France's leading journalists, Jean Daniel, then foreign editor of the weekly news magazine *L'Express*. Couve de Murville had been in Washington, and Kennedy was in a discouraged but philosophical mood about Franco-American relations. He said to Daniel, who rightly put their talk on the record after Kennedy's death:

> Both Couve de Murville and I had to admit that we were not in agreement on anything. And we both accepted the fact that this total disagreement should not damage the friendship between two great western countries. I have come to the conclusion that the strategy of General de Gaulle, which I do not quite understand, needs a certain tension between France and the United States. Apparently he thinks that only this tension can give the Europeans the will to think for themselves instead of relying lazily on American dollars and political leadership. But we are going to give less and less occasion for France to create this tension.

When Kennedy was assassinated, the outpouring of pro-American sentiment in France was extraordinary. But de Gaulle waited until well into the following day to announce that he would attend the funeral, according to Bohlen "to see what the other leaders did, and when it became clear that the King of the Belgians and the British Prime Minister were going, he decided to go too." In his brigadier's uniform, he walked in the cortege behind the coffin.

But his brief stay was marked by an immediate diplomatic spat with the new president, Lyndon Johnson. In a brief conversation with de Gaulle after the funeral, Johnson warmly renewed a Kennedy invitation for an official visit to Washington that de Gaulle had tentatively accepted for the following April. In a mixup involving both translation and understanding, Johnson thought that de Gaulle had agreed, when he had only made a polite pro-forma response.

Almost immediately, Johnson told newsmen that de Gaulle would be making a Washington visit as planned with Kennedy. Within an hour or two de Gaulle had the French embassy issue a clarification that he had not agreed to come. When he got back to Paris he then elaborated this refusal by adding through his official spokesman that since he was senior in office to Johnson it would be up to the

American president to visit him in Paris first. So they never did meet again—apart from a second rather frigid and brief handshake at the funeral of Konrad Adenauer in Cologne Cathedral in April 1967. Seeking understanding with American presidents was no longer on de Gaulle's agenda.

From this unpromising start, Johnson and de Gaulle were soon at loggerheads. Moreover, by 1964 the Vietnam War was beginning to engulf the United States, and de Gaulle was accelerating his diplomatic efforts not merely to take his distance and independence from Washington, but to oppose Washington openly across the board within the NATO alliance over the MLF proposal, which was still alive, over economic policies, gold and the dollar, in his self-proclaimed leadership of the Third World, and in America's own backyard, Latin America.

With much fanfare he recognized Red China in January 1964—a move regarded in Washington as tantamount to aid and comfort to the American enemy in the Vietnam War. In March he made an official visit to Mexico, where he proclaimed the virtues of independent foreign policy and resistance to hegemony from any power bloc. Johnson sent word that he would be glad to receive de Gaulle in Washington if he wished to stop off on his way back from Paris. But de Gaulle sent word back that he would be glad to receive Johnson on French territory in Martinique—a tit-for-tat to settle that old score over Roosevelt's "summoning" him to Algiers after the Yalta meeting in 1945.

When de Gaulle got back to Paris from his Mexican trip, he made yet another defense of his nuclear policy and dig at the United States, telling a news conference that without its own nuclear arms "France would be relying entirely upon a foreign protectorate, *and for that matter an uncertain one* [italics added], for her defense and thereby for her very existence and policy— No, we are worth more than that!" Two weeks later he announced that France was withdrawing all its naval officers from the various NATO command headquarters. Since the French Fleet had already been withdrawn from assignment to NATO the year before, this was no great surprise. But at the same time, French officers were also withdrawn from SEATO, the Southeast Asia Treaty Organization, military staff at Bangkok.

On the twentieth anniversary of D-Day, the British and Americans thought the occasion would offer an opportunity to smooth things over with a display of Allied amity. Accordingly, joint plans were made with a French veterans' organization for a massive commemoration on the Normandy beaches to be attended by many of the old commanders. But de Gaulle turned his back, refusing to take any notice of the occasion or even allow Premier Georges Pompidou or any other minister except the minister for veterans' affairs to attend. The Americans and British had landed in France without him and they could commemorate their dead without him. Instead, he ostentatiously took Pompidou off to the Riviera on August 15, 1964, to celebrate the twentieth anniversary of the French landings on the Mediterranean coast to liberate southern France.

Then, in September, de Gaulle set off on a month-long trip around South America by air and a French Navy cruiser, taking him to every capital in the hemisphere—something no American president has ever attempted. His theme everywhere was the familiar one of independence from the hegemony of power

368 / CHARLES DE GAULLE

blocs and the emergence of the Third World, with France its most ardent and understanding champion.

Back in Paris in October 1964, de Gaulle opened a concerted effort to scuttle the American MLF nuclear force project in NATO, which Johnson was still pushing nearly a year after Kennedy's death. Brusquely, he put the heat on West Germany's new chancellor, Ludwig Erhard, telling him he had to choose between European unity with France or unity with the Americans over the MLF. Meanwhile, the project, which never had elicited much enthusiasm in Europe, was floundering elsewhere. The Turkish foreign minister made a visit to Moscow and soon after announced that Turkey was abandoning its support. Norway pulled out on the grounds that it wanted nothing to do with nuclear weapons anyway. Finally, under French pressure, the Germans issued a statement in Bonn to the effect that "there is no reason from the German side to press for an acceleration of an agreement on the MLF," which was a polite way of shelving the program. After that, Manlio Brosio, the astute NATO secretary-general, gave a formal opinion to the NATO Council that the multilateral nuclear force could not be deployed within NATO without consent of all its members. At the regular semiannual meeting of NATO foreign ministers held in Paris in December 1964, the Americans threw in the towel, abandoned the effort. De Gaulle did not conceal his satisfaction that he had successfully blocked the Americans on the MLF just as he had opposed the earlier European Army plan.

By now, Lyndon Johnson had come to share Kennedy's view that "General de Gaulle needs a certain tension between France and the United States." But Johnson put his conclusion in characteristically coloquial metaphor: "When General de Gaulle winds up to pitch, I step out of the batter's box."

*

Despite de Gaulle's open and widening breach with the Anglo-Saxons and his espousal of a Europe free of power blocs "from the Atlantic to the Urals," he had not yet attracted all that much response from the Soviet Union. The reality was that even after the Cuban missile crisis—even because of the Cuban missile crisis—Nikita Khrushchev remained a great deal more concerned by and absorbed in his superpower relationship with President Kennedy than he was in fooling around with General de Gaulle. This was manifested in the nuclear test ban treaty, and in Khrushchev's own deep personal reaction to the Kennedy assassination. But when Khrushchev was overthrown in October 1964 and replaced in the Kremlin by Leonid Brezhnev, Soviet interest in de Gaulle began to pick up.

A new ambassador was sent to Paris to replace Vinogradov in April 1965— Valerian Zorin, an odious Stalinist who had run the Communist takeover of Czechoslovakia in 1948, was at the UN during the Cuban crisis and had been the first Soviet ambassador to Bonn when diplomatic relations were established in 1956. He was a hardened senior figure in the Communist Party Central Committee, who regularly turned up on important diplomatic assignments when some turning-point assessment of Kremlin policy might be involved. Soon after Zorin took over the Paris embassy, Foreign Minister Andrei Gromyko arrived on an

official visit to France, which was to pave the way for a de Gaulle visit to the
Soviet Union. Of course men like Zorin and Gromyko had no interest whatsoever
in seeing their power bloc in Eastern Europe dissolve into some vague Atlantic-to-
the-Urals mélange of nineteenth-century independent nation-states. But they
were prepared to listen to de Gaulle and flatter him for casting off the
"hegemony" of the United States in Western Europe and opposing the American
intervention in Vietnam.

Meanwhile de Gaulle opened up a new flank attack on the United States. At a
news conference in February 1965, he called for a reform of the Bretton Woods
world monetary system, with a return to the gold standard as the basis for a new
international financial arrangement. De Gaulle was not the most sophisticated of
men when it came to understanding global economics. He held to simple virtues—a balanced national budget and the fascination of a French peasant with the
possession of gold, "which does not change in its nature, which can be shaped
equally into bars, ingots or coins, which has no nationality, which is eternally and
universally accepted as the unalterable fiduciary value par excellence," as he told
his news conference. Just as he was determined to break out of NATO, so now he
also saw the world strangled by "dollar hegemony," which France must combat.
But he refused to accept that there are other measures of a nation's wealth and the
strength of its currency besides the mere possession of gold. He could not
understand that putting the entire world monetary system back into a straitjacket
based on the price of one metal would disastrously restrict monetary liquidity,
credit flows, economic expansion and world trade. For de Gaulle, it was as if John
Maynard Keynes had never lived and the world needed to get back to where it
was in the 1920s.

Nevertheless, his *démarche* struck an exposed American nerve—as was intended. The financing of the Vietnam War was beginning to have its impact on the
American balance of payments, and American gold reserves were declining. De
Gaulle twisted the screw by announcing two weeks after his news conference that
henceforth France would convert all of its balance-of-payments surplus dollars
and other foreign currency holdings into gold. In due course this meant a physical
transfer of upward of $5 billion from American gold holdings to the Bank of
France.

Next, in June 1965, France withdrew from participation in the tripartite
American-British-French Central Bank gold pool that operated to keep the gold
price pegged at $35 per ounce (what ancient times!). These combined moves
constituted a direct speculative attack against the dollar by the French government—buy gold cheap from the Federal Reserve Bank and then force up the
world market price. But the system remained stronger than de Gaulle—for the
time being at least. Washington responded by launching a policy of demonetizing
gold—treating it simply as another metal on the world market rather than as a
currency base. They gave up free-market intervention to hold down the bullion
trading price while continuing for the time being to maintain a price of $35 in
official dealings.

Nevertheless, de Gaulle had made a hole in the dike of gold that finally burst in

1971, when Nixon was forced to suspend the conversion of dollars into gold and in effect declare this commitment under the Bretton Woods agreement to be finished. By this time, of course, Charles de Gaulle was dead. In the 1970s gold took off on the free market, fueled as well by the oil crisis, and eventually soared past $800 per ounce. This wild fluctuation proved for all time how impossible it would have been to try to go back to basing the world currency system on the gold standard.

Meanwhile there were other jabs for President Johnson. In February 1965 de Gaulle addressed a personal letter of sympathy and support to the Vietnamese Communist leader, Ho Chi Minh, condemning foreign intervention in Vietnam and the escalation of the fighting. It was a letter that Ho Chi Minh would probably have found even more welcome had it been sent by de Gaulle when he was ruling France in 1945 instead of twenty years later.

Then, in May 1965, the French delegate to the United Nations was instructed by de Gaulle to vote with the Soviet Union to condemn the Johnson intervention in the Dominican Republic. The French, of course, could and did point to the fact that the United States had voted with the Soviet Union in the UN against France and Britain at the time of the Suez War in 1956. But in this atmosphere Washington and Paris were scarcely on speaking terms any longer.

De Gaulle's European partners were by no means immune from his scorn and attack. He barely concealed an attitude bordering on contempt for Ludwig Erhard. Although he went through the motions of twice-yearly Franco-German summit meetings as called for in the treaty he had signed with such a flourish in January 1963, these had become mechanical exercises for de Gaulle because the Germans palpably declined to share his anti-NATO passion. The United States still mattered more to the security of West Germany than France, and the Germans still held to their European beliefs in supranationalism and integration in the vision of Jean Monnet.

In particular, these German convictions and attitude toward the building of Europe were personified in Dr. Walter Hallstein, who had been Adenauer's confidant and had become the first president of the Common Market Commission in Brussels. In this post, Hallstein was deliberately pursuing policies and programs to enlarge the supranational role of the commission and push the pace of European economic integration to the limits of interpretation of the Treaty of Rome. This put him on a collision course with de Gaulle, who struck back in a ferocious counterattack against the Common Market in July 1965.

Using as an excuse the failure of a round of negotiations in Brussels on common agricultural policy, de Gaulle abruptly announced that France was suspending its participation in all Common Market activities. The French permanent representative was withdrawn from Common Market headquarters, and France began a long boycott of all meetings of foreign ministers, finance and agricultural ministers and all the many Brussels working committees and other consultation meetings. Instead of going on to a new round of agricultural negotiations, de Gaulle simply demanded that the rest of the Common Market bow to France's terms for agreement. At the same time he declared that the Treaty of Rome would have to be amended to get rid of many of its supranational commitments, and less openly he passed the word that he wanted Hallstein replaced as commission president.

But this time he had overplayed his hand. It was one thing for him to feud with the United States over NATO and pull out bit by bit from the Allied military command structure. But it was a different political game when he sought to scuttle France's commitments under the Treaty of Rome. He had taken on some pretty tough-minded and experienced European leaders—in particular Joseph Luns of The Netherlands and Paul Henri Spaak of Belgium. To them, the treaty was almost as sacred as the constitution of the United States is to Americans. They believed in its idealism, Spaak had presided over its drafting, and they were deeply committed to its workings. The other five Common Market partners countered by refusing even to discuss de Gaulle's demands for a treaty revision, and determined to sit him out. Their response was that nothing could be done until France ended its boycott and returned to fulfilling its treaty obligations. A long, long stalemate lasting six months ensued.

At first the French tried to entice the other European partners into a special negotiation on de Gaulle's demands away from Brussels and outside the Common Market framework. But Luns and Spaak saw at once that if they agreed to this they would in effect have been lured into a first concession on changing the Rome Treaty. De Gaulle wanted the benefits of the treaty without its obligations. Yet he could not pull out of the Common Market without direct economic and political damage to France, whether he liked the terms he was saddled with or not. So he found himself outmaneuvered by the silent resistance of his partners. They would neither listen to him nor discuss with him until he ended his boycott, and the longer he boycotted the more it would hurt France.

Meanwhile his first seven-year presidential term was nearing its end. He had fixed December 5, 1965, as polling date for the first round of voting that would be the first direct election of a president by popular mandate in French history. In 1962 he had amended the Fifth Republic constitution to do away with the traditional system of choosing a president through a "grand council of electors"— mayors, members of parliament, city councilors, regional assembly members. Now he would present himself directly to the people, and he had no doubt whatsoever of the outcome.

When de Gaulle launched his attack on the Common Market in July, he probably calculated that the Europeans would knuckle under and give in to his demands and that it would all be over in a matter of weeks, giving him another nationalistic political victory and agriculture agreement to parade before the electorate. Instead, when the other five partners dug in their heels, his boycott began to backfire politically. By the time the presidential campaign got under way, his opponents had an issue of principle as well as national interest, in which de Gaulle was increasingly seen to be not only pretty highhanded with France's closest partners, but also wrong.

Despite seven years of Gaullist scorn and diatribe about integration and su-pranationalism, there was still a lot of European idealism in France. Jean Monnet was not dead and his intellectual influence was still very much alive. If de Gaulle insisted on staging boycotts and feuds with the Europeans as well as the Anglo-Saxons, what friends would France have left? As Jean Lecanuet, presidential candidate of the old MRP Catholic Party, said in a windup campaign speech: "We will avoid the fate of being a satellite of Russia or the foreman of the American bosses only if we are part of the power of a European camp." But de Gaulle plunged toward re-election full of confidence, with his power still cresting in the land and no one of any comparable stature opposing him. To him, the European issue seemed politically insignificant, as he sought to turn it upside down and convince the voters that he was, as always, acting in the national interest of France. He asked the French for "a massive vote of confidence."

He did not get it. On the first round of balloting, de Gaulle drew only 44 percent of the votes cast—a considerable blow to his prestige, and more especially his political *amour propre*. Of his five opponents on the ballot paper, the runner-up was François Mitterrand, at the head of a combined left ticket with both Socialist and Communist backing. Mitterrand finally became a de Gaulle successor as president of the Fifth Republic sixteen years later in the election of 1981.

De Gaulle had fully expected an outright majority victory over the entire field on the first round of voting. He was taken aback, embittered and angry at the result. There were even rumblings from the Élysée Palace reaching the press the morning after that he was so infuriated with the French voters for inflicting this humiliation that he might withdraw once again from public life altogether.

He waited three days before informing his Cabinet that "naturally" he would be a runoff candidate on the second round of voting on December 19, 1965. He then dropped his rather aloof campaign manner of the first round and came out fighting with a combative television appearance, an interview program with hand-picked journalists, always his most effective form of political dialogue and projecting himself to the French. The runoff was never in doubt.

The final result was a comfortable 54 percent victory for de Gaulle over Mitterrand, and a second seven-year term to last through 1972. The first-round setback was wiped out, or at least so it seemed. His mandate of power had been renewed, unimpeded and unchecked by domestic political restraints. But when de Gaulle started his second term of office, he was no longer quite as tall as he had been.

NINETEEN

ALONE AT LAST, 1966–67

As a first act of his new term of office, President de Gaulle dispatched his foreign minister, Maurice Couve de Murville, to a Common Market meeting in Luxembourg in January 1966 to end his six-month boycott and patch up the counterproductive and politically damaging feud with his European partners. But there would be no revision of the Treaty of Rome as he had demanded. Instead some face-saving compromise interpretations of the treaty were arranged. It was agreed that a provision of the treaty to make decisions by majority voting, which technically came into force on January 1, 1966, would be applied only on minor questions. Unanimity—and hence the right of veto—would continue to be the rule on major issues. Everyone also felt that it was time to nudge Walter Hallstein into dignified retirement after seven years as commission president. In future, it was decided, the presidency would rotate among the member States with a maximum term of four years. In future also commission presidents would be expected to behave as the servant of governments and not like the equal of heads of governments. Supranational trimmings would be done away with, for example, in the way commission presidents would receive foreign ambassadors. None of this made any great practical difference in the powers, the functioning or the effectiveness of the Common Market Commission, only its style. But it enabled Charles de Gaulle to satisfy himself that he had succeeded in cutting the Brussels bureaucracy down to size. By the end of February the French had returned to full participation in Brussels, to take up the agricultural negotiation where de Gaulle had impetuously and imperiously broken it off the previous July.

There was an important paradox in this outcome, and a lesson for de Gaulle, whether he accepted it as such or not.

The paradox was that the very economic success France had registered in de Gaulle's first term of office had made the Common Market and economic integration with Europe basic and vital to the nation's growth, expansion and strength in the world. The lesson was that de Gaulle had run up against limits of both power and independence—two elements he cherished above all else.

De Gaulle had lunged out against the Common Market with much the same tactics and the same objectives that he was using with virtual impunity against NATO, seeking to impose his will and force change. If he had come to power any earlier than 1958, there probably would never have been a Common Market, certainly not with the powers and form that he inherited in the Treaty of Rome, already signed, sealed and ratified. But in the end, against the Common Market he shot his bolt. What he gained was largely a victory of shadow, while the substance of the treaty remained intact and unchanged. He had to settle his feud with Brussels because in the end the Common Market was more important to France than Gaullist independence. He found that his fiat of power had run out somewhere between Paris and Brussels.

De Gaulle's interest in economics and the actual running of his country was limited to say the least. As president of France, his focus was almost entirely on foreign policy and creating a role or an impact in the world for France. Naturally a strong France was vital to strong Gaullist foreign policy. But basically the internal management and running of the country and the economy was the domain of de Gaulle's prime ministers—Michel Debré from 1959 to 1962; Georges Pompidou from 1962 to 1968, and finally Maurice Couve de Murville for the last ten months of his rule.

For France, or from France, de Gaulle wanted simple things: strength, order and governmental efficiency first of all, a balanced budget, ample resources for the development of the *force de frappe* and nuclear arms, ready funding of prestige projects such as the Concorde supersonic airliner, generous aid for former French colonies in Africa to keep them dependent and responsive to France's leadership as a kind of French flagship in the Third World. Beyond that, he dealt only with the broad outlines of government economic policy and strategy—budget totals, the balance of spending among various departments, general allocations of funds, priorities for his own pet projects. The rest was up to the prime minister, the finance minister and the able technicians of the French Treasury and the bureaucracy.

During de Gaulle's entire period of power, the industrial world was enjoying the greatest unbroken economic expansion and growth of international trade in all history, with only occasional brief periods of slowdown or national recession here and there. The key to the great expansionist success of the French economy in the de Gaulle years lay not in any innovative Gaullist policies, but simply in the imposition of Gaullist order and the healthy world economic environment. Indeed, the groundwork for France's expansion had been laid under the much-maligned Fourth Republic, through the work of the Commissariat du Plan under Jean Monnet, through effective use of Marshall Plan aid and direction of government investment in the postwar recovery period, and then through creation of the European Coal and Steel Community, which began opening up the wide vistas of trade expansion across practically the entire Western European continent. In the eight years from 1949 to 1957 before de Gaulle's return to power, French gross national product increased by 50 percent and French living standards by 22 percent. This expansion then continued at almost the identical rate for the next ten years under de Gaulle from 1958 to 1968, when gross national product rose by another 63 percent.

Meanwhile, France's European partners—West Germany, Italy and Benelux—were all registering much the same record of economic growth in the expansionist decade of the 1960s, with varying ups and downs. The French economic success was therefore neither exceptional nor was it any particular achievement of Gaullist policies—except the political atmosphere of de Gaulle's firm and autocratic leadership and rule, the essential condition of stability in which growth and expansion could confidently be pursued by both government and industry. To begin with, the growth rate in France that began in the Fourth Republic could never have been maintained if de Gaulle had not returned to the scene to extricate the nation from the Algerian War and transform the French Empire into an association of self-governing (but dependent) states. Once the Empire was converted from a political liability into an asset, once the Algerian abscess was drained from the French economic and political body, the economy basically was sound and well run, and more or less took care of itself, with firm direction at the top to be sure but without much innovation, prodding or special measures beyond good technical management.

At the same time, profound and far-reaching changes were taking place in the structure of French society and the French economy. A slow transformation, or evolution, of France from a largely agricultural economy into a modern industrial state began to accelerate. After World War I, over 9 million Frenchmen worked the land, and in 1946 after World War II there were still 7.5 million French farmers, 36 percent of the work force. But by 1968 this had dropped to 3 million, down to 15 percent of the work force, and today it is below 8 percent.

In the de Gaulle decade from 1958 to 1968, French exports increased from 10 percent of gross national product to 15 percent. Today France is the fourth-largest exporting nation in the world behind the United States, Japan and West Germany. When de Gaulle returned to power, the French colonies were taking well over one-third of French exports, with only 22 percent going to her neighbors in Europe. But by 1968, thanks to the Common Market, 43 percent of French exports were being sold in Europe, with Germany by far the predominant customer, and exports to the former colonies were down to 13 percent of the total. With steady economic growth averaging about 6 percent annually, France passed Great Britain in 1963 in per capita income, and today the French enjoy nearly double the average income per head of population of the British.

Movement from farms into cities, movement into new service industries, movement from traditional markets into new markets, movement from protectionism to free trade within the Common Market, the arrival of new large immigrant contingents from Algeria, Africa, Spain and Portugal to take up the slack supply at the bottom of the labor market all added up to a dynamic change in French society. But most volatile of all was the big push upward of the postwar baby boom. Before World War II, the French university student enrollment averaged about 60,000 in a population of 42 million. But by 1958 this had already swollen to 175,000 students—and in the ensuing decade this became a true population explosion. By 1968 the university enrollments had reached 500,000 out of a total population of 50 million—more than tripling in a single decade.

As de Gaulle's second term of office began, the French university system was heading into a state of crisis, almost a breakdown of overloaded teaching staffs, ancient buildings, lack of amenities and facilities, and the growing demands of France's burgeoning middle-class society with its increasing wealth and social expectations.

But de Gaulle's eyes were on the horizons and not the sidewalks. In the soaring confident atmosphere of economic expansion of the mid-1960s, it was easy to assume that continuous growth in the end would take care of everything from university buildings to annual overproduction of artichokes. Because politics and political parties played no role at all in the direction of the French government in the de Gaulle years, there was no political early-warning system against the pressures building up as a consequence of the successes of expansion and growth. True, there was a Gaullist Party in the National Assembly, the Union for a New Republic (UNR), and there was a strong Gaullist political movement and organiza-tion in the country at large. But de Gaulle himself remained fiercely aloof, above party, disdaining politics. Politics, like the running of the economy, was the province of the prime minister. All de Gaulle wanted of the UNR was loyalty and votes in the National Assembly—not advice. He chose his ministers for personal loyalty, not party rank or standing or political influence. Behind the ministers was the powerful and efficient civil service—the real instrument of Gaullist power in running France.

Moreover, when de Gaulle returned to power in 1958, a new elitist group was just beginning to emerge at the top of the civil service—a group that in a sense was his own creation, the graduates of the École Nationale d'Administration (ENA) that de Gaulle founded in Paris after the liberation in 1945. Just as Napoleon created the famous École Polytechnique in 1802 to train a new breed of military officers in the sciences of engineering, so de Gaulle saw the need to produce a new elite trained in modern government administration. In part the aim was to supersede and neutralize the collaborationist image that clung to the bureaucracy after the Vichy period by bringing an entirely new generation, a new layer of professionals, rapidly to the top of the civil service.

Establishment of the ENA, entrusted in 1945 to Michel Debré as the school's first director, turned out to be one of de Gaulle's most far-reaching decisions. Only about 100 students a year are admitted to the school, after the most rigorous sifting of thousands of application examinations. At the end of a three-year course, an ENA diploma guarantees immediate placement among the top specialist ranks of the civil service. Only by graduating from ENA, for example, is it possible to enter the French diplomatic service or become an *inspecteur des finances* and join the inner circle of the French Treasury. By 1958 the early postwar crop of *énarques,* as the graduates are called, had begun to reach the upper levels of the civil service. One was Valéry Giscard d'Estaing, who graduated in 1952, became an *inspecteur,* was named by de Gaulle the youngest finance minister in French history in 1959, and then eventually was elected president of France in 1974. Today, as de Gaulle intended, *énarques* infuse the entire French power structure. Virtually all the French ambassadors overseas are now ENA graduates. All the top administrative positions in government departments are filled by ENA men, as are all the senior personal staff advisers to Cabinet ministers. Outside the government, ENA graduates are on the boards of all the big banks and all the nationalized industries such as Renault automobiles, the steel, gas, electricity and nuclear industries, Air France and the aircraft manufacturer Aérospatial. The *énarques* are a formidable power elite with influence far exceeding their numbers. Even today there are not yet 4,000 ENA graduates since 1946, but the ENA diploma is the brass ring of success on the French merry-go-round.

Gaullism and a strong civil service went hand in hand. Under the General, the prime minister functioned as an efficient chief of staff to a commanding officer, and below the civil servants were the subordinate unit commanders, nominally under Cabinet ministers but largely responsible for carrying out the power orders from on high.

The virtual absence of any "political factor" in the process of government decision-making while de Gaulle was in power was a dreamworld come true for civil service planners. As one example, for years successive French governments looked at plan after plan from the civil service to move the wonderful but hopelessly outdated, inefficient and overcrowded central fruit and vegetable market out of Les Halles in the heart of Paris. But no government ever lasted long enough to have the time and political will to take the decision. When de Gaulle came to power, at last a decision could be taken. Planning was approved and funds flowed without interruption to build a vast new wholesale produce market with modern refrigerated warehouses and railroad sidings and trucking facilities alongside a main highway on the outskirts of the city near Orly Airport. The project took eight years to complete. There were tears of nostalgia from the lovers of early-morning onion soup when Les Halles at last went out of business late in 1968, but after a century and a half in the center of Paris, it could no longer properly supply the growing city.

Regional investment and development and distribution of industry were stimulated along with the great projects that began moving for Paris. Planning and construction got under way on an eight-lane Boulevard Périphérique that rings the capital, dipping under a lake in the Bois de Boulogne. The vast redevelopment of the La Défense area at the edge of the city began, transforming a nondescript residential district into a high-rise office complex to take the commercial pressure off the heart of Paris. Land acquisition, planning and start of construction were authorized on the huge new airport to the north of Paris that today bears Charles de Gaulle's name. Beneath the city, work began on the high-speed Métro lines tunneled below the existing system, which then rise to the surface and serve the Paris suburbs east, west, north and south with the finest public transportation network of any major city in the world.

Most striking to visitors to Paris in the 1960s was the cleaning and scrubbing of the city's splendid buildings, an enforcement by the de Gaulle government of a city ordinance long on the statute books but ignored or forgotten during the Fourth Republic. De Gaulle galvanized and invigorated his country in many ways, and this cleaning of the Parisian buildings and monuments became part of the transformation of France, both practical and symbolic. His exercise of power, permeating to the roots of France, stimulated a whole new tone and vigor to the life of the nation, wiping away at last the chagrin of military defeat and the shambles of political incertitude.

*

With the tone of the national confidence and purposeful vigor went Gaullist grandeur and pageantry. Charles de Gaulle remained extremely modest in his personal tastes and living habits—no extravagance, no wealth, no display, no luxury, no ostentation. But he could slip on the robes of state with the royal *grandeur* of Louis XIV. Scarcely a month seemed to go by without the Champs-Élysées being festooned with a new set of banners, and the mounted band of the Garde Républicaine jogging and jangling by to escort some visiting potentate up to the Arc de Triomphe for a wreath-laying ceremony at the tomb of the unknown soldier. De Gaulle planned and supervised these visits in close detail. Equally, the social rituals of the Élysée Palace were an integral part of the exercise of power. Who was invited and who was not was watched the way stockbrokers follow profit-and-loss statements. The length of time de Gaulle would accord a guest passing in the receiving line, whether he would recognize a person, the form of greeting he would use, the names he would remember, and the hidden meanings and significance of his brief and often pointed or cutting remarks were all matters of animated observation and discussion.

As in the days of absolute monarchy, citizens approached the throne always with a mixture of excitement and apprehension. De Gaulle's power and authority were absolute over those who served him, and a deliberate element of fear was part of his exercise of power. On one occasion, an information chief from the Foreign Ministry went through a receiving line at the Élysée Palace to be greeted by de Gaulle by name, and the remark: *"Faites attention, vous parlez beaucoup!"* (Watch out—you talk too much.) White and shaken that he must have offended the president of the Republic in some fashion, he went to his superior next morning, told him what de Gaulle had said and submitted his resignation. He was told to forget it, that he should be pleased that the General had greeted him by name, and the rest was only his sense of humor.

An elderly French lady gushed to de Gaulle at a reception that she had been a Gaullist ever since his call to resistance from London on June 18, 1940. "There is one better," de Gaulle said, and then presented his wife to the lady with the remark: *"Madame, voilà la première femme Gaulliste!"*

All of this palace gossip and intrigue was parodied in the humorous Paris weekly Le Canard Enchaîné in a feature column titled "La Cour," which was wittily and often wickedly written in the style of the famous diaries of Saint-Simon of the Versailles court in the days of Louis XIV. "La Cour," avidly read, was one of the few works of facetious *badinage* to survive throughout the entire de Gaulle era. Of course, Charles de Gaulle physically was a godsend to cartoonists. But in France it is generally true that politics is regarded as far too serious a business to be debased by humor. Along with scrubbing the buildings of Paris, there was also an extraordinary rise in the enforcement of a law of 1881, making it an offense punishable by fine or imprisonment to insult the head of state.

It is impossible to know the extent to which de Gaulle himself inspired the sharp rise in prosecutions under this law or how much was the work of overzealous Gaullist officials in the Ministry of Justice. But the facts are that in sixtynine years of the Third Republic there were only six convictions under the act, and in fourteen years of the Fourth Republic there were only three. But in the ten years of de Gaulle's rule from 1958 to 1968 there were more than 350 convictions, including writers, cartoonists, publishers and even ordinary citizens who booed when the General came on the movie screen or shouted "Down with de Gaulle!" when his motorcade drove down the Champs-Élysées. A manufacturer of ashtrays who produced a model in an unflattering form of de Gaulle's face had his entire stock confiscated and was fined 5,000 francs. A well-known French author, Alfred Fabre-Luce, an unreconstructed Vichyite, published a book in 1962 titled *Haute-Cour* (published in English as *The Trial of Charles de Gaulle*), in which the General was portrayed on trial in a High Court for his breaches of French law and the constitution from 1940 on—a parody of the Pétain trial. He was convicted of insulting the head of state and the entire stock of his book was confiscated, although he was fined only a nominal sum. His publishers then cleverly retaliated against the State by publishing a transcript of the trial in book form with a preface by the convicted author.

Certainly there was no lack of free speech or free thought or political freedom in France under de Gaulle. Nonetheless, apart from the period of Pétain and Vichy fascism, not since Napoleon III in the mid-nineteenth century was the law so assiduously applied to shield a head of state from public offense.

The de Gaulles were a very straitlaced couple. In rectitude and morality, the atmosphere they created was more like the court of Queen Victoria than that of Louis XIV. Madame de Gaulle, known colloquially to the French as "Tante Yvonne," was reputed to censor the invitation lists at the Élysée Palace to ensure that no one was received if there was a divorce or scandal in his or her background. Equally it was said that she held a veto over the General's appointing anyone to his government who was divorced. Madame de Gaulle never gave a press interview in her life, or permitted the private living quarters of the Élysée Palace to be photographed. She was totally self-effacing and utterly simple in her tastes and routines. She was a close reader of newspapers and magazines, and she loved to knit—and those were her principal occupations. She had her close and closed family circle but no friends of her own outside, no bridge games, no social life except at the General's side. Even her clothes for official functions, purchased mostly from the fashionable Paris dressmaker Jacques Heim, were vetted by her husband. Petite and plain, she was not a Frenchwoman who stood out in a crowd or was readily recognized, and she shopped regularly on her own and largely unnoticed at fancy food-stores around the Place de la Madeleine, or at the very bourgeois department store Au Bon Marché, where she had bought clothes and household needs ever since the early days of her marriage. Her food shopping was usually for small specialties to round out the weekend table at Colombey-les-Deux-Églises or for the dinners she shared alone with the General in their private apartment in the Élysée Palace. In particular she would often buy a couple of obscure cheeses that her husband liked, a strong reddish cheese from northern France called *mi-mollette* and a hard blue cheese made from sheep's milk from the southwest, *brebis de Pyrénées*.

"In the early days it must have been hell for her," a retired French general who knew de Gaulle from his years as a cadet told a Gaullist chronicler. "He was then very like the man he was in later life—regarding himself as a superior being, above all petty contingencies. The difference was that whereas he became president of France, then he was an obscure colonel whose theories were largely ignored, and who was disliked by most of the General Staff for his arrogance and his rudeness. At home he was practically a tyrant."

But in later years, particularly after his return to power, Charles de Gaulle played the grand paterfamilias in the privacy of his own home at Colombey-les-Deux-Églises. His family circle all speak of his affection and solicitousness for his grandchildren, the stimulation and humor of his conversation, his attention to details about the house and garden, an atmosphere of warmth and relaxation in his company that others, outsiders, seldom if ever saw. Nevertheless, this side of de Gaulle was a compartmentalized role that he would assume as family duty when the occasion presented itself, and then return abruptly to the impersonal role of head of state. Moreover, even as he played paterfamilias, the family kept a certain distance, followed fairly precise routines in his company and observed household protocol.

Privacy at Colombey-les-Deux-Églises was complete, the routines simple and unchanging. Every weekend when de Gaulle was not traveling or officially engaged, and every summer from mid-July to the end of August, he would head for his country home. There was a cook, a housemaid and de Gaulle's official chauffeur. The garden was looked after by a man from the village. Security was largely unobtrusive but complete. An *aide de camp* would also stay at the house if needed.

La Boisserie, today open to the public, is a comfortable home but scarcely spacious or imposing. Apart from rooms for servants, there are five main bedrooms, but only one full bathroom with tub. Bedrooms were set aside for de Gaulle's son and daughter and their spouses and children. Often there would be a big family weekend meal with in-laws and grandchildren, but seldom did others penetrate. Madame de Gaulle liked to drive her little French car in the country, and usually did her own shopping in the village, making the rounds of the butcher, the baker, the *épicerie* for groceries.

In the morning, de Gaulle was served a *petit déjeuner* in his bedroom. He would read the morning newspapers and then dress and go to his study to continue reading or tend to paperwork or write letters or prepare a speech or press conference. When he finished whatever tasks he had allocated to himself, he would join the family for lunch. He was a substantial eater, although not greatly interested in food, rapidly disposing of whatever was put in front of him without much comment or appreciation. Still, his wife saw to it that the menu followed his likes, and adventurous or elaborate French dishes outside the routine were avoided.

After lunch he and Yvonne and sometimes others of the family would be driven to some nearby beauty spot where they would then walk in the woods and hills and fields for an hour or so. After years of residence and years of walking near Colombey-les-Deux-Églises, he knew every footpath for miles around. He liked to gather mushrooms in season on his walks, in particular the pungent *girolles* for the family table. But if grandchildren were with him, they were forbidden this pleasure because they might not know what was edible and what was not.

Back in his living room, he would sometime settle down to a card table for a game of solitaire—to his own rules, as in most things de Gaulle did. His son-in-law, General Alain de Boissieu, has related:

> The card-table was a place where he relaxed, and when he was playing cards nobody could speak to him. For success, he had his own system with his own rules, which allowed him to obtain good results without too much difficulty. Thus he could preserve his *liberté d'esprit* [contentment]. But he kept his statistics all the same. He had a little box containing a sheet of graph paper where he inscribed his wins and his losses. He compared his percentages daily, but he told us that from one week to the next the averages were practically the same.

In the evening before dinner, he always watched the television news at 8 P.M. After dinner he would often have a small armagnac or cognac. Very occasionally he would drink a scotch and water. He usually retired by 10:30 or 11 P.M. Never in his life, except occasionally during the war years and once in the Algerian crisis of 1961, was he ever disturbed at night after he had gone to bed.

*

The two major items on Charles de Gaulle's agenda for 1966 after settling his differences with the Common Market were France's final withdrawal from NATO military cooperation and his long-contemplated visit to the Soviet Union. NATO clearly had to be dealt with first. It would not look good for General de Gaulle to go to Moscow and *then* announce such a decisive break with his Western Allies. On the other hand, it would be propitious from his standpoint to prepare for his Moscow visit by freeing himself finally from his NATO military commitments and doing his bit once again to "dissolve the power blocs." He had similarly paved the way for his visit to Moscow in 1944 to meet Stalin by first granting a pardon to French Communist leader Maurice Thorez for desertion from the French Army so Thorez could return to France from his wartime haven in the Soviet Union.

Ever since 1958, de Gaulle had steadily pursued his policy of "being in NATO less and less." By early 1966, the American embassy in Paris was aware that studies were under way at the Quai d'Orsay on a possible French request for changes in the various Franco-American bilateral agreements on American bases and stationing of troops in France. But in a conversation with Ambassador Bohlen in late January, de Gaulle took a deliberately misleading line. "I will do nothing precipitate. We shall take our time on this and examine everything closely, but I shall certainly do nothing suddenly," he told Bohlen, who adds: "Once again I was fooled by de Gaulle."

Three weeks later, at a new conference on February 22, de Gaulle talked about wanting all NATO headquarters and foreign troops out of France by the end of the first twenty-year period of the NATO treaty, which would have put the deadline three years hence in April 1969. But he couched this more as a warning than an edict, and still he had done nothing precipitate. Then, on the weekend of March 7, he retired to Colombey-les-Deux-Églises to prepare the final blow.

De Gaulle's study at Colombey was on the ground floor of a hexagonal tower he had added to the old stone house after the war. From a straight-backed armchair with a red-leather seat at a red-topped table-desk in the Second Empire style that had been crafted for him after he left office in 1946, he had a view out across his garden and the silent rolling countryside. Here on that weekend he wrote out in longhand a personal letter to President Johnson. (He also wrote in hand in similar terms to the heads of government of West Germany, Great Britain and Canada, which then had troops stationed in France, but in a typical touch he sent only a typewritten letter to the Italian premier.) He returned to Paris, and on Monday, March 8, Bohlen was summoned by Foreign Minister Couve de Murville to the Quai d'Orsay and handed the de Gaulle letter in a regal green-leather flat folder, in the style of a monarch communicating with a fellow sovereign. Bohlen read only a few lines, and then looked at Couve de Murville and said: "This is a sad day. I will not attempt to argue the case with you now, but I am saddened to have to transmit this message to my President."

De Gaulle's letter said:

> In three years our Atlantic Alliance will complete its first term. I am anxious to tell you that France appreciates the extent to which the solidarity of defense thus established between fifteen free peoples of the West contributes to assuring their security, and especially what essential role the United States of America plays in this respect. Accordingly France intends from now on to remain party to the treaty signed at Washington on 4th April 1969. This means that, except in the event of developments which might occur in the course of the next three years to change the fundamental factors of East-West relations, she will be, in 1969 and thereafter, determined, even as today to fight at the side of her allies in case one of them will be the object of unprovoked aggression.
>
> However, France considers the changes which have taken place or are in the process of occurring since 1949 in Europe, Asia and elsewhere, as well as the evolution of her own situation and her own forces, no longer justify insofar as that concerns her the arrangements of a military nature adopted after the conclusion of the alliance, whether in common under the form of multilateral conventions or whether by special agreement between the French Government and the American Government.

It is for this reason that France proposes to recover the entire exercise of her sovereignty over her territory, presently impaired by the permanent presence of allied military elements or by constant utilization which is made of her air space, to terminate her participation in the "integrated" commands and no longer place her forces at the disposal of NATO. . . .

The de Gaulle letter was translated and transmitted urgently from the Paris embassy to the White House, where it arrived very early Monday morning. Johnson sent an immediate brief acknowledgment that same afternoon. He told de Gaulle that he was initiating immediate discussions with the other NATO Allies and added that "I would be less than frank if I did not inform you that your action raises grave questions regarding the whole relationship between the responsibilities and benefits of the Alliance."

But the Quai d'Orsay moved into high gear to implement de Gaulle's decision with a series of formal notes and aide-mémoires of concrete action to the United States and the other principal Allies. These announced that five bilateral agreements with Washington were being unilaterally abrogated by France. The Allies were informed that at the end of the month all French officers would be withdrawn from SHAPE outside Paris and from all other NATO commands as well. On April 1, 1966, French forces in Germany and elsewhere would cease to come under NATO command. The Allies were given one year from that date to remove SHAPE and all other NATO headquarters, bases, foreign troops and storage depots and clear out of French territory.

A considered reply on all this from Johnson to de Gaulle on March 23 had an almost wistful quality about it:

I am puzzled by your view that the presence of allied military forces on French soil impairs the sovereignty of France. Those forces have been there at French invitation pursuant to a common plan to help insure the security of France and her allies. I have always viewed their presence as a wise and far-seeing exercise of French sovereignty. . . . We do not intend to ignore the experience of the past 20 years. Indeed we find it difficult to believe that France, which has made a unique contribution to western security and development, will long remain withdrawn from the common affairs and responsibilities of the Atlantic. As our old friend and ally, her place will await France whenever she decides to resume her leading role.

But once again de Gaulle had presented his allies with a *fait accompli,* and there was nothing to discuss or negotiate. Bohlen returned to Washington for consultations and found, particularly at the Pentagon, that there were those who wanted to challenge de Gaulle, primarily on the technicality that France's bilateral agreements with the United States provided for two years' notice of termination. But Bohlen argued that there was not the slightest possibility of budging de Gaulle, and to challenge him would only make a bad situation worse. Johnson agreed, and gave firm orders to clear out of France lock, stock and barrel—a vast logistical operation involving shifting some 800,000 tons of supplies and equipment to new depots and bases in Britain, West Germany and Benelux. Meanwhile the Belgians offered a site for a new Supreme Allied Headquarters near the city of Mons. A German contractor undertook construction work at top speed. On March 31, 1967, de Gaulle's deadline was met. To the roll of drums from a British military band, fourteen flags of the Atlantic Alliance were lowered for the last time in front of the Paris SHAPE headquarters and raised the next morning at the new headquarters in Belgium. On de Gaulle's orders the French flag had disappeared the year before.

General de Gaulle's expulsion order had not directly affected the political headquarters of the Atlantic Alliance, but the Allies soon concluded collectively that he was no longer a friendly or hospitable landlord. Therefore the NATO Permanent Council of Ambassadors and the Secretariat of the Alliance moved out of Paris the following year to a new headquarters complex near Brussels, where it continues to function today in its fourth decade—the longest any alliance has ever lasted in peacetime history.

As disruptive and even destructive as de Gaulle's final blow against NATO had been, the treaty and its institutions were stronger than France. In the long run it could even be said that NATO gained in cohesion and effectiveness after France's withdrawal. For the military planners, the loss of a direct French contribution and commitment in common defense, and the loss of the use of French territory were setbacks and a handicap, but this was not fatal to the effective forward defense of Western Europe. By walking out of the NATO military structure, de Gaulle removed his own thorn from the side of the Allies—and a very large thorn it had been. NATO ministerial meetings in the 1960s had regularly turned into semian-nual semantic catfights between France and the rest of the Allies over the wording of every paragraph of the final communiqués—with Couve de Murville under implacable instructions from de Gaulle to reject any text or declaration that in any way implied a NATO role in French foreign policy or any remote or imagined infringement on French independence. French officers assigned to NATO head-quarters were equally kept on a short lead and marked down if they showed too much enthusiasm for integrated defense.

Initial shock and regret over de Gaulle's action gave way to a certain sense of relief as the rest of the Allies settled into their new political and military headquar-ters in Belgium to get on with the business at hand without the French. Some important reforms and changes were carried out in the organization to improve the integrated military structure—changes that could never have been attempted while France was still "cooperating" with the command. In the end, as de Gaulle insisted that France would play only by its own rules, it was better all around that she withdraw and play alone.

*

General de Gaulle was alone at last. But from the time he withdrew France from the military side of the NATO Alliance, his foreign policy became more and more like one of those famous French son et lumière productions of music, lights and historical narrative that are regularly performed against the façades of its cathedrals and famous buildings. De Gaulle moved from one stage to the next in a kind of diplomatic *mise en scène* of official visits, press conferences, public declarations, speeches and private advice to the world that regularly captured headlines, dramatized and entertained. But at the end, each performance then faded, leaving little of substance, while other realities remained, like the cathedrals and châteaux that the *son et lumière* productions are designed to enhance on late summer evenings.

As de Gaulle prepared for his first visit to the Soviet Union since 1944, the first in this new *son et lumière* series, Ambassador Bohlen reported to the State Department in a long analytical dispatch:

> The only basis on which de Gaulle seems to rest his policy is his belief that the Soviets have really changed and have abandoned any idea of military force and further expansion of Communism. Although this suits his purposes, it is hardly necessary to emphasize the extreme weakness of this point, and I may add that almost all Frenchmen that I know who are knowledgeable about Soviet affairs disagree with him with great violence.

Nevertheless, there can be little doubt that de Gaulle was openly playing for some big change or turn in Soviet foreign policy and in the Soviet bloc to match his own breach in the ranks of NATO. He had made this clear in his letter to Johnson when he said that France would remain in the Alliance until 1969 and thereafter "except in the event of developments which might occur in the course of the next three years to change the fundamental factors of East-West relations." So he set off for Moscow in June 1966, prepared to push for changes "in the fundamental factors of East-West relations." But when the *son et lumière* faded on his return, the hard realities that Bohlen cited still remained.

To be sure, de Gaulle was received by the Soviet leadership like no other Western leader since the end of World War II. On a twelve-day visit, he saw and did things never seen or done before. He was the first foreigner ever to witness a space launch from the Soviet space center at Baikonur. He returned to Stalingrad—rechristened "Volgograd" by Khrushchev in 1961—which he had visited when it was in ruins in 1944. Before an audience of Soviet officers assembled in front of the vast war memorial on the heights of the city looking across the Volga River, he delivered an extraordinary lecture on the Battle of Stalingrad without a note. Next in Leningrad on a Sunday he insisted that he must attend Mass, and a Russian Orthodox Church was hastily repainted for the occasion.

And of course he spent hours at the Kremlin in talks with Leonid Brezhnev, Aleksei Kosygin, Nikolai Podgorny and Andrei Gromyko hovering in the background. Here the hard realities of Soviet policy were reiterated and the talks were largely unproductive. The Russians demanded a European peace treaty based on the division of Germany, mutual recognition of the two German States, a special status for West Berlin and continued membership of the two Germanies in the Warsaw Pact and NATO respectively. This of course would merely solidify the division of Europe as it existed, and de Gaulle did not have to travel all the way to Moscow to discover that this was Soviet policy.

But it was not de Gaulle's policy. He countered, according to the account of Couve de Murville, who was present, by seeking to convince the Soviets that the threat to peace arose in Europe because Germany was an area of confrontation for the superpowers. He argued, therefore, that the superpowers should pull back, withdraw their forces from Germany and allow some kind of reunification to develop. This Germany would then be neutralized outside either NATO or the Warsaw Pact and would renounce nuclear weapons and accept existing post–World War II frontiers. Apparently de Gaulle thought this would be a price the Soviets would be willing to pay in order to get a United States withdrawal from Europe.

At best, this was more nineteenth-century romanticism than twentieth-century realism on his part. Moreover, there was absolutely nothing that de Gaulle himself or France could possibly deliver toward such a policy for Germany and Europe except the theory—and this the Russians were not about to buy. The Soviet Union always prefers to hold on to what it has already got. Indeed, did de Gaulle really believe in his own proposal? Is not a divided Germany preferable for France, just as it is for the Soviet Union?

In any case, de Gaulle had once again used the technique of posing an impossible policy in order to establish his own independence. He had done this in 1958 with his triumvirate proposal to Eisenhower and Macmillan, knowing that it would be rejected, thus giving him the excuse to start his disengagement from NATO. Now he proposed to Brezhnev and the Soviet Union a policy for Germany and Central Europe that he must have known they were unlikely to accept. However, if they decided to play along with him, he would achieve one aim. If they rejected his policy or ignored it, as they did, then de Gaulle once again would be seen to be standing independent and alone.

Accordingly, the results of the visit, apart from the *son et lumière,* were meager. There was an agreement to establish a Moscow–Paris hot-line communications link, as a status symbol for de Gaulle to match the Moscow–Washington line. A special bilateral commission was set up to increase trade. Regular political consultation meetings were agreed upon. There was an agreement to collaborate in space research, which eventually lead to a French cosmonaut orbiting in a Soviet space satellite in 1982. All of this was more than enough to fulfill de Gaulle's purpose of the imagery of a new opening to the east in his policy, while retaining or even enhancing his independence.

At the end of August 1966, soon after his visit to the Soviet Union, de Gaulle set off on a trip around the world. It began somewhat embarrassingly when riots and independence demonstrations broke out at his first stopping place in French Somalia on the Red Sea coast. But this was rapidly left behind when he flew on to the Cambodian capital of Phnom Penh. There he addressed a crowd of 80,000 in the city's sports stadium in the company of Prince Norodom Sihanouk, and delivered his strongest public condemnation yet of the American intervention in neighboring Vietnam. It was, he said, "ever more menacing to world peace."

He flew on to the Central Pacific to witness a nuclear test on an island atoll of a trigger device for building a French hydrogen bomb. Back in Paris in October, he told a news conference that "friendship for America has from the beginning led us ceaselessly to try to turn her away from the deadly enterprise" of the Vietnam War.

Meanwhile, Couve de Murville was dispatched to try to water the stony ground of Eastern Europe with de Gaulle's ideas of independence and dissolution of the power blocs. The foreign minister made a round of visits to Prague, Warsaw, Budapest and Bucharest to prepare the way for later possible visits by the General himself. In December Premier Kosygin visited Paris to reinforce the trade and economic ties that de Gaulle was so anxious to foster between the two nations.

By now, NATO and relations with the United States counted for very little any longer in de Gaulle's perspective. His focus was entirely on the East and the Third World. To be sure, NATO and America remained France's distant guarantee of security. In fact, they guaranteed his independence and enabled him to pursue his diplomatic games in the world on the pretext that he was beholden to no power and resistant to all.

*

But at home in France, as the calendar turned into 1967, the country was in an economic slowdown—the first really noticeable check in its long and successful record of sustained growth ever since the days of Marshall Plan aid. Moreover, to a large extent this was de Gaulle's own responsibility, with his rigid and simplistic insistence on balanced budgets, the accumulation of gold reserves, and maintaining a high value for the franc. But the price of a tight economy was a slowdown in investment and growth, and for the first time since the war, unemployment was rising, not falling.

In March the French voters went to the polls to elect a new National Assembly for a five-year term. The result was a major setback for de Gaulle—as decisive as it was unexpected. It was particularly jarring because the Gaullists appeared to be doing well on the first round of voting. But on the second round, the voters unexpectedly switched to opposition or non-Gaullist candidates, and even the Communists gained an extraordinary thirty-two Assembly seats at the expense of the Gaullists. At the end, the Gaullist coalition with the Independent Republicans headed by Valéry Giscard d'Estaing clung to their Assembly majority by only one seat—and that thanks to the overseas vote in Martinique, Guadeloupe and Ré-union.

The voting setback was a clear sign of the unrest and political malaise that burst on de Gaulle and his government in full force a year later. But for the moment it was swept under the carpet when Prime Minister Georges Pompidou, with de Gaulle's blessing, drove through the new Assembly an emergency powers act that permitted the government to rule by decree on economic and social questions for six months. The bill passed by only eight votes. It relieved Pompidou of the tedious problem of fighting the legislature step by step for a series of new economic measures. But it also stored up trouble for 1968 by closing off parliamentary debate and concentrating even greater power in de Gaulle's government—and therefore even greater ultimate responsibility for the declining economic situation, rising unemployment and rising social and political tensions.

But General de Gaulle had other things on his mind. In May 1967, Great Britain again knocked on the door to enter Europe. This time it was a Labour prime minister, Harold Wilson, newly converted to the European cause and determined to show up Macmillan and the Tories. Boldly declaring that he "would not take no for an answer," Wilson dispatched an unambiguous letter of application to Brussels to join the Common Market and accept the Treaty of Rome, and sat back to await the crucial response from de Gaulle.

More immediate for de Gaulle was the deteriorating situation in the Middle East. Egyptian President Nasser had ordered the United Nations peacekeeping force withdrawn from the Sinai and was preparing to close the Straits of Tiran and blockade the Israeli port of Elat. Events were rapidly heading for the Six Day War, which finally broke out on June 5. As tensions mounted, de Gaulle first tried to use his newfound "special relationship" with Moscow to attempt to control events. On May 24 he proposed a special four-power consultation to head off a conflict by imposing a Great Power solution. To his diplomatic embarrassment, his proposal was accepted by Britain and the United States but turned down by the Soviet Union.

Two days later, Israeli Foreign Minister Abba Eban stopped off in Paris on his way to the United Nations in New York and had a stormy confrontation with de Gaulle. At this time the French were still the largest arms supplier to Israel—a continuation of their arms deal that triggered the Suez War in 1956. In particular, French Mirage aircraft were the backbone of the Israeli Air Force. Eban found de Gaulle in a state of some agitation over the prospect of another Middle East war, fearful in particular after his rebuff from the Russians that the superpowers might get sucked into a new confrontation that would endanger peace and security for Europe and the world. He coldly informed Eban that whichever party launched the war would be the guilty party in France's eyes. Eban argued that Egypt was already committing aggression and creating a state of war against Israel, but de Gaulle brushed this aside, since no shots had yet been fired. His final words to Eban were "Do not make war."

On Wednesday, May 31, de Gaulle abruptly announced an immediate suspension of all French arms shipments to Israel. But Pompidou, a former director of the Rothschild Bank in Paris, managed to fiddle the paperwork so that a number of heavily loaded cargo planes still got away for Israel on June 1.

On Monday, June 5, the Israeli Air Force took off with the rising sun to decimate the Egyptian Air Force in the first four hours of conflict. The Mirage fighter-bombers skimmed low over the Mediterranean, well away from the Egyptian coast, and then made a U-turn to swoop back across over land and strike the Egyptian bases from the rear, their aircraft still sitting naked on the runways. The results were devastating, and the war effectively was over by noon, although the ground fighting went on for six days until the Israeli Army was firmly on the banks of the Suez.

This knockout success by the Israeli Air Force, incidentally, triggered quick repercussions in the North Atlantic Treaty forces in Europe. By the end of the year, NATO began preparations for a crash program to build bombproof "hangarets" on its air bases all the way from northern Norway to Turkey, to disperse and protect individual aircraft against the possibility of such preemptive attacks.

Whatever this powerful advertisement for the Mirage, de Gaulle was incensed at the Israelis. He announced to Ambassador Bohlen at their next meeting: "I told Mr. Eban when he was en route through Paris that Israel should not ever have recourse to arms. What do you think they did with my advice? They completely ignored it!" Bohlen commented that if a nation felt its existence was at stake it might find it impossible to follow the best advice with the best intentions, and asked rhetorically: "Suppose you were an Israeli?" To which de Gaulle stiffly replied: "But I am not an Israeli."

Nevertheless, de Gaulle paid an immediate price with French public opinion, which was overwhelmingly on the Israeli side. The provocative acts by Nasser that led up to the conflict had been abundantly clear in the daily headlines, and there was great public outcry over de Gaulle's arms embargo. In particular, this was a last straw with American public opinion and American Jews—not that de Gaulle ever bothered himself much about his public standing in the United States.

But when the dust settled, the central fact was that de Gaulle had used the Middle East conflict as a chance to make yet another decisive break in the foreign policy alignments and posture that he had inherited from the Fourth Republic. Ever since the Suez War, France had been seen in Arab eyes as a leading supporter of Israel and a mainstay of Israeli military strength. It was a position that de Gaulle regarded as unnatural for France, and did not like. In the Six Day War he found his opportunity to change sides with maximum publicity—and from that time on France has continued to be identified preeminently with the Arab cause.

*

General de Gaulle still had another score to settle in the New World as well. Canada in 1967 was observing the 100th anniversary of the establishment of the Canadian Confederation. Along with a succession of other friendly heads of state, de Gaulle had fixed the last week of July for an official visit to mark the occasion—but it was not going to be a very friendly visit. His focus was not on the old British colony that had evolved into a British dominion and then a fully independent member of the Commonwealth. His sole concern was French Canada and Quebec Province, which the French had been obliged to surrender to the British in 1763 after Wolfe defeated Montcalm on the heights of Quebec City. To be sure, the durability and survival of the French Canadians for two centuries had been remarkable—with very little attention from France itself. To de Gaulle, this was a historical wrong that he intended to put right. He therefore carefully arranged his official visit to Canada in a French warship by sea rather than by air, so he would sail up the St. Lawrence (calling at Saint-Pierre and Miquelon on the way) and arrive in Quebec and then visit French-speaking Montreal before going on to the country's capital in Ottawa, where British tradition held sway.

By 1967 the Quebec separatist movement had become the dominant force in provincial politics. De Gaulle was well aware of this and was determined from the time he sailed for Canada to do all that he could to galvanize it toward French-Canadian independence. At the first state dinner on his arrival in Quebec, he praised the *Québecois* as "a people who intend to dispose of themselves and take their destiny in hand in all domains." With this warmup, buoyed by enthusiastic crowds every time he appeared in public, de Gaulle moved on to Montreal on July 24, where a cheering throng assembled in front of the Hôtel de Ville.

He greeted the crowd with his typical gesture of arms outstretched above his head, fists clenched, and told them: "This evening here, and all along my route today, I found myself in an atmosphere of the same kind as that of the Liberation." With this allusion to French Canada as an occupied nation, he wound up his speech with the electrifying cry: *"Vive le Québec libre!"*

If this was not exactly a revolutionary shot heard round the world, it was certainly a cry heard all across Canada. Next day the Canadian Cabinet, under Premier Lester Pearson, spent the entire day discussing how it should react to what amounted to a foreign head of state lending his support to separatism if not insurrection in the country to which he was making a friendly official visit. At the end of the day, a formal statement was issued in Ottawa declaring that de Gaulle had made statements that were "unacceptable" to the Canadian government.

De Gaulle, still in Montreal, immediately ordered his plane to prepare for his return to Paris and canceled the rest of his program to visit Ottawa—no doubt to the relief of his irritated hosts. When he flew into Orly in the early-morning hours of July 27, his entire Cabinet had been rounded up to greet him. Another big *son et lumière* performance was over.

Next he was off to Poland, in September, where he had served as a young officer in 1919–20 when the Poles decisively defeated the Red Army on the Vistula. The Polish regime, like the Canadian government, had reason to be uneasy about their outspoken guest. In Poland above all the states of Eastern Europe, de Gaulle could readily find all those enduring nationalist strengths and fundamental virtues of the nation-state surviving the vicissitudes of history—including communism. In Gdansk he told the Poles: "You are a great nation. You don't need the advice of France. But we hope you will perhaps look a little further and think rather bigger than you have been allowed to do till now. The obstacles that you think are insurmountable today, you will without any doubt surmount them. You know what I mean."

They certainly did. Not once while in Poland did de Gaulle make any reference to the Soviet Union. But at the same time he gave public endorsement—the first from a Western leader—to permanent recognition of Poland's post–World War II frontiers, in particular the Oder-Neisse rivers in the west. This was all pretty heady stuff for Poland—a little too heady for Premier Wladyslaw Gomulka, who told de Gaulle in a private conversation please not to try to rush things—"give us time, do not expect too much, we have to take account of realities."

Back in Paris at a November news conference, de Gaulle turned his full attention to the new British application to join the Common Market, which had been on the table in Brussels for nearly six months. From the outset, the omens for Harold Wilson and his ebullient and unstable foreign secretary, George Brown, had not been good. Frosty politeness was the best they had gotten from the French, but as usual, de Gaulle waited to act in his own good time. For months, the Quai d'Orsay had been applying a kind of negative drip-treatment to the British bid, so that the second de Gaulle veto was scarcely a surprise.

Couching his verdict in terms reminiscent of his first veto of Britain nearly four years earlier, de Gaulle announced that "for the British to link up with the continent, a profound transformation must take place." Unctuously he added that "those, like me, who have proven by their acts the attachment, the respect they feel for England, strongly wish to see her one day choose and accomplish the immense effort which would transform her." Meanwhile he went through a familiar litany of the "incompatibility" of the British economy with Europe, the weakness (then) of pound sterling, the size of the British trade and budget deficit, etc., etc. The British application had been under discussion among the six Common Market members in preparation for a negotiation. This time the French imposed their veto by simply refusing to allow the Common Market to open any negotiation at all. Nevertheless, the application to join from the British Labour Government remained on the table and valid. De Gaulle remarked impatiently to a French visitor: "One day the British will join the Common Market, but I will not be around to see it." It was another of his self-fulfilling prophecies.

As it happened, this news conference on November 27 turned out to be the General's last appearance before the press until long after he was nearly engulfed by the events of May 1968. He had just turned seventy-seven and was in extraordinarily vigorous form and good humor, talking for more than an hour and a half without even a sip of water. He continued to ride some of his old hobby-horses, lashing out at the Yankee dollar, American investment trying to take over Europe, the Vietnam War, the American deficit, and calling again for a return to the gold standard. In particular he delivered a long and colorful defense of his "Quebec caper," blandly outlining his own ideas for a reform of the Canadian constitution, so that Quebec could be "set free" but still avoid "being overpowered by the United States."

But the remarks which burned most deeply and lasted longest from that press conference were the pronouncements that General de Gaulle volunteered about the Jews. It was his first press conference since the Six Day War, and naturally he used the occasion to defend his condemnation of Israel.

> One might ask oneself, in fact, and even many Jews do ask, whether the establishment of this community on territories acquired by more or less justifiable means, and in the midst of the Arab peoples who were fundamentally hostile, would not involve innumerable and interminable causes of friction and conflict. . . . Some have even wondered whether the Jews, who in the dispersion remained what they have always been, *an elite people, self-confident and domineering* [italics added], would not, when once reunited, transform the vaulting ambition of a conqueror into the hopes which they so

392 / CHARLES DE GAULLE

movingly cherished for nineteen centuries: Next year in Jerusalem. . . .
Despite the wave, sometimes rising, sometimes falling, of ill-will provoked,
or more exactly inspired, by the Jews in certain countries and certain
periods, they accumulated a certain balance of interest, even of sympathy, in
their favor, especially, it goes without saying, in Christendom. . . .

It is quite possible that coming from anyone but President de Gaulle, the
description of the Jews as "an elite people, self-confident and domineering" would
be taken on the whole as complimentary, if a little barbed. But from de Gaulle, on
top of his actions in the Six Day War, it suddenly posed a painful question: Was
the French president opening the floodgates of anti-Semitism in France?

David Ben-Gurion, full of anxiety and despair, wrote a fourteen-page letter to
de Gaulle. He got a stiff reply, rebuking Israel once again for "disregarding the
warnings given at the proper time by the French Republic" against going to war,
and declaring: "There was nothing offensive in underlining the character, thanks
to which this strong people had been able to remain themselves after 19 centuries
spent in unheard of conditions."

Raymond Aron, France's most noted political commentator of the postwar era,
next responded with a slim little book entitled *The General and the Jews.*

> I defy any man of good faith [Aron wrote] to contradict me when I say that
> General de Gaulle could not possibly have not foreseen the emotional
> reactions which he provoked. The Jews of France (or rather of the entire
> world) immediately realized the historic significance of the words pro-
> nounced by the President of the French Republic. The anti-Semites received
> from the head of the State the official authority to speak again in the same
> language as before the great massacre. State-approved anti-Semitism at one
> blow became *salonfähig,* as the Germans say. What has been said cannot be
> unsaid. But tomorrow either explanation or silence will establish the ulti-
> mate meaning of the few words which, in part at least, will define the last
> stage of Gaullism.

To accuse General de Gaulle of deliberate anti-Semitism would be far-fetched,
totally out of keeping with his own integrity, intelligence and honor, and his sense
of honor of the French nation. His own father set this example for him by
defending Dreyfus when the whole nation was aroused at the turn of the century.
De Gaulle was not anti-Semitic—but he certainly was insensitive in this as in so
many other matters.

*

At the end of the year, the French chief of the defense staff, General Charles
Ailleret, published an important article in the *Revue de Défense Nationale,* the text of
a lecture he had delivered to the Superior War College. France, it seemed, needed
a new strategic doctrine of defense to go with de Gaulle's alone-at-last posture in
the world, and Ailleret provided it. From now on, he told the War College and

the much wider audience that publication of his remarks was designed to impress, France must be prepared to defend herself *mondial et tous azimuts*—world wide and from all points of the compass.

The last time in history that France had been militarily threatened from "all points of the compass" was in the days of Napoleon, when the forces of Prussia, Russia and Austria closed in from the east while Wellington mounted the Peninsular Campaign in Portugal and Spain to enter France from the southwest. Meanwhile the British Fleet was blockading France in the English Channel, the Atlantic coast and the Mediterranean. Did General de Gaulle and General Ailleret now seriously think that in the days of NATO, more than 150 years later, France had to be prepared to face a military threat from allies in the west as well as from the east? Was the United States threatening to seize the port of Bordeaux, or were the British going to try to land on the Normandy beaches all over again. Yet *tous azimuts* was solemnly declared to be the strategic basis on which the defense of France must now be planned. Once again, the *son et lumière* was more impressive than the reality.

In this baffling French atmosphere of high purpose and artificial mistrust, of fierce independence and gratuitous advice, of hard truths and tenaciously held fallacies, Ambassador Bohlen came to the end of the most difficult five years that any American envoy ever spent in the French capital. Across that time, he had held private meetings with General de Gaulle thirty-two times, an average of once every two months, much more frequently than any other ambassador assigned to Paris. No matter how tense or difficult relations were between Paris and Washington, Bohlen always found de Gaulle "one of the most polite men I ever knew," and their conversations were always conducted on a high plane of mutual respect—considerably enhanced by the fact that Bohlen spoke beautiful and impeccable French. De Gaulle was a great admirer of professionalism, and he did Bohlen the unusual honor of awarding him on his departure France's highest decoration for foreigners, the Grand Cross of the Legion of Honor.

In his own last public appearance in Paris before returning to Washington, Bohlen diplomatically avoided any criticism or expression of anguish about the state of Franco-American relations except to remark rather pointedly that "I think it can fairly be said that the United States has never acted against the interests of France," and let it go at that. He then added in a typical flash of humor: "Of course France possesses one diplomatic advantage that no other country enjoys, and that is the beauty of the city of Paris. It is impossible to live here and walk around this city and stay mad at the French for very long."

But to Secretary of State Dean Rusk, he penned a rather different final appraisal:

> Given the attitude of de Gaulle, there would seem to be very little chance of any real improvement in Franco-American relations. Even if the war in Vietnam is brought to the negotiating table, which should help in public opinion, nevertheless I feel that de Gaulle's basic interpretation of American

power—which compels the French to withdraw from support of us in any given circumstance short of all-out war—really does not offer much hope or room for improvement by actions of the American Government or even by those of the French Government. I can offer little encouragement to any belief in a change in our relations with France until after the departure of de Gaulle.

TWENTY

LA CHUTE, 1968-70

*It is truly with confidence that I envisage for the next twelve months the existence of our
country. . . . In the midst of so many lands shaken by so many jolts, ours will continue to
give the example of efficiency in the conduct of its affairs.*

PRESIDENT DE GAULLE
NEW YEAR'S BROADCAST
DECEMBER 31, 1967

At the apogee of his power as 1968 began, General de Gaulle's view of France and
the world was serene, secure and not a little smug. He looked out loftily on the
political upheavals and economic unrest of others, and saw History moving his
way. He exuded vigor and confidence and relished the unassailable independence
that he proclaimed so ceaselessly toward the rest of the world. In his own domain
there was little he perceived that could not be contained or controlled or cor-
rected by strong government and firm leadership.

Across the Atlantic, the United States was bogged down in the Vietnam War,
racked by growing peace demonstrations, racial disorders and rising student
unrest. Faced with a soaring balance-of-payments deficit, America was forced in
the first week of 1968 to take massive measures to defend the almighty dollar by
curtailing the outflow of overseas investment and even asking American tourists to
stay home. President Johnson, in the face of these multiple pressures, was edging
slowly, reluctantly, but steadily toward the negotiating table with North Vietnam
to begin the process of getting out of a war that America could not win. All this
was observed with a certain sense of historical satisfaction by de Gaulle.

Across the Channel, Prime Minister Wilson, rebuffed by de Gaulle in his bid to
join Europe, had also given up fighting to protect pound sterling with bravado and
little else. Britain had finally been forced to devalue its currency. Against the
Anglo-Saxons, the French were accumulating gold, and the franc looked strong
and steady.

Across the Rhine in West Germany, a new coalition was in power, with Socialist Willy Brandt as foreign minister, and a dynamic new force on the European scene. Although Brandt's new *Ostpolitik* opening to the east would clearly take the initiative from de Gaulle's efforts at *détente* with the Soviet Union, here was the birth of a new German policy that was both European and independent and not overly welcomed in Washington. It therefore had de Gaulle's blessing. De Gaulle said to Brandt in a wide-ranging conversation on December 15, 1967:

Communism as an ideology has, after all, substantially declined. Russia has changed and is bound to change. France is trying to take advantage of this. She is entering into contact with Russia, striving for *détente* and even, perhaps, for practical cooperation. It is above all the best policy for Western Europe and, in my view, the best policy for Germany as well. If Germany so desires, France will help her along this path. . . .

The prime essential is that each country should have a policy of its own. France must have a French policy and Germany must have a German policy and it is up to Germany to create one. A French or German or British policy which was an American policy would not be a good policy. France is not opposed to America. On the contrary, she is America's friend, but nothing can be worse for Europeans than an American hegemony which enfeebles Europe and prevents the Europeans from being themselves. Such a hegemony also hinders agreement with the East—in fact, it hinders absolutely everything. The Americans are Americans, not Europeans. I realize that the Alliance with the United States was concluded at a time of acute danger. The Alliance is still justified today, though to a smaller extent, because one must always be careful. But the situation has changed, and American hegemony inhibits faith in self and inhibits others from faith in the countries of Europe. It has to be realized that France exists, and Britain and Germany. . . .

Across the Elbe in Eastern Europe, de Gaulle could also see beginning to stir beneath the suffocating conformity of communism and Soviet hegemony those historic forces of nationalism and a reassertion and reappearance of the life of nation-states, as he had long espoused in his "Atlantic to the Urals" vision of Europe. In January 1968 in Prague, the Czechoslovak Communist Party suddenly ousted Moscow's protégé, Antonin Novotny, as party and government leader. In a palace coup, the Czech Central Committee picked its own new leader, Alexander Dubcek. This was the first time since Stalin imposed Communist governments on Eastern Europe that any country in the Soviet bloc had chosen a leader who did not have Moscow's approval—except of course for Marshal Tito, whom Stalin tried and failed to oust in 1947. Dubcek was a loyal Communist, to be sure, but he was also a Czech nationalist, and he set out at once on his experiment with "Communism with a human face." For the Soviet Union under Brezhnev, this was a mortal challenge. For de Gaulle, it was historical inevitability—the decline of communism, the breakup of the power blocs.

To keep the process going, de Gaulle found fresh opportunity to reassert his own independence and lash out at American hegemony, real or imagined. In mid-March 1968 the United States and the Soviet Union, negotiating in the framework of the seventeen-nation Geneva Disarmament Conference, completed after six years of patient effort the draft of a treaty to halt the spread of nuclear weapons in the world. France, working at that point to develop its own megaton hydrogen warheads, promptly made clear that it would stand aside and have nothing to do with the nonproliferation treaty and would continue to conduct its own nuclear policy and its own nuclear deals in the world as it saw fit.

Next came a new de Gaulle attack against "dollar hegemony." The United States, after intensive consultation with the "Group of Ten" leading monetary nations of the world, had evolved a scheme to increase the financial resources of the International Monetary Fund by creating a new supplemental reserve of "special drawing rights"—a credit of paper gold. Each member of the IMF puts up a basic contribution of gold and dollars to a central reserve. Members then borrow from this fund when they have financial or balance-of-payments diffi-culties. The special drawing rights plan was designed to increase the fund's lending power through creation of new credits without anyone putting up any more gold or dollar cash. France, as a member of the Group of Ten, had been fully aware of the scheme as it evolved at IMF headquarters in Washington. A final meeting was scheduled to take place in Stockholm at the end of March 1968 for adoption of the plan.

One week before the meeting de Gaulle lashed out with a formal statement declaiming against an "unfair and unworkable" monetary system based on the dollar as a "privileged" currency, and again called for a return to gold as the basis for international reserves and currency exchanges. He then dispatched the ultra-loyalist Michel Debré to Stockholm with rigid instructions to use all possible means to block adoption of the SDR plan. The French tried to rally the other Common Market members to their side, but the West Germans, the Italians, the Dutch and the Belgians were not about to follow General de Gaulle down this dead end. He could declaim against the dollar and extoll the virtues of gold, but he could not win support and he could not exercise a veto. The SDR scheme was adopted by nine of the Group of Ten and then by the IMF as a whole—and has continued to expand and function ever since.

The assault on the IMF was Charles de Gaulle's last big *son et lumière* show before his proud tower all but fell apart in the epic upheavals of May 1968. Barely three months after the Stockholm meeting, Finance Minister Debré was forced into an ironic volte-face when he had to knock on the door of the IMF for an emergency loan to tide France over a massive foreign exchange hemorrhage that drained considerably more than one billion dollars out of the Treasury during the student uprising and general strike. France, despite General de Gaulle, was a vulnerable country like all the rest.

*

The proverbial little cloud no larger than a man's hand had already formed over the French scene, had anyone in authority been alert and intuitive enough to perceive it. The same week that de Gaulle was concentrating his fire against the IMF and the dollar, a student demonstration against the Vietnam War took place on March 22 in the heart of Paris at the Place de l'Opéra. Windows of the American Express Company were smashed, and in a short sharp police action, five students were arrested. They were from a branch of the University of Paris, the Sorbonne, located in a dreary western appendage of the city, Nanterre, where a hastily constructed collection of concrete-and-glass buildings had been thrown together to take a student overflow and had already swollen from an original 2,000 to 10,000 enrollment. The jailing of the five Nanterre students galvanized a whole catalogue of unrest and emotions into formation next day of a spontaneous protest organization calling itself the "Mouvement du 22 Mars." At a campus rally, someone suggested they occupy the ultimate seat of authority at Nanterre, the university's professorial council chamber. Students swept into the administration building and staged a six-hour sit-in around the council table that lit a sputtering fuse under the de Gaulle government.

It was in the nature of de Gaulle's rule to ignore or anodize the evidence or recognition of blots or blemishes on the image of a strong and stable France. The General himself had yet again set this tone with his complacent 1968 New Year's broadcast to the nation. France was to be seen always as secure within and immune from without to the troubles of less fortunate lands. His own authoritarian style meant that often instead of anticipating domestic problems, or attempting to defuse them, they would be allowed to accumulate—finally to be resolved on high by more or less despotic decree, in a manner that in turn enhanced the image of strong government. Efficiency and order counted for everything—not the exposure of what was wrong, critical inquiry or public admission of errors, faults or blunders, or candid debate about things that needed to be put right.

Nevertheless, as 1968 began to gain speed as an extraordinary year of civil violence, France did indeed share one common problem with other democracies—and that was the population explosion in the universities. In the decade from 1958 to 1968, university enrollment in America jumped from 2.6 million to 7 million. In Britain it went up from 216,000 to 418,000, and in West Germany from 115,000 to 250,00. In France, where university study is free to those who can pass the qualifying baccalauréat, enrollment had leaped from 200,000 to more than 500,000. Moreover, facilities had woefully failed to keep up with the numbers. Nowhere were there adequate lecture halls, libraries, dormitories, laboratory facilities or teaching faculties. Above all, the centralized French education system, which went back to Napoleon, reinforced by the authoritarian atmosphere of the de Gaulle regime, was badly out of touch with and divorced from the intellectual ferment, the needs and ideas, of students in the second half of the twentieth century.

The universities of France, controlled and directed from Paris, had become pressure cookers of unrest. French students knew perfectly well what was already going on in the United States, from Columbia to Berkeley; in West Germany at Heidelberg, Frankfurt, Freiburg, Göttingen, Tübingen, and the Free University in West Berlin; in Britain at Leicester, Sussex, Liverpool, Essex and even the famed London School of Economics; in Franco's Spain at the University of Madrid; and in Communist Poland at the University of Warsaw. Added to the physical and practical causes of student unrest were political causes—the Vietnam War, right-wing governments, the suppression of freedom under facism or communism. Finally, a new leftist ideology was at hand in the form of Maoism, with its creed of civil violence unleashed by China's Red Guards in the Cultural Revolution. Here was communism to satisfy those fed up with Stalinist discipline and Moscow orthodoxy, tired of waiting for the dawn of revolution that never came. In the name of Mao Tse-tung, it was now correct for students, intellectuals, workers to rise and storm the barricades of existing order any day in the week.

On top of this ferment at Nanterre and throughout the university system, the French economy was continuing to slump. The de Gaulle government continued to pursue its conservative course of a balanced budget, the accumulation of gold, the maintenance of a strong exchange rate for the franc, tight credits, and along with this a new campaign by de Gaulle to discourage American investment in France. Accordingly, in 1968 the growth rate had dropped from a high of 7 percent annually to less than 4 percent, and unemployment, at 450,000, had reached a postwar high. Housing starts were down by nearly 40 percent. Prime Minister Pompidou, ruling by decree, had imposed a tight stabilization policy to fight inflation, but this had meant a slowdown in wage increases, leaving the workers convinced that they were on the short end of the inevitable wage-price spiral.

The economic and social fabric of France that spring of 1968 had become like dry tinder, ready for a spark to set it off. Nonetheless, de Gaulle's ministers were getting ready to stage a national celebration of the General's tenth anniversary of return to power, with André Malraux enthusiastically in charge. De Gaulle himself was preparing for another foray into Eastern Europe to visit Roumania, where Communist leader Nicolai Ceausescu pursued a mildly independent foreign policy vis-à-vis Moscow while running the tightest Stalinist police state in the Soviet bloc.

The majestic order of the Gaullist State was not to be disturbed by a handful of university students. So the rector at Nanterre, after telephoning the Ministry of Education, closed the school in the wake of the sit-in protest in his professorial council chamber. It was a major error. The university faculty immediately sided with the students against the administration, to demand that the university be reopened and the grievances aired. Moreover, the students had a leader—a fiery, redheaded leftist revolutionary named Daniel Cohn-Bendit, who disdained any-one's discipline and who became a folk hero of the events of May. Danny the Red, as he was known among the students, was born in France of a German-Jewish father and a French mother. His father managed to submerge himself as a refugee in France throughout the Vichy period, but both Danny's parents died in the 1950s. He then returned to Germany to take his citizenship from his father, and had come back to the land of his birth on a scholarship to study sociology. He had a quick and agile mind, a sharp sardonic wit, a crowd-pleasing comedian's sense of timing and a voice that could reach the rafters in three languages. He was a total iconoclast of the left, who was "very anti-Lenin," found "nothing new" in Marx and laughed off "trying to make a myth out of Mao." His idealism was simple. He was against State repression, authoritarianism and hierarchy. He found plenty to combat in France.

Under student and faculty pressure, Nanterre was reopened after two days, but academic order and discipline disappeared completely, to be replaced by a sort of continuous talkfest of dissatisfied youth. At least the situation had not turned violent. But then in mid-April the minister of education, an ambitious and arrogant young disciple of de Gaulle's, Alain Peyrefitte, announced that in order to relieve the pressure on university enrollment, future admissions would be on the basis of special examination instead of automatic for anyone passing the famous baccalauréat. Since this clearly would favor upper-class youth at the expense of the sons and daughters of the working class, it was like waving a red flag at the students. By the end of April the situation had become so explosive and chaotic at Nanterre that Peyrefitte himself prodded the rector into again closing the school. At the same time, Cohn-Bendit was ordered to appear before a disciplinary council at the higher headquarters of the university on the precincts of the Sorbonne.

On the morning of May 5, a Friday, Cohn-Bendit headed for his rendezvous with authority in revolutionary style—at the head of a procession of Nanterre students who walked with him on a three-hour trek, across the Seine to the Sorbonne. At this judicious moment, Prime Minister Pompidou, leaving the situation to Peyrefitte and not deigning to take it seriously, departed the country with Couve de Murville on a long-arranged official visit to Iran and Afghanistan.

But as the Nanterre students walked to the Sorbonne, a right-wing group calling itself "Occident" formed up in the university quadrangle to meet them—a hardcore group of anti-Communist Algerian War veterans, many with OAS connections, still taking university courses. They began breaking up tables and chairs to arm themselves for battle.

On Friday afternoon, the rector of the Sorbonne, Jean Roche, acting with the blessing if not the urging of the government, went to the fatal extreme of calling in the police to keep order. It is a tradition of French universities that the police never enter the buildings or the precincts, no matter what is going on, except when asked in—a very extreme step. Moreover, in this case the government sent not the regular gardiens de la paix, but the special riot squad shock troops of the menacing CRS Republican Security Companies. As the heavy CRS trucks poured into the Latin Quarter, Roche took his next wrong turn of the day and did what only the Nazi occupiers of Paris had done before in seven hundred years. He declared the entire university closed.

At the end of the afternoon on Friday there was a brief period of what seemed to be a truce as the CRS surrounded the main Sorbonne building and negotiated to allow the students to leave peacefully. But as they began trickling out, they were seized, roughed up, pitched into police vans and driven away. All this had taken place in brilliant spring weather, and was watched by growing crowds of other students and the rest of the population of the crowded Latin Quarter. When the other students realized what was happening, stones began to fly at the police. Within an hour the Quarter turned into a running battlefield—and for the next six weeks France rocked in a state of near anarchy.

*

There was nothing planned, premeditated or organized about the Paris student uprising. It was a spontaneous product of tensions and provocation—the brutal overkill of authority against the country's frustrated youth. Perhaps in the nature of things in Gaullist France it was inevitable. Certainly it became inevitable when the government chose to send in the CRS instead of opening its doors for dialogue and discussion.

It is possible, too, that the Gaullist authorities were lulled by the attitude of the Communist Party during the buildup to the events of May. On the morning of the first fateful clash at the Sorbonne, the party paper, L'Humanité, blossomed with a full-page spread under the by-line of party leader Georges Marchais with a banner headline: FALSE REVOLUTIONARIES TO BE UNMASKED. There followed a vituperative condemnation of Cohn-Bendit as "a German anarchist" and his Nanterre followers as "mostly sons of les grands bourgeois, contemptuous of students of working-class origin." Marchais condemned the students for "pretending to give lessons to the labor movement" and complained that "more and more they are to be found outside factory gates or in centers of immigrant workers distributing leaflets and other means of propaganda."

It had not been unusual in France under General de Gaulle for the Communist Party to come to the support of the regime in its own indirect and roundabout way. Now Marchais and the party leaders were thrown off stride by a leftist movement that they did not and could not control. Even the party's own captive student movement, the Union des Étudiants Communistes de France (UEC), had temporarily fallen into the hands of young new-left intellectuals who refused to toe the line of the French Politbureau. They had finally been purged after a two-year leadership struggle that left the UEC badly demoralized. Marchais and the Communist leaders did not like to see "control of the streets" slipping from their hands any more than did the de Gaulle government.

But if anything, the public stance taken by Marchais and L'Humanité, there for all to read openly, served only to spur on Cohn-Bendit and a handful of other maverick new-left leaders—notably Alain Geismar, of the University Teachers Union, who called himself an independent Marxist, and Alain Krivine, who proclaimed himself a Trotskyist.

In the clashes of the first Friday, there had been 596 arrests. Across a weekend of sullen and menacing atmosphere in the Latin Quarter, student leaders got together and decided on a mass demonstration on Monday to protest the arrests and demand reopening of the university and withdrawal of the CRS and the police. The Communist leaders notably held back, but this in no way dampened either the turnout or the militancy. As the protest march got under way from the

Place Denfert-Rochereau, the CRS got orders to halt the demonstration. There was a wild CRS baton charge, backed up by concussion grenades and tear gas—and a running battle was on lasting twelve hours well into the night. Another 422 arrests were logged and a staggering number of at least 600 students injured. Most of these were cared for in makeshift treatment to avoid the injured falling into the hands of the police.

There was no quarter from the government and the police—and no surrender from the students, who took to the streets again on Tuesday. On Wednesday Peyrefitte appeared before the National Assembly and loftily echoed the Communist Party line that the disturbances were "the work of specialists in agitation and elements foreign to the university." He promised that "if order is restored, everything is possible—if not, nothing is possible." Order was the first requisite of Gaullism.

Meanwhile, on Friday, May 10, the long-awaited Vietnam peace talks began on the peaceful side of Paris in the Hôtel Majestic conference center, just off the Champs-Élysées. Ambassador W. Averell Harriman represented the United States, and the North Vietnamese delegation was headed by a former foreign minister, Xuan Thuy. It was to have been an occasion of historic satisfaction and international prestige for Charles de Gaulle. But, alas, it was totally overclouded by the tear gas and the concussion grenades on the Left Bank. That Friday night was the most violent yet.

By now more experienced in street tactics and better organized, the students fought the CRS to a standstill, meeting their baton charges with barricades of overturned automobiles and showers of heavy paving stones from the cobbled streets. On that Friday night, 188 cars had been rolled into the streets and set on fire on the boulevard Saint-Michel and other Latin Quarter streets. There had been another 460 arrests and at least 367 injured before the students broke off on Cohn-Bendit's radioed instructions well after midnight. Meanwhile, student demonstrations had now broken out all over France at the universities of Strasbourg, Lille, Lyon, Toulouse, Rennes, Tours, and other cities.

In the faraway Afghanistan capital of Kabul, Prime Minister Pompidou, in touch with Paris on a fading radio-telephone, decided that he had better get home. "When I got back to Paris, my name will be unsullied," he said complacently to an aide accompanying him. By the time his plane touched down on Saturday afternoon, he had already drafted a speech which he intended to deliver that evening. He went first to see de Gaulle, who throughout these tumultuous days had remained remote and silent, telling his ministers: "The chief of state should not be in the front line. He does not act under the compulsion of circumstances when things are at their hottest." It was up to ministers first to restore order.

In effect, the speech that Pompidou had prepared was a repudiation of the policy of confrontation that ministers had been pursuing in his absence. Louis Joxe, who had been deputizing for Pompidou (and whose son was fighting with the students on the other side of the barricades), had wanted to make a gesture of compromise but had been turned down by de Gaulle. Nevertheless, when Pompidou now proposed a speedy release of the arrested students and reopening of the Sorbonne, de Gaulle agreed, telling the prime minister: "It's your turn to play. If you win, so much the better. France wins with you. If you lose, too bad for you."

And so Pompidou went on the air on Saturday night to announce that release of the students would be speeded up by the Court of Appeals and that the Sorbonne would reopen on Monday. It was a virtual capitulation—but it was too little and too late. After a week of watching and listening over the radio to the students battling the CRS, the French labor movement would put up no longer with the hands-off attitude of the Communist Party leadership. In the face of rising pressures for a show of support for the students, the Communist-dominated trade union federation, the CGT, finally changed course and called for a "solidarity demonstration" and a one-day general strike on Monday, May 13—which also happened to be the anniversary of the start of events that had brought General de Gaulle back to power in 1958. Now the slogan was to be: "Ten years is enough."

On Monday some 800,000 students and workers formed up at the Place de la République and moved across the Seine to the Place Denfert-Rochereau, with Danny the Red and the other student leaders in the front line and Georges Marchais, Waldek Rochet and the Communist leaders following somewhat glumly behind. But on Pompidou's orders there was to be no interference with a peaceful march, and the demonstration passed off quietly. It was only a brief pause.

When the Sorbonne reopened on Monday afternoon, instead of resuming classes, students immediately occupied the buildings in a victory celebration that turned into a permanent round-the-clock sit-in and talkfest of grievances and leftist philosophy.

That same afternoon Pompidou persuaded de Gaulle that "the tempest is really over" and he should go ahead and leave Paris early next morning for Bucharest and his long-planned official visit to Roumania. The Sorbonne was reopened and the one-day general strike would be over. Pompidou argued that "if you don't leave, people will think that the whole affair has not yet ended." It hadn't.

De Gaulle was scarcely airborne on Tuesday morning when a new development far from Paris altered everything. A one-day token strike was not enough for the workers at the nationalized Sud Aviation plant at the city of Nantes, far to the west of Paris near the Atlantic coast. Taking a cue from the student occupation of the Sorbonne and the Odéon Theater, the workers decided spontaneously to turn the strike into a factory sit-in. To drive the point home, they welded shut the iron gates of the plant and hoisted a red flag over the factory roof, reminiscent of the Paris Commune of 1871.

All day Tuesday and Wednesday the factory sit-in movement spread across the entire country. At the giant Renault automobile plant in Paris at Boulogne-Billancourt, workers related that it started with a young apprentice suddenly shouting, "I've had enough!" and throwing down his tools. "The oldies said we should wait for the union—wait, wait, wait. Well, in half an hour the whole plant downed tools. We decided to occupy the place like the students. The unions followed along." So by mid-week, a one-day protest action had been transformed into a national general strike with no one in control.

In Roumania at the end of the week, General de Gaulle concluded that he had had enough of receiving bouquets of flowers from pretty girls in embroidered blouses, inspecting spruced-up collective farms and specially selected factories. He cut short his visit by eighteen hours and returned to Paris on May 18 in a fury. As soon as he arrived back, he called his ministers together and announced that he wanted the CRS to clear the students out of the Sorbonne. Christian Fouchet, the interior minister and an old Gaullist, pleaded with him that it could not be done without the police firing into the crowds, and there would be student casualties and deaths. Pompidou warned of a disastrous chain reaction to any killings. Three hours later, after pacing his office and reflecting, de Gaulle relented and canceled the instruction, now furious at being overridden.

Next de Gaulle announced that he would address the nation on the following Friday, May 24. Meanwhile there were now 2 million workers on strike. The airports were all shut down, as were the railroads and Paris Métro and busses. Gasoline supplies dried up; electricity and gas were cut off. Mail delivery had halted completely. The banks had no clerks to clear checks. Tourists could not even travel to France if they were inclined to try, with no air or rail services. Hotels and restaurants in Paris began closing for lack of business.

De Gaulle's television appearance was a political and public relations disaster. He came on the screen a quavering old man of seventy-eight, pleading almost pathetically for Frenchmen to remember all he had done and to return to work and stop messing up the Fifth Republic. Finally he resorted to his favorite tactic and announced that he would call another national referendum "to give the State, and above all its Chief, a mandate for renovation." This renovation, he declared, would take the form of a new law to establish "worker participation" in the ownership and management of both private and State enterprises—long a de Gaulle pet idea. If the referendum failed, he would step aside.

While de Gaulle spoke there had been a pause in the street activity. But as soon as he faded from the television screens, the violence in the streets of the Latin Quarter reached an unbelievable pitch. The CRS had been sent back to keep order, and by Saturday morning the boulevard Saint-Michel and the rue Gay-Lussac looked like scenes out of World War II. There were 795 arrests, seventy-two large trees had been cut down for street barricades, and twelve hundred square yards of paving stones ripped up. Countless automobiles had been overturned and fired, windows shattered for blocks, and more than five hundred injured—including 212 CRS and police. How could this go on? But it did.

*

France had now been gripped by social turmoil plus economic paralysis for three weeks—yet no one in the de Gaulle government from the General on down had yet begun to address the *causes* of the unrest instead of its affects. So far the government's only policy was to restore order. But after the failure of de Gaulle's television broadcast, the spread of the general strike, and the upsurge of fighting in the Latin Quarter, Pompidou moved to the negotiating table. He summoned the leaders of France's three big trade union groups (the Communist-dominated CGT, the Socialist-led CFDT and the independent Force Ouvrière) together with the leaders of the Patronat (manufacturers' association) to a nonstop roundtable negotiation over which he would preside, to hammer out an overall wage package settlement to end the general strike. Meanwhile, he also gave orders to the CRS to "disperse all demonstrations with the greatest energy and to execute orders without weakness or delay."

The weary students rested on the weekend, and the wage negotiations began on Saturday afternoon at the Ministry of Social Affairs on the rue de Grenelle. It continued without a break overnight and all day Sunday and that night as well, with the participants catnapping in relays, until agreement was announced at 7:30 A.M. on Monday, May 27. The final package, called the Grenelle Agreements, gave all French workers an immediate 7 percent wage boost plus another 3 percent to follow in six months, along with fringe benefits in social security from the government to sweeten the total up to around 15 percent overall. Finally there was an increase in the basic minimum wage of the lowest-paid workers.

For the moment, Pompidou appeared to be the hero of the crisis, but not for long. That very afternoon, the Renault workers at the Boulogne-Billancourt plant hooted down the Communist CGT union leader when he arrived to present the agreement and urge a return to work. The crisis was by no means over.

Meanwhile, Finance Minister Michel Debré complained to de Gaulle that Pompidou had sold out in the Grenelle Agreements and given away too much, that social security funds would be depleted and the wage increases would weaken France's competitive position in the world. How on earth Debré would have gotten France back to work if he had still been prime minister is impossible to imagine or understand. At any rate, Pompidou next urged de Gaulle to forget about calling a national referendum after the sour reception he had gotten from the television viewers, and instead dissolve the National Assembly and call new legislative elections.

Sound as this advice was, Pompidou was in fact driving nails into his own coffin as far as de Gaulle was concerned. On his decision the Sorbonne had been reopened—only to be occupied by a student sit-in. On his decision, the Grenelle Agreements had been concluded—giving away too much, only to be rejected by the workers with no visible return to work yet. Pompidou had opposed de Gaulle's orders to the CRS to clear the students from the Sorbonne even if it meant gunfire, and now he was opposing de Gaulle's plan to call another national referendum.

In this increasingly rancorous atmosphere of continuing national crisis and chaos along with palace-guard infighting, de Gaulle was scheduled to preside as usual over the regular weekly Cabinet meeting at the Élysée Palace on Wednesday morning, May 29. But shortly after 9 A.M. he summoned his secretary-general, Bernard Tricot, and abruptly directed him to cancel the meeting. His only explanation was that "I'm too tired and it will show if I try to preside." It was a decision that stunned his staff, his ministers and the nation—the first time in ten years that de Gaulle had ever cancelled a Cabinet meeting on short notice, the first time he ever appeared to be flinching under pressure in the exercise of power.

In the next twenty-four hours, the last great drama of Charles de Gaulle's life played to a last triumphant climax. The bare outlines of what happened can be quickly summarized, but are scarcely the full story.

Shortly after 11 A.M., de Gaulle left the Élysée Palace with Madame de Gaulle, telling Tricot that he was going to Colombey-les-Deux-Églises to get some rest for twenty-four hours. Instead he drove to an Air Force helicopter base in the Paris district of Issy-les-Moulineaux and took off heading east. From this moment he was literally lost. He did not land at Colombey, and no one at the Élysée Palace, no one in Paris, knew where he was. He flew secretly to Baden-Baden in the Black Forest of West Germany, where he spent two hours in deep discussion across a luncheon table with General Jacques Massu, commander of French forces in Germany. Finally around 6 P.M., he arrived at Colombey, telephoned Tricot and told him that he would return to the Élysée Palace next day and to arrange a Council of Ministers meeting for 3 P.M. By this time Paris was wild with rumors that the General's disappearance meant that he was abdicating and had left the capital for good. But on Thursday he was driven back from Colombey by car, entering the Élysée by a side gate. The Cabinet meeting lasted less than half an hour. At 4:30 P.M. he went on the air over the State radio network (not television this time) to deliver in less than five minutes, with all his old vigor and decisiveness, a brief declaration to the nation that effectively turned the crisis:

> Being the custodian of national and republican sovereignty, I have envisaged for the past twenty-four hours all eventualities, without exception, that might allow me to maintain it. I have taken my decisions. In present circumstances, I shall not retire. I have a mandate from the people; I shall fulfill it. I shall not change the Prime Minister, whose valor, solidity, capacity merit the homage of all. . . . I dissolve the National Assembly this day.

De Gaulle concluded with an unusual passage in which he warned that "France is threatened by dictatorship that could only be from totalitarian communism," and finally the ringing words: "*Eh bien! Non!* The Republic shall not abdicate."

This briefly is what happened—yet a certain mystery still surrounds the whole affair and always will. The mystery is locked forever with Charles de Gaulle himself. Did he really contemplate an abdication from power when he left Paris, or was he merely throwing up a tactical smokescreen, as he had so often done in the past, to confuse and allow things to simmer while he contemplated his next moves and prepared to seize the initiative? Why did he choose of all people to visit Massu, with whom he had not by any means always been on good terms? Even among those closest to the events, there are differences of nuance, of facts and interpretation.

To begin with, de Gaulle had arranged for his departure in deep secrecy at least twenty-four hours in advance through his naval aide, Captain Flohic, and was also in contact with his son-in-law, General Alain de Boissieu, who was then commanding a tank division in the eastern French city of Mulhouse. But no one else at the Élysée Palace, no minister or anyone on the civilian side of the government, knew anything of what was afoot. He first flew to an air force base near Saint-Dizier. Here he was met by Boissieu. In Boissieu's account, de Gaulle intended to meet Massu on French soil at Strasbourg, but this had to be abandoned because of communications difficulties due to the general strike. De Gaulle's son, Admiral Phillipe de Gaulle, says it was cancelled because of bad weather around Strasbourg. In any case, from Saint-Dizier a message was sent to Massu to expect the General, who then flew on to Baden-Baden.

Just before leaving the Élysée Palace, de Gaulle made an unusual personal call to Pompidou to tell him that he was going to Colombey to get some rest "and be face to face with myself." He said nothing about going to Baden-Baden. When Pompidou made a response that in effect questioned whether the General would return to Paris next day, de Gaulle's comment was somewhat enigmatic. First he assured Pompidou that "I shall be back tomorrow," but then he said elliptically, "In any case, there is the future, and you are on the side of the future, there's no reason for you to worry." He then ended the conversation most unusually with "I embrace you."

Pompidou's account of these events, written soon after de Gaulle dropped him as prime minister in July, and published by his wife in 1982, long after his death, says:

> I was extremely worried. I had known for a long time the General's psychological crisis and his periodic temptation to leave [the presidency]. I knew that the atmosphere at Colombey was highly conducive to that temptation, and that Madame de Gaulle had already been hoping for several years the General would retire. . . . In fact, the General had a fit of despair. Believing all was lost, he had chosen retreat. Arriving at Baden-Baden, all was prepared for a long stay. Philippe de Gaulle and his family were also there. The French Ambassador had been summoned to receive instructions to warn the German government. It was General Massu who, by his courage of expression, his reminder of the past, and his assurances of the loyalty of the Army, succeeded in modifying the General's determination and subsequently in making him change his mind completely. France on account of that day owes a lot to General Massu.

Pompidou quotes de Gaulle as saying to him later: "For the first time in my life I had a breakdown. I am not proud of myself."

General Massu's account agrees generally with Pompidou's, but differs in some particulars and interpretations. He has recounted:

> On debarking from the helicopter, General de Gaulle said to me: "Massu, tout est foutu" [It's all over]. He then asked me, "Can I go to Strasbourg?" and I answered that I could get him there right away. But de Gaulle did not follow up on the project, for which he gave me no explanation. He then asked me to warn François Seydoux, our ambassador in Bonn, of his arrival,

which I did discreetly. It was in my eyes useless that the Federal Government of Germany know that de Gaulle had arrived in Baden.

The truth is that General de Gaulle had chosen to retire. He had not come to Baden to chat with me, nor did he come for only two hours. He came to rest, and he came to stay at least for some time. It seemed to me that family influence, notably that of Madame de Gaulle, had played an important role in the notion of retiring. Just a few days before, Madame de Gaulle had been insulted in a large department store in Paris by people who recognized her. The General and she had been very affected by this lamentable incident.

It is correct that General de Gaulle decided to return to France after having listened to me. I will say nothing about the actual exchange with the President of the Republic. In my will I shall leave my account to my children, who will be free to decide on its publication. But my objective was to send him back to Paris. He was a stricken man, and I had a frank talk with him. As soon as I convinced him, de Gaulle was impatient to leave right away for Colombey. But as the helicopter was initially intended to stay in Baden, nothing was ready and he had to wait for the crew to refuel. In the meantime he asked my staff, "Am I right to return?" but in fact he was not interested in their answers. He knew that with his return he would win.

Philippe de Gaulle says "it is only a legend" that his father had a lot of baggage with him for a long stay in Baden, pointing to the fact that in any case the original plan was for a meeting not in Germany but on French soil in Strasbourg. He adds, loyally, "I do not know if General de Gaulle was losing his control, but I know that he caught himself and he was the only one who was able to save himself."

De Gaulle's son-in-law, General Boissieu, gave this account of the meeting at the airfield at Saint-Dizier:

The General personally, in front of me, suggested three alternative hypothesis. The first was to go to Colombey, and there to address the French nation, and to return to Paris only when the situation had stabilized. The second was directed to installing a government in Alsace, a relatively calm region. The third consisted of going to see the military and returning immediately after this discussion to Paris.

I must admit that the first hypothesis frightened me because I could discern in it a device for wanting to give up power. During my talk with the General I did everything to discourage this possibility. It was not a good one. The second one I did not like either, because the General would look as if he were forming a refugee government in a region where there was deployed a division commanded by one of his own relatives [Boissieu's tank division at nearby Mulhouse]. So he adopted the third, which was the good one.

But it should be noted that he was not originally supposed to meet General Massu at Baden but at Strasbourg. It was a breakdown of international telephone communications which obliged General de Gaulle to cross the Rhine.

As for Pompidou, he did not know the truth of what he had been told. General Massu might have let himself be impressed by General de Gaulle, who made a big apocalyptic scene. But in truth the only really important thing is that General Massu succeeded with much dexterity in making General de Gaulle understand that the only dignified solution was for his return to Paris, to power, and to make an energetic speech.

Balanced against these accounts, differing somewhat in nuance and emphasis but all agreeing on the importance of Massu's talk with de Gaulle, is the fact that de Gaulle had *already* assured both Tricot and Pompidou that he would return to Paris. In the end, a reasonable supposition would be that the General knew all along what he should do, what he wanted to do and what he intended to do. But he wanted time to work out precisely what to do and how he would do it. By throwing up a smokescreen around his intentions, he was simply inviting persuasion and reassurance from loyalists for a course he would take anyway.

*

When de Gaulle's broadcast ended on Thursday afternoon, a vast crowd of Gaullist loyalists began surging to the Place de la Concorde. Gaullist deputies to the National Assembly came running across the Concorde bridge after hearing the formal announcement that the president of the Republic had dissolved parliament and new elections would be held. The throng swelled to half a million men and women, who then took off on a mass march up the Champs-Élysées, led by redoubtable Gaullist barons—André Malraux, Olivier Guichard, Jacques Foccart, Michel Debré. It was the "bourgeois backlash," demonstrating against the left-wing chaos that had gripped France for a month, a right-wing surge of excitement and emotion that the General was back and they would now win—as indeed they did. But not at once.

On Friday, Pompidou, with a renewed mandate and basking in the General's praise, reorganized his Cabinet and cleared the decks for a quick election campaign. At the same time, armed police moved into the Central Post Office in the city of Rennes in the first direct police action to break the sit-ins and the general strike. The Communists were almost as anxious to get the workers back under control as was de Gaulle. But the first big break did not come until June 5 when workers in the nationalized Électricité de France signed a contract based on the Grenelle Agreements and began going back to work. The strike was beginning to break up, but there was one more eruption of violence. The tireless CRS was sent to a Renault factory outside of Paris, and in a familiar baton charge against strikers, a seventeen-year-old boy was either pushed or fell into the Seine and was drowned. That night, June 10, the Latin Quarter again erupted.

Across the next two nights there were some fifteen hundred arrests, seventy-two CRS and policemen were injured and several hundred students were treated in their own first-aid stations. Seventy-five cars were wrecked, ten police vans damaged, twenty-five more trees cut down for barricades, five district police stations attacked, three hundred fire alarms set off, two dozen traffic lights destroyed and three newly opened Gaullist election campaign offices smashed.

Pompidou now issued an edict banning all demonstrations. Physical and emotional exhaustion was also taking hold. On Sunday, June 16, six weeks after the troubles at the Sorbonne began, the CRS surrounded the main university building to eject the students from their long sit-in. Even the students had grown weary—and smelly. There was a brief effort to rouse last-gasp resistance, but few had any energy for yet another fight. By 8 P.M. the Sorbonne had been forcefully but peacefully cleared, with students singing "Auld Lang Syne" as they left. Danny the Red was picked up and expelled from France. At last Gaullist order again prevailed.

The prime minister now threw himself vigorously into the election campaign, which produced an extraordinary Gaullist landslide. In two rounds of voting that concluded on Sunday, June 30, the Gaullists and their allies, the Independent Republicans under Giscard d'Estaing, won an incredible total of 349 out of 482 seats in the new National Assembly. The narrow Gaullist margin after the 1967 election was thereby transformed into the biggest single-party majority in French parliamentary history for the next five years. But, as Pompidou had ruefully remarked during the crisis, "Things will never be the same again." In particular this applied to Pompidou himself. Ten days after the election de Gaulle abruptly dismissed him.

Georges Pompidou was one of the oldest and closest of de Gaulle's collaborators. He came from solid French bourgeois stock, the son of teachers in the Auvergne region of the southwest of France. He was a brilliant and hardworking scholar who made it into the École Normale on competitive examination and took honors in Greek and Latin. He then became a teacher. Demobilized from the Army after the fall of France, he took a teaching post in Paris. He had no Resistance record apart from patriotic yearning for victory. But he did have well-placed friends from his class at the École Normale, and when General de Gaulle returned to Paris in August 1944, through one of these friends he was recruited to a lowly secretarial post on de Gaulle's personal staff. He had qualities that de Gaulle appreciated—intelligence, efficiency, and tirelessness, and he was self-effacing and secretive. After de Gaulle left power in 1946, Pompidou continued in a key civil service post on the Conseil d'État and then went into business with the Rothschild Bank. But he kept his contacts with de Gaulle on an ever more personal basis. He negotiated the book contract for publication of the War Memoirs. He set up and administered the Anne de Gaulle Foundation trust fund that de Gaulle established to aid handicapped children, and became a personal financial adviser to the General. When de Gaulle returned to power in 1958, he made Pompidou his *directeur de cabinet* and trusted chief of staff for the crucial first six months. Next Pompidou handled the first secret peace contacts with the Algerian FLN rebels. Finally he came out into the open and succeeded Debré as prime minister in April 1962.

Given de Gaulle's totally personal style and concept of power, there was an inevitability about the dismissal of Pompidou from office after the events of May and more than six years as prime minister. Pompidou had already come to feel a certain estrangement, a coolness, an end to former intimacy between himself and de Gaulle well before the crisis broke. It had done him no good that he had opposed de Gaulle at key times in the handling of the crisis and had been right where de Gaulle was wrong. Finally, the great election victory had been a Pompidou victory—not a de Gaulle victory. The National Assembly was Pompidou's arena. De Gaulle was still determined, when it was over, that he had to have a personal renewal of his power mandate in the form of a national referendum by the people. All the same, the manner of Pompidou's going showed Charles de Gaulle at his most malevolent.

On several occasions during the May crisis, and again before the election, Pompidou discussed resignation with de Gaulle—who brushed it aside. In fact, he still needed Pompidou, and hence his words of praise for the prime minister in his May 30 crisis broadcast. After the election, Pompidou once more told de Gaulle that it was time that he quit, but de Gaulle replied: "We have won together. We must continue. Think it over for two days. I will need you." Yet at that very time, de Gaulle had already secretly told Foreign Minister Couve de Murville to begin preparing himself to take Pompidou's job. Pompidou did "think it over" seriously for several days, and then sent word to de Gaulle through Bernard Tricot that he would stay on. Next day, having heard nothing, he telephoned Tricot to be told: "I gave the General your message but it was too late. Steps had already been taken. Couve was appointed prime minister last night after dinner."

General de Gaulle never left anyone in doubt as to who wielded power.

The end for Pompidou had come with brutal ill-grace. But he had won a seat in the National Assembly in the General Election that he would have had to give up had he remained prime minister. So he now automatically assumed the role of leader of the enormous Gaullist parliamentary majority, with a very strong power base of his own. He was indeed the man of the future. Dismissed from office, he was more than ever de Gaulle's logical successor. Not only had de Gaulle's rule been shaken to its foundations, but there was a replacement in the wings.

Couve de Murville, who took over the premiership, was an admirable ice-cold technician, a complete Gaullist loyalist, no politician and by no stretch of the imagination any threat to de Gaulle as a possible successor. He had to face the onerous task of sorting out the economic and political aftermath of the uprising: a loss of more than $1 billion in foreign exchange, an estimated loss of some $3 billion in industrial production during the strike, a supplementary budget of $1.5 billion to meet the cost of increased salaries in the nationalized industries, tax increases totalling $500 million, and as new education act for university reform.

The image of France invulnerable—stable, strong and secure—had been shattered. Then, in August, de Gaulle's détente foreign policy took a heavy blow from the Soviet Union. The Red Army rolled into Prague, to snuff out Alexander Dubcek's brief experiment with "communism with a human face." So much for de Gaulle's hopes for or belief in, the ideological decline of communism, the change in Russia, the historical inevitability of a new détente alignment of European nation-states, and a fading away of the power blocs. It was a hope and a vision that had been crushed by the Soviets in Budapest in 1956, and would be crushed again thirteen years later in Warsaw, in 1981, after de Gaulle.

The stage on which General de Gaulle had performed with such freedom and *éclat* had largely collapsed. His rule or reign seemed to be coming to some Shakespearean end—an aging King battered by storms of his realm, a vigorous Dauphin banished from the court but waiting inexorably for the inevitable hour when power would at last drop into his hands. At this point, in October 1968, salacious rumors about Pompidou and his wife began to circulate in the political demimonde of Paris. A young Yugoslav immigrant named Stefan Markovic was found murdered under sordid circumstances. It would have been just another *fait divers* but for the fact that he had served as a bodyguard and kind of personal factotum to the young, popular film star Alain Delon. As the police investigation got under way, there were reports of wild sex parties that Markovic had arranged for Delon and his friends. Blackmail looked like a reason for bumping off the Yugoslav, and hints followed that there was an effort to hush up the affair because of involvement of someone high up in French politics. Finally the word began to spread: Madame Pompidou had attended, participated in and been photographed at the Markovic-Delon sex parties.

A dossier on the Markovic case with the accusations involving the Pompidous had in fact reached the Élysée Palace, and de Gaulle had been informed. His reaction had been, "Let justice take its course." But instead of speeding up justice, or seeking proof or corroborating evidence, or warning against rumors, or even questioning Madame Pompidou herself, the whole affair was allowed to seep and spread by poisonous innuendo. It was a very useful way to smear and undercut the only visible political challenger or possible successor to General de Gaulle.

Pompidou and his wife were vulnerable to the extent that, unlike the de Gaulles, they did mix with artists and film stars and they did know Delon and had seen him socially. The rest was calumny. Moreover, Pompidou knew it was fully within the power and authority of the government to quash such rumors in a hurry if it wanted to. He largely blamed Couve de Murville for allowing it to go on, but twice he saw de Gaulle privately to complain about the rumors. Both times he came away with sympathy and little else. Finally, when a new spate of headlines broke in January 1969, Pompidou issued a formal statement that he and his wife "know nothing about this news item." Until then he had kept a cold furious public silence, but he seethed to his close friends. After his statement, it was announced almost at once that President de Gaulle had invited the former prime minister and his wife to dinner at the Élysée Palace. It is a measure of the shallowness of the whole affair that this gesture by de Gaulle was enough to bring it entirely to a halt. The rumors abruptly stopped, but no one was ever charged with the Markovic murder. The dinner on March 12, 1969, was a very strained and heavy affair. Debré, with a heavy cold, also attended with his wife. Madame de Gaulle was ill at ease and Madame Pompidou scarcely said a word. Pompidou and de Gaulle kept up a desultory exchange, and the Pompidous departed at 9:30, the hour of minimum courtesy. It was the last time he saw Charles de Gaulle.

*

General de Gaulle still contrived on occasion to lunge out in his old way to reassert French independence or charge at one of his old windmills. In November

1968 the Western World plunged once again into one of its periodic monetary crises, and the Group of Ten leading financial nations gathered in Bonn to work out a new currency alignment. In three days of very difficult technical negotiations, the finance ministers hammered out agreement on a series of adjustments, including a standby credit of some $2 billion for France, along with a devaluation of the franc by nearly 10 percent. The agreement was concluded in the early hours of Saturday morning. The French finance minister at that period, François-Xavier Ortoli, flew from Bonn to Paris at once to present the package to President de Gaulle and his Cabinet. Most of the ministers, including Couve de Murville, were in favor of devaluation, but one in particular was not—Jean Marcel Jeanneney, an old Gaullist loyalist and budget minister. Couching his arguments in terms of national discipline, independence and the virtues of standing firm in the midst of crisis, which were all themes the General wanted to hear, Jeanneney convinced de Gaulle that he could and should avoid devaluation. And so that Saturday afternoon, de Gaulle again grabbed the headlines and startled the world with a one-sentence announcement: "The President of the Republic makes known that following a cabinet meeting, the following decision has been taken: The present parity of the French franc will be maintained."

It was, however, a costly decision, for it made it more difficult than ever for French exports to compete on world markets and had to be accompanied by a new round of budget cuts and austerity measures with the country still wallowing in the economic aftermath of the May uprising. But de Gaulle was elated at having stood up alone once again against the Group of Ten.

In February 1969 de Gaulle staged a last backhanded attack against the Common Market. Sensing that Great Britain might be preparing yet another effort to get a negotiation going in Brussels, he invited the new British ambassador, Christopher Soames, to lunch and an intimate talk. It ought to be possible, de Gaulle told Soames, for Britain and France to move closer together by changing the Treaty of Rome, to loosen its more onerous aspects of supranationalism and integration and thus make it more acceptable to both countries. De Gaulle, in short, was maneuvering to use the British to help him gain what he had failed to achieve by frontal attack on the Common Market in 1965. For good measure de Gaulle went on to sketch to Soames how a new loose agreement on European collaboration could also enable Europe to organize its own defense arrangements, with NATO to continue and the Americans to remain allies, but no longer present in Europe! Finally, he told Soames, all these matters could be explored between the two governments in secret bilateral talks if the British were interested and would take the initiative in asking for discussions.

The British Foreign Office, with a long memory of tilts and maneuvers of General de Gaulle going back nearly thirty years, saw a large diplomatic booby trap in this unexpected overture. Britain, after all, had an application lying on the table in Brussels to join the Common Market and accept the Treaty of Rome as it stood. How would it now look to the Germans or the Dutch or the Belgians or the Italians if they learned that Britain had asked for "secret talks" to go behind their backs and agree with de Gaulle on changes in the treaty? What would Washington think if it learned that Britain was discussing seriously some new Gaullist gimmick for a European defense organization to supersede NATO?

Accordingly, London, with a certain Machiavellian touch, maneuvered back. Instead of responding to de Gaulle's beckoning finger and requesting secret bilateral talks with the French, the British deliberately informed the West German government (and later other EEC governments) in detail of what de Gaulle was proposing to their ambassador in Paris. This not only torpedoed the de Gaulle "initiative," but also exposed him to diplomatic embarrassment and some pointed inquiries from his Common Market partners. The French were furious at this thrust from *perfide Albion,* and life in Paris for Ambassador Soames was made very chilly and difficult indeed for many weeks.

But these were acts and gestures of spent and fading leadership. General de Gaulle had declared his determination to hold another national referendum to renew his mandate, and everything else was simply treading water, marking time, sideplay until events ran their course on the General's chosen path. Everything waited and depended on the terms of the referendum and its date.

In early March, President Richard Nixon arrived in Paris on an official visit. It was the first face-to-face conversation de Gaulle had held with an American president since John F. Kennedy in May of 1961, eight years before. Nixon had shared with de Gaulle the experience of "traversing the political desert," and he had regularly sought out and talked with the General on visits to Paris while he was working his way back after his defeat by Kennedy in 1960. The Nixon visit was the last big official function of de Gaulle's presidency. He even did the new president the honor of accepting an invitation to dine at the American embassy for the first time ever. They spent eight hours in all in private talks—de Gaulle primarily urging Nixon to recognize Red China and get out of Vietnam. In his final weeks in office, it seemed as if de Gaulle again needed good relations with Washington, and Nixon wanted to show that he could turn a new page in relations with Paris.

At last the referendum date was fixed for April 27, 1969—almost exactly one year after Danny Cohn-Bendit had marched with the Nanterre students to the Sorbonne. De Gaulle's ministers had always been apprehensive about the probable result, and had dragged their feet as long as they could to postpone the General's last rendezvous with the French people.

In the meantime Pompidou had infuriated de Gaulle by dropping all reticence about his availability as a successor. To a group of French journalists while on a visit to Rome, when the question of a successor was posed, Pompidou, instead of ducking as usual, said: "It is no secret that I will be a candidate." A few weeks later, before Swiss television cameras on a visit to Geneva, he said: "The question of succession has not been raised, but this said, it must be added that someday elections for a President of the Republic will have to be held." To de Gaulle and his entourage, these remarks by Pompidou in public—and in foreign cities— were little short of treason and betrayal. State television network was given orders to ban the former prime minister forthwith from the nation's screens.

There was no necessity to hold a referendum. The Gaullists had more than enough votes in the National Assembly to push through any kind of reform the General wanted. For de Gaulle, the point of the referendum was not reform—but renewal of a power mandate. He decided to pose two questions. He asked the voters to approve an amendment to the Fifth Republic constitution to abolish the Senate (the upper legislative chamber) and secondly to approve a program of restructuring the government to give greater authority and autonomy to France's regional and local governing bodies. De Gaulle wanted a renewal of power from the people or he wanted out. In retrospect, it appears that he probably wanted out, and therefore chose to pose referendum questions that produced his dismissal.

Pompidou, waiting in the wings, gave loyal if desultory support to de Gaulle in the referendum campaign—but Giscard d'Estaing urged his Independent Republican followers to vote no, and they could have provided the margin of defeat. On Friday afternoon, April 25, President de Gaulle recorded a final broadcast appeal to the nation. When he finished, he got up from the table and muttered to his staff aides, as he had to General Massu in Baden-Baden ten months before: *"C'est foutu!"* He left the Élysée Palace almost immediately by car for the last time with Madame de Gaulle for Colombey-les-Deux-Églises to await the Sunday results.

Within fifteen minutes of the polls' closing at 8 P.M., it was clear that the referendum would be defeated. The final result was a no vote of 53 percent. Shortly before midnight de Gaulle spoke to Couve de Murville and instructed him to announce at once that he was resigning the presidency. The prime minister went on the television screens twenty minutes later, speaking gravely, calmly: "Tomorrow a new page in our history will be turned. General de Gaulle was at the center of our national and political life. We remain faithful to him. A difficult period, perhaps a period of trouble, now lies before us. For the moment the government will ensure continuity of public powers in accordance with the constitution. It will naturally do its duty."

*

"Après moi le deluge!"—but there was no deluge. At the Élysée Palace, the faithful Tricot was instructed by de Gaulle to remove all personal files and papers and every trace of his presence from the building immediately. When Alain Poher, president of the Senate, arrived at the Élysée on Tuesday to take up the function of interim president of the Republic as provided by the constitution, there was not even letterhead paper in the presidential office.

Election dates for a new president were fixed in accordance with the Fifth Republic constitution, and when the campaign got under way de Gaulle sent a personal letter of support to Pompidou. But it was couched in terms of near mockery that Pompidou could not possibly make public, noting with a typical de Gaulle sardonic touch that "you, yourself" have alluded to your qualifications for high office. In order to be away from France during the voting, he and Madame de Gaulle flew to Ireland for a month's vacation during June. Pompidou did get a brief telegram of congratulations from Ireland, which he could make public when he was elected president on a runoff ballot on June 15.

Now the old weekend routines at Colombey-les-Deux-Églises became permanent. Charles de Gaulle never returned to Paris. The gates at La Boisserie were closed except for the comings and goings of the family and a few old loyalists who would be invited in turn for lunch once or twice a month—Couve de Murville, Pierre Messmer, André Malraux, Michel Debré, Marcel Jeanneney, Jacques Foccart. There would be reading—Aeschylus, Sophocles, Shakespeare, a little of Paul Claudel, the French classics—and then correspondence to be dealt with. After that the long daily walk in the countryside, the game of solitaire to his own rules, the evening television news, dinner and rest.

He began work on a projected three volumes of Memoirs of his second period of power, with researchers providing him with papers and raw material from his files, which were stored in offices that he never visited, in Paris, on the rue Solferino. In the summer of 1970 he and Madame de Gaulle visited Spain—a visit he could not make for political reasons while he was president of the Republic. Now he could meet and hold a long talk with Generalissimo Francisco Franco.

His mood—whether real or contrived for visitors—was always sardonic and pessimistic. Charles de Gaulle was never a man who looked backward with satisfaction or forward with enthusiasm. *"Ce pauvre Pompidou,"* that unfortunate Pompidou, as the new president was now invariably called at de Gaulle's table, was already "giving way" to pressures from the English and the other Europeans. Malraux records a last conversation with de Gaulle, undoubtedly embellished with the novelistic touch, that nevertheless must be taken as an accurate reflection of both mood and style:

> I have tried to set France upright against the end of the world. Have I failed? It will be for others to see later on. We are certainly present at the end of Europe. Why should parliamentary democracy (involving as it does here in France the distribution of tobacco shops!), which is on its last legs everywhere, create Europe! Good luck to this federation without a federator! Why should a type of democracy that nearly killed us, and isn't capable of assuring the development even of Belgium, be sacred when it is a question of overcoming the enormous obstacles confronting the creation of Europe? You know as well as I do that Europe will be a compact between the states, or nothing. Therefore nothing. We are the last Europeans in Europe that was Christianity. A lacerated Europe, which all the same did exist. The Europe whose nations hated one another had more reality than the Europe of today. It is no longer a matter of wondering whether France will make Europe—it is a matter of understanding that she is threatened with death through the death of Europe. . . .
>
> To be sure, nothing is final. What would happen if France became France again? I have learned to my cost that the gathering together of the French has always to be done over again. But perhaps this time the stake hardly concerns her. When all is said, I shall have done what I could. If we must watch Europe die, let us watch: It doesn't happen every day. . . .

*

On November 9, 1970, General de Gaulle worked in his study in the morning on the third chapter of the second volume of his Postwar Memoirs. He had a talk with a young neighbor farmer about the use of a tract of land adjoining La Boisserie. He wrote a brief letter to a cousin and lifelong friend, Henri Maillot.

He had settled at his card table for a game of solitaire before the evening television news when suddenly he gasped: "I have a pain—a pain here, in my back!" and slumped unconscious on the table. The housemaid, Charlotte, rushed in from the study, where she had been drawing the curtains, and Madame de Gaulle said, "A doctor—the doctor." The chauffeur, Maroux, was called, and quickly dragged a mattress into the room from upstairs and lifted the unconscious General out of his chair and stretched him out. The local doctor reached the house fifteen minutes later, and by this time the local priest was also on the way. There was barely time for the last rites before it was all over. Charles de Gaulle died only thirteen days short of his eightieth birthday.

Phillipe de Gaulle, commanding a naval station at Brest on the Brittany peninsula, was telephoned, but rather than commandeer a plane at that hour, he instead caught a night sleeping-car train to Paris, arranging to be picked up at the station early in the morning and driven to Colombey. Meanwhile, de Gaulle's death remained a family secret overnight. His daughter Elizabeth and her husband, General de Boissieu, arrived in the early hours, and at 7 A.M. Phillipe de Gaulle formally notified Michel Debré, then minister of defense, that General de Gaulle was dead. The news agency flashes began moving about an hour later.

President Pompidou now took from his personal safe a sealed envelope of instructions that de Gaulle had entrusted to him in the early days of their long association, when relations were close and intimate. Dated January 16, 1952, and written in de Gaulle's sloping, free-flowing hand, the instructions read:

> I desire my funeral to take place at Colombey-les-Deux-Églises. If I die elsewhere my body must be taken home without any public ceremony whatever.
>
> My grave shall be that in which my daughter Anne lies and where, one day, my wife will also rest. Inscription: Charles de Gaulle (1890–   ). Nothing else.
>
> The ceremony shall be arranged by my son, my daughter, my daughter-in-law, assisted by members of my personal staff, in an extremely simple manner. I do not wish for a State funeral. No president, no ministers, no parliamentary delegations, no representatives of public bodies. Only the armed forces may take part officially, as such, but their participation must be on a very modest scale, without bands or fanfares or trumpet calls.
>
> No oration shall be pronounced, either at the church or elsewhere. No funeral oration in parliament. No places reserved during the ceremony except for my family, my comrades who are members of the Order of Liberation, the municipal council of Colombey. The men and women of France may, if they wish, do my memory the honor of accompanying my

body to its last resting place. But it is in silence that I wish to be taken there.

I declare that I refuse in advance any distinction, promotion, dignity, citation, decoration whether French or foreign. If any whatsoever were conferred upon me, it would be in violation of my last wishes.

C. de Gaulle

In death as in life, General, de Gaulle's instructions were again carried out. The great of the world came to Paris to attend a memorial Mass at Notre-Dame Cathedral on the morning of Thursday, November 12. That afternoon at three o'clock, church bells began tolling in every parish church in France from the sunlit Côte d'Azur to the bleak Brittany peninsula as the final service began at the de Gaulle family church at Colombey.

At six o'clock that Thursday evening, the great avenue des Champs-Élysées was closed to traffic, and the president of the municipal council of Paris asked all citizens who wished to pay final tribute to General de Gaulle to join in a march to the Arc de Triomphe. They came not in hundreds or thousands, but in tens of thousands, scores of thousands, to walk in silence, broken only by a heavy falling rain, where General de Gaulle had walked on that great day of the liberation of Paris in August 1944.

An enormous Cross of Lorraine now stands on a little hill overlooking the village of Colombey-les-deux-Églises.

General de Gaulle's tall figure will forever cast its shadow over the land.

SELECTED BIBLIOGRAPHY

ALEXANDRE, PHILLIPE. *The Duel—de Gaulle and Pompidou.* Boston: Houghton Mifflin Company, 1972.

AMBROSE, STEPHEN E. *The Supreme Commander.* Garden City, N.Y.: Doubleday, 1969.

ARDAGH, JOHN. *The New French Revolution.* London: Secker & Warburg, 1968.

ARON, ROBERT. *De Gaulle Before Paris.* London: Putnam & Co., 1962.

————. *De Gaulle Triumphant.* London: Putnam & Co., 1964.

————. *An Explanation of de Gaulle.* New York: Harper & Row, 1966.

ASHCROFT, EDWARD. *De Gaulle.* London: Odhams Press, 1962.

BARBER, NOËL. *The Week France Fell.* London: Macmillan, 1976.

BARKER, ELISABETH. *Churchill and Eden and War.* London: Macmillan, 1978.

BARRÈS, PHILIPPE. *Charles de Gaulle.* London: Hutchinson, 1942.

BOHLEN, CHARLES E. *Witness to History.* New York: W. W. Norton, 1973.

BRANDT, WILLY. *People and Politics.* Boston: Little, Brown, 1978.

BURNS, JAMES MACGREGOR. *Roosevelt, Soldier of Freedom,* 1940–45. London: Weidenfeld & Nicolson, 1970.

CHURCHILL, WINSTON S. *The Second World War.* London: Cassel, 1948–54.

COLLINS, LARRY, and DOMINIQUE LAPIERRE. *Is Paris Burning?* New York: Simon and Schuster, 1965.

COOPER, ALFRED DUFF. *Old Men Forget.* London: Rupert Hart Davis, 1957.

CRAWLEY, AIDAN. *De Gaulle.* London: Literary Guild, 1969.

CROZIER, BRIAN. *De Gaulle.* New York: Charles Scribner's Sons, 1973.

DE CARMOY, GUY. *The Foreign Policies of France, 1942–1968.* Chicago: University of Chicago Press, 1970.

DE GAULLE, CHARLES. *The Army of the Future.* Paris: Berger Levrault, 1934, and London: Hutchinson, n.d.

————. *The Edge of the Sword.* Paris: Berger Levrault, 1932, and London: Faber & Faber, 1960.

————. *Memoirs of Hope, 1958–62*. Paris: Plon, 1970, and London: Weidenfeld & Nicolson, 1971.

————. *The War Memoirs, 1940–46*. 3 vols. Paris: Plon, 1954–59, and New York: Simon & Schuster, 1964.

EISENHOWER, DWIGHT D. *Crusade in Europe*. Garden City, N.Y.: Doubleday, 1967.

FOOT, M. R. D. *Resistance*. London: Eyre Methuen, 1976.

————. *SOE in France*. London: H.M. Stationery Office, 1966.

FUNK, ARTHUR LAYTON. *Charles de Gaulle, the Crucial Years, 1943–44*. Norman, Oklahoma: University of Oklahoma Press, 1959.

GALANTE, PIERRE. *The General*. London: Leslie Frewin, 1969.

GRINNEL-MILNE, DUNCAN. *The Triumph of Integrity*. London: Bodley Head, 1961, and New York: Macmillan, 1962.

HOFFMANN, STANLEY. *Decline or Renewal: France Since the 1930s*. New York: Viking, 1974.

HORNE, ALISTAIR. *To Lose a Battle*. London: Macmillan, 1969.

————. *A Savage War of Peace*. London: Macmillan, 1977.

KERSAUDY, FRANÇOIS. *Churchill and de Gaulle*. London: Collins, 1981.

LANGER, WILLIAM L. *Our Vichy Gamble*. New York: Alfred A. Knopf, 1947.

LASH, JOSEPH P. *Roosevelt and Churchill, 1939–41*. London: André Deutsch, 1977.

LAVAL, PIERRE. *The Unpublished Diary of Pierre Laval*. London: Falcon Press, 1948.

LECOUTRE, JEAN. *De Gaulle*. London: Hutchinson, 1963 & 1969.

LEDWIDGE, BERNARD. *De Gaulle*. London: Weidenfeld & Nicolson, 1982, and New York: St. Martin's Press, 1982.

MACMILLAN, HAROLD. *Memoirs of Harold Macmillan*. 6 vols. London: Macmillan, 1965–73.

MALRAUX, ANDRÉ. *Fallen Oaks*. London: Hamish Hamilton, 1972.

MARRUS, MICHAEL R., and ROBERT O. PAXTON. *Vichy France and the Jews*. New York: Basic Books, 1981.

MATTHEWS, RONALD. *The Death of the Fourth Republic*. London: Eyre & Spottiswood, 1954.

MAURIAC, CLAUDE. *The Other de Gaulle*. London: Angus & Robertson, 1973.

MENGIN, ROBERT. *No Laurels for de Gaulle*. New York: Farrar, Straus and Giroux, 1966.

MONNET, JEAN. *Memoirs*. Garden City, N.Y.: Doubleday, 1978.

MURPHY, ROBERT. *Diplomat Among Warriors*. Garden City, N.Y.: Doubleday, 1964.

PAXTON, ROBERT O. *Vichy France, Old Guard and New Order*. New York: W. W. Norton, 1972.

PICKLES, DOROTHY. *The Fifth French Republic*. London: Metheun, 1960.

PONVIEILLE-ALQUIER, FRANÇOIS. *The French and the Phoney War, 1939–40*. London: Tom Stacey, 1971.

PRIAULX, ALLAN, and SANFORD J. UNGAR. *The Almost Revolution, France, May 1968*. New York: Dell, 1969.

ROY, JULES. *The Trial of Marshal Pétain*. New York: Harper & Row, 1968.

SCHOENBRUN, DAVID. *Three Lives of Charles de Gaulle*. New York: Atheneum, 1965.

SHERWOOD, ROBERT. *White House Papers of Harry L. Hopkins*. 2 vols. London: Eyre & Spottiswood, 1948.

SHIRER, WILLIAM L. *The Collapse of the Third Republic*. New York: Simon & Schuster, 1969.

SINGER, DANIEL. *Prelude to Revolution: France in May 1968*. London: Jonathan Cape, 1970.

SPEARS, EDWARD. *Assignment to Catastrophe*. 2 vols. London: William Heinemann, 1954.

————. *Two Men Who Saved France, Pétain and de Gaulle*. London: Eyre and Spottiswood, 1966.

TOURNOUX, JEAN-RAYMOND. *Pétain and de Gaulle*. London: William Heinemann, 1966.

WERTH, ALEXANDER. *De Gaulle*. London: Penguin Books, 1965.

————. *The de Gaulle Revolution*. London: Robert Hale, 1960.

————. *France, 1940–55*. London: Robert Hale, 1957.

WEYGAND, MAXIME. *Recalled to Service*. London: William Heinemann, 1952.

INDEX